BLACK SOCIETY
IN THE NEW
WORLD

BLACK SOCIETY IN THE NEW WORLD

Edited,

with Introductions by

RICHARD FRUCHT

University of Alberta, Canada

Random House New York

For my teachers: the people;
history's hastening agents

Library of Congress
Catalog Card Number: 76–141962
Standard Book Number: 394-31005-5
Manufactured in the United States of America:

Typography by Jack Meserole

First Edition
987654321

Preface

This anthology is more than a collection of articles giving comparisons of certain aspects of social life among the black population of the New World. A quick scan of the contents will show that there are few "one-to-one" comparisons of these aspects. For example, although I have included an article on the plantation systems of Brazil, I have not included one on those same systems in the Caribbean or in the United States. Instead, I have assembled various selections on different facets of social life in the three major areas of the New World with black populations in order to show the similarity in social conditions among these populations wherever they are found. Since, with few exceptions, all of the readings are descriptive, and though I connect them with my own arguments, it should not be difficult to integrate them with other descriptive materials (for more pointed comparisons) and with other theoretical points of view.

I have elected to emphasize only certain, often neglected, aspects of black social life. In sociology and anthropology, whenever black society is the subject, there appears to be a heavy emphasis on the family and household and on processes of socialization and personality formation as well as on aspects of folk culture—oral narrative, music, ritual—and their African, European, or syncretic origins. Thus, we describe and analyze the public and private behavior of black people often without describing and analyzing the larger social context within which this behavior occurs.

The focus of the argument, or theme, I use to connect the readings in this book is on the social relationships that make up the larger context within which behavior occurs. It is, so to speak, a focus on the external aspects of life rather than on the internal or psychological aspects. It does not attempt to describe what it is like to be a black man. It does attempt to describe those conditions, both social and historical, of which black society is a product. These conditions are, primarily, the material aspects of life, *i.e.*, technology, economics, and the division of labor, which affect the development of race and class relations, family relations, and the forms of the household, religious ideological, and religious organization, political ideology and political organization.

Thus, the underlying assumption of this argument can be simply stated: the New World was colonized and exploited for its resources and its potential by a capitalist economic and social system based on private property and the private accumulation of wealth, and in which labor and labor power were bought and sold as any other commodity. African slaves were brought to the New World and exploited for their labor. Their descendants continue to be exploited for their labor power, if it is needed at all. Most other features of the relationships within and between the black working class and the black peasantry and the national societies of which they are a part derive from this complex fact. The readings herein outline and give content to the structure of social relationships among this black underclass.

The social and economic position of black peasantries and black working classes in the New World is similar whether one looks at the United States or Jamaica or Brazil. They are economically and politically exploited, they work for wages or must pay rent in order to live on the land, and they are cursed by their color because of racist beliefs. They suffer a similar history as well in that their ancestors were slaves brought from Africa.

It is obvious that blacks are not the only representatives of the underclass under capitalism. This underclass exists over a good part of the world and is comprised of many different kinds of groups, cultural and ethnic, black, and white. This is a crucial realization. It tells us that whatever our analysis of the situation in the New World, or merely in one country, any attempt at changing it can be worldwide.

It would be naive to maintain that the material conditions of life constrain or limit behavior in some predetermined manner. Quite often, as current events are showing, rapid changes in technology, knowledge, and social relations are responsible for new forms of consciousness and innovative, revolutionary behavior. When people begin to recognize that these changes can potentially bring about material improvements, but people are hindered from realizing them by traditional patterns of life and exploitation, this new consciousness and innovative behavior can effect new social relationships in order to meet that potential. Thus, we speak of the social tensions and contradictions that changing circumstances generate and out of which new relationships develop.

A study of the black peasantry and working class exposes ever more clearly the kinds of social tensions and contradictions capitalism has wrought in the New World for 400 years. In the United States, for example, there is great technological potential for material improvement, but great poverty as well; a democratic ideology and mechanisms for political representation, but mass powerlessness and manipulation of the many by the few; adoption of the Enlightenment values of liberty, equality, fraternity, but also racism and oppression. These tensions are characteristic of the entire society and not only of the black underclass. It is the black underclass, however, that has lately become truly conscious of the nature of these tensions and therefore has become an agent in hastening changes in the conditions which engender them.

Although the readings in Part II describe the specific differences between black peasants and workers based on technological and organizational conditions, *i.e.,* plantation versus small holding, urban versus rural, the common forms of exploitation and oppression are also described. The readings in Part III describe the similar results of racism in different countries, namely the relegation of black people, the descendants of African slaves, to the lowest ranks of society. The selections in Parts IV and V show how both family and religion respond to the economic and political demands of the larger social context. Part VI deals with the problems of developing a black ideology and black political power. That is, in spite of the differences of language (*e.g.*, English, Spanish, French, Portuguese) and style of life (*e.g.*, industrial, agrarian, metropolitan, rural) there must develop a mode of communicating the experience and consciousness of the black underclass among all its national manifestations for the purpose of overcoming that which they all share: exploitation, oppression, and the effects of racism.

In all of these sections I have tried to include materials illustrative of various New World societies, with special emphasis on the United States, the Caribbean and Brazil. I am sure other selections and other arrangements could be justified. My hope is that the foregoing words and the subsequent introductions justify my intentions in bringing these readings together. I leave it to students and instructors to integrate this book into their own courses and plans of study.

Finally, I would like to thank all the authors who gave permission to reprint their works. I am also indebted to Charles Brant, Pieter de Vries, David Bai, Sydney Sharpe, and Elaine Wade for various kinds of help, and to Edith DuVal of Random House for editorial assistance. I am, of course, solely responsible for any intellectual shortcomings in my arguments.

Contents

PART SIX · BLACK IDEOLOGY AND BLACK POWER

PART ONE
SLAVERY

In order to understand the relationships of black people to the national societies of which they are a part, we can start with the question, why were Africans brought as slaves to the New World. The answer is simple, although its implications are not always easily grasped: Africans were brought to the New World to serve as labor in a burgeoning capitalist plantation economy based on manual technology. Plantation technologies in the New World, until recently, were labor intensive: massed hands instead of massed machines. The tools of cultivation and reaping were hoe, pitchfork, and machete; the power behind the tools, human muscle.

As Eric Williams points out in the first selection, there was an attempt to utilize the labor power of American Indians, followed by poor whites from Europe who came to the New World under different forms of unfreedom: convict labor, indenture, and contract. This became costly to the planters because of the difficulties in obtaining convicts, the incidence of white runaways, and the end of contracts and indenture periods. Thus, the planters turned to an already existing traffic in African slaves, previously monopolized by the Portuguese and Spanish, necessitated by the demands and costs of plantation production and reinforced by their attitudes about the inferiority of blacks.

Williams' article is important for two other reasons. First, he dismantles the myth about climate, i.e., the tropics and subtropics, being responsible for the necessity for black labor. Second, he places the history of the New World in its context, as part and parcel of the capitalist expansion of European nations.

The result of the plantation economy operated with slave labor was a distinctive way of life or culture, with a characteristic technology, social organization, and ideology: manual labor; agricultural production for profit; restricted ownership of land, tools, and labor; a class system including slavery; and a set of ideas, beliefs, and attitudes stipulating the inferiority of blacks and rationalizing the system of profit making and slavery. Kenneth Stampp, a historian with an appreciation of the anthropological approach, documents the nature of slave-based society in the American South. In the selection here, Stampp demonstrates that the constraints of slavery were not merely economic, but were found in the daily and personal lives of the slaves. Despite the instances of kindness between master and slave and the slave's attempt to associate himself with the master, according to Stampp, the slave lived under the whim and the whip of his master. And yet, in spite of this dehumanizing attempt to circumscribe every aspect of the slave's life, the slaves developed their own responses to the situation. Whether one explains this as a result of the strength of African custom, the number of slaves on the plantations, or the variable intensity and severity of the master's control, it is clear that slave life was not disorganized. Stampp describes two aspects of this part-society of slaves: social differentiation based on occupation or position within the slave system and the variations in the definition and existence of family units and in sexual relationships among the slaves.

In an attempt to explain the apparent differences in the position of blacks in the United States and in Brazil, some historians have emphasized the ideological differences between the master classes, leading to differential treatment of slaves. Thus, the Protestant English were harsher in their treatment than were the Catholic Portuguese, who also experienced the Moorish conquest, which further relaxed their attitudes towards blacks and slaves.

Marvin Harris, an anthropologist, takes issue with these explanations. He emphasizes the economic functions of slavery and discusses the evidence that shows that the Brazilian master was as cruel to his slaves as the English and American.

The conditions described by Stampp and Harris often resulted in a terrorized slave population. There is, however, a long and substantial history of slave rebellions in the New World, especially well documented for the United States and Brazil. Mary Reckord's article describes a slave rebellion in the British West Indian slave society of Jamaica. She emphasizes the use of religious institutions and ideology to support the rebellion and the use of missionaries as allies. The institutions of the old society were used to reconstruct, radically, a new society. Thus, blacks have their revolutionary history and heroes around which to organize and support their modern-day demands.

2

Eric Williams
THE ORIGIN OF
NEGRO SLAVERY

When in 1492 Columbus, representing the Spanish monarchy, discovered the New World, he set in train the long and bitter international rivalry over colonial possessions for which, after four and a half centuries, no solution has yet been found. Portugal, which had initiated the movement of international expansion, claimed the new territories on the ground that they fell within the scope of a papal bull of 1455 authorizing her to reduce to servitude all infidel peoples. The two powers, to avoid controversy, sought arbitration and, as Catholics, turned to the Pope—a natural and logical step in an age when the universal claims of the Papacy were still unchallenged by individuals and governments. After carefully sifting the rival claims, the Pope issued in 1493 a series of papal bulls which established a line of demarcation between the colonial possessions of the two states: the East went to Portugal and the West to Spain. The partition, however, failed to satisfy Portuguese aspirations and in the subsequent year the contending parties reached a more satisfactory compromise in the Treaty of Tordesillas, which rectified the papal judgment to permit Portuguese ownership of Brazil.

Neither the papal arbitration nor the formal treaty was intended to be binding on other powers, and both were in fact repudiated. Cabot's voyage to North America in 1497 was England's immediate reply to the partition. Francis I of France voiced his celebrated protest: "The sun shines for me as for others. I should very much like to see the clause in Adam's will that excludes me from a share of the world." The king of Denmark refused to accept the Pope's ruling as far as the East Indies were concerned. Sir William Cecil, the famous Elizabethan statesman, denied the Pope's right "to give and take kingdoms to whomsoever he pleased." In 1580 the English government countered with the principle of effective occupation as the determinant of sovereignty.[1] Thereafter, in the parlance of the day, there was "no peace below the line." It was a dispute, in the words of a later governor of Barbados, as to "whether the King of England or of France shall be monarch of the West Indies, for the King of Spain cannot hold it long. . . ."[2] England, France, and even Holland, began to challenge the Iberian Axis and claim their place in the sun. The Negro, too, was to have his place, though he did not ask for it: it was the broiling sun of the sugar, tobacco and cotton plantations of the New World.

REPRINTED FROM *Capitalism and Slavery* (CHAPEL HILL: UNIVERSITY OF NORTH CAROLINA PRESS, 1945) BY PERMISSION OF THE PUBLISHER AND THE AUTHOR.

According to Adam Smith, the prosperity of a new colony depends upon one simple economic factor—"plenty of good land."[3] The British colonial possessions up to 1776, however, can broadly be divided into two types. The first is the self-sufficient and diversified economy of small farmers, "mere earth-scratchers" as Gibbon Wakefield derisively called them,[4] living on a soil which, as Canada was described in 1840, was "no lottery, with a few exorbitant prizes and a large number of blanks, but a secure and certain investment."[5] The second type is the colony which has facilities for the production of staple articles on a large scale for an export market. In the first category fell the Northern colonies of the American mainland; in the second, the mainland tobacco colonies and the sugar islands of the Caribbean. In colonies of the latter type, as Merivale pointed out, land and capital were both useless unless labor could be commanded.[6] Labor, that is, must be constant and must work, or be made to work, in co-operation. In such colonies the rugged individualism of the Massachusetts farmer, practising his intensive agriculture and wringing by the sweat of his brow niggardly returns from a grudging soil, must yield to the disciplined gang of the big capitalist practising extensive agriculture and producing on a large scale. Without this compulsion, the laborer would otherwise exercise his natural inclination to work his own land and toil on his own account. The story is frequently told of the great English capitalist, Mr. Peel, who took £50,000 and three hundred laborers with him to the Swan River colony in Australia. His plan was that his laborers would work for him, as in the old country. Arrived in Australia, however, where land was plentiful—too plentiful—the laborers preferred to work for themselves as small proprietors rather than under the capitalist for wages. Australia was not England, and the capitalist was left without a servant to make his bed or fetch him water.[7]

For the Caribbean colonies the solution for this dispersion and "earth-scratching" was slavery. The lesson of the early history of Georgia is instructive. Prohibited from employing slave labor by trustees who, in some instances, themselves owned slaves in other colonies, the Georgian planters found themselves in the position, as Whitefield phrased it, of people whose legs were tied and were told to walk. So the Georgia magistrates drank toasts "to the one thing needful"—slavery—until the ban was lifted.[8] "Odious resource" though it might be, as Merivale called it,[9] slavery was an economic institution of the first importance. It had been the basis of Greek economy and had built up the Roman Empire. In modern times it provided the sugar for the tea and the coffee cups of the Western world. It produced the cotton to serve as a base for modern capitalism. It made the American South and the Caribbean islands. Seen in historical perspective, it forms a part of that general picture of the harsh treatment of the underprivileged classes, the unsympathetic poor laws and severe feudal laws, and the indifference with which the rising capitalist class was "beginning to reckon prosperity in terms of pounds sterling, and . . .

becoming used to the idea of sacrificing human life to the deity of increased production."[10]

Adam Smith, the intellectual champion of the industrial middle class with its new-found doctrine of freedom, later propagated the argument that it was, in general, pride and love of power in the master that led to slavery and that, in those countries where slaves were employed, free labor would be more profitable. Universal experience demonstrated conclusively that "the work done by slaves, though it appears to cost only their maintenance, is in the end the dearest of any. A person who can acquire no property can have no other interest than to eat as much, and to labour as little as possible."[11]

Adam Smith thereby treated as an abstract proposition what is a specific question of time, place, labor and soil. The economic superiority of free hired labor over slave is obvious even to the slave owner. Slave labor is given reluctantly, it is unskilful, it lacks versatility.[12] Other things being equal, free men would be preferred. But in the early stages of colonial development, other things are not equal. When slavery is adopted, it is not adopted as the choice over free labor; there is no choice at all. The reasons for slavery, wrote Gibbon Wakefield, "are not moral, but economical circumstances; they relate not to vice and virtue, but to production."[13] With the limited population of Europe in the sixteenth century, the free laborers necessary to cultivate the staple crops of sugar, tobacco and cotton in the New World could not have been supplied in quantities adequate to permit large-scale production. Slavery was necessary for this, and to get slaves the Europeans turned first to the aborigines and then to Africa.

Under certain circumstances slavery has some obvious advantages. In the cultivation of crops like sugar, cotton and tobacco, where the cost of production is appreciably reduced on larger units, the slaveowner, with his large-scale production and his organized slave gang, can make more profitable use of the land than the small farmer or peasant proprietor. For such staple crops, the vast profits can well stand the greater expense of inefficient slave labor.[14] Where all the knowledge required is simple and a matter of routine, constancy and cooperation in labor—slavery—is essential, until, by importation of new recruits and breeding, the population has reached the point of density and the land available for appropriation has been already apportioned. When that stage is reached, and only then, the expenses of slavery, in the form of the cost and maintenance of slaves, productive and unproductive, exceed the cost of hired laborers. As Merivale wrote: "Slave labour is dearer than free *wherever abundance of free labour can be procured.*"[15]

From the standpoint of the grower, the greatest defect of slavery lies in the fact that it quickly exhausts the soil. The labor supply of low social status, docile and cheap, can be maintained in subjection only by systematic degradation and by deliberate efforts to suppress its intelligence. Rotation of crops and scientific farming are therefore alien to slave societies. As

Jefferson wrote of Virginia, "we can buy an acre of new land cheaper than we can manure an old one."[16] The slave planter, in the picturesque nomenclature of the South, is a "land-killer." This serious defect of slavery can be counter-balanced and postponed for a time if fertile soil is practically unlimited. Expansion is a necessity of slave societies; the slave power requires ever fresh conquests.[17] "It is more profitable," wrote Merivale, "to cultivate a fresh soil by the dear labour of slaves, than an exhausted one by the cheap labour of free-men."[18] From Virginia and Maryland to Carolina, Georgia, Texas and the Middle West; from Barbados to Jamaica to Saint Domingue and then to Cuba; the logic was inexorable and the same. It was a relay race; the first to start passed the baton, unwillingly we may be sure, to another and then limped sadly behind.

Slavery in the Caribbean has been too narrowly identified with the Negro. A racial twist has thereby been given to what is basically an economic phenomenon. Slavery was not born of racism; rather, racism was the consequence of slavery. Unfree labor in the New World was brown, white, black, and yellow; Catholic, Protestant and pagan.

The first instance of slave trading and slave labor developed in the New World involved, racially, not the Negro but the Indian. The Indians rapidly succumbed to the excessive labor demanded of them, the insufficient diet, the white man's diseases, and their inability to adjust themselves to the new way of life. Accustomed to a life of liberty, their constitution and temperament were ill-adapted to the rigors of plantation slavery. As Fernando Ortíz writes: "To subject the Indian to the mines, to their monotonous, insane and severe labor, without tribal sense, without religious ritual, . . . was like taking away from him the meaning of his life. . . . It was to enslave not only his muscles but also his collective spirit."[19]

The visitor to Ciudad Trujillo, capital of the Dominican Republic (the present-day name of half of the island formerly called Hispaniola), will see a statue of Columbus, with the figure of an Indian woman gratefully writing (so reads the caption) the name of the Discoverer. The story is told, on the other hand, of the Indian chieftain, Hatuey, who, doomed to die for resisting the invaders, staunchly refused to accept the Christian faith as the gateway to salvation when he learned that his executioners, too, hoped to get to Heaven. It is far more probable that Hatuey, rather than the anonymous woman, represented contemporary Indian opinion of their new overlords.

England and France, in their colonies, followed the Spanish practice of enslavement of the Indians. There was one conspicuous difference—the attempts of the Spanish Crown, however ineffective, to restrict Indian slavery to those who refused to accept Christianity and to the warlike Caribs on the specious plea that they were cannibals. From the standpoint of the British government Indian slavery, unlike later Negro slavery which involved vital imperial interests, was a purely colonial matter. As Lauber writes: "The home government was interested in colonial slave conditions and legislation only when the African slave trade was involved. . . . Since it (Indian slavery) was never sufficiently extensive to interfere with Negro slavery and the slave trade, it never received any attention from the home government, and so existed as legal because never declared illegal."[20]

But Indian slavery never was extensive in the British dominions. Ballagh, writing of Virginia, says that popular sentiment had never "demanded the subjection of the Indian race *per se,* as was practically the case with the Negro in the first slave act of 1661, but only of a portion of it, and that admittedly a very small portion. . . . In the case of the Indian . . . slavery was viewed as of an occasional nature, a preventive penalty and not as a normal and permanent condition."[21] In the New England colonies Indian slavery was unprofitable, for slavery of any kind was unprofitable because it was unsuited to the diversified agriculture of these colonies. In addition the Indian slave was inefficient. The Spaniards discovered that one Negro was worth four Indians.[22] A prominent official in Hispaniola insisted in 1518 that "permission be given to bring Negroes, a race robust for labor, instead of natives, so weak that they can only be employed in tasks requiring little endurance, such as taking care of maize fields or farms."[23] The future staples of the New World, sugar and cotton, required strength which the Indian lacked, and demanded the robust "cotton nigger" as sugar's need of strong mules produced in Louisiana the epithet "sugar mules." According to Lauber, "When compared with sums paid for Negroes at the same time and place the prices of Indian slaves are found to have been considerably lower."[24]

The Indian reservoir, too, was limited, the African inexhaustible. Negroes therefore were stolen in Africa to work the lands stolen from the Indians in America. The voyages of Prince Henry the Navigator complemented those of Columbus, West African history became the complement of West Indian.

The immediate successor of the Indian, however, was not the Negro but the poor white. These white servants included a variety of types. Some were indentured servants, so called because, before departure from the homeland, they had signed a contract, indented by law, binding them to service for a stipulated time in return for their passage. Still others, known as "redemptioners," arranged with the captain of the ship to pay for their passage on arrival or within a specified time thereafter; if they did not, they were sold by the captain to the highest bidder. Others were convicts, sent out by the deliberate policy of the home government, to serve for a specified period.

This emigration was in tune with mercantilist theories of the day which strongly advocated putting the poor to industrious and useful labor and favored emigration, voluntary or involuntary, as relieving the poor rates and finding more profitable occupations abroad for idlers and vagrants at home. "Indentured servitude," writes C. M. Haar, "was called into existence by two different though complementary forces: there was both a positive attraction from the New World and a negative repulsion from the Old."[25] In a state paper delivered to James I in 1606 Bacon emphasized that by emigration England would gain "a double commodity, in the avoidance of people here, and in making use of them there."[26]

This temporary service at the outset denoted no inferiority or degradation. Many of the servants were manorial tenants fleeing from the irksome restrictions of feudalism, Irishmen seeking freedom from the oppression of landlords and bishops, Germans running away from the devastation of the Thirty Years' War. They transplanted in their hearts a burning desire for land, an ardent passion for independence. They came to the land of opportunity to be free men, their imaginations powerfully wrought upon by glowing and extravagant descriptions in the home country.[27] It was only later when, in the words of Dr. Williamson, "all ideals of a decent colonial society, of a better and greater England overseas, were swamped in the pursuit of an immediate gain,"[28] that the introduction of disreputable elements became a general feature of indentured service.

A regular traffic developed in these indentured servants. Between 1654 and 1685 ten thousand sailed from Bristol alone, chiefly for the West Indies and Virginia.[29] In 1683 white servants represented one-sixth of Virginia's population. Two-thirds of the immigrants to Pennsylvania during the eighteenth century were white servants; in four years 25,000 came to Philadelphia alone. It has been estimated that more than a quarter of a million persons were of this class during the colonial period,[30] and that they probably constituted one-half of all English immigrants, the majority going to the middle colonies.[31]

As commercial speculation entered the picture, abuses crept in. Kidnaping was encouraged to a great degree and became a regular business in such towns as London and Bristol. Adults would be plied with liquor, children enticed with sweetmeats. The kidnapers were called "spirits," defined as "one that taketh upp men and women and children and sells them on a shipp to be conveyed beyond the sea." The captain of a ship trading to Jamaica would visit the Clerkenwell House of Correction, ply with drink the girls who had been imprisoned there as disorderly, and "invite" them to go to the West Indies.[32] The temptations held out to the unwary and the credulous were so attractive that, as the mayor of Bristol complained, husbands were induced to forsake their wives, wives their husbands, and apprentices their masters, while wanted criminals found on the transport ships a refuge from the arms of the law.[33] The wave of German immigration developed the "newlander," the labor agent of those days, who traveled up and down the Rhine Valley persuading the feudal peasants to sell their belongings and emigrate to America, receiving a commission for each emigrant.[34]

Much has been written about the trickery these "newlanders" were not averse to employing.[35] But whatever the deceptions practised, it remains true, as Friedrich Kapp has written, that "the real ground for the

emigration fever lay in the unhealthy political and economic conditions.
. . . The misery and oppression of the conditions of the little (German)
states promoted emigration much more dangerously and continuously than
the worst 'newlander.' "[36]

Convicts provided another steady source of white labor. The harsh
feudal laws of England recognized three hundred capital crimes. Typical
hanging offences included: picking a pocket for more than a shilling; shop-
lifting to the value of five shillings; stealing a horse or a sheep; poaching
rabbits on a gentleman's estate.[37] Offences for which the punishment pre-
scribed by law was transportation comprised the stealing of cloth, burning
stacks of corn, the maiming and killing of cattle, hindering customs officers
in the execution of their duty, and corrupt legal practices.[38] Proposals made
in 1664 would have banished to the colonies all vagrants, rogues and
idlers, petty thieves, gipsies, and loose persons frequenting unlicensed
brothels.[39] A piteous petition in 1667 prayed for transportation instead of
the death sentence for a wife convicted of stealing goods valued at three
shillings and four pence.[40] In 1745 transportation was the penalty for the
theft of a silver spoon and a gold watch.[41] One year after the emancipation
of the Negro slaves, transportation was the penalty for trade union activity.
It is difficult to resist the conclusion that there was some connection between the law and the labor needs of the plantations, and the marvel is
that so few people ended up in the colonies overseas.

Benjamin Franklin opposed this "dumping upon the New World of
the outcasts of the Old" as the most cruel insult ever offered by one nation
to another, and asked, if England was justified in sending her convicts to
the colonies, whether the latter were justified in sending to England their
rattlesnakes in exchange?[42] It is not clear why Franklin should have been
so sensitive. Even if the convicts were hardened criminals, the great increase of indentured servants and free emigrants would have tended to
render the convict influence innocuous, as increasing quantities of water
poured in a glass containing poison. Without convicts the early development
of the Australian colonies in the nineteenth century would have been
impossible. Only a few of the colonists, however, were so particular. The
general attitude was summed up by a contemporary: "Their labor would
be more beneficial in an infant settlement, than their vices could be
pernicious."[43] There was nothing strange about this attitude. The great
problem in a new country is the problem of labor, and convict labor, as
Merivale has pointed out, was equivalent to a free present by the government to the settlers without burdening the latter with the expense of importation.[44] The governor of Virginia in 1611 was willing to welcome
convicts reprieved from death as "a readie way to furnish us with men
and not allways with the worst kind of men."[45] The West Indies were prepared to accept all and sundry, even the spawn of Newgate and Bridewell,
for "no goale-bird [sic] can be so incorrigible, but there is hope of his
conformity here, as well as of his preferment, which some have happily
experimented."[46]

The political and civil disturbances in England between 1640 and 1740 augmented the supply of white servants. Political and religious non-conformists paid for their unorthodoxy by transportation, mostly to the sugar islands. Such was the fate of many of Cromwell's Irish prisoners, who were sent to the West Indies.[47] So thoroughly was this policy pursued that an active verb was added to the English language—to "barbadoes" a person.[48] Montserrat became largely an Irish colony,[49] and the Irish brogue is still frequently heard today in many parts of the British West Indies. The Irish, however, were poor servants. They hated the English, were always ready to aid England's enemies, and in a revolt in the Leeward Islands in 1689[50] we can already see signs of that burning indignation which, according to Lecky, gave Washington some of his best soldiers.[51] The vanquished in Cromwell's Scottish campaigns were treated like the Irish before them, and Scotsmen came to be regarded as "the general travaillers and soldiers in most foreign parts."[52] Religious intolerance sent more workers to the plantations. In 1661 Quakers refusing to take the oath for the third time were to be transported; in 1664 transportation, to any plantation except Virginia or New England, or a fine of one hundred pounds was decreed for the third offence for persons over sixteen assembling in groups of five or more under pretence of religion.[53] Many of Monmouth's adherents were sent to Barbados, with orders to be detained as servants for ten years. The prisoners were granted in batches to favorite courtiers, who made handsome profits from the traffic in which, it is alleged, even the Queen shared.[54] A similar policy was resorted to after the Jacobite risings of the eighteenth century.

The transportation of these white servants shows in its true light the horrors of the Middle Passage—not as something unusual or inhuman but as part of the age. The emigrants were packed like herrings. According to Mittelberger, each servant was allowed about two feet in width and six feet in length in bed.[55] The boats were small, the voyage long, the food, in the absence of refrigeration, bad, disease inevitable. A petition to Parliament in 1659 describes how seventy-two servants had been locked up below deck during the whole voyage of five and a half weeks, "amongst horses, that their souls, through heat and steam under the tropic, fainted in them."[56] Inevitably abuses crept into the system and Fearon was shocked by "the horrible picture of human suffering which this living sepulchre" of an emigrant vessel in Philadelphia afforded.[57] But conditions even for the free passengers were not much better in those days, and the comment of a Lady of Quality describing a voyage from Scotland to the West Indies on a ship full of indentured servants should banish any ideas that the horrors of the slave ship are to be accounted for by the fact that the victims were Negroes. "It is hardly possible," she writes, "to believe that human nature could be so depraved, as to treat fellow creatures in such a manner for so little gain."[58]

The transportation of servants and convicts produced a powerful vested interest in England. When the Colonial Board was created in 1661, not the least important of its duties was the control of the trade in indentured servants. In 1664 a commission was appointed, headed by the King's brother, to examine and report upon the exportation of servants. In 1670 an act prohibiting the transportation of English prisoners overseas was rejected; another bill against the stealing of children came to nothing. In the transportation of felons, a whole hierarchy, from courtly secretaries and grave judges down to the jailors and turnkeys, insisted on having a share in the spoils.[59] It has been suggested that it was humanity for his fellow countrymen and men of his own color which dictated the planter's preference for the Negro slave.[60] Of this humanity there is not a trace in the records of the time, at least as far as the plantation colonies and commercial production were concerned. Attempts to register emigrant servants and regularize the procedure of transportation—thereby giving full legal recognition to the system—were evaded. The leading merchants and public officials were all involved in the practice. The penalty for man-stealing was exposure in the pillory, but no missiles from the spectators were tolerated. Such opposition as there was came from the masses. It was enough to point a finger at a woman in the streets of London and call her a "spirit" to start a riot.

This was the situation in England when Jeffreys came to Bristol on his tour of the West to clean up the remnants of Monmouth's rebellion. Jeffreys has been handed down to posterity as a "butcher," the tyrannical deputy of an arbitrary king, and his legal visitation is recorded in the textbooks as the "Bloody Assizes." They had one redeeming feature. Jeffreys vowed that he had come to Bristol with a broom to sweep the city clean, and his wrath fell on the kidnapers who infested the highest municipal offices. The merchants and justices were in the habit of straining the law to increase the number of felons who could be transported to the sugar plantations they owned in the West Indies. They would terrify petty offenders with the prospect of hanging and then induce them to plead for transportation. Jeffreys turned upon the mayor, complete in scarlet and furs, who was about to sentence a pickpocket to transportation to Jamaica, forced him, to the great astonishment of Bristol's worthy citizens, to enter the prisoners' dock, like a common felon, to plead guilty or not guilty, and hectored him in characteristic language: "Sir, Mr. Mayor, you I meane, Kidnapper, and an old Justice of the Peace on the bench. . . . I doe not knowe him, an old knave: he goes to the taverne, and for a pint of sack he will bind people servants to the Indies at the taverne. A kidnapping knave! I will have his ears off, before I goe forth of towne. . . . Kidnapper, you, I mean, Sir. . . . If it were not in respect of the sword, which is over your head, I would send you to Newgate, you kidnapping knave. You are worse than the pick-pockett who stands there. . . . I hear the trade of kidnapping is of great request. They can discharge a felon or a traitor, provided they will go to Mr. Alderman's plantation at the West Indies." The mayor was fined one thousand pounds, but apart from the loss of dignity and the fear aroused in their hearts, the merchants lost nothing—their gains were left inviolate.[61]

According to one explanation, Jeffreys' insults were the result of intoxication or insanity.[62] It is not improbable that they were connected with a complete reversal of mercantilist thought on the question of emigration, as a result of the internal development of Britain herself. By the end of the seventeenth century the stress had shifted from the accumulation of the precious metals as the aim of national economic policy to the development of industry within the country, the promotion of employment and the encouragement of exports. The mercantilists argued that the best way to reduce costs, and thereby compete with other countries, was to pay low wages, which a large population tended to ensure. The fear of overpopulation at the beginning of the seventeenth century gave way to a fear of underpopulation in the middle of the same century. The essential condition of colonization—emigration from the home country—now ran counter to the principle that national interest demanded a large population at home. Sir Josiah Child denied that emigration to America had weakened England, but he was forced to admit that in this view he was in a minority of possibly one in a thousand, while he endorsed the general opinion that "whatever tends to the depopulating of a kingdom tends to the impoverishment of it."[63] Jeffreys' unusual humanitarianism appears less strange and may be attributed rather to economic than to spirituous considerations. His patrons, the Royal Family, had already given their patronage to the Royal African Company and the Negro slave trade. For the surplus population needed to people the colonies in the New World the British had turned to Africa, and by 1680 they already had positive evidence, in Barbados, that the African was satisfying the necessities of production better than the European.

The status of these servants became progressively worse in the plantation colonies. Servitude, originally a free personal relation based on voluntary contract for a definite period of service, in lieu of transportation and maintenance, tended to pass into a property relation which asserted a control of varying extent over the bodies and liberties of the person during service as if he were a thing.[64] Eddis, writing on the eve of the Revolution, found the servants groaning "beneath a worse than Egyptian bondage."[65] In Maryland servitude developed into an institution approaching in some respects chattel slavery.[66] Of Pennsylvania it has been said that "no matter how kindly they may have been treated in particular cases, or how voluntarily they may have entered into the relation, as a class and when once bound, indentured servants were temporarily chattels."[67] On the sugar plantations of Barbados the servants spent their time "grinding at the mills and attending the furnaces, or digging in this scorching island; having nothing to feed on (notwithstanding their hard labour) but potatoe roots, nor to drink, but water with such roots washed in it, besides the bread and tears of their own afflictions; being bought and sold still from one planter to another, or attached as horses and beasts for the debts of their masters, being whipt at the whipping posts (as rogues,) for their masters' pleasure, and sleeping in sties worse than hogs in England. . . ."[68]

As Professor Harlow concludes, the weight of evidence proves incontestably that the conditions under which white labor was procured and utilized in Barbados were "persistently severe, occasionally dishonourable, and generally a disgrace to the English name."[69]

English officialdom, however, took the view that servitude was not too bad, and the servant in Jamaica was better off than the husbandman in England. "It is a place as grateful to you for trade as any part of the world. It is not so odious as it is represented."[70] But there was some sensitiveness on the question. The Lords of Trade and Plantations, in 1676, opposed the use of the word "servitude" as a mark of bondage and slavery, and suggested "service" instead.[71] The institution was not affected by the change. The hope has been expressed that the white servants were spared the lash so liberally bestowed upon their Negro comrades.[72] They had no such good fortune. Since they were bound for a limited period, the planter had less interest in their welfare than in that of the Negroes who were perpetual servants and therefore "the most useful appurtenances" of a plantation.[73] Eddis found the Negroes "almost in every instance, under more comfortable circumstances than the miserable European, over whom the rigid planter exercises an inflexible severity."[74] The servants were regarded by the planters as "white trash," and were bracketed with the Negroes as laborers. "Not one of these colonies ever was or ever can be brought to any considerable improvement without a supply of white servants and Negroes," declared the Council of Montserrat in 1680.[75] In a European society in which subordination was considered essential, in which Burke could speak of the working classes as "miserable sheep" and Voltaire as "canaille," and Linguet condemn the worker to the use of his physical strength alone, for "everything would be lost once he knew that he had a mind"[76]—in such a society it is unnecessary to seek for apologies for the condition of the white servant in the colonies.

Defoe bluntly stated that the white servant was a slave.[77] He was not. The servant's loss of liberty was of limited duration, the Negro was a slave for life. The servant's status could not descend to his offspring, Negro children took the status of the mother. The master at no time had absolute control over the person and liberty of his servant as he had over his slave. The servant had rights, limited but recognized by law and inserted in a contract. He enjoyed, for instance, a limited right to property. In actual law the conception of the servant as a piece of property never went beyond that of personal estate and never reached the stage of a chattel or real estate. The laws in the colonies maintained this rigid distinction and visited cohabitation between the races with severe penalties. The servant could aspire, at the end of his term, to a plot of land, though, as Wertenbaker points out for Virginia, it was not a legal right,[78] and conditions varied from colony to colony. The serf in Europe could therefore hope for an early freedom in America which villeinage could not afford. The freed servants became small yeomen farmers, settled in the back country, a democratic force in a society of large aristocratic plantation owners, and were the pioneers in westward expansion. That was why Jefferson in America, as Saco in Cuba, favored the introduction of European servants instead of African slaves—as tending to democracy rather than aristocracy.[79]

The institution of white servitude, however, had grave disadvantages. Postlethwayt, a rigid mercantilist, argued that white laborers in the colonies would tend to create rivalry with the mother country in manufacturing. Better black slaves on plantations than white servants in industry, which would encourage aspirations to independence.[80] The supply moreover was becoming increasingly difficult, and the need of the plantations outstripped the English convictions. In addition, merchants were involved in many vexatious and costly proceedings arising from people signifying their willingness to emigrate, accepting food and clothes in advance, and then suing for unlawful detention.[81] Indentured servants were not forthcoming in sufficient quantities to replace those who had served their term. On the plantations, escape was easy for the white servant; less easy for the Negro who, if freed, tended, in self-defence, to stay in his locality where he was well known and less likely to be apprehended as a vagrant or runaway slave. The servant expected land at the end of his contract; the Negro, in a strange environment, conspicuous by his color and features, and ignorant of the white man's language and ways, could be kept permanently divorced from the land. Racial differences made it easier to justify and rationalize Negro slavery, to exact the mechanical obedience of a plough-ox or a cart-horse, to demand that resignation and that complete moral and intellectual subjection which alone make slave labor possible. Finally, and this was the decisive factor, the Negro slave was cheaper. The money which procured a white man's services for ten years could buy a Negro for life.[82] As the governor of Barbados stated, the Barbadian planters found by experience that "three blacks work better and cheaper than one white man."[83]

But the experience with white servitude had been invaluable. Kidnaping in Africa encountered no such difficulties as were encountered in England. Captains and ships had the experience of the one trade to guide them in the other. Bristol, the center of the servant trade, became one of the centers of the slave trade. Capital accumulated from the one financed the other. White servitude was the historic base upon which Negro slavery was constructed. The felon-drivers in the plantations became without effort slave-drivers. "In significant numbers," writes Professor Phillips, "the Africans were latecomers fitted into a system already developed."[84]

Here, then, is the origin of Negro slavery. The reason was economic, not racial; it had to do not with the color of the laborer, but the cheapness of the labor. As compared with Indian and white labor, Negro slavery was eminently superior. "In each case," writes Bassett, discussing North Carolina, "it was a survival of the fittest. Both Indian slavery and white servitude were to go down before the black man's superior endurance, docility, and labor capacity."[85] The features of the man, his hair, color and dentifrice, his "subhuman" characteristics so widely pleaded, were only the later rationalizations to justify a simple economic fact: that the colonies needed labor and resorted to Negro labor because it was cheapest and best. This was not a theory, it was a practical conclusion deduced from the personal experience of the planter. He would have gone to the moon, if necessary, for labor. Africa was nearer than the moon, nearer too than the more populous countries of India and China. But their turn was to come.

This white servitude is of cardinal importance for an understanding of the development of the New World and the Negro's place in that development. It completely explodes the old myth that the whites could not stand the strain of manual labor in the climate of the New World and that, for this reason and this reason alone, the European powers had recourse to Africans. The argument is quite untenable. A Mississippi dictum will have it that "only black men and mules can face the sun in July." But the whites faced the sun for well over a hundred years in Barbados, and the Salzburgers of Georgia indignantly denied that rice cultivation was harmful to them.[86] The Caribbean islands are well within the tropical zone, but their climate is more equable than tropical, the temperature rarely exceeds 80 degrees though it remains uniform the whole year round, and they are exposed to the gentle winds from the sea. The unbearable humidity of an August day in some parts of the United States has no equal in the islands. Moreover only the southern tip of Florida in the United States is actually tropical, yet Negro labor flourished in Virginia and Carolina. The southern parts of the United States are not hotter than South Italy or Spain, and de Tocqueville asked why the European could not work there as well as in those two countries.[87] When Whitney invented his cotton gin, it was confidently expected that cotton would be produced by free labor on small farms, and it was, in fact, so produced.[88] Where the white farmer was ousted, the enemy was not the climate but the slave plantation, and the white farmer moved westward, until the expanding plantation sent him on his wanderings again. Writing in 1857, Weston pointed out that labor in the fields of the extreme South and all the heavy outdoor work in New Orleans were performed by whites, without any ill consequences. "No part of the continental borders of the Gulf of Mexico," he wrote, "and none of the islands which separate it from the ocean, need be abandoned to the barbarism of negro slavery."[89] In our own time we who have witnessed the dispossession of Negroes by white sharecroppers in the South and the mass migration of Negroes from the South to the colder climates of Detroit, New York, Pittsburgh and other industrial centers of the North, can no longer accept the convenient rationalization that Negro labor was employed on the slave plantations because the climate was too rigorous for the constitution of the white man.

A constant and steady emigration of poor whites from Spain to Cuba, to the very end of Spanish dominion, characterized Spanish colonial policy. Fernando Ortíz has drawn a striking contrast between the role of tobacco and sugar in Cuban history. Tobacco was a free white industry intensively cultivated on small farms; sugar was a black slave industry extensively cultivated on large plantations. He further compared the free Cuban tobacco industry with its slave Virginian counterpart.[90] What determined the difference was not climate but the economic structure of the two areas. The whites could hardly have endured the tropical heat of Cuba and succumbed to the tropical heat of Barbados. In Puerto Rico, the jíbaro, the poor white peasant, is still the basic type, demonstrating, in the words of Grenfell Price, how erroneous is the belief that after three generations the white man cannot breed in the tropics.[91] Similar white communities have survived in the Caribbean, from the earliest settlements right down to our own times, in the Dutch West Indian islands of Saba and St. Martin. For some sixty years French settlers have lived in St. Thomas not only as fishermen but as agriculturalists, forming today the "largest single farming class" in the island.[92] As Dr. Price concludes: "It appears that northern whites can retain a fair standard for generations in the trade-wind tropics if the location is free from the worst forms of tropical disease, if the economic return is adequate, and if the community is prepared to undertake hard, physical work."[93] Over one hundred years ago a number of German emigrants settled in Seaford, Jamaica. They survive today, with no visible signs of deterioration, flatly contradicting the popular belief as to the possibility of survival of the northern white in the tropics.[94] Wherever, in short, tropical agriculture remained on a small farming basis, whites not only survived but prospered. Where the whites disappeared, the cause was not the climate but the supersession of the small farm by the large plantation, with its consequent demand for a large and steady supply of labor.

The climatic theory of the plantation is thus nothing but a rationalization. In an excellent essay on the subject Professor Edgar Thompson writes: "The plantation is not to be accounted for by climate. It is a political institution." It is, we might add, more: it is an economic institution. The climatic theory "is part of an ideology which rationalizes and naturalizes an existing social and economic order, and this everywhere seems to be an order in which there is a race problem."[95]

The history of Australia clinches the argument. Nearly half of this island continent lies within the tropical zone. In part of this tropical area, the state of Queensland, the chief crop is sugar. When the industry began to develop, Australia had a choice of two alternatives: black labor or white labor. The commonwealth began its sugar cultivation in the usual way—with imported black labor from the Pacific islands. Increasing demands, however, were made for a white Australia policy, and in the twentieth century non-white immigration was prohibited. It is irrelevant to consider here that as a result the cost of production of Australian sugar is prohibitive, that the industry is artificial and survives only behind the Chinese wall of Australian autarchy. Australia was willing to pay a high price in order to remain a white man's country. Our sole concern here with the question is that this price was paid from the pockets of the Australian consumer and not in the physical degeneration of the Australian worker.

Labor in the Queensland sugar industry today is wholly white. "Queensland," writes H. L. Wilkinson, "affords the only example in the world of European colonization in the tropics on an extensive scale. It does more; it shows a large European population doing the whole of the work of its civilization from the meanest service, and most exacting manual labor, to the highest form of intellectualism."[96] To such an extent has science exploded superstition that Australian scientists today argue that the only condition on which white men and women can remain healthy in the tropics is that they must engage in hard manual work. Where they have done so, as in Queensland, "the most rigorous scientific examination," according to the Australian Medical Congress in 1920, "failed to show any organic changes in white residents which enabled them to be distinguished from residents of temperate climates."[97]

Negro slavery, thus, had nothing to do with climate. Its origin can be expressed in three words: in the Caribbean, Sugar; on the mainland, Tobacco and Cotton. A change in the economic structure produced a corresponding change in the labor supply. The fundamental fact was "the creation of an inferior social and economic organization of exploiters and exploited."[98] Sugar, tobacco and cotton required the large plantation and hordes of cheap labor, and the small farm of the ex-indentured white servant could not possibly survive. The tobacco of the small farm in Barbados was displaced by the sugar of the large plantation. The rise of the sugar industry in the Caribbean was the signal for a gigantic dispossession of the small farmer. Barbados in 1645 had 11,200 small white farmers and 5,680 Negro slaves; in 1667 there were 745 large plantation owners and 82,023 slaves. In 1645 the island had 18,300 whites fit to bear arms, in 1667 only 8,300.[99] The white farmers were squeezed out. The planters continued to offer inducements to newcomers, but they could no longer offer the main inducement, land. White servants preferred the other islands where they could hope for land, to Barbados, where they were sure there was none.[100] In desperation the planters proposed legislation which would prevent a landowner from purchasing more land, compel Negroes and servants to wear dimity manufactured in Barbados (what would English mercantilists have said?) to provide employment for the poor whites, and prevent Negroes from being taught to trade.[101] The governor of Barbados in 1695 drew a pitiful picture of these ex-servants. Without fresh meat or rum, "they are domineered over and used like dogs, and this in time will undoubtedly drive away all the commonalty of the white people." His only suggestion was to give the right to elect members of the Assembly to every white man owning two acres of land. Candidates for election would "sometimes give the poor miserable creatures a little rum and fresh provisions and such things as would be of nourishment to them," in order to get their votes—and elections were held every year.[102] It is not surprising that the exodus continued.

The poor whites began their travels, disputing their way all over the Caribbean, from Barbados to Nevis, to Antigua, and thence to Guiana and Trinidad, and ultimately to Carolina. Everywhere they were pursued and dispossessed by the same inexorable economic force, sugar; and in Carolina they were safe from cotton only for a hundred years. Between 1672 and 1708 the white men in Nevis decreased by more than three-fifths, the black population more than doubled. Between 1672 and 1727 the white males of Montserrat declined by more than two-thirds, in the same period the black population increased more than eleven times.[103] "The more they buie," said the Barbadians, referring to their slaves, "the more they are able to buye, for in a yeare and a halfe they will earne with God's blessing as much as they cost."[104] King Sugar had begun his depredations, changing flourishing commonwealths of small farmers into vast sugar factories owned by a camarilla of absentee capitalist magnates and worked by a mass of alien proletarians. The plantation economy had no room for poor whites; the proprietor or overseer, a physician on the more prosperous plantations, possibly their families, these were sufficient. "If a state," wrote Weston, "could be supposed to be made up of continuous plantations, the white race would be not merely starved out, but literally squeezed out."[105] The resident planters, apprehensive of the growing disproportion between whites and blacks, passed Deficiency Laws to compel absentees, under penalty of fines, to keep white servants. The absentees preferred to pay the fines. In the West Indies today the poor whites survive in the "Red-legs" of Barbados, pallid, weak and depraved from in-breeding, strong rum, insufficient food and abstinence from manual labor. For, as Merivale wrote, "in a country where Negro slavery prevails extensively, no white is industrious."[106]

It was the triumph, not of geographical conditions, as Harlow contends,[107] but of economic. The victims were the Negroes in Africa and the small white farmers. The increase of wealth for the few whites was as phenomenal as the increase of misery for the many blacks. The Barbados crops in 1650, over a twenty-month period, were worth over three million pounds,[108] about fifteen millions in modern money. In 1666 Barbados was computed to be seventeen times as rich as it had been before the planting of sugar. "The buildings in 1643 were mean, with things only for necessity, but in 1666, plate, jewels, and household stuff were estimated at £500,000, their buildings very fair and beautiful, and their homes like castles, their sugar houses and negroes huts show themselves from the sea like so many small towns, each defended by its castle."[109] The price of land skyrocketed. A plantation of five hundred acres which sold for £400 in 1640 fetched £7,000 for a half-share in 1648.[110] The estate of one Captain Waterman, comprising eight hundred acres, had at one time been split up among no less than forty proprietors.[111] For sugar was and is essentially a capitalist undertaking, involving not only agricultural operations but the crude stages of refining as well. A report on the French sugar islands stated that to make ten hogsheads of sugar required as great an expenditure in beasts of burden, mills and utensils as to make a hundred.[112] James Knight of Jamaica estimated that it required four hundred acres to start a sugar plantation.[113] According to Edward Long, another planter and the historian of the island, it needed £5,000 to start a small plantation of three hundred acres, producing from thirty to fifty hogsheads of sugar a year, £14,000 for a plantation of the same size producing one hundred hogsheads.[114] There could be only two classes in such a society, wealthy planters and oppressed slaves.

The moral is reinforced by a consideration of the history of Virginia, where the plantation economy was based not on sugar but on tobacco. The researches of Professor Wertenbaker have exploded the legend that Virginia from the outset was an aristocratic dominion. In the early seventeenth century about two-thirds of the landholders had neither slaves nor indentured servants. The strength of the colony lay in its numerous white yeomanry. Conditions became worse as the market for tobacco was glutted by Spanish competition and the Virginians demanded in wrath that something be done about "those petty English plantations in the savage islands in the West Indies" through which quantities of Spanish tobacco reached England.[115] None the less, though prices continued to fall, the exports of Virginia and Maryland increased more than six times between 1663 and 1699. The explanation lay in two words—Negro slavery, which cheapened the cost of production. Negro slaves, one-twentieth of the population in 1670, were one-fourth in 1730. "Slavery, from being an insignificant factor in the economic life of the colony, had become the very foundation upon which it was established." There was still room in Virginia, as there was not in Barbados, for the small farmer, but land was useless to him if he could not compete with slave labor. So the Virginian peasant, like the Barbadian, was squeezed out. "The Virginia which had formerly been so largely the land of the little farmer, had become the land of Masters and Slaves. For aught else there was no room."[116]

The whole future history of the Caribbean is nothing more than a dotting of the i's and a crossing of the t's. It happened earlier in the British and French than in the Spanish islands, where the process was delayed until the advent of the dollar diplomacy of our own time. Under American capital we have witnessed the transformation of Cuba, Puerto Rico and the Dominican Republic into huge sugar factories (though the large plantation, especially in Cuba, was not unknown under the Spanish regime), owned abroad and operated by alien labor, on the British West Indian pattern. That this process is taking place with free labor and in nominally independent areas (Puerto Rico excepted) helps us to see in its true light the first importation of Negro slave labor in the British Caribbean —a phase in the history of the plantation. In the words of Professor Phillips, the plantation system was "less dependent upon slavery than slavery was upon it. . . . The plantation system formed, so to speak, the industrial and social frame of government . . . , while slavery was a code of written laws enacted for that purpose."[117]

Where the plantation did not develop, as in the Cuban tobacco industry, Negro labor was rare and white labor predominated. The liberal section of the Cuban population consistently advocated the cessation of the Negro slave trade and the introduction of white immigrants. Saco, mouthpiece of the liberals, called for the immigration of workers "white and free, from all parts of the world, of all races, provided they have a white face and can do honest labor."[118] Sugar defeated Saco. It was the sugar plantation, with its servile base, which retarded white immigration in nineteenth century Cuba as it had banned it in seventeenth century Barbados and eighteenth century Saint Domingue. No sugar, no Negroes. In Puerto Rico, which developed relatively late as a genuine plantation, and where, before the American regime, sugar never dominated the lives and thoughts of the population as it did elsewhere, the poor white peasants survived and the Negro slaves never exceeded fourteen per cent of the population.[119] Saco wanted to "whiten" the Cuban social structure.[120] Negro slavery blackened that structure all over the Caribbean while the blood of the Negro slaves reddened the Atlantic and both its shores. Strange that an article like sugar, so sweet and necessary to human existence, should have occasioned such crimes and bloodshed!

After emancipation the British planters thought of white immigration, even convicts. The governor of British Guiana wrote in glowing terms in 1845 about Portuguese immigrants from Madeira.[121] But though the Portuguese came in large numbers, as is attested by their strength even today in Trinidad and British Guiana, they preferred retail trade to plantation labor. The governor of Jamaica was somewhat more cautious in his opinion of British and Irish immigrants. Sickness had broken out, wages were too low, the experiment could only be partially useful in making an immediate addition to the laboring population, and therefore indiscriminate importation was inadvisable.[122] The European immigrants in St. Christopher bewailed their fate piteously, and begged to be permitted to return home. "There is not the slightest reluctance on our part to continue in the island for an honest livelihood by pleasing our employers by our industrious labour if the climate agreed with us, but unfortunately it do not; and we are much afraid if we continue longer in this injurious hot climate (the West Indies) death will be the consequence to the principal part of us. . . ."[123]

It was not the climate which was against the experiment. Slavery had created the pernicious tradition that manual labor was the badge of the slave and the sphere of influence of the Negro. The first thought of the Negro slave after emancipation was to desert the plantation, where he could, and set up for himself where land was available. White plantation workers could hardly have existed in a society side by side with Negro peasants. The whites would have prospered if small farms had been encouraged. But the abolition of slavery did not mean the destruction of the sugar plantation. The emancipation of the Negro and the inadequacy of the white worker put the sugar planter back to where he had been in the seventeenth century. He still needed labor. Then he had moved from Indian to white to Negro. Now, deprived of his Negro, he turned back to white and then to Indian, this time the Indian from the East. India replaced Africa; between 1833 and 1917, Trinidad imported 145,000 East Indians* and British Guiana 238,000. The pattern was the same for the other Caribbean colonies. Between 1854 and 1883, 39,000 Indians were introduced into Guadeloupe; between 1853 and 1924, over 22,000 laborers from the Dutch East Indies and 34,000 from British India were carried to Dutch Guiana.[124] Cuba, faced with a shortage of Negro slaves, adopted the interesting experiment of using Negro slaves side by side with indentured Chinese coolies,[125] and after emancipation turned to the teeming thousands of Haiti and the British West Indies. Between 1913 and 1924 Cuba imported 217,000 laborers from Haiti, Jamaica and Puerto Rico.[126] What Saco wrote a hundred years ago was still true, sixty years after Cuba's abolition of slavery.

Negro slavery therefore was only a solution, in certain historical circumstances, of the Caribbean labor problem. Sugar meant labor—at times that labor has been slave, at other times nominally free; at times black, at other times white or brown or yellow. Slavery in no way implied, in any scientific sense, the inferiority of the Negro. Without it the great development of the Caribbean sugar plantations, between 1650 and 1850, would have been impossible.

Notes

1. C. M. Andrews, *The Colonial Period of American History* (New Haven, 1934–1938), I, 12–14, 19–20.

2. N. M. Crouse, *The French Struggle for the West Indies, 1665–1713* (New York, 1943), 7.

3. Adam Smith, *The Wealth of Nations* (Cannan edition, New York, 1937), 538. To this Smith added a political factor, "liberty to manage their own affairs in their own way."

4. H. Merivale, *Lectures on Colonization and Colonies* (Oxford, 1928 edition), 262.

5. *Ibid.*, 385. The description is Lord Sydenham's, Governor-General of Canada.

6. Merivale, *op. cit.*, 256.

7. *Ibid.*

8. R. B. Flanders, *Plantation Slavery in Georgia* (Chapel Hill, 1933), 15–16, 20.

9. Merivale, *op. cit.*, 269.

* This is the correct West Indian description. It is quite incorrect to call them, as is done in this country, "Hindus." Not all East Indians are Hindus. There are many Moslems in the West Indies.

10. M. James, *Social Problems and Policy during the Puritan Revolution, 1640–1660* (London, 1930), 111.

11. Adam Smith, *op. cit.*, 365.

12. J. Cairnes, *The Slave Power* (New York, 1862), 39.

13. G. Wakefield, *A View of the Art of Colonization* (London, 1849), 323.

14. Adam Smith, *op. cit.*, 365–366.

15. Merivale, *op. cit.*, 303. Italics Merivale's.

16. M. B. Hammond, *The Cotton Industry: An Essay in American Economic History* (New York, 1897), 39.

17. Cairnes, *op. cit.*, 44; Merivale, *op. cit.*, 305–306. On soil exhaustion and the expansion of slavery in the United States see W. C. Bagley, *Soil Exhaustion and the Civil War* (Washington, D. C., 1942).

18. Merivale, *op. cit.*, 307–308.

19. J. A. Saco, *Historia de la Esclavitud de los Indios en el Nuevo Mundo* (La Habana, 1932 edition), I, Introduction, p. xxxviii. The Introduction is written by Fernando Ortíz.

20. A. W. Lauber, *Indian Slavery in Colonial Times within the Present Limits of the United States* (New York, 1913), 214–215.

21. J. C. Ballagh, *A History of Slavery in Virginia* (Baltimore, 1902), 51.

22. F. Ortíz, *Contrapunteo Cubano del Tabaco y el Azúcar* (La Habana, 1940), 353.

23. *Ibid.*, 359.

24. Lauber, *op. cit.*, 302.

25. C. M. Haar, "White Indentured Servants in Colonial New York," *Americana* (July, 1940), 371.

26. *Cambridge History of the British Empire* (Cambridge, 1929), I, 69.

27. See Andrews, *op. cit.*, I, 59; K. F. Geiser, *Redemptioners and Indentured Servants in the Colony and Commonwealth of Pennsylvania* (New Haven, 1901), 18.

28. *Cambridge History of the British Empire*, I, 236.

29. C. M. MacInnes, *Bristol, a Gateway of Empire* (Bristol, 1939), 158–159.

30. M. W. Jernegan, *Laboring and Dependent Classes in Colonial America, 1607–1783* (Chicago, 1931), 45.

31. H. E. Bolton and T. M. Marshall, *The Colonization of North America, 1492–1783* (New York, 1936), 336.

32. J. W. Bready, *England Before and After Wesley—The Evangelical Revival and Social Reform* (London, 1938), 106.

33. *Calendar of State Papers, Colonial Series,* V, 98. July 16, 1662.

34. Geiser, *op. cit.*, 18.

35. See G. Mittelberger, *Journey to Pennsylvania in the year 1750* (Philadelphia, 1898), 16; E. I. McCormac, *White Servitude in Maryland* (Baltimore, 1904), 44, 49; "Diary of John Harrower, 1773–1776," *American Historical Review* (Oct., 1900), 77.

36. E. Abbott, *Historical Aspects of the Immigration Problem, Select Documents* (Chicago, 1926), 12 n.

37. Bready, *op. cit.*, 127.

38. L. F. Stock (ed.), *Proceedings and Debates in the British Parliament respecting North America* (Washington, D. C., 1924–1941), I, 353 n, 355; III, 437 n, 494.

39. *Calendar of State Papers, Colonial Series,* V, 221.

40. *Ibid.*, V. 463. April, 1667 (?).

41. Stock, *op. cit.*, V, 229 n.

42. Jernegan, *op. cit.*, 49.

43. J. D. Lang, *Transportation and Colonization* (London, 1837), 10.

44. Merivale, *op. cit.*, 125.

45. J. D. Butler, "British Convicts Shipped to American Colonies," *American Historical Review* (Oct., 1896), 25.

46. J. C. Jeaffreson (ed.), *A Young Squire of the Seventeenth Century. From the Papers (A.D. 1676–1686) of Christopher Jeaffreson* (London, 1878), I, 258. Jeaffreson to Poyntz, May 6, 1681.

47. For Cromwell's own assurance for this, see Stock, *op. cit.*, I, 211. Cromwell to Speaker Lenthall, Sept. 17, 1649.

48. V. T. Harlow, *A History of Barbados, 1625–1685* (Oxford, 1926), 295.

49. J. A. Williamson, *The Caribbee Islands Under the Proprietary Patents* (Oxford, 1926), 95.

50. *Calendar of State Papers, Colonial Series,* XIII, 65. Joseph Crispe to Col. Bayer, June 10, 1689, from St. Christopher: "Besides the French we have a still worse enemy in the Irish Catholics." In Montserrat the Irish, three to every one of the English, threatened to turn over the island to the French (*Ibid.*, 73. June 27, 1689). Governor Codrington from Antigua preferred to trust the defence of Montserrat to the few English and their slaves rather than rely on the "doubtful fidelity" of the Irish (*Ibid.*, 112–113. July 31, 1689). He disarmed the Irish in Nevis and sent them to Jamaica (*Ibid.*, 123. Aug. 15, 1689).

51. H. J. Ford, *The Scotch-Irish in America* (New York, 1941), 208.

52. *Calendar of State Papers, Colonial Series,* V, 495. Petition of Barbados, Sept. 5, 1667.

53. Stock, *op. cit.*, I, 288 n, 321 n, 327.

54. Harlow, *op. cit.*, 297–298.

55. Mittelberger, *op. cit.*, 19.

56. Stock, *op. cit.*, I, 249. March 25, 1659.

57. Geiser, *op. cit.*, 57.

58. E. W. Andrews (ed.), *Journal of a Lady of Quality; Being the Narrative of a Journey from Scotland to the West Indies, North Carolina and Portugal, in the years 1774–1776* (New Haven, 1923), 33.

59. Jeaffreson, *op. cit.*, II, 4.

60. J. A. Doyle, *English Colonies in America—Virginia, Maryland, and the Carolinas* (New York, 1889), 387.

61. MacInnes, *op. cit.*, 164–165; S. Seyer, *Memoirs Historical and Topographical of Bristol and its Neighbourhood* (Bristol, 1821–1823), II, 531; R. North, *The Life of the Rt. Hon. Francis North, Baron Guildford* (London, 1826), II, 24–27.

62. Seyer, *op. cit.*, II, 532.

63. *Cambridge History of the British Empire,* I, 563–565.

64. Ballagh, *op. cit.*, 42.

65. McCormac, *op. cit.*, 75.

66. *Ibid.*, 111.

67. C. A. Herrick, *White Servitude in Pennsylvania* (Philadelphia, 1926), 3.

68. Stock, *op. cit.*, I, 249.

69. Harlow, *op. cit.*, 306.

70. Stock, *op. cit.*, I, 250. March 25, 1659.

71. *Calendar of State Papers, Colonial Series,* IX, 394. May 30, 1676.

72. Sir W. Besant, *London in the Eighteenth Century* (London, 1902), 557.

73. *Calendar of State Papers, Colonial Series,* V, 229. Report of Committee of Council for Foreign Plantations, Aug., 1664 (?).

74. G. S. Callender, *Selections from the Economic History of the United States, 1765–1860* (New York, 1909), 48.

75. *Calendar of State Papers, Colonial Series,* X, 574. July 13, 1680.

76. H. J. Laski, *The Rise of European Liberalism* (London, 1936), 199, 215, 221.

77. Daniel Defoe, *Moll Flanders* (Abbey Classics edition, London, n.d.), 71.

78. T. J. Wertenbaker, *The Planters of Colonial Virginia* (Princeton, 1922), 61.

79. Herrick, *op. cit.*, 278.

80. *Ibid.*, 12.

81. *Calendar of State Papers, Colonial Series,* V, 220. Petition of Merchants, Planters and Masters of Ships trading to the Plantations, July 12, 1664.

82. Harlow, *op. cit.*, 307.

83. *Calendar of State Papers, Colonial Series,* IX, 445. Aug. 15, 1676.

84. U. B. Phillips, *Life and Labor in the Old South* (Boston, 1929), 25.

85. J. S. Bassett, *Slavery and Servitude in the Colony of North Carolina* (Baltimore, 1896), 77. On the docility of the Negro slave, see *infra*, pp. 201–208.

86. Flanders, *op. cit.*, 14.

87. Cairnes, *op. cit.*, 35 n.

88. Callender, *op. cit.*, 764 n.

89. Cairnes, *op. cit.*, 36.

90. Ortíz, *op. cit.*, 6, 84.

91. A. G. Price, *White Settlers in the Tropics* (New York, 1939), 83.

92. *Ibid.*, 83, 95.

93. *Ibid.*, 92.

94. *Ibid.*, 94.

95. E. T. Thompson, "The Climatic Theory of the Plantation," *Agricultural History* (Jan., 1941), 60.

96. H. L. Wilkinson, *The World's Population Problems and a White Australia* (London, 1930), 250.

97. *Ibid.*, 251.

98. R. Guerra, *Azúcar y Población en Las Antillas* (La Habana, 1935), 20.

99. Williamson, *op. cit.*, 157–158.

100. *Calendar of State Papers, Colonial Series*, X, 503. Governor Atkins, March 26, 1680.

101. *Ibid.*, VII, 141. Sir Peter Colleton to Governor Codrington, Dec. 14, 1670. A similar suggestion came from Jamaica in 1686. Permission was requested for the introduction of cotton manufacture, to provide employment for the poor whites. The reply of the British Customs authorities was that "the more such manufactures are encouraged in the Colonies the less they will be dependent on England." F. Cundall, *The Governors of Jamaica in the Seventeenth Century* (London, 1936), 102–103.

102. *Calendar of State Papers, Colonial Series*, XIV, 446–447. Governor Russell, March 23, 1695.

103. C. S. S. Higham, *The Development of the Leeward Islands under the Restoration, 1660–1688* (Cambridge, 1921), 145.

104. Harlow, *op. cit.*, 44.

105. Callender, *op. cit.*, 762.

106. Merivale, *op. cit.*, 62.

107. Harlow, *op. cit.*, 293.

108. *Ibid.*, 41.

109. *Calendar of State Papers, Colonial Series*, V, 529. "Some Observations on the Island of Barbadoes," 1667.

110. Harlow, *op. cit.*, 41.

111. *Ibid.*, 43.

112. Merivale, *op. cit.*, 81.

113. F. W. Pitman, *The Settlement and Financing of British West India Plantations in the Eighteenth Century*, in *Essays in Colonial History by Students of C. M. Andrews* (New Haven, 1931), 267.

114. *Ibid.*, 267–269.

115. *Calendar of State Papers, Colonial Series*, I, 79. Governor Sir Francis Wyatt and Council of Virginia, April 6, 1626.

116. Wertenbaker, *op. cit.*, 59, 115, 122–123, 131, 151.

117. R. B. Vance, *Human Factors in Cotton Culture: A Study in the Social Geography of the American South* (Chapel Hill, 1929), 36.

118. J. A. Saco, *Historia de la Esclavitud de la Raza Africana en el Nuevo Mundo y en especial en los Países America-Hispanos* (La Habana, 1938), I, Introduction, p. xxviii. The Introduction is by Fernando Ortíz.

119. T. Blanco, "El Prejuicio Racial en Puerto Rico," *Estudios Afrocubanos*, II (1938), 26.

120. Saco, *Historia de la Esclavitud de la Raza Africana* ... Introduction, p. xxx.

121. *Immigration of Labourers into the West Indian Colonies and the Mauritius*, Part II, *Parliamentary Papers*, Aug. 26, 1846, 60. Henry Light to Lord Stanley, Sept. 17, 1845: "As labourers they are invaluable, as citizens they are amongst the best, and rarely are brought before the courts of justice or the police."

122. *Papers Relative to the West Indies, 1841–1842, Jamaica-Barbados*, 18. C. T. Metcalfe to Lord John Russell, Oct. 27, 1841.

123. *Immigration of Labourers into the West Indian Colonies* . . . , 111. William Reynolds to C. A. Fitzroy, August 20, 1845.

124. These figures are taken from tables in I. Ferenczi, *International Migrations* (New York, 1929), I, 506–509, 516–518, 520, 534, 537.

125. The following table illustrates the use of Chinese labor on Cuban sugar plantations in 1857:

PLANTATION	NEGROES	CHINESE
Flor de Cuba	409	170
San Martín	452	125
El Progreso	550	40
Armonía	330	20
Santa Rosa	300	30
San Rafael	260	20
Santa Susana	632	200

The last plantation was truly cosmopolitan; the slave gang included 34 natives of Yucatan. These figures are taken from J. G. Cantero, *Los Ingenios de la Isla de Cuba* (La Habana, 1857). The book is not paged. There was some opposition to this Chinese labor, on the ground that it increased the heterogeneity of the population. "And what shall we lose thereby?" was the retort. *Anales de la Real Junta de Fomento y Sociedad Económica de La Habana* (La Habana, 1851), 187.

126. Ferenczi, *op. cit.,* I, 527.

Kenneth Stampp
ASPECTS OF SLAVE LIFE IN THE UNITED STATES

1

The ante-bellum South had a class structure based to some extent upon polite breeding but chiefly upon the ownership of property. Superimposed upon this class structure was a caste system which divided those whose appearance enabled them to claim pure Caucasian ancestry from those whose appearance indicated that some or all of their forebears were Negroes. Members of the Caucasian caste, regardless of wealth or education, considered themselves innately superior to Negroes and "mulattoes" and therefore entitled to rights and privileges denied to the inferior caste. They believed in "white supremacy," and they maintained a high degree of caste solidarity to secure it.

The slaves were "caste conscious" too and, despite the presence of some "white man's Negroes," showed remarkable loyalty toward each other. It was the exception and not the rule for a slave to betray a fellow slave who "took" some of the master's goods, or shirked work, or ran away. In Tennessee, for example, Jim killed Isaac for helping to catch him when he was a fugitive; and he clearly had the sympathy of the other slaves. At Jim's trial the judge observed that "Isaac seems to have lost *caste. . . .* He had combined with the white folks . . . no slight offense in their eyes: that one of their own color, subject to a like servitude, should abandon the interests of his *caste,* and . . . betray black folks to the white people, rendered him an object of general aversion." Former slaves testified that when a newly purchased chattel was sent to the quarters he was immediately initiated into the secrets of the group. He was told what he "had better do to avoid the lash."[1]

In the quarters the bondsman formed enduring friendships. He became attached to the community—to the soil on which he labored and to the people who shared his hardships and fears, his hopes and joys. Between the slaves on a plantation there developed, one Southerner observed, "a deep sympathy of feeling" which bound them "closely together." It was back to old friends and familiar places that the runaway often fled. As a Kentucky slave began a dash for freedom, he "took an affectionate look at the well-known objects" on his way and confessed that sorrow was mingled with his joy. The slave, explained Frederick Douglass, had "no choice, no goal, no destination; but is pegged down to a single spot, and must take root there or nowhere."[2]

FROM PP. 331–349 OF *The Peculiar Institution,* BY KENNETH STAMPP (NEW YORK: ALFRED A. KNOPF, 1956). COPYRIGHT © 1956 BY KENNETH STAMPP. REPRINTED BY PERMISSION OF THE AUTHOR AND THE PUBLISHER.

This was why estate and execution sales were such tragedies; for each of them involved, besides the breakup of families, the disintegration of a community, the dispersion of a group of people who might have lived together for a generation or more. After the death of a Tennessee planter, one of the heirs noted that the slaves were "much opposed to being broken up." While Fanny Kemble resided on her husband's Georgia plantation, slaves came to her to express their gratitude that she had had children. They regarded the children as security "against their own banishment from the only home they knew, and separation from all ties of kindred and habit, and dispersion to distant plantations."[3] These fears might have caused a group of slaves to grieve at the death of even a severe master.

Although slaves were generally loyal to their caste and fond of their communities, they, like the whites, had their own internal class structure. Their masters helped to create a social hierarchy by giving them specialized tasks for the sake of economic efficiency, and by isolating domestics and artisans from the field-hands as a control technique. But the stratification of slave society also resulted from an impelling force within the slaves themselves—a force which manifested itself in their pathetic quest for personal prestige. Slaves yearned for some recognition of their worth as individuals, if only from those in their own limited social orbit; for to them this wholly human aspiration was, if anything, more important than it was to the whites. Each slave cherished whatever shreds of self-respect he could preserve.

The bondsmen, of course, were cut off from the avenues which led to success and respectability in white society. The paragon of virtue in materialistic nineteenth-century America—at least in its white middle-class segment, both urban and rural—was the enterprising, individualistic, freedom-loving, self-made man. Ideally he was the head of a family which he provided with the comforts and luxuries that symbolized his material success. He sought through education to give his children culture and social poise; he emancipated his wife from household drudgery; and he subscribed to the moral code of the Victorian age. Southern masters more or less conformed to this pattern and thus gained dignity and prestige; but the white caste's whole way of life was normally far beyond the reach of slaves. In slave society, therefore, success, respectability, and morality were measured by other standards, and prestige was won in other ways. The resulting unique patterns of slave behavior amused, or dismayed, or appalled the whites and convinced most of them that Negroes were innately different.

Many domestics did adopt part of the white pattern of respectability, were proud of their honesty and loyalty to the white family, and frowned upon disobedient or rebellious behavior. Some bondsmen at times seemed to fear or disapprove of a trouble-maker lest he cause them all to suffer the master's wrath. But most of them admired and respected the bold rebel who challenged slave discipline. The strong-willed field-hand whom the overseer hesitated to punish, the habitual runaway who mastered the technique of escape and shrugged at the consequences, each won personal triumphs for himself and vicarious triumphs for the others. The generality of slaves believed that he who knew how to trick or deceive the master had an enviable talent, and they regarded the committing of petit larceny as both thrilling and praiseworthy. One former slave recalled with great satisfaction the times when he had caught a pig or chicken and shared it with some "black fair one." These adventures made him feel "good, moral, [and] heroic"; they were "all the chivalry of which my circumstances and condition of life admitted."[4]

The unlettered slaves rarely won distinction or found pleasure in intellectual or esthetic pursuits. Theirs was an elemental world in which sharp wits and strong muscles were the chief weapons of survival. Young men prided themselves upon their athletic skills and physical prowess and often matched strength in violent encounters. Having to submit to the superior power of their masters, many slaves were extremely aggressive toward each other. They were, insisted a Georgian, "by nature tyrannical in their dispositions; and if allowed, the stronger will abuse the weaker; husbands will often abuse their wives, and mothers their children." Slave foremen were notoriously severe taskmasters and, when given the power, might whip more cruelly than white masters. Fanny Kemble discerned the brutalizing effects of bondage in the "unbounded insolence and tyranny" which slaves exhibited toward each other. "Everybody, in the South, wants the privilege of whipping somebody else," wrote Frederick Douglass.[5]

Each community of slaves contained one or two members whom the others looked to for leadership because of their physical strength, practical wisdom, or mystical powers. It was a "notorious" fact, according to one master, "that on almost every large plantation of Negroes, there is one among them who holds a kind of magical sway over the minds and opinions of the rest; to him they look as their oracle. . . . The influence of such a Negro, often a preacher, on a quarter is incalculable." A former slave on a Louisiana plantation remembered "Old Abram" who was "a sort of patriarch among us" and was "deeply versed in such philosophy as is taught in the cabin of the slave." On a Mississippi plantation everyone stood in awe of "Old Juba" who wore about his neck a half dozen charms and who claimed to have seen the devil a hundred times. On Pierce Butler's Georgia plantation Sinda prophesied the end of the world, and for a while no threat or punishment could get the hands back to work. A Louisiana planter noted angrily that "Big Lucy" was the leader who "corrupts every young negro in her power."[6] These were the self-made men and women of slave society.

Slaves who lacked the qualities which produce rebels or leaders had to seek personal gratification and the esteem of their fellows in less spectacular ways. They might find these things simply by doing their work uncommonly well. Even some of the field-hands, though usually lacking the incentive of pecuniary gain, were intrigued by the business of making things grow and enjoyed reputations as good farmers. To be able to plow a straight furrow, to master the skills required in cultivating one of the southern staples, to know the secrets of harvesting and preparing it for market—these activities brought personal rewards which might not be completely lost because all was done for another man's profit. Patsy, for example, was "queen of the field" on a small Louisiana plantation, since the "lightning-like motion" of her fingers made her the fastest cotton picker. Whatever she thought of bondage, Patsy was absorbed in her work and found pleasure in her own special kind of creativeness.[7]

This was still more true of slave artisans whose work often won great admiration. An English visitor affirmed that their aptitude for the mechanical arts should "encourage every philanthropist who has had misgivings in regard to the progressive power of the race." Again it was pride in craftsmanship, not monetary rewards, which gave most carpenters, blacksmiths, coopers, cobblers, and wheelwrights their chief incentive. The carpenters on a North Carolina plantation must have gained additional satisfaction from the knowledge that a white laborer had asked for permission to work with them "for the sake of Instruction." In Louisiana, a white engineer who was training a slave gave the master a favorable report: "I have seldom met with a Negro who shewed more anxiety to learn everything pertaining to a Steam Engine . . . and I have no hesitation in saying that with a little more practice, he will make a competent careful Engineer."[8]

The well-trained domestic also obtained a pleasant feeling of self-importance from the tactful performance of his services. A first-rate plantation cook wallowed in admiration; a personal servant who could humor his master and bandy innocuous pleasantries with him possessed the rare talent of a diplomat. Most domestics were proud of their positions of responsibility, of their fine manners and correct speech, and of their handsome clothing and other badges of distinction. They were important figures in their little world.

Indeed, the domestics, artisans, and foremen constituted the aristocracy of slave society. "I considered my station a very high one," confessed an ex-slave who had been his master's body servant. Many visitors to the South commented on how the domestics flaunted their superiority over "the less favored helots of the plough"—"their assumption of hauteur when they had occasion to hold intercourse with any of the 'field hands.' " And former slaves described the envy and hatred of the "helots" for the "fuglemen" who "put on airs" in imitation of the whites.[9]

Thus, ironically, a slave might reach the upper stratum of his society through intimate contact with the master, by learning to ape his manners, and by rendering him personal service, as well as by being a rebel or a leader of his people. And a bondsman, in his own circle, was as highly sensitive to social distinctions as ever was his master. In a society of unequals—of privileged and inferior castes, of wealth and poverty—the need to find some group to feel superior to is given a desperate urgency. In some parts of Virginia even the field-hands who felt the contempt of the domestics could lavish their own contempt upon the "coal pit niggers" who were hired to work in the mines.[10]

Everywhere, slaves of all ranks ridiculed the nonslaveholders, especially the poor whites—the dregs of a stratified white society—whom they scornfully called "po' buckra" and "white trash." Those who belonged to a master with great wealth and social prestige frequently identified themselves with him and looked disdainfully upon those who belonged to humbler masters. "They seemed to think that the greatness of their masters was transferable to them," wrote Frederick Douglass. "To be a slave, was thought to be bad enough; but to be a *poor man's* slave, was deemed a disgrace, indeed." Another former slave criticized the "foolish pride" which made them love "to boast of their master's wealth and influence. . . . I have heard of slaves object to being sent in very small companies to labor in the field, lest that some passer-by should think that they belonged to a poor man, who was unable to keep a large gang." A northern visitor described the house servant of a wealthy planter as "full of his master's wealth and importance, which he feels to be reflected upon himself." A domestic on a Louisiana sugar plantation was once asked to attend a sick overseer. "What do you think he says," reported the irritated mistress, "he aint used to waiting on low rank people."[11]

Many whites also heard slaves boast of the prices their masters had paid for them, or of the handsome offers their masters had rejected from would-be purchasers. A thousand-dollar slave felt superior to an eight-hundred-dollar slave. "When we recollect that the dollars are not their own," wrote an amused traveler, "we can hardly refrain from smiling at the childlike simplicity with which they express their satisfaction at the high price set on them."[12] But this attitude was not as simple as it seemed. Seeing the master exhibit his wealth as evidence of his social rank, the slave developed his own crass measure of a man's worth and exhibited his price tag.

But the most piteous device for seeking status in the slave community was that of boasting about white ancestors or taking pride in a light complexion. In the eyes of the whites the "mulatto" was tainted as much as the "pure" Negro and as hopelessly tied to the inferior caste; but this did not prevent some slaves of mixed ancestry (not all) from trying to make their Caucasian blood serve as a mark of superiority within their own caste. Fanny Kemble told of a slave woman who came to her and begged to be relieved from field labor "on *'account of her color.'* " This slave made it evident that, "being a mulatto, she considered field labor a degradation."[13] Such an attitude may have been sheer opportunism, or it may have indicated that some slaves had been effectively indoctrinated with the idea of their racial inferiority. But in many cases it was merely another example of the bondsman's search for dignity and self-respect.

2

In Africa the Negroes had been accustomed to a strictly regulated family life and a rigidly enforced moral code. But in America the disintegration of their social organization removed the traditional sanctions which had encouraged them to respect their old customs. Here they found the whites organized into families having great social and economic importance but regulated by different laws. In the quarters they were usually more or less encouraged to live as families and to accept white standards of morality.

But it was only outwardly that the family life of the mass of southern slaves resembled that of their masters. Inwardly, in many crucial ways, the domestic regimes of the slave cabin and of the "big house" were quite different. Because the slaves failed to conform to the white pattern, the master class found the explanation, as usual, in the Negro's innate racial traits. Actually, the differences resulted from the fact that slavery inevitably made much of the white caste's family pattern meaningless and unintelligible—and in some ways impossible—for the average bondsman. Here, as at so many other points, the slaves had lost their native culture without being able to find a workable substitute and therefore lived in a kind of cultural chaos.

The most obvious difference between the slave family and the white family was in the legal foundation upon which each rested. In every state white marriages were recognized as civil contracts which imposed obligations on both parties and provided penalties for their violation. Slave marriages had no such recognition in the state codes; instead, they were regulated by whatever laws the owners saw fit to enforce.

A few masters arbitrarily assigned husbands to women who had reached the "breeding age"; but ordinarily they permitted slaves to pick their own mates and only required them to ask permission to marry. On the plantations most owners refused to allow slaves to marry away from home and preferred to make additional purchases when the sexes were out of balance. Thus an Alabama overseer informed his employer that one slave was without a wife and that he had promised to "indever to git you to Bey a nother woman sow he might have a wife at home."[14] Still, it did frequently happen on both large and small estates that husbands and wives were owned by different masters. Sometimes, when a slave wished to marry the slave of another owner, a sale was made in order to unite them.

Having obtained their master's consent, the couple might begin living together without further formality; or their master might hastily pronounce them man and wife in a perfunctory ceremony. But more solemn ceremonies, conducted by slave preachers or white clergymen, were not uncommon even for the field-hands, and they were customary for the domestics. The importance of the occasion was sometimes emphasized by a wedding feast and gifts to the bride.

After a marriage many masters ignored the behavior of the couple so long as neither husband nor wife caused any loud or violent disturbances. Others insisted that they not only live together but respect their obligations to each other. A Louisianian made it a rule that adultery was to be "invariably punished." On a Mississippi plantation, the husband was required to provide firewood for his family and "wait on his wife"; the wife was to do the family's cooking, washing, and mending. Failure to perform these duties was "corrected by words first but if not reformed . . . by the whip." According to a Georgian, "I never permit a husband to abuse, strike or whip his wife. . . . If the wife teases and provokes him . . . she is punished, but it sometimes happens that the husband petitions for her pardon, which I make it a rule not to refuse, as it imposes a strong obligation on the wife to . . . be more conciliating in her behavior."[15] Some masters apparently ran domestic relations courts and served as family counselors.

Divorce, like marriage, was within the master's jurisdiction. He might permit his slaves to change spouses as often and whenever they wished, or he might establish more or less severe rules. A Louisiana master granted a divorce only after a month's notice and prohibited remarriage unless a divorcee agreed to receive twenty-five lashes. James H. Hammond inflicted one hundred lashes upon partners who dissolved their marriage and forced them to live singly for three years. One day in 1840, Hammond noted in his diary: "Had a trial of Divorce and Adultery cases. Flogged Joe Goodwyn and ordered him to go back to his wife. Dito Gabriel and Molly and ordered them to come together again. Separated Moses and Anny finally. And flogged Tom Kollock . . . [for] interfering with Maggy Campbell, Sullivan's wife."[16] While one master might enforce divorce laws as rigid as these, his neighbor might tolerate a veritable regime of free love—of casual alliances and easy separations. Inevitably the rules on a given estate affected the family life of its slaves.

Not only did the slave family lack the protection and the external pressure of state law, it also lacked most of the centripetal forces that gave the white family its cohesiveness. In the life of the slave, the family had nothing like the social significance that it had in the life of the white man. The slave woman was first a full-time worker for her owner, and only incidentally a wife, mother, and home-maker. She spent a small fraction of her time in the house; she often did no cooking or clothes making; and she was not usually nurse to her husband or children during illness. Parents frequently had little to do with the raising of their children; and children soon learned that their parents were neither the fount of wisdom nor the seat of authority. Thus a child on a Louisiana farm saw his mother receive twenty-five lashes for countermanding an order his mistress had given him.[17] Lacking autonomy, the slave family could not offer the child shelter or security from the frightening creatures in the outside world.

The family had no greater importance as an economic unit. Parents and children might spend some spare hours together in their garden plots, but, unlike rural whites, slaves labored most of the time for their masters in groups that had no relationship to the family. The husband was not the director of an agricultural enterprise; he was not the head of the family, the holder of property, the provider, or the protector. If his wife or child was disrobed and whipped by master or overseer, he stood by in helpless humiliation. In an age of patriarchal families, the male slave's only crucial function within the family was that of siring offspring.

Indeed, the typical slave family was matriarchal in form, for the mother's role was far more important than the father's. In so far as the family did have significance it involved responsibilities which traditionally belonged to women, such as cleaning house, preparing food, making clothes, and raising children. The husband was at most his wife's assistant, her companion, and her sex partner. He was often thought of as her possession ("Mary's Tom"), as was the cabin in which they lived.[18] It was common for a mother and her children to be considered a family without reference to the father.

Given these conditions—the absence of legal marriages, the family's minor social and economic significance, and the father's limited role—it is hardly surprising to find that slave families were highly unstable. Lacking both outer pressures and inner pulls, they were also exposed to the threat of forced separations through sales. How dispersed a slave family could be as a result of one or more of these factors was indicated by an advertisement for a North Carolina fugitive who was presumed to be "lurking in the neighborhood of E. D. Walker's, at Moore's Creek, who owns most of his relations, or Nathan Bonham's who owns his mother; or, perhaps, near Fletcher Bell's, at Long Creek, who owns his father." A slave preacher in Kentucky united couples in wedlock "until death or *distance* do you part." When Joshua and Bush asked for permission to marry, their Virginia master read them a statement warning that he might be forced to separate them, "so Joshua must not then say I have taken his wife from him."[19] Thus every slave family had about it an air of impermanence, for no master could promise that his debts would not force sales, or guarantee that his death would not cause divisions.

If the state did not recognize slave marriages, the churches of the Protestant South might have supplied a salutary influence, since they emphasized the sanctity of the home and family. The churches did try to persuade their own slave members to respect the marriage sacrament and sometimes even disciplined those who did not. But they were quite tolerant of masters who were forced by "necessity" to separate husbands, wives, and children. For example, in 1856, a committee of the Charleston Baptist Association agreed that slave marriages had "certain limitations" and had to be "the subject of special rules." Hence, though calling these marriages "sacred and binding" and urging that they be solemnized by a religious ceremony, the committee raised no objection to the separation of couples against their wills. Apparently the only sinful separation was one initiated by the slaves themselves.[20]

The general instability of slave families had certain logical consequences. One was the casual attitude of many bondsmen toward marriage; another was the failure of any deep and enduring affection to develop between some husbands and wives. The South abounded in stories of slaves who elected to migrate with kind masters even when it meant separation from their spouses. "Ef you got a good marster, foller him," was the saying in Virginia, according to an ex-slave. An equally common story, which was often true, was that chattels were not severely disturbed by forced separation and soon found new husbands or wives in their new homes. All who were familiar with the Negro, wrote a South Carolinian, understood how difficult it was "to educate even the best and most intelligently moral of the race to a true view and estimation of marriage."[21] Here, presumably, was proof that separations through the slave trade caused no real hardship.

Still another consequence was the indifference with which most fathers and even some mothers regarded their children. An angry Virginian attributed the death of a slave infant to "the unnatural neglect of his infamous mother"; he charged that another infant was "murdered right out by his mother's neglect and barbarous cruelty." Fanny Kemble observed the stolid reaction of slave parents to the death of their children. "I've lost a many; they all goes so," was the only comment of one mother when another child died; and the father, "without word or comment, went out to his enforced labor."[22] Many slaveholders complained that mothers could not be trusted to nurse their sick children, that some showed no affection for them and treated them cruelly. This, of course, was not a manifestation of Negro "character" as masters seemed to think. How these calloused mothers could have produced the affectionate slave "mammies" of tradition was never explained. But one master spoke volumes when he advocated separating children from their parents, because it was "far more humane not to cherish domestic ties among slaves."[23]

The final consequence of family instability was widespread sexual promiscuity among both men and women. The case of a Kentucky slave woman who had each of her seven children by a different father was by no means unique. This was a condition which some masters tried to control but which most of them accepted with resignation, or indifference, or amusement. As to the slave's moral habits, wrote one discouraged owner, "I know of no means whereby to regulate them, or to restrain them; I attempted it for many years by preaching virtue and decency, . . . but it was all in vain." Olmsted cited numerous instances of masters who regarded the whole matter with complete unconcern; and masters themselves rarely gave any sign of displeasure when an unmarried slave woman became pregnant. A Virginia planter kept a record of the fathers of his slave children when he knew who the fathers were, but often he could only guess—and sometimes he suggested that the child was sired "by the Commonwealth," or "by the Universe," or "God knows who by." Overseers were generally even less concerned; as one overseer explained, the morals of the slaves were "no business of his, and he did not care what they did." Nor was the law concerned. In Mississippi, when a male slave was indicted for the rape of a female slave, the state Supreme Court dismissed the case on the ground that this was not an offense known to common or statute law.[24]

If most slaves regarded the white man's moral code as unduly severe, many whites did too. Indeed, the number of bastardy cases in southern court records seems to confirm the conclusion that women of the poor-white class "carried about the same reputation for easy virtue as their sable sisters." Marriage, insisted Frederick Douglass, had no existence among slaves, "except in such hearts as are purer and higher than the standard morality around them." His consolation was that at least some slaves "maintained their honor, where all around was corrupt."[25]

That numerous slaves did manage somehow to surmount the corrupting influences everywhere about them, their masters themselves freely admitted. A South Carolinian admired the slave mother's "natural and often ardent and endearing affection for her offspring"; and another declared that "sound policy" as well as humanity required that everything be done "to reconcile these unhappy beings to their lot, by keeping mothers and children together." The majority of slave women were devoted to their children, regardless of whether they had been sired by one or by several fathers. Nor was sexual promiscuity a universal trait of southern Negroes even in bondage. Many slave couples, affirmed a Georgian, displayed toward each other a high degree of "faithfulness, fidelity, and affection."[26]

Seldom, when slave families were broken to satisfy creditors or settle estates, was a distinction made between those who were indifferent to the matter and those who suffered deeply as a consequence. The "agony at parting," an ex-slave reminded skeptics, "must be seen and felt to be fully understood." A slave woman who had been taken from her children in Virginia and sent to the Southwest "cried many a night about it; and went 'bout mazin' sorry-like all day, a wishing I was dead and buried!" Sometimes the "derangement" or sudden rebelliousness of a slave mother was attributed to "grief at being separated from her children." Often mothers fought desperately to prevent traders from carrying off their children, and often husbands and wives struggled against separation when they were torn apart.[27]

But the most eloquent evidence of the affection and devotion that bound many slave families together appeared in the advertisements for fugitives. A Virginian sought a runaway whose wife had been transported to Mississippi, "and I understand from some of my servants, that he had been speaking of following her." A Maryland master was convinced that a female fugitive would attempt to get back to Georgia "where she came from, and left her husband and two children." Even when fugitives hoped to reach the free states, husbands often took their wives and parents their children, though this obviously lessened their chance of a successful escape. Clearly, to many bondsmen the fellowship of the family, in spite of its instability, was exceedingly important.

Some of the problems that troubled slave families, of course, had nothing to do with slavery—they were the tragically human problems which have ever disturbed marital tranquility. One such domestic dilemma involved a slave whose wife did not return his devotion. "He says he loves his wife and does not want to leave her," noted the master. "She says she does not love him and wont live with him. Yet he says he thinks he can over come her scruples and live happily with her."[28] For this slavery was not the cause nor freedom the cure.

But other kinds of family tragedies were uniquely a part of life in bondage. A poignant example was the scene that transpired when an overseer tied and whipped a slave mother in the presence of her children. The frightened children pelted the overseer with stones, and one of them ran up and bit him in the leg. During the ruction the cries of the mother were mingled with the screams of the children, *"Let my mammy go—let my mammy go."*[29]

Notes

1. Catterall (ed.), *Judicial Cases,* II, pp. 522–23; Douglass, *My Bondage,* p. 269; Drew, *The Refugee,* p. 199.

2. Harrison, *Gospel Among the Slaves,* p. 102; Josiah Henson, *Father Henson's Story of His Own Life* (Boston, 1858), p. 107; Douglass, *My Bondage,* p. 176.

3. Allen Brown to Hamilton Brown, December 7, 1834, Hamilton Brown Papers; Kemble, *Journal,* pp. 165–66.

4. Henson, *Story,* pp. 21–23.

5. *Southern Cultivator,* XII (1854), p. 206; Drew, *The Refugee,* p. 45; Kemble, *Journal,* p. 239; Douglass, *My Bondage,* pp. 69–72, 74–75, 129–32.

6. *Southern Cultivator,* IX (1851), p. 85; Northup, *Twelve Years a Slave,* pp. 186–87; Ingraham (ed.), *Sunny South,* pp. 86–87; Kemble, *Journal,* p. 84; Davis (ed.), *Diary of Bennett H. Barrow,* p. 191.

7. Northup, *Twelve Years a Slave,* pp. 188–89.

8. C. P. Phelps to Ebenezer Pettigrew, March 2, 1831, Pettigrew Papers; Lyell, *Second Visit,* I, p. 360; John B. Clarkson to Phanor Prudhomme, February 3, 1854, Phanor Prudhomme Papers.

9. Thompson, *Life of John Thompson,* pp. 24–25; Ingraham (ed.), *Sunny South,* p. 35; Steward, *Twenty-Two Years a Slave,* pp. 30–32.

10. Bancroft, *Slave-Trading,* pp. 153–55.

11. Douglass, *My Bondage,* p. 118; Steward, *Twenty-Two Years a Slave,* p. 101; [Ingraham], *South-West,* II, p. 248; Sitterson, *Sugar Country,* p. 91.

12. Lyell, *Travels,* I, pp. 182–83.

13. Kemble, *Journal,* pp. 193–94.

14. J. B. Grace to Charles Tait, April 25, 1835, Charles Tait and Family Papers.

15. *De Bow's Review,* XXII (1857), pp. 376–79; Plantation Rules in William Erwin Ms. Diary and Account Book; *Southern Agriculturalist,* IV (1831), p. 351.

16. Sitterson, *Sugar Country,* p. 58; Hammond Plantation Manual; Hammond Diary, entry for December 26, 1840.

17. Marston Diary, entry for June 12, 1829.

18. Johnson, *Sea Islands,* pp. 135, 137–38; *id., Ante-Bellum North Carolina,* p. 535.

19. Wilmington (N.C.) *Journal,* May 2, 1851; Coleman, *Slavery Times in Kentucky,* pp. 58–59; Massie Slave Book, entry for September 24, 1847.

20. Charleston *Courier,* August 5, 1857.

21. Smedes, *Memorials,* p. 48; Olmsted, *Seaboard,* pp. 556–57; Charleston *Courier,* September 15, 1857.

22. Massie Slave Book; Kemble, *Journal,* p. 95.

23. Lyell, *Travels,* I, p. 184.

24. Brown, *Narrative,* p. 13; *De Bow's Review,* X (1851), p. 623; Olmsted, *Back Country,* pp. 89, 113, 154; Massie Slave Book; Catterall (ed.), *Judicial Cases,* II, pp. 544–45; III, p. 363.

25. Avery O. Craven, "Poor Whites and Negroes in the Ante-Bellum South," *Journal of Negro History,* XV (1930), pp. 17–18; Douglass, *My Bondage,* p. 86.

26. *De Bow's Review,* XVII (1854), pp. 425–26; Abbeville District, South Carolina, Judge of Probate Decree Book, 1839–1858, May term, 1841; Catterall (ed.), *Judicial Cases,* II, p. 314.

27. Henson, *Story,* pp. 10–11; Ingraham (ed.), *Sunny South,* p. 439; Catterall (ed.), *Judicial Cases,* I, p. 298; III, p. 632; V, pp. 229–30; Loguen, *Narrative,* pp. 112–20; Andrews, *Slavery and the Domestic Slave Trade,* pp. 128–33.

28. Gustavus A. Henry to his wife, December 11, 1839, Henry Papers.

29. Douglass, *My Bondage,* pp. 92–95.

Marvin Harris
THE MYTH OF THE FRIENDLY MASTER

The argument . . . has been that differences in race relations within Latin America are at root a matter of the labor systems in which the respective subordinate and superordinate groups became enmeshed. I have already attempted to show how a number of cultural traits and institutions which were permitted to survive, or were deliberately encouraged under one system, were discouraged or suppressed in the other. It remains to be shown how the specific combinations of features which characterize lowland race relations more narrowly construed can be accounted for by the same set of principles.

At present, probably the majority of American scholars who have found a moment to ponder the peculiar aspects of the Brazilian interracial "paradise" are devoted to an opposite belief. What could be more obvious than the inadequacy of a materialist explanation of the Brazilian pattern? How can plantation slavery be made to explain anything about the lack of interracial hostility in Brazil? Was it not a plantation system in the United States South which bred a condition contrary in every detail to that of Brazil?

The current vogue of opinion about this contrast derives in large measure from the work of Frank Tannenbaum, a noted United States historian, and Gilberto Freyre, Brazil's best known sociologist. The theories of these influential scholars overlap at many points. It is their contention that the laws, values, religious precepts and personalities of the English colonists differed from those of the Iberian colonists. These initial psychological and ideological differences were sufficient to overcome whatever tendency the plantation system may have exerted toward parallel rather than divergent evolution.

Freyre's theories, originally proposed in his classic study of Brazilian plantation life, *Casa grande e senzala,* have remained virtually unchanged for over thirty years. What most impresses Freyre about Brazilian slavery is the alleged easy-going, humanized relations between master and slave, especially between master and female slave. Slaves, while subject to certain disabilities and although sometimes cruelly treated, frequently came to play an emotionally significant role in the intimate life of their white owners. A high rate of miscegenation was one of the hallmarks of this empathy between the races. The Portuguese not only took Negro and mulatto women as mistresses and concubines, but they sometimes spurned

REPRINTED FROM *Patterns of Race in the Americas* (NEW YORK: WALKER & CO., 1964) BY PERMISSION OF THE AUTHOR AND THE PUBLISHER.

their white wives in order to enjoy the favors of duskier beauties. Behind these favorable omens, visible from the very first days of contact, was a fundamental fact of national character, namely, the Portuguese had no color prejudice. On the contrary, their long experience under Moorish tutelage is said to have prepared them to regard people of darker hue as equals, if not superiors:

> The singular predisposition of the Portuguese to the hybrid, slave-exploiting colonization of the tropics is to be explained in large part by the ethnic or, better, the cultural past of a people existing indeterminately between Europe and Africa and belonging uncompromisingly to neither one nor the other of the two continents.[1]

Other colonizers were not as successful as the Portuguese because their libidos were more conservative. Especially poorly endowed sexually were the "Anglo-Saxon Protestants."

> The truth is that in Brazil, contrary to what is to be observed in other American countries and in those parts of Africa that have been recently colonized by Europeans, the primitive culture—the Amerindian as well as the African—has not been isolated into hard, dry indigestible lumps . . . Neither did the social relations between the two races, the conquering and the indigenous one, ever reach that point of sharp antipathy or hatred, the grating sound of which reaches our ears from all the countries that have been colonized by Anglo-Saxon Protestants. The friction here (in Brazil) was smoothed by the lubricating oil of a deep-going miscegenation . . .[2]

The next and fatal step in this line of reasoning is to assert that the special psychological equipment of the Portuguese, not only in Brazil but everywhere in "The World the Portuguese Created,"[3] yields hybrids and interracial harmony. In 1952, after a tour of Portuguese colonies as an honored guest of the Salazar government, Freyre declared that the Portuguese were surrounded in the Orient, America and Africa with half-caste "luso-populations" and "a sympathy on the part of the native which contrasts with the veiled or open hatred directed toward the other Europeans."[4]

How Freyre could have been hoodwinked into finding resemblances between race relations in Angola and Mozambique and Brazil is hard to imagine. My own findings, based on a year of field work in Mozambique, have since been supported by the field and library research of James Duffy.[5] If any reasonable doubts remained about the falsity of Freyre's luso-tropical theory, tragic events in Angola should by now have swept them away. The fact is that the Portuguese are responsible for setting off the bloodiest of all of the recent engagements between whites and Negroes in Africa (including the Mau Mau). And the Portuguese, alone of all the former African colonial powers, now stand shoulder to shoulder with the citizens of that incorrigible citadel of white supremacy, the Republic of South Africa, baited and damned from Zanzibar to Lagos.

It is true that the Portuguese *in Portugal* tend to be rather neutral on the subject of color differences, if they ever think about such things at all. But this datum can only be significant to those who believe that discrimination is caused by prejudice, when the true relationship is quite the opposite. When the innocent Portuguese emigrants get to Africa, they find that legally, economically and socially, white men can take advantage of black men, and it doesn't take long for them to join in the act. Within a year after his arrival, the Portuguese learns that blacks are inferior to whites, that the Africans have to be kept in their place, and that they are indolent by nature and have to be forced to work. What we call prejudices are merely the rationalizations which we acquire in order to prove to ourselves that the human beings whom we harm are not worthy of better treatment.

Actually the whole issue of the alleged lack of racial or color prejudice among the Portuguese (and by extension among the Spanish as well) is totally irrelevant to the main question. If, as asserted, the Iberians initially lacked any color prejudice, what light does this shed upon the Brazilian and other Latin American lowland interracial systems? The distinguishing feature of these systems is not that whites have no color prejudices. On the contrary, color prejudice as we have seen is a conspicuous and regular feature in all the plantation areas. The parts of the system which need explaining are the absence of a descent rule; the absence of distinct socially significant racial groups; and the ambiguity of racial identity. In Portuguese Africa none of these features are present. The state rules on who is a native and who is a white and the condition of being a native is hereditary:

> Individuals of the Negro race or their descendants who were born or habitually reside in the said Provinces and who do not yet possess the learning and the social and individual habits presupposed for the integral application of the public and private law of Portuguese citizens are considered to be 'natives.'[6]

As for miscegenation, the supposedly color-blind Portuguese libido had managed by 1950 to produce slightly more than 50,000 officially recognized mixed types in an African population of 10 million after 400 years of contact.[7] This record should be compared with the product of the monochromatic libidos of the Dutch invaders of South Africa—in Freyre's terms Anglo-Saxon Protestants to the hilt—a million and a half official hybrids (coloureds).[8] It is time that grown men stopped talking about racially prejudiced sexuality. In general, when human beings have the power, the opportunity and the need, they will mate with members of the opposite sex regardless of color or the identity of grandfather. Whenever free breeding in human population is restricted, it is because a larger system of social relations is menaced by such freedom.

This is one of the points about which Tannenbaum and Freyre disagree. Tannenbaum quite correctly observes that "the process of miscege-

nation was part of the system of slavery, and not just of Brazilian slavery.
. . . The dynamics of race contact and sex interests were stronger than
prejudice. . . . This same mingling of the races and classes occurred in the
United States. The record is replete with the occurrence, in spite of law,
doctrine, and belief. Every traveler in the South before the Civil War
comments on the widespread miscegenation. . . ."[9] But it should also be
pointed out that there is no concrete evidence to indicate that the rank and
file of English colonists were initially any more or less prejudiced than the
Latins. It is true that the English colonists very early enacted laws intended
to prevent marriage between white women and Negro men and between
white men and Negro women. Far from indicating a heritage of anti-Negro
prejudices, however, these laws confirm the presence of strong attraction
between the males and females of both races. The need for legal restriction
certainly suggests that miscegenation was not at all odious to many of the
English colonists.

The idea of assigning differential statuses to white indentured servants
and Negro workers was definitely not a significant part of the ideological
baggage brought over by the earliest colonists, at least not to an extent
demonstrably greater than among the Latin colonists. It is true, as Carl
Degler has shown, that the differentiation between white indentured servants and Negro indentured servants had become conspicuous before the
middle of the seventeenth century even though the legal formulation was
not completed until the end of the century. But who would want to suggest
that there was absolutely no prejudice against the Negroes immediately
after contact? Ethnocentrism is a universal feature of inter-group relations
and obviously both the English and the Iberians were prejudiced against
foreigners, white and black. The facts of life in the New World were such,
however, that Negroes, being the most defenseless of all the immigrant
groups, were discriminated against and exploited more than any others.
Thus the Negroes were not enslaved because the British colonists specifically despised dark-skinned people and regarded them alone as properly
suited to slavery; the Negroes came to be the object of the virulent prejudices because they and they alone could be enslaved. Judging from the very
nasty treatment suffered by white indentured servants, it was obviously not
sentiment which prevented the Virginia planters from enslaving their fellow
Englishmen. They undoubtedly would have done so had they been able to
get away with it. But such a policy was out of the question as long as there
was a King and a Parliament in England.

The absence of preconceived notions about what ought to be the
treatment of enslaved peoples forms a central theme in Tannenbaum's
explanation of United States race relations. According to Tannenbaum,
since the English had gotten rid of slavery long before the Discovery, they
had no body of laws or traditions which regulated and humanized the
slave status. Why this legal lacuna should have been significant for the
course run by slavery in the United States is quite obscure. Even Degler,
who accepts the Freyre-Tannenbaum approach, points out that it was

"possible for almost any kind of status to be worked out."[10] One might reasonably conclude that the first settlers were not overly concerned with race differences, and that they might have remained that way (as many Englishmen have) had they not been brought into contact with Negroes under conditions wholly dictated by the implacable demands of a noxious and "peculiar" institution.

Let us turn now to the main substance of Tannenbaum's theory. Tannenbaum correctly believes that the critical difference between race relations in the United States and in Latin America resides in the physical and psychological (he says "moral") separation of the Negro from the rest of society. "In spite of his adaptability, his willingness, and his competence, in spite of his complete identification with the *mores* of the United States, he is excluded and denied. . . ." Also, quite correctly, Tannenbaum stresses the critical role of the free Negro and mulatto in Latin America. Manumission appears to have been much more common, and the position of the freed man was much more secure than elsewhere. Free Negroes and mulattoes quickly came to outnumber the slaves. However, according to Tannenbaum, this phenomenon came about because the slave was endowed with "a moral personality before emancipation . . . which . . . made the transition from slavery to freedom easy and his incorporation into the free community natural."[11] The Negro and mulatto were never sharply cut off from the rest of society because the Latin slave was never cut off from the rest of humanity. This was because slavery in southern Europe and Latin America was embedded in a legal, ethical, moral and religious matrix which conspired to preserve the slave's individual integrity as the possessor of an immortal human soul. The "definition" of the slave as merely an unfortunate human being, primarily according to state and canonical code, is given most weight:

> For if one thing stands out clearly from the study of slavery, it is that the definition of man as a moral being proved the most important influence both in the treatment of the slave and in the final abolition of slavery.[12]

Note that it is not merely being claimed that there was a critical difference between Latin American and United States race relations during and after slavery, but that the very institution of slavery itself was one thing in the United States and the British West Indies and another thing in Latin America:

> There were briefly speaking, three slave systems in the Western Hemisphere. The British, American, Dutch, and Danish were at one extreme, and the Spanish and Portuguese at the other. In between these two fell the French. . . . If one were forced to arrange these systems of slavery in order of severity, the Dutch would seem to stand as the harshest, the Portuguese as the mildest, and the French in between. . . .[13]

The contention that the condition of the average slave in the English colonies was worse than that of the average slave in the Latin colonies obscures the main task which confronts us, which is to explain why the treatment of the free mulatto and free Negro were and are so different. To try to explain why the slaves were treated better in Latin America than in the United States is a waste of time, for there is no conceivable way in which we can now be certain that they were indeed treated better in one place than the other. It is true that a large number of travelers can be cited, especially from the nineteenth century, who were convinced that the slaves were happier under Spanish and Portuguese masters than under United States masters. But there was plenty of dissenting opinion. Tannenbaum makes no provision for the fact that the English planters had what we would today call a very bad press, since thousands of intellectuals among their own countrymen were in the vanguard of the abolitionist movement. The West Indian and Southern planters, of course, were in total disagreement with those who preferred slavery under foreign masters. Actually all of the distinctions between the Anglo-American and Latin slave systems which Tannenbaum proposes were already the subject of debate at the beginning of the eighteenth century between Anglo-American abolitionists and Anglo-American planters. For example, in 1827, the Jamaican planter Alexander Barclay responded to the English critics of his island's slave system as follows:

> According to Mr. Stephen [author of *Slavery of the British West India Colonies*] there exists among his countrymen in the West Indies, an universal feeling of hatred and contempt of the Negroes. . . . It is by this assumed hatred and contempt, that he strives to give probability to the most incredible charges of cruelty and oppression; and indeed, in many cases, this alleged feeling of aversion and abhorrence on the part of the whites, is the sole ground for supposing that the charges should be made, and the sole proof of them. Such things must have happened, because the colonists hate the Negroes. Now, I most solemnly affirm, not only that I am unconscious of any such surely unnatural feelings having place in my own breast, but that I have never seen proof of its existence in the breasts of others.[14]

All slave-owners of whatever nationality always seem to have been convinced that "their" slaves were the happiest of earthly beings. Barclay claims that the Jamaican slaves celebrated the cane harvest with an interracial dance:

> In the evening, they assemble in their master's or manager's house, and, as a matter of course, take possession of the largest room, bringing with them a fiddle and tambourine. Here all authority and all distinction of colour ceases; black and white, overseer and book-keeper, mingle together in the dance.[15]

At Christmas time the same thing happens. The slaves

> . . . proceed to the neighboring plantation villages, and always visit the master's or manager's house, into which they enter without ceremony, and where they are joined by the white people in a dance.[16]

Concludes Barclay:

> All is life and joy, and certainly it is one of the most pleasing sights that can be imagined.[17]

In the United States, equally rapturous descriptions of the slave's lot were a conspicuous part of the ideological war between North and South. Many planters felt that their slaves were better off than the mass of Northern whites, and Southern poets did not hesitate to cap their comparisons of free and slave labor with panegyrics

> . . . on the happy life of the slave, with all his needs provided, working happily in the fields by day, enjoying the warm society of his family in the cabin at night, idling through life in "the summer shade, the winter sun," and without fear of the poorhouse at its close . . . until we finally find the slave "luxuriating" in a "lotus-bearing paradise."[18]

If one were so inclined by lack of an understanding of the nature of sociological evidence, it would not be difficult to paint a picture in which the position of the Anglo-American slave system was promoted from last to first place. Freyre himself provides enough material on cruelty in the Brazilian plantations to fill at least a corner in a chamber of horrors:

> And how, in truth, are the hearts of us Brazilians to acquire the social virtues if from the moment we open our eyes we see about us the cruel distinction between master and slave, and behold the former, at the slightest provocation or sometimes out of mere whim, mercilessly rending the flesh of our own kind with lashes?[19]
>
> There are not two or three but many instances of the cruelties of the ladies of the big house toward their helpless blacks. There are tales of *sinhámoças* who had the eyes of pretty *mucamas* gouged out and then had them served to their husband for dessert, in a jelly-dish, floating in blood that was still fresh. . . . There were others who kicked out the teeth of their women slaves with their boots, or who had their breasts cut off, their nails drawn, or their faces and ears burned.[20]

Another Brazilian observer, Arthur Ramos, goes even further:

> During the period of slavery, suppression and punishment prevented almost any spontaneous activity. . . . The number of instruments of torture employed was numerous and profoundly odious. . . . There was the *tronco*, of wood or of iron, an instrument which held the slave fast at the ankles and in the grip of which he was often kept for days on end; the *libambo* which gripped the unfortunate victim fast at the neck; the *algemas* and the *anjinhos*, which held the hands tightly, crushing the thumbs. . . . Some plantation owners of more perverted inclinations used the so-called *novenas* and *trezenas*. . . . The Negroes tied face down on the ground, were beaten with the rawhide whip on from nine to thirteen consecutive nights. . . .[21]

The testimony of the travelers, poets, planters, abolitionists and scholars in this matter, however, is worthless. Better to dispute the number of angels on a pinhead than to argue that one country's slavery is superior to another's. The slaves, wherever they were, didn't like it; they killed themselves and they killed their masters; over and over again they risked being torn apart by hounds and the most despicable tortures in order to escape the life to which they were condemned. It is a well known fact that Brazil was second to none in the number of its fugitive slaves and its slave revolts. In the seventeenth century one successful group held out in the famous *quilombo* of Palmares for sixty-seven years and in the nineteenth century scarcely a year went by without an actual or intended revolt.[22]

In a recent book, the historian Stanley M. Elkins attempts to save Tannenbaum's theory by admitting that slavery in the United States (at least by 1850) "in a 'physical' sense was in general, probably, quite mild" and that there were very "severe" sides to the Spanish and Portuguese systems.[23] Elkins assures us, however, that even if slavery had been milder here than anywhere else in the Western Hemisphere, "it would still be missing the point to make the comparison in terms of physical comfort. In one case we would be dealing with cruelty of man to man, and, in the other, with the care, maintenance, and indulgence of men toward creatures who were legally and morally *not* men—not in the sense that Christendom had traditionally defined man's nature."[24] It is devoutly to be hoped that Elkins shall never be able to test his exquisite sense of equity by experiencing first thirty lashes dealt out by someone who calls him a black man and then a second thirty from someone who calls him a black devil. But if there be such talents as Elkins' among us, we had better take a closer look at the proposition that the Negro was regarded as a human being by the Latin colonists but not by the Anglo-Saxons. The principal source of evidence for this resides in the law codes by which the respective slave systems were theoretically regulated. Admittedly, these codes do show a considerable difference of legal opinion as to the definition of a slave. The Spanish and Portuguese codes were essentially continuations of medieval regulations stretching back ultimately to Roman law. The British and American colonial codes were the original creations of the New World planter class, developed first in the West Indies (Barbados) and then copied throughout the South.[25] Although the Constitution of the United States said that slaves were persons, state laws said they were chattels—mere property. "Slaveholders, legislators, and judges were forever trying to make property out of them . . . They simply did not regard them as human beings."[26] On the other hand, Spanish and Portuguese slave laws did, as Tannenbaum claims, specifically preserve the human identity of the slave: "The distinction between slavery and freedom is a product of accident and misfortune, and the free man might have been a slave."[27] From this there flowed a number of rights, of which Fernando Ortiz identifies four as most significant: (1) the right to marry freely; (2) the right to seek out another master if any were too severe; (3) the right of owning property; and (4) the right to buy freedom.[28] Tannenbaum shows how all of the U. S. slave states denied these rights. He goes further and shows how the U. S. slaves were virtually left without legal remedy for harms committed upon them, and he emphasizes the casual fines which protected the life of a slave under the early laws,[29] and the total lack of legal recognition given to the slave's affinal or consanguine family. Indeed, for every favorable section in the Spanish law, both Elkins and Tannenbaum readily find an unfavorable section in the Anglo-Saxon codes.

What the laws of the Spanish and Portuguese kings had to do with the attitudes and values of the Spanish and Portuguese planters, however, baffles one's imagination. The Crown could publish all the laws it wanted, but in the lowlands, sugar was king. If there were any Portuguese or Spanish planters who were aware of their legal obligations toward the slaves, it would require systematic misreading of colonialism, past and present, to suppose that these laws psychologically represented anything more than the flatus of a pack of ill-informed Colonel Blimps who didn't even know what a proper cane field looked like. Ortiz leaves no room for doubt in the case of Cuba. Yes, the slave had legal rights, "But these rights were not viable . . . if they contrast with the barbaric laws of the French and above all, of the English colonies, it was no less certain that all of these rights were illusory, especially in earlier times. . . ." Sanctity of the family? "Man and wife were permanently separated, sold in separate places, and separated from their children."[30] "How many times was a son sold by his father!" and "Pregnant or nursing slaves were sold with or without their actual or future offspring."[31] Protection of the law? "The sugar and coffee plantations were in fact feudal domains where the only authority recognized was that of the master. . . . Could the Negroes hope in these circumstances to change masters? The rawhide would quiet their voices. . . ." Rights to property? "From what I have said in relation to the work of the rural slave, to speak of his right to hold property and to buy freedom, is futile. . . ." "But I repeat, the plantation slave was treated like a beast, like a being to whom human character was denied. . . ."[32]

Tannenbaum makes much of the fact that there was no set of ancient slave laws to which the Anglo-Saxon planters or the slaves could turn for guidance. He prominently displays the meager penalties attached to murder of slaves as examples of their sub-human status in the eyes of the Anglo-Saxon colonists. But Ortiz informs us that "it was not until 1842 that there was any specific legal regulation of the form of punishment which a Cuban master could give his slave."[33] Actually it turns out that "the state did not concern itself with the limitation of the arbitrary power of the master in relation to the punishment of his slave until after the abolition of slavery [1880]."[34]

In Brazil, as everywhere in the colonial world, law and reality bore an equally small resemblance to each other. Stanley Stein's recent historical study of slavery in the county of Vassouras during the last century yields a picture almost totally at variance with that drawn by Gilberto Freyre for the earlier plantations. The Vassouras planters went about their business, methodically buying, working, beating and selling their slaves, in whatever fashion yielded the most coffee with the least expense. The master's will was supreme. "It was difficult to apply legal restraints to the planter's use of the lash."[35]

> Typical is an eyewitness account of a beating told by an ex-slave. On order from the master, two drivers bound and beat a slave while the slave folk stood in line, free folk watching from further back. The slave died that night and his corpse, dumped into a wicker basket, was borne by night to the slave cemetery of the plantation and dropped into a hastily dug grave. *"Slaves could not complain to the police, only another fazendeiro* [master] *could do that,"* explained the eyewitness.[36] [Italics are mine.]

If Stein's picture of nineteenth-century Vassouras is accurate—and it is the most carefully documented study of its kind in existence—then the following recent pronouncement from Charles Boxer will have to be accepted minus the time restriction:

> The common belief that the Brazilian was an exceptionally kind master is applicable only to the 19th century under the Empire, and it is contradicted for the colonial period by the testimony of numerous reliable eyewitnesses from Vieira to Vilhena, to say nothing of the official correspondence between the colonial authorities and the Crown.[37]

Of special interest in Boxer's refutation of the myth of the friendly master is the evidence which shows that Brazilian planters and miners did not accept the legal decisions which awarded human souls and human personalities to the slaves. The Brazilian slave owners were convinced that Negroes were descended from Cain, black and "therefore not people like ourselves." Making due allowance for exceptions and the special circumstances of household slaves, Boxer concludes that "it remains true that by and large colonial Brazil was indeed a 'hell for blacks.' "[38]

Notes

1. Freyre 1956:4.
2. *Ibid.*:181–182.
3. Freyre 1940.
4. Freyre 1952:39.
5. Harris 1958; 1959; Duffy 1962; 1959. "Colonial authorities speak of Portugal's civilizing mission, but the realities of life for the Africans in the Colonies are grim. They are subject to an abusive contract labor system. . . . The standard of wages is among the lowest in Africa. . . . Social services for Africans are either minimal or nonexistent. *And, perhaps, most important of all, Africans have become*

the object of a growing racial prejudice created by the rapid influx of white settlers." (Duffy 1961:90. Italics are mine.)

6. Estatuto Indigena, May 1954, quoted in Harris 1958:7.

7. Jack 1960:7; *Recenseamento Geral,* 1953, Província de Mocambique, p. xxxi.

8. Vilakazi 1955:313.

9. Tannenbaum 1947:121–123.

10. Degler 1960:51. This article is an attack on Handlin and Handlin's (1950) theory that the differentiation between Negro and white indentured servants developed gradually during the seventeenth century and that initially there was little specifically anti-Negro discrimination or prejudice. Degler contends that "the status of the Negro in the English colonies was worked out within a framework of discrimination; that from the outset, as far as the available evidence tells us, the Negro was treated as an inferior to the white man, servant or free" (52). Degler suffers from the illusion that early examples of discriminatory treatment of Negroes in the English Colonies are relevant to the Tannenbaum (-Freyre) explanation of Latin American race relations. Somehow or other Degler has received the impression that in Latin America there was not an equally early display of discrimination. But of course, in both cases, slavery was reserved for Negroes, Indians and half-castes. Neither English nor Iberian whites were ever enslaved in the New World; surely this is an instance of discriminatory treatment. Degler explicitly accepts the Tannenbaum (-Freyre) point of view, despite the fact that his article really amounts to a denial of the significance of ideological and psychological factors in the explanation of race relations. The early *de facto* enslavement of Negroes, even when there was no body of law sanctioning slavery, is certainly a rather negative comment on Tannenbaum's use of law as evidence of behavior (see below). To conclude that slavery ". . . was molded by the early colonists' discrimination against the outlander" (66) is to confirm that prejudice followed discrimination, whereas it is essential for the Tannenbaum (-Freyre) point of view that the causality be reversed.

11. Tannenbaum 1947:42; 100.

12. *Ibid.:*vii.

13. *Ibid.:* note p. 65.

14. Barclay 1827:xi-xii.

15. *Ibid.:* 10.

16. *Ibid.:*11.

17. *Ibid.*

18. Mandel 1955:99.

19. Freyre 1956:392, quoting Lopes Gomes.

20. *Ibid.:*351.

21. Ramos 1939:34-35.

22. *Ibid.:*43 ff.

23. Elkins 1959:78.

24. *Ibid.*

25. Dumond 1961:8.

26. *Ibid.:*251.

27. Tannenbaum 1947: 46.

28. Ortiz 1916:303.

29. Actually, quite severe laws regulating punishment of the slaves were eventually passed by the slave states. (Cf. Stampp 1956:217-221.)

30. Ortiz 1916:303-304.

31. *Ibid.:*173.

32. *Ibid.:*303-304.

33. *Ibid.:*265.

34. *Ibid.:*267.

35. Stein 1957:135.

36. *Ibid.:*136.

37. Boxer 1962:173.

38. Boxer 1963:114.

References

BARCLAY, ALEXANDER. *A Practical View of the Present State of Slavery in the West Indies.* London: Smith, Elder & Co., 1827.

BOXER, CHARLES. *The Golden Age of Brazil.* Berkeley: University of California Press, 1962.

———— *Race Relations in the Portuguese Colonial Empire, 1425–1825.* Oxford: Clarendon Press, 1963.

DEGLER, CARL. "Slavery and the Genesis of American Race Prejudice," *Comparative Studies in Society and History,* Vol. 2 (1960).

DUFFY, JAMES. *Portuguese Africa.* Cambridge: Harvard University Press, 1959.

———— *Portugal in Africa.* Cambridge: Harvard University Press, 1962.

DUMOND, DWIGHT LOWELL. *Antislavery.* Ann Arbor: University of Michigan Press, 1961.

ELKINS, STANLEY M. *Slavery.* Chicago: University of Chicago Press, 1959.

FREYRE, GILBERTO. *Os Mundo que o português criou.* Rio de Janeiro: J. Olympio, 1940.

———— *Um brasileiro em terras portuguêsas.* Lisbon: Livros do Brasil, 1952.

———— *The Masters and the Slaves.* New York: Alfred A. Knopf, 1956.

HARRIS, MARVIN. *Portugal's African "Wards."* New York: American Committee on Africa, 1958.

———— "Labour Emigration Among the Mozambique Thonga," *Africa,* Vol. 19 (1959).

JACK, HOMER. *Angola: Repression and Revolt in Portuguese Africa.* New York: American Committee on Africa, 1960.

MANDEL, BERNARD. *Labor: Slave and Free.* New York: Associated Authors, 1955.

ORTIZ, FERNANDO. *Los Negros Esclavos.* Havana, 1916.

RAMOS, ARTURO. *The Negro in Brazil.* Washington: Associated Publishers, 1939.

STAMPP, KENNETH. *The Peculiar Institution.* New York: Alfred A. Knopf, 1956.

STEIN, STANLEY. *Vassouras.* Cambridge: Harvard University Press, 1957.

TANNENBAUM, FRANK. *Slave and Citizen.* New York: Alfred A. Knopf, 1947.

VILAKAZI, ABSOLOM. "Race Relations in South Africa," in Andrew Lind (ed.), *Race Relations in World Perspective.* Honolulu: University of Hawaii Press, 1955.

Mary Reckord

THE JAMAICA SLAVE
REBELLION OF 1831

On Tuesday, the 27th of December, 1831, a fire on Kensington estate in St. James, one of the most important sugar growing parishes in Jamaica, marked the outbreak of a slave rebellion which swept the western parishes of the island. The rebellion was precipitated by circumstances which comparison with negro slave rebellions in the United States suggests were classic ingredients for revolt: political excitement stirred by rumours of emancipation, economic stress, a revolutionary philosophy circulating among the slaves and the presence of a group of whites whom the slaves could identify as their allies.[1] The Jamaican rebellion, however, was characterized by the fact that the missions were the source of the slaves' philosophy and the missionaries themselves were cast in the role of the slaves' allies. Further, a network of independent religious meetings which had developed round the mission churches served the slaves as a ready made political organization and thus supplied an element for which there is no parallel in American slave revolts.

Violent protest against slavery in the form of riot or rebellion had been endemic in eighteenth-century Jamaica; the outbreaks occurred on average every five years, and two such efforts, the Maroon wars of 1738 and 1795, secured freedom for small communities of ex-slaves in the mountain districts. The abolition of the slave trade in 1808 and the stabilization of areas of settlement produced more settled conditions; the Negro villages were no longer dominated by immigrant Africans and a creole slave society emerged. It was not until the 1820s, under the influence of the anti-slavery agitation in England, that further disturbances took place. The most important was in Demerara in 1823; in Jamaica itself slave conspiracies were discovered in 1823 and 1824.

The comparative quiescence of the slaves made no substantial difference to the administration of the slave system. The white ruling class, a dwindling minority of some 30,000 in a slave population ten times greater, disciplined and degraded their slaves in the traditional manner. The exclusion of slaves as witnesses in the courts, for example, underlined the assumption that they were creatures of inferior intelligence. Family life was discouraged to demonstrate the intrinsically animal nature of the Negro. The whip as an instrument of punishment and a badge of authority symbolized the whole tenor of slavery, and cases of excessively brutal

REPRINTED FROM *Past and Present, a Journal of Historical Studies,* NUMBER 40, JULY, 1968, BY PERMISSION OF THE SOCIETY AND THE AUTHOR. WORLD COPYRIGHT: THE PAST AND PRESENT SOCIETY, CORPUS CHRISTI COLLEGE, OXFORD.

punishments came to the attention of the imperial government as long as the system lasted. The imperial government's programme for the reform of slavery, suggested in 1823, touched on all these features of the system and won no effective support in the island.[2]

In such a society christian missions to the slaves were inevitably regarded as a dangerous innovation and the missionaries themselves as agents of Wilberforce. Missions were only established in the island through the good offices of individual whites, and expanded under the indirect auspices of the imperial government which promoted the activity of the established Anglican church among the slaves as part of the amelioration programme. The missionaries, mindful of their position, geared their teaching to promote obedience, but this did not prevent the slaves from seeing in the doctrine of spiritual equality sanctions for political discontent. It is significant, therefore, that the rebellion took place in the western parishes[3] where the missions were most numerous and independent religious meetings proliferated. The Baptists were particularly influential in St. James where Thomas Burchell, a popular and enterprising missionary, had been in charge of the Montego Bay station from its foundation in 1824 and had built up a number of flourishing out-stations. The Wesleyans were also represented at Montego Bay and Lucea and the Moravians were active in the parishes of Manchester, St. Elizabeth and Westmoreland. The missions played a rôle in the slave rebellion in some respects analogous to that of the Methodist churches in working-class movements in England. In England, also, areas of intense political activity coincided with areas of intense religious activity: for example, the Wesleyan church and the Chartist movement flourished simultaneously in the West Riding of Yorkshire.[4] The ideal of christian obedience and rewards in heaven proved unsatisfactory to chattel-slave and wage-slave alike. The missions therefore, unknown to the missionaries, provided both inspiration and—indirectly—organization for a rebellion which exceeded in scale and duration any American slave enterprise.

The current of political excitement which sparked off the rebellion derived from the campaign for the immediate abolition of slavery launched in the House of Commons in April 1831. It was obvious to the Colonial Office that this campaign was likely to create disturbances in the slave colonies and, in June 1831, the precaution was taken of supplying the West Indian governors with a royal proclamation to quiet signs of unrest. But the white population in Jamaica showed no such prescience. Intent only on expressing their unqualified opposition to abolition, they exacerbated the impact of the campaign by holding a series of public protest meetings throughout the island between July and November. Inflammatory speeches were made and duly published in the newspapers. Armed revolt was advocated and the possibility of securing assistance from the United States was openly discussed.[5] Plans were made to set up a new governing body, independent of the crown, consisting of delegates from the parish meetings to meet concurrently with the Assembly in November 1831. This scheme had no immediate results,[6] but the Assembly itself, meeting in November, marked its unrelenting opposition to any mitigation of the slave system by refusing, almost unanimously, to discuss a proposal to abolish flogging for women, a reform introduced in the Crown colonies in 1824. The governor, the Earl of Belmore, commented that the parish meetings seemed calculated "to disturb the minds of the slaves",[7] but he made no effort to restrain them and the royal proclamation was not published until December by which time the rebellion had virtually begun.

The slaves were therefore exposed to the full effect of these events. Comparatively few were able to understand the precise nature of events in England and the colonists' response, but the gist of the political situation was translated into easily remembered and amended anecdote, circulated endlessly among the population. A well-known St. James magistrate and attorney, James Grignon, was said to have told his fellow whites: "The king is going to give black people free: but he hopes that all his friends will be of his mind and spill our blood first". It was rumoured that the whites in the House of Assembly were planning to keep the women and children in slavery, while they took out the men and shot them like pigeons. Reports of the intentions of the "high buckra" were confirmed by the conduct of their underlings. Baptist members told Knibb: "When busha [i.e., overseer] and book-keeper flog us they say we are going to be free and before it comes they will get it out of us".[8] The missionaries reported in July from Kingston that "the expectation of the slaves has been raised to the very highest point with reference to freedom". The same month, at the other side of the island, Knibb wrote from Falmouth: "The slaves believe they are soon to be free, and are anxiously waiting till King William sends them their free paper".

Political awareness was sharpened by economic distress. A six-month drought early in the year, followed by heavy rains in May, affected the harvest of ground provisions in many areas. Smallpox and dysentery were rife.[9] Hard times made the existing system less tolerable for the slaves and the prospect of emancipation the more desirable.

Political discontent found expression in religious groups which had developed side by side with the mission churches. The groups reflected primarily the slaves' religious interests, and mingled christianity with traditional African religious forms to produce a type of worship which satisfied their emotional needs more completely than did mission services. But, in a society where religious meetings were the only form of organized activity permitted, such meetings became the natural focal point for all the slaves' interests not served by estate organization. Freed from the supervision of the missionary and his emphasis on conformity and obedience, the slaves were also able to express their political interests and to use religion as a sanction for their hopes.

The same process has been observed in Africa, both among industrial workers in South Africa subjected to the political restrictions of apartheid and in the Congo under the Belgians. Throughout these areas separatist christian sects have proliferated under the leadership of Africans, which combine religious functions, cleansing from sin and protecting from witch-craft, with political aspirations, looking forward to the end of white domination.[10] Even in nineteenth-century England, where church members could carry their concern for justice into a range of political associations, brotherhoods and unions, churches became political clubs. In Huddersfield the New Connection Methodists were known as the Tom Paine Methodists since they discussed Tom Paine at chapel meetings together with the works of their founder, Alexander Kilham; and in Halifax a group of Methodists purchased their own chapel and ran it as a Jacobin chapel. The Primitive Methodist sect identified their church so closely with the trade-union move-ment as to make it practically a labour religion, and the church supplied almost all the trade-union leaders for the agricultural labourers and the Durham and Northumberland miners throughout the century.[11]

The religious groups among the slaves fell into three categories: groups consisting chiefly of mission members meeting on the estates and modelling themselves primarily on the mission churches; groups formed by mission converts, often church leaders, among slaves who did not attend mission churches; and, thirdly, groups run by leaders who were independent of the missions, or repudiated them outright, while associating themselves with christianity—these latter tending to call themselves Baptists, "native" or "spirit" Baptists.

Each mission had a satellite of such groups. Slaves and coloured people took up preaching and in some instances became known for the influence they exercised over the slaves on a particular estate. Political thinking developed to some extent along racist lines. But the slaves' over-whelming political concern was not race but freedom, and with the anti-slavery campaign in England reaching new heights, political discontent overflowed from these groups into the mission churches. Hope of a better life in the world to come became hope of a better life in the world after abo-lition. In the last months of 1831 there was what the missionaries described as "a great outpouring of the Spirit" in the North Coast parishes. The chapels were crowded out with hearers, and membership figures rapidly expanded.[12] After the rebellion it became clear that

> many churches and congregations had been swelled by a host anticipating freedom, who, now that their hopes were disappointed, fell away. It was common for a backslider to answer an exhortation thus: "It is no use minister; what can church and prayers do for we again? . . .".[13]

Out of this political ferment emerged leaders who directed the wide-spread excitement and discontent into action, utilizing religious meetings and the authority of the missionaries to promote the cause of freedom. The most outstanding rebel leader was Sam Sharpe, a domestic slave who worked in Montego Bay and was a member of the Baptist church there. Sharpe was literate, intelligent and ambitious and, like many of his kind, he found an outlet and a stimulant for his ambition in a mission church.

As a convert, he displayed a talent for eloquent and passionate preaching which won him a position as leader, entrusted with the spiritual care of a class of other converts. Sharpe, however, was not content to serve simply within the church; he built up an independent connection with the "native" Baptists among whom he figured as a "daddy" or "ruler". At the same time he found mission teaching on obedience unsatisfactory. From his own reading of the Bible he became convinced that the slaves were entitled to freedom.[14] This conviction, combined with the development of the emancipation campaign in England, of which Sharpe kept himself well informed, led him to believe that the slaves must make a bid for freedom. In recruiting aides, Sharpe naturally turned to other Baptist slaves of whom George Taylor, another church leader, Johnson, George Guthrie, Thomas Dove and Robert Gardner all became leaders in the rebellion.[15]

Sharpe, according to the account he gave the Wesleyan missionary, Henry Bleby, who had several conversations with him when he was in jail, did not plan armed rebellion, but mass passive resistance. After the Christmas holidays when the cane harvest was due to begin, the slaves were to sit down and refuse to work until their masters acknowledged that they were free men and agreed to pay them wages. Sharpe expected that the whites would try to intimidate the strikers by shooting hostages as examples; but the slaves were not expected to fight back, simply to continue passive resistance.[16]

It became evident, however, that plans were also made for armed revolt. Several leaders in the rebellion, including Gardner and Dove, took military titles and led a slave regiment. They claimed that Sharpe himself had planned armed rebellion and timed it for Christmas so that, with the whites away in the towns, the slaves could easily collect arms from the estates.[17] Possibly the intention was that the majority of the slaves should strike while some undertook military action to back up the passive resistance.

Whatever the case, plans for rebellion were promulgated at religious meetings among mission members and among the "native" Baptists. The usual practice was to hold a regular prayer meeting after which a selected few were asked to remain behind; Sharpe's aide then explained the plan and tried to persuade all present to swear on the Bible not to work after Christmas. Sharpe himself was a speaker who appeared to have "the feelings and passions of his hearers completely at his command"; when he spoke against slavery they were "wrought up almost to a state of madness".[18] His language, a combination of religious imagery and political message, was no doubt the language of radical Methodists in England. As one wrote of the pre-Reform government:

> Unequal laws and a partial administration plant a thorn in every breast and spread gloom in every countenance . . . . It may justly be said of such rulers, Their vine is the vine of Sodom and the fields of Gommorrah; their grapes are the grapes of gall . . . .

And the oaths sworn by the slaves were probably like the oaths of their English counterparts, based on the Bible: "Thus saith the Lord God: remove the Diadem and take off the Crown . . . exalt him that is low and abase him that is high . . .".[19]

The arguments used to encourage the slaves to take action included the notion, common to the Jamaican disturbances of December 1823 and June 1824, and the Demerara rebellion of 1823, and to several American slave disturbances, that freedom had already been granted and was being withheld by the slave owners.[20] Sharpe, though too well-informed to hold the belief himself, was said to have told his followers that the legislation had passed in March 1831. As a natural extension of this idea, it was also said that the king's troops would not fight the slaves since they were only claiming their rights, or even, that the king's troops would fight with the slaves. During the rebellion some of the slaves believed that the "black sand", or gunpowder, landed from a naval ship at Savannah-la-Mar, was for their use.[21]

The main body of arguments, however, related to religion, and Christianity came to provide a positive justification for action. Sharpe and his aides proclaimed the natural equality of men and, on the authority of the Bible, denied the right of the white man to hold the black in bondage. The text, "No man can serve two masters", persistently quoted by Sharpe, became a slogan among the slaves. To protest against slavery was a matter of "assisting their brethren in the work of the Lord . . . this was not the work of man alone, but they had assistance from God".[22] The authority of the missionaries themselves was used to sanction the protest: it was widely believed that the missionaries favoured freedom for the slaves. Sharpe's pastor, Burchell, of the Montego Bay Baptist mission, who had left for England in May 1831, was made in his absence into a political leader. Messages attributed to him circulated among the slaves: that he would be a pillar of iron to them, but they must shed no blood, for life was sweet, easy to take away, but very hard to give. Slaves who were unconvinced that freedom was already legally theirs, adopted the pleasing and plausible expectation that Burchell, who was due to return at Christmas 1831, would bring the free paper with him.[23]

Preparations for the Christmas rebellion probably started about August 1831, in the interval between the arduous work of cane holing and the cane harvest, and were a parallel development to the white population's parish meetings. Given the network of religious meetings and a ready-made following among the slaves, Sharpe and his aides were able during that time, to spread their influence through St. James, parts of Hanover and Trelawny and into Westmoreland, St. Elizabeth and Manchester, an area of six hundred square miles.

It was not until the missionaries met their congregations for the Christmas services that they learnt of the plans for rebellion and of the political rôle with which they had been endowed. Naturally, the missionaries made every effort to keep their converts from any form of violence or disobedience, and demonstrated by their arguments that the slaves must not look to them for support. The Presbyterian missionary, George Blyth, who had just returned to the island from a visit to England, strove to assure his congregation that he was in possession of the latest news. He argued the case against rebellion on grounds of principle and policy, describing

> the bloodshed, anarchy and injury to religion which would be the consequence of insurrection . . . I also described to them the great improbability of the slaves obtaining their liberty by such means on account of the want of unanimity, arms, etc. . . . .

On the 27th of December, at the opening of a new Baptist chapel at Salters Hill, St. James, Knibb used the occasion to warn the people:

> I learn that some wicked persons have persuaded you that the King has made you free. Hear me, I love your souls.—I would not tell you a lie for the world. What you have been told is false—false as Hell can make it. I entreat you not to believe it, but go to your work as usual. If you have any love to Jesus Christ, to religion, to your ministers, to those kind friends in England who have given money to help you build this chapel, be not led away by wicked men.

A Wesleyan meeting at Ramble on the 26th of December was conducted in the same tone: the day-long services admonished the people that religion meant love to God and men.[24]

The slaves' reaction to such advice, however, reflected their profound disappointment. When it became clear that the missionaries were solely concerned with law and order, they became sullen, and some openly angry. At Hampden, Blyth's congregation was "not only disappointed but offended" with him. At Salters Hill the Baptist congregation was:

> perfectly furious and would not listen to . . . dissuasions from engaging in such a perilous enterprise. . . . They accused their ministers of deserting them, and threatened to take revenge upon them.[25]

From the outset of the rebellion it was clear that the preparations Sharpe and the other conspirators had made were inadequate for success. In the first place, the rebellion proper was presaged by a number of false alarms which served to put the white population and the government on guard. A week before Christmas there was a labour dispute on Salt Spring estate near Montego Bay: the St. James magistrates sent for troops from Falmouth as a precaution, and the governor, Belmore, on the 22nd of December sent warships to Montego Bay and Black River and belatedly issued the proclamation received from England the previous June. On the 23rd of December in Trelawny, the trash house was fired on one estate, and on two others the slaves went on strike. Receiving this news on the 28th of

December, the governor in council decided to send troops to Montego Bay. These troops were ready to embark when news of the rebellion reached Spanish Town and martial law was immediately declared.[26]

The firing of the trash house on Kensington estate, St. James on the evening of the 27th of December, 1831, which served as a signal for the rebellion, was symptomatic of confusion among the slaves. The destruction of property formed no part of Sharpe's original plan and may have been started accidentally; on the other hand, the owner of Kensington estate was warned by a neighbour on the morning of the 27th of December that the slaves planned to burn the estate that evening. It was said that the properties to be fired were numbered and Kensington was first because, set on a hill, it served as a beacon.[27] In the event, the rebellion comprised all forms of protest action: armed rebellion, withdrawal of labour, destruction of property, while amid the confusion some slaves simply stuck to estate routine.

The rebels' military core was the Black Regiment, about one hundred and fifty strong with fifty guns among them.[28] The Black Regiment, under the command of Colonel Johnson of Retrieve estate, fought a successful action on the 28th of December 1831 against the Western Interior militia, which had retreated from its barracks in the interior to Old Montpelier estate, near Montego Bay. From there, the Black Regiment forced a further retreat to Montego Bay and put the country between Montego Bay, Lucea and Savannah-la-Mar in rebel hands. The Black Regiment then carried rebellion into the hills, invading estates and inviting recruits, burning properties on the border of St. James and setting off a trail of fires through the Great River Valley in Westmoreland and St. Elizabeth. Its commanders, "Colonels" Dove and Gardner, set up headquarters at Greenwich, Gardner's estate on the border of Hanover and Westmoreland, and from there a sketchy organization held sway over the surrounding estates. The slaves were organized into companies, each responsible for guarding its estate boundaries and holding allegiance to Gardner and Dove at Greenwich. This sort of activity was carried on by a number of rebel leaders, also Baptist members, notably Captain Dehany operating in the Salters Hill area, and Captain Tharp in the interior.[29] Their work was supplemented by the activity of self-appointed leaders, who took the opportunity to roam the country collecting recruits, looting and destroying and intimidating other slaves, enjoying a little brief authority.

There appears, however, to have been no co-operation among these various groups. They were short of arms, no special arrangements having been made to secure guns or ammunition.[30] Moreover, the slaves had no experience of military operations and in their contacts with the soldiers showed no skill in guerilla warfare. The scene of a typical skirmish between the rebels and their trained opponents was described by the Wesleyan missionary, Bleby:

The insurgent slaves, with little judgment had posted themselves on the side of a hill commanding the narrow mountain road; and when the soldiers came in sight, they discharged upon them a volley of musketry and stones. . . . They then ran and attempted to gain the brow of the hill, but in so doing exposed themselves fully to the unerring aim of the military. . . . Sixteen bodies, dragged into the road, were putrefying in the sun when we passed by . . . carrion crows were feeding upon them.[31]

The main rebel forces were rapidly disposed of. By the first week in January, armed rebellion was virtually at an end.

Strike action was effectively organized in some areas. In Trelawny, for example, the slaves on Carlton estate "sat down" firmly after Christmas. The Presbyterian missionary, Rev. Waddell, went to the estate to persuade them they were not yet free, but they accused him of being paid by the magistrates to deceive them. The strikers were equally firm in dealing with a gang of rebels who invaded the estate; they did not allow them to burn the property or plunder the stores, arguing that if they were to be free they would want rum and sugar for themselves.[32]

Successful strike action, however, demanded the co-operation of large numbers of estates, and it proved impossible to organize widespread passive resistance with the help of a few aides and a proliferation of meetings where the converted kissed the Bible and swore allegiance. A strong nucleus of strike leaders, working with the headman, or one of the drivers on each plantation, with weeks of careful instruction for all the slaves on the precise form the strike was to take, would have been necessary for there to be any hope of success. In the circumstances the authorities, instead of being confronted by thousands of slaves over a wide area refusing to work, had to deal only with isolated groups; and pacification consisted of forcing the slaves to choose between martyrdom and submission. On Georgia estate, Trelawny, where the slaves put up a determined and well disciplined opposition, the negro village was subjected to a daybreak attack by the militia using a fieldpiece; when they still refused to move, they were dragged out, one by one, and one man was shot as an example.[33] Sharpe had warned his followers that the whites would try to intimidate them by shooting hostages; but only the consciousness of being part of a solid strike resistance, involving hundreds of estates, could have given the slaves the confidence to accept the necessity for such martyrs. In the circumstances they were intimidated and returned to work.

Most of the estates involved in the rebellion were neither part of the rebels' rudimentary military organization, nor organized for passive resistance. Their rebellion consisted chiefly in the destruction of white property, and a brief heady disregard for routine combined with assertions of freedom. Some indulged in isolated acts of defiance: one woman put down her washing at the water tank to toss a fire stick into the trash house as the militia passed the estate. Many, caught in the excitement, took the opportunity to kill and cook the estate hogs, or hamstring the estate cows. The head driver of one estate allowed a party of rebels to burn the great house and celebrated his new-found independence by galloping round the property on his owner's horse wearing his owner's hat.[34] In some cases, faction developed between the law-abiding slaves and those who claimed their freedom. Judging by the testimonies of witnesses at the Courts Martial, this split often occurred along class lines: where the head driver and the skilled workers were for the rebellion, the field slaves stood by "buckra", and vice-versa. On Burnt Ground penn, St. James, for example, the head driver tried to prevent the buildings being burnt, but an obstreperous field slave, one Henry James, who had recently served a three month workhouse sentence, prevailed on the slaves to fire them. At Moor Park, however, the slaves who wanted to protect the master's property from the rebels were prevented from doing so by the head driver.[35]

On estates where the rebel cause had no representative, confusion reigned. The slaves were intimidated by the fires and by the appearance of rebel bands wanting to loot and burn the property. Some left their homes and went into hiding in the woods. Others kept their nerve and organized guards to keep out the rioters; and in some cases, as on the estates observed by a missionary in Hanover, they carried on with the cane harvest, "making sugar and rum as good as they usually do without any white supervision".[36]

The failure of the rebellion left the slaves exposed to white vengeance. The military authorities, represented by Sir Willoughby Cotton, the commander-in-chief, were concerned simply to restore order and combined retribution against slaves caught in rebellious acts with free pardon for all who returned to work on the estates. A proclamation to this effect was issued by Cotton on his arrival in Montego Bay, and a hundred of the rebel prisoners were released to circulate it on the estates.[37] But for the overseers and attorneys-turned-militiamen, pacification involved not only restoring order, but vengeance for their losses and humiliation. After the defeat at Old Montpelier, the militia had been pinned in Montego Bay until the military arrived—watching estates go up in flames, anxiously patrolling the streets for fear of rebel incursion, their women and children stowed away for safety on ships in the harbour. Pacification took place amid the charred and blackened ruins of a countryside which a few days before had been ripe for harvest. It was estimated that the damage in St. James alone amounted to six hundred thousand pounds.[38] The militia were bent on vengeance and among them were individuals whose political rancour approached insanity. They raided and burnt negro villages on rebel estates, driving neighbouring slaves to take refuge in the woods for fear it was their turn next.[39] Suspected ring-leaders and known troublemakers were shot out of hand, despite the proclamation. In one case all the slaves on an estate in Trelawny had been pardoned by Cotton in person when, an hour later, a militia detachment under the command of the estate's attorney, John

Gunn, arrived. The slaves were again called out and the attorney-turned-lieutenant ordered the second driver of the gang to be shot. On this occasion the attorney was court-martialled, and acquitted; the court martial was unique, such executions not unusual. The Wesleyan missionary, Bleby, watched the militia arrive at an estate where the slaves, in accordance with the proclamation, were at work. Two men, a boy and a woman, were taken from their work and sent for trial in Montego Bay where the men were condemned and shot.[40] Cases such as this cast grave doubt on the official figure for slaves killed in the rebellion: 207, compared with 14 whites. As a Presbyterian missionary commented, "In the rage for making examples [the colony] lost many able hands it could ill spare".[41]

The Courts Martial hastily constituted of militia men on the warrant of the commander-in-chief[42] were equally ruthless. At Montego Bay, ninety-nine slaves were tried of whom eighty-one were executed; at the Slave Courts, instituted when martial law was lifted, eighty-one were tried of whom thirty-nine were executed; in all 626 slaves were tried of whom 312 were executed.[43] The trials at Montego Bay, where the greatest number of slaves were tried, followed a regular pattern: it was established that the slaves on a particular estate were rebellious, the prisoner was proved to belong to this estate and a witness found to claim the prisoner had been seen to commit an offence which could be considered a rebellious act, or even to have heard him claim to have committed one. Witnesses were, from time to time, condemned by interested attorneys and owners as "great rascals", "liars", "notorious runaways", and the trial records suggest they often had private grievances to pay off, or were turning witness to keep themselves out of the dock. Prisoners were condemned for trivial offences; one man, arrested while cooking one of the estate hogs, was executed for this; another, accused of ham-stringing a cow and having said he had snapped a gun five times, was hanged. The courts made no attempt to assess the degree of guilt, or even to distinguish between prisoners who had taken some sort of leading rôle in estate disturbances and those merely caught up in events. Cases were personally known to the missionaries where slaves had acted under provocation, or were condemned apparently to settle private grievances. The Presbyterian missionary, Blyth, felt justified in exerting himself on behalf of a Presbyterian candidate for membership who had complained bitterly to him before the rebellion of the harsh conduct of the overseer; he was found guilty of helping to cut a bridge and breaking into the estate stores, and executed. The Wesleyan missionary, Murray, saw a slave who was a leader in the Wesleyan church executed—condemned, Murray believed, because his religious convictions made him "obnoxious to those over him".[44]

The executions bore final witness to white vengeance. In Montego Bay

PARISH	TOTAL TRIED	TOTAL EXECUTED
Hanover Courts Martial	58	27
Hanover Civil Courts	82	60
Trelawny Courts Martial	70	24
St. James Courts Martial	99	81
St. James Civil Courts	81	39
Westmoreland Courts Martial	26	12
Westmoreland Civil Courts	52	20
St. Elizabeth Courts Martial	73	14
Portland Courts Martial	23	7
Portland Civil Courts	5	5
St. Thomas in the Vale Courts Martial	9	—
Manchester Courts Martial	15	13
Manchester Civil Courts	16	7
St. Thomas in the East Courts Martial	12	1
St. Thomas in the East Civil Courts	5	2
TOTALS	626	312

The gibbet erected in the public square in the centre of the town was seldom without occupants, during the day, for many weeks. Generally four, seldom less than three, were hung at once. The bodies remained stiffening in the breeze, till the court martial had provided another batch of victims . . . [The executioner] would ascend a ladder . . . and with his knife sever the ropes by which the poor creatures were suspended and let them fall to the ground. Other victims would then be . . . suspended in their place and cut down in their turn . . . the whole heap of bodies remaining just as they fell until the workhouse negroes came in the evening with carts, and took them away, to cast them into a pit dug for the purpose, a little distance out of town.

At Lucea, the condemned men were put into an ox-cart, their arms pinioned, a rope round their neck and a white cap on their heads.

In this way they were carried up under a strong guard into the midst of the burned properties, distances of twelve to thirty miles and the sentence was carried into effect on the estates as they successively arrived at them. On each of the melancholy occasions, the unfortunate men met their death, with a fortitude and cool deliberation that astonished all who beheld them.[45]

The rebellion, though unsuccessful, demonstrated some degree of political maturity among the slaves. They had created a protest movement, partly inspired by christianity and organized through religious meetings, in which religion had been subordinated to political aims. A predominantly religious protest would have produced a millenarian movement in which the leaders regarded themselves as prophets announcing the will of God and their followers expected a new world to be established "by divine revelation". The Nat Turner rebellion of 1831 in Virginia was tinged with millenarianism: Turner saw himself as a prophet "ordained for some great purpose in the hands of the Almighty", and raised rebellion in response to signs from heaven, first divulging his intention to other slaves after an eclipse of the sun in February 1831. The original date for the outbreak, the 4th of July, was chosen for political reasons, but when Turner fell sick on that day the conspirators waited for another sign from heaven and found it manifested on the 13th of August, 1831, in the greenish blue colour of the sun. Turner's rebellion started as a crusade, the prophet leading six disciples,[46] which apparently aimed to carry vengeance, sanctioned by heaven, against the white population; a vengeance that Turner inaugurated by first killing his master's family. In the Jamaican protest movement, the most important leader, Sam Sharpe, made extensive use of the Bible, but he seems to have regarded himself more as a political leader than as a prophet. The movement he organized did not aim to establish a new world, but to make specific and limited changes in Jamaican society: the slaves were to establish their right to sell their labour for wages.

The slaves' activities in the rebellion were geared to the achievement of this political end. Though they indulged in widespread destruction of property, there was no hint of a crusade against the whites in their activity. Their attempts at strike action were intended to win freedom with a minimum of disorder and bloodshed. Even the armed rebels fought only those whites who attacked them; whites who offered no opposition met with no harm. The overseer of Ginger Hill estate, for example, in the centre of the St. Elizabeth rebellion area, was held prisoner under threat of death, but the slaves were content to make him sign a declaration divesting himself of authority on the estate.[47] There were only two crimes of violence against white people throughout the rebellion.[48] The fact that the slaves formed an overwhelming majority of the population, of course, contributed to their confidence in dealing with the white people. Moreover, the temptation they were exposed to was limited, in that the majority of whites took refuge in the towns when the fires started. Their restraint was, however, remarked on by contemporaries. A Presbyterian missionary wrote:

> Had the masters when they got the upper hand been as forbearing, as tender of their slaves' lives as their slaves had been of theirs it would have been to their lasting honour, and to the permanent advantage of the colony.[49]

It seems fair to conclude that such conduct was not entirely circumstantial, but reflected the nature of the movement.

The only millenarian element in the Jamaican rebellion was the tendency of the slaves to turn the Baptist missionary, Burchell, into a

Messianic figure whose arrival was expected to herald freedom. But even so, the figure was equipped with a political document: Burchell was expected to bring the act of parliament announcing emancipation.

The rebellion contributed indirectly to the abolition of slavery. The whites blamed the missionaries for the rebellion and in the aftermath of the revolt chapels were destroyed, missionaries tried for direct complicity with the rebels and preaching brought to an end. The Baptist and Wesleyan missionaries, on whom enmity chiefly focused, concluded that their work could only continue in the island if slavery was abolished— and delegates were sent to England to explain the situation. The delegates were immediately caught up in the emancipation campaign and proved invaluable propagandists. Thomas Fowell Buxton, who led the final stages of the campaign, attributed their presence in England to "the over-ruling hand of Providence, which had turned the intolerance of the [slave] system to its own destruction";[50] but credit was more directly due to the rebel slaves. Further, the missionaries' testimony against the slave system was vitally influenced by their experiences in the rebellion. As public speakers and as witnesses before the Parliamentary committees on slavery, they not only expressed their confidence in the Negro population and supported its claim to freedom, but also threatened that delay could only promote further rebellion.[51] The precise impact of this threat on government circles and on public opinion has yet to be established; but certainly it convinced no less a person than the parliamentary Under Secretary to the Colonial Office, Lord Howick, of the need for immediate action. His plan for emancipation, considered by the Cabinet in January 1833 provided for complete abolition of slavery from 1 January 1835.[52] The slaves had demonstrated to some at least of those in authority that it could prove more dangerous and expensive to maintain the old system than to abolish it.

The 1831 revolt was the last substantial rebellion in Jamaican history. Emancipation was celebrated with religious services and holiday festivities; the hardships of apprenticeship provoked no protest and the final transition to wage labour in 1838 took place without incident. In 1865, in a period of acute depression, a riot in one of the parishes became known as a rebellion, but the label reflected the scale of the government's reprisals and the potential for violence in the desperate condition of the people rather than the size of the popular movement. Discontent in the twentieth century has, so far, been manifested in the "back to Africa movement" started by Marcus Garvey, or been channelled into trade unionism and party politics. Constitutional politics have achieved political independence for the island; it remains to be seen whether these means can also achieve the economic and social reconstruction which are as necessary for the mass of the people now as in 1831.

Notes

1. H. Aptheker, *American Negro Slave Revolts* (Columbia U.P., 1944), chaps. iv and v. Aptheker also specifies an increase in the slave population, a point irrelevant to Jamaica where the slaves formed an overwhelming majority of the population.

2. The proposals also included, the abolition of Sunday markets, the removal of obstacles to manumission, the regulation of sales for debt, the prohibition of sales separating members of the same family and the institution of savings banks. C[olonial] O[ffice] 854/I, Circ. despatch, 9 July 1823, pp. 160–4.

3. An independent conspiracy was formed among the head people on a small group of estates in Portland, and slaves from estates in St. Thomas in the East near Manchioneal planned to abscond to the bush where they built a hide-out village: C.O., 137/185, Courts Martial Portland, St. Thomas in the East.

4. E. J. Hobsbawm, "Methodism and the Threat of Revolution in Britain", *History Today,* Feb. 1957, pp. 120–1. E. P. Thompson, *The Making of the English Working Class* (London, 1963), discusses the connection in chapter xi.

5. Parl. Papers, House of Commons (hereafter referred to as P.P.) 1831–2, vol. xlvii, no. 285, *Despatches Relative to the Recent Rebellion,* pp. 263, 266–8: Petitions of Freeholders and others. W. L. Burn, *Emancipation and Apprenticeship* (London, 1937), p. 91.

6. Belmore was advised that such a meeting would only be unconstitutional if it had a seditious intention. Belmore avoided any direct action by letting it be known that if the Assembly corresponded with the delegates he would dissolve the House. C.O., 137/179, Belmore to Goderich, 17 Dec. 1831, no. 130.

7. P.P., 1831–2, vol. xlvii, no. 285, p. 263: Belmore to Goderich, 20 July 1831.

8. H. Bleby, *Death Struggles of Slavery* (London, 1853), pp. 112, 114; J. H. Hinton, *Memoir of William Knibb* (London, 1847), pp. 115, 113.

9. Methodist Missionary Society archives, letters from missionaries in Jamaica to the society in London (hereinafter referred to as M.M.S. letters), Pennock, Kingston, 11 July 1831; Edney, Grateful Hill, 22 Sept. 1831; Duncan, Kingston, 7 June, 1831.

10. B. Davidson, *The African Awakening* (London, 1955), pp. 156–61; M. Gluckman, "The Magic of Despair", *The Listener,* Apr. 29, 1954, p. 725.

11. E. P. Thompson, *op. cit.,* pp. 44–5; Hobsbawm, *art. cit.,* p. 118 and his *Primitive Rebels* (Manchester, 1959), p. 138.

12. M.M.S. letters, Edney, Grateful Hill, 22 Sept. 1831, referring to Guys Hill; Wood, St. Ann's Bay, 1 Oct. 1831. Revivals of this sort occurred periodically; in 1828 and 1826 the mission churches had benefited in a similar way. Such movements might reflect an outburst of purely religious enthusiasm, but there seems no doubt that the revival of 1831 represented political interests. M.M.S. letters, Ratcliffe, Bellemont, 10 Nov. 1826; Orton, Montego Bay, 13 July 1828.

13. H. M. Waddell, *Twenty-nine years in the West Indies and Central Africa* (London, 1865), pp. 70–1.

14. Bleby, *op. cit.,* p. 116.

15. P.P., 1831–2, vol. xlvii, no. 561, *Report of the House of Assembly on the Slave Insurrection,* p. 214, confession of T. Dove; p. 211, confession of Ed. Morrice. Gardner belonged to Greenwich estate, on the borders of St. James and Westmoreland. In 1825 it had been reported to the Colonial Office that a negro preacher held sway over the slaves there.

16. Bleby, *op. cit.,* p. 116.

17. P.P., 1831–2, vol. xlvii, no. 561, p. 217, Confession of R. Gardner; p. 210, Confession of J. Davis.

18. Bleby, *op. cit.,* pp. 111–2, 115, quoting R. Gardner.

19. Thompson, *op. cit.,* p. 393 quoting a minister of the Independent Methodists; p. 392, the oath taken in a Lancashire conspiracy, 1801.

20. This belief was also current during slave disturbances in Virginia, 1830, North Carolina 1825, Alabama 1840. For a full discussion see H. Aptheker, *op. cit.*

21. P.P., 1831–2, vol. xlvii, no. 561, p. 215, Confession of T. Dove; no. 285, p. 286, Deposition of W. Anand.

22. *Ibid.*, p. 218, Confession of R. Gardner; no. 285, p. 295, Deposition of W. Anand. Bleby, *op. cit.*, p. 111.

23. *Ibid.*, no. 285, p. 286, Deposition of W. Anand; no. 561, p. 188, Evidence of H. R. Wallace. Bleby, *op. cit.*, pp. 2–3.

24. *Scottish Missionary Society and Philanthropic Register* (hereinafter referred to as *S.M.S.*), March 1832, p. 98, Blyth, Falmouth, 2 Jan. 1832; Baptist Missionaries, *A narrative of recent events connected with the Baptist Mission in this island* (Kingston, Jamaica, 1833) (hereinafter referred to as *Narrative Account*), p. 29; M.M.S. letters, Murray, Montego Bay, 10 Mar. 1832.

25. *S.M.S.*, Mar. 1832, pp. 98, 101, Blyth, Falmouth, 2 Jan. 1832.

26. P.P., 1831–2, vol. xlvii, no. 285, pp. 272–3, Belmore to Goderich, 6 Jan. 1832.

27. *Ibid.*, no. 561, p. 200, Evidence of J. H. Morris. Bleby, *op. cit.*, p. 116.

28. C.O., 137/185, Courts Martial, St. James, vol. i, f. 42, Evidence of Angus McNeil. Bleby, *op. cit.*, p. 11.

29. C.O., 137/185, Courts Martial, St. James, vol. i, f. 20, Evidence of Philip; vol. ii, ff. 46–7, trial of Tharp; vol. iii, ff. 37–40, trial of Dehany. Baptist Missionary Society Archives, Brief on behalf of Francis Gardner, pp. 5–6.

30. Caches of guns and ammunition were found in negro huts on Ginger Hill estate, St. Elizabeth, and at Catadupa estate, between Lucea and Montego Bay: P.P., 1831–2, vol. xlvii, no. 285, p. 284; Major-Gen. D. Robertson to Belmore, 1 Jan. 1832; Belmore to Goderich, 16 Jan. 1832. One of the rebel leaders claimed that a white man on Lethe estate had taught some of them to make cartridges: *ibid.*, no. 561, p. 218, Confession of R. Gardner.

31. Bleby, *op. cit.*, p. 18.

32. Waddell, *op. cit.*, pp. 56–7.

33. C.O., 137/185, Courts Martial, Trelawny, ff. 12–15, trial of Edmund Grant.

34. *Ibid.*, Courts Martial, St. James, vol. iii, f. 51, trial of Jinny; vol. i, f. 6, trial of James Guy; vol. ii, ff. 20–1, trial of Thomas Linton; vol. i, ff. 17–18, trial of Alick Gordon.

35. *Ibid.*, vol. ii, ff. 35–6, trial of Henry James; vol. i, ff. 17–18.

36. *S.M.S.*, March 1832, pp. 198–9, Watson, Lucea, 7 Feb. 1832.

37. P.P., 1831–2, vol. xlvii, no. 285, p. 288, proclamation 2 Jan. 1832: "Negroes, You have taken up arms against your masters. . . . Some wicked persons have told you the King has made you free. . . . In the name of the King I come amongst you to tell you that you are misled. . . . All who are found with the rebels will be put to death without mercy. You cannot resist the King's troop. . . . All who yield themselves up provided they are not principals and chiefs in the burnings that have been committed will receive His Majesty's gracious pardon, all who hold out will meet with certain death".

38. P.P., 1831–2, vol. xlvii, no. 561. Sum total of losses in the rebellion in Jamaican currency:

St. James:	£606,250
Hanover:	£425,818
Westmoreland:	£47,092
St. Elizabeth:	£22,146
Trelawny:	£4,960
Manchester:	£46,270
Portland:	£772
St. Thomas in the East:	£1,280

39. Waddell, *op. cit.*, p. 61.

40. C.O., 137/185, Courts Martial, Trelawny, ff. 131–6, trial of Lieut. John Gunn. Bleby, *op. cit.*, pp. 48–54, 17.

41. Waddell, *op. cit.*, p. 66.

42. The Courts Martial at Montego Bay were ordered by Col. George McF. Lawson of the St. James Regiment of Foot Militia on Sir Willoughby Cotton's warrant. It is not clear exactly by what authority they sat. C.O., 137/185, Abstract of the Courts Martial at Montego Bay, p. 1.

43. C.O., 137/185, Parish Returns. See table, p. 122 below.

44. C.O., 137/185, Courts Martial, St. James, vol. i, f. 6, trial of James Guy; vol. ii, ff. 20–1, trial of Thomas Linton. *S.M.S.* April 1832, p. 149, Blyth, 10 Jan. 1832. M.M.S. letters, Murray, Montego Bay, 28 May 1832.

45. Bleby, *op. cit.,* pp. 26–7; Waddell, *op. cit.,* p. 66, quoting letter from Watson, Lucea, 8 May 1832.

46. Hobsbawm, *Primitive Rebels,* pp. 58–9. Aptheker, *op. cit.,* pp. 296–8.

47. P.P., 1831–2, vol. xlvii, no. 285, p. 286, deposition of W. Anand.

48. Bleby, *op. cit.,* p. 43. C.O., 137/183, Mulgrave to Goderich, 14 Dec. 1832, no. 45, enclosing Return of persons killed: total of white casualties, 14.

49. Waddell, *op. cit.,* p. 66.

50. T. F. Buxton, *Memoirs,* ed. Chas. Buxton (London, 1849), pp. 305–6.

51. The House of Lords select committee on the laws and usages of the West Indian colonies in relation to the slave population and the House of Commons select committee on the extinction of slavery throughout the British dominions, met from May to August 1832. P.P., 1831–2, vol. cccvi, pp. 430–1, 636–8, 668; vol. xx, pp. 75, 117, 112.

52. D. J. Murray, *The West Indies and the Development of Colonial Government, 1801–34* (Oxford, 1965), pp. 194–5.

PART TWO
RELATIONS OF
PRODUCTION

In order to grasp clearly the definition and the position of the black underclass we must understand where black people stand with respect to the processes and organization of production in New World societies. That is, we must ask: What do they do in order to survive and make a living? Who controls the land, tools, and materials used? Who benefits? Who reaps the fruits of labor?

The emancipation of slaves in different countries and at different times has led to similar results: the formation of a black rural proletariat and a black peasantry. The former exists insofar as black people are forced to subsist by selling their labor power, since they lack access to the land and the tools and techniques necessary to exploit it. The peasantry exists insofar as land is available for settlement in a geographical situation far enough away from the demands of the plantations. Whereas the proletariat lives by selling its labor power to the plantations for wages in cash or in kind, the peasantry lives by cultivating food crops with use of household and cooperative labor for home consumption and for sale in urban areas through internal marketing arrangements. The peasantry often cultivates cash crops for sale within an international economic context, e.g., sugarcane, cotton, coffee, tobacco, nutmeg. Furthermore, while many peasants own the land they work, others must pay various forms of rent to landlords of large holdings or defunct plantations or to the State. The hallmark of this poor peasantry is the *minifundia,* small holdings barely enabling subsistence and found, for example, in the American South after the passing of the plantations, and in the marginal regions of the larger Caribbean islands.

Thus, for a long time after emancipation, and even today in the Caribbean and in Brazil, the black underclass was part of the rural masses, working on plantations or eking out a marginal existence on the land. In all instances they were economically as well as socially dependent. The whim and whip of the master was replaced by the wage of the employer and rent of the landlord.

Harry Hutchinson's detailed description of two sugar plantations in northeast Brazil documents these relationships. His distinction between the *engenho,* or small privately-owned plantation, and the *usina,* or corporately-owned field and factory combine, is not limited to Brazil. In some of the small islands of the West Indies the *engenho*-type still operates, and in the larger islands the *usina* is characteristic. The differences between these two types are not merely academic, since the paternalism and frequent personal contacts between workers and owners on the *engenho*-type often circumscribe the political attitudes and organizations of the workers, whereas the impersonality and size of the *usina*-type may yield quite different and radical approaches to politics among the workers. Such relationships were pointed out originally by anthropologists and are important subjects for social and political research in these societies.

In order to make workers totally dependent upon the plantation for existence, a major problem for the plantation is control of the workers, not only on the job, but in almost every other aspect of life. In the article on "Intimidation of Labor", Allison Davis and the Gardners describe the terrorization of workers on an American cotton plantation. Although I have eschewed an emphasis on "experience", this chapter does expose one major aspect of the black experience in the United States.

Richard Frucht makes it obvious that while the distinction between proletariat and peasantry may be analytically clear once the characteristic relationships of each have been defined, the distinction is not always manifestly clear. That is, many households exhibit or engage in *both* proletarian and peasant relationships. Thus, the "peasant" households of Nevis often send their members to work on nearby plantations or as emigrant laborers across the seas. Occupational multiplicity is characteristic of marginal economic existence. In Nevis, the combination of peasantlike and proletarianlike relations is a function of sharecropping, which is an organization of production found in situations of cash shortage and economic depression.

Both the system of production and the economic relationships operating within a society have effects on the family and household level of organization. R. T. Smith's comments on the "Economic Features of the Household Group" document variations in the form and activities of the household among the black underclass of British Guiana. (Now called Guyana, this former colony received its independence in 1966.) Much of his analysis holds true for the Caribbean area as a whole, especially his remarks on the nature of the Guianese "peasantry". Smith's contribution should be read again in connection with the selections in Part IV on "Family and Interpersonal Relations".

The black rural proletariat and the black peasantry (terms now used with all of the qualifications referred to above) still exist in the Caribbean and Brazil. In the United States, however, almost three-quarters of the black population live in urban areas, and whereas there is usually no hesitancy in referring to the black underclass as an urban or industrial proletariat, the question of whether or not they are at all integral to the rapidly changing technological and occupational structure has been infrequently posed. It is, however, consistently posed in the remaining selections.

Harry Dillingham and David Sly document and describe the mechanization of the southern U.S. cotton plantation and the resulting migration of blacks to the cities in search of jobs. They end with a cautionary note on the future of technological change and black employment. The selection from Elliot Liebow's exposition of the social relations and attitudes of the black underclass in Washington, D.C., continues the story begun by Dillingham and Sly. Liebow implicitly describes the effects and reinforcement of racism. Opportunities for employment are limited by racist expectations about blacks to heavy work, long hours, and low wages. In weighing the alternatives before them, the men often refuse to work or engage in activities to supplement their low wages. To racists and employers, this provides ample proof of their most firmly held beliefs. This behavior, however, is the result of racism and the treatment of labor as a commodity. Clearly, the men of Tally's corner are not participating in the technological potential of American society and, indeed, seem to be victims of it.

Unlike white immigrants from Europe, blacks in American cities have not proceeded rapidly nor risen far up the scale of social mobility and economic success. In spite of constitutional guarantees and an ideology of equality of opportunity, the disengagement of blacks from the processes and fruits of production has resulted in what Paul Baran and Paul Sweezy refer to as a "subproletariat." The class structure of capitalist society in America—and elsewhere—based as it is on the private ownership of property and capital, does not include a black ruling or super-rich class. It does, however, include a black bourgeoisie. The importance of this group toward maintenance of the larger social and economic system and in the exploitation of the black underclass is underscored in this selection. Again, the question of whether or not blacks are redundant to the processes of production is posed. For an answer, Baran and Sweezy should be read in connection with Blauner's and Allen's contributions in Part VI.

Harry Hutchinson
PLANTATION LIFE

The Golden Age of the sugar industry was typified by the plantation complex, which was accompanied by a definite way of life. The final breakdown of this complex came at the end of the nineteenth century with the creation of the large central mill. Changes in the agricultural practices, however, have only begun to take place. Almost all the emphasis of change in the past was placed on the development of the technical aspects of processing the cane, and very little attention was given to the agricultural side of the industry.

Modern plantations continue to be relatively self-sufficient units, just as the *engenhos* were. The factories brought almost no change in the land settlement patterns of the area. Since they were established on the site of former plantations, they did not create new nuclei; rather, they simply enlarged the old centers. Some of the former slave population moved to those factories which needed more workmen. But in subsequent years there was a gradual resettlement of the former slaves on the old plantations, in the same locations and even at times in the same buildings.

The disappearance of the small smokestacks of many plantation mills and the appearance of the more widely scattered but far larger ones of the factories, together with the appearance of networks of narrow gauge railways radiating out from the factories, mark the major changes in the landscape of the Recôncavo. The outlines of the new plantations and their boundaries remain much the same as they were a hundred or more years ago. The former small mills are frequently still used as workshops and sheds for the oxcarts.

The following discussion will examine one of the five private plantations in the community of Vila Recôncavo and will then describe the network of factory plantations in the same community.

THE PRIVATE PLANTATION: FAZENDA DAS MOÇAS

The Fazenda das Moças . . . is typical of a privately owned plantation in all respects but one. Its owner is a lady who assumed active direction of the plantation after her husband's death. At first there was some difficulty in persuading the overseer of the plantation to take

REPRINTED FROM *Village and Plantation Life in Northeastern Brazil* (SEATTLE: UNIVERSITY OF WASHINGTON PRESS, 1957) BY PERMISSION OF THE AUTHOR AND THE PUBLISHER. THE AUTHOR CAUTIONS US THAT THE SYSTEM DESCRIBED HERE IS NOW A HISTORICAL SITUATION IN BAHIA, ALTHOUGH IT CONTINUES IN THE STATES OF PERNAMBUCO AND TO SOME EXTENT IN SAO PAULO.

orders from a woman, for he felt his prestige was lowered in the eyes of the workmen as well as the overseers of neighboring plantations. However, after three or four years, Dona Sinhá, in cooperation with "Seu"[1] Paulo, the overseer, has made an outstanding success of her plantation, and the original friction between the two has greatly diminished. Below is an inventory of the Fazenda das Moças:

Extent:	930 *tarefas*,[2] mostly of *massapê*, 450 of which are under sugar-cane cultivation, the rest consisting of pasture and small gardens
Water:	4 drinking tanks for livestock
	2 small freshwater streams
	(Drinking water must be brought from a neighboring plantation, which has a spring well known in the area for the salubrious qualities of its water.)
Houses:	45 workers' houses
	Owner's house, with living room, dining room, 4 bedrooms, kitchen, bathroom, 2 maids' rooms, 2 other dependencies, veranda; surrounded by orchard
	1 overseer's house
	1 house formerly used as a school
	1 new, rural school, with rooms for classes and living quarters for teacher, constructed by the state on land donated by Dona Sinhá
Value of the plantation:	Cr$1,500,000.00.[3]
Equipment:	1 Caterpillar tractor, model D2
	1 John Deere plow
	1 jeep
	2 four-wheeled, rubber-tired wagons
	9 *juntas* of oxen (the *junta* equals ten oxen, eight in use and two resting)
	9 two-wheeled carts drawn by oxen—the antique and most used transportation in the Recôncavo
	30 burros for carrying cane
	12 saddle horses
	35 milk cows and breeding mares
	78 cattle for breeding purposes

The Fazenda das Moças is unusual in its possession of a tractor, a mechanical plow, and a jeep. (Even more recently a second tractor and a mechanical cultivator have been added.) More commonly the *pai adão* (Father Adam) plow is used, drawn by eight oxen. According to Pinho the plow was introduced into Brazil in the late eighteenth century. Before this all cultivation was done with the hoe.[4] For the past 150 years the *pai adão* has been used primarily to open the rows in which the sugar cane is planted. All the rest of the cultivation is done by hand, with the hoe and billhook. The *pai adão* is a simple plow with a single plowshare. When it is drawn by oxen, a driver is needed, plus a small boy helper and another man to manage the plow. When it is drawn by tractor, only two men are needed, the driver and the plowman. Various properties of the soil, such as its hardness in the summer when it dries, its swamplike character during the rainy season, and the danger of turning up the infertile *tauá* which underlies the shallow layer of *massapê,* have made plowing difficult in the Recôncavo. So far only the *pai adão* has been able to fulfill the plowing requirements. Lately, however, tractors with caterpillar tread have been introduced and, when used carefully with disk plows, have given excellent results. But the old standby is still commonly in use, hitched to eight, ten, twelve, or as many as twenty oxen.

The owner's house with its park stands on a small hilltop and is visible from afar because of its imperial palms. Nearby, on another hilltop, is the settlement of workers, a long street with houses on either side, the barracks, a small store, and the ever-present *casa de farinha,* the house where manioc is always being ground, pressed, and roasted to make the farina which is the staple food of the area. Also on this street is the overseer's house, which stands out from the others because of its large size and its veranda. The houses of the workmen are small and built for the most part under one long, common roof. Each house is really an apartment consisting of a front living room and a long corridor going back to the kitchen, with one or two bedrooms leading off the corridor. Other houses, under separate roofs, have similar interior arrangements. The roofs are of red tiles, the rest of the house of clay mud (*taipa*) slapped on both sides of a bamboo framework. After the mud has dried a coat of whitewash is applied. The houses are built and kept in repair by the plantation owner and do not belong to the workers. The floors are of beaten earth, difficult to keep clean. At night, when only a tiny oil lamp is burning, the houses look dark and gloomy.

After dark one has the impression of hearing much more than one can see. Kerosene is expensive to burn, no one reads, and most of life is geared to doing in the daytime those tasks which require light. At night the workmen and their families sit in the dark talking, or perhaps go to the *casa de farinha* where a fellow workman and his family may be grinding their manioc. This building is softly lit with kerosene lamps and there is a cheerful glow from the roasting fire. More recently the overseer's house has been equipped with electricity, and now it is always well lighted at night. His new radio has become a center of attraction and small groups form about his veranda, listening. At the other end of the street, during harvest time, there is always a bonfire in front of the barracks where the migrant workers are sheltered. On special occasions there may be a *samba* (dance), perhaps in the plantation owner's house. Then everyone dons his best and the women dance while the men play the drums, tambourines, and *cavaquinhos* (a ukelelelike instrument) or simply stand around watching, gossiping and "passing the *branquinha*" (the local white rum).

There is a hierarchy of personnel on the plantation, which starts with the owner, Dona Sinhá, and her family. On other plantations the owner is also sometimes a lawyer, doctor, or engineer whose main interests, both economic and social, are in the city of Salvador. This is not always the case, however, for many owners are only rural proprietors, as is Dona Sinhá. But it is always considered a sacrifice to be obliged to spend the winter on one's plantation. It has been a traditional prerogative of the plantation master to spend the winter in the city, and it is one of the traditions kept up today by the planters. However, as soon as the rains show signs of abating in August or September, Dona Sinhá appears on the scene, generally grateful for her release from the city and from the round of anniversaries, parties, and official functions she feels called upon to attend while there.

This aspect of partial absenteeism has given rise to the next rung in the hierarchical ladder: the overseer. As such he is a relatively new phenomenon, but he has actually been part of the scene for a long time. At the time of the *engenho,* the *feitor-mor,* or head foreman, frequently occupied the place of today's overseer. Seu Paulo is the focal point for most activities on Fazenda das Moças. It is he who puts into action Dona Sinhá's plans, for he has the greatest contact with the workers in the fields and at home, on the *arruado* (the street on which the houses are located). During the time Dona Sinhá is away he is ruler of the plantation (*dono da terra*).

Seu Paulo rose from the workers' ranks; he is familiar with all aspects of sugar-cane cultivation, and is able to handle men and to deal with the owner as well as with the workers. He is a dark mulatto, about forty-six years old, with a large family. He is sought after by the workers as godfather to their children. He rents a small piece of land on which he raises his own sugar cane. He has his own burros, oxen, and carts, which he rents to Dona Sinhá during the harvest season. Although unable to read or write, he can do figures in his head in an astounding fashion. He dresses well, in what is sometimes thought to be an attempt to imitate the plantation master of bygone days, while Dona Sinhá and her family have adopted a more comfortable garb for the country—"*modo americano.*" He spends most of his day in the saddle, riding from one point of operation to another; going to the sugar mill to straighten out this or that matter, such as the nonappearance of railroad cars at the plantation loading point; caring for the troubles of the workers; and looking to his own interests.

Below these two figures of authority is a salaried man who stands only slightly apart from the bulk of the workers, the foreman (*feitor*), Asclepiades. It is his duty to keep track of how much work is done each day and by whom. He walks about the plantation, from field to field, measuring with the six-foot stick he carries and marking down in his notebook the amount of work done by each man. The plantation laborers are paid according to how much each of them weeded, or planted, or to how many tons of cane each cut or conducted to the factory. Asclepiades writes it down in his little black book, and it appears on the daily work sheet which in turn is transferred to the fortnightly payroll. During harvest time the records of who was the driver and who the guide, of how much sugar cane was cut and by whom, are kept at each end of the plantation where the carts must pass to be weighed before the cane is transferred to the factory. It is Seu Paulo's duty every morning to assign tasks to the workmen, while Asclepiades keeps track of how much is done but does not see that it gets done, for this is the duty of the overseer. The foreman is paid a monthly salary of one thousand *cruzeiros*, and although he does not occupy the position of prestige which the overseer has there is always the chance that he may become an overseer either on that plantation or on another.

There is one other salaried person on the plantation—the cowboy (*vaqueiro*) João who receives four hundred *cruzeiros* a month, plus room and board. João takes care of the cattle, milk cows, and saddle horses. He must also inspect the fences constantly and report any breaks, and whenever possible retrieve animals which have broken out of the pasture and wandered into the cane fields, where they cause great damage. As a rule the pastures are fenced, as are new cane plantations, but the established cane fields are left unguarded. Fences do not last more than one season, for the posts rot because of the wet soil, and the barbed wire rusts quickly. João is also the constant companion of the plantation owner when she is present, accompanying her or her children or guests on pleasure rides, meeting the train or boat with horses for guests or business acquaintances, and getting the mail from the post office in the town of Vila Recôncavo. João lives in the owner's house, enjoying her confidence to a greater degree than anyone else except perhaps the overseer. This is frequently the cause of friction between the cowboy and overseer, and this fact is not helped by the fact that João is an inlander (*sertanejo*), a true cowboy, taciturn and independent, from the cattle country to the north of Recôncavo. When Dona Sinhá is away, he occupies a different position, subject to the orders of Seu Paulo unless Dona Sinhá has left definite instructions for him. When Dona Sinhá is present he receives orders directly from her, bypassing the overseer. João is in a position to check on much of the plantation activity, bringing to the owner's attention any necessary works forgotten by Seu Paulo.

Below the owner, overseer, foreman, and cowboy are the bulk of the resident workmen (*moradores*). On the Fazenda das Moças, there is a population of slightly over two hundred men, women, and children, providing a working force of between sixty and seventy men and boys, plus a few women who occasionally do light work in the fields.

Below is an extract from one of the fortnightly pay sheets of the plantation. A brief explanation of the list, beginning at the top, will give a good idea of at least a part of the work on a plantation in this community. The "second weeding of a cane field" indicates that the man worked in a field which had already been weeded once since planting. Depending upon the amount of sunshine and rain and the quality of the weeding done, a field may have to be weeded as many as seven times between harvests. A cane field (*taboleiro*) varies from ten to twenty *tarefas,* and each field is numbered. Seu Paulo can therefore assign a man to weed a certain field, and they will both know whether it is the first, second, third, or other weeding. The weedings become progressively more difficult so that the amount paid per unit increases with the number of weedings. Weeding constitutes one of the major expenditures on Fazenda das Moças, as it is done slowly with a hoe. As with all other tasks on the plantation, there is a set price for this work.

"Carrying seed" indicates the transference of bundles of tops of sugar-cane stalks from a field where they are cut to another where they are planted. The amount paid per trip increases with the distance the man must travel between fields. As a rule, several fields of cane are planted to be used exclusively for seed. The next item on the list, "cutting seed," indicates work done in these fields. The top of the stalk just below the leaves is used as seed.

"Cutting out cattle" refers to selecting cattle from the herd to be used for the day's transportation. The "trip to neighboring plantation" means that Malaquias was sent to another plantation on an errand either for Dona Sinhá or for Seu Paulo on some plantation business, such as to get the payroll sheets, which are made up by a resident of another plantation. "Planting" means the first planting of sugar cane, while "replanting" means planting cane in the spaces where the first seed did not grow, either because it was buried too deeply, or because after planting it received too much sunshine or too much rain. Such spaces are always filled in when the new cane reaches a height of several inches.

"Carpentering," a craft, commands a higher salary than agricultural work. Sometimes a plantation keeps a carpenter on a regular salary; at other times he is hired from the factory, as is the case here. His work may be on the wooden carts used for transportation or on any of the many houses of the plantation.

An *estiva* is a type of makeshift bridge crossing a drainage ditch or a low spot on the road where water collects during the rainy season. It is usually no more than four or five yards long and a yard or two wide. The lengthwise pieces are bamboo with other pieces of the same material laid across them close together. Then earth is placed on top and smoothed off. These bridges require constant repair work. During the height of the rainy season they often break up entirely and float away. They are often quite perilous for horses, burros, and oxen, whose legs sometimes go through the bamboo latticework.

"Catching escaped cattle" requires some agility on the part of the person who does it. It is usually done on foot, and if the ox or cow is in a cane field it must be worked out carefully in order not to destroy too much of the standing sugar cane. "Repairing fences" accompanies catching escaped cattle, for the animals often break through the fences enclosing their pastures. The fence posts are usually of bamboo, which rots quickly

				Cr$	Cr$
Ricardo Teixeira	2nd weeding of cane field	13½ braças*	at	3.50	47.25
Julio Bispo	digging drainage ditch	30 meters	at	1.50	45.00
Paulo Manoel	carrying seed	12 trips	at	0.80	9.60
José Santo	cutting seed	5 loads	at	0.80	4.00
S. Santo	cutting out cattle	1 day	at	15.00	15.00
Malaquias Ario	trip to neighboring plantation	1 trip	at	10.00	10.00
Mario Adriano	3rd weeding of cane field	249 braças	at	3.70	921.30
F. Cramosa	planting	3½ braças	at	2.20	7.70
Cecilio Argolo	replanting	65 braças	at	1.50	97.50
Paulo Manoel	carpentering	3 days	at	23.00	69.00
Sancho Santiago	repairing estiva	1 day	at	12.00	12.00
Paulo Souza	1st weeding of cane field	35 braças	at	3.20	112.00
Agostinho Batista	catching escaped cattle	2	at	10.00	20.00
Mario Serra	repairing fences	250 braças	at	0.15	37.50
Maria das Dores	gathering cane leaves for animal fodder	4 cartloads	at	2.00	8.00
Francisco Julião	loading railway wagon with sugar cane	½ day	at	7.50	7.50
Pedro Julio	cutting bamboo	12 mãos†	at	5.00	60.00
Francisco Brito	conducting load of wood	1 load	at	15.00	15.00
Crispim Argolo	repairing barracks	2½ days	at	12.00	30.00
Domingos Moura	gardening	12 days	at	10.00	120.00
Osorio Ancieto	burying a burro	1 day	at	12.00	12.00
Pedro Julio	carrying water	1 day	at	10.00	10.00

*The braça equals 6 feet and is the measurement always used locally in the cane fields.
†Mão is a bundle of fifty and is used locally in speaking of fence posts and ears of corn.

and must be constantly watched and replaced as it shows signs of weakening. "Cutting bamboo" is done for many different ends. Most plantation boundary lines are marked by rows of graceful bamboos whose wood is used for fence posts and *estivas,* as well as for the wicker framework of the mud-covered houses.

Maria das Dores, whose name is listed as "gathering cane leaves for animal fodder," does the only type of work on the plantation done by women other than housework and gardening. When a field of cane is cut, the tops of the stalks and the long leaves are cut off and left on the ground. The very tip of the stalk is used as seed, while the heavier part is loaded on carts and sent to the factory. When natural pasturage gives out because of overgrazing or drought, the cattle's diet is supplemented with the freshly cut, green cane leaves; if the tender tips are not required for seed, they are also fed to the cattle. Gathering the leaves and stalk tips is relatively light work, and if a woman on the plantation wants to supplement her husband's income this is the task assigned her. Few women on this plantation do it, however, for it is a point of pride with any husband that he is capable of supporting his wife without her having to do gainful work. Only a small number of leaves are gathered up, and the remainder are burned as they lie in the field. Burning is done at night when there is little or no wind, and often during the summer fires which extend for acres dot the countryside. Burning is a traditional practice. Although professional agronomists insist that it is injurious to the cane roots and the new shoots, planters continue to burn the unwanted leaves, feeling that the ash provides some fertilization.

"Gardening" refers to work done in the vegetable garden which supplies Dona Sinhá's house. This garden stands in contrast to the *roças,* which are planted by the workers as well as by Dona Sinhá, and which are reserved for beans, manioc, corn, and some tobacco. Such plants as lettuce, tomatoes, cabbage, carrots, and other vegetables are disdained by the workers and are grown only for Dona Sinhá.

"Carrying water" is usually work reserved for a small boy. Mounted on a donkey with four wooden kegs he rides to the neighboring plantation, Pedras, which belongs to the factory, fills the kegs at the spring, and returns to Fazenda das Moças where he puts the water into the various large clay containers in the kitchen and washrooms of the owner's house. "Oh, Pedro, there's no water" is a common cry heard in Dona Sinhá's house.

There are few rules restricting the workers. Their services must be at the disposal of Dona Sinhá whenever required. Other than that, if during a slack season a man finds an opportunity to work somewhere else, he is free to do so. If he has a burro, or oxen, he has the right to pasture them on the lands of the plantation, renting them to Dona Sinhá at harvest time for transport. Often a family has one or two pack horses or burros which can be used to transport cane or, at other times of the year, water or firewood. A worker also has the right to a plot to raise food crops. If the man in the household dies or deserts his family, the woman who is left can do one of several things: go to work in the field herself, the least popular alternative; send her children out to work if they are old enough; find another husband, which is not too difficult, for there is a scarcity of women in this rural zone; or return to her father's house.

A group of workers who are essential to the well-being of the plantation, but who are not residents, are the *caatingueiros* (migrant workers from the scrubby forest area which borders on the Recôncavo and extends into the desert to the north). Hundreds of these men are available during the harvest season, a time when not only the plantations but the factories as well need more men than the resident population provides. The town of Vila Recôncavo, the other small rural towns, and the capital city do not supply agricultural workers to the rural areas. The plantations use instead the migrants from the north. A system has grown up whereby each plantation and factory has a man who can contact these migrant laborers. This man is called the *empreiteiro,* a contractor who has a system of contacts in the north usually through family and godparent relationships. The migrant workers are housed in the barracks, and generally keep themselves well apart from the residents. Only men come, leaving their families at home to care for their small farms and livestock while they earn money in the Recôncavo. None of these men appears on the plantation payroll. It is the *empreiteiro* who contracts with the overseer to have the required work done by the migrant laborers. Usually this work consists only of weeding, which must be done constantly but which at harvest time the resident workers cannot do. On the list of jobs and wages, above, there appears the name of Mario Adriano, who received 921.30 *cruzeiros* for weeding 249 *braças*. This man is the *empreiteiro,* who is paid for work done by fifteen, twenty, or more men. He in turn pays the migrant laborers, giving them less than the price for which he agreed with the overseer to do the work. In this way the contractor earns a living. Throughout the harvest season he gets work for about seventy-five to one hundred migrants, who camp in and about the barracks and have little to do with the residents. At the end of the season they can be seen walking along the paths of the Recôncavo toward the north, each man carrying over his shoulder a stick from which is suspended a cloth bundle containing his few possessions.

One prominent aspect of the relationships between people in this hierarchy is the intimacy and familiarity which has for so long characterized the Recôncavo. While slavery was not a benign institution anywhere, there was a softness in the relations between the Brazilian and his slaves which seems to have been absent in other slave areas. This quality persists today on private plantations such as Fazenda das Moças between the owner and the workers. Dona Sinhá knows the residents by name or nickname, knows their background and present condition; the worker knows Dona Sinhá's family background, her children, and her extended family.

The former master is now the patron. It is she who arbitrates any differences between workers, or between a worker and Seu Paulo. It is her task to protect the worker against injustices, to provide medical care, to aid at weddings and baptisms, in short to do all the things the worker is unable to do through ignorance, fear, or poverty.

The relationship between Dona Sinhá and Seu Paulo is a curious one, for neither one of them can do without the other. The role of overseer came into being for several reasons, the primary one being the absenteeism of the owner. In order to keep the plantation running properly all year long it was necessary for someone with knowledge and authority to be present all the time; so the former *feitor-mor* became known as the overseer, with a house larger and better than that of anyone else on the plantation except the owner. As time went on, the overseer gathered more and more rights and privileges unto himself, until today he is the veritable owner of the plantation in all but the legal sense. He has the confidence and loyalty of the workmen, without which he would be a failure. He eventually becomes related to nearly all of them through the system of godparentship; in fact, he is more sought after than the owner for this purpose. On the Fazenda das Moças, the overseer is paid a higher salary than any other overseer in the area—as much as Cr$1,500.00 a month in comparison with Cr$1,000.00 or less for the others. In addition he receives a bonus at the end of the year, one *cruzeiro* for each ton of sugar cane the plantation produced during the year.

Dona Sinhá and other plantation owners feel that a plantation cannot be successful without a good overseer, and they also feel that the white man does not make a good overseer. They say he cannot stand the heat of the summer and the rain and mud of the winter when spending entire days in the saddle overseeing the work. Only the indefatigable *mestiço* is supposed to be able to take such punishment. The owners also say that only he can deal properly with the *mestiço* workers—that, being one himself, he knows their "foibles and tricks." To a certain extent the *mestiço* population seems to agree with this, for orders from the overseer are much more promptly obeyed than orders from the owner, and most of the workmen prefer to have the overseer explain what is wanted. It is also believed that the *mestiço* is stronger. For example, if Dona Sinhá has made a hard trip in the winter to get to the plantation the workers will sympathize with her, saying, "You came through all that rain and mud, and at night!" when the same trip may be a daily one for the overseer, the cowboy, or any of the workers.

However, the creation of the position of overseer has also created a series of new problems for the owners. All owners now suspect their overseers of cheating them, and the control of the overseer is a subject which comes up frequently at social gatherings. Since the owner is absent from the plantation about half the year, there are many things which the overseer must do without consulting his employer. The owners will interpret independent action on the overseer's part as good management, mismanagement, or cheating, depending upon the results of the action. When the results are doubtful and there is any suspicion that the overseer might have gained money by his action, it is considered cheating. Very often the owners claim that the overseer and the foreman are "partners" working together against him.

On one plantation in the community of Vila Recôncavo, the owner decided he would be his own overseer. He was young and had been born and brought up on the plantation. Within a few years his harvest had dropped to almost nothing, and lately he has changed to raising milk cows, at which he has not been particularly successful either. He himself, and all his friends, blame his lack of success on the lack of an overseer, saying that even though the old overseer had cheated and helped himself to what was not his, the plantation as a whole had not suffered as badly as it did without him.

As a result, owners have to be satisfied with higher costs than they feel necessary and less profit than they think possible, the difference going to the overseer, rather than accept the complete failure of the plantation. Overseers, foremen, and owners are all aware of the situation, but politeness, the traditional respect patterns, and the unwillingness to compete openly keep the situation covert.

Nevertheless, on Fazenda das Moças, in spite of these difficulties there is considerable cooperation between Dona Sinhá and Seu Paulo. The duties of the overseer are confined generally to the plantation itself— seeing that the work is done, the cane planted, cultivated, harvested, and delivered to the factory as expediently as possible. The duties of Dona Sinhá are mainly concerned with finance, with arranging ready funds to meet the current expenses of the plantation. The practice of mortgaging crops did not end with the abolition of slavery, and it is the owner's task to juggle funds, loans, and interest so she will have enough money to improve and increase the yield of her plantation. In general the owners of single plantations rarely have enough funds to carry them through the year. Payrolls are met throughout the year with advances on the estimated harvest made by the factory, by the banks, or by the Cooperative of Sugar-Cane Growers and Suppliers. Thus when the season ends the owner is already in debt, part of which he must pay off in order to finance the coming year. There are two problems constantly present in the struggle to increase the size of the harvest: cost of production, and the antiquated methods used on the private plantations, where practically all work is done by hand.

Table 1 shows production, costs, and profits for the harvests of the years 1947–48, 1948–49, and 1949–50 at Fazenda das Moças. The drop in production and the rise in costs in the years 1948–49 were attributed to a slackening of the vigilance of Dona Sinhá and to a poor overseer. It was at the end of this year that Seu Paulo assumed the position of overseer of the plantation. The following year showed a great improvement which has continued, for the 1950–51 harvest produced 6,000 tons, the highest output of any private plantation in the Recôncavo. Future harvests are expected to go well above this. In addition to changing the overseer, and in the following year the foreman, Dona Sinhá was able to borrow enough money to purchase the tractor mentioned earlier. The next year, as a result of the evident success of the new combination, two four-wheeled carts were added which could be drawn by the tractor, thus cutting down transportation costs. Recently a jeep was acquired to pull the carts, and a second tractor equipped with the mechanism to cultivate cane fields was purchased.

Still, the plantation is heavily in debt, and any profits are immediately used for improvements or for paying off debts. Moreover, the cost of tractors, jeeps, and fertilizer is very high since they are imported products. Because of the dollar exchange rate their cost is extravagantly high in Brazil, compared with the United States. In addition, the plantation is still burdened with the old equipment and the necessity of pasture for the oxen, which cuts down the acreage available for planting. Animal traction cannot yet be entirely dispensed with, because of the condition of the soil in winter. The problem of maintaining the old system of work as well as introducing the new, which can only slowly pay for itself, is considerable. Dona Sinhá is faced with the dilemma of difficult natural conditions which, while good in many ways for sugar cane, impede the application of modern techniques. She is also faced with personnel problems in relation to the overseer. One solution is clearly apparent and has been adopted by Dona Sinhá: to spend more and more time on the plantation, sharing more and more work with Seu Paulo. This of course is a complete break with the past traditions of the plantation master. It is a difficult break for both parties concerned. Dona Sinhá misses her city life, and Seu Paulo resents the continued presence of the owner and the consequent lessening of his authority.

Along with their feeling of pride and love for the Recôncavo, many landowners recognize clearly the difficulties with which they are faced.

TABLE 1   *Production, Costs, Profits: Fazenda Das Moças*

1947–1948	
4,000 tons of cane at the selling price of Cr$81.40 a ton	Cr$325,600.00
Cost of production	206,244.00
Profit	119,356.00
1948–1949	
2,500 tons of cane at Cr$88.90	222,250.00
Cost of production	225,198.00
Loss	32,948.00
1949–1950	
5,000 tons of cane at Cr$107.40	537,000.00
Cost of production	319,248.00
Profit	217,751.00

The following excerpt from the diary of Dona Sinhá, which I was allowed to read, illustrates the outlook of a sugar-cane planter of the Recôncavo:

. . . "Dona Sinhá, there is a man here looking for you." "What is it, my son?" "I have some boils coming out all over my body." Some sulfa and a little ointment do the trick, and just in time, for here comes Seu Paulo, the overseer.

"The oxen of Pedras, the neighboring plantation, invaded the cane fields last night. Also those of Seu Cosme." "I'll telephone the *usina* immediately." "Also, there are no wagons at the loading point." "I'll find out about that too."

The tractor driver comes, complaining that there is no oil. I get that from the storeroom. Now there are two men on the veranda wanting to know about the last payday, when they claim their money "came out wrong." Going through the pay sheets, that was straightened out.

Now, while there is no one else, I'll go out and look over the fields. I look at the plantings, feel the earth which I love. But it doesn't satisfy me. Something is missing. We are backward and retrogressing, passively. This place puts an inertia in the heart of a person, a desire to stop fighting, to find everything fine and as it should be—the ragamuffin Negroes, poorly fed, ignorant and rude, their dirty children with protruding stomachs and the white pretending that there is progress, his house full of company, electricity, radio, telephone, horseback rides, poetry of Baudelaire, Verlaine, philosophy of Voltaire, Carlyle, etc.—but in the end, zero! Sometimes I feel a tremendous anguish, I feel that nothing can be done in the Recôncavo and I want to leave this paralyzed land, poisoned with tradition, with its ruined *sobrados*. And we today hold fast to these fantasies and want to relive the opulent past. Deep down there is a clash against these indefatigable overseers, mulattoes, and Negroes with their boots, *senhores da fazenda*.

The entire harvest is done with great sacrifice, my head wearied by accounts; 6,000 tons of cane, over CR$600,000.00—a lot of money, enough for all the expenses, and still some left over. What a mistake! The general costs, the extraordinary costs, house repairs, etc., will take it all. So we start again—new plantings, larger fields, all for more money. But we lack the courage to stop planting sugar cane and plant corn or coffee, anything else. We were born hearing of *senhores de engenho,* of trays and trays of silver service, of Negro slaves, of everything which has disappeared into the past. But it still burns in our blood, and deep down we want to have lands, to order and be obeyed. We like the humble and servile vassalage of the Negro, which makes us feel important, the dispensers of favors.

I think of this as old Saturno goes along, step by step. There is Paulos Santos coming along the road, with his little burro and two baskets, going to get manioc for the ever-present *farinha.* "Good morning, Patron!" What affection I feel for each one of them! Pedro Manuel with so many little children; Zé Julião with his sick wife, Conceição with his air of secular servility. But affection resolves nothing! Money and action do! I could knock down those miserable hovels and make good hygienic houses.

Once home I fall into the hammock, reading Proust and forgetting everything.

THE USINA: USINA SÃO PEDRO

The Sociedad Anonima, the corporation which operates this factory, represents the new pattern in the Recôncavo. There are now nine factories functioning in the Recôncavo, for the trend has been to close the small ones which could not function economically. Five of the nine belong to one corporation, which holds extensive lands and receives the cane of many suppliers. We will describe the smallest of the four independent factories, which has a rated capacity of seventy-two thousand sacks of sugar as compared with the two hundred thousand of one of the larger mills (a sack equaling 60 kilograms). The legal capacity of the Usina São Pedro—which it has never reached—is fifty-two thousand sacks, as determined by the Institute of Sugar and Alcohol. At the present time, however, the factory is undergoing a reformation which will raise its capacity to over one hundred thousand sacks, and the legal capacity will be readjusted.

Usina São Pedro, although the smallest, is representative of the others and experiences the same problems and difficulties. It differs from some in that it is a family enterprise. The stockholders are nearly all members of the Conde family, and the operations are directed by two members of the family. The factory itself was one of the three built by the state government in 1900 on land controlled by the Navy,[5] on the edge of the Bay, which provides excellent year-round transportation facilities. The mill was acquired in 1909 by the Conde family with two plantations, to which the family has since added four other contiguous plantations. The corporation has a total area of slightly over four thousand acres, mostly of rich *massapê* soil. The factory receives cane from the plantation of Dona Sinhá, who is also a member of the Conde family by birth and by marriage. It also gets cane from four other plantations within the community and four outside the community, which send their cane by the traditional sailboat. In addition, the factory owns a 2,324-acre plantation in the county of Purificação which is used for grazing and raising cattle and for supplying wood for the factory fires. There is direct water transportation between the factory and the plantation in Purificação.

The designation *usina* has several meanings which are quite similar to the meanings of the older term, *engenho*. In its larger context, *usina* means the entire land-factory combination, including the mill and all the plantations belonging to the corporation. More specifically, *usina* means the factory building itself. In another context, *usina* simply indicates the population nucleus, including the factory, the owner's house, and the other buildings.

The *usina* or factory nucleus roughly follows the same settlement pattern of the old plantations. The point of orientation is the factory building, near which stand the chalet and other homes of the owning family, which are grouped together in a park of royal palms and mango trees. Usually a small chapel or oratory is included in one wing of the chalet, where a Mass can be celebrated for the family when a priest is available.

Situated nearest the chalet are the houses of the general overseer, the chief mechanic of the factory, the major office employees, and the director of the factory store. Next in order are the houses of the technical personnel of the factory. Behind them and farthest from the center are the homes of the agricultural workers who work on the plantation nearest the factory nucleus. The regional overseer of this plantation also lives among his plantation workers. The school and the store are located just outside the small park of the chalet.

The chalet has replaced the former *solar* (mansion) of the plantation masters. Its style differs from the earlier type and its name is derived from the fact that it is a modified copy of a Swiss chalet. In a different way it is as ornate as the old *solar*, but more up-to-date, with running water and electricity.

The personal, paternal aspect of the private plantation obviously cannot function on the *usina*, which has 1,350 people living on its lands. There is, nevertheless, an attempt at just such relations. The owning family spends vacations in the chalet. They also spend Christmas, *Carnaval*, and *Botada*[6] there, and at those times there are parties for the workers, Christmas presents for them and for their wives and children, dances, and ball games. The *Coronel* (Colonel, an honorary title now going out of use), the patriarch of the family, now incapacitated, still receives visits from the older workmen who used to have daily contact with him. His son and son-in-law, present directors of the enterprise, make their presence felt throughout the factory and the six plantations as best they can. As on the private plantation, the final arbitration of any difficulty lies with the *usineiro,* and no worker considers himself too far removed to go to him if he cannot get satisfaction from his overseer. However, the strongest relationships, both business and personal, lie between overseer and worker—employee and employee—rather than between employee and employer.

The private plantation presents a far better appearance than any plantation belonging to the factory, for it is usually "home" to the owner, who is interested in keeping it as pleasant as possible, while the factory plantation in charge of an overseer is simply a business project existing only to produce sugar cane.

At the Usina São Pedro, as stated earlier for the Recôncavo generally, the consolidation of land by the corporations has not turned the entire property into one large plantation. Instead, each plantation has retained its old boundaries, indeed complete autonomy, following only the general policies of the factory directory. The Usina São Pedro happens to be situated in a central position in relation to its six plantations. This is not always the case, for frequently the lands of a factory are scattered far from the plant itself, creating difficulties of administration and transportation.

Each of the plantations has its own nucleus, the street of workers' houses oriented toward the house of the overseer. Each of these little villages has its own small store, usually a private enterprise of the overseer. The largest plantation, Pedras, has a chapel and a school. None of the plantations has an electric power line, but each has a telephone in the overseer's house. The feeling of isolation and abandonment is strong, as indeed it is on almost all overseer-directed plantations belonging to a factory. There is a general feeling of pity for the residents who are situated so far from their *patrão* and whose first recourse must be the overseer, a man like themselves, with little or no education and little interest in the people other than to keep them working. In other words, the factory plantation lacks the paternal hand of the owner. In other respects it is similar to the private plantation in that it has an overseer, a foreman, a cowboy, and resident workmen.

The bulk of the agricultural direction of the São Pedro plantations is in the hands of the general overseer, Seu Pipiu. It is his duty to direct and supervise the activities of all six plantations. He is a man of no small status. He is practically independent in his actions, for the directors of the factory tell him how much cane they feel they need in the forthcoming harvest, and it is up to him to produce it. The methods and problems in doing this are left up to him. Seu Pipiu gives orders to each of the regional overseers, whose duties are the same as those of the overseer on a private plantation. The only difference is that they are dealing with a superior employee, instead of with the owner in person. The general overseer is entitled to the same rights and privileges as any other worker: a house, land on which to grow subsistence crops, and the use of the owner's pastures for his oxen, burros, and horses. The horses used in his work are supplied by the corporation, as are those of the other overseers. His salary is high: Cr$2,000.00 a month, plus a bonus of one *cruzeiro* for each ton of cane produced on all six plantations. The regional overseers receive Cr$800.00 a month, plus a bonus of half a *cruzeiro* per ton of cane produced on their plantation. Seu Pipiu has been general overseer of Usina São Pedro for twenty-five years, during which time he has accumulated a good deal of property. He is a mulatto, somewhat lighter skinned than the six administrators who are under him. Two of his sons work in the factory office, and a third runs the store on one of the plantations. In addition he is a small farmer, renting some forty acres from the factory, on which he plants sugar cane. He pays 25 per cent of the harvest to the factory for the use of the land.

The *usineiros* have the same complaints against their general overseers that private plantation owners have against theirs. At the same time, after many years of service such an official becomes indispensable, or is thought to be, and is allowed to go his way—quiet, well dressed, well mounted, ruler of all he surveys—while the *usineiro* watches and mutters to himself.

So far the rural properties of the factories have led the private plantations in the field of mechanization, as they have greater funds for purchasing equipment and can get more use out of each piece. Mechanization, however, is used as yet only in preparing the soil for planting. The ground is plowed and replowed, and grooves are made to receive the cane shoots. Also, planting in unplowed land is still common—grooves are opened for the seed with the simple plow, and no soil preparation is done at all. Here mechanization ends, and all further cultivation, as well as the cutting and harvesting of the cane, is done by hand. Narrow-gauge railway tracks reach out from the mill to loading points on the six plantations, where the cane is transferred from the oxcarts to the railroad wagons to be drawn to the mill. Approximately two thousand acres are under cultivation; the remaining land is used as pasture or as garden plots by the workers, in accordance with a rotation system.

Financially the two units—factory and plantation—are run separately. One set of books is kept for the agricultural part, and one set for the factory. The six plantations combined produced eighteen thousand tons of cane in 1950, although they had planned on twenty-three thousand. The fall in the expected harvest was due to several things. First, less new cane was planted, because of the activities of the petroleum workers who were invading the cane fields of the factory and drilling oil wells. (The first time a field is cut, the percentage of cane is higher than that obtained by cuts during the next four or five years. The same amount of land, therefore, will produce more cane if it is replanted regularly. The factory, however, deemed it wiser to be content with the older plantings for one year because of the oil workers' invasion, for newly planted cane is more subject to damage than an established field.) Second, during that year there was a serious drought which affected adversely the growth of sugar cane. There is no irrigation in the Recôncavo, and during the drought seasons which come periodically a partial crop loss nearly always occurs. In addition one entire *taboleiro* caught fire and burned to the ground, causing the loss of many tons of cane.

The agricultural cycle and the work on a plantation may be divided into two broad epochs, summer and winter. Summer is the busiest season, for it is harvest time and all hands are occupied, including the migrant workers. The cutters with their machetes cut an average of three to four tons a day apiece, which must be quickly loaded and carried to the factory and milled, for the longer the lapse of time between the two operations, the greater the loss of sugar content. After a field has been cut, one of two things occurs. If it is to be turned into pasture, it is fenced, and the draft animals are turned loose in it. Otherwise the leaves which were cut from the top of the plant and left lying on the ground are burned, and within a short time the roots start sending up new shoots. This old planting (*soca*) each year gives a decreased yield. As a rule a field is cut and burned three to four years before being turned into pasture. In the days of the old plantations, when the soil was more vigorous, cane of twelve years was considered "new cane." Now, however, the yield is so decreased by the increasing poverty of the soil that three to four years is the best, depending upon the amount of rain. During the summer, if land is prepared and there are prospects of heavy showers, "summer plantings" may be made. They are never as good as those done in the winter, for the sun frequently kills the new shoots. Toward the end of summer, the pastures or garden plots which are to be made into new plantations (*rêgo novo*) are prepared, for such work is usually done in accordance with conditions of the land rather than only at the time of planting. New plantings yield an average of thirty to forty tons per acre. Cutting, transporting, burning, and planting are done by the resident workers, while the weeding and general cultivating are carried out by the migrant laborers.

Work in the winter period can usually be handled by the resident workers alone. The planting of cane goes on throughout the year, but the most favorable time is during July and August, when the rains begin to diminish in constancy and the sun shines longer. Cane planted at this time gives the greatest yield. The seed used is the top part of the cane itself, the "eye" which appears just below the leaves. As a rule each plantation furnishes most of its own seed. That for the summer planting comes from the cane which is cut to go to the factory, and that for the winter from small plantings made previously for the purpose. The state government also maintains an agricultural station in the area, from which the planters can get seed. During the winter all repairs are made on houses, fences, and equipment, and of course the necessary drainage ditches must be built or repaired and seasonal cultivation and clearing work must be done.

The *usineiros* maintain that the agricultural operations pay more than does the factory. The factory plantations sell their cane at the same price as the private suppliers, a price fixed by the Institute of Sugar and Alcohol. This price has gradually gone up as have all the factory costs. But the ceiling price of sugar, which is Cr$166.00 a sack, has not increased. In 1951 the cost per sack of sugar at Usina São Pedro was Cr$132.00. Each year the costs rise, creeping nearer and nearer to the selling price. So while the books show that each plantation is making more money for its cane, the factory's books show a slackening of profits. At the moment, most of the factories in the Recôncavo are engaged in refining their processes in order to get a higher percentage of sugar out of each ton of cane. The Usina São Pedro is only able to get an average of eighty kilograms of sugar per ton of cane, while the largest factory gets one hundred kilograms per ton. The factory also loses money because it pays for the cane by the ton of dead weight, and not by the percentage of sucrose the cane contains. As a result the planters are interested in raising a heavy cane and increasing their tonnage rather than in raising the quality of the cane. There is a movement under way to change the payment method to payment by percentage of sucrose, but it seems to be gaining little headway.[7]

The factory of the Usina São Pedro is directed personally by two members of the Conde family, while most other factories have a paid employee, a general manager, who is the industrial counterpart of the general overseer. There are approximately eighty salaried employees in this factory, who are paid by the day and who work all year long. The factory operates from September till February—the harvest season—in two shifts of twelve hours each. During the harvest season over a hundred migrant workers are added to the payroll under the direction of the contractor, and usually work on the endless belt and in the unloading operations.

The resident factory worker, in addition to receiving a house, also has the right to electric light and to firewood. These workers are trained in the factory, and many of them have been there for a long time. The Usina São Pedro is especially proud of the loyalty of its men, many of whom remained there during the war when they were being enticed away with higher wages by the federal government to build military installations. The Usina São Pedro has experienced no labor difficulties as have some other larger factories, which have had riots and demonstrations caused by labor unions. This is due partly to the small size of the factory, and partly to the continued atmosphere of paternalism, to which many other factories are now making a determined effort to return.

Thus paternalism stands out as one of the major factors in the complicated organizational hierarchy of plantation life. The former master is now simply the patron, but in this role he carries out almost the same functions as did the master in relation to the well-being of his slaves. The patron of today has the same ethical responsibilities toward his workmen as did the former master. In general these responsibilities include care of the workmen beyond the mere payment of a salary, such as care of the sick and the old. Paternalism today is found at its highest degree on the private, family-run plantation and at its lowest degree on the overseer-run, corporation plantation. At its highest level it is a form of unwritten social security which works well, supplementing the low wages which are paid throughout the area. Even on the factory plantations there is a mild form of paternalism, which is stronger in plantations nearer to the factory and to the home of the *usineiro*.

The migrant workers, however, do not fit into the pattern of paternalism, mostly because they do not seek it. Indirectly they receive its benefits, for if one of them is ill he can go to the contractor who will then go to the plantation owner or *usineiro* for medicine or whatever is needed. But in general the migrant laborers stay by themselves and ask little or nothing of their employers.

In addition to the protection provided by a paternalistic system, the workers have the right to at least half an acre of land on the plantation where they can plant and raise their subsistence crops. Often they also plant tobacco, both in these plots and in the small areas throughout the plantation where no sugar cane is planted, such as corners where the plow cannot penetrate. The tobacco is sold to traveling buyers who scour the area at the tobacco harvest season. The money thus gained belongs to the workers, and many of them say that cash earned in such a way provides

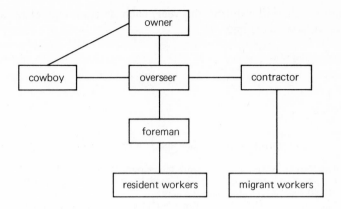

**Fig. 1. Hierarchical diagram of the private plantation
(Fazenda das Moças)**

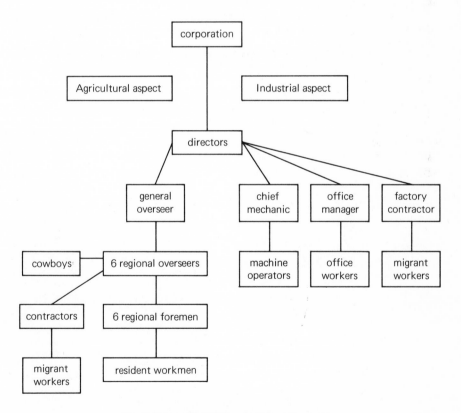

**Fig. 2. Hierarchical diagram of the *usina* system
(Usina São Pedro)**

the "extras" they like during the year, such as rum, cigarettes, a pair of earrings, or some perfume.

Notes

1. "Seu" is a corruption of Senhor and is a title often given to persons of some prestige.

2. The *tarefa* is the unit of land measurement used in Bahia. It equals 900 square *braças*. The *braça* equals 6 feet, which gives the *tarefa* 32,400 square feet. This is 11,160 square feet less than one acre.

3. The *cruzeiro* (Cr$) is the Brazilian monetary unit and equals roughly five cents in United States currency. Thus the value of the plantation is approximately $75,000.00.

4. de Araujo Pinho, *Historia de um engenho do Recôncavo, 1522–1944* (Rio de Janeiro, 1946), p. 243.

5. The shoreline bordering salt water is controlled to the depth of 33 meters by the Brazilian Navy.

6. *Botada* is the annual blessing of the factory machinery, performed on the first day of the grinding season. It is a traditional ceremony formerly carried out on the plantations.

7. Jayme V. B. Machado, *Industria acucareira na Bahia* (Bahia, 1950).

Allison Davis, Burleigh Gardner,
and Mary Gardner
INTIMIDATION OF LABOR

In an area where most tenants are colored and most landlords white, the caste system is a powerful aid to landlords in enforcing economic sanctions upon their laborers. When the deferential and obedient behavior which the caste system demands of the colored tenant is not observed, the landlord often resorts to the intimidation of the colored tenant, either by beating or shooting him or by threatening to do so. The use of threats for this purpose is universal among white landlords. The actual beating or shooting of tenants is much less common, chiefly for the reason that the frequent use of such violent sanctions would increase the difficulty which landlords already experience in maintaining a sufficient number of tenants. The evidence which was presented on this point, in the section dealing with the supply of labor, showed that one of the bases of competition between landlords for tenants was the landlord's reputation among tenants with regard to his use of physical violence.[1] At the same time, the field evidence reveals that the use of threats of violence by white planters is one of the basic controls upon labor, just as it has previously been demonstrated that intimidation is fundamental in maintaining the restrictions of caste.

Before proceeding to the evidence of the control of workers by intimidation, it is necessary to distinguish between the use of intimidation by the planter and its use by gangs or mobs, usually from the towns, who have motives other than the planters', his need being the maintenance of a steady and adequate supply of workers. When the White Shirts were beating and killing colored individuals near the close of the period of Reconstruction in Rural County to prevent them from voting, white planters often protected their colored tenants. During this period, a white plantation-manager in Rural County killed six white men in a gang which was terrorizing and shooting his colored tenants. In the same county in 1933 white planters still refused to allow white gangs to beat their colored tenants, unless the planters themselves had decided upon the whipping as a means of enforcing their control. A member of a whipping-gang cited a case of a landlord protecting his colored tenant in 1933:

> You bet the whites look after their own niggers. I went out with a party just last June to whip a nigger. I thought then, and still think, he

REPRINTED BY PERMISSION FROM *Deep South* (CHICAGO: UNIVERSITY OF CHICAGO PRESS, 1941), COPYRIGHT 1941 BY THE UNIVERSITY OF CHICAGO. ALL RIGHTS RESERVED. PUBLISHED OCTOBER 1941.

needed it; but just as we got to the place, the owner sent us word to leave the nigger alone, and that was the end of it. We just went home. We figured the owner of the place had to put up with the nigger, and it was his own lookout, and he could do what was necessary.

INTIMIDATION AND CASTE

When we turn to the evidence concerning the use of intimidation by planters themselves, to perfect the economic and occupational control of their workers, we find that the caste system and the economic system constantly reinforce one another. Most cases of terrorization which occur in the rural areas of both counties arise from conflicts between landlords and tenants with regard to the management of the farm and stock or the settlement of accounts.[2] An analysis of a large body of interview materials gathered from both planters and tenants in both Old and Rural counties reveals that practically all cases of intimidation result either (1) from the landlord's charge that the tenant has stolen property, deserted his crop, hurt or killed stock, refused to perform work at the time when the landlord wished it done, or damaged plantation roads or (2) from the tenant's charge that the landlord has cheated him in the settling of accounts for the year. Some instances of the use of intimidation to enforce the taboos of caste do occur, however. Although the caste system usually insures deference to the landlord's every wish, on the part of the colored tenant, some colored tenants occasionally refuse to accord such deference to their white landlords. When such a tenant is "impudent" or "too smart," the use of intimidation helps oil the wheels of the caste system.[3] One white landlord in Old County stated that he had told his sons who were managing his plantation to shoot or hang such a tenant on a neighbor's plantation.[4]

> There was one [colored tenant] out our way not long ago—he was on a place near ours—who was getting smart. I told my boys that if he didn't behave they ought to take him out for a ride, and tend to him, and tell him that if he didn't stop talking and acting so big, the next time it would be either a bullet or a rope. That is the way to manage them when they get too big—take them in hand before any real trouble starts.

Another large white planter in Rural County stated that he had beaten one of his tenants who "didn't do anything, but he had that insolent kind of manner about him." A very influential government official in Rural County felt that, "when a nigger gets ideas, the best thing to do is to get him under ground as quick as possible."

ECONOMIC CONTROL BY INTIMIDATION

In most cases of intimidation of tenants by landlords the purpose is not merely to enforce the caste taboos but also to maintain the economic system prevailing on the plantation. The wife of a large white planter in

Rural County who frequently whipped his colored tenants stated that whipping was the best method of controlling farm hands.

> That [whipping] is the way they usually do with farm hands. It is the best way. They can't afford to send them to jail because they need them on the farms; so they just take them out and give them a good beating, and that teaches them. It is a good way. It frightens them and they are all right after that. If they just whip one, it frightens the others enough. The boys [whipping group] were at it again last night, but I don't think they got any one. A lot of the men from here went down to help them, Mr. Corliss and some others. That is the way they do, help each other that way.

For Stealing. The most common reason advanced by landlords in both counties for the use of intimidation was the punishment of tenants who had stolen the landlord's property. A white planter in Rural County said that he always whipped colored tenants who stole his hogs or chickens; he then gave a detailed account of the beating of a colored man who had stolen goods from the plantation store. It is the custom in Rural County, he stated, for the landlord whose property has been stolen to invite a group of his social equals to help him whip the suspected tenant. He insisted, as did several other landlords, that the poor-whites and town loafers were not invited to these whipping-parties.

Some planters whipped their tenants without the aid of a gang. A very large landholder in Rural County said that he did not allow whipping-parties on his plantations but that he himself whipped tenants who stole from him.

Tenants' Attitudes Toward Stealing. A large number of additional accounts of whippings of tenants charged with stealing are available, but it is not necessary to continue these descriptions. The fact that stealing is the charge upon which most beatings are justified is the result both of the fact that the ownership of property is the basic principle of the society and of the fact that stealing is the most frequent offense of tenants. Many colored tenants do not regard the taking of small amounts of stock or cotton from their landlords as stealing but rather as a just compensation for the money stolen from them by their landlords in the reckoning of accounts or for the beatings administered to them by their landlords. Under the systems of economic control and intimidation exercised by the landlord, the colored tenant often justifies his thefts on the grounds that his only means of securing his fair share of the proceeds from his crop is by the use of stealth. This attitude was expressed by many colored workers both in Old City and on the farms. The fullest expression, however, came from two large colored landlords, who were interpreting the Negro tenants' behavior. One of these stated, in a conversation with another colored landlord, that a white planter once had asked him why colored tenants frequently stole from their landlords. He replied:

The white man has beat him, and kicked him and shot him, and hurt him, and lynched him, and cheated him, and stolen from him for so long, that the Negro feels that anything he can steal or cheat the white man out of is no more'n what's been done to him! The white man has made him crooked and immoral.

The white planter then said: "You know, I believe you're right about that!"

In a conversation between two large colored planters and a colored manager for a white planter the talk centered upon recent thefts from the white planter by his colored tenants. One of the colored landlords, who had lived in the county for more than forty years, said:

> That's why you hear white people say the Negro's an inveterate liar and thief. But really, I can't blame him. You see that is his only protection. Of course *you* can't do anything with him. He isn't afraid of you. You're colored. But a white man will ride over his place with a Winchester across his saddle, and if they talk that way to him, he'll shoot them, and claim they started back here [*putting his hand toward his hip pocket*] on him. And that will be all to it, because they control the courts and everything else. Well, the Negro knows that, so he uses a different method. He doesn't consider he's stealing from the white man. He considers that he's taking his part. He lies and flatters the white man as a way of getting around him.

The speaker then related the experience of a colored tenant who had recently shown his white landlord, by reference to his own account book, that the landlord had paid him $100 less than he owed him; the landlord had threatened to shoot him if he did not leave the plantation before nightfall.

> So there was nothing for him to do but leave. Well, that's just an example to show you how the Negro has to work in order to live. He's got to get his by his wit, his cunning. I don't blame him. He isn't naturally a thief; it's the system he has to live under which makes him that way.

To Make Tenants Work. A second reason for the use of intimidation by white landlords is to force colored tenants to perform the specific work which the landlord wants done at the time when he wishes it done, or to punish them if they refuse. One white planter in Old County stated that he had forced a colored tenant to pick his cotton, even though the weevil and rain had reduced the yield to the point where the tenant would receive nothing for his year's work. The tenant was a "good, hard-working Negro." He had wanted to begin other work in Old City, but the landlord stated he had to "make the Negro pick the cotton" in order to get his rent.

Because he cut timber instead of pulling corn as he had been ordered, another colored tenant was shot by his white landlord in Old County. The tenant, fatally wounded, then shot the landlord, who also died. In a similar case, a white landlord told his colored tenant that he was going to kill him because he had not picked his cotton when he had been ordered to do so. The landlord went to the tenant's cabin with his shotgun, but the tenant shot first, killing the landlord. In a fourth case, corroborated by a relief agency, a white landlord severely beat a colored woman who had refused to continue work in the fields when her baby was about to be born.

For Harming Stock. A third economic or property motive for the intimidation of workers was to punish them for maltreatment of stock. Particularly frank and vivid accounts of whippings on this score were furnished by a white planter in Rural County. He stated that he had whipped one of his colored tenants for beating mules which belonged to the landlord. "He started to run, but before he could get away, I hit him so hard with the whip that the shock just stopped him in his tracks. I then gave him a half a dozen good ones." The same landlord also related how he had whipped another colored worker for chasing calves instead of driving them in slowly, and a third worker for an action which had really been committed by a relative of the landlord.

> One day he [the relative] had gone to town in a wagon with a Negro, and when they got back I noticed that the mule had a long whip-cut on his back. I called the Negro up and told him I was going to whip him for cutting the mule—he knew I wouldn't stand anything like that. I took a piece of grass plow-line and thrashed him a bit with it. Afterward he told me that my cousin had cut the mule. He should have told me that before, and I wouldn't have hit him.

Over Credit and Settlements. A fourth economic motive for the intimidation of workers is to force them to pay for supplies furnished by landlords and to accept the landlord's reckoning of accounts in all matters pertaining to credit and the selling of the crop. A Negro tenant who questions a white landlord's reckoning is always regarded as a "bad Negro" and a danger to the operation of the plantation system itself. He is usually driven off the plantation before he can "spoil" the other tenants. A large white landlord in Old County stated that, when a colored tenant had refused to indorse his subsidy check from the federal government in the landlord's favor, in payment for supplies furnished him, he had called the tenant up before the other tenants, shown him a clasp knife, and told him that he "was going to cut his throat from ear to ear" unless he signed the check immediately. The tenant indorsed the check in favor of the landlord. The landlord, who used a knife in this case, said that he usually carried an automatic revolver when he rode his plantations.

Instances of the shooting of landlords by tenants who had objected to the landlords' reckoning of accounts were cited by colored informants.

Other Reasons. Intimidation was also used to preserve peace among tenants themselves. A planter in Rural County stated that he had forced two colored tenants, who often fought each other in "quarters," to fight for a whole hour and had allowed them to stop only when both had been severely beaten. In 1935 a use for intimidation which had not previously arisen, occurred in regard to the abortive efforts of colored tenants to organize a Huey P. Long Share-Our-Wealth Club. A large white planter said that he had told the wife of the colored tenant who was the leader of this group that he "would hate to have to help hang" her husband but that he would be forced to unless the man discontinued his efforts to organize the club. The tenant fled.

Whipping Women. The dogma of the caste system does not permit the extension of the code of chivalry to the women of the lower caste. Although colored women are usually allowed to escape unharmed when they have committed certain minor infractions of the taboos of caste (for which colored men would be beaten or shot), they also may be the victims of intimidation. Many colored women have been beaten, shot, or lynched by white individuals or mobs in the South—some of them in the area we are studying.

An instance of the beating of a pregnant tenant-woman by her landlord, when she refused to work, has already been cited. Other instances were described in detail by a white planter in Rural County. He related the story of his having beaten a colored woman for stealing, until "her head was all covered with blood." In a second case, he had whipped an old colored woman because she had insisted upon coming between the landlord and her son, whom he was trying to whip. "I didn't want to whip the old woman, but I finally had to. I just let her have it with the whip and gave her a good beating. Then I whipped the boy."[5]

IMPORTANCE OF "EXAMPLE"

The function of whippings and shootings such as these is to intimidate all colored farm workers in the area to the point where they will not object, either as individuals or as an organized group, to the economic and caste domination of the white landlords. One such incident is an effective warning to all colored tenants in the neighborhood. Interviews with colored workers show that an actual beating, shooting, or lynching serves as an "example" to most colored individuals in the area for years afterward. In most cases of conflict between a white landlord and a colored tenant, however, the landlord makes use only of threats. Threats are usually as effective as the use of violence because colored workers realize that the threats of white landlords are supported by the whole caste system, including the law officers and the courts.

Notes

1. According to the statement of an individual who had a large part in the negotiations to prevent the lynching of a colored man in the Delta in 1935, a lynching did not occur because the white planters did not wish colored tenants to leave the area in the midst of the cotton-planting season.

2. An officer of a relief agency of the federal government in a large neighboring city stated that most of their clients from the rural areas of Mississippi and Louisiana had fled as a result of conflicts with planters over these economic relations.

3. A large planter in Rural County stated that he had made the fathers of colored children whip them for infractions of the rules of caste or of the plantation system. "It often makes good Negroes out of them."

4. Although more than one hundred instances of the terrorization of colored workers by their white employers were cited by colored informants, all except three of the instances referred to in the following account were cited by white landlords themselves or by members of their families.

5. In the light of the above evidence of the widespread use of intimidation by planters in both counties, and of their entire willingness to describe beatings such as those cited in this account, it is necessary to attribute the following statement by a planter with regard to the treatment of colored workers in the past to an exaggerated form of the "Yankee hatred" which is still an extremely important factor in the politics, caste system, and myth of the South.

"I'm glad they've freed them [colored people] now, but the northerners all had the wrong idea about it. Of course, there were some hard masters, but most of the people were kind to their slaves and treated them just like members of the family. There were quite a number of what we call 'absent owners' here then, though. They owned the land, but they weren't here to manage it; so they had overseers to manage the Negroes for them. Those overseers were pretty cruel, a lot of them. But it was mostly northerners who were the absent owners, though. But most of the southern owners were kind to the slaves, and treated them like real members of the family."

Richard Frucht

A CARIBBEAN
SOCIAL TYPE:
NEITHER "PEASANT"
NOR "PROLETARIAN"[1]

Studies and commentaries on Caribbean societies have made it clear that such concepts as "peasant" and "proletarian" are not categorical, but variable.[2] In this paper I attempt to show that what may also be of importance in understanding Caribbean societies besides the nature of the category ("peasant" or "proletarian") is the nature of the variable relationships characterizing the society. I want to show that particularly for the smaller islands, such as Nevis,[3] the people are categorically neither peasants nor proletarians. Rather the situation may be comprehended by making use of Marx's analytic distinction between the *means of production,* that is, the tools and techniques, and *relations of production,* that is, what we usually mean by the social division of labour as well as the articulation of the productive economy and the social organization, including property and power relations. More specifically, I want to show that during the period after slave emancipation in 1834 and until the end of the second World War, Nevisian society could be characterized as exhibiting a *peasant-like* means of production along with *proletarian-like* relations of production. The argument here rests on discriminating between kinds of sharecropping or *metayage* relationships.

Most of our discussions about peasantry and proletariat in the Caribbean have been based on work carried out in the Greater Antilles[4]—Jamaica, Haiti and Puerto Rico—and in some of the more important Lesser or Eastern Antilles[5] such as Martinique and Trinidad, as well as Guyana. At the risk of over-simplifying, such peasantries are to be found in communities on lands marginal to the needs of the plantations, in the highlands and sometimes in the arid lowlands. A primary characteristic of peasantry is household production of subsistence crops on small plots, with cash crops produced according to location and market conditions.[6] Occasional involvement in wage labour on plantations in order to supplement cash needs is also a feature of Caribbean peasantries. They are usually contrasted with the part-societies of plantation labourers, the rural proletariat, who live on or near plantations and whose livelihood depends primarily upon the sale of their labour to the plantations and supplemented by desultory cultivation of subsistence crops on garden plots, when and if available.[7]

REPRINTED FROM *Social and Economic Studies,* VOL. 16, 1967, BY PERMISSION OF THE INSTITUTE FOR SOCIAL AND ECONOMIC RESEARCH, UNIVERSITY OF THE WEST INDIES.

I want to point out that the word "peasant" is not to be here understood as a categorical concept describing a subculture or kind of community. It is not to be so understood because the so-called peasantry of Nevis has always been inextricably bound to the plantation system or to some other system of wage labour in more than an occasional sense. This is an artifact of geography, of economic history, and of the economic and political predominance of the industrial, colonial power.[8]

In essence I want to make what I hope is not a too simplified distinction: that in Nevis, whereas there is a peasant-like *means* of production, which includes cultivation of small plots with the use of household labour and traditional manual technology,[9] the *relations* of production are proletarian, that is, based on the sale of labour for wages either paid in cash or in kind, and the latter through systems of sharecropping, farming-out, and under conditions of male labour emigration. Finally, the existence together and in alternation of seemingly disparate *means* and *relations* of production is an adaptation to the vicissitudes of a marginal economy.

The development of a peasant-like means of production—household production—began after the emancipation of slaves in 1834, because of geographical and economic factors. In the first place, free villages of the type founded in Jamaica, for instance, did not develop in the Leeward Islands since there was no land available either for slaves or freedmen. All the land was alienated and under the control of the plantation-owners. The post-emancipation villages established on free-hold or lease-hold tenure grew on estate boundaries, along the sides of steep ravines, too steep for profitable sugar-cane cultivation, on the arid lowlands, and on the steep upper slopes of the central mountain masses. In short, the villages were founded on land marginal to the plantations' uses, but on or near them so that they served, in effect, as dormitories for the labourers. Such villages are still found in St. Kitts and Antigua where plantations predominate. In Nevis, however, the plantation economy slowly became a small-holders' economy through the failings of the sugar—and, later, the cotton—markets. But the small-holders' economy in this island is not a peasant economy—that is, it is *not always* and has never been *only* a peasant economy.

To some extent, the economy based on household production of subsistence and cash crops on small plots was instituted in order to preserve a way of life based on the social relations of plantation production. In Nevis, for instance, the end of the apprenticeship period in 1838 and the final emancipation of slaves, together with the threatened position of the entire West Indian sugar industry led to a call for debt payments on the part of the factors and creditors of plantation operators. The resulting cash shortage and the necessity of maintaining plantation operations for the benefit of the planters and absentee-owners resident in England led to the adoption of forms of sharecropping as the means by which sugar-cane cultivation could be carried on. The hallmark of sharecropping is the use of household labour, but the share which remains with the labourer can be considered a form of wage payment—not in cash, but in kind. In other words, the freed slaves were forced to remain on plantation lands, and the lack of cash with which to pay these freedmen even low wages impelled the planters to pay their labourers in kind—through the means of what may be referred to as the share-wage.

The share-wage is one form of sharecropping. It refers to a situation in which the cropper, or labourer, supplies the tools—in this case hoe and pitch-fork—and the labour—his own and that of his household. The landowner, on the other hand, supplies the seed, the fertilizer, the insecticide, and supervision in the person of a "chargehand" or overseer. Furthermore, within this relationship it is the owner who decides which crop shall be cultivated. In this way the share which remains with the sharecropper or labourer can be considered a form of wages in kind.[10]

The other form of sharecropping is what I refer to as the share-rent, and is similar to the share-tenant relationship characteristic of the American south.[11] Under these conditions, the tenant supplies tools, seed, fertilizer, labour, etc., the landowner merely lets the use of his land. The decision as to what to cultivate remains with the tenant, and he may hire labourers to work his plot for him. The share given to the landowner, then, can be considered a form of rent in kind. In Nevis, the share-rent relationship was engaged in primarily and perhaps only by what I have previously referred to as Special People[12]—an upper lower class composed of millhands, carters, overseers, mechanics and other skilled or semi-skilled individuals able to accumulate cash wages. The share-wage relationship was never engaged in by this type, but always by households of agricultural labourers.

The use of household labour on small plots for the benefit of the plantation was further reinforced during the middle of the nineteenth century in spite of conditions of available cash, because of new techniques of intensive cultivation of sugar cane introduced from Barbados. Under this farming-out system, sugar cane planting was carried out by gangs hired by the estate after which households were given one to two-acre plots to care for, for which they were paid a weekly wage. The cane cutting was done by gangs which invariably included men from the households who were given farms. This system gave the advantage of intensive care which produced greater yields and was even more eminently suited to the cultivation of cotton, a more delicate crop, which was introduced at the beginning of this century. But the farming-out system was common on the few large, well-capitalized estates, while the many smaller estates still relied on sharecropping.

Finally, another factor in the instituting of peasant-like adaptations or household production is the emigration of male labourers which began during the depression of the 1880's and which continued to the end of the first quarter of this century. During the eighties and nineties there was emigration to the gold fields of Venezuela, and to other islands in search of employment. According to the 1891 census there were 83 males for every 100 females in Nevis. After the turn of the century, opportunities for overseas male employment increased. In 1911 there were 74 males for every

100 females in Nevis, and in 1921, 68 males per 100 females. Female predominance under sharecropping and farming-out worked as well if not better with cotton, which was introduced in 1904. Demands of cotton cultivation are not as great as those of sugar cane. Weeding and picking cotton was primarily the work of women, children and elderly men; a division of labour which exists to this day. In a real sense, during the early part of this century women engaged in peasant-like means of production, although both they and the emigrant male labourers were engaged in proletarian *relations* of production: wage labour, either for cash or for kind.

The co-existence of peasant means of production and proletarian relations of production continued until the end of the second World War, which saw the end of sharecropping and farming-out as predominant systems of production due to the slump in the sugar and cotton markets and the selling out of plantations to local speculators who then divided these estates and sold to small holders for the wealth which the latter were able to accumulate during the wartime prosperity and high wages. Opportunities for emigration were reduced; Nevisian males stayed at home on their small plots and cultivated subsistence crops, some sugar cane, and some cotton for whatever price they were able to receive. Household labour predominated, pitch-fork and hoe were still used. The government bought defunct estates and initiated expanded land settlement schemes in order to encourage the development of a yeomanry. The immediate post-war period of Nevis was the season of peasantry, both in modes and means of production.

After 1955 opportunities for emigration opened up again, not only to England, but to the U. S. Virgin Islands, where the tourist industry had begun to flower and, with it, demands for labourers in construction and the service occupations multiplied. And, as the cotton market rose for a short time and subsequently went into a steady decline, Nevisian labouring class households were again dependent upon cash remittances sent by emigrants, this time both male and female, while desultory cultivation of cotton and subsistence crops was carried on by the grandmothers, grandfathers and youngsters left behind. In 1962, more than 70 per cent of the adult population was not cultivating at all, save for a garden plot of yams, sweet potatoes, and garden vegetables on freehold and leasehold land. In the same year well over $600,000 BWI in postal and money orders were cashed, an amount greater than the proceeds cotton growers received during their biggest crop year since 1942. As I have stated elsewhere, remittances replace agricultural production as the main and most important source of wealth, by a wide margin.[13]

Accompanying this trend towards agricultural non-production and the increasing influx of wealth is the increasing availability of land. Estates are purchased, divided and resold in small parcels to foreign speculators in the tourist business as well as to Nevisians. To the latter, it would appear, land is considered more as a commodity rather than as capital for further productive use. Land is an investment, not only insuring social prestige, but economic independence, in the way of ensuring bank loans for further emigration. In this present period of Nevisian social and economic history, the means of peasant production are present, but are not used; the source of wealth is the cash wages of emigrant labourers. The cash is often invested in land, in shops, in cars and other consumer goods. Today in Nevis there is a curious mixture of dependence upon proletarian-like relationships, peasant-like holdings, and bourgeois aspirations and consumer behaviour. In any event, theirs is a marginal economy, and since there is now some question about whether they can continue to send emigrants abroad—to say nothing of the ability of the emigrants to continue to send remittances—they will be forced to seek out any means of making a livelihood by their own labour, whether for themselves or for others.

In the foregoing pages I have tried to point out that the development of seemingly disparate means and relations of production is possible, especially within the context of marginal, and perhaps only capitalist, economies. In the specific case of Nevis, a former British Caribbean colony, my argument has not been with the *concepts* of peasantry or proletarian *per se,* but with the categorical use of such concepts, since certain forms of production, e.g., sharecropping, may yield proletarian-like relationships in association with peasant-like techniques. In a different context this argument has been already made. Sidney Mintz suggests three historical contexts for the development of Caribbean peasantries: the early yeomen cultivators; a " 'proto-peasantry' which evolved under slavery", i.e., slaves who were allowed to cultivate and market food crops, and peasantries which developed in opposition to the slave plantation, e.g., Bush Negroes and Maroons.[14] There is some evidence that a "proto-peasantry" developed in the Leeward Islands and especially on Nevis,[15] but it did not become a "reconstituted peasantry"[16] after emancipation as in Jamaica. The small size of the Leeward Islands and the lack of open areas into which they could go forced the freed slaves/"proto-peasants" into wage labour and sharecropping relations. In terms of the means of production they remained "proto-peasants". Peasant-like production and marketing in these situations may be interpreted as the means by which planters reduced their costs of production by having the slaves provide for themselves, and later, under sharecropping, as the means by which plantation production was carried on in the face of cash shortage. In terms of the relations of production and the social division of labour, the slaves remain slaves, and the sharecroppers remain proletarian.

Furthermore, I am not arguing that Nevisian society is wholly proletarian (though because of its historic tradition and its pattern of labour migration a strong argument could be made for this case), but that the increasing wealth and rising standard of living invites thinking of the present day situation in terms of a *petit bourgeois* style of life. Such circumstances make it difficult categorically to apply terms like "peasant" or "proletarian". The special conditions noted here have to be taken into account, for instance, if attempts are made to organize Nevisian sentiment into political action. The rise of new, non- or anti-Labour Government political parties might be expected under these conditions.

Finally, comparisons of these materials for Nevis with those for other islands such as Montserrat, or even other areas, such as the lower Danubian basin described by Doreen Warriner,[17] may enable us to stipulate other sociological and ideological components accompanying the apparent disparities between peasant-like means of production and proletarian-like relations of production. One possible implication of such an attempt is that we will have to shift our attention from peasant and proletarian *community,* and describe and analyze peasant and proletarian *relations* in all their variety. This is to reiterate the point that peasantry and proletariat can be conceived of as both class *and* culture.[18]

Notes

1. The data on which this article is based were collected in 1961 and 1962–63 during fieldwork supported by Brandeis University and the Research Institute for the Study of Man. This article was read as a paper before the American Anthropological Association in Pittsburgh, 1966.
2. See, for instance, Sidney Mintz, Foreword to *Sugar and Society in the Caribbean,* by R. Guerra y Sanchez, Yale University Press, New Haven, 1964, especially pages xxiv–xxxviii, also, A. Norton and G. Cumper, 'Peasant,' 'Plantation' and 'Urban' Communities in Rural Jamaica: A Test of the Validity of the Classification, *Social and Economic Studies,* 15:4:338–352, 1966.
3. Nevis is a unit of the former British Caribbean colony of St. Kitts-Nevis-Anguilla in the northern Lesser Antilles. It has an area of 36 square miles, and a population of approximately 13,000. Sugar-cane and Sea Island cotton were the major cash crops.
4. A comprehensive bibliography of the British and formerly British Caribbean, edited by Lambros Comitas is forthcoming. Herewith are some references I have found useful. M. Horowitz, "A Typology of Rural Community Forms in the Caribbean", *Anthropological Quarterly* 33:4:177–187, 1960; S. Mintz, "Historical Sociology of the Jamaican Church-Founded Free Village System", *De West Indische Gids* 38:46–70, 1958; A. Metraux, *Making a Living in the Marbial Valley* (Haiti), UNESCO, 1951; J. Steward (ed.), *The People of Puerto Rico,* University of Illinois Press, 1956.
5. M. Horowitz, *Morne Paysan: Peasant Village in Martinique,* Holt, Rinehart and Winston, Inc., New York, 1967; M. Freilich, *Cultural Diversity Among Trinidadian Peasants,* Ph.D. Dissertation, Columbia University, 1960; R. Farley, "Rise of a Peasantry in British Guiana", *Social and Economic Studies* 2:4, 1954.
6. Support for this emphasis on household production within the peasant type can be found in: Eric Wolf, *Peasants,* Prentice-Hall, Englewood Cliffs, 1966, especially pages 13–15; Janet Fitchin, "Peasantry As A Social Type", in *Proceedings of the 1961 Annual Spring Meeting of the American Ethnological Society,* Seattle, 1961, especially page 115; Teodor Shanin, "The Peasantry as a Political Factor", *Sociological Review* 14:1:5–27, 1966, especially pages 6–10.
7. Sidney Mintz, "The Folk-Urban Continuum and the Rural Proletarian Community", *American Journal of Sociology* 59:136–143, 1953; Eric Wolf and Sidney

Mintz, "Haciendas and Plantations in Middle America and the Antilles", *Social and Economic Studies* 6:3:380–412, 1957.

8. This theme is elaborated in R. Frucht, *Community and Context in a Colonial Society*, Ph.D. Dissertation, Brandeïs University, 1966.

9. Based on use of pitch-fork and hoe, wielded equally well by men and women.

10. See C. Y. Shephard, *Peasant Agriculture in the Leeward and Windward Islands*, Imperial College of Tropical Agriculture, Trinidad, 1945, pp. 5–10.

11. R. Vance, *Human Factors in Cotton Culture*, University of North Carolina Press, 1929, pp. 253–271.

12. R. Frucht, "Remittances and the Economy in a Small West Indian Island", read before the American Anthropological Association, 1963.

13. R. Frucht *Ibid.;* see also R. Manners, "Remittances and the Unit of Analysis in Anthropological Research", *Southwestern Journal of Anthropology* 21:3:179–195, 1965.

14. Sidney Mintz, "The Question of Caribbean Peasantries: A Comment," *Caribbean Studies* 1:31–34, 1961, especially page 34.

15. See, for instance, Elsa Goveia, *Slave Society in the British Leeward Islands at the End of the Eighteenth Century*, Yale University Press, New Haven, 1965.

16. Sidney Mintz, Foreword to R. Guerra y Sanchez, *op. cit.,* p. xx.

17. D. Warriner, *The Economics of Peasant Farming*, Oxford University Press, 1939.

18. Sidney Mintz, "The Folk-Urban Continuum and the Rural Proletarian Community," *op. cit.,* especially page 141; T. Shanin, *op. cit.,* especially page 17; Eric Wolf, *op. cit.,* especially pages 91–92.

Raymond T. Smith
ECONOMIC FEATURES OF THE HOUSEHOLD GROUP

In considering headship of the household we have been led into an examination of the organizational features of the household group as a functioning system, and one of the primary fields in which this organization comes to life is in the handling of everyday economic problems. It is also in this field that many of the inter-relations of the household to the wider social system are most clearly seen, and to some extent we shall try to keep these two aspects separate for the purpose of analysis.

Since it is common practice in British Guiana to refer to a 'Negro peasantry' and make the assumption that villages are peasant communities, composed of small farmers and their families struggling to make a living from the soil, it is necessary to stress time and again the fact that the household in a rural Negro village community is not by any means the kind of corporate productive unit encountered in the general run of peasant societies. It is not tied to a farm which is the basis of its existence, and the productive activities of its members do not fall into place as parts of a total pattern of exploitation of a *natural* environment. For any particular household the overriding consideration is the acquisition of cash income, and cash is in turn the means of acquiring necessary goods and services. Subsistence crops and the unsold portion of products accruing from agricultural activity generally, are regarded as supplementary to the money income of the group, in the same way that kitchen garden produce is regarded in this country. A striking example of the truth of this statement is to be seen in the fact that all magical practices concerned with acquiring wealth are directed towards getting money, or 'gold', and not towards ensuring the productivity of farms or the increase of animal stock. No instance of anyone employing any kind of supernatural aids to farming was encountered during the course of field-work. On the other hand, rational techniques for improving the yields of farms and the quality of produce are extremely difficult to introduce into the Negro communities, and the methods of agricultural production are just about as rudimentary as they could be. This is a generalization of course, and the few exceptions to the rule do not invalidate it. Where better methods are employed one's immediate reaction is to find out if the operator is a non-Negro, and in the majority of cases this is so.

Men are expected to earn money. Within the context of the household this is easily their most important function in the economic field, and to

REPRINTED FROM *The Negro Family in British Guiana* (NEW YORK: HUMANITIES PRESS INC. AND LONDON: ROUTLEDGE & KEGAN PAUL LTD., 1956) BY PERMISSION OF THE PUBLISHERS.

this end they spend considerable periods of time away from the house, and in most cases, away from the village. The occupations which they pursue are such as to preclude their working in family units with a degree of authoritarian control over a team of sons. Furthermore the avenues of employment which are open are mainly for unskilled labour where there is very little differentiation in rates of pay as between one man and another, irrespective of age.

After leaving school at the age of 14 or 15 years a youth continues to do odd jobs on the farm lands and around the house, as well as taking care of stock. These are all jobs he has been introduced to since his boyhood, and which he is able to do with a minimum of direction from his father. He may begin to work at a trade as apprentice to a carpenter, tailor, blacksmith or shoe-maker, and if he does, it is most unlikely that the man he will work with will be his father. He gets no pay apart from an occasional 'pocket-piece' from his master, and it is more than likely that he will only be one of a number of 'apprentices'. In any case it is only in a minority of cases that he will persevere and become a full-time tradesman himself. There is no rigid apprenticeship system which requires a tradesman to serve his time before becoming a recognized craftsman, just as there is no overall standard of skill in the various trades. A youth is much more likely to flit from job to job in the village and spend only a small part of his time working with his master. The village tailor in August Town had various boys 'apprenticed' to him, but one did not often find them in the shop, and it is significant that the tailor had plans for his sons to take up quite different occupations.

By the time a young man reaches the age of 18 to 20 years, he is ready to begin earning money in the same way as the adult males. He goes to work on the sugar estates, or moves to the bauxite mines in search of a job. The money he earns does not come under the control of the male head of the household to which he belongs, and any money he contributes to household expenses is given to his mother, presuming of course that she is alive, as in a typical household.

A man sets up his own household when he is able to assume responsibility for a spouse and children, and assuming responsibility means providing a house, food and clothing. That he delays this move for a considerable period of time is clear . . . and the fact that Perseverance men establish separate households at an earlier age than in the other two villages demonstrates that the difficulty involved in a man's accumulating enough money to provide a house is not the only operative factor. It is certainly one factor to be considered and is often enough advanced as a reason for delaying the establishment of a separate household.

The observed fact remains that the majority of young men remain nominal members of their parents' households during the whole of their twenties. This does not mean that they are living at home during this period though, and in the case of August Town, one of the most noticeable facts about the village is the almost complete absence of young men, the majority of them being at the bauxite mines. There they can earn relatively high wages, but more important still, they are responsible for themselves. They no longer depend on their father to provide for them, and they can actually contribute to their mother's support. If the mother is sole head of the household then the son will feel a definite pride in being a major contributor to the running of the household, and he will in all likelihood assume responsibility for the payment of the rates on the land and in many ways take the place of the male head of the group. Such a state of affairs will often lead to his postponing the setting up of his own household, based on a conjugal tie, until his mother dies. There are a large number of female household heads who depend mainly on their sons for support in this way and the sons may have a number of children of their own with a woman, or women, with whom they have never lived.

· · ·

In households where there is no man present as male head several situations may exist. A female household head who is a widow or common-law widow probably receives cash from her adult children. In addition she may have daughters and their children living with her in which case there is probably some cash income from the fathers of the children, no matter how sporadic it may be. This money is paid to the mother of the child, who gives the mistress of the house either a part of the money, or buys food herself to hand over for the common pot. If the father of the child contributes no money, then it is not unusual for the maternal grandmother to assume full responsibility for the care of the child, including buying its clothes. This is all the more likely if the child's mother has left the village or has left a child when she goes off to set up house with a man. However, the child's mother will generally attempt to raise enough money to contribute a fair share of the cost of keeping it, and more particularly will she endeavour to buy the child's clothes. In order to do this she may go out to work, either on the sugar estates or in domestic service, or she may take odd jobs carrying earth for the contractors who burn heaps to make brick for the road. In such a situation there is always a delicate balance between the amount of money the young woman can earn or acquire to contribute to the support of her child, and the degree of authority she exercises over it, or the amount of 'motherhood' she can claim in relation to it.

A woman who is left alone with small children is in a much more difficult position for she has to raise cash as well as try to look after her children, and the likelihood is that she will not only work for pay, but she will also have a series of liaisons with men who give her presents in exchange for her sexual favours, if she is young enough. She may have men coming to live with her, but such unions are generally short-lived owing to the fact that the man never really becomes effective head of the household in a situation where the young woman already has a large measure of independence. Such women may depend on a brother for occasional help but there is never any suggestion that the woman is being kept by her brother.

It is clear that in any household group there is always one woman who is the manager of the internal economy of the group and this is a part of her general function as a leader in domestic activities. In Bales' terminology relating to small group interaction patterns, she would be primarily an 'expressive leader', but she is also an 'instrumental leader' in many important respects. Instrumental leadership may be divided amongst a number of individuals at certain stages of the development of the household group, but the rôle of husband-father as head of the household, responsible for the group and being the chief provider of cash and economic resources is well established in the system and those households which are headed by females are almost by definition without a male head. Thus women will often say that they are poor and have to work hard because they have no husband to take care of them. The absence of a male is thought of as a deficiency in this sense.

At this stage it will be useful in presenting a picture of the over-all configuration of the household economy to examine one or two particular cases selected on the basis of the type of household group involved and its stage of development.

CASE NO. 1

The first case is that of a household group consisting of a man aged 46 years, his wife aged 40 years and eight children ranging in age from 18 months to 13 years. They live in a three-roomed wooden house which has a corrugated iron roof and an attached kitchen, but the house is very sparsely furnished and the floor of the bedroom needs repair. It was built in 1936 and is now beginning to deteriorate. The head of the household owns the house and the lot on which it stands, and he also owns two other unoccupied house lots in the village, the three having a total area of .549 acres. He also owns two beds of land in the cultivation area. The first has an area of .992 acres and half of it is planted in corn, the other half being abandoned to bush. The second is .278 acres and is planted in mixed provisions for household use. In addition to this the head rents 1.5 acres of rice land on an adjoining estate, and this is all planted in rice. The rental for this land is $6.00 per acre per crop, and since only one crop per year is planted the rent is $9.00. Once the crop has been reaped the owner is free to rent it to someone else for the small crop, or to graze cattle on it, so that the tenant only has rights to the use of the land for that period during which his rice is actually growing on it. The wife of the household head has planting rights in a Perseverance cultivation lot which is registered in the name of her mother's sister's daughter. This woman (the title holder) does not live in the village and so the land is used by the head's wife and her brother. The total area of the lot is 1.462 acres and the head's wife has about one quarter of it planted in rice, the rest being planted by her brother.

The total amount of land operated by this household (actually planted) is then, approx. 2 acres of rice land, .278 acres of mixed provisions and .496 acres of corn. Scattered throughout the holdings mentioned (including house lots) are twenty coconut trees, two orange trees, ten banana trees, eight mango trees and two star-apple trees. The household group also possesses eight goats and twenty fowls of which ten are hens over 6 months of age. They possess no other livestock.

Just in front of the house is a small cake shop operated by the head, or his wife, in which they sell bottled drinks, cakes, bread, matches, cigarettes, sweets, and various home-made drinks such as ginger beer. This shop makes a maximum profit of $4.00 per week. The household head refers to himself as being a carpenter, but in fact he rarely works at his trade. He spends most of his working time on a fishing boat which operates from the village, fishing off-shore and selling the bulk of the catch in Georgetown. For this he gets a share of the cash made on the catch, and this may amount to as much as $15.00 to $20.00 in one week though the pay fluctuates considerably according to the catches and the market prices, and according to the amount of time which has to be spent on repairing nets. Since this man does not own the boat he need not always join the crew as there are other men who can take his place on some trips, and in any case he rarely spends more than three or four days per week on the boat. His wife does not normally work for money apart from keeping an eye on the cake shop, but during the rice harvest she works as a cutter, and during November 1952 she made $14.00 at this work.

The family has very few debts. The head owes $10.00 to the Co-operative Credit Bank which he borrowed to help to pay for planting his rice, and he will pay this back out of the proceeds from the sale of padi, plus an interest of 3½ per cent per annum. The wife has a small running debt with the grocery shop which she clears every week if possible, and this rarely exceeds $5.00. The head has $60.00 in the Post Office Savings Bank which is a reserve in case of sickness etc., and he also keeps a canister with money which is used for running expenses. Two of the children have sums in the School Savings Society of $1.68 and $1.00 respectively. The wife has no savings of her own, generally spending what money she gets almost as soon as she gets it. She estimates that she needs to spend $14.00 per week on food etc. for the whole family, over and above that which comes from the farm. From the 1951 rice crop they reaped sixteen bags of clean padi, of which ten bags were kept for domestic consumption and seed, but in 1952 they planted a little more, though the unfavourable weather conditions meant that the yield was approximately the same. During November 1952 the head's wife spent $17.48 on clothes for herself and the children, and the bulk of this was money she earned by cutting rice.

Other expenses for the whole household were such things as rates, which amounted to about $17.00, and the rent for the rice land which is another $9.00. During the 1952 rice harvest the head had to pay men to assist him with the beating of the padi as well as paying cutters, and his total expenditure on this was in the region of $50.00.

Small subsidiary sources of income are from selling farm produce such as coconuts, bananas, corn, and an occasional goat or fowl. Over a whole year it is doubtful whether the total income from these sources amounts to more than about $100.00 at the most. What is quite clear is that the household cannot function at its present level without the wages of the household head. If for some reason he loses his job on the fishing boat he will have to go and seek work on the estates or elsewhere. This man has worked on the estates and in the gold fields at one time or another, and he does not regard his job on the boat as his permanent job. It is just the thing that he is doing at the moment. In fact he considers himself to be a carpenter, and this is undoubtedly what he would put down on any census return as his 'occupation'. This is a family where the woman is still largely dependent on her husband's earnings, but even so she organizes the whole of the spending for the household in connexion with food, and her own and the children's clothes. The head takes care of the farm and all expenditure connected with it, and he gives his wife money as he can afford it and she needs it. She has very little scope for earning money herself, apart from during the rice harvest, and if she needs clothes or wishes to travel to see a relative or buy a present for someone, she either has to ask her husband for the money or take it out of the money she handles for the housekeeping. Eight children and two adults consume quite a large quantity of food and there is very little margin for extra expenditure. Her husband has one outside child towards whose support he contributed a little money until the child was 16 years old, and that was an extra drain on the income.

CASE NO. 2

The second case is a household with a female head who is 52 years of age. She is illiterate and was very uncertain about the dates of the birth of her children, and even her own age. However, she got her first child when she was very young, certainly before she was 18 years old, and when she became pregnant she went to live with the father of her child. They lived together for 22 years in a common-law union and during this time she had eleven children, of which four died, three of them in infancy. Her last pregnancy resulted in a miscarriage at 5 months. Shortly after this her common-law husband left her to go and live with another woman in the same village, and she says that he was beginning to be very troublesome and she got tired of the way in which he would be perpetually going about with other women. For the past twelve or thirteen years she has been running her household alone, and it now consists of herself, her two adult daughters who are 21 and 23 years of age, and four small children. Three of the children aged 8, 4 and 1 year are the children of the elder daughter, each one having a different father, and the other one aged 9 years is the child of the daughter aged 21 years. The head also has two sons aged 21 and 17 years, both of whom work away from the village, sending no money to their mother, but they come home occasionally and help her with the farm work, and they do give her presents now and again with which she buys clothes. Another daughter lives in a small house on the same lot with a common-law husband, but she cooks separately and runs a separate household.

The house is a two-roomed thatched cottage with a separate kitchen, all in a bad state of repair. There are no furnishings apart from a small wooden bench and an old wagonette which serves as a table. The lot on which the house stands belongs to the head, and this is the only house lot which she owns. Her own estimate of the value of the house is $20.00. She has recently bought .845 acres of land in the provision area, but has not yet obtained title to it. This is planted in mixed provisions and scattered over the lot are eight coconut trees, four mango trees, one star-apple tree, and there are forty banana trees planted. This woman also rents two acres of rice land on an estate which is three or four miles from the village, and she pays $8.00 per acre per crop for it. In all then, the household group cultivates .845 acres of mixed provisions and two acres of rice. The household head also owns one pig, one donkey, two hens and five dogs, and she possesses one hoe, one cutlass and an agricultural fork.

This household depends to a large extent on the produce of the farm for food, but even so it is estimated that they spend about $4.00 every week on food from the shop. Some of this money comes in the form of intermittent payments for child maintenance from the fathers of the daughters' children, which theoretically totals $8.00 per week for the four children. However, these payments are not regular, and one of the fathers went to prison during the period of the study for failure to pay, being many months in arrears. Neither of the adult daughters has a regular job, but all three women work on the farm, and they will take odd jobs such as carrying wood or cutting rice whenever they can get them, which is not often. The bulk of the cash comes from the sale of provisions and bananas, which the household head takes several miles to market on a donkey cart. During the crab season which lasts from mid-July to mid-September, the whole household group catches crabs on the village foreshore and the head carries them to market. Crabs bring a fairly high price, selling for as much as twenty cents for three or four crabs. The money obtained from the sale of produce and crabs is almost invariably spent as soon as it is obtained. The general practice is for women to crowd the stores on market day buying cloth and various items of clothing with the money they have made. Some food, such as fresh meat or fish, may be bought and a little money will be saved for the food requirements of the next few days, but certainly this woman spends most of her money as soon as she gets it, and she is fairly typical in this respect. No member of this household group has any savings.

The household head used to operate as a village midwife, but this source of income has stopped since a government midwife began to work in the district. Despite the poverty of the group, the head is renowned as a woman with taste for clothes and she somehow manages to buy these fairly regularly. She does not buy clothes for her daughters' four children, for each daughter gets whatever she can from men friends or the fathers of their children for this purpose. The head owes $65.00 to the Co-operative Credit Bank which is the outstanding balance of a loan contracted for the purpose of repairing the house, and for paying for the provision land which she finally bought. She has no debts at the shop, and always tries to pay as she goes. Her two daughters often do the cooking and they also buy food as it is required with any money they may have. She is generous to her daughters when she has money, and out of $70.00 she made from the sale of padi in 1952 she gave them $10.00 each to buy clothes. They, of course, contributed their labour freely during the cutting of the rice.

One cannot draw up a precise balance sheet for the income and expenditure of a group such as this, for existence is a continuing process and resources are balanced against expenditure in a complex and piece-meal way. This woman has managed, and manages, to keep a household together and she does it effectively despite the low standard of living which the group enjoys.

CASE NO. 3

The final case we shall quote is slightly more complex, and although the family still belongs to the village group, and the lower class, it is in the slightly 'better off' category now. The household group consists of a man aged 57 years, his wife aged 52 years, and eight children ranging in age from 28 years to 8 years. The group occupies two house buildings, but one is practically unfurnished and merely serves as a dormitory for the older sons, having only one room. The other building has two rooms and an attached kitchen, and is reasonably well furnished with a large double bed, washstand and trunks in the bedroom; table, four chairs, a small sideboard and a meat safe in the living room. Light is provided by a wick-burner oil lamp, and cooking is done on an open hearth in the kitchen. There is also a pit latrine, a bathroom, a rice room and a small animal pen on the lot. The head of the household is a 'driver', or contractor, on a sugar estate about ten miles from the village, and this is a fairly permanent job. Tasks such as trench cleaning or making up dams, cutting cane, etc., are given to this man by the European manager or overseers, and he in turn employs labourers to carry out the work. The estate authorities pay him for the job, and he pays the men according to the amount of work each one has done. Two sons who are members of the household group, aged 28 and 25 years respectively, work regularly for their father and he pays them in exactly the same way that he pays all the other men working under his command. One other son aged 17 years does not work on the estate as yet, but he has a part-time job delivering newspapers which brings him $3.00 per month. The head's wife sometimes does washing in order to earn a little money for her own personal use. Some friends of hers take in washing from the East Indians of a neighbouring village, and they will always give her a part of the total if she wants it, and she does her share in their yard, not at her own home.

It was impossible to ascertain how much money is earned each week by the head of the household, partly because the amount is irregular, and partly because he only spends a portion of his income on his family. At the time of the study there was a 21-years-old daughter (unmarried and childless) living at home, and she was doing most of the cooking and running the finances for the feeding of the group. Every week the head of the household would bring approximately $7.00 worth of food from a shop on the estate where he worked, and in addition he handed over about another $7.00 in cash to the daughter for the purpose of buying food. This was rarely handed over in one sum, but was given in smaller amounts spread over the week. The head also gives his wife $3.00 per week for her own personal use. There is a household canister which contains money which theoretically is kept in case of sickness, but it acts as a central fund, and also serves in some sense as a symbol of the authority of the household head. The head himself puts varying amounts of money into this canister. Sometimes he will put as much as $10.00 per week, or he will put in a lump sum when he sells a pig. The two adult sons earn between $9.00 and $15.00 each week during the busiest seasons on the estate. The eldest son contributes absolutely nothing to household expenses, nor does he give any money to his mother. He often sleeps away from the house with friends and never seems to save anything at all. The other adult son pays nothing towards food, but he gives his mother $1.50 every week for her personal use, and he also puts between $3.00 and $5.00 per week in the canister when his wages are good. In addition to this he 'cares' one of his younger brothers aged 13 years, buying most of his clothes and school books and giving him small sums of money to spend on sweets, etc. He also has a bank account of his own and takes a great pride in saving. The 17-years-old son who delivers newspapers puts the bulk of his money in the canister.

This is a household group with a relatively high, and comparatively stable, income, but even so we can see that both income and expenditure are diffused according to the various statuses and relationships within the group. The head is personally responsible for paying the rates on all the land (three house lots and one provision bed), and the provision of food for the group is unequivocally his responsibility. The one provision bed is worked by the adult son who contributes to the group canister, and the produce is used by the group. This son also keeps fowls but those are his own private property and the money he obtains by selling them, and their eggs, is his alone. The canister in this household is a stable core of the whole economy in one sense, but the fact that the only person who is allowed to take money out of it is the head himself, emphasizes his authority. The daughter who was doing most of the housekeeping could 'get away' with removing small amounts from the canister for food, but this was only because she was a great favourite of the head, and she never abused the privilege by taking too much or too frequently. The head's wife always knew how much was in the canister, and when the head removed a large amount in order to pay for timber to build a new kitchen for one of his 'girl friends' in another village, his wife created a great fuss. She was particularly indignant because part of the money had been obtained from the sale of some pigs which she had originally bought with her own money. Because the head paid for the feed for these pigs he had claimed them as his own, but she did not consider that this gave him the right to spend the money from their sale on anything except the needs of his own household group. Money from the canister would be used for buying clothes for the children, except for the boy who was being kept by the adult son. The head's wife bought her own clothes and she also bought most of the clothes for her favourite daughter aged 10 years out of her own money.

The head always kept a great deal of his earnings for himself and he had quite a number of 'outside' children which he helped to support. At the time of the study he had a paramour with whom he would spend several nights per week, and his wife accepted the situation, though she never hesitated to complain about it in public. If he ever failed to give her the weekly allowance which she considered her due, then she would certainly create a great fuss and make life as unpleasant as possible for him, even to the extent of 'shaming' him by complaining to his European employers.

Although this woman handled practically none of the money used for the day-to-day running of the household, there was no doubt that she was the centre of the household group, and she was its main unifying force. Even her married daughters looked to her for guidance, and when they were hungry or short of money they would come to her for food or small gifts of cash. They would also ask their father for money, and he would occasionally give them a little.

This household is not a 'farming' family at all, and although the head keeps a few pigs and goats (there are seven goats which nominally belong to an eight-years-old son, but the head decides when they shall be sold and receives the money from the sale), and one son keeps fowls and works a small bed of provisions, the group would not be considered a 'farm family' even for the purposes of the agricultural census. The total income of all members of the group is higher than for most village families and yet this household is not differentiated in any way from the poorer families. Its members share the common village culture and participate in all normal village activities. It does not use its cash income to build up an accumulation of 'display' possessions such as furniture, a radio, etc., and the household dwelling is indistinguishable from any other of its type. Nor is the money used to purchase more land, and land has very little value as capital unless it is actually being worked, in this village at any rate.

These three cases have been cited in order to give a concrete demonstration of the way in which domestic economy is organized. The three households are not necessarily 'typical', but the manner in which they handle their finances and resources is comparable to that obtaining in the majority of lower-class rural Negro homes.

Harry C. Dillingham and
David F. Sly

THE MECHANICAL COTTON-PICKER, NEGRO MIGRATION, AND THE INTEGRATION MOVEMENT

Two viewpoints about the integration movement seem to predominate within the larger society. The more dominant one is that the recent integration movement, dating from about 1955, resulted from slow changes in the *geist* or *weltanschaung* of Negroes as well as many whites, which reached a threshold in the mid-50's and boiled over. This viewpoint is more often implicit than explicit. It is implied in phrases such as, "Freedom now," and "We have waited long enough." It is implied in the white Southerners' attribution of the Negro problem to "those outside agitators."

Whether from the viewpoint of the Negro attacking, or the white defending, the system, the problem is seen in terms of a transcendent morality. The major recourse by both sides is to legal machinery, quasi-legal actions such as boycotts, police brutality, etc., with a flanking movement of educational efforts (propaganda) to change public opinions concerning justice and morality. This conception does not readily lend itself to sociological investigation, although this is not ruled out. One can envision a study having a general orientation similar to that of *The Authoritarian Personality* or *The Lonely Crowd,* focusing on the type of personality most disposed to be "moral," as appropriately defined.

The second viewpoint has been expressed in print only twice, to our knowledge, though we have not exhaustively reviewed the literature. In a perceptive article, "Who Needs the Negro," Willhelm and Powell say,

> The tendency to look upon the racial crisis as a struggle for equality between Negro and white is too narrow in scope. The crisis is caused not so much by the transition from slavery to equality as by a change from an economics of exploitation to an economics of uselessness.[1]

A similar viewpoint is expressed by Ray Marshall:

> Measures to combat unemployment are very important because the great unemployment among Negroes since 1953 undoubtedly has been one of the main causes of increased intensity of racial unrest.[2]
>
> Discrimination—by unions and in the larger society—has declined markedly since 1940 and significantly since 1960. However, technological

REPRINTED FROM *Human Organization,* VOL. 25, 1966, BY PERMISSION OF THE AUTHORS AND THE PUBLISHER.

change and depressed economic conditions have eroded the Negro's overall economic condition, relative to whites, faster than it has been improved
through migration out of agriculture, falling racial barriers, and improved
training and education.[3]

Neither of these studies has documented the impact of technological
change upon the Negro, which it is our intention to do here in a limited
way. In addition, we believe that Marshall may have been misleading in
his implication that "migration out of agriculture" would improve the
"Negro's overall economic condition"; for our data suggest that it is precisely technological innovations *in agriculture* which are a major source
of the Negro's poor economic condition. In the present paper we shall
attempt to document this thesis by presenting evidence concerning the
adoption of tractors and mechanical cotton-pickers on Southern farms with
a subsequent, and consequent, out-migration of Negro tenant farmers.

When the study was first formulated we thought that data on mechanical cotton-pickers would be critical. After a considerable search turned up
no usable data, we settled on the more accessible data on tractors. Later
we did obtain a small amount of data on mechanical cotton-pickers, the
analysis of which has confirmed our expectations. We shall discuss both
tractors and mechanical cotton-pickers here, because they supplement one
another in shedding light on Negro unemployment.

The adoption of tractors by Southern cotton growers has been slow
compared to their adoption rates by most other growers. The reasons for
this retarded rate of adoption have to do with the total labor requirements
of Southern cotton-growing and its technology. There are several interrelated features. One feature is the long growing season required for
maturation in a warm, humid climate, which promotes the growth of
competitive weeds. A second feature is the delicacy of the cotton plant
itself which makes it very susceptible to injury by mechanical weeding
devices. A third feature is (was) the large amount of hand labor involved
in hand-hoeing and picking the individual cotton-bolls.

In the face of these features, the cotton grower traditionally has had
to rely on a relatively larger hand-labor force than other crop producers.
This labor force has been recruited from two sources, some areas relying
more on one source than the other. The more traditional source has been
resident sharecroppers. Predominantly Negroes, these men lived in houses
on the owner's land and cultivated a fixed proportion of that land in
return for the value of half the crop they produced. The other source of
labor has been wage-hands who worked by the hour (or an equivalent
scale) but who lived in nearby towns or villages and were trucked to work
and back each day.

The sharecropper, under annual contract, living on the land with his
family the year around, offered the most reliable work force. The wage-
hand was a less predictable but more flexible source of labor who could
be hired or fired as needed.

Confronted with the necessity of (1) having land plowed and planted, (2) having the plants individually weeded several times during the growing season (three to seven times), and (3) having the cotton picked by hand (three times), the cotton grower had to provide enough total working time to enough laborers to insure that a sufficient number would stay with him or be available when called.

Labor has been a very high cost to cotton producers, compared to labor costs of other crop producers; but this high cost has not meant high wages for the laborer, himself. Cotton is sold on a world competitive market and does not command a high price; also, the work is seasonal—the Negro tenant *averages* only *100* working days per year. These conditions impose a very low limit on the income of the numerous laborers required in cotton production.

Workers with low wage scales and severely limited work opportunities are prone to migrate. In the South, however, the white monopoly of regional political power has certainly been a contributing factor in the inhibition of Negro out-migration. But even if this coercive power is thought of as relatively constant for the past sixty years, we may note that twice there have been heavy waves of Negro migration, each coincident with war-economy job expansions in the North. In other words, the pull of superior economic opportunities can overcome ordinarily restraining forces.

Complementing this fact is another, well known to the cotton grower: if the total wages (for work done) that are available to the potential labor force fall significantly below the standards of a given period, then the labor force may *perceive* better job opportunities elsewhere. In the areas of intensive cotton-growing, the Negro cotton laborer's average family income is around $800 per year, including remuneration for the large amount of field work done by his wife and children (over ten years). The level of living permitted by such an income has no room to drop without dropping into the starvation level. The grower was reluctant to reduce the number of mule-team drivers by introducing tractors, because this would alienate a portion of his work force necessary for weeding and picking. Even when tractors were purchased they might be infrequently operative, being reserved for emergency use. This is why technological agricultural innovations came to the South both late and slow.

However, tractors were adopted by some growers even before World War II with a commensurate, but slow, shift toward the more flexible wage-labor. More were adopted after the war, partly in response to the general tightening of labor as many Negroes had migrated to the industrial North during the war years. And economies of tractor operation attracted cotton growers to other crops that required much less hand labor than cotton.

Our first data concern the increases in tractor use in 70 Southern counties. These counties were selected by the criterion of having a Negro population of at least 20,000 in 1910. These were at that time the most heavily Negro counties, and, by presumption, the most committed to cotton-growth. These 70 counties were ranked according to the increases in the number of tractors between 1950 and 1959. The differences in the number of tenants in the counties in 1950 and in 1959 were then computed for each county and ranked. The Spearman rho is .32, p = <.003 (one tail). This relationship is a modest one but strong enough to lend support to the hypothesis that increasing mechanization drives Negro tenants away from their county.

As noted above, cotton growers were reluctant to adopt tractors since maximal use would reduce the earnings of the labor force sufficiently to force many of their tenants to seek employment elsewhere; and this would leave the growers without the labor necessary for weeding and picking. However, we should note that a tractor is a very versatile machine, permitting the owner to perform some tasks impossible for men and mules alone, e.g., laying down drain tiles, applying liquid fertilizers, deep plowing, etc. Tractor adoption therefore *need not* make serious inroads on the employment of tenant labor.

While the adoption of tractors seems to be only loosely correlated with Negro out-migration, the adoption of the mechanical cotton-picker was expected to correlate much higher. This machine, unlike the tractor, has but a single purpose. It also replaces much more hand labor than does the tractor.

The adoption of mechanical pickers began in 1943, when the first machines were marketed. Their widespread adoption was hindered by the same kind of considerations that affected tractor adoption. Two factors, however, have facilitated recent adoption in large numbers. One of these is the fact that by the early 1950's many cotton growers had acquired tractors (and the more mechanical equipment acquired or available to the farmer, the greater the temptation to realize the economies possible with such equipment); the other factor has been the development (beginning in the early 1950's) of chemical weed-killers. Even though the weed-killers do not destroy weeds as efficiently as hand-hoeing, they do permit the economies of tractor use *and* mechanical pickers to be fully realized: this combination sounded the death knell of the Negro hand-laborer.

Our data on the use of mechanical cotton-pickers are not nearly as adequate as we should like, being restricted to 17 Arkansas counties, only 15 of which had large Negro tenant populations, two indeed having none. Nevertheless, these counties have the merit of having been chosen by the Extension Cotton Specialist of that state as being the ones which might be most pertinent for a study of the adoption of such machines. In any event the data are all that we have found after an intensive search among state agricultural experts in the South.[4]

From the county agents in each of these counties we obtained an estimate of the number of mechanical pickers for each year from 1952 through 1963. The data must be regarded as crude since the figures given by some agents show equal increments of annual increase, and/or there is a tendency for figures to be in multiples of five. With these reservations, the data show a striking increase over the eleven-year period. In 1952, these 17 counties had 482 mechanical pickers or an average of 28.3 per county. By 1963, the total had grown to 5,061 and the average to 297.7.

The data for tenants, white and Negro, cover the period of 1950-1959. By 1959, the number of mechanical pickers had grown to 3,254 and the average to 191.4 per county. It is these latter figures that will be used, rather than the figures for 1963, since they correspond to the date of the census of agriculture in 1959.

In Table 1 we show the basic data. Fifteen counties are ranked by the magnitude of Negro tenant loss between 1950 and 1959. The rank order correlation (Spearman rho) is .74, $p = <.014$ (one tail).

In Table 2 we have identical measures for white tenants; $rho = .39$, $p = <.30$.

The differences between the rhos are in the expected direction; the Negro tenants were more often doing the kind of unskilled labor which is displaced by a more efficient technology. The size of the Negro tenant correlation, .74, is high enough to lend strong support to the hypothesis that the mechanical picker displaces Negro tenants.

The potential impact of adopting mechanical pickers is indicated by the fact that the smaller-sized picker can harvest an acre of cotton in six man-hours compared to 74 man-hours of hand-labor.[5] The tenant laborer

TABLE 1   *Loss of Negro Tenants in Fifteen Arkansas Counties, 1950–59, By Number of Mechanical Cotton-Pickers in 1959*

COUNTIES	NEGRO TENANTS				MECHANICAL PICKERS	
	1950	*1959*	*Difference*	*Rank*	*1959*	*Rank*
Crittenden	4188	1057	3131	1	295	4
St. Francis	2835	810	2025	2	185	9
Jefferson	2560	559	2001	3	350	1
Phillips	2226	778	1448	4	197	8
Mississippi	2176	734	1442	5	325	2
Desha	1429	290	1139	6	280	5
Lee	1814	773	1041	7	300	3
Cross	1030	290	740	8	180	10
Lonke	684	189	495	9	276	6
Monroe	884	415	469	10	230	7
Woodruff	705	280	425	11	110	13
Pulaski	537	143	394	12	27	15
Poinsett	434	170	264	13	170	11
Jackson	208	46	162	14	140	12
Prairie	152	53	99	15	44	14
Total	21,862		15,275		3,109	

rho = .74

TABLE 2   *Loss of White Tenants in Seventeen Arkansas Counties,*
1950–59, By Number of Mechanical Cotton-Pickers in 1959

COUNTIES	WHITE TENANTS				MECHANICAL PICKERS	
	1950	*1959*	*Difference*	*Rank*	*1959*	*Rank*
Mississippi	3458	1184	2274	1	325	2
Poinsett	2772	991	1781	2	170	11
Crittenden	1004	308	696	3	295	4
Cross	1006	414	652	4	180	10
Lonke	1062	418	644	5	276	6
Desha	911	276	635	6	280	5
St. Francis	903	303	600	7	185	9
Jackson	1032	472	560	8	140	12
Clay	1231	699	532	9	130	13
Jefferson	820	334	486	10	350	1
Woodruff	848	373	475	11	110	14
Phillips	718	282	436	12	197	8
Lawrence	873	441	432	13	15	17
Lee	731	394	337	14.5	300	3
Pulaski	480	143	337	14.5	27	16
Monroe	522	268	254	16	230	7
Prairie	411	182	229	17	44	15
Total	18,842		11,360			

$rho = .39$

is supporting more than four other family members. These figures make it possible to understand how the presence of a hundred mechanical pickers in a county could lead to the emigration of several hundred, and even thousands, of persons. Median Negro family size is over five persons in these counties, and many of the emigrating tenants take their families with them.

In 1958, 27 percent of the Mississippi Delta cotton crop was harvested by mechanical pickers. Six years later (1964) this percentage had increased to 81.[6] This must mean a staggering reduction in Negro tenancy in that area, and very similar figures can be expected for the other Southern areas of intensive cotton culture and Negro tenancy.

While we do not have comparable figures for all of the sampled Arkansas counties, we do know that in two of them, Mississippi and Crittenden, 24 percent of the cotton crop was harvested by machines in 1958. This is so close to the figures for the Delta area of Mississippi that we expect the Arkansas counties also expanded the percentage of their crop that was machine-harvested to about 81 percent by 1964. Parenthetically, fifty percent of the Mississippi Delta crop was machine-harvested in 1959. The area of the state of Mississippi that is called the Delta lies just east of the Mississippi River from the middle of the state to the northern border. This area and the 17 Arkansas counties we studied are agriculturally similar, lying in the valley on opposite sides of the Mississippi River.

The data we have presented—on the differential degree of impact of the adoption of tractors and the adoption of mechanical cotton-pickers on Negro tenancy—are not as comparable as we would like since they do not apply to identical counties. In an effort to increase the comparability of the data we computed the rank order correlation between the adoption of tractors in the Arkansas counties and the Negro tenancy decline in those counties.

The correlation (rho) between the increase in the number of tractors from 1950-1959 in the fifteen Arkansas counties having Negro tenants and the decline in the number of Negro tenants in those counties between 1950-1959 is .34 (Table 3). This is so close to the figure of .32 obtained in the similarly computed correlation for the 70 Southern counties reported above that it gives some confidence in predicting from the Arkansas counties to the other cotton counties of the South.

The correlation was also computed between the increase in the number of tractors in these fifteen counties for 1945-1950 and the decrease in their tenants for 1950-1959. This correlation is .52.

TABLE 3   *Loss of Negro Tenants in Fifteen Arkansas Counties, 1950–59, By Increase in Number of Tractors 1945–50 and 1950–59*

| COUNTIES | DIFF. IN NO. OF TRACTORS | | | | DIFF. IN NO. OF NEGRO TENANTS | |
| | 1945–50 | | 1950–59 | | 1950–59 | |
	Number	Rank Order	Number	Rank Order	Number	Rank Order
Mississippi	2456	1	591	9	1442	5
Poinsett	1557	2	1077	1	264	13
Lonke	1437	3	473	11	495	9
St. Francis	1214	4	601	8	2025	2
Jefferson	1208	5	227	13	2001	3
Crittenden	1157	6	776	4	3131	1
Cross	1133	7	702	6	740	8
Phillips	822	8	896	2	1448	4
Lee	808	9	794	3	1041	7
Desha	694	10	738	5	1139	6
Jackson	686	11	513	10	162	14
Woodruff	571	12	297	12	425	11
Pulaski	558	13	168	15	394	12
Prairie	544	14	194	14	99	15
Monroe	488	15	608	7	469	10
Total	15,333		8,655		15,275	

col. 2 - col. 6, rho = .52
col. 4 - col. 6, rho = .34

That the number of tractors adopted in the earlier five-year period is a more accurate index of the declines in Negro tenancy between 1950-1959 than the number of tractors adopted between 1950-1959 was predicted from our more detailed knowledge of the manner in which tractors were put to use on Southern cotton farms. They were not utilized to maximal efficiency when first adopted. They are very flexible machines which permitted them to be used in part for functions which had a minimal effect on Negro tenant labor until combined with the chemical weed-killers and mechanical cotton-pickers in the 1950's.

Another factor about the adoption of tractors is relevant for the adoption of mechanical cotton-pickers. While the cotton-pickers became available in 1943, the adoption rate was very slow during the first seven years of availability. But after 1950, they were adopted at a very rapid rate. But more tractors were adopted between 1945-1950 than between 1950-1959. We see then that by 1950 sufficient mechanization had occurred in the form of tractor adoption to permit, and encourage, the wholesale adoption of mechanical cotton-pickers, which, in conjunction with the tractor and chemical weed-killers, permitted the *immediate,* drastic decline in the employment of Negro tenant labor.

The hypothesized relationships between the adoption of mechanical cotton-pickers in some Southern counties, Negro emigration, and the nationwide integration movement cannot be experimentally demonstrated. We propose, nevertheless, to defend this hypothesis.

Two arguments may be raised against the hypothesis that mechanization caused the continuing large emigration of Negroes from the rural South. One argument might be that much of this migration could be attributed to the forty percent reduction in cotton acreage imposed by federal government programs in 1953. The argument would be that the consequent reduction of labor requirements produced the out-migration, rather than the increasing mechanization. The second argument would be even more devastating and would propose that mechanization followed, rather than preceded, emigration, and was a response to a *short labor supply.*

We will dispose of the second argument first. The reduction of cotton acreage noted in the first argument created a *large labor surplus.* Several studies of Mississippi show the decade to be one of a constantly *declining* cotton labor force and a *high surplus* of workers in that same labor force *after* the decline.[7] In the face of such data the hypothesis that mechanization in the 1950's was caused by emigration is scarcely tenable.

The first argument, that the emigration of the 1950's is attributable to the federally-instigated reductions in cotton acreage, is obviously a tenable hypothesis. It is necessary, however, to qualify this hypothesis by placing it in a broader perspective. Let us put three facts together: (1) adoption of mechanical cotton-pickers began before the imposition of acreage controls; (2) the rate of adoption throughout 1950 shows no variation around the year 1953; (3) by 1964 the use of mechanical pickers was extensive enough to have replaced all of the workers displaced by acreage reduction *and more.*

We interpret these facts to mean that the economies of mechanization were sufficiently great to warrant the purchase and use of machines even when the available labor force was abundant and wage costs as low as they could fall. From this perspective, whatever the emigration attributable to acreage reduction, *it would have occurred anyway, and very soon,* if acreage reduction had not occurred.[8]

These Negro emigrants had to look for work elsewhere, and we can be certain the "elsewhere" was urban places. Some evidence *suggests* that most of these emigrants went to urban areas in the South. These Southern urban places in turn have been losing a large number of emigrants to urban places in the North. Our deduction is that this latter stream of emigrants was propelled Northwards by the increased competition for available urban jobs in the South, imposed by the rural migrants entering these Southern urban places.

We deduce that this Northward stream was propelled, rather than attracted, since evidence is lacking for any substantial expansion of job opportunities for Negroes in the urban North. The evidence of the continuing high rates of unemployment in most of the nation during most of this period and the known increases in automation of Northern industries strongly suggest that opportunities for Negroes have been declining in the North, or expanding at a declining rate.

The Northern Negroes possess local, as well as national, political power. They utilize this power to achieve welfare benefits as well as access to jobs that are directly disposable by political organizations, e.g., civil service; but *direct* action upon economic organizations to achieve more jobs is impossible. Therefore, the political power is used for direct assaults upon the intervening social structure which exclude them from jobs.

This is evident in the pressures exerted in New York and Cleveland for access to construction jobs by applying federal governmental pressures to *unions* to permit Negro membership. It is also reflected in the pressures in Chicago and New York for an abolition of segregated schools. The assumption is that white students in the classrooms will raise the educational achievement of the Negroes and make them more efficient in competing for jobs requiring such education.[9]

In the Southern states the movement has focused on a more modest goal: the abolition of Jim Crow legislation and traditional segregation practices that touch on job opportunities very tangentially. This movement has had some success. The desegregation of lunch counters and city buses and the hiring of some additional Negro workers has occurred where the local Negro population has been able to boycott certain establishments in sufficient numbers to affect total sales. Desegregation of interstate travel media has been solely due to federal intervention, however.

The movement to achieve political power through the franchise has had a limited success in Southern urban areas. The proportion of Negroes registered to vote in the South has scarcely increased in the last few years. In the near future success will probably require even stronger federal intervention.[10]

The possibility of utilizing the franchise in the South, if obtained and exercised, to facilitate access to Southern jobs seems remote.[11] Political power itself constitutes an indirect means of access to the structures that can directly allocate jobs to Negroes; and the urban economic technology (both North and South) is automating at such a speed that even the more skilled white population is not able to maintain satisfactory employment rates.

ADDENDUM

Since this was written in February and March of 1965, several developments have occurred which bear on the thesis of this paper. Presented at the Population Association meeting in April, 1965, it was subsequently summarized by the New York Times. Several civil rights organizations and government bodies requested reprints. Both the McCone report on the Watts riot and the report of the President's Commission on Technology, Automation and Manpower seem to have accepted the thesis that the changing cotton technology had had a massive impact on Negro migration and joblessness.

Some civil rights organizations, themselves, have radically changed their goals and are placing heavy, if not primary, emphasis upon the acquisition of economic power:

> The man who brought the "black power" cry into the Negro movement is Stokely Carmichael, 25-year-old head of S.N.C.C. . . . Mr. Carmichael has given several interpretations of "black power." One of his interpretations is that it means basically, political power—"and maybe, using that as a steppingstone, we can get to economic power, which is really the crucial problem."
>
> Most Negro leaders belittle the "war on poverty." They demand government help on a far larger scale. Says Dr. King, "It would take at least one hundred billion dollars over the next ten years to really bring the Negro to the point where he is able to stand on his own two feet."
>
> The new and militant director of CORE, Floyd B. McKissick said, ". . . I'm saying that where you have a great number of Negroes concentrated in ghettos—as you have in the urban North—with large numbers of unemployed, then that increases the danger."[12]

It would appear that much of the Negro population is in basic agreement that civil rights legislation with or without implementation does not take the place of jobs and does not lead to jobs for more than a token few. A jobless, urban proletariat is a very volatile mass.

But Mr. Carmichael's definition of black power seems basically wistful, for, like the recipe for tiger soup, one must first get a tiger. The Negro population cannot get a tiger, and this basic fact is foremost in the minds of the NAACP and the Southern Christian Leadership Conference. Indeed, the probability of retaining the goodwill or even tolerance of many white people was jeopardized by a rash of summer riots in 1966.

We concluded an earlier version of this paper with the statement that, "The future looks bleak for the Negro's access to employment." In the interim, the national rates of unemployment have declined rapidly. Prosperity, partially "war"-induced, has grown much brighter; but, it has scarcely affected the Negro. Automation is awesome indeed, and the future appears as bleak as before.

Notes and References

1. Sidney M. Willhelm and Edwin H. Powell, "Who Needs the Negro," *Trans-Action*, 6 (September-October, 1964), pp. 3–6.

2. Ray Marshall, *The Negro and Organized Labor,* John Wiley and Sons, New York, 1965, p. 302.

3. *Ibid.*, p. 303.

4. Roughly, these counties lie along the west bank of the Mississippi River between the northern and southern boundaries of Arkansas. Mr. William E. Woodall, Ext. Cotton Specialist, Cooperative Extension Work in Agriculture and Home Economics, Little Rock, Arkansas, provided the data.

5. Daniel F. Capstick, "Economics of Mechanical Cotton Harvesting," *Bulletin 622 of the Agricultural Experiment Station,* University of Arkansas, Fayetteville, Arkansas, March, 1960, p. 4.

6. Personal communication from the Cooperative Extension Service Mississippi State University, State College, Mississippi, December 1, 1964.

7. Nelson L. LeRay, George L. Wilber, and Grady B. Crowe, "Plantation Organization and the Resident Labor Force, Delta Area, Mississippi," *Bulletin 606 of the Agricultural Experiment Station,* Mississippi State University, State College, Mississippi, October, 1960, pp. 18–19: "Chopping and picking cotton are the major hand operations connected with making a cotton crop. . . . Cotton chopping or picking, or both, was the major type of farmwork engaged in by 69 percent of the males and all of the females who did farmwork. . . . Workers with 100 days or more of farmwork included 37 percent of the tractor drivers, 80 percent of the mechanics, but only about 12 percent of those who had cotton chopping and picking as their major type of farmwork during 1957. These figures indicate that in terms of total days worked, there is a source of labor on large plantations in the Delta area available for additional employment."

"Net migration in Mississippi 1950 to 1960," *Bulletin of the Agricultural Experiment Station,* Mississippi State University, State College, Mississippi: "Most of the migration, both within and beyond the state's borders, was an expression of a vigorous population's efforts to adjust to a changing economy. The streamlining of farming enterprises plus the expanding of industries in the cities, have spurred thousands of Mississippi's rural youth to seek new homes and new occupations in the nation's burgeoning urban areas."

Nelson LeRay and Grady B. Crowe, "Labor and Technology on Selected Cotton Plantations in the Delta Area of Mississippi, 1953–1957," *Bulletin 575 of the Agricultural Experiment Station,* Mississippi State University, State College, Mississippi, April, 1959, p. 19: "There are both economic and non-economic reasons why the resident labor force did not decline in proportion to the reduction in labor requirements. The primary economic reasons are: (1) those cotton production operations with peak labor requirements have not been completely mechanized; and (2) plantation operators hesitate to depend on seasonal off-farm labor for picking and chopping cotton. Non-economic reasons for maintaining excess labor vary but, in general, they are related to paternalistic attitudes that have developed between plantation operators and resident croppers and day hands on the plantations. Many individuals and their families have long histories of service on Delta plantations. Plantation operators do not displace these individuals with machines; instead, they are replaced by machines through a process of attrition."

8. N. LeRay and G. Crowe, "Labor and Technology on Selected Cotton Plantations," *loc. cit.*, p. 19. These authors measured the reductions in labor requirements during the five-year interval of 1953–1957. Their data and the data on the proportion of the cotton crop harvested by machine from 1952 to 1964 support our conclusion concerning the relative impacts of acreage controls and mechanization.

9. Thomas Pettigrew, "White-Negro Confrontations," in Eli Ginzberg, (ed.), *The Negro Challenge to the Business Community,* McGraw-Hill, New York, 1964, p. 47.

10. D. R. Mathews and J. W. Prothoo, "Negro Voter Registration in the South," in Allan P. Sindler, (ed.), *Change in the Contemporary South,* Duke University, Durham, N.C., 1963, p. 123: "In 1956, the Southern Regional Council estimated that about 25 percent of the Negro adults were registered. Four years, two Civil Rights Acts, and innumerable local registration drives later, the proportion of Negro adults who were registered had risen to only 28 percent, as compared with about 60 percent for the adult whites in the region."

11. J. J. Spengler, "Demographic and Economic Change in the South, 1940–1960," in Sindler, *op. cit.,* p. 32: "Nonagricultural employment on satisfactory terms was not (and probably could not be) expanded fast enough in the South to absorb both the natural growth of the nonagricultural population and all the migrants from farms."

12. *U. S. News and World Report,* July 18, 1966, pp. 32–40.

Elliot Liebow
MEN AND JOBS

A pickup truck drives slowly down the street. The truck stops as it comes abreast of a man sitting on a cast-iron porch and the white driver calls out, asking if the man wants a day's work. The man shakes his head and the truck moves on up the block, stopping again whenever idling men come within calling distance of the driver. At the Carry-out corner, five men debate the question briefly and shake their heads no to the truck. The truck turns the corner and repeats the same performance up the next street. In the distance, one can see one man, then another, climb into the back of the truck and sit down. In starts and stops, the truck finally disappears.

What is it we have witnessed here? A labor scavenger rebuffed by his would-be prey? Lazy, irresponsible men turning down an honest day's pay for an honest day's work? Or a more complex phenomenon marking the intersection of economic forces, social values and individual states of mind and body?

Let us look again at the driver of the truck. He has been able to recruit only two or three men from each twenty or fifty he contacts. To him, it is clear that the others simply do not choose to work. Singly or in groups, belly-empty or belly-full, sullen or gregarious, drunk or sober, they confirm what he has read, heard and knows from his own experience: these men wouldn't take a job if it were handed to them on a platter.[1]

Quite apart from the question of whether or not this is true of some of the men he sees on the street, it is clearly not true of all of them. If it were, he would not have come here in the first place; or having come, he would have left with an empty truck. It is not even true of most of them, for most of the men he sees on the street this weekday morning do, in fact, have jobs. But since, at the moment, they are neither working nor sleeping, and since they hate the depressing room or apartment they live in, or because there is nothing to do there,[2] or because they want to get away from their wives or anyone else living there, they are out on the street, indistinguishable from those who do not have jobs or do not want them. Some, like Boley, a member of a trash-collection crew in a suburban housing development, work Saturdays and are off on this weekday. Some, like Sweets, work nights cleaning up middle-class trash, dirt, dishes and garbage, and mopping the floors of the office buildings, hotels, restaurants, toilets and other public places dirtied during the day. Some men work for

REPRINTED FROM *Tally's Corner* BY ELLIOT LIEBOW, BY PERMISSION OF LITTLE, BROWN AND CO. COPYRIGHT © 1967 BY LITTLE, BROWN AND CO.

retail businesses such as liquor stores which do not begin the day until ten o'clock. Some laborers, like Tally, have already come back from the job because the ground was too wet for pick and shovel or because the weather was too cold for pouring concrete. Other employed men stayed off the job today for personal reasons: Clarence to go to a funeral at eleven this morning and Sea Cat to answer a subpoena as a witness in a criminal proceeding.

Also on the street, unwitting contributors to the impression taken away by the truck driver, are the halt and the lame. The man on the cast-iron steps strokes one gnarled arthritic hand with the other and says he doesn't know whether or not he'll live long enough to be eligible for Social Security. He pauses, then adds matter-of-factly, "Most times, I don't care whether I do or don't." Stoopy's left leg was polio-withered in childhood. Raymond, who looks as if he could tear out a fire hydrant, coughs up blood if he bends or moves suddenly. The quiet man who hangs out in front of the Saratoga apartments has a steel hook strapped onto his left elbow. And had the man in the truck been able to look into the wine-clouded eyes of the man in the green cap, he would have realized that the man did not even understand he was being offered a day's work.

Others, having had jobs and been laid off, are drawing unemployment compensation (up to $44 per week) and have nothing to gain by accepting work which pays little more than this and frequently less.

Still others, like Bumdoodle the numbers man, are working hard at illegal ways of making money, hustlers who are on the street to turn a dollar any way they can: buying and selling sex, liquor, narcotics, stolen goods, or anything else that turns up.

Only a handful remains unaccounted for. There is Tonk, who cannot bring himself to take a job away from the corner, because, according to the other men, he suspects his wife will be unfaithful if given the opportunity. There is Stanton, who has not reported to work for four days now, not since Bernice disappeared. He bought a brand new knife against her return. She had done this twice before, he said, but not for so long and not without warning, and he had forgiven her. But this time, "I ain't got it in me to forgive her again." His rage and shame are there for all to see as he paces the Carry-out and the corner, day and night, hoping to catch a glimpse of her.

And finally, there are those like Arthur, able-bodied men who have no visible means of support, legal or illegal, who neither have jobs nor want them. The truck driver, among others, believes the Arthurs to be representative of all men he sees idling on the street during his own working hours. They are not, but they cannot be dismissed simply because they are a small minority. It is not enough to explain them away as being lazy or irresponsible or both because an able-bodied man with responsibilities who refuses work is, by the truck driver's definition, lazy and irresponsible. Such an answer begs the question. It is descriptive of the facts; it does not explain them.

Moreover, despite their small numbers, the don't-work-and-don't-want-to-work minority is especially significant because they represent the strongest and clearest expression of those values and attitudes associated with making a living which, to varying degrees, are found throughout the streetcorner world. These men differ from the others in degree rather than in kind, the principal difference being that they are carrying out the implications of their values and experiences to their logical, inevitable conclusions. In this sense, the others have yet to come to terms with themselves and the world they live in.

Putting aside, for the moment, what the men say and feel, and looking at what they actually do and the choices they make, getting a job, keeping a job, and doing well at it is clearly of low priority. Arthur will not take a job at all. Leroy is supposed to be on his job at 4:00 P.M. but it is already 4:10 and he still cannot bring himself to leave the free games he has accumulated on the pinball machine in the Carry-out. Tonk started a construction job on Wednesday, worked Thursday and Friday, then didn't go back again. On the same kind of job, Sea Cat quit in the second week. Sweets had been working three months as a busboy in a restaurant, then quit without notice, not sure himself why he did so. A real estate agent, saying he was more interested in getting the job done than in the cost, asked Richard to give him an estimate on repairing and painting the inside of a house, but Richard, after looking over the job, somehow never got around to submitting an estimate. During one period, Tonk would not leave the corner to take a job because his wife might prove unfaithful; Stanton would not take a job because his woman had been unfaithful.

Thus, the man-job relationship is a tenuous one. At any given moment, a job may occupy a relatively low position on the streetcorner scale of real values. Getting a job may be subordinated to relations with women or to other non-job considerations; the commitment to a job one already has is frequently shallow and tentative.

The reasons are many. Some are objective and reside principally in the job; some are subjective and reside principally in the man. The line between them, however, is not a clear one. Behind the man's refusal to take a job or his decision to quit one is not a simple impulse or value choice but a complex combination of assessments of objective reality on the one hand, and values, attitudes and beliefs drawn from different levels of his experience on the other.

Objective economic considerations are frequently a controlling factor in a man's refusal to take a job. How much the job pays is a crucial question but seldom asked. He knows how much it pays. Working as a stock clerk, a delivery boy, or even behind the counter of liquor stores, drug stores and other retail businesses pays one dollar an hour. So, too, do most busboy, car-wash, janitorial and other jobs available to him. Some jobs, such as dishwasher, may dip as low as eighty cents an hour and others, such as elevator operator or work in a junk yard, may offer $1.15 or $1.25. Take-home pay for jobs such as these ranges from $35 to $50 a week, but a take-home pay of over $45 for a five-day week is the exception rather than the rule.

One of the principal advantages of these kinds of jobs is that they offer fairly regular work. Most of them involve essential services and are therefore somewhat less responsive to business conditions than are some higher paying, less menial jobs. Most of them are also inside jobs not dependent on the weather, as are construction jobs and other higher-paying outside work.

Another seemingly important advantage of working in hotels, restaurants, office and apartment buildings and retail establishments is that they frequently offer an opportunity for stealing on the job. But stealing can be a two-edged sword. Apart from increasing the cost of the goods or services to the general public, a less obvious result is that the practice usually acts as a depressant on the employee's own wage level. Owners of small retail establishments and other employers frequently anticipate employee stealing and adjust the wage rate accordingly. Tonk's employer explained why he was paying Tonk $35 for a 55-60 hour workweek. These men will all steal, he said. Although he keeps close watch on Tonk, he estimates that Tonk steals from $35 to $40 a week.[3] What he steals, when added to his regular earnings, brings his take-home pay to $70 or $75 per week. The employer said he did not mind this because Tonk is worth that much to the business. But if he were to pay Tonk outright the full value of his labor, Tonk would still be stealing $35-$40 per week and this, he said, the business simply would not support.

This wage arrangement, with stealing built-in, was satisfactory to both parties, with each one independently expressing his satisfaction. Such a wage-theft system, however, is not as balanced and equitable as it appears. Since the wage level rests on the premise that the employee will steal the unpaid value of his labor, the man who does not steal on the job is penalized. And furthermore, even if he does not steal, no one would believe him; the employer and others believe he steals because the system presumes it.

Nor is the man who steals, as he is expected to, as well off as he believes himself to be. The employer may occasionally close his eyes to the worker's stealing but not often and not for long. He is, after all, a businessman and cannot always find it within himself to let a man steal from him, even if the man is stealing his own wages. Moreover, it is only by keeping close watch on the worker that the employer can control how much is stolen and thereby protect himself against the employee's stealing more than he is worth. From this viewpoint, then, the employer is not in wage-theft collusion with the employee. In the case of Tonk, for instance, the employer was not actively abetting the theft. His estimate of how much Tonk was stealing was based on what he thought Tonk was able to steal despite his own best efforts to prevent him from stealing anything at all. Were he to have caught Tonk in the act of stealing, he would, of course, have fired him from the job and perhaps called the police as well. Thus, in an actual if not in a legal sense, all the elements of entrapment are present. The employer knowingly provides the conditions which entice (force) the employee to steal the unpaid value of his labor, but at the same time he punishes him for theft if he catches him doing so.

Other consequences of the wage-theft system are even more damaging to the employee. Let us, for argument's sake, say that Tonk is in no danger of entrapment; that his employer is willing to wink at the stealing and that Tonk, for his part, is perfectly willing to earn a little, steal a little. Let us say, too, that he is paid $35 a week and allowed to steal $35. His money income—as measured by the goods and services he can purchase with it—is, of course, $70. But not all of his income is available to him for all purposes. He cannot draw on what he steals to build his self-respect or to measure his self-worth. For this, he can draw only on his earnings—the amount given him publicly and voluntarily in exchange for his labor. His "respect" and "self-worth" income remains at $35—only half that of the man who also receives $70 but all of it in the form of wages. His earnings publicly measure the worth of his labor to his employer, and they are important to others and to himself in taking the measure of his worth as a man.[4]

With or without stealing, and quite apart from any interior processes going on in the man who refuses such a job or quits it casually and without apparent reason, the objective fact is that menial jobs in retailing or in the service trades simply do not pay enough to support a man and his family. This is not to say that the worker is underpaid; this may or may not be true. Whether he is or not, the plain fact is that, in such a job, he cannot make a living. Nor can he take much comfort in the fact that these jobs tend to offer more regular, steadier work. If he cannot live on the $45 or $50 he makes in one week, the longer he works, the longer he cannot live on what he makes.[5]

• • •

Furthermore, the man does not have any reasonable expectation that, however bad it is, his job will lead to better things. Menial jobs are not, by and large, the starting point of a track system which leads to even better jobs for those who are able and willing to do them. The busboy or dishwasher in a restaurant is not on a job track which, if negotiated skillfully, leads to chef or manager of the restaurant. The busboy or dishwasher who works hard becomes, simply, a hard-working busboy or dishwasher. Neither hard work nor perseverance can conceivably carry the janitor to a sitdown job in the office building he cleans up. And it is the apprentice who becomes the journeyman electrician, plumber, steam fitter or bricklayer, not the common unskilled Negro laborer.

Thus, the job is not a stepping stone to something better. It is a dead end. It promises to deliver no more tomorrow, next month or next year than it does today.

Delivering little, and promising no more, the job is "no big thing." The man appears to treat the job in a cavalier fashion, working and not working as the spirit moves him, as if all that matters is the immediate satisfaction of his present appetites, the surrender to present moods, and the indulgence of whims with no thought for the cost, the consequences, the future. To the middle-class observer, this behavior reflects a "present-time orientation"—an "inability to defer gratification." It is this "present-time" orientation—as against the "future orientation" of the middle-class person—that "explains" to the outsider why Leroy chooses to spend the day at the Carry-out rather than report to work; why Richard, who was paid Friday, was drunk Saturday and Sunday and penniless Monday; why Sweets quit his job today because the boss looked at him "funny" yesterday.

But from the inside looking out, what appears as a "present-time" orientation to the outside observer is, to the man experiencing it, as much a future orientation as that of his middle-class counterpart.[6] The difference between the two men lies not so much in their different orientations to time as in their different orientations to future time or, more specifically, to their different futures.[7]

The future orientation of the middle-class person presumes, among other things, a surplus of resources to be invested in the future and a belief that the future will be sufficiently stable both to justify his investment (money in a bank, time and effort in a job, investment of himself in marriage and family, etc.) and to permit the consumption of his investment at a time, place and manner of his own choosing and to his greater satisfaction. But the streetcorner man lives in a sea of want. He does not, as a rule, have a surplus of resources, either economic or psychological. Gratification of hunger and the desire for simple creature comforts cannot be long deferred. Neither can support for one's flagging self-esteem. Living on the edge of both economic and psychological subsistence, the streetcorner man is obliged to expend all his resources on maintaining himself from moment to moment.[8]

As for the future, the young streetcorner man has a fairly good picture of it. In Richard or Sea Cat or Arthur he can see himself in his middle twenties; he can look at Tally to see himself at thirty, at Wee Tom to see himself in his middle thirties, and at Budder and Stanton to see himself in his forties. It is a future in which everything is uncertain except the ultimate destruction of his hopes and the eventual realization of his fears. The most he can reasonably look forward to is that these things do not come too soon. Thus, when Richard squanders a week's pay in two days it is not because, like an animal or a child, he is "present-time oriented," unaware of or unconcerned with his future. He does so precisely because he is aware of the future and the hopelessness of it all.

Sometimes this kind of response appears as a conscious, explicit choice. Richard had had a violent argument with his wife. He said he was going to leave her and the children, that he had had enough of everything and could not take any more, and he chased her out of the house. His chest still heaving, he leaned back against the wall in the hallway of his basement apartment.

"I've been scuffling for five years," he said. "I've been scuffling for five years from morning till night. And my kids still don't have anything, my wife don't have anything, and I don't have anything.

"There," he said, gesturing down the hall to a bed, a sofa, a couple of chairs and a television set, all shabby, some broken. "There's everything I have and I'm having trouble holding onto that."

Leroy came in, presumably to petition Richard on behalf of Richard's wife, who was sitting outside on the steps, afraid to come in. Leroy started to say something but Richard cut him short.

"Look, Leroy, don't give me any of that action. You and me are entirely different people. Maybe I look like a boy and maybe I act like a boy sometimes but I got a man's mind. You and me don't want the same things out of life. Maybe some of the same, but you don't care how long you have to wait for yours and *I—want—mine—right—now.*"[9]

Thus, apparent present-time concerns with consumption and indulgences—material and emotional—reflect a future-time orientation. "I want mine right now" is ultimately a cry of despair, a direct response to the future as he sees it.[10]

In many instances, it is precisely the streetcorner man's orientation to the future—but to a future loaded with "trouble"—which not only leads to a greater emphasis on present concerns ("I want mine right now") but also contributes importantly to the instability of employment, family and friend relationships, and to the general transient quality of daily life.

Let me give some concrete examples. One day, after Tally had gotten paid, he gave me four twenty-dollar bills and asked me to keep them for him. Three days later he asked me for the money. I returned it and asked why he did not put his money in a bank. He said that the banks close at two o'clock. I argued that there were four or more banks within a two-block radius of where he was working at the time and that he could easily get to any one of them on his lunch hour. "No, man," he said, "you don't understand. They close at two o'clock and they closed Saturday and Sunday. Suppose I get into trouble and I got to make it [leave]. Me get out of town, and everything I got in the world layin' up in that bank? No good! No good!"

In another instance, Leroy and his girl friend were discussing "trouble." Leroy was trying to decide how best to go about getting his hands on some "long green" (a lot of money), and his girl friend cautioned him about "trouble." Leroy sneered at this, saying he had had "trouble" all his life and wasn't afraid of a little more. "Anyway," he said, "I'm famous for leaving town."[11]

Thus, the constant awareness of a future loaded with "trouble" results in a constant readiness to leave, to "make it," to "get out of town," and discourages the man from sinking roots into the world he lives in.[12] Just as it discourages him from putting money in the bank, so it discourages him from committing himself to a job, especially one whose payoff lies in the promise of future rewards rather than in the present. In the same way, it discourages him from deep and lasting commitments to family and friends or to any other persons, places or things, since such commitments could hold him hostage, limiting his freedom of movement and thereby compromising his security which lies in that freedom.

What lies behind the response to the driver of the pickup truck, then, is a complex combination of attitudes and assessments. The streetcorner man is under continuous assault by his job experiences and job fears. His experiences and fears feed on one another. The kind of job he can get— and frequently only after fighting for it, if then—steadily confirms his fears, depresses his self-confidence and self-esteem until finally, terrified of an opportunity even if one presents itself, he stands deflated by his experiences, his belief in his own self-worth destroyed and his fears a confirmed reality.

Notes

1. By different methods, perhaps, some social scientists have also located the problem in the men themselves, in their unwillingness or lack of desire to work: "To improve the underprivileged worker's performance, one must help him to learn *to want* . . . higher social goals for himself and his children. . . . The problem of changing the work habits and motivation of [lower class] people . . . is a problem of changing the goals, the ambitions, and the level of cultural and occupational aspiration of the underprivileged worker." (Emphasis in original.) Allison Davis, "The Motivation of the Underprivileged Worker," p. 90.

2. The comparison of sitting at home alone with being in jail is commonplace.

3. Exactly the same estimate as the one made by Tonk himself. On the basis of personal knowledge of the stealing routine employed by Tonk, however, I suspect the actual amount is considerably smaller.

4. Some public credit may accrue to the clever thief but not respect.

5. It might be profitable to compare, as Howard S. Becker suggests, gross aspects of income and housing costs in this particular area with those reported by Herbert Gans for the low-income working class in Boston's West End. In 1958, Gans reports, median income for the West Enders was just under $70 a week, a level considerably higher than that enjoyed by the people in the Carry-out neighborhood five years later. Gans himself rented a six-room apartment in the West End for $46 a month, about $10 more than the going rate for long-time residents. In the Carry-out neighborhood, rooms that could accommodate more than a cot and a miniature dresser—that is, rooms that qualified for family living—rented for $12 to $22 a week. Ignoring differences that really can't be ignored—the privacy and self-contained efficiency of the multi-room apartment as against the fragmented, public living of the rooming-house "apartment," with a public toilet on a floor always different from the one your room is on (no matter, it probably doesn't work, anyway)—and assuming comparable states of disrepair, the West Enders were paying $6 or $7 a month for a room that cost the Carry-outers at least $50 a month, and frequently more. Looking at housing costs as a percentage of income—and again ignoring what cannot be ignored: that what goes by the name of "housing" in the two areas is not at all the same thing—the median income West Ender could get a six-room apartment for about 12 percent of his income, while his 1963 Carry-out counterpart, with a weekly income of $60 (to choose a figure from the upper end of the income range), often

paid 20–33 percent of his income for one room. See Herbert J. Gans, *The Urban Villagers*, pp. 10–13.

6. Taking a somewhat different point of view, S. M. Miller and Frank Riessman suggest that "the entire concept of deferred gratification may be inappropriate to understanding the essence of workers' lives" ("The Working Class Subculture: A New View," p. 87).

7. This sentence is a paraphrase of a statement made by Marvin Cline at a 1965 colloquium at the Mental Health Study Center, National Institute of Mental Health.

8. And if, for the moment, he does sometimes have more money than he chooses to spend or more food than he wants to eat, he is pressed to spend the money and eat the food anyway since his friends, neighbors, kinsmen, or acquaintances will beg or borrow whatever surplus he has or, failing this, they may steal it. In one extreme case, one of the men admitted taking the last of a woman's surplus food allotment after she had explained that, with four children, she could not spare any food. The prospect that consumer soft goods not consumed by oneself will be consumed by someone else may be related to the way in which portable consumer durable goods, such as watches, radios, television sets or phonographs, are sometimes looked at as a form of savings. When Shirley was on welfare, she regularly took her television set out of pawn when she got her monthly check. Not so much to watch it, she explained, as to have something to fall back on when her money runs out toward the end of the month. For her and others, the television set or the phonograph is her savings, the pawnshop is where she banks her savings, and the pawn ticket is her bankbook.

9. This was no simple rationalization for irresponsibility. Richard had indeed "been scuffling for five years" trying to keep his family going. Until shortly after this episode, Richard was known and respected as one of the hardest-working men on the street. Richard had said, only a couple of months earlier, "I figure you got to get out there and try. You got to try before you can get anything." His wife Shirley confirmed that he had always tried. "If things get tough, with me I'll get all worried. But Richard get worried, he don't want me to see him worried. . . . He *will* get out there. He's shoveled snow, picked beans, and he's done some of everything. . . . He's not ashamed to get out there and get us something to eat." At the time of the episode reported above, Leroy was just starting marriage and raising a family. He and Richard were not, as Richard thought, "entirely different people." Leroy had just not learned, by personal experience over time, what Richard had learned. But within two years Leroy's marriage had broken up and he was talking and acting like Richard. "He just let go completely," said one of the men on the street.

10. There is no mystically intrinsic connection between "present-time" orientation and lower-class persons. Whenever people of whatever class have been uncertain, skeptical or downright pessimistic about the future, "I want mine right now" has been one of the characteristic responses, although it is usually couched in more delicate terms: e.g., Omar Khayyam's "Take the cash and let the credit go," or Horace's *"Carpe diem."* In wartime, especially, all classes tend to slough off conventional restraints on sexual and other behavior (i.e., become less able or less willing to defer gratification). And when inflation threatens, darkening the fiscal future, persons who formerly husbanded their resources with commendable restraint almost stampede one another rushing to spend their money. Similarly, it seems that future-time orientation tends to collapse toward the present when persons are in pain or under stress. The point here is that, the label notwithstanding, (what passes for) present-time orientation appears to be a situation-specific phenomenon rather than a part of the standard psychic equipment of Cognitive Lower Class Man.

11. And proceeded to do just that the following year when "trouble"—in this case, a grand jury indictment, a pile of debts, and a violent separation from his wife and children—appeared again.

12. For a discussion of "trouble" as a focal concern of lower-class culture, see Walter Miller, "Lower Class Culture as a Generating Milieu of Gang Delinquency," pp. 7, 8.

Paul Baran and Paul Sweezy
MONOPOLY CAPITALISM
AND RACE RELATIONS

1

As always happens in social science, answering one question leads to another. What social forces and institutional mechanisms have forced Negroes to play the part of permanent immigrants, entering the urban economy at the bottom and remaining there decade after decade?[1]

There are, it seems to us, three major sets of factors involved in the answer to this crucially important question. First, a formidable array of private interests benefit, in the most direct and immediate sense, from the continued existence of a segregated subproletariat. Second, the socio-psychological pressures generated by monopoly capitalist society intensify rather than alleviate existing racial prejudices, hence also discrimination and segregation. And third, as monopoly capitalism develops, the demand for unskilled and semi-skilled labor declines both relatively and absolutely, a trend which affects Negroes more than any other group and accentuates their economic and social inferiority. All of these factors mutually interact, tending to push Negroes ever further down in the social structure and locking them into the ghetto.

Consider first the private interests which benefit from the existence of a Negro subproletariat. (a) Employers benefit from divisions in the labor force which enable them to play one group off against another, thus weakening all. Historically, for example, no small amount of Negro migration was in direct response to the recruiting of strikebreakers. (b) Owners of ghetto real estate are able to overcrowd and overcharge. (c) Middle and upper income groups benefit from having at their disposal a large supply of cheap domestic labor. (d) Many small marginal businesses, especially in the service trades, can operate profitably only if cheap labor is available to them. (e) White workers benefit by being protected from Negro competition for the more desirable and higher paying jobs. Hence the customary distinction, especially in the South, between "white" and "Negro" jobs, the exclusion of Negroes from apprentice programs, the refusal of many unions to admit Negroes, and so on.[2] In all these groups— and taken together they constitute a vast majority of the white population —what Marx called "the most violent, mean, and malignant passions of the human breast, the Furies of private interest," are summoned into action to keep the Negro "in his place."

REPRINTED FROM PP. 263–280 OF *Monopoly Capital* BY PERMISSION OF MONTHLY RE-VIEW PRESS. COPYRIGHT © 1966 BY PAUL M. SWEEZY.

With regard to race prejudice, it has already been pointed out that this characteristic white attitude was deliberately created and cultivated as a rationalization and justification for the enslavement and exploitation of colored labor.[3] But in time, race prejudice and the discriminatory behavior patterns which go with it came to serve other purposes as well. As capitalism developed, particularly in its monopoly phase, the social structure became more complex and differentiated. Within the basic class framework, which remained in essentials unchanged, there took place a proliferation of social strata and status groups, largely determined by occupation and income. These groupings, as the terms "stratum" and "status" imply, relate to each other as higher or lower, with the whole constituting an irregular and unstable hierarchy. In such a social structure, individuals tend to see and define themselves in terms of the "status hierarchy" and to be motivated by ambitions to move up and fears of moving down.[4] These ambitions and fears are of course exaggerated, intensified, played upon by the corporate sales apparatus which finds in them the principal means of manipulating the "utility functions" of the consuming public.

The net result of all this is that each status group has a deep-rooted psychological need to compensate for feelings of inferiority and envy toward those above by feelings of superiority and contempt for those below. It thus happens that a special pariah group at the bottom acts as a kind of lightning rod for the frustrations and hostilities of all the higher groups, the more so the nearer they are to the bottom. It may even be said that the very existence of the pariah group is a kind of harmonizer and stabilizer of the social structure—so long as the pariahs play their role passively and resignedly. Such a society becomes in time so thoroughly saturated with race prejudice that it sinks below the level of consciousness and becomes a part of the "human nature" of its members.[5] The gratification which whites derive from their socio-economic superiority to Negroes has its counterpart in alarm, anger, and even panic at the prospect of Negroes' attaining equality. Status being a relative matter, whites inevitably interpret upward movement by Negroes as downward movement for themselves. This complex of attitudes, product of stratification and status consciousness in monopoly capitalist society, provides an important part of the explanation why whites not only refuse to help Negroes to rise but bitterly resist their efforts to do so. (When we speak of whites and their prejudices and attitudes in this unqualified way, we naturally do not mean all whites. Ever since John Brown, and indeed long before John Brown, there have been whites who have freed themselves of the disease of racial prejudice, have fought along with Negro militants for an end to the rotten system of exploitation and inequality, and have looked forward to the creation of a society in which relations of solidarity and brotherhood will take the place of relations of superiority and inferiority. Moreover, we are confident that the number of whites will steadily increase in the years ahead. But their number is not great today, and in a survey which aims only at depicting the broadest contours of the current social scene it would be wholly misleading to assign them a decisive role.)

The third set of factors adversely affecting the relative position of Negroes is connected with technological trends and their impact on the demand for different kinds and grades of labor. Appearing before a Congressional committee in 1955, the then Secretary of Labor, James P. Mitchell, testified that unskilled workers as a proportion of the labor force had declined from 36 percent in 1910 to 20 percent in 1950.[6] A later Secretary of Labor, Willard Wirtz, told the Clark Committee in 1963 that the percentage of unskilled was down to 5 percent by 1962.[7] Translated into absolute figures, this means that the number of unskilled workers declined slightly, from somewhat over to somewhat under 13 million between 1910 and 1950, and then plummeted to fewer than 4 million only twelve years later. These figures throw a sharp light on the rapid deterioration of the Negro employment situation since the Second World War. What happened is that until roughly a decade and a half ago, with the number of unskilled jobs remaining stable, Negroes were able to hold their own in the total employment picture by replacing white workers who were moving up the occupational ladder. This explains why, as Table 1 shows, the Negro unemployment rate was only a little higher than the white rate at the end of the Great Depression. Since 1950, on the other hand, with unskilled jobs disappearing at a fantastic rate, Negroes not qualified for other kinds of work found themselves increasingly excluded from employment altogether. Hence the rise of the Negro unemployment rate to more than double the white rate by the early 1960's. Negroes, in other words, being the least qualified workers are disproportionately hard hit as unskilled jobs (and, to an increasing extent, semi-skilled jobs) are eliminated by mechanization, automation, and cybernation. Since this technological revolution has not run its course—indeed many authorities think that it is still in its early stages—the job situation of Negroes is likely to go on deteriorating. To be sure, technological trends are not, as many believe, the *cause* of unemployment: that role . . . is played by the specific mechanisms of monopoly capitalism.[8] But within the framework of this society technological trends, because of their differential impact on job opportunities, can rightly be considered a cause, and undoubtedly the most important cause, of the relative growth of Negro unemployment.

2

All the forces we have been discussing—vested economic interests, socio-psychological needs, technological trends—are deeply rooted in monopoly capitalism and together are strong enough to account for the fact that Negroes have been unable to rise out of the lower depths of American society. Indeed so pervasive and powerful are these factors that the wonder is only that the position of Negroes has not drastically worsened. That it has not, that in absolute terms their real income and consuming power have risen more or less in step with the rest of the population's, can only be explained by the existence of counteracting forces.

One of these counteracting forces we have already commented upon: the shift out of Southern agriculture and into the urban economy. Some schooling was better than none; even a rat-infested tenement provided more shelter than a broken-down shack on Tobacco Road; being on the relief rolls of a big city meant more income, both money and real, than subsistence farming. And as the nation's per capita income rose, so also did that of the lowest income group, even that of unemployables on permanent relief. As we have seen, it has been this shift from countryside to city which has caused so many observers to believe in the reality of a large-scale Negro breakthrough in the last two decades. Actually, it was an aspect of a structural change in the economy rather than a change in the position of Negroes within the economy.

But in one particular area, that of government employment, Negroes have indeed scored a breakthrough, and this has unquestionably been the decisive factor in preventing a catastrophic decline in their relative position in the economy as a whole. Table 1 gives the essential data (all levels of government are included).

Between 1940 and 1962, total government employment somewhat more than doubled, while non-white (. . . more than 90 percent Negro) employment in government expanded nearly five times. As a result non-white employment grew from 5.6 percent of the total to 12.1 percent. Since non-whites constituted 11.5 percent of the labor force at mid-1961, it is a safe inference that Negroes are now more than proportionately represented in government employment.[9]

Two closely interrelated forces have been responsible for this relative improvement of the position of Negroes in government employment. The first, and beyond doubt the most important, has been the increasing scope and militancy of the Negro liberation movement itself. The second has been the need of the American oligarchy, bent on consolidating a global empire including people of all colors, to avoid as much as possible

TABLE 1   *Non-white Employment in Government, 1940–1962—*
(Figures are for April, in Thousands)

	1940	1956	1960	1961	1962
Government employees, total	3,845	6,919	8,014	8,150	8,647
Non-white government employees	214	670	855	932	1,046
Non-white as percent of total	5.6	9.7	10.7	11.4	12.1

Source: United States Department of Labor, *The Economic Situation of Negroes in the United States,* Bulletin S-3, Revised 1962, p. 8.

the stigma of racism. If American Negroes had passively accepted the continuation of their degraded position, history teaches us that the oligarchy would have made no concessions. But once seriously challenged by militant Negro struggle, it was forced by the logic of its domestic and international situation to make concessions, with the twin objectives of pacifying Negroes at home and projecting abroad an image of the United States as a liberal society seeking to overcome an evil inheritance from the past.

The oligarchy, acting through the federal government and in the North and West through state and local governments, has also made other concessions to the Negro struggle. The armed forces have been desegregated, and a large body of civil rights legislation forbidding discrimination in public accommodations, housing, education, and employment, has been enacted. Apart from the desegregation of the armed forces, however, these concessions have had little effect. Critics often attribute this failure to bad faith: there was never any intention, it is said, to concede to Negroes any of the real substance of their demand for equality. This is a serious misreading of the situation. No doubt there are many white legislators and administrators to whom such strictures apply with full force, but this is not true of the top economic and political leadership of the oligarchy— the managers of the giant corporations and their partners at the highest governmental levels. These men are governed in their political attitudes and behavior not by personal prejudices but by their conception of class interests. And while they may at times be confused by their own ideology or mistake short-run for long-run interests, it seems clear that with respect to the race problem in the United States they have come, perhaps belatedly but none the less surely, to understand that the very existence of their system is at stake. Either a solution will be found which insures the loyalty, or at least the neutrality, of the Negro people, or else the world revolution will sooner or later acquire a ready-made and potentially powerful Trojan horse within the ramparts of monopoly capitalism's mightiest fortress. When men like Kennedy and Johnson and Warren champion such measures as the Civil Rights Act of 1964, it is clearly superficial to accuse them of perpetrating a cheap political maneuver. They know that they are in trouble, and they are looking for a way out.

Why then such meager results? The answer is simply that the oligarchy does not have the power to shape and control race relations any more than it has the power to plan the development of the economy. In matters which are within the administrative jurisdiction of government, policies can be effectively implemented. Thus it was possible to desegregate the armed forces and greatly to increase the number of Negroes in government employment. But when it comes to housing, education, and private employment, all the deeply rooted economic and socio-psychological forces analyzed above come into play. It was capitalism, with its enthronement of greed and privilege, which created the race problem and made of it the ugly thing it is today. It is the very same system which resists and thwarts every effort at a solution.

3

The fact that despite all political efforts, the relative economic and social position of Negroes has changed but little in recent years, and in some respects has deteriorated, makes it a matter of great urgency for the oligarchy to devise strategies which will divide and weaken the Negro protest movement and thus prevent it from developing its full revolutionary potential. These strategies can all be appropriately grouped under the heading of "tokenism."

If we are to understand the real nature of tokenism, it is necessary to keep in mind certain developments within the Negro community since the great migration from the Southern countryside got under way. As Negroes moved out of a largely subsistence economy into a money economy and as their average levels of income and education rose, their expenditures for goods and services naturally increased correspondingly. Goods were for the most part supplied by established white business; but segregation, *de jure* in the South and *de facto* in the North, gave rise to a rapidly expanding demand for certain kinds of services which whites would not or could not provide or which Negroes could provide better. Chief among these were the services of teachers, ministers, doctors, dentists, lawyers, barbers and beauty parlors, undertakers, certain kinds of insurance, and a press catering to the special needs of the segregated Negro community. Professionals and owners of enterprises supplying these services form the core of what Franklin Frazier called the black bourgeoisie.[10] Their ranks have been augmented by the growth of Negro employment in the middle and higher levels of the civil service and by the rapid expansion of the number of Negroes in the sports and entertainment worlds. The growth of the black bourgeoisie has been particularly marked since the Second World War. Between 1950 and 1960 the proportion of non-white families with incomes over $10,000 (1959 dollars) increased from 1 percent to 4.7 percent, a rate of growth close to three times that among whites. During the same years, the total distribution of income among Negro families became more unequal, while the change among white families was in the opposite direction.[11]

The theory behind tokenism, not often expressed but clearly deducible from the practice, is that the black bourgeoisie is the decisive element in the Negro community. It contains the intellectual and political elite, the people with education and leadership ability and experience. It already has a material stake in the existing social order, but its loyalty is doubtful because of the special disabilities imposed upon it solely because of its color. If this loyalty can be made secure, the potential revolutionizing of the Negro protest movement can be forestalled and the world can be given palpable evidence—through the placing of loyal Negroes in prominent positions—that the United States does not pursue a South African-type policy of *apartheid* but on the contrary fights against it and strives for equal opportunity for its Negro citizens. The problem is thus how to secure the loyalty of the black bourgeoisie.

To this end the political drive to assure legal equality for Negroes must be continued. We know that legal equality does not guarantee real equality: the right to patronize the best hotels and restaurants, for example, means little to the Negro masses. But it is of great importance to the well-to-do Negro, and the continuation of any kind of disability based solely on color is hateful to all Negroes. The loyalty of the black bourgeoisie can never be guaranteed as long as vestiges of the Jim Crow system persist. For this reason we can confidently predict that, however long and bloody the struggle may be, the South will eventually be made over in the image of the North.

Second, the black bourgeoisie must be provided with greater access to the dominant institutions of the society: corporations, the policy-making levels of government, the universities, the suburbs. Here the oligarchy is showing itself to be alert and adaptable. A *New York Times* survey found that:

> Business and industry here, in the face of the civil rights revolution, have been reassessing their employment policies and hiring Negroes for office and other salaried posts that they rarely held before.
>
> Many national concerns with headquarters in New York City have announced new nondiscrimination policies or reaffirmed old ones. Personnel officers are taking a new look at their recruiting methods and seeking advice from Negro leaders on how to find and attract the best qualified Negroes.
>
> On a nationwide basis, about 80 of the country's largest companies enrolled under Plans for Progress of the President's Committee on Equal Opportunity have reported substantial increases in the hiring of Negroes for salaried positions. . . .
>
> The latest figures for the 80 companies that filed reports in the last year . . . showed that non-whites got 2,241 of the 31,698 salaried jobs that opened up. This represented an increase of 8.9 percent in the number of jobs held by nonwhites in those companies.[12]

The same thing has been happening in government, as already noted; and in addition to being hired in larger numbers in the better-paying grades, Negroes are increasingly being placed in executive jobs at or near the cabinet level, in federal judgeships, and the like. And as Negroes are brought into the economic and political power structure, they also become more acceptable in the middle- and upper-class suburbs—provided of course that their incomes and standard of living are comparable to their neighbors'.

Not many Negroes are affected by these easings of the barriers separating the races at the upper economic and social levels—in fact, it is of the essence of tokenism that not many should be. But this does not deprive the phenomenon of its importance. The mere existence of the possibility of moving up and out can have a profound psychological impact.

Third, the strategy of tokenism requires not only that Negro leadership should come from the black bourgeoisie but that it should be kept dependent on favors and financial support from the white oligarchy. The established civil rights organizations—the National Association for the Advancement of Colored People, the Urban League, and the Congress of Racial Equality—were all founded on a bi-racial basis and get most of their funds from white sources; they therefore present no potential threat. But it is always necessary to pay attention to the emergence of new and potentially independent leaders. Where this occurs, there are two standard tactics for dealing with the newcomers. The first is to co-opt them into the service of the oligarchy by flattery, jobs, or other material favors. Noel Day, a young Boston Negro leader who ran for Congress in the 1964 election, comments on this tactic:

> Although the system is rotten it is nevertheless marvellously complex in the same way as the chambered Nautilus, beautiful in its complexity. The co-opting begins at birth; the potential for co-optation is built into the system. It is part of what we are taught is good. We have been taught to feel that the couple of thousand dollars a year more is what is desirable. The Negro and most other minority groups have been taught to desire entrance into the mainstream, they have not been taught to look to themselves and develop any sense of pride within their group, they have been taught to aspire to become mainstream Americans. In the case of the Negro, to aspire to become white. . . . One way of becoming white is by having a higher salary, or a title or a prestige position. This is not a very simple thing, but it is one of the evil beauties of the system. It has so many built-in checks and controls that come into operation—some of these are vitiating the energy of the freedom movement already. The official rhetoric has changed—in response to the dislocations and pressures we are witnessing an attempt at mass co-optation similar to the mass co-optation of the labor movement. The reaction of American business, for instance, is fantastic. The integration programs of some of the major companies are quick and adept—the fact that the First National Bank of Boston two months ago had about fifty Negro employees and now has over a thousand. Under pressure by CORE, they gave in to CORE's demands within *two weeks. Two months later* one of their top personnel men came into my office and said—now we are really concerned about developing a program for dropouts. What he was saying is that they are so adaptable, so flexible, in maintaining the balance of American business, in substituting reform as an antidote to revolution, that they will even go beyond the demands of the civil rights movement.[13]

If co-optation fails, the standard tactic is to attempt to destroy the potentially independent leader by branding him a Communist, a subversive, a trouble-maker, and by subjecting him to economic and legal harassments.

The reference in Noel Day's statement to developing a program for dropouts points to a fourth aspect of tokenism: to open up greater opportunities for Negro youths of all classes who because of luck, hard work, or special aptitudes are able to overcome the handicap of their background and start moving up the educational ladder. For a "qualified" Negro in the

United States today, there is seemingly no limit to what he may aspire to. A report in the *New York Times* states:

> Dr. Robert F. Goheen, president of Princeton University, said yesterday that the competition among colleges and universities for able Negro students was "much more intense" than the traditional competition for football players. . . . Dr. Goheen said: "It certainly is very clear that the number of able colored who have also had adequate educational opportunities is very small. And we find we are all extending our hands to the same relatively few young men and women." [14]

Here we can see as under a magnifying glass the mechanics of tokenism. With the country's leading institutions of higher learning falling over themselves to recruit qualified Negro students—and with giant corporations and the federal government both eager to snap them up after graduation—the prospects opened up to the lucky ones are indeed dazzling. But as President Goheen stresses, their number is very small, and it can only remain very small as long as the vast majority of Negroes stay anchored at the bottom of the economic ladder.

The fact that the great mass of Negroes derive no benefits from tokenism does not mean that they are unaffected by it. One of its purposes, and to the extent that it succeeds one of its consequences, is to detach the ablest young men and women from their own people and thus to deprive the liberation movement of its best leadership material. And even those who have no stake in the system and no hope of ever acquiring one may become reconciled to it if they come to believe there is a chance that their children, or perhaps even their children's children, may be able to rise out of their own degraded condition.

4

It would be a great mistake to underestimate the skill and tenacity of the United States oligarchy when faced with what it regards—and in the case of race relations, rightly regards—as a threat to its existence. And it would be just as serious a mistake to underestimate the effectiveness, actual and potential, of the strategy of tokenism. Yet we believe that in the long run the real condition of the Negro masses will be the decisive factor. If some improvement, however modest and slow, can be registered in the years ahead, a well conceived policy of tokenism may be enough to keep Negroes from developing into monopoly capitalism's "enemy within the gates." But if the trends of the recent past continue, if advances are canceled out by setbacks, if the paradox of widespread poverty and degradation in the midst of potential abundance becomes ever more glaring, then it will be only a matter of time until American Negroes, propelled by the needs of their own humanity and inspired by the struggles and achievements of their brothers in the underdeveloped countries, will generate their own revolutionary self-consciousness.

If this assessment of the situation is correct, it becomes a matter of great importance to know whether the kinds of reforms which are possible within the framework of the existing system—the kinds advocated by the established civil rights organizations and their white supporters—are likely to yield any real benefits to the Negro masses.

It seems clear to us that the answer is negative; that the chief beneficiaries of reforms of this type are the black bourgeoisie; and that, regardless of the intentions of their sponsors, their objective effect is merely to supplement the policy of tokenism.

This might be thought not to be the case with prohibitions against discrimination in the hiring of labor, which unquestionably helped open up many new jobs to Negroes during the war. In a period of heavy and growing unemployment, however, no such effect can be expected. Even if color is not the reason, Negroes will be discriminated against because of their inferior qualifications. Only those with special talents or training will benefit, and they are already set apart from the ghettoized masses.

Nor can the ghetto dwellers hope to gain from anti-discrimination measures in the field of housing. The only kind of housing that would benefit them would result from construction on a large scale of low-rent units for those who most need it where they need it. Under existing conditions, there is no chance that such housing could be integrated. Attempts to build low-rent housing in marginal neighborhoods and to keep it occupied on a bi-racial basis necessitate the enforcement of so-called "benevolent quotas"—in other words require that Negro occupancy be kept low and hence that few Negroes benefit. As to the prevention of discrimination in the sale of private housing, either by law or by judicial nullification of restrictive covenants, this certainly helps well-to-do Negroes to move into previously all-white neighborhoods. As far as low-income Negroes are concerned, however, the most that can be said is that it facilitates expansion of the ghetto itself through what has been called the "invasion-succession sequence." In this strictly limited sense, anti-discrimination measures do help low-income Negroes; after all, they have to live somewhere. But it does nothing to raise their status or to promote racial integration in the lower reaches of the social structure.

With appropriate modifications, the story is not different in the case of school integration. Where neighborhoods are racially mixed, school integration follows naturally and is unquestionably good for all concerned. But this affects few Negroes, mostly of the higher-income group. The real problem is the ghetto schools. Some upgrading of schools attended by ghetto dwellers may be achieved by placing them on the margins of the ghetto and drawing school districts so as to include both black and white areas. But this does not touch the problem of the ghetto schools themselves, and here all the forces of tradition, inertia, prejudice, and privilege come into play to block or abort attempts at reform. Programs of driving a certain number of Negro children by bus from the ghetto areas to white schools elsewhere merely evade the problem, and there is considerable evidence that they increase the insecurity and self-distrust of the children involved.[15]

There is really no mystery about why reforms which remain within the confines of the system hold out no prospect of meaningful improvement to the Negro masses. The system has two poles: wealth, privilege, power at one; poverty, deprivation, powerlessness at the other. It has always been that way, but in earlier times whole groups could rise because expansion made room above and there were others ready to take their place at the bottom. Today, Negroes are at the bottom, and there is neither room above nor anyone ready to take their place. Thus only individuals can move up, not the group as such: reforms help the few, not the many. For the many nothing short of a complete change in the system —the abolition of both poles and the substitution of a society in which wealth and power are shared by all—can transform their condition.

Some will say that even if this is true, it does not mean that the Negro masses will necessarily become aware of the causes of their degradation, still less that they will achieve a revolutionary self-consciousness. May they not be blinded by the mystifications of bourgeois ideology and paralyzed by a leadership drawn from the tokenized elite? After all, there have always been oppressed classes and races, but the achievement of revolutionary self-consciousness is a rare historical event. Why should we expect American Negroes to do what so few have done before them?

There are, we believe, two reasons, equally compelling.

First, American Negroes live in a society which has mastered technology and advanced the productivity of labor beyond anything dreamed of even a few years ago. True, this has been done in search of profits and more perfect means of destruction, but the potential for human abundance and freedom is there and cannot be hidden. Poverty and oppression are no longer necessary, and a system which perpetuates them cannot but appear to its victims ever more clearly as a barbarous anachronism.

Second, the tide of world revolution against imperialist exploitation, which in our time is simply the international face of monopoly capitalism, is flowing strong, much too strong to be turned back or halted. Already, the rise of independent African nations has helped to transform the American Negro's image of himself. As Africans—and Asians and Latin Americans—carry their revolutions forward from national independence to socialist egalitarianism, the American Negro's consciousness will be transformed again and again—by his own knowledge and experience and by the example of those all over the world who are struggling against, and increasingly winning victories over, the same inhuman system of capitalist-imperialist oppression.

The Negro masses cannot hope for integration into American society as it is now constituted. But they can hope to be one of the historical agents which will overthrow it and put in its place another society in which they will share, not civil rights which is at best a narrow bourgeois concept, but full human rights.

Notes

1. "The Negro population," says the Commission on Race and Housing, "in spite of its centuries of residence in America, has at present some of the characteristics of an incompletely assimilated immigrant group." *Where Shall We Live?* pp. 8–9.

2. "There has grown up a system of Negro jobs and white jobs. And this is the toughest problem facing the Negro southerner in employment." Leslie W. Dunbar, Executive Director of the Southern Regional Council, in testimony before the Clark Committee. *Equal Employment Opportunities,* p. 457.

3. Among colored peoples, race prejudice, to the extent that it exists at all, is a defensive reaction to white aggression and therefore has an entirely different significance. It may serve to unify and spur on colored peoples in their struggles for freedom and equality, but once these goals have been achieved it rapidly loses its *raison d'être.* As Oliver Cox has pointed out: "Today communication is so far advanced that no people of color, however ingenious, could hope to put a cultural distance between them and whites comparable to that which the Europeans of the commercial and industrial revolution attained in practical isolation over the colored peoples of the world. And such a relationship is crucial for the development of that complex belief in biological superiority and consequent color prejudice which Europeans have been able to attain. Therefore, we must conclude that race prejudice is not only a cultural trait developed among Europeans, but also that no other race could hope to duplicate the phenomenon. Like the discovery of the world, it seems evident that this racial achievement could occur only once." *Caste, Class, and Race,* pp. 348–349. The other side of this coin is, since the colored races obviously can and will attain cultural and technological equality with whites, that the race prejudice of modern whites is not only a unique but also a transitory historical phenomenon. It needs to be added, however, that completely eliminating it from the consciousness of whites, even in a predominantly non-exploitative (that is, socialist) world, may take decades rather than months or years.

4. The crucial importance of the status hierarchy in the shaping of the individual's consciousness goes far to explain the illusion, so widespread in the United States, that there are no classes in this country, or, as the same idea is often expressed, that everyone is a member of the middle class.

5. At this level of development, race prejudice is far from being reachable by public opinion polls and similar devices of "sociometrics" which remain close to the surface of individual and social phenomena. Incidentally, we have here another reason for believing that the eradication of race prejudice from whites will be, even in a rational society, a difficult and protracted process.

6. *Automation and Technological Change.* Hearings Before the Subcommittee on Economic Stabilization of the Joint Committee on the Economic Report, 84th Cong., 1st Sess., pursuant to Sec. 5(a) of P. L. 304, 79th Cong., Oct. 14, 15, 17, 18, 24, 25, 26, 27, and 28, 1955, p. 264.

7. *Nation's Manpower Revolution,* Part 1, May 20, 21, 22, and 25, 1963, p. 57.

8. Under socialism there is no reason why technological progress, no matter how rapid or of what kind, should be associated with unemployment. In a socialist society technological progress may make possible a continuous reduction in the number of years, weeks, and hours worked, but it is inconceivable that this reduction should take the completely irrational form of capitalist unemployment.

9. If the data were available to compare income received from government employment by whites and non-whites, the picture would of course be much less favorable for Negroes since they are heavily concentrated in the lower-paying categories. But here too there has been improvement. A study made by the Civil Service Commission showed that between June 1962 and June 1963 Negro employment in the federal government increased by 3 percent and that "the major percentage gains had been in the better-paying jobs." *New York Times,* March 4, 1964.

10. E. Franklin Frazier, *Black Bourgeoisie: The Rise of a New Middle Class in the United States,* Glencoe, Illinois, 1957.

11. All data from Herman P. Miller, *Trends in the Income of Families and Persons in the United States: 1947 to 1960,* Bureau of the Census Technical Paper No. 8, Washington, 1963, Table 9, pp. 168–189. The measure of inequality used by Miller is the so-called Gini coefficient which increased for non-white families from .402 in 1950 to .414 in 1960, while for white families it was declining from .372 to .357.

Apart from the direction of change, the greater degree of income inequality for non-whites which these figures indicate should not be interpreted to mean that there is really a greater degree of equality of material circumstances among whites than among Negroes. In the upper reaches of the social structure, income is less significant than property; and while we know of no data on Negro property ownership, it seems beyond doubt that the disparity between Negroes and whites in this regard is immeasurably greater than in incomes.

12. *New York Times,* November 12, 1963.

13. "Symposium: New Politics," *Studies on the Left,* Summer 1964, pp. 44–45.

14. *New York Times,* October 21, 1963.

15. See A. James Gregor, "Black Nationalism: A Preliminary Analysis of Negro Radicalism," *Science & Society,* Fall 1963, pp. 427–431. Gregor also presents valuable evidence on the negligible importance to the Negro masses of anti-discrimination programs in housing.

PART THREE
RACE AND
CLASS RELATIONS

The structure of national societies in the New World can best be understood by reference to the categories of race and class. There is physical diversity among the populations of the New World and there are obvious differences among individuals in terms of skin color and physiognomic features. Differential access to and control over resources, property, and wealth results in class stratification. Race and class, however, are not mutually independent, and race here refers not to a biological construct, but to a definition of a social group based on physical characteristics. Thus, as Morton Fried argues in the first article, the term race has no scientific or objective validity, and its importance is not biological but sociological; that is, as an expression of social tensions and contradictions such as those mentioned in the foregoing pages.

In discussing the problem of racial classifications of social groups in modern society, Kenneth Little pinpoints the sources and perpetuation of racism in capitalist social and economic relations. In this social and economic system, founded on unequal access to the means and fruits of production, and operating with an ideology of individual achievement toward access, one of the major criteria for determining access is based on ascribed biological factors over which the individual has no control. Thus, *ancestry* and *skin color* determine social and economic position; they are marks of race. Racial discrimination, along with sexual discrimination, stands as one major contradiction in capitalist societies and a source of social and political tension which is indeed generating conditions for change.

In Brazil, the darker one's skin color, the lower his social position and the more difficult his access to a share of the national wealth. In the United States, known descent or ancestry from African slaves, no matter the skin color, is enough to ensure one's disengagement from the processes of production. The results are the same: the formation of a black underclass.

Skin color, a mark of race in Brazil and the Caribbean, is often socially defined; thus, the common Brazilian and West Indian expression, "money whitens." In Brazil, as Wagley's contribution indicates, physical appearance determines social position. Yet, there is a multiplicity of categories based on color and other physiognomic features *and* on certain social and economic considerations such that a wealthy, well-educated man with dark skin is referred to by a term different from those describing the black underclass. The higher up the social and economic scale, the lighter the perception of skin color. Gordon Lewis, in discussing color and society in Puerto Rico, refers to this as "racial intermediacy" and he explains the ways in which it keeps people in their place.

149

Moreover, the intricacies of race and class in Brazil and the Caribbean have led some scholars to distinguish public relations from private relations in order to expose the racist thinking and discrimination that pervade these societies in spite of appearances to the contrary. Thus, a well-to-do Negro is invited to a political reception, but he is hardly invited to dinner; and, ". . . well, after all, one must consider one's sister!"

A distinguishing feature between these societies and that of the United States is the criterion used for race/class categories. In the phrases of Oracy Noguiera, in the former societies there is "color prejudice of mark", i.e., skin color, and in the United States "color prejudice of origin", i.e., the rule of descent or ancestry. These differences seem to be associated with the size and importance of a middle class of intermediate color and mixed ancestry. In the West Indies, for example, the intermediate color of the mulatto or "colored" descendants of slave women and white masters justifies their intermediate social position. Daniel Guérin, after describing race relations in the Caribbean, documents the effects of this colored middle class on the life of the region. He takes this middle class to task for its failures, especially in preventing the development of a West Indian culture or consciousness. Marvin Harris argues that the small size and relative unimportance of this intermediate, colored class is, *inter alia,* part of an explanation for the origin of a categorical descent rule in the United States as against the development of the variable use of skin color in Brazil. Against a background of intense competition for economic resources and social position among the lower classes and between them and the upper classes, the rigid criterion of descent—the virulent racism of America—as applied to emancipated slaves ensured their existence as an underclass, separated them from the white underclass and paved the way for the upward mobility of the latter. Harris' critique of the Tannenbaum thesis appears in Part I of this reader.

The remaining chapters in this part discuss the relations of black society in Canada and the United Kingdom. Robin Winks maintains that Canadian attitudes toward blacks reflect those of white America. The social and economic status of the black underclass, especially in Nova Scotia, reflects the same productive processes and social relations of class and race found in other New World societies. An extension of the black underclass of the New World to the Old, the Caribbean community in Britain, is, as Claudia Jones points out, no improvement in their position or condition. This example should teach us that the problems emphasized in this reader are not peculiar to the New World. They are not an aspect of geography but an aspect of a distinctive social and economic system.

Morton H. Fried
A FOUR-LETTER WORD
THAT HURTS

Taking the great white race away from today's racists is like taking candy from a baby. There are sure to be shrieks and howls of outrage. But it will be very hard to take away this piece of candy, because, to drop the metaphor, nothing is harder to expunge than an idea. The white race is not a real, hard fact of nature; it is an idea.

In 1959 a young anthropologist named Philip Newman walked into the very remote village of Miruma in the upper Asaro Valley of New Guinea to make a field study of the Gururumba. It was late that first afternoon when it began to dawn upon his native hosts that he had made no move to leave. Finally a man of some rank plucked up his courage and said, "How long will you stay, red man?"

Most people are probably amused, but a few will be puzzled and chagrined to know that what passes in our own culture as a member of the great white race is considered red by some New Guineans. But when did anyone ever really see a *white* white man? Most so-called white men are turned by wind, rain, and certain kinds of lotion to various shades of brown, although they would probably prefer to be thought bronze. Even the stay-in who shuns the sun and despises cosmetics would rarely be able to be considered white in terms of the minimal standards set on television by our leading laundry detergents. His color would likely be a shade of the pink that is a basic tint for all Caucasoids. (That, like "Caucasian," is another foolish word in the service of this concept of race. The Caucasus region, as far as we know, played no significant role in human evolution and certainly was not the cradle of any significant human variety.)

Actually, even the generalization about pink as a basic skin tint has to be explained and qualified. In some people the tint of the skin is in substantial measure the result of chemical coloring matter in the epidermis; in others there is no such coloring matter, or very little, and tinting then depends on many factors, including the color of the blood in the tiny capillaries of the dermis. Statistically, there is a continuous grading of human skin color from light to dark. There are no sharp breaks, no breaks at all. Since nobody is really white and since color is a trait that varies without significant interruption, I think the most sensible statement that can be made on the subject is that there is no white race. To make this just as true and outrageous as I can, let me immediately add that there never *was* a white race.

REPRINTED FROM *Saturday Review*, OCTOBER 2, 1965, BY PERMISSION OF THE AUTHOR AND THE PUBLISHER. COPYRIGHT 1965 SATURDAY REVIEW, INC.

While at it, I might as well go on to deny the existence of a red race, although noting that if there was such a thing as the white race it would be as least esthetically more correct to call it the red race. Also, there is not now and never has been either a black race or a yellow race.

To deny that there are differences between individuals and between populations is ridiculous. The New Guineans spotted Dr. Newman as an off-beat intruder as soon as they clapped eyes on him. Of course, they were noticing other things as well and some of those other things certainly helped to make the distinctions sharper. After all, Newman was relatively clean, he had clothes on, and, furthermore, he didn't carry himself at all like a Gururumba—that is to say like a human being. I was spotted as an alien the first time I showed up in the small city of Ch'uhsien, in Anhwei province, China, back in 1947. Even after more than a year in that place, there was no question about my standing out as a strange physical type. During the hot summer, peasants who had never seen anything like me before were particularly fascinated by my arms protruding from my short-sleeved shirt, and I almost had to stop patronizing the local bath house. I am not a hirsute fellow for someone of my type, but in Ch'uhsien I looked like a shaggy dog, and farmers deftly plucked my hairs and escaped with souvenirs. Another time, a charming young lady of three scrambled into my lap when I offered to tell her a story; she looked into my eyes just as I began and leaped off with a scream. It was some time before I saw her again, and in the interval I learned that in this area the worst, bloodthirsty, child-eating demons can be identified by their blue eyes.

Individual differences are obvious, even to a child. Unfortunately, race is not to be confused with such differences, though almost everybody sees them and some people act toward others on the basis of them. I say "unfortunately," because the confusion seems so deeply embedded as to make anyone despair of rooting it out.

Most laymen of my acquaintance, whether tolerant or bigoted, are frankly puzzled when they are told that race is an idea. It seems to them that it is something very real that they experience every day; one might as well deny the existence of different makes and models of automobiles. The answer to that analogy is easy: cars don't breed. Apart from what the kids conjure up by raiding automobile graveyards, and putting the parts together to get a monster, there are no real intergrades in machinery of this kind. To get a car you manufacture parts and put them together. To get our kind of biological organism you start with two fully formed specimens, one of each sex, and if they are attracted to each other, they may replicate. Their replication can never be more than approximate as far as either of them, the parents, is concerned, because as we so well know, each contributes only and exactly one-half of the genetic material to the offspring. We also know that some of the genetic material each transmits may not be apparent in his or her own makeup, so that it is fully possible for a child to be completely legitimate without resembling either side of the family, although he may remind a very old aunt of her grandfather.

The phenomenon of genetic inheritance is completely neutral with regard to race and racial formation. Given a high degree of isolation, different populations might develop to the point of being clearly distinguishable while they remained capable of producing fertile hybrids. There would, however, be few if any hybrids because of geographical isolation, and the result would be a neat and consistent system.

Much too neat and consistent for man. Never in the history of this globe has there been any species with so little *sitzfleisch*. Even during the middle of the Pleistocene, way down in the Lower Paleolithic, 300,000 or more years ago, our ancestors were continent-hoppers. That is the only reasonable interpretation of the fact that very similar remains of the middle Pleistocene fossil *Homo erectus* are found in Africa, Europe, and Asia. Since that time movement has accelerated and now there is no major region of this planet without its human population, even if it is a small, artificially maintained, nonreproductive population of scientists in Antarctica.

The mobility so characteristic of our genus, Homo, has unavoidable implications, for where man moves, man mates. (Antarctica, devoid of indigenous population, is perhaps the only exception.) This is not a recent phenomenon, but has been going on for one or two million years, or longer than the period since man became recognizable. We know of this mobility not only from evidence of the spread of our genus and species throughout the world, but also because the fossils of man collected from one locality and representing a single relatively synchronic population sometimes show extraordinary variation among themselves. Some years ago a population was found in Tabun Cave, near Mt. Carmel, in Israel. The physical anthropologists Ashley Montagu and C. Loring Brace describe it as "showing every possible combination of the features of Neanderthal with those of modern man." At Chouk'outien, a limestone quarry not too far from Peking, in a cave that was naturally open toward the close of the Pleistocene geological period, about 20,000 years ago, there lived a population of diverse physical types. While some physical anthropologists minimize them, those who have actually pored over the remains describe differences as great as those separating modern Chinese from Eskimos on one hand and Melanesians on the other. All of this, of course, without any direct evidence of the skin color of the fossils concerned. We never have found fossilized human skin and therefore can speak of the skin colors of our ancestors of tens of thousands of years ago only through extrapolation, by assuming continuity, and by assuming the applicability of such zoological rules as Gloger's, which was developed to explain the distribution of differently pigmented birds and mammals.

The evidence that our Pleistocene ancestors got around goes beyond their own physical remains and includes exotic shells, stones, and other materials in strange places which these objects could have reached only by being passed from hand to hand or being carried great distances. If our ancestors moved about that much, they also spread their genes, to put it euphemistically. Incidentally, they could have accomplished this spreading of genes whether they reacted to alien populations peacefully or hostilely; wars, including those in our own time, have always been a major means of speeding up hybridization.

Even phrasing the matter this way, and allowing for a goodly amount of gene flow between existing racial populations through hundreds of thousands of years of evolution, the resulting image of race is incredibly wrong, a fantasy with hardly any connection to reality. What is wrong is our way of creating and relying upon archetypes. Just as we persist in thinking that there is a typical American town (rarely our own), a typical American middle-class housewife (never our wife), a typical American male ("not me!"), so we think of races in terms of typical, archetypical, individuals who probably do not exist. When it is pointed out that there are hundreds of thousands or millions of living people who fall between the classified races, the frequently heard rejoinder is that this is so now, but it is a sign of our decadent times. Those fond of arguing this way usually go on to assert that it was not so in the past, that the races were formerly discrete.

In a startlingly large number of views, including those shared by informed and tolerant people, there was a time when there was a pure white race, a pure black race, etc., etc., depending upon how many races they recognize. There is not a shred of scientifically respectable evidence to support such a view. Whatever evidence we have contradicts it. In addition to the evidence of Chouk'outien and Tabun mentioned above, there are many other fossils whose morphological characteristics, primitivity to one side, are not in keeping with those of present inhabitants of the same region.

Part of the explanation of the layman's belief in pure ancestral races is to be found in the intellectually lazy trait of stereotyping which is applied not only to man's ancestry but to landscape and climate through time as well. Few parts of the world today look quite the way they did 15,000 years ago, much less 150,000 years ago. Yet I have found it a commonplace among students that they visualize the world of ages ago as it appears today. The Sahara is always a great desert, the Rockies a great mountain chain, and England separated from France by the Channel. Sometimes I ask a class, after we have talked about the famous Java fossil *Pithecanthropus erectus*, how the devil do they suppose he ever got there, Java being an island? Usually the students are dumbfounded by the question, until they are relieved to discover that Java wasn't always cut off from the Asian mainland. Given their initial attitudes and lack of information, it is not surprising that so many people imagine a beautiful Nordic Cro-Magnon, archetypical White, ranging a great Wagnerian forest looking for bestial Neanderthalers to exterminate.

Once again, there is no evidence whatsoever to support the lurid nightmare of genocide that early *Homo sapiens* is supposed to have wreaked upon the bumbling and grotesque Neanderthals. None either for William Golding's literary view of the extirpation of primitive innocence and goodness. The interpretation that in my view does least damage to the evidence is that which recognizes the differences between contemporary forms of so-called Neanderthals and other fossil *Homo sapiens* of 25,000 to 100,000 years ago to have been very little more or no greater than those between two variant populations of our own century. Furthermore, the same evidence indicates that the Neanderthals did not vanish suddenly but probably were slowly submerged in the populations that surrounded them, so that their genetic materials form part of our own inheritance today.

Then, it may be asked, where did the story come from that tells of the struggle of these populations and the extinction of one? It is a relatively fresh tale, actually invented in the nineteenth century, for before that time there was no suspicion of such creatures as Neanderthals. The nineteenth century, however, discovered the fossils of what has been called "Darwin's first witness." After some debate, the fossil remains were accepted as some primitive precursor of man and then chopped off the family tree. The model for this imaginary genealogical pruning was easily come by in a century that had witnessed the hunting and killing of native populations like game beasts, as in Tasmania, in the Malay peninsula, and elsewhere. Such episodes and continuation of slavery and the slave trade made genocide as real a phenomenon as the demand for laissez–faire and the Acts of Combination. It was precisely in this crucible that modern racism was born and to which most of our twentieth-century mythology about race can be traced.

In the vocabulary of the layman the word "race" is a nonsense term, one without a fixed, reliable meaning, and, as Alice pointed out to Humpty Dumpty, the use of words with idiosyncratic meanings is not conducive to communication. Yet I am sure that many who read these words will think that it is the writer who is twisting meaning and destroying a useful, common-sense concept. Far from it. One of the most respected and highly regarded volumes to have yet been published in the field of physical anthropology is *Human Biology,* by four British scientists, Harrison, Weiner, Tanner, and Barnicot (Oxford University Press, 1964). These distinguished authors jointly eschewed the word "race" on the ground that it was poorly defined even in zoology, *i.e.,* when applied to animals other than man, and because of its history of misunderstanding, confusion, and worse, when applied to humans.

Similar views have been held for some time and are familiar in the professional literature. Ashley Montagu, for example, has been in the vanguard of the movement to drop the concept of human race on scientific grounds for twenty-five years. His most recent work on the subject is a collation of critical essays from many specialists, *The Concept of Race*

(Free Press, 1964). Frank B. Livingstone, a physical anthropologist at the University of Michigan, has spoken out "On the Non-existence of Human Races" (*Current Anthropology*, 3:3, 1962). In the subsequent debate, opinions divided rather along generational lines. The older scientists preferred to cling to the concept of race while freely complaining about its shortcomings. The younger scientists showed impatience with the concept and wished to drop it and get on with important work that the concept obstructed.

Quite specifically, there are many things wrong with the concept of race. As generally employed, it is sometimes based on biological characteristics but sometimes on cultural features, and when it is based on biological traits the traits in question usually have the most obscure genetic backgrounds. The use of cultural criteria is best exemplified in such untenable racial constructs as the "Anglo-Saxon race," or the "German race" or the "Jewish race." Under no scientifically uttered definition known to me can these aggregates be called races. The first is a linguistic designation pertaining to the Germanic dialects or languages spoken by the people who about 1,500 years ago invaded the British Isles from what is now Schleswig-Holstein and the adjacent portion of Denmark. The invaders were in no significant way physically distinct from their neighbors who spoke other languages, and in any case they mated and blended with the indigenous population they encountered. Even their language was substantially altered by diffusion so that today a reference to English as an Anglo-Saxon language is quaint and less than correct. As for the hyperbolic extension of the designation to some of the people who live in England and the United States, it is meaningless in racial terms—just as meaningless as extending the term to cover a nation of heterogeneous origin and flexible boundaries, such as Germany or France or Italy or any other country. As for the moribund concept of a "Jewish race," this is simply funny, considering the extraordinary diversity of the physical types that have embraced this religion, and the large number that have relinquished it and entered other faiths.

The use of cultural criteria to identify individuals with racial categories does not stop with nationality, language, or religion. Such traits as posture, facial expression, musical tastes, and even modes of dress have been used to sort people into spurious racial groups. But even when biological criteria have been used, they have rarely been employed in a scientifically defensible way. One of the first questions to arise, for example, is what kind of criteria shall be used to sort people into racial categories. Following immediately upon this is another query: how many criteria should be used? With regard to the first, science is still in conflict. The new physical anthropologists whose overriding concern is to unravel the many remaining mysteries in human evolution and to understand the role that heredity will play in continuing and future evolution are impatient with any but strictly genetic characters, preferably those that can be linked to relatively few gene loci. They prefer the rapidly mounting blood factors, not only the ABO, Rh, MNS, and other well-known series, but such things as Duffy, Henshaw, Hunter, Kell, and Kidd (limited distribution blood groups named for the first person found to have carried them). Such work has one consistent by-product: the resultant classifications tend to cross-cut and obliterate conventional racial lines so that such constructs as the white race disappear as useful taxonomic units.

Some scientists argue that a classification based on only one criterion is not a very useful instrument. On the other hand, the more criteria that are added, the more abstract the racial construct becomes as fewer individuals can be discovered with all the necessary characteristics and more individuals are found to be in between. The end result is that the typical person is completely atypical; if race makes sense, so does this.

That racial classification is really nonsense can be demonstrated with ease merely by comparing some of the most usual conceptions of white and Negro. What degree of black African ancestry establishes a person as a Negro? Is 51 per cent or 50.1 per cent or some other slight statistical preponderance necessary? The question is ridiculous; we have no means of discriminating quantities of inherited materials in percentage terms. In that case can we turn to ancestry and legislate that anyone with a Negro parent is a Negro? Simple, but totally ineffective and inapplicable: how was the racial identity of each parent established? It is precisely at this point that anthropologists raise the question of assigning specific individuals to racial categories. At best, a racial category is a statistical abstraction based upon certain frequencies of genetic characters observed in small samples of much larger populations. A frequency of genetic characters is something that can be displayed by a population, but it cannot be displayed by an individual, any more than one voter can represent the proportion of votes cast by his party.

The great fallacy of racial classification is revealed by reflecting on popular applications in real situations. Some of our outstanding "Negro" citizens have almost no phenotypic resemblance to the stereotyped "Negro." It requires their acts of self-identification to place them. Simultaneously, tens of thousands of persons of slightly darker skin color, broader nasal wings, more everted lips, less straight hair, etc., are considered as "white" without question, in the South as well as the North, and in all socioeconomic strata. Conversely, some of our best known and noisiest Southern politicians undoubtedly have some "Negro" genes in their makeup.

Why is it so hard to give up this miserable little four-letter word that of all four-letter words has done the most damage? This is a good question for a scientific linguist or a semanticist. After all, the word refers to nothing more than a transitory statistical abstraction. But the question can also be put to an anthropologist. His answer might be, and mine is, that the word "race" expresses a certain kind of unresolved social conflict that thrives on divisions and invidious distinctions. It can thrive in the total absence of genetic differences in a single homogeneous population of common ancestry. That is the case, for example, with the relations between the Japanese and that portion of themselves they know as the Eta.

In a truly great society it may be that the kinds of fear and rivalry that generate racism will be overcome. This can be done without the kind of millenarian reform that would be necessary to banish all conflict, for only certain kinds of hostilities generate racism although any kind can be channeled into an already raging racial bigotry. Great areas of the earth's surface have been totally devoid of racism for long periods of time and such a situation may return again, although under altered circumstances. If and when it does, the word "race" may drop from our vocabulary and scholars will desperately scrutinize our remains and the remains of our civilization, trying to discover what we were so disturbed about.

Kenneth Little
THE SOCIAL FOUNDATIONS
OF RACISM

In any discussion of race and society, it is essential to have a clear understanding of the terms employed. It is history rather than race which is the main factor in producing the differences between the cultures and cultural attainments of the world's population. The fact that such differences exist is not sufficient reason for believing that there are underlying disparities in innate capacity for intellectual and emotional development.

Why, then, if 'racial superiority' is only a myth and lacks any real substance, does 'race' play such a large part in the affairs of modern life? In many parts of the world racial differences are the basis for discriminatory legislation and social practices which signify a flat denial of the scientific view. Moreover, many people—for instance both in the southern part of the United States and in the Union of South Africa—continue to argue that the Negro is biologically inferior to the white man. Many white Southerners claim that he is quite a different being, and many South Africans that he is unfit to live as a member of a white civilization. Australia prohibits the immigration of coloured races, and in a number of other countries black and white are separated, either by law or by custom. Can it be simply that the various fallacies of race are not yet known and understood by the governments and peoples concerned?

The plain answer, of course, is that superstitious and ill-informed thinking is not the primary cause of racial prejudice and of the innumerable laws and customs which govern relations between races. Harmony between persons of different racial origin does not depend upon their being properly informed about the latest findings of modern anthropology! If racial amity did so depend, it would be necessary to explain why racial differences are tolerated in one country and not in another; why they are virtually ignored in, say, Brazil or Hawaii, and why so much attention is paid to them in, say, South Africa or the United States. Brazil has far fewer schools per head of the population than white South Africa, and until the present century many Hawaiians were illiterate.

The fact is that race itself, in the biological sense, is irrelevant to racial attitudes and thinking. No doubt, there are many people with a deep and unreasoning repugnance to an individual of different colour who cannot bear the thought of any kind of physical contact with him. But this does not mean that they were born with such feelings or that such feelings are instinctive. The more likely explanation is that inhibitions of this kind

REPRINTED FROM PP. 7–17 OF *Race and Society* (PARIS: UNESCO, 1965) BY PERMISSION OF THE AUTHOR AND UNESCO.

are acquired, for the most part unconsciously, during early childhood. Children tend to take on the attitudes of those in charge of them at home and in school, and they learn to react emotionally in the same way as those about them. If their parents and friends strongly hold certain beliefs that the members of a particular racial group are unclean, unhealthy, etc., it is not surprising that, growing up in that environment, they come to have the same sort of feeling about that racial group as they do about dirt and disease. In any case, what is much more convincing than any psychological explanation is the fact that although such racial aversions are very common in some places, notably the southern United States and South Africa, they are almost unknown in certain other countries. If feelings of repugnance *were* innate, it would obviously be very difficult to explain how millions of men and women manage to work and to mix together without the slightest difficulty on this score. It would be even harder to account for the fact that miscegenation frequently goes on even in the face of severe penalties against it. The truth is that people can get along together without attributing peculiar qualities to each other, despite wide differences in complexion and variability in the shape and size of noses and heads.

The last point should help us to realize that it is not the existence of racial differences *per se* which gives rise to the problem of racial relations, but the fact that such differences are singled out by the members of a given society. What is important, therefore, is not whether groups of individuals *do*, or *do not*, differ in actual biological terms, but the fact that they conceive themselves as racially different. As it happens, there are national and cultural groups in all parts of the world which are not proper races in the anthropological meaning of the term. This does not prevent their members regarding themselves and other similar groups as races. Without this consciousness of group differences, race relations in the strict sense of the word cannot be said to exist, *however* biologically mixed the given society may be. Race relations depend fundamentally upon the recognition and treatment of individuals as the representatives of a given biological, or supposed biological, group; and in the absence of that kind of recognition a relationship between persons of different race is no different from any other kind of relationship occurring in human society.

The problem of race and society is psychologically complicated. Racial attitudes and feelings do not exist *in vacuo*. As they are not biological in origin, they can only be social. This means that they must be the product not only of existing circumstances, but of the kind of contact which the groups concerned have had with each other in the past. This latter point is important because of the varying extent, as between one society and another, to which racial consciousness is fostered. In some countries the fact that people differ from each other in racial appearance passes unnoticed; in others it is a matter of constant attention. In some cases, it gives rise to special laws against intermarriage; in others it has no social consequences. What is the explanation of this paradox—has culture anything to do with the matter? Can it be that conflict in race relations occurs because the groups concerned have different ways of life? There are many people, indeed, who assert that this is the main factor and that there will always be friction so long as racial differences are linked with differences in language and custom among the members of the same society. But the fact is that there are instances of groups with dissimilar cultures getting along amicably with each other, just as there are examples of hostility between races with similar cultures. And there are examples of racial groups with similar cultures living together in amity, just as there are instances of friction between races with dissimilar cultures. A few illustrations will clarify this point.

Jamaica, in the British West Indies, contains a population which is racially mixed in terms of whites, coloured (i.e., people of mixed blood), and blacks, but has a common religion and language, and is governed by a single system of laws. The wealthier and more prominent people are mainly white or near-white; there is a middle class composed mainly of coloured; the labouring and peasant section is mostly black. A great deal of attention is paid to gradations in colour and it is a considerable social and economic asset for an individual to be light in skin. This is because colour differences are largely linked with class differences. But there is no discrimination on grounds of race (as distinct from colour), and race is no bar to any official position on the island. The children attend the same schools, and at any important social gathering there will be persons of black as well as white complexion.

As in Jamaica, whites and Negroes in the southern United States also have the same general habits and customs, speak the same language, and have the same general outlook on life, but there a rigid separation of the races exists in nearly every sphere. Negroes have separate schools, churches, recreational centres, etc., and are not allowed to mix publicly with white people in any form of social activity. Recently, however, the United States Supreme Court has ruled that segregation in public schools is unconstitutional. School segregation is already disappearing in some of the states chiefly affected, and some Southern state universities, too, have admitted Negro students within recent years. Segregation is upheld partly by law and partly by strong social mores on the side of the whites. It is strictly enforced by legal means, by intimidation or even by physical force. Violent action, such as dynamiting a house, may be taken against Negroes who infringe the code of racial etiquette by trying to improve the subordinate status assigned to them.

These are examples of racially dissimilar groups with similar cultures. In South Africa, the groups concerned are culturally as well as racially and ethnically dissimilar. There are the Europeans, who speak English or Afrikaans and are Christians; the Cape Coloured (people of mixed blood), who speak pidgin-English or Afrikaans and are Christians; the Indians, who speak mainly Hindustani and are Hindus or Muslims; and the native Africans, who speak mainly Bantu languages and follow mainly tribal customs and religions. As will be explained below in more detail, these various groups are socially segregated from each other, and the non-European sections of the population are kept completely subordinate. There is considerable friction and hostility between Europeans and non-Europeans in areas where they meet. In contrast, again, is New Zealand, which also has a racially and culturally mixed population. The majority are people of European descent, mostly British. They are known locally as Pakehas. The minority consists of Maoris, a people of Polynesian descent. The larger part of the Maori population still follows tribal customs, but there is no discrimination. Maoris have full equality under the laws of the Dominion and share the benefits of a social security act in common and equally with white New Zealanders. They are also eligible for, and sit as members of, the House of Representatives. A certain amount of racial mixture goes on, mainly with Pakehas belonging to the lower economic class, and a number of Maoris have settled in the towns. White New Zealanders tend to look down on the latter group, but the more general attitude is tolerant of racial differences, and the average Pakeha takes pride in his Maori compatriots.

An alternative to examining racial attitudes in terms of their cultural context is to compare the *antecedents* of each case with those of others. For example, in the Southern states, it was the institution of plantation slavery which firmly ingrained the notion of Negro subordination in the minds of the white population. In South Africa, it was the social and religious exclusiveness of the early Boer farmers which was largely responsible for native Africans and other non-Europeans being regarded and treated as an 'out-group'. But history is not a conclusive factor. Jamaica also had the institution of Negro slavery, and most of the slaves worked on plantations under conditions similar to those in the Old South. Brazil provides another example. Yet both in Jamaica and in Brazil, race relations took a very different, and more liberal, course than in the United States. Again, the complete subordination of the coloured races of South Africa, which followed their wars with the European settlers, lacks its counterpart in New Zealand. Wars were also fought there between settlers and the native population less than a hundred years ago, but they have resulted in racial parity, not subjugation.

Thus, at first sight it appears as if cultural and historical considerations throw very little light upon the problem. However, if we extend our review of culture and history beyond the area of Western civilization in its modern form, we are confronted by a very significant fact. This is the virtual absence of racial relations as we define the term, before the period of European overseas expansion and exploration. In no other civilization, either ancient or modern, do we find the kind of legal and customary recognition of group differences which characterizes the contact of European peoples with other races. In the Muslim world, for example, the important differences today, as in the past, are those of religion. Muslim people are traditionally 'colour-blind', and Islam insists on the equality of believers, whatever their race or colour. According to Koranic law, all members of a conquered population who embrace Islam become the equals of the conquerors in all respects. Racial considerations are also lacking in the Hindu caste system although some writers claim that it originated in racial diversity. They argue that classical Hindu society was divided into four original *varna*, or colours, and explain this as racial differentiation. However, the word *varna* has quite a different meaning from *caste*, and the basis of exclusion in the caste system is not racial. It is religious and ritual, and both excluders and excluded assent to it and play their part in enforcing it. This is unlike any modern form of racial relations regulated by law and by social pressure on the subordinated group.

In other older civilizations, such as those of Egypt and Greece, the relationship between races was that of captor and captive, or master and slave. There is little evidence of aversion or special prescription on the grounds of race or colour. The Egyptians, for example, spoke scornfully of the Negroes to the south of them, and Egyptian artists sometimes caricatured the Negro's thick lips and woolly hair. But the Egyptians looked upon other foreigners, including blue-eyed Libyans, with equal disdain. Like other earlier peoples, the Egyptians mixed freely with their captives, whatever their colour, and some of the Pharaohs showed in their features signs of their partially Negroid ancestry. The Greeks also knew Negroes as slaves, but most of the slave population of Greece were of the same race as their masters, and there was no occasion to associate any physical type with the slave status. In any case, the kind of distinction which the Greeks made between people was cultural, not racial. They looked down on all barbarians but, provided the barbarian took on Hellenistic characteristics, he does not seem to have been subjected to social exclusion on account of his physical appearance.[1] In Rome, too, the situation was similar. The slave population was drawn from North Africa, Asia Minor, and Western Europe, and it included Nubians and Ethiopians as well as Germans and Britons. Roman citizens thought poorly of the peoples they conquered and spoke disparagingly of them, and of non-Romans in general, irrespective of race. It was considered disgraceful for a Roman soldier to take a barbarian wife, but this was not from any objection to racial differences: it was because such a union disregarded the custom of marriage between citizens. Nevertheless, it is said that nine out of every ten free plebeians at the end of the first century A.D. had foreign blood, and citizenship was given to every free-born man in the empire early in the third century. This conception of common humanity was widened further by the teaching of the Stoics and, above all, by the spread of Christianity.

In the period following the downfall of Rome, the Catholic Church emerged as a powerful political as well as religious institution. The Church fostered the spiritual unity of Christendom, teaching that all who were Christians were the same kind of men. As time went on the Church was more and more conceived as an instrument of international order, the glory of God demanding that the whole world be brought under its sway. With this purpose in view wars were fought against Muslims and 'pagans', the basis of antagonism being entirely religious. Jews were persecuted and Muslims enslaved because they were enemies of the faith, not because they were considered racially different from Christians. Nevertheless, Jews, Muslims, and pagans, in their unlikeness from Christian Europe, serve as forerunners of the modern concept of alien races. In other words, this period between the First Crusade and Columbus' discovery of America was characterized by the religious view of world order, and it established a pattern of dealing with non-Christian peoples which was to be continued—lacking only its religious motivation—to the present day. In the meantime, Italian, Spanish and Portuguese merchants were making their voyages of discovery and meeting new peoples and cultures. The Moors and heathens whom the Portuguese encountered down the African coast were inferior to them as fighters, but this led to no conclusions about racial superiority. Nor was there, as yet, any idea of perpetuating the servile status of black people captured in such raids and forays. On the contrary, their conversion to Christianity was sought with enthusiasm, and this transformation was supposed to make the Africans the human equals of all other Christians. In this way, many of the Africans taken by the Portuguese were assimilated in the general population and a number of them rose to important positions in the Portuguese State.

What changed this easy-going attitude to men of different race was the development of capitalism and the profit-motive as a characteristic feature of Western civilization. The new lands discovered in America provided ideal opportunities for economic exploitation and their native inhabitants were too weak to withstand the well-armed European settler-business man. Tobacco, indigo, rice, cotton, and sugar cane, which could be produced on a large scale and at a considerable profit, were grown for sale in Europe. The difficulty was to recruit the workers required. There was a lack of free labour, and so it became necessary to use slaves. Slavery in the Spanish colonies was at first limited to the aboriginal Indians, but long before the end of the colonial era a large part of the native population was wiped out by harsh treatment or by European diseases. Also, Indian slavery was severely criticized on religious grounds by the Jesuit and other missionaries, including the celebrated priest, Las Casas; and so it was decided to introduce Negroes from Africa. They made better workers and were less restive in captivity.

The first African Negroes were landed in the New World about 1510. As already mentioned, trade in African slaves, including Negroes, was not new in commerce; but before the middle of the fifteenth century it was limited to the Mediterranean. In West Africa, there was not the same excuse for war, but if Christian men had any misgivings, they were allayed by a bull of Pope Nicholas V which authorized the Portuguese 'to attack, subject and reduce to perpetual slavery the Saracens, Pagans, and other enemies of Christ southward from Capes Bajador and Non, including all the coast of Guinea'. The usual condition was attached: all captives must be converted to Christianity.

These elementary methods of securing slaves sufficed while the trade was local, but the rapid exploitation of fresh settlements in the West Indies and on the American mainland greatly stimulated the demands and brought a more elaborate system into being. All along the West African coast trading-stations sprang up, which were stocked by African purveyors, and at which slaves could be procured by barter. The Africans offered for sale were, or were supposed to be, war-captives, condemned criminals, or persons who had sold themselves into slavery. By this convenient rationalization, the Europeans were relieved of moral responsibility, and the supporters of the slave trade even took credit for saving their victims from death. However, the scale of the commerce was too large to escape public attention, and as time went on there was increasing knowledge of the harsh and inhuman conditions on the plantations as well as of the horrors of the Middle Passage. The slave owner and trader had to find some way of justifying themselves or run the risk of losing both property and business. At first, they argued on the grounds of the economic necessity of slavery to national prosperity, and then, as the humanitarian attack was pressed, they offered the ingenuous theory that Negroes were sub-human and incapable of moral feelings; hence there was no obligation to treat them like ordinary human beings.

Mr. Long, in his *History of Jamaica,* published in three volumes in 1774, wrote:

'We cannot pronounce them *unsusceptible of civilization since even apes* have been taught to eat, drink, repose and dress *like men.* But of all the human species hitherto discovered, their *natural baseness of mind* seems to afford the least hope of their being (except by miraculous interposition of Divine Providence) so refined as to think as well as act like *men.* I do not think that an Orang Outang husband would be any dishonour to an Hottentot female.'

What this amounted to was a deliberate attempt to depersonalize a whole group of human beings—to reduce them to mere articles of commerce or economic 'utilities'. The extent to which it was successful may be illustrated by the case of the slave ship *Zong,* when one hundred and thirty slaves were thrown overboard on the plea of lack of water. The law took its course, but the trial was not for murder. It was to decide whether the throwing overboard of the slaves was a genuine act of jettison, for which the insurance company would have to pay, or a fraud on the policy.

However, what is significant about this earlier development of racial prejudice is the fact that efforts to impersonalize human relations in order to exploit men more effectively for economic purposes were not confined to the African slave. The capitalist-entrepreneur of the day was just as ready to use people of his own race in the same way. Indeed, part of the early demand for labour in the West Indies and on the mainland was filled

by white servants, who were sometimes defined in exactly the same terms
as those stereotyping the Negro. Plantation owners bid eagerly for supplies
of convicts from the London prisons, and hundreds of children were kid-
napped and shipped from Scotland. But the white servants were allowed
to work off their bond, while the Negro was gradually pushed into chattel
slavery. His servile status was established by substituting a racial reason
for the previous religious one—by characterizing a whole race as degenerate, degraded, immoral, lacking in intelligence, etc. The religious argument proved insufficient when it came to be a question of continuing
slavery for the convert.

This, then, as Dr. Oliver Cromwell Cox has pointed out, marks the
beginning of modern race relations.

'It was not an abstract, natural, immemorial feeling of mutual antip-
athy between groups, but rather a practical exploitative relationship with
its socio-attitudinal facilitation—at that time only nascent racial prejudice.
Although this peculiar kind of exploitation was then in its incipiency, it
had already achieved its significant characteristics. As it developed and
took definite capitalistic form, we could follow the white man around the
world and see him repeat the process among practically every people of
colour.'[2]

Dr. Cox goes on to quote Earl Grey's description in 1880 of the
motives and purposes of the British in South Africa.

'Throughout this part of the British Dominions the coloured people
are generally looked upon by the whites as an inferior race, whose interest
ought to be systematically disregarded when they come into competition
with our own, and who ought to be governed mainly with a view to the
advantage of the superior race. And for this advantage two things are
considered to be especially necessary: firstly, that facilities should be
afforded to the white colonists for obtaining possession of land heretofore
occupied by the native tribes; and secondly, that the Kaffir population
should be made to furnish as large and as cheap a supply of labour as
possible.'

Dr. Cox's thesis is that racial exploitation is merely one aspect of
the problem of the proletarianization of labour, regardless of the colour
of the labourer. Hence, racial antagonism is essentially political class
conflict. The capitalist exploiter, being opportunistic and practical, will
utilize any convenience to keep his labour and other resources freely
exploitable. He will devise and employ race prejudice when that becomes
convenient. The reason why race relations are 'easier' in most countries
colonized by the Latin nations, viz. Portugal and Spain, is partly because
neither Spain nor Portugal ever attained the industrial development of
Northern Europe. They remained longer under the political and economic
authority of the Church. Also, the capitalist spirit, the profit-making
motive among the sixteenth-century Spaniards and Portuguese, was constantly inhibited by the universal aims and purpose of the Church. This
tradition in favour of the old religious criterion of equality is in contrast

to the objective, capitalistic attitude of Anglo-Saxon and Germanic countries, such as Britain, the Netherlands, and the United States.[3] It might be compared in some respects, however, with the assimilative aims of French colonial policy—to absorb colonial and coloured subjects as part of a 'greater France' on a common basis of culture and citizenship.

What this implies is a direct relationship between racial attitudes and society—*that race relations are, in effect, a function of a certain type of social and economic system.*

Notes

1. cf. Ina C. Brown. *Race Relations in a Democracy,* Harper, 1949.
2. Oliver C. Cox. *Caste, Class and Race,* Doubleday, 1948.
3. *Ibid.,* p. 174.

Charles Wagley
RACE AND SOCIAL CLASS IN BRAZIL

• • •

The social and economic classes of Brazil have been described as if they were racially homogeneous, as if Brazil were not a multiracial society. Actually, one cannot understand social and economic stratification in Brazil without referring to race relations, for in Brazil race and class relations are historically and functionally interrelated. The traditional Brazilian two-class system was closely associated with the twofold racial division of the Brazilian people. The landed gentry, the traditional upper class, was predominantly of Caucasoid ancestry, as its descendants still are. The slaves, the peasants, manual workers, and dependents of all kinds were historically of Negroid, American Indian, or mixed ancestry. In modern Brazil, the newly formed classes and social segments continue to have racial overtones. In general, as one moves down the social hierarchy, the number of racially mixed or otherwise nonwhite individuals gradually increases.

At no point in the social and economic hierarchy does one encounter a homogeneous group. Individuals of mixed ancestry occur even among the upper classes, and many whites are found in the lower social strata. In fact it is one of the most cherished national themes that Brazil is a racial democracy. Since the abolition of slavery in 1888, there has been no legal form of racial discrimination or segregation in Brazil. Innumerable individuals of Negroid or mixed physical appearance have filled important roles in Brazil's national life since the time of the empire. All books on Brazil cite names of Negroes and mulattoes of importance, such as the baroque sculptor Aleijadinho, the great nineteenth-century novelist Machado de Assis, the abolitionist journalist and statesman José do Patrocínio, the politician Nilo Peçanha (who was president of the republic in 1909–10), the twentieth-century poet Mário de Andrade, and the psychiatrist Juliano Moreira, to cite but a few. The world championship soccer team of 1962 covered the whole spectrum of skin color: Pelé, the "King of Soccer," who is a Negro, was injured but was competently replaced by Amarildo, a mulatto. Several players were clearly white. This tradition of racial democracy is a source of great pride to Brazilians. More than any country in the Western world, Brazil is recognized, cited, and applauded as proof that racial democracy can work. But the facts of Brazilian race and class relations are not as simple as that. They require some explanation, sometimes even to Brazilians themselves.

FROM CHARLES WAGLEY, *An Introduction to Brazil*, NEW YORK: COLUMBIA UNIVERSITY PRESS, 1963, PP. 132–147.

Basic to the understanding of race and social class relations is the Brazilian concept of "race." The official statistics use only four categories, namely, *branco* (white), *pardo* (brown), *prêto* (black), and *amarelo* (yellow). However, the people in the street have other racial categories which vary from one region to another. In one small town in the Eastern Highlands described by Marvin Harris, they recognized in addition to "whites" and "Negroes" five other types: *moreno, chulo, mulato, creolo,* and *cabo verde.* Harris describes these types:

> The *moreno* has wavy hair with the skin coloring of a heavily sunburnt white. The *mulato* has crisp, curly hair and is darker than the *moreno.* The *chulo* has crisp, rolled hair and his skin is the "color of burnt sugar or tobacco." The *creolo* has fine wavy hair, is almost as dark as the *chulo,* but has smoother skin. The *cabo verde* has very straight hair and is the color of the Negro.[1]

In some localities the system of popular classification is much more complex[2] while in others it is somewhat simpler, but everywhere in Brazil intermediate types between white and Negro are recognized, these types are ranked in terms of attractiveness and acceptability from the most Caucasoid to the most Negroid, and criteria other than skin color, such as nose shape, hair type, and lip thickness are also used to classify an individual.[3]

The existence of recognized intermediate types is important to the understanding of the Brazilian race-class system and to its functioning. To put it simply, a twofold Jim Crow system could never work in Brazil. A mulatto is not a Negro, and a *moreno* (dark white) is not a mulatto. If Brazilians wanted to install a Jim Crow system, they would have to provide at least four or more sets of schools, hospitals, sections on public transportation, and restaurants. Our North American South can hardly afford a two-race system of segregation, and certainly Brazil could not afford a fourfold or sixfold system.[4]

To be accurate, however, the picture of Brazilian racial democracy must be drawn in relation to the racial composition of the population as a whole and to that of the various social and economic classes. The 1950 census classified 61.6 percent of all Brazilians as white, 11 percent as black, 26.6 percent as brown, and the small remainder as yellow. It should be remembered that the census data reflect racial identity as reckoned by the respondents and sometimes by the census taker; a survey by objective anthropological standards would certainly show a larger percentage of mixed types. A study of color and occupation making use of 1940 census data underlines the correlation between class and color throughout the country.[5] The white 64 percent of the male population over ten years of age accounts for 90 percent of those engaged in the professions, private teaching, and cultural and private administrative activities, for 76 percent of those in public administration, and for 79 percent of those in commercial and financial positions. The Negro 14.7 percent accounts for only 2.5 percent, 8 percent, and 5 percent of these prestige categories, respectively.[6] Another set of data shows equal disproportion. The 342,000 males classified as employers include 3.48 percent of the whites but only 0.74 percent of the browns and 0.55 percent of the blacks. To look at it in a slightly different way, whites account for 81 percent of these employers, browns for 11.8 percent, and blacks for 5.7 percent.[7] There is no reason to believe that these ratios have changed strikingly in the last twenty years or so, although the social mobility of people of color is a noted fact in some parts of the country.

These figures do not tell the entire story, for the population of the various regions of Brazil is dissimilar in racial composition. In the Northeast coastal region and in such areas as the coast of Maranhão, Piauí state, and the São Francisco Valley, the percentage of people of color is unusually high and whites predominate only in the middle and upper classes. On the other hand, in states such as São Paulo, Paraná, Santa Catarina, and Rio Grande do Sul, over four-fifths of the population are white in all social and economic classes. And in the Amazon Valley, where there were few Negro slaves, where Negroes often came as free men and artisans, and where the Indian was the exploited laborer, the majority of people in the lower classes are of the American Indian physical type. But for Brazil as a whole, and speaking generally, the old Brazilian rule of thumb still stands: "The darker the skin the lower the class and the lighter the skin the higher the class."

The claims for a Brazilian racial democracy must be judged also against widely documented color prejudice in almost every part of the nation. This color prejudice is expressed in many ways, some subtle and some overt. Almost all studies of race relations in Brazil have cited the traditional derogatory sayings about Negroes. This example was recorded by Harry W. Hutchinson in a small community of the Recôncavo region of Bahia:

> Negro doesn't marry, he gets together.
> Negro doesn't accompany a procession, he runs after it.
> Negro doesn't sit down, he squats.
> Negro in white clothes is a sign of rain.
> Negro doesn't hear Mass, he spies on it.
> Negro at a white man's party is the first to grab and the last to eat.
> Negro's intelligence is the same size as his hair [i.e., short].[8]

Similar sayings involving derogatory stereotypes have been recorded in widely separate Brazilian communities and are part of the Brazilian cultural heritage. They portray the Negro as inferior in intelligence, dependability, morality, honesty, and physical appearance. Attitude questionnaires and social-distance tests reveal similar prejudice against the Negro, and in a milder and sometimes somewhat different form, against the mulatto as well. White Brazilians indicate in verbal responses some resistance to working with Negroes, living with them, dancing with them, accepting them into the family, and marrying them—generally in about that order of intensity. Many of the overt derogatory statements about Negroes heard in Brazil are as shocking as those heard in the Deep South of the United States, although the social-distance tests show less reluctance to associate with Negroes at all levels.

Furthermore, there have been and still are overt forms of discrimination in terms of skin color, although this is strictly illegal. North American Negroes have been surprised to find that there were no rooms available in Brazilian upper-class hotels, although reservations had been made. Until recently it was well known in Brazil that the Foreign Service excluded people of darker skins (some have now been admitted) and that the traditionally upper-class Naval Academy accepted only white candidates. Certain private schools, both primary and secondary, were until recently homogeneously white or accepted a brilliant mulatto or two on scholarships as a matter of principle. Then, too, there was (now discontinued) a way of warning dark mulattoes and Negroes that they need not apply for openings as clerks or office workers—an advertisement reading "Needed: young lady of good appearance for office position" could be inserted in the newspaper, and it was clearly understood what "good appearance" meant.

The existence of color prejudice and even of discrimination does not mean, for several reasons, that the Brazilian racial democracy is a myth. First, there is obviously a wide gulf in Brazil between what people say and what they do, between verbal and social behavior. The emotional tone surrounding color prejudice is generally lighthearted and amused, and mixed with a liberal sprinkling of earthy appreciation. Oracy Nogueira records the heckling of a football team by fans in racial terms so strong that they would have caused a race riot in the United States.[9] Marvin Harris tells of a white man in the community of Minas Velhas who stoutly maintained that a Negro, even if he was a *doutor* (a professional) should not be associated with, but who bowed and scraped when he actually met a Negro engineer.[10] Also, set against the derogatory attitude, there is a certain pride in the "Brazilian race" and even in the *prêto* (Negro): everyone who visited Brazil in recent years has seen the huge billboard featuring Pelé, the black soccer player, with his arms about a little white boy, obviously his ardent fan. Derogatory attitudes and stereotypes remain in the Brazilian tradition and can be called on in any competitive situation (if there is no other way to get at your competitor you can always call him a *prêto*), but they generally lack conviction as determinants of behavior.

Secondly, many of the stereotypes and attitudes are survivals from slavery times and are shared by the southern United States and the West Indies. There is a vast difference, however, between the social effect of these attitudes and stereotypes in the United States and in Brazil. In the United States, they are aimed against all people of known Negro ancestry, regardless of physical appearance. Thus, such attitudes, derogatory stereotypes, and forms of prejudice and discrimination are aimed against a large group that varies from Caucasoid to Negroid in physical appearance. It is a group determined by ancestry and descent, not by any objective physical anthropological standards of measurement. In Brazil, on the other hand, the criterion is physical appearance. As the Brazilian sociologist Oracy Nogueira puts it, in Brazil there is "race prejudice of mark" (i.e., prejudice of appearance) rather than "race prejudice of origin." Color and other physical characteristics such as hair, lip, and nose type are visible marks and symbols of one's social class, and probably of one's slave ancestry. But through miscegenation succeeding generations can and do become lighter. Color prejudice or "prejudice of mark" decreases as the skin lightens.[11]

In fact demographic figures indicate that the numbers of whites and browns are increasing at the expense of the blacks. From 1940 to 1950, for example, the percentage of those classified as *prêto* was reduced from 14.6 percent to 10.9 percent. This has been called the bleaching process in the Brazilian population. Much of it can be ascribed to the tendency of census takers to "classify lighter," but some of it is biological. The chance has always been very good at all levels of the social and economic hierarchy for frequent licit and illicit sexual unions between people of different colors. This does not mean that unions between very dark-skinned and very light-skinned individuals are common. Such unions, whether in marriage or concubinage, are considered socially undesirable and cause embarrassment to the individuals concerned. Rather, it is common for an upward-moving individual, generally a male, to take a spouse several shades lighter. Color differences between spouses are most acceptable in the lower classes, but tolerance for marriages between white and not-quite-white partners is a traditional and enduring part of Brazilian national culture.

Thirdly, perhaps the most important difference between race relations in Brazil and in the United States is that color is but one of the criteria by which people are placed in the total social hierarchy. Before two Brazilians decide how they ought to behave toward each other, they must know more than the fact that one is dark-skinned and the other light-skinned. A Brazilian is never merely a white man or a man of color; he is a rich, well-educated white man of a good family or a poor, uneducated white man from the *povo*; he is a well-educated mulatto with a good job, or a poor, uneducated Negro. Other criteria, such as income, education, family connections, and even personal charm and special abilities or aptitudes come into play when placing a person in terms of the prestige hierarchy or even of social class. Above all, these multiple criteria determine who will be admitted to hotels, restaurants, and most social clubs; who will get preferential treatment in stores, churches, nightclubs, and travel conveyances; and who will have the best chance among a number of marriage suitors.

As a matter of fact, a Brazilian's perception of an individual's racial classification is influenced by all these social criteria. I have told elsewhere

how people in a small Amazon community refused to classify the most
important lady in town as the dark mulatto she was, but made her white,
and how the same townspeople refused to see the town drunk as "white"
—"How could he be a white?" they said.[12] Brazilians cannot ignore the
obvious, and no one would have the courage to call a wealthy, highly
educated Negro a white, but they might politely call him a *moreno*
(brunet). Yet the amusing Brazilian statement, "Money whitens the skin,"
is not unmeaningful. It is easy to lower or to raise the color status of
people from one grade to another according to criteria other than color.
Thus, a *pardo* who is a professional, has a good income, good manners,
and thus good social connections, will be raised to *branco*. In Bahia, there
are two amusing terms for such people, namely, *branco da Bahia* (white
from Bahia) and *branco da terra* (white from the country). Likewise, a
pardo who is poor, illiterate, and marginal is apt to be classed as a Negro.
It is this interplay between skin color and social criteria that makes
Brazilian census data on race so dubious.

This means, in effect, that there are no Brazilian social groups based
on skin color alone, although, to the casual visitor, this would not seem to
be true. Are not the "Samba Schools," the beautifully costumed groups
who come down from the *favelas* and the suburbs of Rio de Janeiro to
dance during Carnival, homogeneously Negro? It seems that all the participants in a *candomblé* ceremony in Bahia are Negroes. One can visit
social clubs throughout the country in which all of the members are
exceedingly dark in skin color. There is in Brazil an Association of Men
of Color, and St. Benedict is the patron saint of many religious brotherhoods whose members are black or nearly so. However, if one looks
closely at the members of these associations, it becomes apparent that there
are different shades of darkness, and even a few very light-skinned people.
But that is not the point. The essential point is that these are people of the
same social class and incidentally of similar skin color.

Generally, when an individual improves his social and economic
situation, he soon moves upward to another club or association more in
keeping with his new status. The Brazilian sociologist Fernando Henrique
Cardoso makes this point in an article describing the results of his studies
of race relations in southern Brazil. He describes the pride shown when
one of the members of a club made up of Negroes graduates from normal
school or another school of higher learning or is appointed to an important
position. The members of the club hold a dance or a luncheon in his
honor. "The orator," he writes, "recalls that the success of the young
doutor is also a success for the Negro race. The young *doutor*, who is now
called by this title, will in all probability soon stop coming to the club
which is thus honoring him, since henceforth he will formally act as if he
belonged to another social level."[13]

Thus, in Brazil, race relations and social class are intertwined in an
intricate manner. They are not separate phenomena as they are apt to be
elsewhere. There is no middle-class Negro society separate from white

middle-class society. But this does not mean that color prejudice and dis-crimination can be entirely reduced to class prejudice; it is not simply that the colored populations have not improved their status because the socioeconomic system of Brazil has afforded them few opportunities for upward mobility. It would seem that their physical appearance is an added disability, although negligible as compared to other countries. For nowhere in Brazil does one's physical appearance, one's race, constitute an impos-sible barrier to upward mobility.

Race discrimination is thus relatively mild and equivocal in Brazil, but class discrimination produces disabilities and inequalities of a sharp, incisive nature that can be shocking to North Americans. Some of the more subtle aspects of the relations between the upper and lower classes have been described by the Brazilian anthropologist Thales de Azevedo for the traditional city of Salvador in Bahia. He writes:

> The people of the lower class are obliged to address the superior group with the title *Dona* for women and *O senhor* for men, terms which indicate subordination in this context, no matter what the physical type or age of the speaker might be. In the inverse situation [i.e., upper class addressing lower class] the title *Dona* is much less used because it ex-presses subordination of the speaker, but *O senhor* remains obligatory because it keeps anyone at a distance. An "inferior" person cannot, except with offensive intent, use *você* [second person for "you" and less intimate than *tu*] to address the members of the superior group—a mode of address common in horizontal and intra-class relations. . . . The greetings with kisses among women, the little goodbye signal made with the fingers, the handshake and embrace between men are rarely employed in asymetrical relations [between classes]. They always require the initiative of the superior and in these cases the inferior always limits himself to letting the superior take his hand without responding with a clasp of his own. Other mechanisms . . . regulate the spatial relations of people and limit the expressions of intimacy. A member of the lower class may be received into the house of the upper- or middle-class person, but rarely will he sit in the living room or at the dinner table; if food is offered him, he eats in the kitchen, in the pantry, or even at the dining table—but separately, after or before the others.[14]

Azevedo stresses the fact that marriages seldom cross class lines, that clothing is different, that speech is different, and that treatment before public authorities differs for the two groups:

> A *popular* [i.e., member of the lower class] caught in a crime by a policeman is taken to a filthy prison without facilities where he may be treated with brutality and where his companions are criminals, bums, alcoholics, and beggars. The individual of the upper class . . . in the same circumstances almost always finds a way of avoiding immediate arrest; if arrested, however, he is taken to the police station discreetly in an auto-mobile . . . he may then be taken to the hospital rather than the prison on the pretext that he is ill . . . while persons with higher educational degrees have the legal right to be held in a special prison.[15]

These are but a few details of class discrimination, and they could be extended at length. Such details, however, are reflections of a profound gulf between the Brazilian middle and upper classes and the masses of the people. More important are the differences in living standards and in access to education and other services. While the middle class suffers from its inability to acquire the accessories of modern living, and the upper class spends less than it used to in Paris and New York, the masses of the Brazilian people cannot afford the basic essentials of life. They cannot buy bread, meat, clothes, shoes, education, shelter, and medicines for themselves and their children. Under such conditions the issue of racial discrimination is scarcely a vital one. Lower-class whites and lower-class colored people are both segregated and discriminated against. Brazil is accurately described as a racial and political democracy, but by no stretch of the imagination is it as yet a social democracy.

Thus, the cleavage between social and economic classes works strongly for diversity in Brazilian national culture. One would think that Brazil would be ripe for a violent class revolution and that interclass tension and conflict would be widespread and intense. Although there are signs of peasant uprisings in the Northeast and some lower-class discontent throughout the country, the lower classes of Brazil are surprisingly passive, resigned, and tolerant. They are hungry, but they participate in religious processions and in Carnival, and they share the enthusiasm of the rest of the country for soccer. They accept the traditions and the ideal behavior patterns formed by the middle and upper classes. They would like to (but cannot for pecuniary reasons) live like their more fortunate compatriots, marry like them, dress like them, and eat like them. They do not have a culture apart from the upper class—they share in Brazilian culture, although largely in a vicarious way.

Notes

1. Harris, *Town and Country in Brazil,* p. 119n.
2. See H. W. Hutchinson, *Village and Plantation Life in Northeastern Brazil,* pp. 118–20.
3. See Wagley, ed., *Race and Class in Rural Brazil.*
4. The hierarchy of types in Brazil is very much like that prevailing among North American Negroes, who accord each other beauty and prestige to the extent that their skin color and type of hair, lips, and nose, approximate that of the whites.
5. *Estudos sôbre a composição da população do Brasil segundo a côr,* IBGE.
6. *Ibid.*
7. *Ibid.*
8. H. W. Hutchinson, *Village and Plantation Life in Northeastern Brazil,* p. 122. A slightly modified version of the same was recorded by Marvin Harris for the Eastern Highlands (*Town and Country in Brazil,* p. 118).
9. Oracy Nogueira, "Relações raciais no município de Itapininga," in Bastide and Fernandes, eds., *Relações raciais entre negros e brancos em São Paulo,* p. 507.
10. Harris, *Town and Country in Brazil,* p. 125.

11. Nogueira, "Skin Color and Social Class," in *Plantation Systems of the New World,* pp. 164–79.

12. Wagley, *Amazon Town,* p. 134.

13. Cardoso, "Os brancos e a ascenção social dos negros em Pôrto Alegre," *Anhembi,* XXXIX (August, 1960), 585.

14. Azevedo, "Classes sociais e grupos de prestígio na Bahia," *Arquivos da Universidade da Bahia,* V (1956), 86.

15. *Ibid.,* p. 89.

Gordon K. Lewis
COLOR AND SOCIETY
IN PUERTO RICO

The characteristic trilogy of the Caribbean social drama has been family, religion and color. The frontier conditions of Caribbean life made the family a fragile institution at best. The sugar and slave economy, uprooting whole generations from their African background, gave rise to the esoteric cult religions—voodoo, obeah, the saint cults—of the Afro-Caribbean variety. Racial intermixture, finally (the inevitable consequence wherever the sex drive finds itself in a slavery environment), produced the massive complexes of color psychology in the regional life, with serious results both for the quality of personal self-esteem and of social life.

There is a widespread belief in Puerto Rico that whatever the family and religious situations may be there is no local problem of race prejudice. The belief usually adopts one of two methods of evidence. The first is to argue (as José Celso Barbosa and Tomás Blanco have done) that if there is discrimination it exists only in "social" or "class" areas, a phenomenon plausible enough, perhaps, in the light of the cultural heritage of Spanish pride of class. The second is, overtly or by implication, to accept the North American criteria of discrimination, based as they are upon an open black-white dichotomy, and then apply them to Puerto Rican conditions: the method is implicit, for example, in the 1959 Civil Liberties Committee report on racial discrimination. The general consequence of both modes of argument is to facilitate an optimistic tone whenever the problem is discussed. The optimism is frequently accepted uncritically by outside observers or even resident Americans as proof that all is well; thus, Professor Henry Wells can sweepingly assert that there is "an almost total absence of deep-rooted value conflicts: the island has always been notably free of racial tension, religious controversy, and class antagonism."[1] The reluctance of the individual Puerto Rican to discuss racialism, in particular with Americans, is in part justified, perhaps, by his suspicion that most Americans are prejudiced in one degree or another. It does not fully explain, however, the quite powerful taboo on such discussion within the local community itself. Nor does it in any way justify the conclusion that, if prejudice exists, it must be due to the growing influence of American attitudes.

What, in truth, is the position? To begin with, insular history has been such as to ameliorate the harsher features of race relations. The rapid

REPRINTED FROM *Puerto Rico: Freedom and Power in the Caribbean* (NEW YORK: MONTHLY REVIEW PRESS, 1963) BY PERMISSION OF THE PUBLISHER AND THE AUTHOR. COPYRIGHT © 1963 BY GORDON K. LEWIS.

growth of the free mulatto class and the degree of racial intermarriage have already been noted, facilitating, in part, the emergence of the new social order of post-slavery Caribbean life, the Creole society of the classic form, even before the advent of legal emancipation. It is true that slave rebellions were not unknown and that Spanish liberalism, as compared with British or Dutch policies, must not be exaggerated. It is true nonetheless that none of those rebellions reached the grim magnitude of the St. Johns revolt of 1833 or that of St. Croix in 1848. And it is an astonishing fact, as the Spanish Cortes was told in the 1873 debates on emancipation, that Puerto Rican slaveowners themselves petitioned for emancipation, against the inclination of the mother country.[2] All of these factors contributed to a marked improvement in the social role of the freed Negro in the second half of the nineteenth century, as compared with worsening conditions throughout the first half. The names of Barbosa, Morell Campos, Carrión Maduro and Pedro Timothee testify to his social mobility. He was still debarred from the police, the magistracy, and business. But the independent professions welcomed him, and at the proletarian level there were real opportunities. Henry Carroll reported in 1900 that of the eleven working class representatives who testified before him at that time nine were Negroes, all of whom, with one exception, could read and write and were decently clothed.[3] The observation takes on some further significance in the light of the fact that white labor tended to survive in the Puerto Rican coffee and tobacco economies and worked side by side without friction with Negro labor, encouraging thereby a widespread habit of intermarriage, especially after 1900, between the white highland laborers and the colored coastal people. The *hidalgo*-like contempt for manual labor was there, of course; but at least colored and white workers shared the opprobrium together. Equally, the fact helped to shatter the myth—an article of faith in all of the apologetic literature on slavery—of the innate inability of the white person to undertake physical labor in the tropics.

These factors help to explain the contemporary situation. They accelerated an amalgamative process between the races, so that there has grown up an entire vocabulary (as throughout Latin America) of terms indicating with nice exactitude the degree of color discoverable in any given person. There is very little, in the Puerto Rican Negro, of the belligerent militancy of his counterpart in the United States. The term "Negro" itself is more one of endearment in personal relations, even between whites, than it is one of derogation; significantly, too, there are no equivalents in Spanish of the opprobrious epithets "nigger" and "coolie" that are in such common use throughout the former British West Indies. There is full political equality for Negroes, to the extent that where there are colored Puerto Ricans in the Legislature, like Leopoldo Figueroa or the late Ernesto Ramos Antonini, they are there not as trustees of a supposed "Negro" vote but as high-ranking members of the leading political parties. Creole society in the island has many features in common with the social structure of a southern American state like Louisiana, but it is markedly different in that there is no elaborate complex of political oppression against the Negro citizen to make possible the emergence of a white paternalistic "nigger lover" like the late Governor Earl Long. Both the local Socialist Party and, after it, the *Popular* Party have been instrumental in widening employment opportunities for dark-skinned Puerto Ricans in, for example, the teaching profession and the police force, including the higher echelons of the latter group. In the field of religion, again, there admittedly is a temptation on the part of light-colored groups to equate witchcraft and magic with Negro groups; but at the same time the Negro middle class is an accepted part of congregations, both Catholic and Protestant. African elements, if any, have been assimilated, not isolated. At least one of the most revered patron saints of the island, the Virgin of Monserrate, is unmistakably dark-colored and the fact has entered some of the popular devotional verse:

> Virgen de Monserrate,
> Virgen de Hormigueros,
> dime quien te ha dado
> tu color moreno.

And all this, finally, is reinforced by the fact that there is an increasing degree of racial anonymity going on as anatomic characteristics popularly designated as Negroid become less and less conspicuous in the individual heavily colored person, with the exceptions of certain population pockets in the island.

But how far does all this amount to a genuine racial democracy? Very little, perhaps, in any complete way. For racial tensions do not have to assume the forms of physical violence or of overt segregationism or even of open political expression before they can be said to exist. In Puerto Rico, as elsewhere in the Caribbean, they express themselves more subtly through the vehicle of racial intermediacy, the discreet yet very real sense of color snobbishness based upon the awareness of "shades." So, whereas in the United States one drop of "colored" blood designates one as a Negro, in Latin America and the Caribbean one drop of "white" blood can launch an individual on the road to social acceptance as white. The consequence of this difference is of course to protect the Caribbean colored person from the evils of "white supremacy." At the same time, it also serves to impose upon him a heavy burden of emotional insecurity. For the American Negro, save for the tiny minority who "pass," remains a defined Negro; he is what he is; he knows where he stands; his Puerto Rican brother is daily confronted with the torture of an ambivalent racial identity. "If the mulatto looks more like a white person than a Negro," Dr. Rogler has noted, "he is socially defined as a white person, providing his accomplishments so rate him." His self-appraisal therefore revolves around his success in obtaining that badge of social recognition. In a more mysterious procedure, perhaps, he shares with the American Negro the half-conscious envy of "whiteness," the conviction of its utter desirability. If he is curiously silent about it all, it is because he fears the problem and therefore attempts to hide it within himself. But that he is quite right to be aware of race mixture, and of its social penalties, is evident enough in the number of popular sayings that are illustrative of an attitude of, at best, genial contempt towards the colored person: Professor Rosario has collated them and put them together in his study of 1940.[4] The ramifications of the attitude run deep and wide throughout the society. As early as 1901 an American social service worker could report that in the charity schools of the island it was looked upon as a degradation for any but Negroes to do housework.[5] An American visitor could write in a home journal in 1922 that it was curious that Puerto Rican Negroes seemed to be Republican in their political sympathies; and the local rival party press was quite willing to reprint the observation as a means of taunting its opponents.[6] During the 1930's and 1940's, again, an important psychological reason for the widespread recruitment into the extremist Nationalist Party was the insecurity feeling of the mulatto who could never determine whether he hated the white American or the obvious Puerto Rican Negro more. The type furnished material for many of the party's leaders. Styling themselves white and vehemently denying Negro ancestry, they were clearly enough victims of a virulent sense of racial shame, disguising itself under a spurious and comic invocation of things Spanish. They perhaps saw themselves as the custodians of the old Spanish colonial tradition, without appreciating that a Spanish grandee, had he ever witnessed their aping of his manner, would have dismissed them as arrogantly as the Napoleonic nobility of the First Empire discounted the abilities of the Haitian black leadership after 1800. The sentiment led them into a grotesque perversity of values, as when, for example, they could attack Senator Chavez of New Mexico as a "cultural hybrid" who had betrayed his own Mexican "race" in order to seek success in North American politics.[7] More recently, the trilogy of plays produced by the playwright Francisco Arriví has dramatically portrayed the trauma of race shame that afflicts the mulatto group; in *Sirena* the figure of the mulatto girl who undergoes facial plastic surgery in order to win the love of the white man she adores speaks eloquently for the emotional price the group has to pay for living in a multi-racial society not yet come to satisfactory terms with its color question.

The characteristic form of racial discrimination thus is "shade" discrimination. It is not less real because it is more difficult to decipher than the American forms of discrimination. Nor does it make it any less illiberal to call it, as does Tomás Blanco in his essay of 1942, "social" and not "racial." Nor indeed does the use, however charming, of characteristic euphemisms to refer to racial admixture—*pardo, moreno, trigueño*—disguise the fact that social acceptance goes hand in hand with the degree of whiteness in skin texture. "A person who has marked Negro physical characteristics," Dr. Raymond Scheele writes of the upper class, "and is therefore described as a Negro, may have high income, great political power, and advanced education, yet on racial grounds may be excluded from the inner circles of intimate family life, Greek letter sorority or fraternity membership, and the more select social clubs. He may attend political affairs, be a guest at the governor's palace, and be invited to political cocktail parties, because people wish to cultivate his friendship, but he would probably not be asked to a girl's engagement party or other more private functions."[8] Wealthy white men may marry light-skinned mulatto women without loss of status, but their wives will rarely achieve equal social recognition. The wives in other unions may bring wealth to the husband, if he is comparatively poor, in exchange for which they will receive the socially desirable attribute of whiteness. Correspondingly, marriages of white men to dark mulatto or Negro women can carry with them a strong moral stigma not so easily overcome; and, significantly enough, a great many of such unions tend to be undertaken by resident Americans of liberal leanings. There is, then, no absolute bar on marital admixture, so that the society has not given birth to the class of "poor whites" so prevalent in the Leeward and Windward Islands groups, where the ravages of consanguine degeneracy can be seen today in the modern descendants of the seventeenth-century French and English emigrants. The real bar in Puerto Rico comes from the existence of an elaborate and subtle system of informal social pressures and prohibitions based upon an ambivalent attitude to color. There are alumni groups of professional men of dark color who "feel more at home" with each other than they would with their white associates. There is, of course, no open denigration of color. On the contrary, there is almost an official code of feminine beauty that applauds the favorite style of the woman who is neither too dark nor too white; as the song goes:

> Lo mas que me gusta el café
> Que de la trigueña me cuela.

But neither, on the other hand, is there a complete and harmonious acceptance of color. That is perhaps why the colored Puerto Rican will sometimes seek refuge in the claim that he is "Indian" or "Spanish" or "Latin." That is perhaps why too a poet like the late Luis Palés Matos, who identified himself in his work with the Afro-Antillean Negro cultural tradition and thus broke away from the traditional aping of European poetic forms, has been attacked by his fellow countrymen as an artist who sought to deny that Puerto Rico, unlike the other Caribbean islands, was "white by blood and by culture."[9] It is not then surprising that the colored Puerto Rican has rarely responded, in any number, to the invitation of men like Betances and Barbosa to adopt an attitude of open racial pride. He prefers, still, to remain—in the phrase of Pedro Timothee—a pampered servant in an alien house than to become master in his own. The pride of race yields, still, to the atmosphere of color worship.

All this, in turn, threatens to become worse, not better, as the society becomes more industrialized. For industrialization everywhere, and especially in its early stages, works to unloosen the nuts and bolts that hold a traditionalist society together. Spanish feudal traditions (which include slavery and anti-Moorish feelings) tended, as Professor Rogler has pointed out, to perpetuate a closed caste system in the colony and by its discourage- ment of the competitive process and spirit to play down sharp racial and class struggle. That has changed; and is certain to change even more as industrialization speeds up the appeal to individual self-interest and self- assertion. Even before 1940 there was evidence to suggest a great deal of frustration on the part of colored university students who found their pro- fessional advancement limited by prejudice.[10] They could move up the social scale through personal achievement. But the movement was always relative; their final position rarely corresponded to that of the white person of comparable achievement; and only too often white persons of inferior social standing obtained privileges denied to colored persons of superior standing. The readiness to accept all this is certain to become diluted as the percentage of candidates for professional preferment (via mass educa- tion) grows. The Puerto Rican who told Christopher Rand that "on the mainland, there has always been a lot of social mobility and a lot of color discrimination, here there has been little social mobility and little color discrimination" quite properly was emphasizing a connection between the two phenomena that is sure to increase in its effects as sharpened economic competitiveness and heightened social ambitions throw people more and more together. The volume of discriminatory practices discovered by the investigators of the Civil Liberties inquiry of 1959—in the college frater- nities and sororities, in certain private schools, in the luxury tourist hotels, in the higher-priced housing developments—shows that prejudice has reached serious proportions and by no means justifies the rather tepid con- clusions of the inquiry itself in its General Report.[11] The legislative enquiry during the summer of 1963 added further evidence concerning discriminatory employment practices on the part of local banks.

It is of some interest to note, in this respect, the puzzled conclusions of the authors of the Princeton University study on social mobility. Their refined statistical analyses yield, for them, little evidence that skin color matters in Puerto Rican life, but the "testimony of common sense," they confess, suggests otherwise: being Negro or white clearly does matter when dealing with status-conscious members of the middle and upper classes.[12] As American forms of discrimination press upon these more ambivalent forms the Puerto Rican who regards himself as white will increasingly find himself in the cruelly ironic position of being himself subjected to the prejudicial techniques he has hitherto utilized against the dark-colored persons of his own society. He will then have to decide whether he will accept that position as a necessary price of retaining political and economic ties with the United States or whether he will join forces with those per- sons in a common front against prejudice. If, of course, those ties are retained then it follows that the decisive factor in the shaping of future race relations in the island will be the development of race relations in the United States.

This raises, finally, the question of immediate public policy. The Civil Liberties report has advised against the extended use of the public police power. Speaking of discrimination in the "private" field of *casinos* and some civic associations, it argues that government pressure would be "unnecessary" and would only arouse feelings of "hostility."[13] Similar language is employed by the Princeton University study to arrive at a similar cautious conclusion: the attention paid to skin color, they assert, is "heightened to critical awareness at the fringes and the interstices of personal relations, where public policy is not an issue, and where public controls are not available."[14] The argument deserves two comments. In the first place, it runs counter to the principle, emphasized most recently by the American courts in the cases relating to the administrative applications of the desegregation rulings of 1954, that the vitality of constitutional rights cannot be allowed to yield simply because of disagreement with them, nor their practical exercise be nullified by threats of public disturbance. To argue otherwise is to hold up the application of the law to ransom by any group that allows its feelings of "hostility" to get the better of it.[15] Secondly, as far as Puerto Rico is concerned, the Commonwealth government has itself already legitimized the use of the public power in this field with the passage of the Civil Rights Act of 1943, reinforced later with the constitutional guarantees of the 1952 Bill of Rights. The tendency of all modern legislation is clearly to enlarge the scope of "public" as against "private" jurisdictions in the whole area of the liberty of the subject; indeed the very definition of what constitutes "private" relationships is rapidly changing as it becomes clear that the distinction between "private" and "public" behavior is psychologically and sociologically unsound, since all "private" acts are imbued with "public" consequences. To take another Puerto Rican example, Chancellor Benítez entertains the visiting Negro writer James Baldwin at a well-publicized luncheon, but the powers of the University Chancellorship are not used to crush the discriminatory practices of a number of the University fraternities. There is little reason to believe that discrimination will of itself disappear without the more coercive machinery of the state being invoked through the medium of statutory measures adequately enforced. It is worth noting increasing parliamentary and public sentiment for such measures in Great Britain following the outbreak of the Notting Hill race riots of 1959. It is difficult to believe that the Puerto Rican experience will point to any other conclusion.

Notes

1. Henry Wells, "Administrative Reorganization in Puerto Rico," *Western Political Quarterly* (June 1956), p. 486. For a more judicious estimate of Puerto Rican social problems, including that of racial prejudice, see Pablo Morales Otero, *Nuestros Problemas* (San Juan, Biblioteca de Autores Puertorriqueños, 1947), especially pp. 191–196. An additional rationalization sometimes advanced by Puerto Rican patriotic sources is that racial prejudice, if it exists, is of American origin. See, for example, Movimiento Pro-Independencia, *Tesis Política: La Hora de la Independencia* (San Juan, Movimiento Pro-Independencia, 1963), pp. 87–88.

2. Cayetano Coll y Toste, ed., *Boletín Histórico de Puerto Rico* (San Juan, Cantero Fernández, 1923), Vol. 10, p. 72.

3. Henry K. Carroll, *Report on the Island of Porto Rico*, p. 51. This liberal tradition in racial matters has been a part of the Puerto Rican radical spirit, as, for example, in the figure of Ramon Betances. For Betances, see Maria Luisa de Angelís, *Ramon E. Betances: Su Vida y Su Labor Política* (San German, Maria Luisa de Angelís, 1913), pp. 15–17.

4. José Colombán Rosario and Justina Carrión, *Problemas Sociales: El Negro* (Rio Piedras, Universidad de Puerto Rico, 1940), pp. 125–126.

5. Trumbull White, *Porto Rico and Its People* (New York, Stokes, 1938), p. 258.

6. Exchange of correspondence between Mary Weld Coates and Charles W. St. John, *Current History* (April-September 1922), pp. 650–651.

7. *Puerto Rico Libre* (San Juan), February 26, 1944.

8. Raymond Scheele, "The Prominent Families of Puerto Rico," in Julian Steward, ed., *The People of Puerto Rico* (University of Illinois Press and Social Sciences Research Center, University of Puerto Rico, 1949), pp. 424–425.

9. Salvador Arana Soto, "Refutando a Luis Palés Matos," *El Mundo*, May 25, 1959. For a more sympathetic treatment of Palés Matos, see Tomás Blanco, *Sobre Palés Matos* (San Juan, Biblioteca de Autores Puertorriqueños, 1950). Yet even such a humanist spirit as Tomás Blanco is still obviously puzzled by his compatriot's identification, as a white Puerto Rican artist, with the Caribbean Afro-Negroid cultural tradition. The Puerto Rican Negro, in his uniquely Hispanized milieu, as distinct from the Haitian or the Martiniquan Negro, has been later treated by the poet Cesáreo Rosa-Nieves, *Diapasón Negro* (San Juan, Editorial Campos, 1960). For the leading present-day Negro poet, Victorio Llanes Allende, see Juan Diáz de Andino, *El Mundo, Suplemento Sabatino,* December 1, 1962.

10. José Colombán Rosario and Justina Carrión, *Problemas Sociales: El Negro,* pp. 144–158.

11. Commonwealth Government of Puerto Rico, Civil Liberties Committee, *Informe sobre Discrímenes por Motivo de Raza . . .,* pp. 1–18.

12. Melvin M. Tumin and Arnold Feldman, *Social Class and Social Change in Puerto Rico* (Princeton University Press, 1961), p. 233.

13. Commonwealth Government of Puerto Rico, Civil Liberties Committee, *Informe sobre Discrímenes por Motivo de Raza . . .,* p. 8.

14. Tumin and Feldman, *Social Class and Social Change in Puerto Rico,* p. 233.

15. *Brown v. Board of Education,* 349 U.S. 294, 300 (1954); and the text of the brief of the National Association for the Advancement of Colored People to the United States Supreme Court in the *New York Times,* September 11, 1958.

Daniel Guérin

RACIAL PREJUDICE AND THE FAILURE OF THE MIDDLE CLASSES IN THE WEST INDIES

I

We come then to the 'burning' question of race relations in the West Indies.

It would perhaps be best to begin with a few figures. From one Caribbean territory to another the proportion of whites, blacks and various grades of mulattos differs widely. In Guadeloupe and Martinique the whites constitute a tiny minority (1 per cent of the population). But the mulattos are far more numerous in Martinique than in Guadeloupe.

As for the British West Indies, the whites form, on an average, 3 or 4 per cent of the population, save in Barbados, where they are 7 per cent, and in Sain Kitts, where they are 6 per cent. In Jamaica the whites comprise 2 per cent of the population, Negroes 78 per cent, mulattos 17 per cent. Some estimate Puerto Rico's coloured population at from 25 to 33 per cent, others at between 30 and 50 per cent.* The average Puerto Rican is comparatively light skinned. In Haiti, Negroes form a good 90 per cent of the population, mulattos the rest, whites having almost completely vanished since the San Domingo uprising. The situation in the adjacent Dominican Republic is very different: here, 14 per cent of the people are white, 18 per cent black, and 68 per cent mulatto. In Cuba the majority are white (or reputed to be) and the percentage of coloured people falls between 27 and 33 per cent. The observations which follow apply to those of the West Indies (the only ones I personally visited) where the Negro element predominates and where the whites form a tiny minority.

The fact that the latter are so very few in number prevents West Indian racial tension from ever assuming the acute and glaring forms which it often does in the United States and which, when I visited America, I had good occasion to study at first hand.[2] No segregation in the West Indies, no legally codified discrimination; but the Caribbean brand of racial prejudice, sneaking about under a mask of hypocrisy, is more irritating and, psychologically, more demoralizing than if it nakedly showed itself for what it is.

In Martinique the hermetic caste of white islanders (degenerate and

---

* It would seem that the Puerto Rican census compilers have deliberately reduced the percentage of coloured people in order to flatter the susceptibilities of influential families who prefer to be classified as 'white'.[1]

REPRINTED FROM *The West Indies and Their Future* (LONDON: DENNIS DOBSON, 1961) BY PERMISSION OF THE AUTHOR. COPYRIGHT © 1961 BY DANIEL GUÉRIN.

asleep on their feet), which economically dominates the territory, continues to avoid any social intercourse with the coloured people. The men have cordial business relations with their darker colleagues; they even go so far as to dine together, but these meals are almost never taken at home.[3] The white Creoles, or *békés*, frequent exclusive private clubs, such as the Lido, not far from Fort-de-France, where I was forbidden entry up till the moment it was made clear that I was a visitor from the mother country (and hence white); therewith the management was all apology and confusion. A vain Guadeloupe mulatto who occupies an important commercial post proudly gave me to understand that he was a welcome guest anywhere; race problem? My good sir! Was he not living proof that no such thing exists in the West Indies? But as chance would have it, a few hours later I met some young gentlemen belonging to Fort-de-France's Creole set. And these precious little idiots, while admitting that reasons of business constrained them to 'welcome' the said personage, further confessed, grief's accents in their voices, that they did so most reluctantly. The conversation having wandered off upon matters having to do with sex, as one man they affirmed that it was not without an undeniable pleasure they now and then 'welcomed' a coloured girl into their arms; then alluded to the taboo which strictly forbids interracial marriage.

There is a certain ship that flies the colours of the Compagnie Générale Transatlantique—whose mission is to maintain a regular service connecting France and France's Caribbean islands—aboard which the upper echelons of the personnel appear to have been recruited for their racist dispositions and who all too often treat coloured passengers to stupid affronts.*

In Barbados, which like Martinique has kept its tight little band of white natives, the planters' snobbery and racism can be nothing short of grotesque.[4] The same caste mentality lives on in the descendants of aristocratic French families who took refuge in Trinidad after the San Domingo revolt and who have melted into the island's no less ludicrous British 'élite'. This is the glittering *beau monde* one finds at Port of Spain's

---

* An example: at the time of the Mendès-France government, M. Jean Joseph, president of the Martinique Conseil Général, made a vehement protest, by radiogram, against the refusal of the *Antilles'* master to allow the large group of West Indian students travelling second class to attend a ball that was held in the first class. Following this incident, M. Joseph declined an invitation to sit at the captain's table. The racism current among the French steamship line's Officers and Gentlemen derives, as well as from a reactionary political attitude, from principles of good business: they fancy that, in order to attract a rich English, American and Venezuelan clientele, it is only fitting that they discriminate against coloured French citizens. And thus it is that, in the West Indies as elsewhere, France is busily throwing large monkey-wrenches into her own future.

† 'A Dutch official,' Eric Williams writes, 'was appointed to my staff. . . . . He asked a West Indian typist to type a letter in which he said that every time he walked down Frederick Street on a Saturday morning he was conscious of the inherent superiority of the white race.'[5]

sumptuous and needless to say restricted Country Club.† The greater part of Jamaica's 'better' hotels (built for American tourists) are invariably 'filled up' when a coloured client applies for a room.

In Puerto Rico racial discrimination decides which guests are to be admitted into the first-class hotels and restaurants and night-clubs. It is also manifest in the shape of exclusive clubs. Despite a 1943 law which penalizes any infraction of the principle of racial equality, the coloured people, rather than encounter any unpleasantness, prefer to avoid going to certain hotels and cabarets.

Trinidad's banks practise discriminatory employment methods, systematically refusing posts to coloured applicants; so do Trinidad's oil companies. When I visited the giant refinery at Pointe-à-Pierre, near San Fernando, I found that the employees are neatly divided into two categories: there is a higher, almost altogether made up of whites, and enjoying enormous material advantages; and there is a lower, made up of coloured workers, who must make do with a minimal wage. In Puerto Rico the banks, the sugar companies, the airways and shipping companies, the large department stores employ only white—or the whitest possible—personnel.

But the Caribbean air is polluted by yet another relic of slavery, even more lamentable than the racial prejudice that infects the minds of the whites. Associating the notion of whiteness with those of wealth and power, slavery inculcated a prejudice in the coloured man, a prejudice against himself: slavery turned him into a 'Negrophobe'.[6]* He was made to feel the full social importance of being white, he was made to loathe his own ebony or bronze skin, he was made to understand that it is an individual's fairness which makes him lovable. And so racial discrimination operates within coloured society itself, everyone as best he can contriving to be admitted into the company of, to pay court to, to marry persons who in colour are as far away from black as possible; and those whose skins are truly black are generally avoided.[9] If he chances to be born with a light skin, the child enters life under a happier star than if born black. Even within its own family, the light-skinned child receives greater attention, greater affection. Nothing seems more natural to the family than that, later on, every door will be opened to the fairer son, whilst they will be universally closed to his brother upon whom the unpredictable operation of Mendel's laws has bestowed a darker hue.

Darkness of skin and other attributes of 'negritude'—frizzy hair, flattened nose, thick lips—automatically place an individual at the bottom of the social scale. Girls struggle desperately to straighten the kinks out of their hair and, with the aid of special lotions and creams, to modify the colour of their skin. Ebony-coloured lads, often magnificent, are tormented

* Similarly, Richard Wright has described the 'psychological suicide' of a black woman destroyed by her shame over her colour.[7] Franklin Frazier has written a brilliant analysis of the 'self-hatred' from which all well-to-do American Negroes suffer.[8]

to find themselves scorned by girls whose one guiding idea and desire is to keep company with boys a shade or two lighter than themselves. At Haiti's famous Cabane Choucoune, in Pétionville, I overheard a young mulatto rebuke his brother for dancing with a young lady who was somewhat darker than he; 'to betray one's caste' was the term employed.*

Just like the whites, coloured employers consider pigmentation the crucial factor in deciding a candidate's fitness for a job; the mulatto is regularly chosen over the darker man.

Many a West Indian mother's dream is to have an illegitimate child by a white man even if the father afterwards refuses to give his name to their offspring. The half-breed child will, as Zobel says, enjoy a 'flying start' as he enters the world.

As a rule lighter-skinned, the Martiniquais will often exhibit contempt for the Guadeloupan; and the latter, inversely, sometimes tries to pass himself off as a Martiniquais.[10]

The results of these equally subtle and ridiculous racial distinctions is that the colour of a man's skin determines where he fits into which West Indian social stratum. Wealth, position, esteem mount as the degree of pigmentation declines. As a whole, the middle classes are for the most part composed of mulattos; the impoverished masses are black.† The sometimes muffled, sometimes open struggle which brings Negroes and mulattos to grips is, in a certain measure, a class struggle.

II

The member of the West Indian middle class pretends, in general, to know nothing about the colour question. He doesn't like to think about it, doesn't like to be reminded of the gulf which, despite his rise in the ranks of society, still separates him from the whites. In the United States, where anyone suspected of having a drop of Negro blood is straightway classified as 'Negro,' all the coloured people, whatever their social status or hue, stand together in resenting the insult of racial prejudice, and the coloured middle class, despite its tendency to divorce itself from the mass of poorer Negroes, cannot feign ignorance of the racial conflict's reality or avoid taking part in it.

In the West Indies, on the other hand, the mulatto has a much vaguer feeling of solidarity with his coloured brothers. White arrogance may cut him to the quick, the whites' privileges may exasperate him, but his ruling desire to become included amongst and to vanish into the white ranks

---

* In reply to the racism of Haitian mulattos, certain Negroes adopt a racism of their own, condemning those Negroes who consort with mulatto women.

† However, a *black* middle class is also in the process of forming and of rising. But its economic position is still far weaker than the mulattos'. Thus, in Jamaica, 85 per cent of the farms of one to under two acres are owned by Negroes while the Negroes own only 11 per cent of those of 1,000 acres and over (mulattos owning 38 per cent and whites 50 per cent of the rest).[11]

makes him swallow his pride. As Zobel writes, the mulatto is only too ready to add 'filthy nigger' to his vocabulary and to send the whole black race to the devil.[12] He lives in terror of hearing the West Indian population's ethnical antecedents mentioned; he is not well disposed towards the study of what remains—and in the islands much does remain—of African culture; he is shocked that anyone can take an interest in Voodoo or other 'semi-pagan' religions. He denies or tries to forget that certain of his ancestors were slaves, and takes extravagant pride in any white blood he has in his veins. If the interests of the white plutocracy and the people appear in an antagonistic juxtaposition, or clash outright, he has no doubts as to where he stands: he's on the side of the whites. In the 'Fort Royal' mulatto circle in Fort-de-France a good number of those present were scandalized when I ended a public talk by reading aloud a scathing poem by Jacques Roumain, 'Sale Nègre' ('Dirty Nigger'), in which the author, identifying himself with the black race, announces to the whites that the heyday of racial oppression is over. 'Poor fellow! You went and put your foot squarely in it. What did you do but say *exactly* what one must never say to them,' Max Petit of Radio Martinique, who was in the audience, told me later on. The same poem, recited in Guadeloupe before a popular and considerably darker group of listeners, subsequently met with the warmest reception.

The extreme poverty of the West Indian masses, the abyss dividing their living conditions from those of the middle class, the need felt by the bourgeois or petty bourgeois to consolidate his rather precarious social position by increasing the distinction between himself and the 'rest of them down there', all these have helped dig a veritable moat between the élite and the mass of the population. The élite are concentrated above all in the cities and keep scrupulously out of all touch with those who labour on the land. In the cities themselves, the élite congregate in residential districts generally situated on well-aired heights and at a respectable distance from the popular suburbs. The élite scorn manual work, even frown upon technical careers; they are given purely classical educations. When they employ the Creole patois, it is when addressing domestics and they forbid their children to use it; they are fond of their faultless French, a passage from Montesquieu or Racine is thought to help an interlocutor forget the colour of the man he is chatting with. The élite show precious little interest in the island of their birth, or in the part of the world where that island lies. Every gaze is fastened on distant places, it is with the mother country the élite identify themselves, and 'over there' is where they hope someday to go and live. In the words of Frantz Fanon, the West Indian thinks of his voyage to France 'as of the last stage in rounding out his personality.'[13]

'There is amongst us a wilful ignorance, a deliberate underestimation of our country, of what may be its notable and original qualities,' writes a Martiniquais student of Marxist leanings. Another student, this time a Catholic, charges the élite with 'desertion': 'Every passing day sees this island decapitated anew,' and the author advises the young Martiniquais who have gone abroad to do their studies 'to think always of returning to their native island' and to devote their energies to solving the social problems which exist there, instead of 'considering themselves foreigners in their birthplace, in this poor, backward and retrograde land', instead of 'parading a lofty arrogance and a cruel contempt' for their home.[14]

An English writer, Kenneth Pringle, accuses the Jamaican of knowing 'even less about the people than the English bourgeoisie about its proletariat. . . . No one in the West Indies talks so glibly of the "lazy" black as his coloured brother.'[15]

In Haiti, whites having disappeared from the island, mulattos occupy the top of the social pyramid where they form a closed, insolent and parasitical caste. An eminent Haitian, Dr Price-Mars, has flayed the élite for its princely world-weariness, its 'languid puffiness around the eyes'; failing 'to mingle with the rest of the nation,' it 'exercises nothing better than a kind of empty mandarinate, atrophying, growing fainter and fainter every day.'[16] In a Haitian novel a member of the élite describes the peasant as that 'unconscious creature, just barely above the level of the beast, and who has nothing human about him but a man's shape' and concludes with the exclamation: 'But what kind of a lunatic must one be in order to sympathize with these contemptible wretches!'[17]

The mulatto élite affect no interest save in what goes on outside Haiti, and their passion for France, sincere as it may be and however much a Frenchman may be moved by it, is not incompatible with a dose of snobbery.

As a consequence of this attitude, until a relatively recent date, no indigenous culture has developed in the West Indies. The vestiges of the old African culture, smothered by slavery and eclipsed by contact with European civilization, have little by little retreated out of the picture. Here, there's almost nothing left; over there, a little yet remains. But everywhere, the further up the social ladder people have clambered, the less of the past they've taken with them. A Caribbean 'renaissance' is dawning today; but up till its eve, to fill the absence created by the largely defunct ancient culture, the intellectual élite supplied nothing save what of metropolitan cultures it could import and imitate.

From elementary school on, the child receives an education that has no relation to the reality which surrounds him and which, as Zobel phrases it, he indifferently and 'heartlessly acknowledges'.[18] He is helped to fabricate an essentially 'white' personality. The history he is taught has nothing to do with his native land; he learns geography, but these rivers and mountains are not his own. He must familiarize himself with the flora and fauna of remote countries; they bear slight resemblance to those of his tropics. He learns to draw apples; to paint pictures of people with white faces; to read pastoral tales where the action takes place in a country of plains and wheatfields; to know all about things pertaining to snow and ice; to speak in his French compositions of 'coming back *pink*-cheeked from the bracing out-of-doors'.[19] And he receives his instruction in a difficult classical language (French or English) while, in the schoolroom, he is not allowed to use his true maternal tongue (Creole in the French Antilles, in Haiti and even in a number of British islands).

Higher education lies even more completely under the influence of metropolitan culture. Whilst Puerto Rico possesses a well-known university, there is nothing of the kind (save for the branch of its law school that the University of Bordeaux opened in 1949 in Fort-de-France) anywhere in the French or Dutch West Indies: the student must cross the ocean. The British West Indies suffered from the same deficiency for a very long time. Only in 1947 did the Colonial Office think to found, in Jamaica, a university open to students from all the British territories. The facilities of this university, which has indeed been built, are splendid. But the instruction given there is far too classical, far too aristocratic and, above all, far too British. University-level education in Haiti is in part provided by the professors, sent over from France, of the Institut Français.

Until but a short while ago, the West Indies could claim few writers or painters of any originality. (True enough, they have, as we shall see, brilliantly made up for lost time.) As Fanon writes, 'the West Indian . . . composed his poems, wrote his novels exactly as a white man would have. . . . Prior to Césaire, West Indian literature is a literature of Europeans.'[20] When then centres of indigenous culture at last began to appear, the Caribbean 'renaissance' located itself *first and most intensively in those islands which enjoy a relative political independence*: in Cuba, in Haiti.[21]* The movement has been slow to take hold in the British West Indies, but has advanced in step with their general acquisition of self-government. The French Antilles—which, of them all, are the islands having the least elbow-room, since they have been purely and simply assimilated into the mother country—trail far behind. Cultural pabulum arrives by boat-mail from France. There is virtually no daily press at all; what there is compares rather shamefully with that of the other Caribbean islands. In the matter of public libraries, the comparison is still more painful. The *Revue Guadeloupéenne*, which, in its day, made a genuine effort to encourage native literature and culture, has shut up shop. As for *Horizons Caraïbes*, which is published in Martinique, the horizons that review displays are often, despite the best intentions, more Parisian than Caribbean. It seems to have been in vain that a young professor of history, recently returned to the island, has attempted to interest teachers and lycée students in starting a Martinique historical studies group. . . .[22]

To be sure, the French islands' cultural honour has finally been rescued by such writers as Aimé Césaire, Joseph Zobel, Frantz Fanon, Edouard Glissant.[23] But these sons of Martinique—of whose remarkable achievement I shall have more to say later on—settled in France have somewhat the look of solitary beacons, and the review *Tropiques,* ani-

---

* Even so, Haitian booksellers continue to give the most prominent place in their shop windows to books published in France rather than to contemporary native authors.

mated by Césaire when he lived in the Antilles, glittered for an instant only, then died out.

To sum up, the Caribbean middle class has not shown itself capable of developing an original and authentic culture; it has been intellectually moulded by the various mother countries which have intruded their presence into the region. From one territory to another, the élites do not speak the same language, do not have the same spiritual outlook, and have established little by way of mutual acquaintanceships. A Caribbean culture only started to come into being when, as we shall see, a minority split away from the middle classes and made contact with the people, turned its attentions to their problems, studied their customs, their beliefs, what of the African inheritance the people have kept alive, and voiced the people's aspirations and anger. And notwithstanding the fact that this new culture expresses itself in a number of languages—French, English, Spanish, sometimes even in Creole—and even though it has been more spontaneously born than deliberately launched, one finds that in its main features it is similar in whichever of the islands one looks for it. Nor is this likeness accidental. It is the product of a common phenomenon: the aspiration towards freedom and towards a whole personality shared by populations whose ancestors were African, who came into the New World because they were dragged there in chains, who, after having been delivered from one bondage, fell into another and became the captives of a capitalist plutocracy, and who are finally discovering that they have a common lot, in their misery and in their revolt.

Notes

1. Williams, Eric, 'Race Relations in Puerto Rico and the Virgin Islands', *Foreign Affairs,* New York, January 1945.

2. Guérin, Daniel, *Où va le Peuple américain?,* Vol. II, Paris, 1951; in English: *Negroes on the March,* London-New York, 1956.

3. Leiris, *Contacts de civilisation en Martinique et en Guadeloupe,* Paris, 1956, p. 129.

4. Lamming, George, *In the Castle of My Skin,* London, 1953.

5. Williams, Eric, *My Relations with the Caribbean Commission 1943–1955,* Port-of-Spain, Trinidad, 1955, p. 48.

6. Fanon, Frantz, *Peau noire Masques blancs,* Paris, 1952, pp. 187–8.

7. Wright, Richard, *The Colour Curtain,* London-New York, 1956, pp. 157–60.

8. Frazier, Franklin, *Bourgeoisie Noire,* Paris, 1955, p. 204.

9. Fanon, *op. cit.,* p. 39.

10. *Ibid.*

11. Henriques, F. M., *Family and Colour in Jamaica,* London, 1953, pp. 173–81.

12. Zobel, Joseph, *La Rue Cases-Nègres,* Paris, 1950, pp. 285, 291.

13. Fanon, *Peau noire . . .,* p. 153.

14. *Trait d'Union,* Paris, February-March, 1955; *Alizés,* Paris, October, 1952 and January, 1955.

15. Pringle, Kenneth, *Waters of the West,* London, 1938, quoted in Williams, *The Negro in the Caribbean,* p. 40.

16. Price-Mars, Jean, *Ainsi parla l'oncle,* New York (in French), 1954 (1st ed., 1928), p. 110.

17. Cinéas, J. B., *La Vengeance de la terre,* Port-au-Prince, Haiti, 1933, pp. 75, 81.

18. Zobel, *op. cit.,* pp. 268–9.

19. Fanon, *Peau noire . . ., op. cit.,* pp. 147, 161.

20. *Ibidem,* p. 268.

21. Williams, Eric, *The Negro in the Caribbean,* London, 1945, pp. 50–52; Chapman, Esther, 'The Truth about Jamaica', *The West Indian Review,* Kingston, Jamaica, 1938, pp. 18–19.

22. *Alizés,* Paris, October, 1954.

23. Cf. Glissant, Edouard, *La Lézarde,* Paris, 1958 (a novel).

Marvin Harris
THE ORIGIN OF
THE DESCENT RULE

At one point, and one point only, is there a demonstrable correlation between the laws and behavior, the ideal and the actual, in Tannenbaum's theory: the Spanish and Portuguese codes ideally drew no distinction between the ex-slave and the citizen, and actual behavior followed suit. The large hybrid populations of Latin America were not discriminated against *solely* because they were descended from slaves; it is definitely verifiable that all hybrids were not and are not forced back into a sharply separated Negro group by application of a rule of descent. This was true during slavery and it was true after slavery. With abolition, because a continuous color spectrum of free men had already existed for at least 200 years, ex-slaves and descendants of slaves were not pitted against whites in the bitter struggle which marks the career of our own Jim Crow.

However, to argue that it was the Spanish and Portuguese slave codes and slave traditions which gave rise to these real and substantial differences in the treatment of the free Negro and mulatto is to miss the essential point about the evolution of the New World plantation systems. If traditional laws and values were alone necessary to get the planters to manumit their slaves, and treat free colored people like human beings, the precedents among the English colonists were surely greater than among the Latins.

If anything, the laws and traditions of England conspired to make its colonists abhor anything that smacked of slavery. And so it was in England that in 1705 Chief Justice Holt could say, "As soon as a Negro comes into England he becomes free."[1] Let it not be forgotten that five of the original thirteen states—New Hampshire, Massachusetts, Connecticut, Rhode Island and Pennsylvania, plus the independent state of Vermont—began programs of complete emancipation before the federal Constitutional Convention met in 1787. Partial anti-slavery measures were enacted by New York in 1788, and total emancipation in 1799, while New Jersey began to pass anti-slavery legislation in 1786.[2] Furthermore, all of the original states which abolished slavery lived up to the declared principles of the Declaration of Independence and the Constitution to a remarkable degree in their treatment of emancipated slaves. "They were citizens of their respective states the same as were Negroes who were free at the time of independence."[3]

REPRINTED FROM *Patterns of Race in the Americas* (NEW YORK: WALKER & CO., 1964) BY PERMISSION OF THE AUTHOR AND THE PUBLISHER.

There were no restrictions prior to 1800 upon Negroes voting in any state which had abolished slavery. They were voting at that time and continued to vote without interruption in New Hampshire, Vermont, Rhode Island, and the two slave states of New York and New Jersey.

It was only later that Connecticut (1814) and Pennsylvania (1837) got around to imposing restrictions. Although the slave codes of New York, New Jersey and Pennsylvania had forbidden slaves to testify in court cases involving white persons these laws were never applied to free Negroes, and "there were no such laws in New England. . . . Nor were there any distinctions whatever in criminal law, judicial procedure, and punishments." In all of the Northern states, therefore, Negroes were citizens "by enjoyment of full political equality, by lack of any statements to the contrary in any constitution or law, by complete absence of legal distinction based on color, and by specific legal and constitutional declaration. . . ."[4]

We see, therefore, that if past laws and values had a significant role to play in the treatment of Negroes and mulattoes, the hounding persecution of the free Negroes and mulattoes should never have occurred in the English colonies. For contrary to the oft-repeated assertion that there was no matrix of English law or tradition into which the slave could fit, it is quite obvious that very specific laws and traditions existed to guide the Anglo-Saxon colonists. These laws and traditions held that all men had natural rights, that the Negroes were men and that slaves ought to become citizens. That the Constitution asserts "all men are created equal" is not some monstrous hypocrisy perpetrated by the founding fathers. It was an expression of a general Northern and enlightened Southern belief that slavery was an institution which was incompatible with the laws and traditions of civilized Englishmen. That the American versions of these laws were later subverted by court decisions and that the Constitution's guarantee of freedom and equality became a grim joke is surely ample testimony to the futility of trying to understand socio-cultural evolution in terms of such factors.

Understanding of the differences in the status of free "non-whites" in the plantation world can only emerge when one forthrightly inquires why a system which blurred the distinction between Negro and white was materially advantageous to one set of planters, while it was the opposite to another. One can be certain that if it had been materially disadvantageous to the Latin colonists, it would never have been tolerated—Romans, *Siete Partidas* and the Catholic Church notwithstanding. For one thing is clear, the slavocracy in both the Latin and Anglo-Saxon colonies held the whip hand not only over the slaves but over the agents of civil and ecclesiastical authority. To make second-class citizens out of all descendants of slaves was surely no greater task, given sufficient material reason, than to make slaves out of men and brutes out of slaves.

Although the slave plantation per se was remarkably similar in its effects regardless of the cultural background of the slaves or slave-owners,[5] the natural, demographic and institutional environment with which slavery articulated and interacted was by no means uniform. It is the obligation of all those who wish to explain the difference between United States and Latin American race relations to examine these material conditions first, before concluding that it was the mystique of the Portuguese or Spanish soul that made the difference.

The first important consideration is demographic. Latin America and the United States experienced totally different patterns of settlement. When Spain and Portugal began their occupation of the New World, they were harassed by severe domestic manpower shortages, which made it extremely difficult for them to find colonists for their far-flung empires. Furthermore, in the New World the conditions under which such colonists were to settle were themselves antithetical to large-scale emigration. In the highlands a dense aboriginal population was already utilizing most of the arable land under the tutelage of the *encomenderos* and *hacendados*. In the lowlands large-scale emigration, supposing there had been a sufficient number of potential settlers, was obstructed by the monopolization of the best coastal lands by the slave-owning sugar planters. Only a handful of Portuguese migrated to Brazil during the sixteenth century. In the seventeenth century, a deliberate policy of *restricting* emigration to Brazil was pursued, out of fear that Portugal was being depopulated. Cried the Jesuit father Antonio Vieira, "Where are our men? Upon every alarm in Alentejo it is necessary to take students from the university, tradesmen from their shops, laborers from the plough!"[6]

The migrations of Englishmen and Britishers to the New World followed an entirely different rhythm. Although the movement began almost a century later, it quickly achieved a magnitude that was to have no parallel in Latin America until the end of the nineteenth century. Between 1509 and 1790 only 150,000 people emigrated from Spain to the entire New World, but between 1600 and 1700, 500,000 English and Britishers moved to the North American territories.

The reason for this accelerated rate of migration is not hard to find:

> As opposed to Spain and Portugal, harassed by a permanent manpower scarcity when starting to occupy the Western Hemisphere, seventeenth-century England had an abundant population surplus, owing to the far-reaching changes affecting the country's agriculture since the previous century.[7]

The changes in question were the enclosures by which much of England's farming population was being forced off the land in order to make way for sheep-raising (in turn stimulated by the manufacture of woolen cloth). The depletion of England's own natural resources, especially its forests, made it convenient to consider establishing overseas companies to produce commodities which were becoming increasingly more difficult to produce in England: potash, timber, pitch, tar, resin, iron and copper. It was to produce these commodities that Jamestown was founded in 1607.

> The staple and certain Commodities we have are Soap-ashes, pitch, tar, dyes of sundry sorts and rich values, timber for all uses, fishing for sturgeon . . . making of glass and iron, and no improbable hope of richer mines.[8]

Manufactures of this sort, plus subsistence agriculture, proved to be the mainstay of the more northerly colonies and were later to establish the United States, at least in the North, as an important industrial power. From Maryland on south, however, the colonists quickly switched to tobacco-growing as their basic commercial activity. Whether agriculture or manufacturing was the principal concern of a given colony, labor, as always, was the main problem. There were plenty of Englishmen eager to settle in the New World but the price of the Atlantic passage was high. The system developed to overcome this obstacle was indentured servitude, whereby the price of passage was advanced, to be worked off, usually in five to eight years, after which the immigrant would be free to do as he might choose. Despite the high mortality rate of the early indentured servants, tens of thousands of English men and women bought passage to the New World in this fashion. The great lure of it was that once a man had worked off his debt, there was a chance to buy land at prices which were unthinkably low in comparison with those of England.

For almost one hundred years, white indentured servants were the principal source of manpower in the Anglo-Saxon colonies. Black slave manpower was a relatively late introduction. The case of Virginia would seem to be the most important and most instructive. In 1624, there were only 22 Negroes in Virginia (at a time when several thousand a year were already pouring into Recife and Bahia). In 1640, they had not increased to more than 150. Nine years later, when Virginia was inhabited by 15,000 whites, there were still only 300 Negroes. It was not until 1670 that Negroes reached 5 per cent of the population.[9] After 1680 slaves began to arrive in increasing numbers, yet it was not until the second quarter of the eighteenth century that they exceeded 25 per cent of the population.

In 1715 the population of all the colonies with the exception of South Carolina was overwhelmingly composed of a white yeomanry, ex-indentured servants and wage earners. Against a total white population of 375,000, there were less than 60,000 slaves in all of the colonies. If we consider the four Southern colonies—Maryland, Virginia, North Carolina and South Carolina—the ratio was still almost 3 to 1 in favor of the whites.[10]

At about the same time, the total population of Brazil is estimated to have been 300,000, of whom only 100,000 were of European origin.[11] In other words, the ratio of whites to non-whites was the exact opposite of what it was in the United States. A century later (1819) in Brazil, this ratio in favor of non-whites had climbed even higher, for out of an estimated total of 3,618,000 Brazilians, only 834,000 or less than 20 per cent were white.[12] At approximately the same time in the United States (1820),

Population of the Colonies, 1715

	WHITE	NEGRO
New Hampshire	9,500	150
Massachusetts	94,000	2,000
Rhode Island	8,500	500
Connecticut	46,000	1,500
New York	27,000	4,000
New Jersey	21,000	1,500
Pennsylvania-Delaware	43,000	2,500
Maryland	40,700	9,500
Virginia	72,000	23,000
North Carolina	7,500	3,700
South Carolina	6,250	10,500

7,866,797, or more than 80 per cent of the people, out of a total population of 9,638,453 were whites. Although the Negro population was at this time overwhelmingly concentrated in the South, Negroes at no point constituted more than 38 per cent of the population of the Southern states.[13] The high point was reached in 1840; thereafter, the proportion declined steadily until by 1940 it had fallen below 25 per cent in the South and below 10 per cent for the country as a whole.

Clearly, one of the reasons why the colonial population of Brazil shows such a preponderance of non-whites during colonial times is that a large part of the population increase resulted not from in-migration but from miscegenation and the natural increase of the European-Negroid-Amerindian crosses. Thus, in 1819, there were almost as many mestizos, free and slave, as there were whites, and by 1870, there were more "mixed bloods" than whites. This situation reversed itself toward the end of the nineteenth century after the first great wave of European immigrants had begun to flood São Paulo and the Brazilian south. According to the 1890 census, there were 6,302,198 whites, 4,638,495 mixed types and 2,097,426 Negroes.[14] This "whitening" trend has continued until the present day, when whites number about 62 per cent of the population, mixed types 27 per cent and Negroes 11 per cent.[15] These figures, of course, should be read with an understanding that many persons classed as "whites" are actually "mixed" in conformity with what has previously been said about the inherent ambiguity of racial classification in Brazil.

There is no doubt that the number of Brazilians of color who were free was always greater than the number of free Negroes in the United States, absolutely and in proportion to the number of slaves. But the disparity may not have been as great as many people believe. Thus in 1819, when there were anywhere from 1,500,000 to 2 million slaves in Brazil, there were about 585,000 free men of color (not counting Indians),[16] while in the United States in 1820, 1,538,000 slaves were matched by

233,634 free Negroes.[17] Conservatively, therefore, one might claim that in Brazil there were only about twice as many free Negroes in proportion to slaves as in the United States. This fact permits us to place the claims for a higher rate of manumission in Brazil in proper perspective and leads us directly to the most important question about the demographic patterns under consideration. The number of free people of color in nineteenth-century Brazil is not at all startling in relationship to the number of *slaves*. What is amazing from the North American point of view is the number of free people of color in relationship to the number of *whites*.

Manumission may have been somewhat more frequent in Brazil than in the United States, but not so much more frequent that one can use it with any certainty as an indication that slavery in Brazil was a milder institution than it was in the United States. It should be borne in mind that the higher ratio of free coloreds to slaves in Brazil might to some extent represent a greater eagerness on the part of the Brazilian masters to rid themselves of the care and support of aged and infirm charges. Since we know nothing about the age distribution of the free Brazilian colored population in comparison with that of the United States free colored population, it is obvious that less importance than is customary should be attached to the ratio of free to slave colored in Brazil.

But the ratio of whites to free colored is indeed astonishing, especially if one admits that many of the "whites" quite probably had non-white grandparents. The central question, therefore, is, why did the Brazilian whites permit themselves to become outnumbered by free half-castes? Several factors, none of them related to alleged special features of the Portuguese national character, readily present themselves.

In the first instance, given the chronic labor shortage in sixteenth-century Portugal and the small number of people who migrated to Brazil, the white slave-owners had no choice but to create a class of free half-castes. The reason for this is not that there was a shortage of white women, nor that Portuguese men were fatally attracted to dark females. These hoary sex fantasies explain nothing, since there is no reason why the sexual exploitation of Amerindian and Negro females had necessarily to lead to a *free* class of hybrids. The most probable explanation is that the whites had no choice in the matter. They were compelled to create an intermediate free group of half-castes to stand between them and the slaves because there were certain essential economic and military functions for which slave labor was useless, and for which no whites were available.

One of these functions was that of clearing the Indians from the sugar coast; another was the capture of Indian slaves; a third was the overseeing of Negro slaves; and a fourth was the tracking down of fugitives. The half-caste nature of most of the Indian-fighters and slave-catchers is an indubitable fact of Brazilian history. Indian-Portuguese *mamelucos* were called upon to defend Bahia and other cities against the Indians, and the hordes of people who were constantly engaged in destroying the *quilombos,* including Palmares, were also half-castes.[18] There was little help from the armed forces of the Crown:

> The land owners had to defend themselves. They were obliged to organize militarily. Within each sugar plantation, in every large estate, in the solitude of every cattle ranch, under the command of the *senhor,* there lived for this reason, a small perfectly organized army.
>
> This rabble of *mestizos* . . . provided the fighting corps charged with the defense of the estates. Out of them came the *morenos,* the *cafusos,* the *mulatos,* the *carijos,* the *mamelucos* . . . to guarantee the safety of the master's mills, plantations, and herds.[19]

A second great interstice filled by free half-castes was the cattle industry. The sugar plantations required for the mills and for the hauling of wood and cane, one ox and one horse per slave. These animals could not be raised in the sugar zone, where they were a menace to the unfenced cane fields and where the land was too valuable to be used for pasturage. As a matter of fact, a royal decree of 1701 prohibited cattle raising within 10 leagues of the coast.[20] The cattle industry developed first in the semiarid portions of the state of Bahia and rapidly fanned out in all directions into the interior. Open-range mounted cowboys, for obvious reasons, cannot be slaves; nor would any self-respecting Portuguese immigrant waste his time rounding up doggies in the middle of a parched wilderness. The *vaqueiros* were a motley crew:

> . . . they were recruited from among Indians and mestizos as well as among fugitives from the coastal centers: escaped criminals, fugitive slaves, adventurers of every type.[21]
>
> The people who bring them [the cattle] are whites, *mulatos* and Negroes and also Indians. . . .[22]
>
> The foundation of cattle ranches . . . opened new possibilities in the interior . . . to these new *sesmarias* . . . there flowed the . . . free mestizo population of every sort.[23]

Although the Brazilian economist Celso Furtado estimates that only 13,000 people were supported by stock raising in its initial phases, the capacity of both the human and the animal population to expand rapidly in response to negative economic trends on the coast is given great emphasis.[24]

It is also a reasonable hypothesis that half-castes were used to help supplement the colony's supply of basic food crops. That there was a perennial shortage of food in the colonial cities and on the sugar plantations is well established. Says Freyre, about the state of alimentation during colonial times: "Bad upon the plantations and very bad in the cities—not only bad, but scarce."[25] It is known that in the West Indies the concentration on sugar was so great that much of their subsistence food requirements had to be met by imports from New England.[26] At least in times of high sugar prices it seems probable that the Brazilian plantations suffered the same fate:

The profitability of the sugar business was inducive to specialization, and it is not surprising . . . that the entrepreneurs avoided diverting production factors into secondary activities, at least at times when the prospects of the sugar market seemed favorable. At such times even the production of food for the sustenance of the slaves was anti-economic. . . .[27]

Who then were the food growers of colonial Brazil? Who supplied Bahia, Recife and Rio with food? Although documentary proof is lacking, it would be most surprising if the bulk of the small farmer class did not consist of aged and infirm manumitted slaves, and favorite Negro concubines who with their mulatto offspring had been set up with a bit of marginal land. There was no one to object in Brazil, if after eight years of lash-driven labor, a broken slave was set free and permitted to squat on some fringe of the plantation.

All those interstitial types of military and economic activities which in Brazil could only be initially filled by half-caste free men were performed in the United States by the Southern yeomanry. Because the influx of Africans and the appearance of mulattoes in the United States occurred only *after* a large, intermediate class of whites had already been established, there was in effect no place for the freed slave, be he mulatto or Negro, to go.

It would be wrong, however, to create the impression that the Southern yeomanry, from whence sprang the "rednecks," "crackers" and hillbillies, were capable of intimidating the lords of the Southern plantations. The brutal treatment suffered by the small white farmers as they were driven back to the hills or into the swamps and pine barrens should suffice to set the record straight. If the slave in the South came less and less frequently to be manumitted and if the freedmen were deprived of effective citizenship, and if mulattoes were forced back into the Negro group by the descent rule, it was not because of the sentimental affinity which Southern gentlemen felt for their own "kind." To be sure, there was an intense feeling of racial solidarity among the whites, but nothing could be more in error than to suppose that the racial camaraderie of planter and yeoman was merely the adumbration of some bio-psychological tendency on the part of racially similar people to stick together and hate people who are different. Race prejudice once again explains nothing; such an explanation is precisely what the planters and yeomen came to agree upon, and what the rest of America has been sold for the last 150 years. There were alternate explanations, but these the American people has never permitted itself to learn.

The most remarkable of all the phenomena connected with the "peculiar institution" in the United States is the failure of the non-slaveholding yeomanry and poor whites who constituted three-fourths of all Southerners to destroy the plantation class.[28] These whites were as surely and as permanently the victims of the slave system as were the free half-castes and Negroes and the slaves themselves. Their entire standard of living was depressed by the presence of the slaves. Artisans, farmers and mechanics all found themselves in competition with the kind of labor force it is impossible to undersell—people who work for no wages at all! In 1860, the average annual wage among the textile workers in New England was $205; in the South, it was $145. "Even in industries that employed no slaves, the threat to employ them was always there, nonetheless."[29] The relationship between the precarious condition of the Southern white yeomen and mechanics and the slave system was known and avidly discussed by many planters, reformers and abolitionists. Some of the planters were perfectly willing to see the poor whites depressed to the level of the slaves, in the conviction that the ruling oligarchy was blessed with a divine mandate to rule over the "mudsills"—"the greasy mechanics, filthy operatives, small-fisted farmers. . . ." The slaveholders, "born to command and trained to ride their saddled underlings, assumed the usual aristocratic disdain for the 'lower order' whether Negro or white. . . ."[30] A South Carolina member of the House of Representatives overtly expressed what was probably a general feeling among the planters: "If laborers ever obtain the political power of a country, it is in fact in a state of revolution, which must end in substantially transferring property to themselves . . . unless those who have it shall appeal to the sword and a standing army to protect it."[31] Another Southern spokesman did not hesitate to admit that the Southern government was based on excluding "all of the lowest and most degraded classes . . . whether slaves or free, white or black."[32] Why this opinion of them did not penetrate the minds of the majority of the poor whites, we shall see in a moment. However, there were thousands of individuals and even organized groups of Southern yeomen and mechanics who understood that they as much as the Negroes were suffering the effects of slavery. Some of them were able to put the story together with breathtaking insight:

> When a journeyman printer *underworks* the usual rates he is considered an enemy to the balance of the fraternity, and is called a *"rat."* Now the slaveholders have *ratted* us with the 180,000 slaves till forbearance longer on our part has become criminal. They have *ratted* us till we are unable to support ourselves with the ordinary comfort of a laborer's life. They have *ratted* us out of the social circle. They have *ratted* us out of the means of making our own schools . . . They have *ratted* us out of the press. They have *ratted* us out of the legislature. . . . Come, if we are not worse than brutish beasts, let us but speak the word, and slavery shall die![33]

But slavery did not succumb at the hands of those who could most easily have killed it, and who, it would seem, had every reason to want it dead. Instead, the Southern yeomanry followed the planters into a war and bled themselves white in defense of the "property" which was the cause of all their sorrow. Why? Were they so loyal to the owners of the slaves because the measure of their hatred for dark skin and curly hair was so great?

They fought because they were prejudiced, but it is no ordinary prejudice that leads a man to kill another over his looks.

It is not surprising that a Negro abolitionist, Frederick Douglass, an ex-slave himself, came so close to the answer, which many Americans, including scholars of high repute, cannot face:

> The slaveholders, with a craftiness peculiar to themselves, by encouraging the enmity of the poor, laboring white man against the blacks, succeeded in making the said white man almost as much a slave as the black man himself. The difference between the white slave, and the black slave, is this: the latter belongs to *one* slaveholder, and the former belongs to *all* the slaveholders, collectively. The white slave has taken from him by indirection, what the black slave has taken from him, directly, and without ceremony. Both are plundered, and by the same plunderers. The slave is robbed by his master of all his earnings above what is required for his bare physical necessities; and the white man is robbed by the slave system, of the just results of his labor, because he is flung into competition with a class of laborers who work without wages. . . . At present the slaveholders blind them to this competition by keeping alive their prejudices against the slaves, as *men*—not against them *as slaves*. They appeal to their pride, often denounce emancipation as tending to place the white working man, on an equality with negroes, and, by this means, they succeed in drawing off the minds of the poor whites from the real fact, that, by the rich slave master, they are already regarded as but a single remove from equality with the slave.[34]

This account of the origin of the Southern race mania betrays an understandable tendency to exaggerate both the diabolism of the masters and the stupidity of the poor whites. It does not suffice to account for the equally virulent anti-Negro sentiments in the North as expressed by the Northern mobs which burned Pennsylvania Hall, destroyed the abolitionist presses, burned down a Negro orphan asylum in New York, and rioted against Negroes in almost every major Northern city during the Civil War. It does not explain why the Civil War was begun ostensibly to "save the Union" and why the Emancipation Proclamation could only be sold to the country as a military measure designed to throw additional manpower against the enemy.[35] The fact is, the Southern planters held a trump. To the abolitionists who warned both the Northern and Southern lower-class farmers and laborers that slavery would eventually drag them all down together, the planters countered that slavery was the only thing that was keeping 4 million African laborers from *immediately* taking the lands, houses and jobs which white men enjoyed. The unleashing of 4 million ex-slaves on the wage market was indeed a nightmare calculated to terrify the poor whites of both regions.

> The guiding principle of the slavocracy was *divide et impera*. Its basic policy followed two lines, the first of which was to convince the white laborers that they had a material interest in the preservation of the chattel system. They were constantly told that, by consigning the hard,

menial and low-paid tasks to slaves, the white workers were led to constitute a labor aristocracy which held the best and most dignified jobs,
and that the latter were lucrative only because they were supported by the
super-profits wrung from the unpaid labor of slaves. Unless abolitionism
was "met and repelled" . . . the whites would have to take over the menial
jobs and the emancipated slaves would be able to compete with them in
every branch of industry.[36]

White laborers, both North and South, believed that emancipation was a
plot of Northern capital to lower wages and enlarge its labor pool. Insis-
tent propaganda pounded this line across; anti-slavery men were called
"Midas-eared Mammonites" who wanted to bring Southern slaves into the
North to "compete with and assist in reducing the wages of the white
laborer."[37] First-hand experience with the use of slaves in the South and
of free Negroes in the North to break strikes made this story quite believ-
able. And indeed, minus the allegation of complicity between abolitionists
and capitalists, there was more than a grain of truth in it.[38]

One more point needs to be made before the freed United States
Negro and mulatto are properly located in relationship to the immense
economic and political forces which were building race relations in their
country as they swept the North and South toward civil war. One gains
the distinct impression that fear of slave uprisings in the United States was
far more pervasive than it was in Brazil, considering the relatively large
number of armed whites who confronted the defenseless, brutalized and
brainwashed slaves. However, this fear was not based on miscalculation
of the enemy. For unlike the case in Brazil, the enemy was not merely the
slave, but an organized, vocal, persistent and steadily increasing group of
skilled abolitionists who from the very day this country was founded dedicated their lives to the destruction of the slave power. Although Brazil was
not entirely devoid of abolitionist sentiment early in the nineteenth century, the scope and intensity of anti-slavery agitation cannot be compared
with the furor in the United States. A congressional investigating committee in 1838 was told that there were 1,400 anti-slavery societies in the
United States with a membership of between 112,000 and 150,000.[39] In
Brazil, the lucky slave fled to a *quilombo,* where cut off from all contact
with the rest of the world, the best he could hope for was that the dogs
would not find him. In the United States, however, the whole North was a
vast *quilombo* in which not only were there escaped slaves but free men of
all colors, actively and openly campaigning to bring an end to the thrall-
dom of the whip. The constant patrolling of Southern roads, the fierce
punishments for runaways, the laws discouraging manumission, the
lumping of free mulattoes with free Negroes, their harassment and persecution and the refusal to permit either of them to reside in some of the
slaveholding states, were all part and parcel of the same problem. One
wonders what effect it would have had in Brazil, if the larger and more
powerful part of the country had been officially dedicated to the proposition that slavery ought to be abolished, and if in every major city in that
region freed Negroes and mulattoes had preached and plotted the over-

throw of the system. In a sense, the Civil War did not begin in 1860, but in 1776. From the moment this country came into existence the issue of Negro rights was caught in a thousand conflicting currents and counter-currents. Under these circumstances, it hardly seems reasonable to conclude that it is our "Anglo-Saxon Protestant heritage" which is at fault. Indeed there are so many more palpable things at which to point, that I hope I will be forgiven for mentioning only the few which seem to me most important.

Notes

1. Dumond 1961:5.
2. *Ibid.:*16 ff.
3. *Ibid.:*120.
4. *Ibid.:*123.
5. Compare these two observations about the effects of slavery on children in the United States and Brazil: "The whole commerce between master and slave is a perpetual exercise of the most boisterous passions, the most unremitting despotism on the one part, and degrading submissions on the other. Our children see this, and learn to imitate it. . . . The parent storms, the child looks on, catches the lineaments of wrath, puts on the same airs in the circle of smaller slaves, gives loose to the worst of passions, and thus nursed, educated, and daily exercised in tyranny, cannot but be stamped by it with odious peculiarities." (Thomas Jefferson, quoted in Dumond 1961:28–29.) "And what are the sons of these sluggards like? . . . The inhumanities and the cruelties that they practice from early years upon the wretched slaves render them all but insensible to the sufferings of their neighbors. . . . No sooner do we acquire intelligence than we observe, on the one hand, the lack of delicacy, shamelessness, dissoluteness, and disorderly conduct of the slaves, and on the other hand the harsh treatment, the thrashings, the blows that these unfortunates receive almost every day from our elders. . . . And what is the inevitable result of all this, if not to render us coarse, headstrong, and full of pride?" (Lopes Gomes, quoted in Freyre 1956:392).
6. Quoted in Diffie 1945:660.
7. Furtado 1959:21.
8. Wertenbaker 1959:15, quoting the Virginia Council in 1608.
9. *Ibid.:*124.
10. Dumond 1961:374, from the Board of Trade. Georgia, which had barely emerged from Spanish control at this time, was very sparsely populated. However, in 1761 there were an estimated 6,100 whites to fewer than 3,570 Negroes. (Greg 1941:100–101.)
11. Furtado 1959:n.81.
12. Cardozo 1960–61:247.
13. Frazier 1949:176.
14. Cardozo and Ianni 1960:247.
15. IBGE 1961:169.
16. Cardozo 1960–61:247.
17. Frazier 1949:39 and 62.
18. Cortesão and Calmon 1956:476; Oliveira Vianna 1937:86; Diffie 1945:668–673.
19. Oliveira Vianna 1937:84.
20. Simonsen 1937:228.
21. Prado Júnior n.d.:45.
22. Simonsen 1937:237, quoting Antonil.
23. *Ibid.:*232.
24. Furtado 1963:63–71.
25. Freyre 1956:57.

26. Furtado 1963:28.

27. *Ibid.:*59.

28. "Nearly three fourths of all free Southerners had no connection with slavery through either family ties or direct ownership. The 'typical' Southerner was not only a small farmer but also a nonslaveholder." (Stampp 1956:30.)

29. *Ibid.:*426.

30. Mandel 1955:38.

31. *Ibid.:*40, quoting F. W. Pichins.

32. *Ibid.:*40, quoting Edmund Ruffin.

33. *Ibid.:*50, quoting Cassius Marcellus Clay.

34. *Ibid.:*59.

35. Lincoln regarded the Thirteenth Amendment as a military measure worth a million soldiers. Williams, L. 1961:187. Wesley (1962) views the confusion over the cause of the Civil War as part of the continuing battle for Negro rights.

36. Mandel 1955:57.

37. Dumond 1961:352, quoting Henry Field James.

38. Cf. Preyes's (1961) description of Negro textile workers.

39. *Ibid.:*258; according to McManus (1961:207), "Practically every American leader during the Revolution favored some plan of emancipation."

References

CARDOZO, MANOEL. "Slavery in Brazil as Described by Americans." *The Americas,* Vol. 17 (1960).

CARDOZO, FERNANDO HENRIQUE AND OCTÁVIO IANNI. *Cor e mobilidade social em Florrianópolis.* São Paulo: Companhia Editôra Nacional, 1960.

CORTESÃO, JAIME AND PEDRO CALMÓN. *Brasil.* Barcelona: Salvat Editores, 1956.

DIFFIE, BAILEY WALLYS. *Latin American Civilization: Colonial Period.* Harrisburg: The Telegraph Press, 1945.

DUMOND, DWIGHT LOWELL. *Antislavery.* Ann Arbor, Mich.: University of Michigan Press, 1961.

FRAZIER, E. FRANKLIN. *The Negro in the United States.* New York: Macmillan, 1949.

FREYRE, GILBERTO. *The Masters and the Slaves.* New York: Alfred A. Knopf, 1956.

FURTADO, CELSO. *Formaçao econômica do Brasil.* Rio de Janeiro: Editôra Fundo de Cultura, 1959.

INSTITUTO BRASILEIRO DE GEOGRAFIA E ESTATÍSTICA (IBGE). *Contribuições para o estudo da demografia do Brasil,* 1961.

MANDEL, BERNARD. *Labor: Slave and Free* (NEW YORK: ASSOCIATED AUTHORS, 1955).

MC MANUS, EDGAR. "Antislavery Legislation in New York." *Journal of Negro History,* Vol. 46 (1961).

OLVEIRA VIANNA, F. J. *Evolución del pueblo Brasileño.* Buenos Aires, 1937.

PRADO JÚNIOR, CAIO. *História econômica do Brasil.* 6th ed. Editôria Brasilense.

PREYES, NORRIS. "The Historian, the Slave and the Antebellum Textile Industry." *Journal of Negro History,* Vol. 46 (1961).

SIMONSEN, R. *História econômica do Brasil,* Vol. 1. São Paulo: Companhia Editôra Nacional, 1937.

WERTENBAKER, THOMAS J. *The Planters of Colonial Virginia.* New York: Russell and Russell, 1959.

WESLEY, CHARLES. "The Civil War and the Negro." *Journal of Negro History,* Vol. 47 (1962).

WILLIAMS, LORRAINE. "Northern Intellectual Reaction to the Policy of Emancipation." *Journal of Negro History,* Vol. 46 (1961).

Robin W. Winks
THE CANADIAN NEGRO:
A HISTORICAL
ASSESSMENT

PART I: THE NEGRO IN THE
CANADIAN-AMERICAN RELATIONSHIP

During the 1960's, English-speaking Canadians often angered those who spoke French by demanding that they "talk white," that is, speak only English.[1] Many Anglo-Canadians would have insisted that no insult to black men was intended by the implication that only the white man's language was civilized, for they would have thought the Negro and his experiences irrelevant to the Canadian scene. But the Negro is not irrelevant to Canada,[2] nor has Canada been irrelevant for the Negro.

The Negro has been present on what today is Canadian soil for nearly as long as on American. The Negro Canadian, like the Negro American, has experienced discrimination, vast uprootings, and the frustrating impotence of potential but badly used political power. Slavery was accepted in British North America long after most Northern states, by their constitutions, judicial decisions, or legislation had ended the practice. Ironically, between 1787 and 1800, fugitive slaves from Canada fled south into New England and the Northwest Territory, reversing the more widely-known direction of flow. Canadians took their place in the broad, continentally-oriented abolitionist movement which culminated in the American Civil War, a war profound in its effects on Canada as well as on the United States. After the war Canadians, too, deferred full equality for the Negro and helped segregate him in his own schools, on occasion into all-Negro communities, and, until World War I, into separate military units. Canadians, too, embraced the racist assumptions so widely held at the turn of the century, which culminated in the United States in the highly restrictive immigration act of 1924. Canadians, too, attempted to bar undesirable races at the gates, or to persuade Negroes, Orientals, and South Asians that they would be unable to tolerate the bleak Canadian climate. The Ku Klux Klan, race rioting, and poll taxes were not unknown to Canadian Negroes in the twentieth century. Canada and the Canadian Negro thus played their part in the centuries of unfolding interracial drama in North America. Patterns of behavior, white and black, primarily

REPRINTED FROM *The Journal of Negro History*, VOL 53, 1968 AND VOL. 54, 1969 BY PERMISSION OF THE AUTHOR AND THE PUBLISHER. THE PAPER, IN BOTH ITS PARTS, WAS FIRST READ TO A SEMINAR AT THE INSTITUTE FOR COMMONWEALTH STUDIES, IN THE UNIVERSITY OF LONDON, IN 1966. THE AUTHOR WOULD LIKE TO THANK THE DIRECTOR OF THE INSTITUTE, PROFESSOR W. H. MORRIS-JONES, FOR GIVING HIM AN OPPORTUNITY TO WORK AT THE INSTITUTE.

associated with the United States proved to be continental in their expression. Canada did not escape involvement in the long Negro story.

While engaged in the writing of a comprehensive history of the Negro in Canada, this writer has found himself entertaining five closely-related questions. To what extent does the Negro experience with Canadian institutions reveal those institutions to differ from or be similar to their counterparts in the United States? In what ways do the Canadian responses to the presence of Negroes support or refute the contention that Canada has failed to develop along paths unique to itself, along paths that would separate it from the United States ideologically and socially as well as politically? How has the Negro, common to both Canada and the United States, influenced relations between the two nations? How do black Canadians differ from black Americans? Should one speak of the Canadian Negro or of the Negro Canadian, of race or of nationality? These questions now demand their answers. That the answers will be incomplete and approximate only, that the answers will change as circumstances change, and that the answers are those of but a single historian should go without saying.

The Expected Negro: Norms. Methods used in studying race relations over time have been determined in part and obviously by prevailing points of view about race itself. The Greeks simply ignored the subject as unworthy; to an extent so did the Middle Ages, since religion and not race then set people apart. From Linnaeus forward a taxonomical view of race produced efforts to classify groups and to measure differences, the differences themselves being accepted with little inquiry. By the late nineteenth century a cultural point of view, in which leopards could change their spots (but probably would not, because of longstanding environmental pressures), opened the path to reform of those institutions that tended to promote the elevation of one race at the expense of another. In the twentieth century a sociological view, relativistic, potentially compassionate, holds forth the assumption that not only must the leopard change some of his spots, but that non-leopards must learn to value leopards. Historians, lost in this maze of metaphor and theory, have tended to write of race relations in terms of concrete data: of wars, native legislation, leadership struggles, and specific instances of conflict. But more recently historians have come to realize that they must know far more about conflict itself and about the nature of social thought, if they are to understand race as an emotional issue that motivates, at least partially, a large proportion of mankind.[3]

In truth, to twentieth century scholarship race became irrelevant except as a subject of popular delusion to be studied in terms of myth. But while scholarship turned up the paths so imaginatively opened by Durkheim and Weber, the popular mind was just beginning to seize upon the real vulgarizations of Darwin and Freud. In the United States the Negro became a stranger, a person close and yet distant, sharing with the white, it was thought, only the most rudimentary biological and social requirements. If race were irrelevant, culture was not, and the Negro was said to have formed a culture of his own, one which set him apart. Within limits this view was true, for the Negro was an entity just as surely as was the Italian-American or the Jew. But other ethnic groups, of whatever definition, passed through the traditional stages of assimilation in the United States, from first to second and ultimately third generation immigrants. The Negro alone remained always of the first generation, for however his cultural traits might in fact alter, his skin did not change, and he remained instantly identifiable as a person apart.

Many of the characteristics of American Negro life that our historians and sociologists have taught us to expect are to be found in the Canadian Negro as well. As in the United States, the Canadian Negro family tends to focus upon the mother as the enforcer of discipline in the home and as the most dependable breadwinner. As in the United States, Negroes in Canada have been, on the whole, underachievers, non-competitive except in athletics, professing to be satisfied with much that they ought not to accept. Self-created ghettos, self-segregated towns, as well as informally enforced white segregation, exist throughout Canadian Negro society. At the same time, centuries of deprivation, of being taught by the dominant white society to think of themselves as second class citizens, decades of intentional and unintentional insults, have led many Negroes into the familiar early stages of paranoia. Racial insults are detected where none were intended, and elaborately conceived plots are discovered against oneself, or one's race. Where persecution is real, delusions of persecution naturally will occur. Accustomed to expect prejudice, Negroes still will detect it even after the prejudicial conditions are removed.[4] Indeed, in these and other equally obvious outward manifestations of racial selfconsciousness, the Canadian Negro in no substantial way differs from the Negro in Massachusetts, or Michigan, or the Dakotas. At first glance, Canada seems to be simply an extension of the American North for him.[5]

Such also is the case for many white Canadians. The patterns of discrimination practiced by whites against blacks in Canada do not differ to any great degree from the patterns of discrimination observed in the Northern states. In 1944 the Swedish scholar, Gunnar Myrdal, in writing of "the rank order of discrimination,"[6] was able to isolate the various racial issues over which whites and Negroes felt most strongly. The highest bar the white raised against the Negro was over intermarriage and sexual intercourse involving white women. Next rose the question of general etiquette and social courtesies, including dancing, swimming, eating, and drinking together. Of slightly less importance to whites was the preservation of discrimination in the use of public facilities, such as schools, churches, and public transport. Political disenfranchisement again stood lower in priorities, followed by discrimination in the law courts and in access to land, credit, jobs, and social welfare. Myrdal found that the

Negroes' own rank order was roughly parallel but inverse: the Negro wanted an end to discrimination in acquiring land, credit, social welfare privileges, and jobs most, and he thought least of intermarriage. When applied to northern communities, Myrdal's hypothesis was found to be a generally accurate portrayal of white fears and Negro wants.[7]

Myrdal's scale also would hold true for Canada, with the one important exception of equality in job opportunities. Passing through longer and often more chronic stages of depression, faced with proportionately larger groups of immigrants to be assimilated, plagued with persistent unemployment, and on the whole less idealistic and philanthropic and less buoyed by ideological and messianic national purposes, Canadians had good reason to place the power to grant or to withhold work higher in the order of discrimination, and Canada moved more slowly than the United States toward recognizing the need for legislation which would assure equality of access to employment. But Myrdal's hypothesis does apply to Canada.[8]

In yet other ways white Canadians reflected a continental norm. They excepted those Negroes who achieved prominence in the areas of spectator sport and public entertainment from discrimination. They believed that Negroes were inherently less intelligent than whites, and the only widely-available intelligence tests administered to Negroes in Canada tended to support this belief.[9] White Canadians considered Negroes lazy, childlike, either rural dullards or urban pseudo-sophisticates.[10] West Indians also were Negroes, although to be viewed as a group apart, for they were aggressive, invariably urban, thought to be morally loose, and sufficiently hard working to constitute a threat. The good Negro was the quiet Negro, the man who knew his place, and who would, as one Negro herself put it, mix but not mingle. "Negroes have no history," remarked a New Brunswick white who had studied the Negro settlement at Loch Lomond for the New Brunswick Historical Society.[11] Somehow it seemed fitting that in 1954 a Negro was voted Hamilton's man of the year: he was a garbage collector who over the years had quietly hauled away the tons of offal Hamilton could not otherwise discharge.[12]

As in the United States, the Negro was a convenient figure around which to shape a moral and sexual mythology. Countless lavatory graffiti testified to the greater attractiveness of what with surpassing vulgarity was called "black meat"; Negro chorus lines were reportedly the most risque of all in Montreal, and a West Indian nightclub singer in Winnipeg was barred before he could perform on the well known principle that Calypso songs are objectionable. Windsor barkeepers designated separate "jungle rooms" for Negroes until 1951. Canadian smut peddlers, weekly tabloids such as *Tab* and *Flash,* missed few opportunities to report of presumably undesirable Negroes, from race track touts to wife beaters, often with lurid and sensational photographs. And white Canadians were certain that the world was not yet ready for the children that would result from interracial marriages.[13]

The Canadian-American Relationship and the Negro. But Canadians are not, after all, Americans, and they have never been more conscious of this political fact, or more eager to demonstrate the contention as a cultural and social reality, than during the recent past. As a result, Canadian attitudes toward the United States also shaped Canadian attitudes toward Negroes. Until the Canadian Labour Congress, through its National Committee on Human Rights, began to turn the intense light of publicity upon repeated instances of racial discrimination, Canadians viewed the United States in the midst of its racial dilemma with a clear assumption of moral superiority, as Canadians often have done when the United States has fallen over its own egalitarian rhetoric. Canadian reactions to the rhetoric tended to be tinged with and supported by anti-Americanism.

Canadians have long felt they were in a position to understand the United States and to explain its peculiarities to the British. As early as 1846 an observant, shrewd British visitor, Richard Henry Bonnycastle, commented on Canada's sense of being an instrument for transmission and translation of American ideas,[14] and over the years Canadians seemed quite willing to accept the rôle of coupling-pin, linch-pin, or golden hinge, as the changing metaphors had it, between the New World and the Old. This was little more than a desire to find a unique function for the 'merging Canadian nation to perform so that it might have an identifiable rôle on the international scene. It is by no means a harmful rôle to have assumed, nor is it an entirely inaccurate one, although it must be classed with those instruments of self-identification which Hans Kohn, one of the leading students of nationalism, has termed "the vital lie."[15] A vital lie is not unnecessarily untrue; indeed, there may be operable truths buried within it. But it is widely accepted, essential to a nation's self esteem, and usually not open to proof. The United States has generated a number of such vital lies, and understandably so too has Canada: for years the linch-pin concept has been one of the most vital.

Most Canadians believe that they understand the American political system and that they are uncommonly well-informed on American matters. There is little evidence to support this belief, but it is the belief that counts. Given this long-standing conviction that matters obscure even to the most astute of the United States's own political and social critics are as uncut crystal to Canadian observers, Canadians not unnaturally have felt free to comment often and at length on America's racial problems. Sometimes the comments are accurate. Usually the comments flatter Canada, again sometimes properly so. But invariably a note of selfrighteousness must enter into any monologue in which one party judges another, and especially so when the party being judged so patently is not listening.[16]

Canadian comments about American racial problems are further colored by the fact that few Canadians are well-informed on Canada's own Negro record. Cowper, in celebrating Justice Mansfield's decision, thought that "Slaves cannot breathe in England: if their lungs receive our air, that moment they are free." This was adequate poetry but inaccurate current events, for Mansfield's decision freed no substantial body of slaves, even in England, and in Imperial Britain they remained enslaved until 1834. Yet to this day most Canadians assume that slavery in British North America was struck down unilaterally by colonial assemblies which, in fact, lacked power to move against such Imperial laws. A standard account of Ontario's history, published in 1898, concluded that because of the passage of Simcoe's Bill (which prohibited the import of slaves) in 1793, "Canadians can therefore claim the proud distinction for their flag . . . that it has never floated over legalized slavery." An extensive guidebook to Canada credits the entire Negro population of Nova Scotia to men "who came north as slaves from the British West Indian colonies . . . , " ignoring totally the Maroon and Refugee elements. An attempt to plumb the character of Canadians found that the Negroes of the Maritime provinces—15,000 in all—were descendants of runaway slaves, when in truth not even half are such.[17] And one of Canada's leading students of race relations, in writing specifically of discrimination against the Negro, asserts that slavery did not exist in British North America in the Nineteenth Century, although slavery was in fact legal until 1833. In short, there is no accurate historical memory in Canada of British North America's own experiences with the Negro, and even a clouded awareness of an earlier Negro presence is slight. Thus, Canadians do not suffer from the usual heavy hand of historical sensitivity that holds the few back from commenting upon the ills of the many.

The effect of this lack of historical awareness in Canada—a lack, indeed, that extends to many more pervasive areas than Negro history—is three-fold. Canadians comment freely and unencumbered by the facts, for what commonly is accepted is apocrypha, and apocrypha are not easily pruned. Finding that their record is clean, and seen to be clean, they may like Caesar's wife be expected to find much ill and little good in those who are so clearly unclean. And action on behalf of the Negro in Canada is slow to find direction, or even expression, since so few are aware of the need for action.

During the decades before the Civil War, the Canadian press was quick to chastise the United States. The Toronto *Globe,* fountainhead of abolitionism in Canada, repeatedly pointed out how Americans spoke much of their liberty and yet imprisoned those who, following the dictates of their conscience, aided slaves to escape. The ills Canada had, the *Globe* opined, were light in comparison. In 1812 pro-slavery senators had conspired to add Canada to the union as free territory in exchange for northern support in acquiring Cuba and portions of Mexico, then ripe for slavery expansion. In 1852 Canadians again were warned that the United States wished to add Canada to its thirty-two stars, and that slavery, the "dread ulcer, eating and destroying the otherwise healthy frame," made this a most unattractive prospect. As thousands of fugitive slaves streamed into Canada West after 1850, Canadians came to hate the United States the more but also to love the Negro less. Nonetheless, Canadians did give refuge to thousands of fugitives, and the mythology of the underground railway, the North Star, and the lion's paw naturally fed the later Canadian assumption that Negroes continued to fare better in Canada than elsewhere.[18]

Yet, Canada was not so much a magnet as the slave states were a propelling force. Slaves fled to wherever freedom was, and the destination changed with the times, and the times changed with European diplomacy. Not only was the Negro imprisoned: even his havens initially were defined in the capitals of far off Europe, and seldom did the defining take the Negroes still in slavery into account. The havens changed: to the Dutch, the Indians, the British army, even Mexico; to the French, the Northern states, to British North America. For the Negro, the provinces were as far away from the slave states as one might go by land. Canada as a congeries of colonies with free institutions did not so much attract as distance itself did, and unfree institutions in the American South propelled.

The Canadian haven was not a nation or a region—it was more of a process than a place. And only one area of British North America actually came to represent a place where the process could be carried out. Canada East, later Quebec, was alien because of the French language. The Maritime Provinces were too distant, perhaps too maritime since most of the Negroes who escaped from the old southwest after 1850 knew little of the sea, and too cold; Negroes believed that in this uttermost extremity of the earth was the land where the wild geese went, and that it was covered over with feathers. The snow stood twelve feet deep and summer, such as there was, came for but a month (and the Jamaican Maroons would have been pleased to confirm this). The West Coast, while ideally distant, was impossible to attain. But Canada West had desirable characteristics besides distance: the winters were less formidable, the people spoke English, the laws were British, it was near the terminal points of the informal escape routes, and it had an agricultural base not unlike some of the upper South. In truth, only Canada West served to any considerable extent as a haven for fugitive slaves, but the whole of the Canadian nation later accepted a mythology arising from but one of its units. By the twentieth century few Canadians had occasion to remember their segregated schools, the inability of the fugitives to find urban employment, or that the United States did, after all, fight a Civil War that, when all revisionism is done, was over slavery.

The British and the Canadians must be praised for their staunch opposition to slavery. No other nation so consistently battled the institution on the sea and in the embassies of the world than Britain, and canadians did provide a haven, whether passively or actively. But anti-Americanism as well as genuine compassion for the fugitive helped to explain Canadian actions. Dislike for the United States as a whole often found its most effective expression in denunciations of slavery and of the Federal government, which appeared to be harboring it, and even Northern travelers in the Canadas were referred to by otherwise intelligent Canadians as slaveholders. As John Charlton, a young abolitionist, noted, prejudice against the United States around Simcoe was so strong that American maps were not allowed in classrooms. The *Globe* argued that Canadians had the "duty of preserving the honour of the continent" against slavery. From its founding in 1846 the Montreal *Witness,* a "weekly review and family newspaper," attacked the United States and slavery as though they were synonymous. For the first volume alone, no fewer than twenty articles, poems, and editorials were written in opposition to slavery. A typical piece related how a young slave girl was hanged in New Orleans for striking her mistress, remarked that the religious press of the North had been silent on the incident, and concluded that the affair was "a hideous offshoot of American Republicanism and American Christianity." The story was not compromised for its readers by its assumption that New Orleans was in Mississippi or because the editor of the *Witness* apparently saw "beneath that dark skin a *white* soul wrung by mortal agony." Charles Stuart, the leading Canadian abolitionist, lost no occasion to emphasize "the deep filth of sin in which [the United States] is now proudly wallowing," and when invited to the United States he found that he could not "dutifully expose my wife and myself to the outrages of of [*sic*] a power so ferocious, so hypocritical, and so base as [America's] present, de facto, government." The entire American people were "democratical-demagogical . . . ." This was in 1840.[19]

If Stuart so wrote in 1840, anti-Americanism remained to color and to confuse Canada's response to its own Negro population into the present century. In 1860 Samuel Gridley Howe noted that ". . . the Canadians constantly boast that their laws know no difference of color; that they make blacks eligible to office and protect all their rights; and the refugees constantly admit that it is so. The very frequency of the assertion and of the admission proves that it is not considered a matter of course that simple justice should be done. People do not boast that the law protects white men."[20] In 1904 a writer for the nationalistic *National Monthly* maundered, "Canada is a wonderful country, one to be proud of; the beginning of a great nation, and Toronto one of its greatest cities. Let us remember that the colors in the maple leaf are brighter every year, and never forget, 'Canada for Canadians' . . . . The most subtle, pertinacious, sneaking, hypocritical foe Canada has is that 'free' and 'enlightened' land that waves the Stars and Stripes . . . . When New York had only a population of 250,000, did she have the magnificent buildings, the beautiful parks, the fine residences, and the excellent colleges that Toronto has? Toronto could outdo her at every turn." In the same issue an article, related in so-called Negro dialogue rife with "gwine be" and "in dere," told of the escape to Canada of two slaves from Maryland who leapt from ice floe to ice floe across Lake Champlain.[21] Canadians had never quite recovered from *Uncle Tom's Cabin.*

Canadian reporting into the mid-twentieth century differed in content but not in kind from these examples. There were eight major race riots in the United States between February, 1942, and August, 1946. All but one—in Los Angeles in 1943—involved white-Negro clashes. The most sanguinary riot, that in Detroit in June, 1943, resulted in 34 deaths and 461 injuries, and in army occupation of the city. In 1943 three Negroes were lynched in the South. The Canadian press neglected none of these developments, and rightly so, for they were news, but the accompanying editorials seldom neglected to invoke the memories of the lion's paw. And in the 1950's the Toronto *Globe and Mail* attacked the segregated services of the American South, again accurately, but without reference to the presence of prejudice in Canada.[22]

Where racial prejudice was found to exist in Canada, it was widely attributed to the "American virus." As the Montreal *Witness* ambivalently observed in 1848, color prejudice was strong in Canada, but if God made Negroes as they were, why should man condemn His work. Yet, God apparently needed help, for "In Canada . . . we must necessarily, trace the prejudice of colour to the neighbouring States . . . ." This evil was to be blocked at the border, the *Globe* argued, for no good Briton would tolerate it. During the immigration debates between the 1890's and the 1920's, Canadians were urged not to acquire American prejudices, but at the same time, Orientals and American Negroes were to be barred if possible, since the presence of any substantial body of Negroes could give rise to discrimination—a clear-cut confession that the Canadian people could not be trusted not to discriminate, infection apparently already having taken place. In the 1950's instances of discrimination in Alberta almost without exception were blamed on the several thousand Americans living in the province.

During the discussions in the late 1950's and early 1960's of lowering the immigration barriers against West Indians, many Canadian newspapers defended the necessity to block out the West Indians, "not from prejudice" but "to prevent Canada from developing a problem" of its own. Canada could help solve the "racial question," the *Globe and Mail* thought, by extending aid to the West Indies so that there would be enough jobs in the islands to keep West Indians home; Canada could be kept white by decreasing motivations for Negroes to come. Why should we want a terrible race problem in Canada, a reader of the same newspaper asked; Negroes could not live in the Canadian climate nor assimilate with Canadian whites. "This is said with no ill will to any Negro or to the colored people as a whole." Speaking at a press conference in Madison, Wisconsin, in May of 1960, Ellen Fairclough, Canada's Minister of Immigration, reported that "Canada has no racial problem. Nor has Canada a racial policy. And that's the way it's going to stay." The "American virus" could be kept out by keeping the black man out as well.[23]

But the nature of the impact of those institutions shaped primarily in the United States upon parallel but frequently dissimilar institutions in Canada has not received the study it deserves. Certainly American ideas, whatever they may be, have their influence in Canada, just as "Americanization," a shorthand term for many of the developments that flow naturally from industrialization, urbanization, and mass democracy, has its influence around the world. But if Canadian institutions and values are themselves strong, and more desirable than their American counterparts, they should be able to resist less attractive, or less valuable, American institutions or values. If one accepts shoddy goods, surely part of the blame falls upon the purchaser. So, too, then does the frequent Canadian argument that racist sentiment in Canada is to be traced to the United States turn back to the more fundamental question, why should Canadians be willing to accept such sentiments if, indeed, they oppose them?

When we speak of "American ideas" thought to be operative in British North America in the pre-Civil War period, in particular, we must speak with caution. America itself still drew many of its ideas from Britain, and later would draw heavily from the continent of Europe, and while in public education, land use, and agricultural policy the United States may have generated new ideas that influenced Canada, in many areas America merely modified British attitudes. It is impossible to tell whether a particular Canadian practice arose from direct contact with Britain or through an American modification, although consciously Canadians tended to look to Britain for guidance in economic policy, relations between church and state, and foreign affairs, and until the turn of the present century political rhetoric was British. Whenever Grits or Tories found something they disliked, they were nearly certain to discover that it stemmed from the baleful American influence. Even scholars, more likely to be attracted to the theory than to the practice of political accommodation, often tended to make an unwarranted leap of faith between the evidence that Canadians talked and wrote about "American" practices and the conclusion that those same Canadians practiced what they preached.

This caution is not to dismiss the general contention that Canada is exposed to an exceptional barrage of cultural artillery from across the border. Canada has but a single immediate neighbor from which to draw ideas, while most nations are influenced and tempered by several diverse national pressures. The majority of Canadians speak approximately the same language as do Americans, adding to the facility with which ideas, and especially simpler ideas, may be transmitted; moreover, they read the same magazines and view the same television programs. For over a century Canadians had cause to watch warily developments in the United States, for they feared an American invasion, and once the fear of physical invasion passed the greater reality of a cultural invasion kept Canadians intent upon the United States.

Canadians see Negroes, then, through an American lens refracted by Canadian institutions. The only Negro a Manitoba farm boy is likely to have seen is at the motion picture theatre.[24] Canadians learn from television and their press of the Congress of Racial Equality, of the Student Non-Violent Coordinating Committee, of sit-ins, civil disobedience, and assassination, and they watch with a dulled, quiet fascination, as this writer knows from many an evening spent watching the watchers in darkened YMCA recreation rooms across Canada. *Life, Newsweek, Time,* and *Look* have effectively championed Negro rights, and readers of these magazines in Canada have learned much of the subject as it relates to the United States. Canadian magazines, too, especially *Maclean's, Saturday Night,* and *Canadian Forum,* have kept their readership well informed of developments with respect to race relations.[25] Indeed, therefore, a portion of the racism to be found in Canada no doubt is to be credited to "American influence," just as the recent Canadian discovery of that racism also is to be credited in part to the rise of concern in the United States for civil rights.

But on the whole white Canadians did not realize that they had amongst them Negroes also in need, Negroes who also had been forced to "think white," Negroes who were the object of Canadian, not imported American, discrimination. By the 1960's some Canadian journals had come to remind Canadians that they should not be self-righteous about racial troubles in the United States, and also to remark that the Canadian pot is not as black as the American kettle, since Canadian Indians, Eskimos and Negroes are not treated as Negroes are treated in Alabama.[26] This healthy middle ground between self-righteousness and hysterical self-contempt, both extreme positions not uncommonly taken today, was evidence of the common sense of most Canadian responses, but it also helped to mute the voices of Canadian reform in racial matters.

Nonetheless, a number of Canadians in responsible or vocal positions at last were aware of a problem at home. The hard glare of publicity given to specific instances of discriminatory acts in rental or sale of property, publicity usually given by newspapers which do not think of themselves as quality productions but which are widely read, such as the Toronto *Star* and *Telegram,* has improved the Negro's situation considerably. The active work of the Committee on Human Rights within the Canadian Labour Congress has resulted in Fair Accommodations and Fair Employment Practices acts in seven of the ten provinces. Former Prime Minister John Diefenbaker's personal desire for a Canadian Bill of Rights has given legal expression to several vaguely held but widely cherished attitudes. Increasingly enlightened welfare agencies, and metropolitan administrations, have worked to undo the effects of generations of ignorance and neglect. "Civil rights" has begun to be a popular phrase upon the lips of college students. Numerous investigations of the Negro, usually by sociologists, have resulted in a fund of statistical information for Halifax, Montreal, and Toronto. Canadian reprint editions of American books on the Negro, including Booker T. Washington's *My Larger Education,* James Baldwin's *Notes of a Native Son,* and Martin Luther King's *Why We Can't Wait,* attest to a growing interest in the Negro problem in the United States.[27] If knowledge must precede action, one may presume that Canadians are ready for action.

But this recent modest growth of knowledge and interest in the Negro too often seemed to lack direction. Baldwin is, after all, good literature, and King was a window into American events. How many Canadians, one wonders, are reading these inexpensive reprints with a view to Canadian affairs? The Negroes of Halifax, and especially of Africville, are one of the most studied groups of people in North America, but the studies seem not to have helped them. If the Toronto and Vancouver press—and a portion of the press in Montreal—are alert to civil rights, the press of Halifax and Fredericton, indeed of the entire Maritime Provinces, seem moribund by comparison. The knowledge thus purveyed often is shallow and simple-minded: ". . . the Negro is *awakening,* as the *colored races* everywhere are. He won't *accept* much longer a status of inferiority," noted a Calgary paper. "Colored Folk Are Like Other People," or so the Chatham, Ontario, *Daily News* discovered for its readers in 1959. There is no discrimination in Canada, we are told by a third, yet young Negro men were leaving Ontario for Detroit since "In Canada, few decent jobs are available for men of color." Even the several theses written in Canadian universities on slavery, fugitives, or more recent developments, are documents of despair, for with but two exceptions— both the work of Negro scholars—they are devoid of understanding. In 1950 when the Canadian Labour Congress distributed its first anti-discrimination pamphlet, "Discrimination Costs You Money," tolerance was presented as a necessary evil, for worker Joe was clumsily asked to work with Negroes, Catholics, and Jews for union solidarity and financial gain. No doubt the Labour Congress knew its audience, and perhaps no appeal to idealism would have worked as well.[28]

Others who had good cause to know better continued to ignore the Negro. In Nova Scotia the Women's Institutes sponsored a provincial volume on the *Canadian Mosaic,* a series of essays on those groups which make up the Canadian nation. The volume contained chapters on Indians, Vikings, Acadians, Germans, United Empire Loyalists, but 12,000 Negroes were unaccountably absent. In 1962 in celebration of Victoria's centennial, the city presented a "pageant-spectacular . . . taken from actual historical records"; time was given to "Ethnic Groups" to perform. Polish, Norwegian, Danish, and Italian communities were represented, but the Negroes were not, so well forgotten was Mifflin Wister Gibbs and the settlers of Salt Spring Island. John Murray Gibbon, in his *Canadian Mosaic,* had no occasion to mention the Negro at all. When an "inquiring sidewalk reporter" in Brantford, Ontario, asked a selection of whites what they thought of discrimination, nearly all responded in terms of the United States: ". . . well I think the States is kind of im-

mature"; "no one [in Canada] can complain. Everyone has equal opportunities." When this writer moved across Canada in 1960 and again in
1965, he met with similar responses. A distinguished historian remarked,
"Surely the Negroes are an unimportant subject!" A television interviewer
dismissed the subject abruptly: "We live in Canada, which is not the
United States." "You know, we're not prejudiced; in fact, some of our
best friends are Negroes," said an Ontario Rotarian unconscious of
cliché. "The coloured always live in a clutter together and they're flashy
and high toned; they won't stay with their own class," remarked a
librarian in New Brunswick. "We have no race problem in our town,"
was the conclusion of a drug clerk in Dresden, although Negroes could
not obtain service in a restaurant across the street. "Hell," said a Vancouver taxi driver, "niggers? I don't even think about 'em. But I try not
to pick one up in my cab. They smell, you know."[29]

By mid-1965, however, an event in the United States appeared at
least temporarily to have jolted a larger group of white Canadians than
ever before into an awareness of needs that existed at home. Demonstrations in Selma, Alabama, were widely covered in all Canadian news
media, and nearly two thousand students in Toronto marched upon the
American consulate there, while students in Vancouver and Windsor
picketed consulates and others massed on Parliament Hill in Ottawa.
Selma became a Canadian synonym for the degradation of the Negro in
America. Premier Ross Thatcher of Saskatchewan, in launching a reform
plan to aid his province's ten thousand Indians and *métis,* suggested that
they were treated "not much better than the [Negroes] of Selma . . . ."
In Nova Scotia a renewed effort to raise living standards for Negroes
throughout the province was announced by the government, "as a result
of Canadian soul-searching inspired by reports of racial discrimination in
Selma . . . ." When interviewed for a Canadian Broadcasting Commission
television film, a Negro spoke more eloquently and more convincingly of
the real issue involved: "I just think we're all tied up in one single gar-
ment of destiny, and when one Negro is lynched a little bit of me is lynched
with him." After generations of apathy, neglect, and ignorance, white
Canadians seemed at least temporarily to have discovered the black man
in their midst.[30]

PART II: THE PROBLEM OF IDENTITY

The black man that Canadians discovered by the 1960's[31] was, in
fact, in many ways very different from the Negro in the United States.
The Canadian Negro, despite his longer period of legal freedom, despite
the lack of any historical memory within most white Canadians of an
indigenous slave period, and despite his comparative scarcity in Canada,
has been considerably less aggressive in seeking out and laying claim to
his rights. This seems at first all the more strange, since a process of
natural selection in all probability sent to Canada more energetic, enter-

prising, and imaginative Negroes than often remained in the American South.

To seek to escape from a slave master was an act in itself enterprising, and to make one's way safely to the far north required courage and energy as well as a large measure of good fortune. The great majority of fugitive slaves, as the overwhelming majority of Loyalist and Refugee Negroes, appear to have been from the states of the upper South, where the slave system and regimented gang labor were less firmly applied. Those who escaped from the upper South had at least some acquaintance with a primitively diversified agriculture and, unlike the Jamaican Maroons, who were taken to Nova Scotia in 1796, they did not expect to find tropical products springing from the Canadian soil. When one reads the scores of fugitive slave narratives, and the many scores of Canadian news reports of fugitive arrivals, one is struck with the number of fugitives who had come from Kentucky, Tennessee, Virginia, and Maryland. One also is struck with the number of fugitives who were designated as "very black." Whether this was a natural Canadian reaction to black skins, having encountered few, or whether the fugitives did tend to be darker than the generality of Negroes cannot be known, but on the whole the cumulative impact of the narratives is to convince one that a higher quality of Negro reached Canada. Certainly those Negroes who moved without the immediate propulsion of slavery—the Vancouver Island settlers of 1859, the western immigrants of the 1920's—were a self-selected and enterprising body of independent farmers, not without education or skill.

Yet the Canadian Negro as a whole does not seem to have shown the cumulative pride, energy, enterprise and courage that the catalog of individual acts of defiance would lead one to expect. In Canada Negroes continued to subscribe to Booker T. Washington's non-militant, essentially separatist, precepts long after W. E. B. DuBois had begun to move his fellow American Negroes toward militancy. Even today the majority of Negroes in Canada object to the word "Negro" and wish to be styled "coloured," a term which American Negroes, despite its retention in the title of their oldest national organization, have come to despise, just as others now reject "Negro" in favor of "black."[32] Racial pride seemed and seems noticeably lacking in all but the few militant urban Negro leaders and, perhaps, in the present generation of school age. As one investigator found, Negroes in Halifax appear to be midway between Southern and Northern American Negroes in their willingness to be submissive in the face of white leadership, and in the mid-1960's the presence of an activist Negro religious leader from Harlem, a leader who by Northern standards could scarcely be considered extremist since he clearly eschewed all resort to violence, initially proved an embarrassment to the majority of Haligonian Negroes. Indeed, Negroes in Nova Scotia were, until the spring of 1965,[33] so reluctant to make "radical" demands upon the closed white leadership of their province, they continued to accept segregated schools, inadequate public transport, and the designation "coloured," and only agitation by "outsiders"—Negroes from the West Indies and the United States—began to move the Nova Scotian Negro away from his general reliance on prayer and passivism.

There is, in fact, no *Canadian* Negro, for the Negroes of Nova Scotia and those of British Columbia have never been brought together in common cause through an organization or a leader. The Canadian Association for the Advancement of Colored People, which has little communication with its American counterpart, is in fact not a national organization at all, and the Nova Scotian Association for the Advancement of Colored People looks to the local Negro churches, and to the white-led Canadian Labour Congress, for guidance rather than to the Canadian Association. Individual Negro leadership nationally is lacking as well. Each community has its own spokesman but those leaders are little known elsewhere. Certainly no one of these men, not even those who have moved high into the administrative echelons of a national organization, such as A. R. Blanchette of the Brotherhood of Sleeping Car Porters or Violet King of the Citizenship Branch of the federal government, has been successful in rallying the Negroes of Canada together. There has been no Canadian Martin Luther King, no national figure to whom Negroes can turn, and perhaps it is their hunger for such a leader that induces the Negroes throughout Canada to speak of the dead, as Marcus Garvey, and of the distant, as Tom Mboya.

Nor is a national leader likely to emerge in Canada in the future, both because of the nature of the leadership Canadian Negroes have grown to accept locally and because of the schisms within the Negro communities themselves. The secular leadership often seems confused and divisive, projecting a contradictory image to the public: Negroes protest newspaper articles that direct attention to the race of a Negro criminal but when a Negro achieves distinction they wish the fact to be advertised in racial terms. They wage small battles to get boxed dates labelled "nigger brand" removed from a Montreal department store, or to force Maritime merchants to give up Pancake Day, an annual celebration in which displays of Aunt Jemima figure prominently[34]—and they ignore the larger war. In Ontario the Negroes attempt to identify with the Protestant community, in Quebec with the Jewish, and almost nowhere do they appear to identify with each other.[35] Where the Canadian Association for the Advancement of Colored People is disassociated from Negro churches, as in Vancouver, membership remains small and attendance at meetings even smaller. Where the associations are directly affiliated with a church, as in Nova Scotia, membership is larger but priorities of action differ preventing effective national cooperation and circumscribing the expression of alternative secular methods.

There are, of course, clear historical reasons why the Negroes of Canada have not brought forward an effective national leadership of their own. Very few Negroes are of the middle class, and those few who have become successful professional men have, on the whole, dispersed themselves into the Canadian community, achieving the assimilation they sought but without carrying any or many of their brethren with them. This is especially true in Montreal and in the prairie provinces, in the latter because there are so few brethren to carry in any case. Concern for sweeping reform is a luxury of the middle class; the lower class will settle for improvement for it is too ill-educated to plan for reform and too preoccupied with daily needs to forward it. Until recently few Negroes in Canada were above, at best, the lower middle class in social or economic standing.

Then, too, since Negro communities in Canada are seldom contiguous, since there is no black belt, no large urban ghetto, each Negro community has been ill-informed of developments by, on behalf of, or against Negroes elsewhere. There is no genuinely national newspaper in Canada to make these developments widely known in any case, and all attempts at founding successful Negro news outlets have foundered. One result has been the persistent tendency of Canadian Negroes to respond to queries about their hopes, plans, and frustrations with what may be called a "back then and over there" hypnosis. In virtually every Negro community the author visited—and between 1961 and 1968 he visited them all—Negro spokesmen would respond that conditions were not as good as they might wish, but that after all, life for them was much better than it had been for their fathers, and that, in any case, if one wished to see a community where conditions were genuinely bad, one should go to place X. In Amherst, Nova Scotia, a Negro thought that Truro was where one would find just how bad things could be; in Truro a Negro respondent suggested that Sydney represented the utter end of Negro degradation; in Sydney Negroes unanimously agreed that Halifax was the worst possible Negro community; in Halifax urban Negroes thought conditions were far worse in Amherst. In Dresden, Ontario, center of national publicity over the refusal of restaurants to serve Negroes in the face of a court order, Negro spokesmen suggested that one should look to the Maritimes for the more burdensome restraints, and in the Maritimes one was reminded that after all things were much worse for the Negro down in the Boston States. Indeed, the whole of the United States constituted a last resort, a monolithic "over there" to which Negroes could point when asked whether they had encountered any prejudice. If one naturally assumes that while conditions are bad they could be much worse, one is loathe to enter upon a path toward change for fear that indeed the much worse may come.

A few individuals among the fragmented and localized Negro leadership were aware of the need for change. These individuals, however, most often chose the path of prayer in seeking that change. Time and again the Negro has been told to cast his burdens upon the Lord, and cast he does Sunday after Sunday. Negro church leaders had every reason to preserve their own churches in order to preserve their power, and one cannot escape the conclusion that, as in the United States, while the Negro churches no doubt provided much consolation, they neither broke nor consumed the cake of custom. The African and British Methodist Episcopal Churches and the African Baptist Association[36] were often self-perpetuating, fundamentalist sects which, by sheering off from their white parent groups, saved everyone much embarrassment in the nineteenth century, when Negro forms of worship differed and when separate churches were the norm. But the continued existence of such churches *qua* organizations deep into the twentieth century, while possibly furthering individual salvation, also furthered segregation. A few leaders within these bodies were aware of this and some, such as Reverend William Oliver in the twentieth century and "Father" Josiah Henson in the nineteenth, moved slowly, very slowly, but sincerely to use the church as an effective tool for Negro material improvement as well as for spiritual uplift.[37] But most did not.

Without his own leadership, the Negro was without voice. Yet he recognized his need for a voice, and from the time of the Jesuit priests forward, he turned to interested whites who would speak for him. But too often whites, however well meaning, however affectionately they regard their Negro friends, however earnest students of Negro mores and problems they may be, are unable to understand the issues involved. London, Ontario, once the Oberlin of Canada, and in the twentieth century still, through Fred Landon, W. Sherwood Fox, and Sir Adam Beck, a center of genuine agitation for Negro equality, could not speak for Halifax any more than Boston may speak for Los Angeles. Perhaps because the Negroes of Canada West were more important to the abolitionist movement, they and their few leaders received prominence and the clusters of Negroes in British Columbia and the Maritimes were ignored. Even the most sincere of Canadian abolitionists—and abolition was for them, as for American abolitionists, but one of a myriad of reforms they advocated—seems not to have looked beyond abolition in the United States itself. Almost never did the religious rhetoric of Thomas Clarkson, the father of English abolitionism, or of Charles Stuart, his chief Canadian follower, cease being precisely that; Clarkson, the grandest of English anti-slavery enthusiasts, led no "life examined," and the abolitionists' religious assumptions about the rôle of the "Christian state" were never translated into action. But Negroes continued to think in terms of this Christian state long after the state had turned toward a secular society. If Clarkson was on occasion an unreliable judge of events, he was a perfectly reliable recorder of sentiments, but events stop and sentiments grow, and by 1900 Negroes still harbored sentiments no longer applicable to their world, and they still turned to whites to express for them their wants. Those few in Canada who, like Benjamin A. Walker, editor of Saint John's magazine *Neith* at the turn of the century, wished to speak for the black man, soon left for the United States, where the chances of being heard seemed greater.

Divided within themselves, Negroes in Canada too frequently depended upon whites and outside circumstances to move them forward. The abolitionists were but one such group. The predominately Jewish leadership of the Canadian Labour Congress was another, and the Congress has done more for Negro civil rights than any other organization in

Canada. Canadian Negroes also have benefited, as elsewhere, from cold war tensions, from the general awakening of Western man to the more obvious absurdities of racism, and from the elevation to public prominence of race conflict as a policy issue for nations. Where personal relations become public relations, the group suffering discrimination usually will gain, and the Negro in Canada has now learned the value of publicity.

But the Negro in Canada remains divided despite these recent forces that would move him together. He has been geographically, historically, and socially set against himself. His degree of sophistication, his knowledge of and response to the outside world, and his material success has differed widely from section to section of the country. He is not a group, for his Nova Scotian experience has differed from his experience elsewhere, at least in degree.

Why were those Negroes who made their way to Nova Scotia and their descendants so consistently less successful and more depressed than those who went to Canada West, to British Columbia, or to the prairie provinces? A portion, but only a portion of the answer lies in the physical environment of the Maritime Provinces, of course: most people in Nova Scotia tended to be poorer than most people in Ontario. This is an oversimplification, but the more hierarchical and older society of Nova Scotia had less room at the top or even in the middle than did the more open and expansive society of Canada West. The experience of white Nova Scotians with Negroes went much further back in time, and the proportion of Negroes to white population was consistently much higher than to the west. Nor on the whole were the Negroes who came to Nova Scotia as enterprising as those who, at a later date, made their way to the Canadas. The Nova Scotian Negroes, did not, in fact, make their way at all for they exercised little choice in the matter: the Loyalist Negroes were carried to the province by their masters, the Maroons were transported by the government of Jamaica, and the Refugees were moved by His Majesty's Navy. There was no substantial influx of self-propelled fugitive slaves at a later date to provide a more independent leadership. All of the earlier Negro groups in Nova Scotia became chronic dependents upon the charity of a province often itself in need of charity. Even today there is rather more *noblesse* and rather less *oblige* in Nova Scotia than in Ontario, and Canada as a whole seems not to have developed the philanthropist as a social type.

There was intermittent prosperity in Nova Scotia, of course, but precisely because of its intermittency, prosperity had little time to trickle down to those so clearly at the bottom of the barrel. One has but to contrast the buying power to be found in Halifax with that in Toronto in any given decade to see the hard economic facts. In Canada West the Negro often arrived with the white pioneers and won at least a modicum of respect early, in a region where land was plentiful, cheap, and productive. In Nova Scotia, except for the Loyalist Negroes, whites were well-established before the Negro arrival, and land while plentiful and in many instances provided by the province was unproductive and distant from markets. Finally, an element of caste was involved in the Nova Scotian relationship which was lacking in the simpler class structure of the Canadas. Yet the Nova Scotian Negro was the most numerous and this helped set the general Canadian stereotype.

These simple facts precede theoretical structures, but if one feels the need for such support, it exists. The theories of John Dollard on frustration and aggression apply well to the economically retarded province of Nova Scotia, while W. Lloyd Warner's class constructions also would be supported by the historical evidence. Marxist theorists would point out that prejudice in Canada West does not occur at the outset of settlement, since Negroes and whites were pioneers together, but during the 1840's and thereafter, when labor was badly needed for building the railroads, a surfeit of Irish immigration led to discrimination against the Negro. And the Irish did prove to be more hostile to the Negro in Canada West, whether along railway lines or elsewhere, than any other ethnic group within the province. In truth, the Negro in Canada became a superfluous man, for successive waves of European immigrants kept him from becoming important as a commodity, labor. The historian's difficulty in relying upon theory to support his mosaic of facts is that he does not know what will happen over the next decades (although he may be willing to guess), and unlike those who bolster their conclusions by reference to theories developed for other times and other places, historians are not armed with a doctrine that they believe will tell them. One observer who began with these theories before examining the data has noted that today Nova Scotian Negroes and Ontario Negroes differ precisely *because* they are in different environments.[38]

But it is not precisely that way at all. More basically, the various identifiable Negro groups in Canada differ because they have continued to preserve far more than have Negroes in the United States their own self-conscious class lines. The Canadian Negro is rent by divisions of his own making, divisions he perpetuates, divisions which to date have foiled every effort to organize Negroes in Canada nationally or to provide them with a single leadership which might be presumed to answer the persistent question, "Who speaks for the Negro?" In Canada no one does, least of all the Negro himself.

Contrary to popular thought, it is not that the Canadian Negro has too little history that holds him back, but that he has too much and that he remembers it too well. Negroes in Canada continue to identify themselves with the particular historical group to which they trace their ancestry. Nova Scotian Negroes have failed to unite, in part only but in large part, because they hold to rigid class lines that break them into four quite separate groups. Negroes who are descended from those who came as slaves with the United Empire Loyalists, or, preferably, as Black Pioneers, pridefully hold themselves to be as fully of the U.E.L. strain as the Sewells, Wentworths, Parrs, or Smiths, and so they are. Loyalist

Negroes today consider themselves superior to all other Negro groups in Canada.

With equal persistence if less cause, descendants of the Maroon Negroes of Jamaica set themselves apart, proud of their distant West Indian past. There are, indeed, very few such Negroes, but there are more who claim the heritage. The descendants of the Refugee Negroes, in all probability the largest number, are viewed by Loyalist, Maroon, and contemporary West Indian Negroes alike with ill-concealed disdain. And in Nova Scotia, Negroes traced from the few fugitive slaves who made their way to the province, and present-day American and West Indian Negroes, are treated as outsiders, warily admitted to the inner circle only if professional qualifications as preachers or school teachers dictate acceptance.

In Quebec province there is a similar cleavage between groups—a cleavage in part closed by the work of the Montreal Community Centre in the city's Negro ghetto revolving about St. Antoine Street—but a cleavage still visible and effective. Most West Indian migrants have gone to Montreal, Ottawa, or Toronto, and by a considerable margin the majority of West Indian students are in Montreal.[39] These West Indians hold themselves apart from the Canadian Negro, and to a considerable extent from each other, since island rivalries often are transferred to the new environment. A number of the remaining Negroes in Montreal are descended from a brief but intense migration of Harlem and urban Northern Negroes from the United States who moved into the city in the 1920's in order to continue the "sporting life" during the American experiment with prohibition. All other groups of Negroes in Canada have, until recently, held themselves aloof from the Harlemites, for the high life too often appeared to be the immoral life. The Canadian Negro tended to be pious, prudish even, for fear that he might behave in precisely the manner whites expected him to behave; to the consternation of the churchly group, the Harlem Negroes did fulfill the white stereotype, for they were for a time touts, pushers, pimps, and prostitutes. No longer is this the case, but the Canadian Negro groups still retain an unpleasant image of the American Negro. They have accepted the common Canadian assumption of moral superiority over the United States.

Nor is there any real sense of unity to the westward. In Ontario, where the majority of Negroes are descended from fugitive slaves, there is a greater degree of cooperation than in any other province, but here too the West Indian has held aloof and the more recent American Negro arrivals have stood apart as well. The residents of the isolated, semi-segregated Negro communities of the western prairies, in Maidstone, Saskatchewan, in Breton, Junkin's Corners, and Amber Valley in Alberta, are fully committed to rural values and too isolated to contribute effectively to the national cause. The Negroes of Calgary, Edmonton, and Winnipeg are highly transient, better-paid than most, and dependent until recently upon the railroads for which they worked, and their urban, mobile lives provided little opportunity for communication with the highly stable farming communities. Nor could the Negroes of Vancouver and Victoria, themselves separated by Juan de Fuca Strait and together separated from the rest of Canada by the Continental Divide, view themselves as other than a community apart. The Gulf Island Negroes, the majority on isolated Salt Spring Island, are even further cut off. While the far western Negroes do have some degree of mobility, and while those of the prairies have in recent years come to see themselves as forming a single group because of their shared historical experience with dryland farming between 1900 and 1920, they find little in common between themselves and Negroes in Ontario or the Maritime Provinces except the color of their skin, which as they rightly say, they are striving to make irrelevant.

There are at least four ways in which minorities may respond to group pressures: they may be pluralistic, assimilationist, secessionist, or militant. The whole of Canada, basically, is a pluralistic society. Dominant groups feel sufficiently secure to allow dissenters a certain leeway; each group in Canada emphasizes its own religious, linguistic, and cultural heritage. Thus, Canadian Negroes take the pluralistic path easily: they are not Black Muslims, or Back-to-Africanists, and seldom are they overtly assimilationist, for this path requires a melting pot mentality against which the entire Canadian ethos militates in favor of a mosaic. On the whole, then, Canadian Negroes do not break into the type of factionalism common among American Negroes: they are not divided, as in the United States, over alternative responses to pressure, with advocates of each response vying for voice, for power, for leadership. In Canada the Negro is divided not over means or ends but over ancestry, something of interest to comparatively few American Negroes, since the great majority are descended from slaves. The Canadian Negro is fully as rent as the American, indeed more so, but for different, and essentially less dynamic, less tension-producing, less productive reasons. Thus, the Canadian Negro is indolent in fighting for his own rights, for there are few active spokesmen creating controversy by presenting Canadian Negroes with alternate means or ends, forcing upon them thought, commitment, and action; and yet, negatively, the Negro in Canada is divided, not by anything productive but by the heaviest of the dead hands of the past, concern with who one's grandparents were.

Here, then, is one of the Canadian Negro's dilemmas. He wishes to be treated as a Canadian, as an individual, and to achieve this he must emphasize his individuality, not his group identity. But he also wishes to be granted the full exercise of his rights, and without a common organization, an organization that will emphasize rather than soften his racial identity, he cannot hope for widespread reform. Understandably, then, the Negro in Canada has tended to rely upon other groups to show the way toward civil liberties, to allow the Canadian Jewish community, itself far more cohesive and self-aware, to find the paths for upward mobility which the Negro may then follow. Widely dispersed nationally, if clustered locally, and brought to Canada in differing waves of immigration, waves which provided little common experience, and well aware that they would best avoid discrimination by attracting as little attention to themselves as possible, Negro Canadians not only failed to unite, they viewed Negro unity as the greater danger.

In the United States the Negro may, on the whole, assume himself to be the product of a common historical experience with slavery, civil war, and reconstruction, and as he wages his civil rights campaign, he does so with at least some sense of historical continuity and of ethnic unity. But in Canada the Negro's position was different from the outset, and the Negro Canadian who emerged from the period of abolitionism, a shared Civil War, and the racist thought of the late nineteenth century differed even more markedly than before from the Negro American.

The general Canadian response to environment, to immigration, and to cultural pluralism has differed in two important respects from the response in the United States, and as a result the Negro has come to occupy a rather different position in Canadian society than he does in American society. The first difference arises from the tendency of many Canadians, especially in the nineteenth century, to think of themselves as transplanted Europeans. While the American consistently and self-consciously asked Crèvecoeur's question, "What then is the American, this new man?" assuming by the query that the American had become, in fact, a new man, many Canadians continued to assert with equal vigor that they were representatives of European man and of European civilization, for white Canadians sought no new man in the New World. Given this feeling, the Negro in their midst was related by them to his origins, as a MacGregor, the O'Farrell, or a Thomas related himself to his Scots, Irish, and Welsh origins. To white Canadians the Negro was and is an African, as they are Europeans, and as such he is a sport, an exotic in a commonly shared but mutually alien environment. In short, while in the United States the Negro became an object of enslavement, discrimination, and even hatred, he came to be viewed (colonizationists aside) as a natural part of the new American social landscape, while in Canada the Negro may ultimately have achieved a measure of equality but he nonetheless was thought to be foreign to that landscape, equal but alien.[40]

A second, related, cultural response of white Canadians to their environment influenced the Negro Canadian as well. One traditional desire of immigrants newly arrived in the United States was to shed the old world and its ethnic badges of identity as quickly as possible. Immigrants to Canada have been far less eager to assimilate into some amorphous, anonymous North Americanism or even Canadianism.[41] A bi-cultural society of English- and French-speaking settlers encouraged what was to become a highly plural society, a society in which each group, and most strikingly the French Canadian, has fought to guard its separate identity. Since most Canadians retain a justifiable pride in their own ethnic and past national heritages, they assume that the Negro Canadian should do so as well, that it is natural that he should be left alone, self-segregated to his own communities. Where segregation in the United States became the hallmark, the visible stain of racial prejudice, to white Canadians ethnic ghettos seemed not at all unnatural. The European-oriented ethnic group in Canada, if Italian, has as its sword and buckler the glory of Rome, the putative discovery of America, and Michelangelo's Adamic hand nearly in touch with God. And while the white Canadian could take pride in his national heritage, march as an Orangeman, thrill to the skirl of the pipes or to tales of Dollard des Ormeaux at the Long Sault, the Negro Canadian thought he had no national heritage to fall back upon for self-identification. He was alone, and his internal divisions, his unwillingness to work together even in the Canadian pattern as a single ethnic group, assured that he would remain alone, for in Canada voice and ultimately power were to be found by embracing the very ethnicity from which the Negroes turned. Unknown, unobserved, unwanted, the Negro in Canada seemed content to wait for other times and other men to do him justice. Paradoxically, until he did that which white ethnic groups had always expected of him—embraced his Negritude—he would remain to most Canadians an invisible man.

Notes

1. With minor changes five paragraphs of this essay are drawn from my article, " 'A Sacred Animosity': Abolitionism in Canada," in Martin B. Duberman, ed., *The Antislavery Vanguard: New Essays on the Abolitionists* (Princeton, 1965), and one paragraph is drawn from an article, "A Century of Misunderstanding: Canadian-American Cultural Relations," *International Educational and Cultural Exchange,* I (Fall, 1965) .

2. The Negro was invoked during 1958 by the former editor of *Le Devoir* of Montreal, Andre Laurendeau, who argued that English Canadians assumed French Canadians would accept a lower standard of political morality because they were like those Africans whom the British controlled through a Negro king. See *Le Devoir,* July 4, 1958 *et seq.*

3. See Donald G. Macrae, "Race and Sociology in History and Theory," in Philip Mason, *et al., Man, Race and Darwin* (London, 1960), pp. 78–86; and Floyd N. House, "Viewpoints and Methods in the Study of Race Relations," *The American Journal of Sociology,* XL (Jan., 1935), 440–52.

4. The writer noted several examples of this problem while interviewing and working with informants throughout Canada. See Morris Davis, "Results of Personality Tests Given to Negroes in the Northern and Southern United States and in Halifax, Canada," *Phylon,* XXV (Winter, 1964), 362–68. Some of the conclusions in this article are open to question, however.

5. The only general studies of the Negro in Canada published by the 1960's were Ida Greaves, "The Negro in Canada," *McGill University Economic Studies,* whole no. 16 (Orillia, Ont., 1930), and Harold H. Potter, "Negroes in Canada," *Race: The Journal of the Institute of Race Relations,* III (Nov., 1961), 39–56. Potter's article, the work of a Negro sociologist, is reprinted in Richard Laskin, ed., *Social Problems: A Canadian Profile* (New York, 1964), pp. 139–47.

6. Myrdal, *An American Dilemma: The Negro Problem and Modern Democracy* (2 vols., New York, 1944), I, 60–61.

7. For example, see W. S. M. Banks II, "The Rank Order of Sensitivity to Discriminations of Negroes in Columbus, Ohio," *American Sociological Review*, XV (Aug., 1950), 529–34.

8. This generalization is based upon more than fifty interviews with Negroes who were prepared to discuss discrimination, on the files of the National Committee on Human Rights of the Canadian Labour Congress, in Montreal, and on over sixty examples of discriminatory acts, drawn from the Canadian press between 1960 and 1965. See, in particular, *Gazette*, Toronto *Globe & Mail*, Windsor *Star*, Winnipeg *Free Press*, and Vancouver *Sun* for this period. It would be tedious for the reader to cite each newspaper article, but the author's clipping file has been given to the Schomburg Collection of the New York Public Library.

9. Perhaps it is symptomatic of the slow growth of white Canadian awareness that the only book on Negro intelligence tests to be found in all twenty of the university libraries checked by the author was Harry Ambrose Tanser's poorly-based pre-war study of Kent County Negroes, while numerous more recent studies of Negro intelligence, all based upon far broader samples taken in the United States, were markedly absent from the same libraries. See Tanser, *The Settlement of Negroes in Kent County, Ontario, and a Study of the Mental Capacity of Their Descendants* (Chatham, Ont., 1939); and "Intelligence of Negroes of Mixed Blood in Canada," *The Journal of Negro Education*, X (Oct., 1941), 650–52. In his book, Tanser reported that Negroes scored an average of 89.6 and whites an average of 105.4 on intelligence tests. In his later investigation of mixed bloods, he used the National, the Pintner Non-Language, and the Pintner-Paterson Performance tests, the last two of which lean toward emphasis on heredity rather than environment to account for levels of attainment. Tanser found "a trend towards positive correlation between intelligence and degree of White blood." Mixed-bloods surpass full Negroes, in other words. But obviously, the lighter skinned have more educational and social opportunities. Tanser's work was cited by Nathaniel Weyl in *The Negro in American Civilization* (Washington, 1960), pp. 188–90, to prove that "... Negro psychometric intelligence remains substantially lower than white." But Weyl described the milieu in which the Tanser survey was taken as one of equality. Kent County was "an example of environmental equalization at a high point in the socio-economic scale. . . ." This is ludicrous. The work of a historian is not the place to debate Negro intelligence, tests, and abstruse statistical data. The point here is that the only information on Negro intelligence to which most Canadian students have been exposed is Tanser's study, and Weyl's book, and that other surveys which tend to discount differences in intelligence on environmental grounds are little known or unavailable in Canada. Weyl based his entire analysis of Negro intelligence on Tanser's small Kent County sample, together with studies conducted by Audrey M. Shuey and Leona E. Tyler in the United States. For a recent examination of this problem, which concludes that "if there are any inherent distinctions they are inconsequential," see Thomas F. Pettigrew, "Negro American Intelligence: A New Look at an Old Controversy," *The Journal of Negro Education*, XXXIII (Winter, 1964), 6–25.

10. Certainly there were elements of truth in the stereotype, but the chief features involved appear to be class and environmental rather than racial. See the work of John Connor and M. V. Marshall, *Three-Five Mile Plains Study: Socio-Economic Indicators*, Acadia University Institute publication, whole no. 16 (Feb., 1965).

11. Interview by telephone, Saint John, Feb. 20, 1960.

12. See Jessie L. Beattie, *John Christie Holland: Man of the Year* (Toronto, 1956).

13. Based on interviews with white informants throughout Canada and with six white girls who were known to be dating Negro boys in Toronto and Montreal, and on the following: Nadine Asante, "A Mixed Marriage," *Manchester Guardian Weekly*, XC (March 19, 1964), 13; a file of *Tab*, volumes I–IV (1957–60), issues of *Flash* for the last six months of 1950; Toronto *Globe & Mail*, Overseas Edition, Aug. 10, 1960; and Marc Crawford, "The Ominous Malcolm X Exits from the

Muslims," *Life,* LVI (March 20, 1964), 40-40A. Typical of the sexual mythology is an account of the conviction of one Jacob Briggs, a Negro, at Sandwich, Canada West, April 15, 1840, for the rape of an eight-year-old white child (PAC, State Papers, Upper Canada; series E: XI, nos. 26, 27). Defense counsel played upon the myth of large male Negro sexual organs by arguing that "it would have been impossible for a full grown man, *particularly a Negro,* to have entered the body of [the child] . . ." (italics added).

14. Bonnycastle, *Canada and the Canadians in 1846* (2 vols., London, 1846), I, 249–50.

15. See Kohn, *The Idea of Nationalism* (New York, 1937).

16. See Robin W. Winks. "Communications in Canadian-American Relations: An Historian's View," [Rev. F. J. Boland, ed.], *Sixth Seminar on Canadian-American Relations at University of Windsor* (Windsor, Ont. [1965]), pp. 85–92.

17. In order, these quotations are from Thomas Conant, *Upper Canada Sketches* (Toronto, 1898), pp. 127–36; Robert S. Kane,, *Canada A to Z* (Garden City, N.Y., 1964), p. 187; Alistair Horne, *Canada and the Canadians* (Toronto, 1961), pp. 11, 39, 120.

18. Toronto *Daily Globe,* July 6, Sept. 8, 1857, Jan. 16, April 27, Sept. 9, 1858; Edmund Patton, *A Glimpse at the United States and the Northern States of America, with the Canadas . . . during the Autumn of 1852 . . .* (London, 1853), pp. 34–35.

19. Ontario Provincial Archives, Toronto, Charlton Papers, MS. autobiography, p. 167; *Witness,* Jan. 5, May 18, July 6, 20, 27, Aug. 3, 10, Sept. 21, Oct. 12, Nov. 16, Dec. 12, 21, 1846 (the quotations are from June 8, p. 190, and June 22, p. 206, italics added), and March 24, 1852; Syracuse University Library, Gerrit Smith Miller Papers: Stuart to Smith, Jan. 8, 1853, Apr. 16, 1855, Sept. 26, 1857.

20. Howe, *Refugees from Slavery in Canada West* (Boston, 1864), p. 49.

21. Hopkins J. Moorehouse, "A Dash for Freedom," *The National Monthly,* IV (April, 1904), 219–21; *ibid.,* "Toronto *vs.* New York," pp. 223–31; P. T. Hodgson, "Reminiscences, 1848–1857," Huron Institute, *Papers and Records,* II (1914), pp. 2, 10.

22. For a typical editorial, see Toronto *Globe & Mail,* Jan. 5, 1952.

23. Montreal *Witness,* III (May 1, 1848), 140; *Globe & Mail,* July 2, 1954; Pembroke (Ont.) *Observer,* Sept. 8, 1958; Toronto *Daily Star,* May 13, 1960; and Carl T. Rowan, "Negroes in Canada," *Ebony,* XV (Aug., 1960), 98.

24. For what he would have seen, read Albert Johnson, "The Negro in American Films: Some Recent Works," *Film Quarterly,* XVIII (Summer, 1965), 14–30.

25. For examples, see *Maclean's* for 1963: LXXVI (July 27), 2–3, 45–46; (Sept. 7), 3–4; (Oct. 19), 28, 34–38; (Nov. 2), 2–3, on Medgar Evers, James Baldwin, justice in Maryland, and apartheid. *Maclean's* published at least forty-three articles or news items on race relations between 1957 and 1962. See *Saturday Night,* LVII (July 18, 1942), 10; and throughout 1957–63.

26. For examples, see Peterborough *Examiner,* Sept. 13, 1956; Toronto *Telegram,* July 25, 1956, Feb. 4, 1958; Toronto *Financial Post,* Sept. 12, 1958; Pembroke *Observer,* Sept. 30, 1959; Cornwall (Ont.) *Standard-Freeholder,* Oct. 5, 1959; Watertown (Ont.) *Review,* Oct. 22, 1959; *Maclean's,* LXXI (Dec. 6, 1958), 46–48, LXXIV (Jan. 7, 1961), 6, and LXXVIII (Apr. 17, 1965); and *Canada Month* II (Feb., 1962), 31–32.

27. As examples, see Washington, *My Larger Education, being Chapters from My Experience* (Toronto, n.d.), John Howard Griffin, *Black Like Me* (Toronto, 1963), James Baldwin, *Notes of a Native Son* (Montreal, 1964), Martin Luther King, *Why We Can't Wait* (Toronto, 1964), and Jay Saunders Redding, *On Being Negro in America* (Montreal, 1964).

28. Calgary *Albertan,* Aug. 19, 1958; Chatham *Daily News,* Oct. 2, 1959; *Ebony,* II (Dec., 1946), 26; Toronto *Daily Star,* Dec. 27, 1957; Canadian Labour Congress, *La discrimination vous coute du Foin!* (Montreal, [1906]).

29. Mrs. W. A. Turner, comp., *Canadian Mosaic: Nova Scotia Volume* (N. S., 1957), p. 51; *Victoria British Columbia Canada Centennial Celebrations 1862–1962*

(Victoria, 1962), program; Gibbon, *Canadian Mosaic: The Making of a Northern Nation* (New York, 1939); Norman Levine, *Canada Made Me* (London, 1958), p. 262; Toronto *Financial Post,* June 3, 1950; Brantford *Expositor,* Sept. 26, 1959; May 7, 10, Aug. 12, 1960, July 10, 12, 1965.

30. *Time* (Canadian edition), LXXXV (March 19), 24, and *ibid.* (May 14, both 1965), 17, 20; *Canada Week,* II (March 26, 1965), 2; Washington *Post,* April 6, 1965; "One More River," *Canadian Forum,* XLIII (June, 1963), 64. Earlier, Canadians had taken considerable interest in the case of Jimmy Wilson, an illiterate Alabama Negro who was to be executed for robbery, and over three thousand Canadians are said to have written to Governor James E. Folsom of Alabama to urge clemency. See especially London (Ont.) *Free Press,* Sept. 15, Montreal *Matin,* Sept. 8, and Granby (Que.) *La Voix de l'est,* Sept. 4, 1958.

31. See Charlotte Brontë Perry, *The Long Road,* I, *The History of the Coloured Canadian in Windsor, Ontario, 1867–1967* (Windsor, 1967 [*i.e.,* 1968]), and H[arold] H. Potter and D. H. [*sic* for G.] Hill, *Negro Settlement in Canada, 1628–1965: A Survey* (mimeographed, a Report presented to the Royal Commission on Bilingualism and Biculturalism, 1966).

32. On earlier Negro objections to the term "colored," see W. A. Domingo, "What Are We, Negroes or Colored People?," *The Messenger,* VIII (June, 1926), 180, 187, and H. C. Brearley, "Race as a Sociological Concept," *Sociology and Social Research,* XXIII (Aug., 1939), 515.

33. Minutes of the Nova Scotia Association for the Advancement of Colored People, V, entries for March 15, 21, April 7, 1965. These Minute Books are kept in the library of the Cornwallis Street Baptist Church, Halifax, and I should like to thank Reverend Charles Coleman for his help while I was working with these and other records.

34. "Report on Activities for improved human relations in the labour field during the month of February 1959, Submitted by the Assistant Secretary to the National Committee on Human Rights of the Canadian Labour Congress" (mimeographed), p. 2, in the offices of the Committee in Montreal; *The Maritime Merchant,* LXVIII (Jan., 1960), 13–14.

35. On the social structure of white Canada see Nathan Keyfitz, "Ethnic Groups and their Behavior," *Annals of the American Academy of Political and Social Science,* CCLIII (1947), 158–63; Bernard R. Blishen, "The Construction and Use of an Occupational Class Scale," *Canadian Journal of Economic and Political Science,* XXIV (Nov., 1958), 519–31; John Porter, *The Vertical Mosaic: An Analysis of Social Class and Power in Canada* (Toronto [1965]); and *Crestwood Heights: a Study of the Culture of Suburban Life* (Toronto, 1956), by John R. Seeley, B. Alexander Sim, and Elizabeth W. Loosley.

36. But in 1964 white students began to provide pastoral care within the African Association. See *Proceedings and Minutes, The Seventh Assembly of the Baptist Federation of Canada, Acadia University, Wolfville . . . 1964 and the Twenty First Council of the Baptist Federation of Canada, Victoria, British Columbia . . . 1965* (Brantford, n.d.), p. 23.

37. The church is not the only source of "consolation" open to the Negro, of course. The writer interviewed three who had become published poets, and six who were artists; all said they took up such activities for consolation.

38. See Ruth Danenhower Wilson, "Negro-White Relations in Canada," in Irving Goldaber and Albert Vorspan, eds., "Race and Racialism" (mimeographed summary of a seminar on the "Race Problem" held at the New School for Social Research, New York, 1948), pp. 27–28; Charlottetown (P. E. I.) *Guardian,* June 13, 1964.

39. Office of Commissioners for the West Indies, British Guiana and British Honduras, *Location List West Indian Students in Canada, 1961–62* (Montreal [1961]). For a West Indian's opinion, see Yvonne Bobb, "Are Canadians Really Tolerant?," *Chatelaine,* XXXII (Sept., 1959), 26, 64, 66.

40. Brian Moore, in *Canada* (New York, 1963), writes that the composite British Canadian believes that other nationalities, except the French, are not really

Canadians. In a country where those of British origin are so strongly in the ascendancy, Moore argues, other groups feel ill at ease and tend to move on to the United States. See also Blishen, "The Construction and Use of An Occupational Class Scale," and Dennis Wrong, "Background for Understanding," in Richard Laskin, ed., *Social Problems: A Canadian Profile* (New York, 1964), pp. 23–30.

41. "The U.S. is a melting pot. Canada is not. . . . I prefer the Canadian mosaic," wrote one observer. In 1960 the Premier of Quebec, Jean Lesage, noted that all Canadians wished to avoid a melting pot, for not only French Canadians but other groups as well wished to retain their separate ethnic identities. See also A. R. M. Lower, "Motherlands," *Dalhousie Review, XVIII* (July, 1938), 143–48.

Claudia Jones
THE CARIBBEAN COMMUNITY IN BRITAIN

Over a quarter of a million West Indians, the overwhelming majority of them from Jamaica, have now settled in Britain in less than a decade. Britain has become, in the mid-1960's, the center of the largest overseas population of West Indians; numerically relegating to second place, the once superior community of West Indians in the United States.

This new situation in Britain has been inimitably described in the discerning verse of Louise Bennett, noted Jamaican folklorist, as, "Colonization in Reverse."

Immigration statistics, which are approximate estimates compiled by the one time functional West Indian Federation office (Migrant Services Division) in Britain, placed the total number of West Indians entering the United Kingdom as 238,000 persons by the year 1961. Of these, 125,000 were men; 93,000 women; 13,200 were children; and 6,300, unclassified. A breakdown of the islands from which these people came showed that during the period of 1955-1961, a total of 142,825 were from Jamaica; from Barbados, 5,036; from Trinidad and Tobago, 2,282; from British Guiana, 3,470; from Leeward Islands, 3,524; from the Windward Islands, 8,202; and from all other territories, the sum total of 8,732.

Distribution of the West Indian population in the United Kingdom indicates that by mid-1962, over 300,000 West Indians were settled in Britain. The yearly immigration and the growth of community settlement illustrates the rate of growth of the West Indian settlement. For example, the emigration of West Indians to the United Kingdom in mid-1955 totalled 24,473 and by 1961, this figure soared to 61,749. Corresponding to the latter was the fear of family separation due to the then impending Commonwealth Immigrants Act.

In the industrial city of Birmingham, by mid-1955, 8,000 West Indians formed the community there, while in mid-1962, this figure stood at 67,000 Similarly in London, where in Brixton the largest settlement of West Indians exist; the mid-1955 figure of 85,000 had by 1961 grown to 135,000.

West Indians were also to be found in the North of England (Manchester, Nottingham, Wolverhampton, Derby and Leeds) and in such cities as Cardiff, Liverpool, Leicester, Bath, Oxford, Cambridge and in other provinces. *What constitutes the chief features of this unprecedented migration to Britain? To what factors may we ascribe this growth of overseas West Indians away from their original homelands?*

REPRINTED FROM *Freedomways Magazine*, VOL. 4, NO. 3, 1964. PUBLISHED AT 799 BROADWAY, NEW YORK CITY.

Emigration from the West Indies has served for over two generations as a palliative, a stop-gap measure to ease the growing economic frustrations in a largely impoverished agricultural economy in which under colonial-capitalist-imperialist relations, the wealth of these islands is dominated by the few, with the vast majority of the people living under unbearable conditions.

It was the outstanding Cuban poet, Nicholas Guillen, who noting a situation (also observed by other West Indian writers) in which the young generation, most of it out of work, 'chafing at the bit,' seeing as their only hope a swift opportunity to leave their islands, lamented thus: *"Scant, sea-girt land, Oh, tight-squeezed land . . ."*

Indeed, as with all migrant populations here is mirrored in extension the existing problems of the nations and territories from which the migrants originally spring. West Indian emigration to the United Kingdom is no exception to this phenomenon. Furthermore, this emigration, as with many other Afro-Asian peoples, has occurred almost immediately prior to the achievement of political independence in two of the largest of the West Indies islands. *It is because prospects have not yet qualitatively improved for the vast majority of the West Indian workers and people, inhibited by the tenaciousness of continued Anglo-American imperialist dominance over West Indian economic life, that this emigratory movement of people from the West Indies continues.* History will undoubtedly evaluate this development as, in part, attributable to the demise of the West Indian Federation and the consequent smashing of wide hopes for the establishment of a united West Indian nation in which freedom of movement would have absorbed some of our disinherited, disillusioned, and unfilled people who were compelled to leave their homelands in order to survive.

Up to a decade ago, West Indian immigration was directed to America rather than to Britain. But this was sharply modified when in 1952 the United States Federal Government enacted the racially-based McCarran-Walter Immigration Law, which unequivocally was designed to protect the white "races' purity," and to insure the supremacy of Anglo-Saxon stock; limited to 100 per year, persons allowed to emigrate to the United States from each individual Caribbean territory. Henceforth all eyes reverted to Britain. This is not to imply that West Indian immigration to Britain was wholly non-reciprocal. Another influence, was that post-war Britain, experiencing a brief economic boom, and full employment, needed overseas and cheap labor to staff the semi-skilled and non-skilled vacancies, the results of temporary postwar economic incline. Britain sought West Indian immigration as an indispensable aid to the British economy; indeed, encouraged it!

The presence of West Indian immigrants (who together with other Afro-Asian peoples total nearly a half million people) represent less than one per cent in an overall Anglo-populace of 52 million. But even this small minority has given rise to a plethora of new sociological and analytical works such as *"Newcomers"; "Colored Immigrants in Britain"; "The Economic and Social Position of Negro Immigrants in Britain"; "Black and White in Harmony"; "Colored Minorities in Britain"; "Colonial Students"; "Report on West Indian Accommodation Problems in the United Kingdom"; "Race and Racism"; "Dark Strangers"; "They Seek a Living,"* and the like.

Extreme manifestations of the racialism which underlies the present status of West Indians in Britain were graphically witnessed in late 1958, when racial riots occurred in Notting Hill and Nottingham. These events, which followed the as yet unsolved murder of a St. Vincentian, Mr. Kelso Cochrane, claimed world headlines. Clashes even occurred between West Indian and other Afro-Asian migrants with white Britons. The firm handling of the provocateurs by the authorities, following the wide protests of immigrants, labor, Communist and progressive forces, and the intervention of the West Indian Federal leaders, for a time quelled the overt racialists, and the "keep Britain white, fascist-propagandists." But the canker of racialism was now nakedly revealed. It exposed also the smugness of official Britain, who hitherto pointed to racial manifestations in "Little Rock" and Johannesburg, South Africa, but continued to deny its existence in Britain.

Today, new problems, underscored by the Tory Government's enactment, and recent renewal of the 1962 Commonwealth Immigration Act (one which ostensibly restricts Commonwealth immigration as a whole, but in fact discriminates heavily against colored Commonwealth citizens) has established a second class citizenship status for West Indians and other Afro-Asian peoples in Britain. Accompanying the general social problems confronting all new migrant workers, West Indians, stemming as they do in large measure from African origins, are experiencing sharper color-bar practices. In common with other workers, the West Indians take part in the struggle for defense and improvement of their working and living standards. But the growing intensity of racialism forces them, as it does other Afro-Asians, to join and found their own organizations. In fact, their status, is more and more a barometer of British intentions and claims of a so-called "Multi-racial Commonwealth." As put in one of the recent sociological studies of the absorption of a West Indian migrant group in Brixton, financed by the Institute of Race Relations and the Nuffield Foundation:

> Now that the whole equilibrium of world power is changing, and the Commonwealth is, by virtue of conscious British policy, being transformed from a family based on kinship, to a wider multiracial *familia,* the presence of colored immigrants in Britain presents a moral and a practical challenge. The people of these islands face the need not only to reformulate their views of Britain's role and status in such a Commonwealth, but also to apply the new relationships in their dealings with colored Commonwealth migrants here at home. And not only the color-conscious migrants themselves, but the newly-independent Afro-Asian

countries and the outside world as a whole, show an inclination to judge Britain's good faith in international relations by her ability to put her own house in order.

from *Dark Strangers,* by Sheila Patterson

THE COMMONWEALTH IMMIGRANTS ACT

Far from heeding the advice even of sociologists whose studies themselves show a neo-colonialist bias in its precepts (the study is full of pragmatic assertions that xenophobia is the "norm" of British life, and hence, by implication "natural," etc.) the Tory Government has shown utter disdain for putting its own house in order.

Faced with the coming general elections in October, having suffered from local government defeats, mounting criticism rises towards its ruinous domestic and foreign policies. Internally, these range from housing shortages and a Rent Act which has removed ceilings on rentals to the failures of providing new houses; high interest rates on loans to the rail and shipbuilding closures, mergers and the effects of automation.

The external policies of the present British Conservative Government also suffer similar criticism. As a junior partner it supports the United States imperialist NATO nuclear strategy, continuing huge expenditures for colonial wars in Malaysia, North Borneo and Aden. Its subservience to U.S. imperialism is also demonstrated in the case of its denial of long over-due independence to British Guiana, on whom it is imposing the undemocratic system of Proportional Representation which aims further to polarize and divide the political life in British Guiana in order to depose the left-wing, thrice-elected People's Progressive Party under Dr. Cheddi Jagan. As an experienced colonizer, shopping around for a scapegoat for its own sins, the British Tory Government enacted in 1962 the Commonwealth Immigrants Act. The Act sets up a voucher system allowing entry only to those who have a job to come to. Some of its sections carry deportation penalties for migrants from the West Indies, Asia and Africa, whom it especially circumscribes. Its passage was accompanied by the most foul racialist propaganda perpetrated against West Indians and other Afro-Asians by Tory and fascist elements. Thus, it coincided with the futile efforts then engaged in by the British Government to join the European Common Market. It was widely interpreted that these twin events demonstrated the dispensability in Britain's eyes of both the needs of the traditional market of the newly independent West Indian territories for their primary products, and the labor supply of West Indians and other Afro-Asian Commonwealth citizens. On the other hand, the doors would close on colored Commonwealth citizens, while open wide to white European workers.

The pious and hypocritical sentimentality accompanying the "bills" passage was further exposed when the Tory legislators removed the non-Commonwealth Irish Republic from the provisions of the Act, revealing its naked color-bar bias. The result, following a year of its operation, showed that eighty to ninety per cent of all Indian and Pakistani applicants were refused entry permits; and West Indian immigration dropped to a little over 4,000, qualifying for entry. The latter occasioned cautious queries, whether the West Indians had either turned their backs on Britain or had become bitter with the Act's passage.

What the figures showed, of course, was that the main blow fell as intended, most heavily on the *colored* Commonwealth citizens. So much for the facile promises of the then Home Secretary, now Britain's Foreign Minister, Mr. R. A. Butler, that *"we shall try to find a solution as friendly to these people as we can, and not on the basis of color alone."* (my emphasis: C.J.)

All Tory claims that the Act would benefit either Britain or the immigrants are, of course, easily refuted. The most widely prevalent Tory argument was that colored immigrants were "flooding Britain." At the time of the Act's passage, the 1961 British population census showed a two and a half million increase, during the very period of the growth of the immigration of West Indians and Afro-Asians, and this increase was easily absorbed by the British economy. The colored migrant is less than one in every hundred people. Yearly emigration of Britons shows that for every single person entering Britain *three* leave its shores.

The shibboleth that "immigrants take away houses and jobs," when viewed in light of Tory responsibility for high interest property rates and the Rent Act makes this claim likewise ludicrous. As for new houses, there is no evidence that West Indians or other colored immigrants have taken away any houses. Allowed largely only to purchase old, dilapidated short-lease houses, it is the West Indian building worker who helps to construct new houses; he makes an invaluable contribution to the building of new homes.

Even the usual last retort of the racial ideologists that West Indians and other colored citizens "lower moral stands" also fails to stand up. The world knows of the exploits of Christine Keeler and the British Ministers of State, an event which occasioned a calypso in the widely-read *West Indian Gazette*. There has been no notable increase in jobs as a result of this Act. In fact, rail and shipbuilding closures, mergers and automation, continue apace. It is widely admitted that withdrawal of colored workers from transport, foundries and hospital services would cause a major economic dislocation in Britain, and that they continue to make a contribution to the British economy. Vic Feather, leading trade union official, reiterated strongly this view at an all-day conference recently in Smethwick, a Birmingham suburb, where a local election campaign slogan was that to elect Labor meant *"having a nigger for a neighbor."* One finally observes regarding the asserted economic social burden of the migrant, that a "tidy" profit has been made by the Ministry of National Insurance from contributions of the surrendered cards of thousands of immigrants who returned home after a few years in Britain.

In the eyes of the world, the Tory record does not stand any better when it is known that nine times they have blocked the Bill to Outlaw Racial Discrimination by the Labor member for Parliament from Slough, Mr. Fenner Brockway. The main provisions of this bill would be to outlaw discrimination in public places, lodgings, inns, dance halls, and other leases; and also put penalties on incitement to racialism. The Bill has now gained the support of the Labor leadership who promised if they achieve office to introduce such a measure (although there are some indications that it may be watered down), as well as from leading Liberal M.P.'s and even from some Tory M.P.'s. Thus, there has been witnessed a reversal of the former open-door policy to Commonwealth citizens, and speciously to colored Commonwealth citizens. The result of all this has been a new degrading status and sufferance accorded to colored immigrants who are likewise saddled with the responsibility for Britain's social evils.

There is a reluctance on the part of virtually all sections of British public opinion to assess the fundamental reasons for the existence of racial prejudice. The citizens of the "Mother of Democracies" do not yet recognize that the roots of racialism in Britain are deep and were laid in the eighteenth and nineteenth centuries through British conquests of India, Africa, and great parts of Asia as well as the British Caribbean. All the resources of official propaganda and education, the superstructure of British imperialism, were permeated with projecting the oppressed colonial peoples as "lesser breeds," as "inferior colored peoples," "natives," "savages," and the like—in short, "the white man's burden." These rationalizations all served to build a justification for wholesale exploitation, extermination, and looting of the islands by British imperialism. The great wealth of present-day British monopoly-capital was built on the robbery of colored peoples by such firms as Unilever and the East Africa company to Tate and Llye and Booker Brothers in the Caribbean.

These artificial divisions and antagonisms between British and colonial workers, already costly in toll of generations of colonial wars and ever-recurrent crises, have delayed fundamental social change in Britain, and form the very basis of color prejudice. The small top section of the working class, bribed and corrupted, and benefiting from this colonial robbery, have been imbued with this racialist "white superiority" poison. On the other hand progressive opinion rallied with the migrants' protests at the Commonwealth Immigrants Act, for the Labor Party leadership had voted in opposition to its enactment; yet allowing its subsequent renewal to go unchallenged, for fear of losing votes in the coming general elections. Labor offered the government an unopposed passage on the condition that it agree to replace the Act with new and improved legislation drawn up "in consultation" with the Commonwealth countries.

The government, which had itself tried this tactic before, to the negative response of West Indian and other affected Commonwealth Governments, refused to give these assurances. The Labor M.P.'s voted against its renewal, but not before they made clear, to the dismay of the overwhelming majority of immigrants, that they too, stood for "quotas" and "controls." In essence, this stand does not differ in principle from the attitude of the Tory Government and the provisions of the Commonwealth Immigrants Act. With the sole exception of the British Communists, who completely oppose the system of "quotas" and "controls" for Commonwealth immigration, all other political parties have capitulated in one or another way to this racialist immigration measure. A recent statement of the Executive Committee of the British Communist Party declared its opposition to all forms of restrictions on colored immigration; declared its readiness to contest every case of discrimination; urged repeal of the Commonwealth Immigrants Act; and called for equality of access for employment, rates of wages, promotion to skilled jobs, and opportunities for apprenticeship and vocational training. It gave full support to the Bill to Outlaw Racial Discrimination and pledged its readiness to support every progressive measure to combat discrimination in Britain. It also projected the launching of an ideological campaign to combat racialism, which it noted, infects wide sections of the British working class.

SOME ISSUES FACING COLORED IMMIGRANTS

That the Tory color-bar Commonwealth Immigrants Bill has been enacted at the time when apartheid and racialism is under attack throughout the world from the African Heads of State, at Addis Ababa, to the half million Civil Rights March on Washington; from the United Nations, and world criticism of South Africa and the demand for application of economic sanctions, to the condemnation of apartheid and Jim Crow racialist practices in the U.S.; bespeak the fantastic blindness of Britain's Tory rulers even to Britain's own national interests. But, as with every exploiting class, as the example of Hitlerism shows, faced with a radical movement of the masses against their rule, they seek to split and divert this anger onto a false "enemy."

Added to the second-class citizenship status foisted by such a measure, West Indians and other Afro-Asians are confronted in their daily lives with many social and economic problems. Forming several settlements in various cities, the overwhelming majority are workers, with a scattering of professionals. There are 3,000 students.

Throughout Britain, the West Indian contribution to its economy is undoubted. As building workers, carpenters, as nurses, doctors and on hospital staffs, in factories, on the transportation system and railway depots and stations, West Indians are easily evidenced. Lest the younger generation be omitted (without commenting here on the social mores "guiding" the cultural orientation of today's youth) one of the most popular current pop singers is a 16 year old girl from rural Jamaica.

Indicative of their bid to participate in the political life of the nation was the recent success of a West Indian doctor on the Labor ticket as London County Councillor for the second time in an area composed, though not solely, of West Indian migrants. For the first time many thousands of West Indian and Afro-Asian voters have registered and will be eligible to vote. It is not accidental therefore, as reflected in an article entitled "The Color of Their Votes" in a leading Sunday periodical, that speculation is growing as to how they will use their vote. One such article entitled "The Color of Their Votes" concluded that they would vote "according to color" but in consonance with their class interests. But this observation is only a half-truth. For the *common* experience of all Afro-Asian-Caribbean peoples in Britain is leading to a growing unison among these communities as they increasingly identify an injury to one as being an injury to all. When added to this, one marks their pride in the growth of national-liberation achievements from the lands of their origin and among other nationally-oppressed peoples, they are likely to be influenced by this bond as much as by their particular mode of production. Most pre-election polls have indicated their leaning, if critical, towards Labor and other Independents.

Many acute problems face West Indians who seek jobs and shelter. There is as yet no overall veritable picture of West Indians' skills. Results from sample polls are given here, bearing in mind the West Indian economic colonial background, to indicate scales in skills. One such poll revealed that of 608 persons sampled for their skills by their own characterization, the results among West Indians were as follows: Professionals-1%; other non-manual-13%; skilled-46%; semi-skilled-13%; agricultural-12%. In a further breakdown the professional and other blackcoated workers predominated in the migrant groups from Trinidad and Tobago, while skilled workers were more numerous from Jamaica and Barbados. Considerable down-grading of skills frequently occurs and many unskilled workers have been unable to acquire skills, many from rural areas having formerly no industrial experience at all. But even where qualifications exist, many find it difficult to obtain jobs commensurate with their skills. Some employers have a secret quota system for the employment of colored workers, based on the chauvinistic view that *"too many colored workers"* even if qualified, will *"rock the boat."* Others, even when inclined to take on colored workers, have had to face English workers, in some cases trade unionists, who have a definite policy of keeping out colored workers. Even Government Employment Exchanges accept orders from employers not to submit "colored" applicants for work. But this too, is being resisted and demands are being made for the Ministry of Labor to rescind these instructions.

In the background is the country-wide pattern of industrial-labor relations; the traditional view of "keeping the labor force small," the better to bargain with the employers, and the real fear by trade unionists that non-union labor will undercut wages. Then, too, there is the ambivalent right-wing trade union view which seeks to reconcile the principles of trade union brotherhood and non-discrimination with the antipathies of a large and vocal proportion of its rank-and-file members.

Even in the early stages of the present West Indian immigration to Britain, struggles had to be waged for the acceptance of West Indian workers into the jobs they now hold. In the transport system, despite the agreements between the British Transport System and the Barbados Government to train and employ workers, sharp struggles by progressive trade unionists, led by Communists, had to be waged for hiring and upgrading of West Indian workers, for their right to work in booking offices, or as shuttle-plate workers in railway depots or for West Indian women to be employed as "clippies" or bus conductors.

Many of these gains are today under fire. A recent vote by the London busmen served notice that they opposed the hiring of any more West Indian workers. What is more, a growing "Blacklist for Jobs" exists, as an article in the *Sunday Observer* states. The article noted that thousands of West Indians born and educated in Britain will "not be content to do shift work on buses" in a society which, "despite their high academic levels treats them as less than human beings," (the article detailed the difficulties experienced by school-leavers particularly in white-collar jobs). In banks, sales staffs, insurance companies, and newspaper staffs, a policy of "tokenism" is operative. As one executive put it: *"If you have one in an office and she's pleasant, she fits in, but you put two or three there and you may find yourself losing some of your white staff."* Facing stiff competition for jobs, they have it both ways: if undertrained, and if efficient, (the *too*-well-trained, may be rejected) in either case, they may face a color bar.

Excluded from skilled jobs and forced into lower paid ones, still another disability must be faced in the field of housing accommodation. In addition to the problems occasioned from the general housing shortage, the West Indian immigrant and other colored Commonwealth citizens are widely rejected as tenants of advertised flats and lodgings on the basis of a color-bar, and are obliged to pay higher rents even than white tenants. *"So sorry, No Colored, No children," "European Only," "White Only,"* signs dot the pages of advertised flats and lodgings. A "color-tax" meets the West Indian purchaser of property, often inferior lease-hold ones. No wonder estate agents, and unscrupulous landlords, some of them colored themselves, have not been averse to exploiting for huge profits this housing shortage. "Rachmanism" is a synonym in present-day England for this type of practice, alluding to the fortunes made by the man so named in North Kensington in the very area of racial riots of a few years ago. Through exorbitant rentals, resale of properties, the shortage of housing is widely exploited and the West Indian, Afro-Asian as well as white workers are the victims.

A Commons inquiry is now pending since the revelation of collusion of estate agents with Big Business when a restrictive color-bar covenant was discovered in Loriel Properties on whose board of directors are two Tory Cabinet Ministers, a leading Conservative Member of Parliament, who led the racist attack in the House of Commons on the Commonwealth Immigration Act. This company has shareholders among the nation's leading universities at Oxford and Cambridge and most of the other directors hail from The Establishment. Thus, the real origin of color-bar practices and policies stems from the City's imperialist financial barons to whom it is highly profitable, both ways. The Commons inquiry, it should be added, has been initiated by Mr. Fenner Brockway who has nine times tabled his anti-discrimination bill to ban discrimination in public housing, leases, inns, pubs, hotels, dance halls, etc. These and other examples more than confirm the urgency for this type of legislation in present-day Britain. Education policy is yet another field in which inroads are being attempted by the racial propagandists. Stemming from their central campaign, now sanctioned by the Commonwealth Immigration Act to oust West Indian Immigrants from Britain, they have fastened on the growth of communities where children of Afro-Asian-Caribbean immigrants are at school. Encouraging the idea of schools segregation, they have attempted the organization of parents to get them to move their children to other schools. In Southall for example, where in two wards 5,000 Indian families live, this type of segregation propaganda began to make headway and the local Council, despite the relatively good stand of the Board of Education began to weaken. Following an appeal however, from the Education Committee to the Minister of Education, Sir Edward Boyle told 400 parents, "there will be no segregation in our schools." A basis was adopted to spread the children over several schools so that there will be no more than one-third Indian children in the schools. Despite this, new calls are being heard for establishment of separate classes for colored children on grounds of "language difficulties," despite the well-known adaptability of children to become bi-lingual. This approach is being strongly resisted by West Indian, Afro-Asian, educational and progressive groups in Britain. For it is feared that such a wedge may establish an American "Jim Crow" pattern of "separate but equal education," an animal, (as we have learned from the Negro liberation struggles that just don't exist). This fear was confirmed anew when a recent White Paper issued by the Commonwealth Conservative Council suggested that children of immigrant parents be regarded as "immigrants" despite being born in the United Kingdom.

Consequently, whether as tenants waging anti-discrimination struggles; clubbing together to purchase homes to house families the large majority of whom were separated for years until the necessary finances were raised; whether as workers fighting for the right to work, or to be upgraded; or as cultural workers engaged in the attempt to use their creative abilities on stage, screen or television, or to safeguard their children's right to an equal education; or as professionals, students, or in business pursuits, the West Indian immigrant community has special problems, as a national minority. While the workers are heaviest hit, the disabilities cut across class lines.

FUTURE PERSPECTIVES

Conscious therefore of the need for alleviation of their second-class citizenship, determined to live and work in human dignity as is their natural right, the resourceful West Indian migrant, in common with all peoples involved (either consciously or not) in anti-imperialist struggles, are also thinking about their ultimate direction. That they are only now at the stage of tentatively formulating their views may be ascribed to three main factors: 1) to the constant pressure and concern with daily problems of survival, 2) to the groping in their own minds for the fundamental significance of their national identity and, 3) to the lack of an organized perspective for a progressive, united West Indies at home. Linked to the first factor is the urgent necessity to organize and unite the West Indian community in Britain around their fundamental demands. The level of organization in Britain is not yet commensurate to fulfill this urgent need. The West Indian worker, in common with all workers, is confronted with the necessity to engage in struggles, supported by their allies, for his own survival in a new environment. This also means engaging in the general struggle for peace, trade unionism, democracy and social change. While clinging strongly to his own roots, he is mindful of the conditions at home and the reasons for his emigration, and mindful too, of the disabilities which face him there. But his economic situation is relatively better and he views as a practicality that his children will grow up in England. If to this is added the recognition that as with all migrations, this too, will form a permanent community, it is only natural that steps should be taken to implement the recognition: that with permanency comes the growth of new institutions with all its accompanying aspects.

It is true, of course, that some measure of organization exists. West Indians are organized largely in social and welfare groups in the United Kingdom, established originally to meet the needs of incoming migrants. Only a smattering have thus far joined political movements or play an active role politically. This is undoubtedly attributable to the false twin ideas that they should only become politically active with their "return home," or the apolitical view that they should eschew politics. More fundamentally it is traceable also to the lack of previous political activity at home and the fact that for most West Indians their political baptism is occurring in their new environment. There exists such organizations as the Standing Conference of West Indian Organizations, a council composed of fifteen social and welfare groups in London boroughs, as well as Freemason Lodges in areas of large West Indian settlements. There are also similar organizations existing in the Midlands, all of which have close supervision by the Migrant Services Division of the Jamaica, Trinidad and Tobago, Barbados, Leeward and Windward Islands government offices in Britain. In addition there are a growing number of inter-racial committees and groups engaged in dealing with the problems of West Indians and other migrants, besides the students organizations.

There are also special organizations based on island origins beginning to develop. The Church forms a center for many religious West Indian groups, choirs and the like. Yet questions are now arising as to whether these organizations fully meet the present needs of this community. This is evidenced in the concern being expressed by West Indians, as to whether integration in British life should be the sole aim in Britain or whether the self-organization of West Indians should not likewise be emphasized. Questions are being posed too, as to how to harness the national identity of West Indians towards this end.

An interesting example of attempts to concert these trends among West Indians on the basis of reliance on their own efforts, was shown in Bristol last year, when in midst of the MCC-West Indian Test Match tour, a young university student graduate led a successful struggle following threats of a bus boycott by West Indians when one of their number was refused a job by the Bristol Bus Company. Here was witnessed too, the classical intervention of "do good" liberals who "advised" the young West Indian militants not to be too "hotheaded" and, themselves sought to designate who were the "good boys" and the leadership to be followed. But this ruse didn't quite succeed. Their action, widely publicized in the press was won when following the intervention of the then High Commissioner for Trinidad and Tobago, Sir Learie Constantine, and Mr. R. C. Lindo, Jamaican High Commissioner, supported by Mr. Robert Lightbourne, Jamaica Minister of Trade and Industry, trade union and student groups, the bus company climbed down and revoked its stand.

A major effort designed to stimulate political and social thinking has been the launching, six years ago, of the progressive news-monthly, the *West Indian Gazette*. This newspaper has served as a catalyst, quickening the awareness, social and political, of West Indians, Afro-Asians and their friends. Its editorial stand is for a united independent West Indies, full economic, social and political equality and respect for human dignity for West Indians and Afro-Asians in Britain, for peace and friendship between all Commonwealth and world peoples. It has campaigned vigorously on issues facing West Indians and other colored peoples. Whether against numerous police frame-ups, to which West Indians and other colored migrants are frequently subject, to opposing discrimination and to advocating support for trade unionism and unity of colored and white workers, W. I. news publications have attempted to emulate the path of progressive 'Negro' (Afro-Asian, Latin-American and Afro-American) journals who uncompromisingly and fearlessly fight against imperialist outrages and indignities to our peoples. The *West Indian Gazette* and *Afro-Asian-Caribbean News* has served to launch solidarity campaigns with the nationals who advance with their liberation struggles in Africa and in Asia. The present circulation and readership of the W. I. publication would be larger, but for the usual welter of problems faced by most progressive journals. A campaign of support for financial aid among its readers and friends has recently been launched to help its expansion to a weekly and to

establish its own printing plant. It counts among its contributors and supporters many West Indian writers, who live in England, trade-unionists,
and members of Parliament.

Underlying what may be termed "the search for a national identity"
is the concern of West Indians to understand their historical and cultural
heritage. This concern which arose with establishment of the now defunct
West Indian Federation has become more widespread. The consequent
polarization of West Indians into Jamaicans, Trinidadians, Barbadians,
Grenadians, etc., has certain unrealities in England where existing problems
among West Indians are shared in common. A consequence of emigration
to England, has been that Afro-Asians and West Indians have come to
know one another as they might not have previously, separated by the distance of their homelands.

Here, reference is not to some pseudo-intellectuals who, ignorant or
unaware of a scientific definition of nationhood, deny the lack of a national
identity on the spurious grounds of lack of a separate (not common)
language. But rather to the leadership need to acquaint West Indians with
their own history, and by a social interpretation of that history, better to
arm them for future struggles by imparting a pride in their origins, struggles and future. This lack of historical perspective is at root, as Dr. Eric
Williams correctly noted, from a society which eulogized the colonialist,
and whose knowledge of West Indian history was limited to that of Anglo-
Saxon conquests, Sir Walter Raleigh, Captain Morgan, and the feats of
royalty. The task remains to enhance the knowledge of the true history:
of the Morant Bay anti-slavery rebellion, the glorious Maroons, the early
anti-colonial struggles of Captain Cipriani, or of Chritchlows trade unionism, or of the significance of the movement towards closer West Indian
federation, all of which early struggles created the preconditions leading
to the contemporary struggle for nationhood, which thus is something less
than that for which West Indian patriots fought and dreamed. Such an
understanding would likewise help to create an awareness of the need for
support and aid to the bitter struggle being waged for British Guianese
independence against U.S. imperialist intervention which fears social
change along Socialist lines.

Related finally to the continued lack of an organized perspective for
an advancing West Indies is the indication of floundering in West Indian
political life since the Federation demise. The present political parties in
the Caribbean advocating a Socialist alternative, the only ultimate course
for the West Indies, are still small and ineffective. But they represent the
hope of the future, if only because they challenge the perspective of the
present bourgeois-nationalist leaders, who heading a titularly independent
West Indies continue to proclaim their reliance on the West, not only
geographically, but in political and social aims even to the shame of all
West Indians, and Jamaicans in particular, of the unprecedented offer of
Jamaica's soil for a U.S. nuclear base.

Such advocacy may ultimately inspire West Indians at home and abroad to leap the shoals of struggle necessary to transform the economy of the West Indies, and consequently to establish a socialist West Indian nation that will play its role in the community of nations.

Such a perspective would win inspiring participation among West Indians in Britain, who abjure the gradualist view voiced by many of their Ministers that the pace of West Indian advancement will be "slow" and that the West Indian immigrant would do well to consider themselves primarily citizens of Britain and to cease to worry about their national identity. This idea is likewise based on the view held towards immigration by many bourgeois nationalist West Indian politicians who encourage migration as a "safety-valve," fearing the growth of militancy for social change, at home, more than they do the loss of their most valuable citizens.

A special importance attaches itself to the Caribbean, where there is evidenced the two paths to national liberation: either the path of obsequiousness to U. S. imperialism and neo-colonialism or the high road to Socialist advance as exemplified by Socialist Cuba. Particularly in the Caribbean, where United States imperialism threatens socialist Cuba; infringes on the national sovereignty of all Latin American peoples; intervenes in the internal affairs of British Guiana and Panama; and whose pretensions of a "free America in a free world" stands exposed before the massive hammer blows of the mounting Negro liberation struggle, which, as shown in our merged protests, Afro-Asians, and Caribbean peoples, held a Solidarity March to the U.S. London Embassy, in support of the Negro peoples' demands, the struggle for national liberation proceeds with singular emphasis.

PART FOUR
FAMILY AND
INTERPERSONAL
RELATIONSHIPS

Family and kinship relations are perhaps the most frequently studied aspects of black society in the New World. R. T. Smith's lengthy bibliographic discussion of these studies, with respect to the Caribbean, together with his concrete discussion of households and production found in Part II, summarizes the major approaches and ideas regarding the dependence of family relations on relations of production and those of social class.

Smith's comments are especially relevant to the view emphasizing the effects of the "disorganized" black family—the high incidence of female-centered, fatherless households among the black underclass—on the conditions of black society. This view seems to imply that once the black family is "organized"—more like the nuclear family households of the middle class— the problems of the black underclass will be abolished. The implications of Smith's contributions contradict this view.

A word should be said about the phenomenon variously known as the Negro family, the Caribbean family, the matrifocal family. This refers to the ways in which households—the units most often enumerated in censuses— are organized. The household organization among the black populations of the New World cannot be represented by a single type; it varies widely. Thus the household organization most often found among the black bourgeoisie or the colored middle class is the nuclear family. This nuclear family household is organized around a married couple and their offspring just as among the white middle class in modern societies. Moreover, according to United States census reports published in the sixties, almost three-quarters of *all* black families (that is, households enumerated) were composed of husband and wife, as against almost nine-tenths of all white families organized in a similar manner. What is more important, however, is that the remaining one-fourth of black families headed by females is found almost wholly in the lowest categories, based on social and economic variables. Although this does not mean that all of the black underclass can be so represented, we can expect to find the matrifocal family household in the poorest of neighborhoods and communities. Thus, family and household organization varies with social class.

This is not the whole of the picture. In my own research, carried out in communities in the West Indies, I have found, as others have, that nuclear family and extended family households and compounds are normally characteristic of peasant and peasantlike relations of production, whereas the female-headed household is most often found among the plantation proletariat. Thus, family and household organization also varies with relations of production. Since social class itself is dependent upon relations of production, as argued earlier, the latter may be taken as the crucial variable for understanding family organization and the changes necessary for its transformation.

Some of the concerns of Smith, and of previous contributions on social class and economic organization, are dramatically and literally brought home in the last selection, from St. Clair Drake and Horace Cayton's classic sociological and ethnographic study of all levels of black society in Chicago.

Raymond T. Smith

CULTURE AND SOCIAL STRUCTURE IN THE CARIBBEAN: SOME RECENT WORK ON FAMILY AND KINSHIP STUDIES

The territories of the circum-Caribbean region contain some of the most complex societies in the world. Their complexity lies not in their size, degree of internal differentiation or technological development, but in the dependent and fragmented nature of their cultures, the ethnic diversity of their populations, the special nature of their dependent economies, the peculiarities of their political development and the apparent incoherence of their social institutions. It has been suggested that many Caribbean societies have no history of their own but should be viewed as an extension of Europe. Dr. Eric Williams, Prime Minister of Trinidad and Tobago, has recently written in reference to his country:

> On August 31st 1962, a country will be free, a miniature state will be established, but a society and a nation will not have been formed.[1]

His words are an almost exact echo of those of a former Governor of Trinidad, Lord Harris, who wrote in 1848:

> As the question now stands a race has been freed but a society has not been formed.[2]

When Lord Harris wrote he was particularly concerned with the problem of creating a society out of a population consisting of recently freed Negro slaves, their white masters and an intermediate group of coloured persons created out of the irregular unions between white men and Negro women. By the time Dr. Williams came to face the same problem Trinidad had acquired a large population of East Indians and sizeable minorities of Chinese and Portuguese. Each Caribbean territory faces something of the same problem that faces Trinidad, but national unity is further compromised by sharp differences in standard of living between rich and poor—standards which often coincide with ethnic divisions. This incoherence of the national and societal image within each unit is to some extent a reflection of the recent growth of the very idea of national independence, and of an attempt to establish an image different from that of the metropolitan

REPRINTED FROM *Comparative Studies in Society and History*, VOL. 6, 1963, BY PERMISSION OF THE AUTHOR AND CAMBRIDGE UNIVERSITY PRESS.

countries, but Haiti and some of the Latin American countries show that the condition is not cured by simple political autonomy.

The study of kinship and family structure reflects these difficulties and uncertainties; throughout the region we find ambiguity in normative prescriptions and variability in behaviour patterns even within ethnic and class units. Most of the work on kinship and family structure has been concentrated upon lower-class Negro groups and a number of recent publications continue this bias.[3] Some general descriptions of non-Negro groups in Puerto Rico have been published but as Mintz says,

> In Puerto Rico, in spite of a large number of papers and books dealing directly or tangentially with rural family life, there is nothing permitting rigorous comparison with the excellent studies of domestic social structure carried out in Jamaica, Trinidad, British Guiana and elsewhere.[4]

Studies of East Indian family structure in Trinidad and British Guiana have not really been brought into the same comparative framework as yet though they are crucial cases for assessing the relative effect of cultural tradition and structural constraint, and for the testing of other hypotheses.[5] Even if analysis is confined to Negro groups the number of variables that have to be taken into account is considerable. A brief discussion of the development of family studies in the region will show that some unsolved problems and unresolved conflicts still dominate present-day discussions.

The first real family studies to be made in the Caribbean were an offshoot of studies of the American Negro, and they were carried out as a result of Professor Herskovits's scheme for plotting the persistence of Africanisms in the New World.[6] They were not studies of Caribbean family structure, nor even of Haitian or Trinidadian family structure, but of family forms among the descendants of Africans, and of the relation of those forms to the general structural features of African societies. Professor Franklin Frazier had formulated some significant generalisations about the effects of slavery upon the family life of American Negroes.[7] Unlike Professor Herskovits he did not regard New World Negroes as being primarily displaced Africans, but rather as Americans trying to build a stable life after the almost total social disorganisation of slavery and in a society which continues to be hostile and discriminatory. He argued that deviations from normal American patterns of behaviour (including normal family patterns) can best be seen as a failure to achieve proper adjustment because of continuing obstruction. Gunnar Myrdal put it even more strongly when he said,

> In practically all its divergencies, American Negro culture is not something independent of general American culture. It is a distorted development, or a pathological condition, of the general American culture.[8]

Myrdal is making a deliberate statement of value which he proposes as a basis for practical action but the general point is similar to that made by Franklin Frazier.

This controversy between Herskovits and Frazier was introduced into the earliest studies in the British West Indies and it fitted itself into the emerging pre-occupation with welfare problems that came with the post-war movement towards greater political autonomy. It was very noticeable, for example, that Jamaica had an illegitimacy rate of over 70% of all live births and this caused considerable concern as soon as a more active interest began to be taken in the well-being of the lower-classes. Was this evidence of massive social disorganisation or was there something wrong with a view that measured 'legitimacy' according to 'English' or 'upper-class' standards? It had long been known that women exhibited a high degree of independence both in the West Indies and among Negroes in the United States and Frazier had referred to the 'matricentric' family based on a mother and her children, and to a 'type of matriarchate' based upon a group consisting of an old woman, her daughters and their children. The primacy of the relationships between mother and children was remarked upon by both Frazier and Herskovits. Frazier saw this unit of mother and children as the one primary group which had persisted throughout the slavery period while Herskovits derived its structural importance from the domestic organisation of African societies where the mother-children group forms a separate cell within the framework of the polygynous family. Both spoke of the destruction of male roles in relation to the domestic group during the slavery period and Frazier tried to show with a wealth of historical material that American Negroes had rebuilt a stable family life with strong paternal authority whenever they had been able to do so. That is, whenever they could get decent jobs which enabled them to provide the economic foundations for a reasonable family life in the American fashion. In looking at West Indian societies it was natural to adopt the points of view developed in these studies since the family arrangements seemed to be quite similar to those described by Frazier, and there was ample evidence of African cultural survivals. But there were other factors involved in the West Indies. The atmosphere of these developing societies was such that it predisposed students to examine the contemporary situation rather than its historical derivation. Professor Simey did as much as anyone to set the pattern for future studies by his use of simple distribution figures for various family 'types', taking his data from a survey conducted by Lewis Davidson in Jamaica.[9] Both Simey and Henriques[10] directed attention to the colour-class system and to the fact that there seemed to be a close relation between colour, occupational or economic level and family type. By the time Henriques' book was published in 1953 the idea was firmly established that there are a number of different family types each of which is 'normal' within the stratum in which it occurs. A slight variant of this idea was put forward by Dom Basil Matthews on the basis of a number of years work in Trinidad.[11] Focussing attention upon what he called 'the non-legal union' he tried to show that the persistence of this form of mating in the New World is related to the continued importance of plantation agriculture which dominates the economies and the social life of so many territories.

He wrote:

> The persistence of the non-legal union has to do essentially with the
> persistence in the social system of those elements which produced it in
> the first instance. On the impersonal or material side, the effective agents
> or factors comprise the geographic, economic, moral and social conditions
> built into the free plantation economy, heir to the physical and social
> traditions of the plantation in slavery. On the personal and formal side,
> the deciding factor was and is, the free choice of the people. It must,
> however, be conceded that in their choice the people were confronted with
> an overmastering set of social and economic conditions which it was
> morally impossible, that is to say, extremely difficult, for them to overcome.
> The social and economic setting and background of the non-legal
> union everywhere suffice to explain its social origins and its social struc-
> ture. And this setting and historical background are the same for all peo-
> ples in the New World, even for those who did not themselves undergo
> the ordeals of slavery.[12]

This was an important variant upon the themes of colour and poverty because it introduced the idea that high illegitimacy rates and unstable family
forms are not peculiar to the Negro lower-classes but are related to the
existence of a form of social organisation found in the non-Negro areas of
Latin America as well. There is also the suggestion here that the plantation
economy produced a peculiar type of social system wherever it occurred, a
type of social system with a distinct value configuration which would affect
all those who became involved in it irrespective of their contact with plantation life itself.

Here then by the early 1950's the main shape of future studies had
been blocked out. This is by no means a complete survey of the work that
had been published up to that time. A fuller bibliography can be assembled from the summaries by Mintz and Davenport contained in *Working
Papers in Caribbean Social Organization*.[13] No attempt has been made
here to examine the often penetrating commentaries by contemporary
writers for the slavery and post-slavery periods. Extracts such as the following show that many of the ideas we work with today are really quite
old:

> I have known them [the slaves] point to things of this description,
> for the purpose of shewing that it is impossible for them to marry. Over
> their children it is obvious that they could have no authority resembling
> that which parents in a free country possess: they could only leave them
> the same wretched inheritance which they received from their ancestors.
> Hence those who have children are careless in respect to the habits they
> form, and the lives they lead. They know they can never sink lower in the
> scale of society than they already find themselves placed, and they have
> no hope of rising. A regular line of orderly conduct may save them from
> the lash but it can effect no radical change in their condition.[14]

By the early 1950's a clear distinction had been made between cultural
persistence as an explanatory device and the study of contemporary struc-

tural arrangements and inter-connections. Some writers like Simey, Henriques and Matthews adopted a two-dimensional approach but without pushing very far in either direction. The obvious need was for more detailed studies, both historical and of contemporary structure; the main emphasis in recent work has been on the latter for the simple reason that material is more easily available. Mr. George Robert's work in demographic problems is perhaps an exception in that he has done considerable research on archival and census material but he too has been concentrating upon surveys to provide supplementary data in recent years.[15] Almost all recent discussions have been based upon the analysis of quantitative data of the kind presented in my own work on British Guiana and in Miss Clarke's study of Jamaica.[16] In the Mintz-Davenport volume, *Working Papers in Caribbean Social Organization,* four·out of the five papers concentrate upon analysis of quantitative material on household composition while M. G. Smith's book *West Indian Family Structure,* is an extended comparison of statistical data on household composition and mating from five samples, two in Jamaica, two in Grenada, and one in Carriacou. One of the reasons for the concentration upon domestic organization was that since it had been usual to speak of lower-class family life as being 'disorganised' it was important to establish whether any patterning existed at all, and whether the 'disorganization' was not primarily a matter of definition. From our general knowledge of other societies we know that unstable marriage, separate residence of spouses, or even the complete whittling away of the marriage relationship as among the Nayar, is not necessarily a sign of social instability or of pathological development. In an important paper published in 1949 Fortes had shown that a wide range of variability in household composition among the Ashanti could be understood as the result of the varying strength of two major forces; the pull of matrilineal kinship ties on the one hand, and the tendency for the nuclear family to establish itself as a separate unit on the oher.[17] It was pointed out that while economic factors and missionary teaching tended to reinforce the claims of nuclear family relationships at the expense of the matrilineal tie, the conflict was not new, but must be rooted in the very nature of matrilineal systems. Audrey Richards made much the same point in an essay on Central African matrilineal societies published in 1950.[18] Fortes also demonstrated that the shape of households is bound to change over time since households are constituted around the process of physical and social reproduction and are therefore tied to biological birth, maturation and death—a point which he has made even more elegantly in a recent publication.[19] Much the same techniques of analysis have been used in recent studies in the Caribbean but the problem has been to determine the forces which are at work giving shape to domestic group structure. Another way to put it is to ask how social reproduction is accomplished and how it fits with other activities which in many societies are embedded in domestic organisation—activities such as mating, domestic services such as cooking, washing, the provision of economic support and so on. In my studies of three Negro villages in British Guiana, *The Negro Family in British Guiana,* I paid particular attention to the developmental cycle of household groups and tried to see the extent to which the ideal form of nuclear family domestic group is realised in practice and what patterning there is in the deviations from this form. Nancie L. Solien drew attention to the fact that in view of the many relationships which seem to exist in some Caribbean societies between individuals who reside in *different* households, including nuclear family relationships, more attention should be given to investigating these relationships and a clear distinction should be made between domestic organisation and family structure.[20] M. G. Smith takes this point and makes it the basis of his analysis, though the nature of much of his survey data, which was collected during brief interviews, makes it impossible for him to deal in depth with extra-residential relationships. As more field studies are made available it is becoming clear that we need to reconsider the whole question of the relation between nuclear family relationships, socialization and domestic structure; new questions have arisen and new investigations will have to be carried out, but unless we are to revise the whole of current family theory it will not be possible to ignore nuclear family relationships as one important constellation of roles which has functional as well as formal implications.

Another major variable, or set of variables, that has been investigated for its effect upon family and domestic organization is 'the economy' or economic factors. Earlier writers such as Frazier, Simey, and Henriques had discussed the effect of 'poverty' in producing or perpetuating unstable family forms. One of Miss Clarke's main objectives in conducting the West Indian Social Survey (which was actually a study of family life and child-rearing in Jamaica) had been to measure the effect of varying economic background upon family structure. In order to do this she chose communities in a) a sugar plantation area, b) a poverty stricken peasant farming area and c) a relatively prosperous community of citrus farmers.[21] Miss Clarke's collaborator in this study, Dr. Madeleine Kerr, transformed the idea of 'poverty' into that of 'social deprivation' by adding other dimensions to it and has since carried out comparative work in a Liverpool slum area which yields surprisingly similar conclusions about the effect of such deprivation upon personality.[22] Most of the conclusions of these studies are incorporated in Davenport's excellent discussion of the Jamaican family system.[23] Cumper's paper on Barbados and Wilson's on Providencia Island both treat of economic and status factors as the prime variable affecting domestic and family relations but none of the papers in *Working Papers in Caribbean Social Organization,* nor M. G. Smith's book, deal adequately with the whole question of status, societal and subcultural norms, mainly because all the studies limit themselves to Negro subsectors of these societies.

The other major variable to receive considerable attention recently is the organisation of mating relations. From one point of view this is an integral part of the discussion of nuclear family relationships. In the Caribbean it must receive special attention because of the prevalence of unstable mating, of a widespread distinction between legal and non-legal unions, and the existence of mating unions which do not involve common residence. Studies by Roberts and Braithwaite,[24] Judith Blake[25] and M. G. Smith's book *West Indian Family Structure* focus upon the variability in mating relations and its effect upon family structure, and M. G. Smith's book raises anew the whole question of African heritage versus slavery by his derivation of present mating forms from slavery. In the following discussion these varying aspects of Caribbean family structure and its social milieu are dealt with one by one in an attempt to take stock of recent contributions.

THE NUCLEAR FAMILY AND KINSHIP STRUCTURES

Since Murdock published his *Social Structure* in 1949 there has been considerable controversy over the question of the universality of the nuclear family and over Murdock's statement that:

> The family is a social group characterised by common residence, economic cooperation, and reproduction. It includes adults of both sexes, at least two of whom maintain a socially approved sexual relationship, and one or more children, own or adopted, of the sexually cohabiting adults.[26]

It has been pointed out that in many cases husbands and wives habitually live in separate households, or that in some societies nuclear families are so absorbed in wider units that they can hardly be said to exist as separate organizational complexes at all. Despite these objections there has been a convergence upon the view that the basic functions of the family are those of socialization and the regulation of personality whatever other activities the family may engage in, and for these functions the role structure of nuclear family relationships seems to be both required and universally present in all societies.[27] According to some variants of this view it is not necessary that every 'family' should be a concrete co-residential nuclear family group, but the role system of nuclear family relationships should be institutionalised and in the normal cases enough interaction should exist to carry out the functions and to maintain the system. In particular cases nuclear family relationships exist across the boundaries of household groups, household groups take on a great many other activities than those of child-care and sexual interaction, and nuclear family roles may be performed by individuals other than 'real' family members, but empirically there seems to be a close correspondence between 'family' activities and domestic group organisation. As Fortes says, "In all human societies, the workshop, so to speak, of social reproduction, is the domestic group."[28] These views would seem to mean that the nuclear family is more than a fortuitous by-product of sexual mating and physical birth; that it has positive functions and is in a sense 'required' if societies of human beings are to continue. Even Leach in his discussion of the variability of ideologies of reproduction and genetic transmission seems to assume that underneath the differing type of relationship of incorporation and alliance actual nuclear family relationships exist.[29] Even if the theory exists that mothers and sons are like affines, they do not engage in sexual intercourse and there would appear to be more to it than the simple fear of committing adultery, even though this might fit very nicely at the formal structural level. There is something more than psychological dogma or the slavish copying of Freud to the idea that the relationship between a mother and her children is of a particularly close kind, even if at other levels of behaviour the relationship is played down. With the father-child relationship the position is rather different and even those theorists who base their arguments for the universality of the nuclear family upon personality theory admit a great deal of variability in this relationship. Apart from their domestic and familial roles, men in most societies have important statuses in wider social systems and therefore the husband-father role is particularly responsive to variations in the external situation.

Analysis of the Caribbean material is affected by these changing views of nuclear family functions and it provides evidence bearing upon those views. Solien's insistence upon the distinction between household and family arose out of her experience of family arrangements among the Black Carib of Guatemala. She says:

> The nuclear family unit among the Carib may be scattered in several different households. For example, the husband-father may be living with his own mother, one or more children may be with their maternal relatives or with non-Caribs, while the mother may be working and "living in" as a maid in one of the port towns.[30]

Her observations could be duplicated from every report that has ever been written on lower-class Negro family life, and it is quite true that the concentration of attention upon the household as a functioning unit of childcare and economic organisation has tended to divert attention from the networks of relationship linking households to each other. It is important that these relationships be studied with as much exactitude as possible but it would be ridiculous to regard the household in a purely negative way, or to forget that 'family' functions require frequent social interaction and not merely a token recognition of consanguineal or deactivated conjugal relationships. It is also important to know the frequency with which the patterns of divided residence occur and the intensity of the relationships which are maintained across household boundaries. This problem is discussed again below in relation to mating.

The study of household composition has shown that a variety of kinship ties may be activated to bring people together into the same dwelling unit, and considerable attention has been given to charting the shape of kinship systems and the strength of the various relationships within them.

Both Davenport and Solien have analysed 'non-unilineal descent groups' as a structural type and Solien has identified such formations among the Black Carib as well as suggesting that they probably exist elsewhere in the Caribbean. M. G. Smith speaks of patrilineages in Carriacou (though his use of the term 'lineage' is somewhat idiosyncratic) and Bastien stresses the importance of patrilineal joint families in Haiti. Davenport's discussion of the lower-class Jamaican Negro kinship system is couched in general terms but provides an excellent overall view which is applicable to most British West Indian territories. He characterises it as being based upon 'kindred organisation'. By this he means that there are no corporate kin groups, as such, that kinship is reckoned bilaterally and that kinship rights and obligations are relative to individuals. What is equally clear is that "Parents, parent's siblings, first cousins, children, sibling's children (both sexes referred to as 'niece') and grandchildren form a hard core of close kin that is sometimes described as 'near family', in order to distinguish it from more distant relatives, called 'far family'. A person's kindred then will be defined as his near family, plus any other kin with whom he may have special relationships."[31] It is clear from this that kindred ties arise out of domestic relations, mating, and local community ties. Within the kindred, relationships are further modified by emphasis upon siblingship and mother-child relations in much the same way as previously described for British Guiana.[32]

So far as Carriacou and its 'patrilineage' organisation is concerned we are dealing with a miniature society with a whole series of special features. Carriacou is an island dependency of Grenada, which is itself dependent upon the British Government's grants even to balance its budget. Carriacou has a population of about 6,800 and an area of 13 square miles. A large proportion of its male inhabitants are off the island working at any one time. As M. G. Smith describes it there is no significant class differentiation within this small population, and of course the island is so small that most people must know each other personally. The majority of households are headed by women but since there are 2½ times as many adult women as men resident on the island this is perhaps not surprising. The 'bloods' or 'patrilineages' appear to be name groups consisting of those agnatic kin between whom extended family relations exist. The development of these groups seems to be related to the stability of local relations, the regulation of mating in a very small community and the performance of family rituals —the family being not only ideally but actually paternalistic. Not dissimilar name lines of even greater depth can be found in isolated and economically stagnant Guianese Negro villages, but the units carrying out ritual activities are the close kindred on the one hand and the whole village community on the other. It is clear from M. G. Smith's descriptions that it is not merely the existence of 'bloods' which makes paternity important within the family system, but also the strong emphasis upon legal marriage and the status conferring functions of paternity plus the channelling of male economic support through the husband-father role. In other words, it is not the 'lineage' that determines male domestic roles, but other variables.

More extensive groups of kin, settled on 'family land' as in Jamaica or constituting extended family clusters as in Haiti, arise out of common interests in land and Davenport offers an excellent summary of the situation in Jamaica. He stresses the fact that 'family land' represents a focus of interest for absent kindred and while rights in family land are vested in all the members of the kindred there is, inevitably, a number of mechanisms for limiting the actual exercise of claims.

To sum up. The kinship system is bilateral and not very extensive. The most important relationships within it arise out of co-residence, co-siblingship, and the coincidence of neighbourhood and kinship ties. The special strength of the mother-child relationship compared to the easy diminution of father-child ties has been noted by all writers but the reasons for this cannot be located merely in the definition of kinship relations. Similarly the emergence of short matri-lines consisting of mother, daughters, and daughter's children is an important feature of the system though M. G. Smith asserts that this has been greatly exaggerated in the literature.[33] Elizabeth Bott's comments on the conditions necessary for the emergence of these female solidarities are interesting especially since they are based upon work in Britain rather than in the Caribbean. She says:

> . . . the psychological consequences of being brought up in a family having marked segregation of parental roles does not of itself produce groups of women within a kinship network. All it produces is a close emotional tie between mother and children, particularly between mother and daughter. Before there can be a group there must also be several related women in the same place at the same time. If groups of grandmother, mothers, and daughters are to be formed, women should get married young, they should have plenty of children, preferably girls, they should live for a long time, and all the women concerned should continue to live in the same local area. The formation of such groups also depends on certain negative factors—on the absence of rights to land or other economic advantages through the father and his relatives. . .
>
> To phrase the discussion in general terms: whenever there are no particular economic advantages to be gained by affiliation with parental relatives, and whenever two or preferably three generations of mothers and daughters are living in the same place at the same time, a bilateral kinship system is likely to develop a matrilateral stress, and groups composed of sets of mothers and daughters may form within networks of kin.[34]

The special relationship between 'two sisters' children' which was reported for British Guiana[35] and which M. G. Smith has included under the more general term 'materterine' kinship (a term first suggested by Schapera[36]) is, in the societies we are dealing with, clearly derivative from the kind of female grouping within bilateral networks that Bott has described. The placement of children with their mother's sister or mother's sister's daughter is a logical procedure once such female groups have existed.

MARRIAGE AND MATING

What is the nature of the mating system and what is the significance of high illegitimacy rates? This is the most vexed question in the whole literature on Caribbean family systems. It would be impossible to discuss it fully here but certain broad features are clear. Legal, christian, monogamous marriage is everywhere accepted as the correct and respectable form of mating relationship by all sections of the population of Caribbean societies, with the exception of the East Indian groups in Trinidad and British Guiana. In practice the majority of children are conceived and born *outside* such marital relationships. Some of these children are born to couples who live together in non-legal unions, and some are born to women who are not in co-residential unions and who enjoy varying degrees of stability in their relations with the father of their children. M. G. Smith refers to all these latter as 'extra-residential unions', ignoring the differences between them except when they become so unstable as to constitute promiscuity, and he further maintains that a specific type of parental role is associated with such a form of mating though he does not tell us what it is. A more sophisticated treatment in quantitative terms has been carried out by Roberts and Braithwaite who use the term 'visiting' union and try to distinguish degrees of stability within this broad category.[37] A recent book by Judith Blake dealing with Jamaica discusses the whole question of extra-residential mating in a clear and lively way.[38] It is obvious that the existence of visiting unions and the birth of children to women in such unions must affect household composition and, despite Dr. M. G. Smith's assumptions to the contrary, this has been recognised by all previous writers on the subject. The problem is—why do extra-residential mating and co-residential non-legal unions occur and how stable are such forms of mating? Among the Ashanti extra-residential mating is a recognised form clearly associated with the strength of matrilineal ties, and it is based upon clearly recognised marital relationships which include properly defined mutual rights, duties and obligations. Among the Nayar it is again related to matrilineal ties and the need for their protection. In the Caribbean extra-residential mating is clearly associated with the *avoidance* of responsibilities and rights and obligations. Full acceptance of responsibility involves co-residence, but even here there is a variation in the degree of assumption of responsibility from the minimum amount involved in short-term unstable unions up to that of stable marital unions. M. G. Smith joins a long, and respectable, line of writers who attribute the non-legal mating patterns of West Indians to customs laid down during slavery, plus (in order to account for the absence of common-law marriage in Carriacou) the varying success of the churches in enforcing lawful marriage in different areas.[39] He is doubtless correct and there is no reason for not recognising also that there is an equal likelihood that West African patterns of extra-residential mating have persisted into the present. Mintz states very clearly the case for further historical research which will have as its object the elucidation of structural relations at various stages of Caribbean history; the progressive development of different types of structural arrangements has been worked out for Puerto Rico but very little along these lines has been done for the British Caribbean as yet. But even if more attention is devoted to historical research (as opposed to speculation) Schapera's point will remain valid—"I do not imagine that we shall ever abandon completely the study of the social present, and in a study of that kind history is at best an aid to understanding and not the only means of understanding."[40] If we recognise the existence of a direct connection between slave society and the present and between the present lower-class Negro family system and that of the slave plantation, what accounts for the persistence of those patterns? Is it cultural inertia or the existence of a separate folk-culture in a plural society, or is something else involved? Numerous answers have been given to this question and their consideration brings us to the next stage of the discussion.

ECONOMIC AND STATUS FACTORS

It has been a matter of common knowledge for a very long time that there is some sort of association between mating patterns and family structure on the one hand and the level of income and status on the other. Frazier made this association the basis of his analysis and both Simey and Henriques laid primary emphasis upon poverty and low status as causal factors in producing mating and family patterns which deviate from the societal ideals. It has always been assumed that in the 'middle' and 'upper' classes (however they may be defined) legal christian marriage is the rule, that it is an essential prelude to child-bearing, and that the typical domestic unit consists of a nuclear family group. As Davenport says, ". . . it will be assumed [for lack of data to the contrary] that the middle and upper-class family systems are homogeneous and indistinguishable from those of comparable class strata in England and the United States."[41] There is good reason to believe that this is not wholly true. In the first place we know that kinship ties are recognised to a much wider degree than in the U.S. or Britain, partly because of the immobility of the higher status groups and their concentration in a few urban centres. There is also a well marked pattern of extra-marital mating on the part of higher status males. Along with the middle-class emphasis upon respectable patterns of behaviour which differentiate them from the lower-classes, there is an old and pervasive pattern of sexual licence for men. The idea of the Caribbean as a place of hot passions, sensuous music and provocative calypso is not something dreamed up by the tourist agencies. The Europeans set the pattern of mating outside marriage by their willingness to take black or coloured mistresses, and the existence of a large population of mixed-bloods testifies to the importance of the pattern set by the upper classes. The ambivalence about stable marriage, for men at least, is probably found at all levels of the society. Certainly more research needs to be done on attitudes toward marriage among the higher status groups in Caribbean societies, and its possible contribution to attitudes of permissiveness at all levels of the society. Judith Blake, in her recent book on Jamaica, argues that her interview data show that the vast majority of Jamaican women wish to marry, that everyone in the society regardless of class level or culture regards marriage as the right framework for mating, but that men are able to exploit the ignorance and the economic insecurity of women to enjoy regular sexual associations without the responsibility of marriage. She considers that the family structure is weak and that the present conditions reinforce this weakness, that there is no sub-norm of preference for non-legal unions, and that if "economic development and adequate opportunities within the system of social stratification" develop then it is possible that the family system will develop enough control to propel people into marriage at the proper time.[42] Before examining this idea further what sort of variation do we actually find according to economic and status differences?

Edith Clarke's work in Jamaica as presented in *My Mother Who Fathered Me* showed that the variation in mating and household types between her three field centres was quite complex and depended upon more than simple differences in income level. The nature of the community structure and the type of economic base on which the family is erected also affect the picture. For example the high incidence of both concubinage and one-person households in Sugartown is not associated simply with low incomes, but with a whole pattern of mobility, casual labour, individualism, absence of wide kinship networks and a particular kind of community authority structure. In both Mocca (the peasant hill community) and Orange Grove (the prosperous farming area) the household group is a unit of agricultural production in addition to any other functions it may have. The extent of co-operation between families was small in Mocca and extensive in Orange Grove, according to Miss Clarke, and it is interesting that the type of community activity found in Orange Grove is that associated with 'development' and is therefore in conformity with wider societal values. The building of a Community Hall, organising a Savings Union, Agricultural Society Branch, Egg Co-operative, Cricket Club and so forth were obviously related to the level of agricultural prosperity and the striving after a greater sense of social worth. Marriage rates were higher in Orange Grove than in the other two centres, but there was also a higher proportion of extended families of all types, including those with a female head. This is related to the fact that in this community there is an adequate economic base for the growth of more extensive kinship units, so that older women as well as men are able to build up sizeable household groups. Without such a base, including a house, it is difficult for households to grow beyond a certain size, and once a family passes a certain socio-economic level there is presumably an incentive to reduce the size of the household in order to alter the style of life and to facilitate upward mobility.

The most detailed treatment of the relation between 'economic' data and household composition is provided by Cumper both in his earlier work on Jamaica and in his "Household and Occupation in Barbados" which is one of the essays in the Davenport-Mintz volume.[43] Although he works with a relatively simple model which relates the household to the occupational system through the boundary role of the household head, he is not simply dealing with "economic" factors as Davenport suggests.[44] His sample of 1,296 Barbadian households (a random sample of 1 in 42 of the island's population) is divided into eight groups based upon the occupation of the household head. While not attempting to measure 'status' apart from income it is clear that in Barbados occupation is a good index to status. For example, the difference in income between skilled workers and non-farm labourers is very small, but skilled workers are probably a higher status group and this is reflected in the higher incidence of common-law marriages among labourers.

It would be impossible to summarise Cumper's very detailed data on Barbados here but certain key points are worth noting. The group of households in which the head is a white-collar worker conform reasonably closely to the societal ideal of a nuclear family group based upon stable legal marriage. Barbados has a large white population and it is possible that the picture for this white-collar group is affected by the fact that there is a large racially white element included. However, Dr. Cumper is of the opinion that the majority of families in this group are non-white though he has no statistical data on this point.[45] At the other end of the comparative scale Cumper places a group of 'peasant proprietors' whose households appear to be typically stable units, a high proportion of them based upon legal marriage, but containing a relatively high proportion of the children of unmarried daughters. (Peasant proprietors in Barbados, like those in British Guiana, generally live in close proximity to sugar plantations and depend upon them for part-time work.) In all peasant households, both male and female headed, male earnings constitute the bulk of household resources and female heads of households are usually widows or women whose spouses are away or have deserted them. Peasant proprietors are a stable population living in their own houses and able on this account, as well as the relative security of their economic base, to sustain three-generation domestic groups. Cumper shows very ingeniously that the intermediate occupational categories and their households can be dynamically related to each other and to the peasant types through a consideration of the life chances and experiences of their members. It is the same method of analysis which Cumper used so successfully in his study of the symbiotic relationship between sugar plantations, hill peasant communities, and urban migration in Jamaica, and it demands a consideration of development over time including occupational mobility.

The intermediate categories with which he deals consist of:

1. "Renters"—a group of agricultural labourers who erect their own moveable houses upon rented land.

2. Landless labourers (agricultural).
3. Domestic servants.
4. Own Account workers.
5. Non-farm labourers.
6. Skilled workers.

What Cumper suggests is that the 'renters' and landless labourer categories are being constantly augmented by young men with their way to make in the world—young men who are incapable of meeting the prescriptions of the role of married household head. Their compromise solution is to enter into non-legal unions of varying degrees of stability; the acquisition of a house without land is, for example, considered to be a sufficient basis for establishing a common-law marriage, or a young man may join the household of a woman and her mother where he can receive various kinds of domestic services as well as enjoy sexual relations in exchange for his contribution to the household economy. The instability of these unions produces female headed households of either the two or three generation type and of the same general nature as those termed 'denuded' by Miss Clarke. Some young men move from the agricultural labourer or peasant groups into skilled labour but in these cases the men concerned are likely to acquire new mobility aspirations and to adopt new cultural norms in relation to marriage and family formation. Or to put it another way they may feel, because of their higher status occupation, that they are better able to live up to the role prescriptions of the family norms accepted by the whole society as being correct. On the other hand many men and women remain in the renter and landless labourer groups for life, and as they grow older they too may try to meet the cultural prescriptions of the total society by getting married. The possession of even a moveable house on rented land seems to increase the potentiality of the household developing into a three generation group but among the landless labourers households are held together mainly by women, who, living in rented or free quarters manage by their own, their children's or their daughters' lovers' labour to provide an economic base for the continued existence of domestic units.

In the non-agricultural sector the categories of 'own account worker' and 'domestic' are in some senses the counterpart of 'renter' and 'landless labourer' occupations. The households with domestics as heads are naturally female headed, since domestic service is a female occupation in the West Indies, but many of these women have been, or are, in unions of some kind. About 10% of the households contain a common-law husband of the head and ". . . a third or more . . . receive some support from a man who is, or has been, the husband or lover of the head."[46] Other important contributions flow in from remittances and pensions. The own-account worker group contains a varied collection of people from small jobbing contractors to seamstresses, petty shopkeepers and female traders. This group is generally economically less secure than any other non-agricultural group despite its economic independence, and it contains a high proportion of older men living alone, and women from broken unions.

Cumper recognises that his material is limited in many respects, but he shows very clearly the sort of control that is necessary before one can generalise about 'urban' and 'rural' groups in the West Indies. If one compares Cumper's work with that of Dr. M. G. Smith, as set out in his *West Indian Family Structure,* one is immediately conscious of the shortcomings of Smith's generalisations about urban and rural patterns in Jamaica. By lumping together the sample populations on a geographical basis and speaking of status only in terms of a 'folk' typology, Smith confuses important differences within these groups if Cumper's arguments are correct. Davenport too recognises the importance of economic and occupational differences in Jamaica when he says:

> Land and wealth are almost synonymous to the lower-class countryman. When he is landless he is poor, with nothing to fall back on in time of need, and no place to go to when wage work is done. Under these dire circumstances, households, as we have seen, tend to be small or incomplete, with their members dispersed throughout related households which are better able to support them.[47]

SOCIAL CLASS AND THE PLURAL SOCIETY

So far we have dealt mainly with studies of family structure among lower status Negro groups for the simple reason that this is where most work has been done. In most societies in the Caribbean Negroes constitute the lowest status groups for historical reasons and it is therefore very difficult to determine whether the pattern of family and mating relations found among them is due to economic and status factors alone or whether residues of African and slave plantation culture constitute the determining factors. What complicates the matter further is that dark skin colour is itself a status factor in all Caribbean societies. This is a contemporary fact and not simply a 'survival'. Theoretically the study of family structure among East Indians should provide us with a crucial test since in Trinidad, British Guiana and Jamaica East Indians constitute (or did until recently) a special low status group. A number of studies have been carried out in recent years which show conclusively that the East Indian family pattern is quite distinct from that of the lower class Negro groups.[48] Morton Klass in his book *East Indians in Trinidad: A Study of cultural persistence* chooses a deliberately cultural bias in his analysis and sees the East Indians of Trinidad as people who have, in the face of considerable difficulty, re-established an Indian village way of life. Studies by Roberts and Braithwaite in Trinidad and by Smith and Jayawardena in British Guiana,[49] show that there are considerable differences between the kinship structure of Indians in these territories and a pure Indian system (if there is such a thing). What is distinctive about East Indian family and kinship structure is the early age at which marriage takes place, the absence of extra-residential mating and the position of the husband-father in the domestic organisation. All these factors are certainly associated with a continuing Indian sub-culture though all of them are also consonant with the ideal pattern of the total society. In practice they are considerably modified by circumstances. Early marriage takes place but it is usually customary religious marriage and not legal marriage and the incidence of break-up of first unions is high both in British Guiana and in Trinidad.[50] Even if these first unions are regarded as proper marriages and not equivalent to common-law marriages among Negroes, subsequent unions are apt to be simple common-law unions. There is also considerable variation in the internal relations of domestic units. Jayawardena shows that in the sugar estate communities paternal authority is considerably modified in situations where sons, wives and daughters contribute substantially to household income.[51] But the crucial point is that the role of husband-father among Indians is defined in a quite different way to its definition in the rest of the society. A household which does not have a man to represent it in community affairs, in religious organisations and at rites-de-passage is socially deficient. The authority and status of the husband-father within the family does not depend solely upon his ability to provide for his family and to achieve a certain standard of consumption, nor does it depend upon his ability to participate in activities characteristic of higher class groups; it depends upon his ability to represent his family within the Indian community and its specialised associations, though the man's earning capacity and his occupational status are becoming more important as Indians become more closely integrated in the societies of which they are now a part.

Various attempts have been made to place the discussion of Caribbean family systems in a wider comparative framework; a framework not of historical comparisons designed to trace cultural derivations, but a structural framework in which cross-cultural comparisons could be made. Such a comparative framework was suggested in *The Negro Family in British Guiana* and a more elaborate comparative scheme was suggested some years ago by William J. Goode in his paper on "Illegitimacy, Anomie and Cultural Penetration".[52] Goode treats illegitimacy as an index to familial disorganization under certain circumstances. In European countries where illegitimacy rates are high this is usually associated with freedom in courtship and delays in getting married rather than with casual or unsanctioned mating. In Africa the high illegitimacy rates are found mainly in urban areas and are to be seen as a result of the effects of migration and the subsequent weakening of tribal community sanctions. In the New World communities of Latin America, the Caribbean and the southern United States special conditions have been created by massive cultural penetration and the destruction of traditional social systems. Goode suggests that a four phase development is likely under such circumstances:

1. Pre-contact situation with low illegitimacy rates.
2. Intense contact in cities with high urban illegitimacy rates.
3. Beginnings of assimilation in the urban areas and spread of contact to rural areas results in a drop in urban illegitimacy rates below those of the rural areas.

4. The development of a unitary social system and uniformly low illegitimacy rates.

In the Americas south of the Rio Grande the destruction of traditional cultures was accompanied by a period of economic stagnation in which there was little opportunity for the development of upward mobility. A relatively integrated western group dominated many anomic communities in which the peasants had a low commitment to western values while their old values had been undermined. Goode also adopts Merton's idea that anomie can result from the failure to master instrumental norms which are necessary for adherence to cultural norms, so that low educational levels, absence of skills and so forth impede social integration around new norms. This paper is a reasonable attempt to generalise over a wide range of data but it necessarily by-passes many difficulties. The problem of measuring national integration is much more difficult than is suggested and continuing sharp status differentiations are often related to the maintenance of given economic and political systems rather than to some disembodied process of cultural contact and assimilation.

Goode's analysis raises the crucial question of what constitutes 'anomie'. Are we dealing with a state of normlessness in badly integrated societies; are these 'plural societies' in which the population segments "mix but do not mingle", as Furnival said; or are they societies of a peculiar type in which a special mode of integration of a differentiated population obtains? This is a fundamental problem for upon its solution depends the kind of analytical framework one adopts for the examination of family structure and mating. Dr. M. G. Smith takes a 'plural society' view so that for him extra-residential mating and common-law marriage are patterns of "folk culture"—at least so long as they appear to have statistical stability. Miss Blake takes the opposite view and, as a result of attitude measurement, concludes that all Jamaicans hold the same values but many are prevented from realising those values in action owing to a breakdown in social control and to the unfavourable position in which women find themselves. The fact is of course that lower-class West Indian Negroes hold contradictory views about what is desirable or possible for them; otherwise one can hardly explain the fact that although couples live together without benefit of clergy they usually do marry eventually or in times of stress.[53] The problem is to uncover the source of this patterned deviance from social values.

There is a fundamental dissonance between the accepted ideals of these societies and the objective possibility of their realisation by the majority of people. This is not due simply to a failure to master instrumental norms; it has to do with the mode of integration of colonial or ex-colonial societies around the acceptance of white superiority while at the same time political power was deployed for the maintenance of a relatively fixed pattern of social and economic relations. It was, and in many cases still is, a far more rigid stratification than that of nineteenth century England and it produced a family system much closer to Engel's picture of proletarian family life than Europe ever did. Even the special position of East Indians is due to their relative isolation on plantations and to a deliberately pursued policy of encouraging them to retain Indian customs instead of becoming christianised, educated and assimilated to creole society; a policy that was only partially successful.

CONCLUSION

The work reviewed here shows that the study of Caribbean kinship and family structure raises a host of general theoretical problems. Most obviously there is the problem of determining just what is the structure of family relations, how it fits into the domestic organisation and how it is related to generalisations about the family as universal social institution. The adoption of statistical measures of frequency in types of domestic, kinship and mating relations and the use of developmental cycle models, has revealed some very complex patterns. It is to be expected that controversy will continue over the question of whether a number of discrete 'types' of family structure or of household composition are involved or whether actual variations can be seen as the resultant of the interaction of a limited number of organisational principles. There is room for considerable refinement in the application of statistical techniques. Most early studies were case studies of particular communities employing 100% surveys or using very large samples. Now that investigators are beginning to work with national samples or at least with samples covering very large populations it is imperative that proper tests of significance be applied. While the tendency to apply statistical measures over a larger area of the social map is a very welcome trend, it is also necessary to extend the study of family and kinship relations in depth by doing more case studies. Although the records of social agencies, mental hospitals and clinics may contain some interesting case material no systematic work has been done on such records. One suspects that the records are really inadequate. Because of the inarticulateness of the lower-classes, the relative dearth of literary work dealing with lower-class life, and the limited number of people who receive any kind of psycho-therapy we know little of a really intimate nature respecting the personal and family life of Caribbean peoples. Field anthropologists have so far been trying to understand a wide range of behaviour and have not had the time for a close study of a limited number of cases. The biographical studies by Mintz,[54] M. G. Smith,[55] and Oscar Lewis[56] are valuable but we need studies comparable to those carried out in England by Elizabeth Bott. This would deepen our understanding of lower-class motives, feelings, frustrations and values. Judith Blake is right in her contention that we do not understand people's values well enough but more is needed than simple, short, attitude surveys especially since there is so much conflicting evidence.

The major problem is what it has always been; to relate patterns of familial, domestic and mating behaviour to other factors in the contemporary social systems and to the cultural traditions of the people concerned. Here progress has been less impressive because we are still unclear about the nature of these societies. William J. Goode speaks about degrees of political integration, Dr. Eric Williams voices his doubts about whether Trinidad is a society at all, and Dr. M. G. Smith asserts that we are dealing with 'plural societies'. These are not mere idle speculations; they determine what factors we shall consider important for their effect upon family relations. It is possible to start with a close look at families and to move outwards, exploring the systems of action in which family members are enmeshed and we can construct theories of the middle range—or models of limited mechanisms. But eventually we shall have to make decisions about such questions as what is the meaning of blackness in societies integrated around the dominance of whiteness? or what is the meaning of being Indian in societies where prestige is defined in terms of Spanish culture? or what does it mean to be an East Indian in Trinidad? To answer these questions calls for models of total social systems no matter what kind of models they may be. It is an urgent task to find out more about the mode of integration of these societies, both for its intrinsic interest and as the proper framework for family and kinship studies.

In the meantime it is a pleasure to record the considerable progress that has been made in recent years and the growing interest in the Caribbean to which the studies reviewed here testify. A special debt of gratitude is due to the Research Institute for the Study of Man, and to its Director Dr. Vera Rubin, for the assistance it has given to most of the recent studies discussed here.

Notes

1. Eric Williams, *History of the People of Trinidad and Tobago* (PNM Publishing Co., Ltd., Port of Spain, Trinidad, 1962), p. 284.
2. W. L. Burn, *Emancipation and Apprenticeship in the West Indies* (Jonathan Cape, London, 1937), p. 370.
3. Sidney W. Mintz and William Davenport (Eds.), *Working Papers in Caribbean Social Organization,* being a special number of *Social and Economic Studies,* Vol. 10, No. 4 (1961).—M. G. Smith, *West Indian Family Structure* (University of Washington Press, Seattle, 1962).
4. Sidney W. Mintz, "A Final Note", *Working Papers in Caribbean Social Organization,* p. 528.
5. Among recent studies the following deal with family structure and mating: R. T. Smith & C. Jayawardena, "Hindu Marriage Customs in British Guiana", *Social and Economic Studies,* Vol. 7, No. 2 (1958).—R. T. Smith & C. Jayawardena, "Marriage and the Family amongst East Indians in British Guiana", *Social and Economic Studies,* Vol. 8, No. 4 (1959).—Chandra Jayawardena, "Marital Stability in Two Guianese Sugar Estate Communities", *Social and Economic Studies,* Vol. 9, No. 1

(1960).—Morton Klass, *East Indians in Trinidad: A study of cultural persistence* (Columbia University Press, New York & London, 1961.—G. W. Roberts & L. Braithwaite, "Mating among East Indian and Non-Indian Women in Trinidad", *Social and Economic Studies,* Vol. 11, No. 3 (1962).—Chandra Jayawardena, "Family Organisation in Plantations in British Guiana", *International Journal of Comparative Sociology,* Vol. III, No. 1 (1962).

6. M. J. Herskovits, *Life in a Haitian Valley* (New York, 1937).—M. J. Herskovits, "Problem, Method and Theory in Afroamerican Studies", *Afroamerica,* Vol. 1 (Mexico, 1945).—M. J. & F. S. Herskovits, *Rebel Destiny: Among the Bush Negroes of Dutch Guiana* (New York, 1934).—M. J. & F. S. Herskovits, *Trinidad Village* (New York, 1947).

7. F. Frazier, *The Negro Family in the United States* (University of Chicago Press, 1939).

8. G. Myrdal, *An American Dilemma* (Harper Brothers, New York, 1944), p. 928.

9. T. S. Simey, *Welfare and Planning in the West Indies* (Oxford University Press, 1946), pp. 82–90.

10. F. Henriques, *Family and Colour in Jamaica* (Eyre & Spottiswoode, London, 1953).

11. Dom Basil Matthews, *Crisis of the West Indian Family* (Trinidad, 1953).

12. *Ibid.,* p. 104.

13. These summaries are contained in the "Introduction" and "Final Note" in the volume *Working Papers in Caribbean Social Organization* edited by Mintz and Davenport, and referred to above.

14. Quoted in *Negro Slavery; or a view of some of the more prominent features of that state of society as it exists in the United States of America and in the colonies of the West Indies especially in Jamaica* (Hatchard & Son, Piccadilly, London, 1823), pp. 57–58.

15. G. W. Roberts, *The Population of Jamaica* (Cambridge University Press, 1957).—G. W. Roberts & L. Braithwaite, "Fertility Differentials in Trinidad", *International Population Conference* (Vienna, 1959).—G. W. Roberts & L. Braithwaite, "Fertility Differentials by Family Type in Trinidad", *Annals of the New York Academy of Sciences,* Vol. 84, Article 17 (1960).—G. W. Roberts & L. Braithwaite, "A Gross Mating Table for a West Indian Population", *Population Studies,* Vol. XIV, No. 3 (1961).—G. W. Roberts & L. Braithwaite, "Mating Patterns and Prospects in Trinidad", *International Population Conference* (New York, 1961).—G. W. Roberts & L. Braithwaite, "Mating among East Indian and Non-Indian Women in Trinidad", *Social and Economic Studies,* Vol. 11, No. 3 (1962).

16. R. T. Smith, *The Negro Family in British Guiana* (London, 1956).—E. Clarke, *My Mother Who Fathered Me* (London, 1957).

17. M. Fortes, "Time and Social Structure: An Ashanti Case Study", *Social Structure: Studies presented to A. R. Radcliffe-Brown* (Edited by M. Fortes) (Oxford University Press, 1949).

18. A. I. Richards, "Some types of family structure amongst the Central Bantu", *African Systems of Kinship and Marriage* (Edited by A. R. Radcliffe-Brown & Daryll Forde) (Oxford University Press, 1950).

19. M. Fortes, "Introduction", *The Developmental Cycle in Domestic Groups* (Edited by Jack Goody), Cambridge Papers in Social Anthropology, No. 1 (1958).

20. Nancie L. Solien, "Household and family in the Caribbean", *Social and Economic Studies,* Vol. 9, No. 1 (1960).

21. E. Clarke, *op. cit.*

22. M. Kerr, *Personality and Conflict in Jamaica* (Liverpool University Press, 1952).—M. Kerr, *The People of Ship Street* (Routledge and Kegan Paul, London, 1958).

23. W. Davenport, "The Family System of Jamaica", *Working Papers in Caribbean Social Organization* (Edited by Mintz and Davenport) (1961).

24. Roberts & Braithwaite. See note 15.

25. Judith Blake, *Family Structure in Jamaica* (Free Press of Glencoe Inc., New York, 1961).

26. G. P. Murdock, *Social Structure* (Macmillan Company, New York, 1949), p. 1.

27. This view is most clearly expressed in T. Parsons & R. Bales, *Family, Socialization and Interaction Process* (Free Press, Glencoe, Illinois, 1955).

28. M. Fortes, "Introduction", *The Development Cycle in Domestic Groups* (Edited by Jack Goody), Cambridge Papers in Social Anthropology, No. 1 (1958). p. 2.

29. E. Leach, *Rethinking Anthropology* (University of London, The Athlone Press, 1961), pp. 17–26.

30. Nancie Solien, *op. cit.,* p. 104.

31. W. Davenport, "The Family System of Jamaica", *op. cit.,* p. 422.

32. R. T. Smith, *The Negro Family in British Guiana* (London, 1956), pp. 151–159.

33. M. G. Smith, *West Indian Family Structure* (University of Washington Press, Seattle, 1962), p. 243.

34. Elizabeth Bott, *Family and Social Network* (Tavistock Publications Ltd., London, 1957), pp. 137–138.

35. R. T. Smith, *op. cit.,* p. 152.

36. I. Schapera, "Marriage and near kin among the Tswana", *Africa,* Vol. XXVII, No. 2 (1957), p. 154.

37. G. W. Roberts & L. Braithwaite, "A Gross Mating Table for a West Indian Population", *Population Studies,* Vol. XIV, No. 3 (1961).

38. Judith Blake, *Family Structure in Jamaica* (Free Press of Glencoe Inc., New York, 1961).

39. M. G. Smith, *West Indian Family Structure* (University of Washington Press, Seattle, 1962), pp. 255–265.

40. I. Schapera, "Should Anthropologists be Historians?", *Journal of the Royal Anthropological Institute,* Vol. 92, Pt. 2 (1962), p. 154.

41. W. Davenport, "The Family System of Jamaica", *Working Papers,* p. 420.

42. Blake, *op. cit.,* p. 147.

43. G. E. Cumper, "The Jamaican Family: Village and Estate", *Social and Economic Studies,* Vol. 7, No. 1 (1958).—"Household and Occupation in Barbados", *Working Papers, op. cit.*

44. W. Davenport, "Introduction" to *Working Papers, op. cit.,* p. 381.

45. Personal communication.

46. G. E. Cumper, "Household and Occupation in Barbados", *op. cit.,* p. 397.

47. W. Davenport, "The family system of Jamaica", *op. cit.,* p. 450.

48. See note 5.

49. *Ibid.*

50. One of the reasons why East Indians in British Guiana are reluctant to accept automatic registration of customary marriages is that it would then be difficult to dissolve the union if the couple prove to be incompatible.

51. C. Jayawardena, "Family Organisation in Plantations in British Guiana", *International Journal of Comparative Sociology,* Vol. III, No. 1 (1962).

52. William J. Goode, "Illegitimacy, Anomie and Cultural Penetration", *American Sociological Review,* Vol. 26, No. 6 (1961).

53. There was a significant jump in the marriage rate immediately following the earthquake in Jamaica in 1907. See G. W. Roberts, *The Population of Jamaica,* Cambridge University Press (1957), pp. 287–288.

54. S. Mintz, *Worker in the Cane: A Puerto Rican Life History* (Yale University Press, New Haven, 1960).

55. M. G. Smith, "Dark Puritan: The Life and Work of Norman Paul" in two parts in *Caribbean Quarterly,* Vol. 5, Nos. 1 & 2 (1957).

56. O. Lewis, *Five Families: Mexican Case Studies in the Culture of Poverty* (Basic Books, New York, 1959).

St. Clair Drake and
Horace Cayton

LOWER CLASS:
SEX AND FAMILY

It was Christmas Eve, 1938. Dr. Maguire had just finished a hard day.[1] Now for a highball, and then to bed. The doctor stepped back and admired the electric star at the top of the Christmas tree and the gifts neatly stacked beneath it. Judy would certainly be a happy girl in the morning when she bounced downstairs to find the dolls and dishes and baby carriage and candy that Santa Claus had brought her. The doctor smiled, drained his glass, and headed for the bathroom. He caught himself musing in the shower. Not so bad, not so bad. Three years out of med school, in the middle of a depression. A pretty wife with smooth olive skin and straight black hair. A sweet little girl, image of her mother. And buying a home. Well, it was just the "breaks"—lucky breaks ever since he quit picking cotton in Georgia and went off to Howard University in Washington. Plenty of other fellows were better students, but a lot of them were still sleeping in their offices. One or two who were supposed to turn out as distinguished surgeons were Red Capping. He reflected a moment. Yes—the breaks. Suppose he hadn't married a woman like Sylvia. He'd be "on the turf," too, perhaps. Dr. Maguire sharply pulled himself to heel. No, he didn't really believe it had been luck. He prided himself on "having some get-up about him," enough ambition to have made his way anyhow. If he could do it, the other fellows could have, too. He looked at his wife, peacefully sleeping, kissed her lightly on the forehead, and crawled into bed.

Man, what a tough day this Christmas Eve had been! Three appendectomies in the morning and a hernioplasty in the early afternoon. Making the rounds in the midafternoon. Then a few minutes out to help distribute baskets for the Christmas Fund; time out to sign some checks for the legal defense committee of the NAACP; and an emergency meeting of the YMCA executive board. That Y meeting had looked as if it were going to last all night. Negroes talk too damn much. He had hoped to be home by ten o'clock, but it was midnight before he parked his Plymouth. Three late emergency calls—TB patients who ought to be in the sanatorium. Not enough beds—Negro quota filled. Damn this country anyhow. Negroes always get the dirty end of the stick. Christmas! Peace on Earth, Goodwill . . . Bull . . . Sometimes I think the Communists are right. And those

old fogies over at the hospital yell "socialized medicine" every time somebody wants to extend medical care. Aw, hell, what am I bellyaching about?
I haven't had it too tough. He shrugged his shoulders and relaxed. He
was just drifting off to sleep when the 'phone rang.

Sylvia bounded from the bed like a tennis ball coming up after a
smash from the net. She was that way, always ready to protect him and
conserve his strength. What would he do without her?

"Are you one of the doctor's regular patients? . . . Well, why don't
you call your regular doctor? . . . I know, but Dr. Maguire is . . ." He
snatched the 'phone from her hand in time to catch the stream of denuncia-
tion: "That's the way you dicty niggers are. You so high 'n' mighty nobody
kin reach ya. We kin lay here 'n' die. White doctor'd come right away.
Yore own people treat ya like dogs."

Dr. Maguire winced. He always shuddered when this happened. And
it happened often. He waited until the hysterical tirade stopped, then
said calmly but firmly: "Now listen, you want me to do you a favor. I'll
come over there, sure. I'm a doctor. That's my business. But I'm not coming unless you have the money. Have you got five dollars?" He hung up
and began to dress wearily.

"Do they have it?" queried his wife.

"I don't know," he snapped, irritated at himself for having to ask
such a question, and at his wife for pressing the point. "You know I'm
going whether they have it or not. I'm a doctor. I always go. But you
might just as well scare them—it'll be hard enough to collect anyhow."
He slammed the door and went down the snowdrifted path that led to
the garage.

When he arrived at the building, the squad car was at the door. He
and the police went in together. Dr. Maguire pushed his way through
the ragged group of children and their excited elders who jammed the
hall of the dilapidated building.

"Right this way, Doc," someone called.

"What is it?" he asked jauntily. "Shooting or cutting?"

"She stabbed him," volunteered a little girl.

"Boy, she shore put that blade in him too!" A teen-age boy spoke
with obvious admiration, while a murmur of corroboration ripped through
the crowd fascinated by tragedy.

For a moment, Dr. Maguire felt sick at his stomach. "Are these my
people?" he thought. "What in the hell do I have in common with them?
This is 'The Race' we're always spouting about being proud of." He had
a little trick for getting back on an even keel when such doubts assailed
him: he just let his mind run back over the "Uncle Tomming" he had to
do when he was a Pullman porter; the turndown he got when he wanted
to interne at the University of Chicago hospital; the letter from the American Medical Association rejecting his application for membership; the
paper he wrote for a white doctor to read at a Mississippi medical conference which no Negroes could attend. Such thoughts always restored his

sense of solidarity with "The Race." "Yeah, I'm just a nigger, too," he mumbled bitterly.

Then he forgot everything—squalor, race prejudice, his own little tricks of psychological adjustment. He was a doctor treating a patient, swiftly, competently, and with composure. Anger and doubt were swallowed up in pride. His glow of satisfaction didn't last long, however, for the woman who had cut the man was now blubbering hysterically. He barked at her, "Shut up. Get a pan of water, quick! He isn't dead, but he will be if you don't help me." He prepared a hypodermic, gave the shot, and dressed the wound.

"How'dja like to have to give that needle, honey?" A teen-age girl shivered and squeezed her boy friend's hand, as she asked the question.

"Me? I ain't no doc. But, girl, he flipped that ol' needle in his shoulder sweet. Just like Baby Chile did when she put that blade in Mr. Ben. You gotta have education to be a doc. Lots of it, too."

"I'm gonna be a doctor, I am." A small, self-confident urchin spoke up. The crowd tittered and a young woman said, "That's real cute, ain't it? You be a good one too, just like Doc Maguire." Dr. Maguire smiled pleasantly. An elderly crone mumbled, "Doctor? Humph! Wid a hophead daddy and a booze houn' mammy. How he ever gonna be any doctah? He bettah get his min' on a WPA shovel." Everybody laughed.

"The old man will be all right, now." Dr. Maguire was closing his bag. "Just let him lie quiet all day tomorrow and send him down to the Provident Hospital clinic the day after Christmas. The visit is five dollars."

Baby Chile went for her purse. There was nothing in it. She screamed a frantic accusation at the crowd. "I been robbed. You dirty bastards!" Then a little girl whispered in her ear, while the crowd tittered knowingly. Baby Chile regained her composure and explained: "Sorry, Doc. I had the money. I was gonna pay you. But them goddam policemen was gonna take me off on a 'sault and batt'ry charge. My little girl had to give 'em the ten dollars I had in this here bag, and the folks out there had to raise another ten to make 'em go away. Them policemen's got it all. I ain't even got a red cent left for Christmas tomorrow. You got anything, Ben?"

The sick man growled: "You know I ain' got nuthin'! You know I can't holp you."

The doctor didn't say a word. He just picked up his bag and left. But he ostentatiously took out a pencil and wrote down the number of the apartment before he went out. The crowd seemed pleased at his discomfiture. One woman remarked: "He got the number. Them doctors don't never disremember."

"What was it, dear?" Mrs. Maguire asked as her husband once more prepared for bed.

"Same old thing. Niggers cutting each other up over nothing. Rotgut whisky and women, I guess. They ought to start cutting on the white folks for a change. I wonder how they got my number?"

"Did you get the five dollars?" his wife asked.

"Nope. Told me some lie about bribing the police. Maybe they did— I don't know. Let's forget it and go to sleep. Judy will have us both up before daybreak. Tomorrow's Christmas."

Mrs. Maguire turned over and sighed. The doctor went to sleep.

Baby Chile crawled into the bed with Mr. Ben. She cried and cried and stroked the bulky dressing on his shoulder. "Honey, I didn't mean to do that. I love you! I do! I do!"

Mr. Ben didn't say a word. The needle was wearing off and his shoulder hurt. But he wasn't gonna let no woman know she'd hurt him. He bit his lip and tried to sleep. He pushed her hand away from his shoulder. He cursed her.

"Hush up, dammit, shet up!" he growled. "I wanna sleep."

Baby Chile kept moaning, "Why'd I do it? Why'd I do it?"

"Shet up, you bitch," Mr. Ben bawled. "I wisht they'da let them creepers take you to the station! Cain't you let me sleep?"

Baby Chile didn't say another word. She just lay there a-thinking and a-thinking. She was trying to remember how it happened. Step by step she reconstructed the event in her mind as though the rehearsal would assuage her feeling of guilt.

She'd been living with Mr. Ben six months now. Of course he was old and he hadn't ever got the country outa him yet. But he had a good job s'long as he kept the furnace fired and the halls swept out. And he got his room free, bein' janitor. She had a relief check coming in reg'lar for herself and her little girl. They could make it all right as long as the case-worker didn't crack down on 'em. But Mr. Ben was so suspicious. He was always watching her and signifyin' she was turning tricks with Slick who helped him with the furnace and slept in the basement. She wouldn't turn no tricks with Slick. He had bad blood and wouldn't take his shots reg'lar. But you couldn't convince old Mr. Ben. Ben didn't treat her little girl right, either. 'Course, it wasn't his child. But he oughta act right. She cooked for him and slept with him and never held her relief check back on him. He could treat her child right. That was the cause of it all, anyhow.

Baby Chile had come home near dark after a day of imbibing Christmas cheer. She must have been a little slug-happy. All she remembered was chasing her little girl outa Mamie's kitchenette next door, telling her to stay outa that whorehouse. "I ain't raisin' you to be a goddammed whore! Why I send you to Sunday school! Why I try to raise you right? For you to lay up in there with them whores?" You just couldn't keep her outa that place listening to the vendor playing boogie-woogie and seein' things only grown folks oughta see. Then she remembered stretching out on the bed. Just before she lay down she'd asked her daughter, "What Ben get you for Christmas, chile?"

"Nothin', Mother Dear."

"Nothin'?"

"No, ma'am."

Her eyes fell on the sideboard covered with new, shiny bottles of whisky and beer and wine—plenty of "Christmas cheer." A turkey was cooking in the stove. "An' that no-'count bastard didn't get *you* nothin'?" She remembered throwing herself on the bed in a rage. The radio was playing Christmas carols—the kind that always made her cry because it sounded like church back down in Mississippi. She lay there half drunk, carols ringing in her ears from the radio, boogie-woogie assailing them from the juke-box across the hall, the smell of turkey emanating from the kitchen, and her little girl whimpering in the corner.

She recalled the "accident" vividly. She was dozing on the bed in the one large room which along with the kitchen made up their home. She woke up when Ben came into the room. She didn't know how long she'd been sleeping. Whisky and beer don't mix anyhow, and when you been in and outa taverns all day Christmas Eve you get enough to lay you out cold.

When Mr. Ben opened the door near midnight she was almost sober, but mad as hell. Her head ached, she was so mad. Ben grunted, walked into the kitchen, and started to baste the turkey. She challenged him:

"You buy Fanny May a present?"

"Naw," he grunted. "I spent my money for the turkey and the drinks. Tomorrow's Christmas, ain't it? What you do with yore relief check? Drink it up? Why'n you get her a present? She's yore chile, ain't she?"

Ben wouldn't have been so gruff, but he was tired and peeved. That damn furnace hadn't been acting right and everybody was stayin' up all night to see Christmas in, and pestering him for more heat. And all the time he was trying to get the turkey cooked, too. Baby Chile oughta been doing it—she had been sashayin' roun' all day drinking other men's liquor. How'd anybody expect him to think about a present for Fanny May? That girl didn't like him and respect him, nohow—always walling her eyes at him, but polite as hell to "Mother Dear." Crap! Mr. Ben didn't say any of this out very loud. He just mumbled it to himself as he bent over the stove basting the turkey.

Baby Chile stood up and stared at him. She felt her hell arising. She didn't say a word. She walked deliberately to the kitchen table and took up a paring knife, studied it for a moment, and then—with every ounce of energy that anger and frustration could pump into her muscles—she sank it between his shoulders and fled screaming into the hall. "Oh, I've killed Mr. Ben! I've killed my old man! I've killed him!"

Her little girl raced over to the noisy room next door and asked Miss Mamie to call the doctor. And Mamie interrupted her Christmas Eve business to help a neighbor.

Now Baby Chile was in bed with Mr. Ben. His shoulder was all fixed. She squeezed him tight, kissed him, and went to sleep.

Everybody had a good time on Christmas Day at Mr. Ben's. Fanny May went to church. The old folks began a whist game in the morning that ran continuously until midnight, with visitors dropping in to take a hand, eat a turkey sandwich, and drink from Mr. Ben's sideboard. The janitor sat in his rocking chair like a king holding court, as the tenants streamed in and out and Baby Chile bustled about making him comfortable. Baby Chile was "high" enough to be lively, but was careful not to get drunk. No one mentioned the tragedy of the night before. Only Slick was uncomfortable.

BRONZEVILLE'S LOWER DEPTHS

Slick felt "left out of things." He had teamed up with Mr. Ben a month before Christmas after his mother and father had evicted him from their two rooms because his drunken escapades were bringing trouble to the household. Nearly thirty, Slick was a floater with two deserted wives behind him, an insatiable appetite for liquor, and spirochetes in his veins. He was not unattractive and he liked women. But he had an ugly scar over his entire left side where wife number one, in a fit of jealous rage, had thrown a bucket of lye on him. "She tried to hit my privates, but I turned over too fast," was Slick's comment. *"Now* what girl wants me? My side's enough to turn her nature." Yet, during the Twenties, when he had a job and money, he had girls. Now, during the Depression, he was, to use his own words, "a bum."

Slick's family had migrated to Chicago from St. Louis where his mother, a lower-middle-class woman who "married a no-'count Negro," had worked as a seamstress. She had tried to make something out of her only son, but according to her, "It didn't take." With a chronic alcoholic for a husband and a delinquent for a son, Slick's mother had resigned herself to being lower-class, although she refused to take a job in domestic service. When the Depression began, she went on the relief. She kept her two rooms and her person spotlessly clean, tried to make the old man hold a WPA job, and in 1938 got a job as housekeeper in a lower-class kitchenette building. But Slick jeopardized her steady income, and she threw him out.

Slick drifted about. Now he was thinking that he'd better move again as soon as Ben's shoulder got well. Ben was beginning to give him the evil eye. Slick hadn't turned a trick with Baby Chile yet, but he was sure she did want "to be with him." He was gonna stay outa trouble. Just as soon as Ben's shoulder got well, he was gonna cut out—danger was on his trail.

Slick had already propositioned Betty Lou about living with him. He had met her at Streeter's Tavern, bought her a few beers, and "jived" her. She had agreed to live with him if one of Slick's employed friends would consent to board with them until Slick could get a WPA job. This would provide a steady income for food. So Slick wheedled ten dollars from his mother and rented a basement room in the center of the Black Belt—three-and-a-half a week for room, bed, chair, and table. Life began— with Betty Lou, though without a stove or even a hot-plate.

Betty Lou, a native of Alabama, had come north to Detroit in the early days of the Depression and entered domestic service. A rather attractive light-brown-skinned girl in her early twenties, fond of good clothes and with a great deal of personal pride, she worked for three years, went to night school intermittently, and then married a common laborer. One year of married life and they separated after a furious fight. She then came to Chicago to stay with a married sister whose husband worked in the steel mills. Later she secured a job in private family and lived "on premises" for several months. She didn't like living with white folks, but when she decided to return to her sister's home, a lodger was sleeping on the sofa in the living-room where she had formerly slept. Betty Lou had to occupy a pallet on the floor in the bedroom with her sister and husband. Slick's offer of a home provided an avenue of escape.

Slick and Betty Lou lived together in the basement for about a month. He made the rounds of various employment agencies, but spent most of his time trying to work his acquaintances for enough money to buy drinks and pay the rent. Betty Lou, faced with the problem of cooking, made a deal with the unmarried janitor who let her use his kitchen in return for a share of the food. She took a great deal of pride in her biscuits and occasional hot rolls. She was enjoying domesticity.

Here, beneath Bronzeville's surface, were a variety of living patterns. The twenty households, sharing four bathrooms, two common sinks in the hallway, and some dozen stoves and hot-plates between them, were forced into relationships of neighborliness and reciprocity. A girl might "do the hair" of a neighbor in return for permission to use her pots and pans. Another woman might trade some bread for a glass of milk. There was seldom any money to lend or borrow, but the bartering of services and utensils was general. Brawls were frequent, often resulting in intense violence. A supper interrupted by the screams of a man with an ice-pick driven into his back might be unusual—but a fight involving the destruction of the meager furniture in these households was not uncommon.

Slick's immediate neighbors were two teen-aged boys, recently discharged from a CCC camp. They were now making their way by robbing laundry trucks and peddling "hot" shirts, towels, socks, and handkerchiefs among the kitchenette dwellers. Each afternoon their room was a rendezvous for schoolgirls—truants and morning-shift pupils—who pooled their lunch money, prepared pots of steaming spaghetti and hot dogs, and spent the afternoon "rug-cutting," drinking whisky, smoking reefers, and "making love." Slick gave strict orders to Betty Lou to "stay outa that reefer den with all them hustlers and reefer smokers."

Betty Lou's best "girl friend" in the basement was Ella, whose husband, "Poke," had recently been jailed for breaking a liquor store window and stealing a pint of whisky. "I just as well not have no ol' man. Stays in jail all the time," Ella confided one day in a pensive mood. Several days later she was living with another man for the interim. "My baby's got to have some milk," she apologized, "an' that damn worker won't get me a job on the WPA 'cause I have a baby. I can run a power-machine, too!"

Down the hall was Joe, a former cook on the railroad who had been fired for stealing Pullman towels and who was now a dishwasher. Living with a waitress, he was currently much agitated because of a letter he had received from his legal wife in Detroit notifying him that she was en route to Chicago. He kept his bags packed.

Strangest of all was Lily, a tall, husky, masculine woman who was subsequently thrown out of the building and warned never to return. "A damn bull-diker[2] who's been messing with the women in here," was Slick's terse comment.

During this period, Slick's mother visited him several times, and professed to be very fond of her son's new common-law wife. Betty Lou's married sister came to visit them too, as did a woman friend who borrowed the room for a few hours each week on her night off so that she could entertain a boy friend. These visitors sometimes brought a little food when they came.

Slick spoke often of wishing to regularize his alliance if he could get an annulment and if Betty Lou could get a divorce. He fantasied too (usually when drunk) about getting on his feet, taking a civil service examination for a post-office job, and showing the world, his boarder, and his mother that he wasn't a derelict.

After two months in the basement, the couple decided to raise their standard of living. Slick had got a $55-a-month WPA job, so they decided to move into a first-floor kitchenette[3] with a stove and an ice-box. Thus began the second phase of their joint life.

From Kitchenette to Penitentiary: The three months in the kitchenette started on a note of confidence and ended in tragedy. During this period Betty Lou's sister and her brother-in-law visited occasionally, made the acquaintance of Slick's family, tried to mediate quarrels, and in general functioned as approving relatives. Betty Lou's conception of her role was that Slick should work and support her. Slick, however, insisted that she too should get a job, and often charged her with running around during the day "turning tricks." Such "signifying" became the focal point for continuous quarrels and occasional fights; it eventually resulted in separation.

Betty Lou was anxious to join a church and a social club, and, as soon as she could, became a member of an usher board at a lower-middle-class church. Slick resented this attempt at mobility, especially since he had neither the personal organization nor the money and clothes to maintain such social connections. He was often torn with doubts about her motives, and on one occasion said, "I think Betty Lou is just tryin' to work me till she gets another man or gets on her feet."

For a month, Slick worked steadily on the WPA labor project, drank far less than usual, and seemed to achieve a moderate amount of emotional stability. He cashed his first check and allowed Betty Lou to purchase groceries and pay the rent. As for the second check, he spent at least half of it on a "good time." After the first month of fairly steady employment, Slick began to miss work frequently, and it was soon evident that he was spending his time watching Betty Lou in an attempt to catch her with other men. This behavior resulted in some serious fights and a threat on the part of her sister to take Betty Lou back home. In one drunken fit, Slick chased her through the building with a butcher knife, and the housekeeper was forced to call a policeman. On another occasion an argument, which began with the passing of mutual insults, ended in Slick's tearing up Betty Lou's clothing and breaking some cherished china souvenirs which she had patiently gathered at a neighboring tavern over a period of several months.

With the approach of Easter, Slick worked steadily in order to make a down payment on some clothing for himself and Betty Lou. On Easter day both were "togged down."[4] Within two days, however, all of Slick's clothes were in a pawn shop and he was again in rags. This contributed to the ultimate breakup of the alliance, since Betty Lou was now able to go to church and to dances, while Slick, lacking clothes, was never able to participate in any public social activities with her except at taverns.

The fights continued. Then one night Betty Lou stormed out, vowing never to return. Slick was in a disorganized and drunken state for several days, plotting vengeance one moment and crying the next. His mother, who had been friendly toward Betty Lou, now insisted that she had always known she was no good, and that she was probably a prostitute anyway. Betty Lou decided a few days later to return to Slick, but what she saw when she entered their apartment permanently estranged her. There in the room was a white girl ensconced in her bed! Betty Lou snatched her clothing from the closet, cursed the woman roundly, reported the incident to the housekeeper, and left. Slick insisted to the housekeeper that he had met the white woman wandering in the cold and like a gentleman had invited her in. To his cronies he proudly told a different story. The woman, he said, was a "hustling woman" he had known when he worked at a North Side "resort." She had befriended him and given him money. Now she was down and out, and when he met her at a Black Belt tavern he decided to bring her in, sleep with her, and to play the role of pimp for a day or two in order to make some extra change. Slick was given three hours to vacate the room under threat of arrest. He moved into a liquor joint for several days and then rented a single room.

One morning several weeks later, a WPA research project in the basement of a church near Slick's lodging place was thrown into an uproar when he rushed through the premises followed by "Two-Gun Dick" and another officer with drawn revolvers. Having met Betty Lou on the street walking with another man, Slick had followed her until her escort left her, and then stabbed her in the breast. His first impulse was to flee to the WPA project, where he had acquaintances who had befriended him in the past. He did not tarry, however, for the police were close behind. He hurried to his mother's home and hid there for the rest of the day. Returning in the evening to the area in which he had committed the crime, he was arrested. His mother borrowed money on her insurance policies for bail and a lawyer. Her only comment on the girl was: "She ought to be glad my boy didn't mark her in the face. She kin get another man since she ain't marked in the face." When it became evident that Betty Lou would recover, the judge sentenced Slick to a mere six months in the Bridewell Prison.

On his release Slick was at the peak of physical condition; regular treatment for his various bodily ailments, disciplined labor, and regular food had made him almost a different person. But within two months he was once more thoroughly disorganized. Another two months and he was back in prison, this time on a charge of stealing. On his release he departed for St. Louis, whence he had originally come to Black Metropolis.

Slick and Betty Lou—Baby Chile and Mr. Ben: there were hundreds of them in Bronzeville during the Lean Years.

Notes

1. This account of a doctor's Christmas experience is based on an actual incident witnessed by one of the authors, when he was a participant-observer in a group of lower-class households for six months, and on interviews with the physician involved and his wife. The principal characters' inner thoughts are obviously fictionalized. But the other quoted material in this chapter, as throughout the book, has been selected from interview-documents gathered by trained interviewers and has not been subjected to imaginative recasting.

2. "Bull-diker"—homosexual woman reputed to have male genitalia.

3. Bronzeville's kitchenettes are single rooms, rented furnished and without a lease. Sometimes a hot-plate is included for cooking, but often there are no cooking facilities despite the name. Hundreds of large apartment buildings have been cut up into kitchenettes to meet the chronic housing shortage in the Black Belt.

4. Exceptionally well-dressed.

PART FIVE

RELIGION

Religion, as practiced and organized among the black underclass, can be seen as an aspect of control of the underclass by the dominant sections of the national societies, and as both an accommodation and response to the relationships of exploitation and conditions of oppression. Religious belief systems are supernatural belief systems and affect the nature of this control, accommodation, and response. My argument so far is that the conditions of the black underclass are a result of historical and contemporary social and economic relationships, namely those of a capitalist society. I have also argued that a change in conditions for the underclass depends on a change in capitalist relations. Consequently, inculcating a supernatural ideology or frame of reference, wherein these conditions become an aspect of God's will, or the result of sinful behavior (such as being black), or the action of evil spirits does not facilitate the necessary changes in the material or natural conditions responsible for misery. Thus, in these cases, religion may be said to give false hope and to reduce awareness of the social environment to the extent that the material, social, and economic conditions are not seen as causes of oppression and, hence, are not attacked. To encourage such a belief system among the populace is an aspect of control in order to maintain social stability and political hegemony.

The imposition of Christian beliefs upon the slaves by their masters is an example of this form of social control, as Kenneth Stampp illustrates in his article. The perpetuation and encouragement of *vodoun* in Haiti by the Duvalier regime is also an aspect of social control, as Rémy Bastien argues in his contribution.

On the other hand, the *organization* of religion may offer the underclass a centripetal focus around which other more instrumental ideologies and activities develop. In Part I, Mary Reckord's analysis of the role Baptist church groups played in the Jamaican slave rebellion is an example of this proposition. The importance of church groups and religious leaders in making demands for social change in the United States is a modern example. Indeed, there may be a contradiction within these groups and among the leaders between the maintenance of supernatural ideology and upholding the necessity for change and engaging in relevant social and political activities. The life of Malcolm X is a lesson in the personal and ideological changes such a contradiction has wrought.

283

There is diffusion of religious ideology and organization and it is not always imposed from without. People often adopt different beliefs and re-form them to meet their own demands; traditional beliefs also change as circumstances change. In Haiti, for instance, as Bastien points out, the development of *vodoun* is syncretic; that is, a mixture of both Christian and African elements. It is, moreover, a result of the failures of Christianity in meeting the needs of a slave population and the resistance of slaves to their masters. Thus, *vodoun* is a black religion in a way that black Christian sects can never be. The history of *vodoun* related here also points to the fact that even where religion develops within a context of resistance, it can, nevertheless, be subsequently used as a means of social control and political manipulation. It is interesting to note that the history of Christianity supports this notion.

To talk of religion as an accommodation or reaction to exploitative relationships and oppressive conditions is not necessarily to talk of religion as encouraging effective action against those relationships and conditions. The action advocated by religion is ritual action. The aim of ritual action is to activate supernatural agents—gods, spirits, culture heroes—to intervene in the affairs of men or to magically effect some desired end. The millennial and magical elements of the various sects and movements which Vittorio Lanternari describes for the black underclass in Jamaica are clearly aimed at overcoming the misery they experience. Thus, we may understand why they uphold these beliefs, and we may recognize that lack of knowledge about the nature of the relationships responsible for their misery may perpetuate these beliefs. It is still relevant, however, to ask what changes will be made while waiting for the millennium or transportation to Ethiopia. As Lanternari maintains, these beliefs are escapist, not revolutionary.

The Ras Tafari movement, as well as other sects and churches characteristic of the black underclass in the New World, is a means of organizing social life in the face of the disintegrative effects of exploitation for profit. The point, however, is to change this situation, and as knowledge increases and as the black underclass begins to act, the organizations may remain, but the relevance of religious ideology may be questioned.

Kenneth Stampp
CHRISTIANITY IN
SLAVE SOCIETY

"I greatly desire that the Gospel be preached to the Negroes when the services of a suitable person can be procured," wrote a Mississippian to his overseer. Religious instruction "not only benefits the slave in his moral relations, but enhances his value as an honest, faithful servant and laborer," affirmed an Alabama judge.[1] Pious masters regarded their bondsmen as human beings with immortal souls and therefore felt an obligation to look after their spiritual life. Many of them also considered Christian indoctrination an effective method of keeping slaves docile and contented.

When the first Africans were imported in the seventeenth century, some purchasers opposed converting them to Christianity lest baptism give them a claim to freedom. After the colonial legislatures provided that conversion would not have this effect, the opposition diminished. Thereafter most masters encouraged Christian proselytizing among their bondsmen, and conversion proceeded rapidly.

A minority, however, continued to be indifferent. Even in the nineteenth century a southern clergyman complained that some, "forgetful of God and eternity," treated their slaves "too much as creatures of profit." In "extensive districts" thousands of bondsmen never heard the voices of those who brought "the glad tidings of salvation to perishing men." Another clergyman was "astonished to find planters of high moral pretensions" who kept their slaves "shut out almost entirely from the privileges of the Gospel."[2]

A few were openly hostile. "Be assured," wrote a North Carolinian, "that religion among the mass of negroes who profess, is nothing more than a humbug." He did not believe "in the efficacy of preaching to negroes and would never contribute a cent for that purpose." A Louisianian considered attempts to convert slaves the "greatest piece of foolishness"; the only way to improve them, he thought, was through "proper discipline." Olmsted met other slaveholders who shared these views. A Mississippian told him that religious exercises excited the slaves so much that it was difficult to control them. "They would be singing and dancing every night in their cabins, till dawn of day, and utterly unfit themselves for work."[3]

Since Nat Turner had been a slave preacher, the Southampton insurrection temporarily increased sentiment of this kind. Its lasting effect was to convince the master class that the religious life of the slaves needed rigid supervision. In December, 1831, James H. Hammond resolved "to break up negro preaching and negro Churches." Many years later another South Carolinian was still warning slaveholders, "Do not, I beseech you, send off your negroes to worship . . . by themselves. I have known great mischief to have grown out of such meetings."[4]

The early attitude of certain Protestant sects toward slavery also accounted for some of the surviving suspicion. In the eighteenth century and early nineteenth century, southern Baptists and Methodists exhibited considerable antislavery sentiment. Many slaveholders were therefore reluctant to have the preachers and missionaries of these denominations work among their slaves. But when the southern wings of these churches changed their positions, when southern clergymen became ardent defenders of slavery, the master class could look upon organized religion as an ally. Church leaders now argued "that the gospel, instead of becoming a means of creating trouble and strife, was really the best instrument to preserve peace and good conduct among the negroes." This was a persuasive argument. "In point of fact," recalled one churchman, "it was this conviction that ultimately opened the way for the gospel on the large plantations."[5]

Through religious instruction the bondsmen learned that slavery had divine sanction, that insolence was as much an offense against God as against the temporal master. They received the Biblical command that servants should obey their masters, and they heard of the punishments awaiting the disobedient slave in the hereafter. They heard, too, that eternal salvation would be their reward for faithful service, and that on the day of judgment "God would deal impartially with the poor and the rich, the black man and the white." Their Christian preceptors, Fanny Kemble noted, "jump[ed] the present life" and went on "to furnish them with all the requisite conveniences for the next."[6]

Numerous slaveholders agreed that this indoctrination had a felicitous effect. A committee of a South Carolina agricultural society reported that religion contributed much to "the government and discipline of the slave population." A traveler in Mississippi met a planter who was himself "a most decided infidel" but who nevertheless saw "the advantage of giving religious instruction to slaves." Many claimed that imparting Christian doctrine to impressionable slave children was especially beneficial. It taught them "respect and obedience to their superiors," made them "more pleasant and profitable servants," and aided "the discipline of a plantation in a wonderful manner."[7]

Others noticed a decline in theft when bondsmen "got religion." A Methodist missionary related a slave's confession that the Gospel "had saved more rice for massa than all the locks and keys on the plantation." Moreover, religious services on Sundays kept idle slaves at home and out of mischief. Indeed, one planter even used a Methodist exhorter as an overseer, with gratifying success; another, hearing of it, tried to get one too.[8]

In 1845, a group of distinguished South Carolina slaveholders published a pamphlet illustrating "the practical working and wholesome effects of religious instruction, when properly and judiciously imparted to our negro peasantry." Each plantation, they believed, ought to become a "religious or parochial family," for religion could play a major role in the perpetuation of slavery. "Precepts that inculcated good-will, forbearance and forgiveness; that enjoin meekness and patience under evils; that demand truth and faithfulness under all circumstances; a teaching that sets before men a righteous judgment, and happiness or misery in the life to come, according to our course of faith and practice in the life that now is, must . . . change the general character of persons thus taught."[9]

The master class understood, of course, that only a carefully censored version of Christianity could have this desired effect. Inappropriate Biblical passages had to be deleted; sermons that might be proper for freemen were not necessarily proper for slaves. Church leaders addressed themselves to this problem and prepared special catechisms and sermons for bondsmen, and special instructions for those concerned with their religious indoctrination. In 1847, for example, Charles Colcock Jones, of Georgia, wrote a book entitled *Suggestions on the Religious Instruction of the Negroes in the Southern States,* which was published by the Presbyterian Board of Publications. From his own experience Jones advised missionaries to ignore the "civil condition" of the slaves and to listen to no complaints against masters or overseers. In preaching to the bondsmen missionaries should condemn "every vice and evil custom," advocate the "discharge of every duty," and support the "peace and order of society." They should teach the slaves to give "respect and obedience [to] all those whom God in his providence has placed in authority over them." Religion, in short, should underwrite the status quo.

Owners had various methods of providing religious training. Most of them believed it "pernicious and evil" for slaves to preach at their own services or prayer meetings.[10] Nevertheless, some permitted it. The master or overseer usually attended such meetings, as required by law—and the preacher, naturally, was a trusted slave. In a number of southern towns the bondsmen attended their own churches. Richmond had four African Baptist Churches before 1860, each controlled by a governing board of whites and served by a white pastor. In Savannah, Andrew Marshall, a free Negro, was the minister of the First African Baptist Church. Until his death in 1856, Marshall was "greatly respected" by the whites and the "idol" of his slave congregation.[11]

In the regions of small slaveholdings whites and blacks commonly belonged to the same churches; on the large plantations only the domestics accompanied their masters to worship. When there were mixed congregations the slaves sat in the galleries, or were grouped together at the rear. Sometimes they attended special services on Sunday afternoon. Whatever the arrangements, whites admitted Negro members to their churches everywhere in the antebellum South.

The white-controlled churches made an important contribution to the governing of their slave communicants. They disciplined or "excluded from fellowship" bondsmen guilty of such offenses as "disorder," thievery, "selling spirits on the Lord's day at meeting," "unchristian conduct," and "immorality." For instance, the slave Peter, a member of a Presbyterian church in Iredell County, North Carolina, confessed that he had forged a pass. Because forgery and falsehood were such "flagrant crimes," he was suspended from membership and "exhorted to repentence and [a] better life." A year later, Peter applied for the restoration of his church privileges, "professing a deep penitence for his sins, and a strong determination to lead hereafter a life of greater watchfulness and more prayer." Peter was forgiven.[12]

Large slaveholders occasionally built churches on their estates and hired clergymen to preach to their bondsmen each Sunday. The proprietor of a Mississippi plantation maintained a "beautiful little Gothic church" where a resident pastor administered to the spiritual needs of both master and slaves. Other planters, depending upon missionaries who visited their estates periodically, made no provision for regular religious services. Their slaves apparently had mixed feelings about the occasional visitations of the white preachers. One divine noted sadly that some of them made it "a settled point to sleep during sermons."[13]

The best system, many agreed, was one in which the master himself assumed responsibility for the religious life of his slaves. Gathering his "people" around him on the Sabbath, he preached to them from one of the handbooks or read to them from the Scriptures. The advantage of this system, according to a South Carolina planter, was that it created "a feeling of interest between the master and the slave." It produced "that happy state of protection on the one part, and obedience on the other."[14]

Whatever form the bondsmen's religious training took, it appeared that piety increased their value. A former slave remembered hearing a Missouri auctioneer expounding the virtues of a female domestic who was up for sale. She was a good cook and an obedient servant. Moreover, "She has got religion!" Why should this have mattered? Because "the religious teaching consists in teaching the slave that he must never strike a white man; that God made him for a slave; and that, when whipped, he must not find fault,—for the Bible says, 'He that knoweth his master's will and doeth it not, shall be beaten with many stripes!' And slaveholders find such religion very profitable to them."[15]

Notes

1. Phillips (ed.), *Plantation and Frontier,* I, pp. 112–15; Catterall (ed.), *Judicial Cases,* III, p. 238.

2. Charles Colcock Jones, *Suggestions on the Religious Instruction of the Negroes in the Southern States* (Philadelphia, 1847), pp. 7–9, 31; *Southern Cultivator,* IX (1851), pp. 84–85.

3. Ebenezer Pettigrew to James C. Johnston, July 16, 1838, Pettigrew Family Papers; Davis (ed.), *Diary of Bennet H. Barrow,* pp. 323–24; Olmsted, *Back Country,* pp. 92–93, 107–108.

4. Hammond Diary, entries for December 15, 16, 1831; *De Bow's Review,* XXIV (1858), p. 64; Luther P. Jackson, "Religious Development of the Negro in Virginia from 1760 to 1860," *Journal of Negro History,* XVI (1931), p. 206.

5. Harrison, *Gospel Among the Slaves,* pp. 149–51.

6. Sir Charles Lyell, *A Second Visit to North America* (London, 1849), II, pp. 2–3; Kemble, *Journal,* p. 57.

7. *De Bow's Review,* VII (1849), p. 221; XXVI (1859), p. 107; *Southern Agriculturist,* IV (1831), pp. 351–52; Jones, *Suggestions on the Religious Instruction of the Negroes,* pp. 34–35.

8. Harrison, *Gospel Among the Slaves,* pp. 205, 210–11; *Farmers' Register,* IV (1837), p. 574; Henry, *Police Control,* p. 139.

9. Quoted in Charleston *Courier,* August 28, 1845.

10. *De Bow's Review,* XXVI (1859), p. 107.

11. Jackson, "Religious Development . . . ," *loc. cit.,* pp. 221–22; Savannah *Republican,* December 15, 1856.

12. Church of Bethany Ms. Session Book.

13. *De Bow's Review,* VII (1849), p. 221; *Southern Cultivator,* IX (1851), p. 85.

14. Northup, *Twelve Years a Slave,* pp. 97–98; Charleston *Courier,* April 15, 1851.

15. Brown, *Narrative,* pp. 83–84.

Rémy Bastien
VODOUN AND POLITICS IN HAITI

1 ORIGINS AND GROWTH OF VODOUN

If we accept the word as generic, Vodoun is no monopoly of Haiti. As a popular religion that syncretized a variety of African cults and Christian elements, it has a broad following in Brazil, was well-entrenched in Cuba, and took a variety of forms in Jamaica; some of its manifestations have been found in Louisiana. Its distribution means that it cropped up in the territories of the main colonial powers, French, Spanish, British, and Portuguese, irrespective of the dominant Catholicism or Protestantism of the metropolises. Its appearance was due to two circumstances created by Negro slavery: (1) the failure of Christianity to provide the Africans with a satisfactory religious life, and (2) the resistance of the African to his lot, and his will to preserve as much of his cultural heritage as possible. Whereas the Spanish colonists had some success in applying missionary methods to the conversion of the great nuclei of Amerindian population in Mesoamerica and the Andean area, the plantation owners in the West Indies, Brazil, and the southern United States did not care to reconcile human exploitation and the quick-profit mentality with religious fervor. The French colonists were known for their lack of religiosity. Elsewhere religious teaching was frowned upon by the masters and, at least before Abolition, the ministers found little incentive to include the slaves among their flocks. No doubt the Jesuits in Haiti (or rather Saint-Domingue) did show some spirit in opening schools for the Negroes but their work was short-lived; expulsion followed soon after. Equally limited were the efforts of Baptists and Moravian Brethren in Jamaica.[1]

Meager as it was, the presence of Christianity was enough to impress the slaves. They borrowed elements from its ritual and dogma and blended them with their own African heritage. The syncretized Afro-religions of the New World simultaneously practiced both Vodoun and Catholicism, with surprising ease at times. While the economic system of the dominant Europeans created tension, antagonism, and violence, the religious system of the slaves successfully created a workable pattern of coexistence. Religious coexistence, however, did not exclude resistance on the political plane. The eradication of their social and political organization did not deter the Africans from trying to regain their freedom. Their attempts, failures, and rare triumphs are an inseparable part of the struggle for liberty in the

REPRINTED FROM PP. 41–48; 56–68 OF *Religion and Politics in Haiti.* ICR STUDIES, NO. 1 (INSTITUTE FOR CROSS-CULTURAL RESEARCH, 4000 ALBEMARLE STREET, N.W., WASHINGTON, D.C. 20016).

Americas, be it in the Palmares in Brazil, the southern part of Dutch Guiana, Jamaica, Mexico, or Haiti. What is of interest to us is the role that magic and religion played in the conflict. Data may be scarce in many cases but its abundance in the history of Haiti allows us to suppose that elsewhere the rebellious leaders used similar methods to fire the imagination and sustain the courage of their followers.

From this it can be seen that the magico-religious complex practiced by the slaves—we may as well call it Vodoun—contained both a social character and a secret or political one. Chroniclers of the eighteenth century often noted the religious dances performed by Negroes on the plantations. Such gatherings were tolerated and at times encouraged by the colonists. Parallel to these open manifestations were the secret meetings of Vodoun adepts whose primary purpose was not to find an outlet to the frustrations of servile life through dancing, but to create cohesion among the participants in plots against the existing social order. We are ready to concede that the religious side of such meetings was incidental to their political goals, but the fact cannot be denied that Vodoun was the cement which bound the members of the conspiracy and that it served as a catalyst when the time for action came.

In the French colony of Saint-Domingue, later known as Haiti, magico-religious power was one of the attributes of many slave leaders. Makandal manipulated poison as successfully as he convinced his followers that he could fade out of sight at will; he was burned alive in 1758. Later, in 1791 a general uprising of slaves was led by Boukman, a powerful man and a Vodoun priest, as well as a *metteur en scène* of no ordinary talent. A week before the outbreak of the revolt which eventually led to the independence of Haiti, he gathered his closest affiliates in a clearing of the Bois Caiman. There, under a raging tropical downpour accompanied by lightning and the cracking of giant trees, he performed a Pétro ceremony. A pig was sacrificed and its blood, mixed with gunpowder, was distributed among participants to strengthen their will to win. Boukman soon was killed in an encounter with the disciplined French forces, but his task was successfully accomplished by new leaders who, unlike Boukman, possessed military genius and little faith in Vodoun.

We mentioned the word Pétro. It refers to one of the two main Vodoun rites, Rada and Pétro. According to an opinion fairly current among believers, but which may not be entirely correct, the two rites have quite distinct origins. The Rada gods, or *loas*, came from Africa and their role during the slavery period was one of appeasers and conformists, giving solace to their "children." The Pétro were born in Haiti and some of them were deified priests and leaders. They were bent on action through fire, poison, and massacre. While Vodoun tradition piously holds that both groups united to guide the faithful to freedom, it also points out the goodness of the Rada in contrast to the violence and addiction to magic of their younger rivals, the Pétro. The contrast may be exaggerated, but one may wonder if it does not in its simplicity reveal the dual character of Vodoun referred to above. Moreover, it is possible that the two rites hold sway alternately over Haitian life and especially over politics according to the circumstances—crisis or peace. Magic, violence, and secrecy are called for on the one hand; piety, conciliation, and thanksgiving on the other.

Many foreign authors have deplored the high price Haiti had to pay for its independence: the quasi-total destruction of the colonial irrigation system, the wrecking of the sugar refineries, the burning of the plantations. But these are material losses. Perhaps more important was the isolation both imposed upon and chosen by the new country. Surrounded by slave colonies, Haiti became a black sheep. Furthermore, the nation's first ruler, Dessalines, concerned about a possible return of the French, decided to maintain only limited commercial relations with the outside world. At one time he even considered razing all the coastal cities except a few seaports and concentrating the decimated population in the mountains where defense would be easier. Haiti's cultural isolation was made acute when the white settlers, whose technological knowledge could have helped greatly in rebuilding the former colony's economic wealth on a non-slavery basis, either fled or were killed. Lastly and most important for the history of Vodoun, the severance of all ties with France meant that the Holy See would neither establish relations with the new republic nor provide for the spiritual needs of its inhabitants for nearly sixty years. It was not until 1860 that the Haitian Government, after repeated efforts, succeeded in signing a concordat with the Vatican. In the interim, defrocked prelates of dubious morality together with downright impostors posing as priests catered to the magical tastes of the peasantry, thus reinforcing the already existing familiarity between Vodoun and Catholicism.

By 1860, a major date in the religious history of the country, Haiti was already facing most of the socio-cultural problems of today. Blacks and mulattos, at odds since colonial times, were fighting for power. Schools were scarce and illiteracy undoubtedly stood where it stands today, above 85 percent. Constitutions and laws were written in French, a language intelligible only to the educated minority. Health conditions were bad. Roads were almost nonexistent and goods were carried either on the heads of women or by coastal shipping. Attempts to create a landed gentry, Black and mulatto, controlling a cheap labor force had failed. This did not mean, however, that large estates disappeared completely; a small number of them survived under the ownership of King Christophe's former aristocrats in the north. There were others in the Cul-de-Sac near Port-au-Prince and in the southern peninsula. But they were to be found chiefly in the lowlands where control, both by the proprietors and the government, was easier.

Yet, the owners did not have their hearts in the business. In the manner of the French colonists they did not live on their estates and they displayed little interest in agricultural innovations to increase productivity. With typical *latifundista* disdain, they considered their estates to be merely a source of revenues which allowed them to enjoy the dubious comforts of Haitian urban life, participate in political intrigue, and educate their sons in Paris. Those who were educated studied the humanities which prepared them for liberal professions, not engineering or agronomy which could have helped them attack the land problems of the nation.

Nevertheless, the state did try to apply an agricultural policy that was simple and to the point: increase the production of exportable goods. Land grants were made on the condition that such goods would be cultivated. The lack of technicians, however, plus a restive labor force, and poor administration, frustrated these efforts.

In sum, the peasant won his battle against the big landowner and the plantation system. At that time, however, the economy of the country rested on a firmer basis than it does today. Land was plentiful for a population of less than a million. Haitian coffee and cotton had few competitors; molasses and dyewood found a sure market in Europe. Since there was no industrialization, urban development was practically nil and the overwhelming majority of the population lived in hamlets or on isolated farms. Vodoun, occasionally persecuted but tolerated or encouraged most of the time, had put its stamp on all facets of peasant life. Such, then, was the general picture facing the first members of the Catholic clergy who landed in Haiti after the Concordat of 1860.

As Alfred Métraux[2] rightly states, however, the Catholic Church showed lack of discernment in coping with the situation confronting it. Since it was well known that the rural masses were attached to "fetichism and superstitions" (in the vocabulary of the time) and that they should be enlightened and brought to the true Faith, this was obviously a task for missionaries. They would have to fight illiteracy, sickness, and "pagan" practices, and provide both physical and spiritual care. Instead, the Church nicely divided the country into parishes on the French model. This division resulted in an undue concentration of priests in the urban areas while the rural population was neglected. Nor were the priests particularly well prepared for missionary work. If some of them displayed devotion and sacrifice in the performance of their duty, others became the victims of apathy and routine. Some even neglected to learn Creole, the language spoken by all Haitians.

A final point must be made clear in order to understand the subsequent relations between Church, state, and Vodoun, as we discuss them. The majority of the Catholic clergy of Haiti until this time had been of foreign origin and, for linguistic purposes, mostly French. The clergy which was soon to become a political force was entrusted with a secret mission: to create a climate of opinion favorable to a voluntary association of Haiti with France. It is only too well known that in the nineteenth century missionaries in Africa and Asia were often the spearhead of economic penetration and colonial rule. It is not strange, then, that patriotic Frenchmen would undertake to combine faith with national glory. In order to carry out the scheme, the French clerics concentrated on the education of the upper class. They opened excellent secondary schools where Haitian students were fully indoctrinated in the grandeur of France and exposed to insinuations about the backwardness of their country and its incapacity for self-rule.

The plan failed and was given up in the late 1890's. But the imported clergy, conservative as usual, maintained an informal alliance with the upper class whose education and interests tended to set it apart from the rest of the population. Little wonder that by 1960 the clergy of Haiti openly took the side of the bourgeoisie. This led the opponent (in this case the government) to take stern measures against the alliance of the bourgeoisie and the clergy, and in the name of nationalism, to look for support from the masses and Vodoun.

2 BELIEFS AND STRUCTURE OF VODOUN

Vodoun is not only a religion but a body of beliefs and practices applied chiefly but not exclusively by the Haitian peasantry in their efforts to survive in their environment. "Sad Tropics," said French anthropologist Claude Lévi-Strauss.[3] This verdict and a low level of technological knowledge explain the predominance of Vodoun in the Haitian way of life. The peasant whose knowledge of science is limited must rely on the available interpretation of the environment and this is mainly a supernaturalistic one.[4] Crop failures, pests, droughts, and floods are not interpreted as natural phenomena but as manifestations of the anger of neglected spirits or the envy of some neighbor. Equally, success is attributed to the protection of the gods or the magical power of an individual. In the valley of Marbial in 1948, most peasants were convinced that with enough money one could "buy" rain and have it fall on one's plot. Sickness and its sequel, death, are seldom thought to be due to natural causes. Souls are stolen and kept in bottles; illnesses are "sent"; magic turns the most healthy man sexually impotent; the blood of babies is sucked at a distance; tuberculosis can be cured by transferring it to a rooster. Proper offerings can secure success in economic, political, and amorous ventures. Since "an ounce of prevention is worth a pound of cure," preventive and counter-magic are available in the form of amulets, "points," special garments and the like.

We would not say that the Haitian peasant lives in a world of "fear and trembling," but we believe that his limited ability to interpret natural phenomena leaves him no other course than to rely heavily on magical practices. But, one may say, magic is not Vodoun. Academically speaking this may be so. In reality, both bodies of belief are so closely interrelated as to constitute only one complex: the magico-religious. For more than 160 years that complex has been the mainstay of Haitian country life. If we have emphasized its magical aspect so far, it is only to underline its weakness and to make clear that we do not consider the magico-religious complex the best of solutions. That an alternative did exist is made evident by the early efforts of Haitian leadership, even prior to 1804, to create institutions and associations capable of giving the country an orientation towards *natural* behavior. However, the isolation that we have described was incompatible with Europeanization. When this isolation is added to the scarcity of resources, the corruption and the incompetence, it becomes clear why Haiti failed to extend to its masses adequate hygiene, education, and technology. Yet, the extent to which the country did survive is due to the relative success of the peasantry in organizing itself without the assistance of the educated urban element and in some instances even *in spite of* that element.

For example, in the field of group relations, a cooperative labor system was formed to accomplish agricultural tasks. Such *sociétés* as they were called, became obsolete with the atomization of rural property. The rural family, under the stern guidance of its eldest member, became a fairly efficient social unit dominated by the spirit of mutual help. The Haitian peasant, like his counterparts elsewhere, was not an enthusiastic innovator or inventor in the field of agriculture. He used some African and colonial techniques but he forgot others. He did not prune his coffee trees, nor did he use fertilizers or systematic crop rotation. He used his limited agricultural skill to good advantage in the volcanic soil and his coffee crop has been the chief source of income to the country since its independence. Today, soil exhaustion, erosion, and demographic pressure call for radical changes in the field of agricultural techniques.

Vodoun is the main achievement of rural Haiti. The conspiratorial cult of colonial times grew and adapted itself to the multiple needs of an isolated agricultural society, offering solutions to its problems, providing it with entertainment and the means to compensate the harshness of daily life. Some of its aspects are dreadful, but its versatility and its positive role are well expressed by Jahn[5] in his quite accurate definition of the *hounfor* or temple as "Sanctuary, clubhouse, dance hall, hospital, theatre, chemist's shop, music hall, court and council chamber in one." Furthermore, the magico-religious complex can be considered as a moderator of violence. At least prior to 1957, murders were a rare occurrence in the Haitian countryside and the few cases that were registered were usually associated with disputes over land ownership. The explanation might be that the Haitian considers magic to be a more sensible weapon to use against his enemy than one which risks jail. The psychological results can be quite satisfactory if the victim comes to suspect that he is bewitched, a conclusion that he will reach only too easily with the help of the magician. As can be seen, however, the moderating effect in turn creates a chain reaction of countermagic which threatens the cohesion of the community and even of the family. *Houngans* and *bocors* live by keeping their clientele on a constant alert and by sustaining belief in the supernatural interpretation of the environment. Should the peasantry, the urban proletariat, and a sector of the bourgeoisie lose their faith in the capacity of the Vodoun clergy to manipulate nature and its phenomena at will, *houngans* and *bocors*[6] would face a serious loss of income and social power. But that loss of faith can come only when education, sanitation, and improved economic conditions alleviate the chronic insecurity. Such a program is well beyond the national resources, both financial and human, of Haiti. As long as these improvements are not introduced, Vodoun will reign supreme over goods and lives. It will operate beyond class lines since it offers to some members of the educated minority a last hope against illnesses which the professional physician cannot cure. As long as insecurity prevails, urbanites and peasants will seek from the *houngan* the secret of wealth and the key to political and social advancement.

Thus, it is hard to see Vodoun in perspective. It unites and divides, cures and kills, protects and persecutes all at once. More than the state it has succeeded in giving to the Haitian masses a sense of belonging. Perhaps more successfully than Creole as a unifying language, Vodoun has erased the tribal differences among the former slaves of the French colony by imposing coexistence on their divers gods. To be sure, traces of tribalism do survive. The Nago rite may be predominant in the north, the Ibo in the southwest, the Congo in the valley of Jacmel, but in some places all their *loas*, with the exception of the dreaded Pétros, dwell peacefully in the same *hounfor*.[7] Yet when all has been said, good and bad, one condemning aspect of Vodoun remains. Historically the religion, like all religions, has evolved and then suffered a process of stagnation which is fatal to the interest of Haiti. It undoubtedly possesses a certain dynamism and undergoes superficial changes.[8] But it has lost its original revolutionary impetus. It has turned into a conservative institution which condones and feeds upon the backwardness of the peasantry. Moreover, Vodoun lacks a hierarchy capable of formulating and imposing a new policy for the benefit of the rural population. It can only thwart or at least remain indifferent to the efforts of the state to initiate changes which might menace the local control of the *houngans* over their flocks. To our knowledge, no *houngan* has ever sponsored the building of a school, promoted a program of community development, sought to introduce new crops, or innovated an agricultural technique. His overspecialization not only guarantees him relative power and wealth, but it also makes him unfit for the kind of *true* leadership which places the material and spiritual welfare of the community above personal advantages. The type of change needed today is beyond the comprehension of Vodoun and contrary to its interests.

Vodoun will remain the bane of Haiti and the arch-enemy of the progressive state until its clergy is curbed by a superior power and learns to cooperate with the rural teacher, the physician, and the agronomist. But should this metamorphosis occur, the *houngan* would cease to be *houngan*; he would turn into a civil servant. The gods would die.

3 *DUVALIER AND VODOUN*

The relationship between Duvalier and Vodoun should be viewed not as one of an individual to a faith, but rather it should be approached from the standpoint of the relations between church and state. For *raison d'État* not a few heads of state will participate in religious ceremonies although they may be agnostics or downright atheists. This is considered to be sound policy. In his *Mémoires* Saint-Simon relates with a touch of bitterness how he vainly prompted the Duke of Orléans, then Regent of France, to show himself at the processions and other celebrations of the Catholic Church in order to gain popular sympathy and confidence for his government. The Regent adamantly declined to perform such a boring duty. He was a poor politician.

Few Haitians, holders or candidates to an elective office, will display such a lack of common sense. They will cultivate the friendship of the key *houngans* of their district, make donations to their temples, offer ceremonies and, in addition, go to Mass every Sunday. They become vulnerable to blackmail on the part of their "friends," but this is the price they must pay for the support and the favorable influence the *houngans* will exercise upon the electorate.

The relations between state and church are a trial of strength, a conflict of interests. In Haiti, as elsewhere, the theory that the state holds "the monopoly of legitimate physical force"[9] is seriously weakened by the existence of groups and institutions wielding other types of forces: economic, social, and religious. The complex interactions of such forces against the state are at the roots of the rise of Vodoun in Haiti since 1957, though Vodoun itself represented a power which more than once had undermined the state. Haiti has too few permanent institutions upon which a government can hope to rest. There are no political parties: there is no continuity in the public service, no "loyal opposition." By 1937, three years after the end of the American Occupation, the Army once more became ill with political fever.

Power then is personal; the state becomes *one* man: the executive, who with little pain can dispose of independent senators and congressmen as if they were caddies. The meager financial resources must be spent on creating supernumerary jobs for partisans, informants, and parasites. A president lasts as long as he can manage to keep the opposition divided, and the opposition is the whole conscious population minus one citizen— the president.

The situation confronting Duvalier in 1957 was not far different from this somewhat pessimistic picture. To be sure, the Army had backed him, but who could trust the Army? The Catholic clergy and the bourgeoisie were openly predicting his fall and flight within a few months. A large sector of the Black intelligentsia was resolutely against him. The rural areas were divided in loyalty and its masses in expectancy. The majority of the businessmen did not trust him, although those who had financed his campaign did hope he would last long enough for them to recover their money or receive compensatory advantages. The United States Department of State and the Episcopal Church were sympathetic, but how long would their interests coincide with the plans and ambitions of Duvalier?

In 1966, nine years later, François Duvalier is sole master of Haiti. By using naked force, murder, cunning, temerity, blackmail, nationalism, and Vodoun he has crushed the Opposition, cowed the Catholic Church, outsmarted the United States Department of State, rendered the Army impotent, and bled business white. If the capacity to remain in power were the sole yardstick by which to measure the skill of a politician, we could say that Duvalier is a success. But his success would mean only the triumph of one man and the rout of a nation. The plight of Haiti is too well known to dwell on it; suffice it to say that many publicists consider today's Haiti as "the poorest country on earth." Nor is it far from the truth to view the tiny Black Republic as being in full regression. However, our concern is for Vodoun, and we cannot understand its resurgency in Haiti properly without setting it in the general political context.

We can safely consider the tenure of office of Duvalier, so far, as a ceaseless struggle against all kinds of foes, and in all fairness some of the negative character of his government can be laid at the door of that bitter opposition. Any other man would have chosen to retire, but stubbornness, tenacity of purpose, and in a sense, the response to the challenge brought the former rural physician to seek and follow the path of absolute power regardless of the cost in suffering and frustration to his fellow citizens. He used the weapons available. To his cause he enlisted all possible allies in defiance of international opinion and with total disregard for future consequences. He has succeeded in building a formidable machine of oppressive control which he, even as a master sorcerer, may now be unable to steer towards constructive action.

Duvalier's battle against the opposition has been fought on simultaneous and connected fronts, but we will emphasize only the one action which is most closely connected with our topic and which sheds light on his whole strategy and its relation to Vodoun. We will discuss the struggle between the state and the churches; we purposefully write *churches* because Catholicism, Vodoun, and Protestantism were parties or victims in the encounter.

A few words about the respective relations of the three creeds with the body social are necessary for a better understanding of the operations. Catholicism is the dominant faith, but its ability to control suffers from a number of limitations. Its principal ally, the mulatto and Black bourgeoisie, is not strong enough to win a favorable decision by itself; it needs the support or, at least, the indifference of the Army.

The peasant practices both Catholicism and Vodoun with hardly a pang of conscience. But the Haitian ruralite is not a religious fanatic; he is tolerant and generally feels no deep attachment to the curate. He fears the civilian authorities, "the State," more than the priests, and he fears the *houngan* even more than the authorities.

The Catholic clergy of Haiti is not united; it is still two-thirds white, while the native third is itself divided between the ever present factions: Blacks and mulattos. The bishoprics and key positions are held by foreigners at a time when nationalism and anti-colonialism are on the rise. Add to these factors the ambition, legitimate or not, of some Haitian prelates and the weakness of the Catholic clergy becomes patent.

Protestantism is not only numerically feeble (involving 10% of the people, it is said), but the presence of various denominations—Baptist, Adventist, Wesleyan—precludes all joint action. The Episcopal Church is fairly strong because of its financial resources, but it can do little more than make its voice heard. Finally, there is Vodoun, the most formidable adversary of the state.

Let us remember that until Duvalier had dealt with that source of nuisance, the Army, he could not stay in power. Lacking in esprit-de-corps and divided into political factions, the rank and file as well as the officer corps were easily purged of suspicious elements.[10] Once the Army had been made toothless by concentrating weapons in the hands of the well-known *Tonton Macoutes* and later the militia, the gradual liquidation of the other sources of opposition was a question of time and opportunity. Duvalier did not provoke them openly; quite the contrary. For the first time, I believe, in the country's history, he appointed a Haitian prelate as Minister of Education. Although this move may have been inspired by respect, it could well have been calculated to mark the beginning of a promising era for the native clergy. In a way, it was a sort of message: "Here is the proof of my nationalism. Rally to my government and reap ecclesiastical promotions." On the other hand, to demonstrate his independence from Catholicism, Duvalier openly courted the Episcopal Church which had given him its blessing jointly with the United States Department of State during the presidential campaign. So far, all was in order.

Although the higher Catholic clergy must have been aware of its own weakness, it chose to show its displeasure with the behavior of the executive. On moral grounds it could not remain silent in front of the increasing wave of murders, abuses, and practice of Vodoun. After preliminary skirmishes during which the Catholic press was muzzled, the final stroke was as swift as it was unexpected: the Archbishop of Port-au-Prince, two bishops, and a number of influential French priests were summarily ejected in quick succession from the country. Shortly afterwards, the head of the Episcopal Church suffered a similar fate: He "was arrested and expelled at gun point on a half hour's notice."[11] The Papal Nuncio was recalled and Duvalier was excommunicated. But this did not impede another Haitian prelate from keeping the Portfolio of Education. He had succumbed evidently to the double call of nationalism and ambition.

What do the men in the street and the peasants think of a president who deals such defiant blows? What is the opinion of a president who stands up to the United States, triumphs over repeated invasions, escapes from attempted assassination, and crushes plots before they hatch? The answers are multiple, but all reveal admiration, grudging or not, and chiefly awe: "He is not afraid of the white man.[12] He is strong, he has *power*, magical power, the *loas* are on his side!" Not in vain did Duvalier woo Vodoun during the twenty years prior to his election. As president, he has openly espoused the popular religion, but we must consider his action a *mariage de raison* and not one of love. Dr. François Duvalier may not be a great scholar, but his long contacts with Haitian life taught him some essential truths: the westernization of Haiti was only superficial. The great masses were still in the grip of the magico-religious way of thought. Since Duvalier must have read Lévy-Bruhl,[13] he may have regarded the mentality of his fellow countrymen as "primitive" and "pre-logical." The real focus of power, the rural masses, had not been exploited by the heads of state, save during the War of Independence. An effectively controlled peasantry could well outweigh the urban minority, including business and the Army. Vodoun was foremost among the tools required to carry out that scheme for absolute power.

Two presidents had reached the same conclusions instinctively, but Soulouque and Simon failed because they *believed* in Vodoun. Their faith easily rendered them the tools of the *houngans*; they were not the masters of their political decisions. Not so with Duvalier! Only if he does *not* believe can he expect to impose his will on his reluctant collaborators. His will is supported by his pretense of conformity, and by the repeated "proofs" that he possesses magical powers to a superlative degree. In the event that his magical prestige does not suffice, he holds a trump card: armed force. As early as 1958 some prominent *houngans* met an untimely death; we do not know whether more of their kind failed to heed the notice that they had a new master.

To deal with Catholicism and Protestantism was child's play. Their futile attempt to bar the road to absolutism required only one blow: "Strike the shepherd and the flock scatters." Vodoun is made of harder stuff, it has a thousand heads, its "bishops" are legion, and this makes the struggle between the state and that particular church only fiercer. It might be enough to disorganize Protestantism momentarily and to divide and confuse the Catholic clergy. The danger of a Catholic schism headed by native elements might demand extra caution in the dealings with the Vatican. But Vodoun had no external support. It had to be dealt with thoroughly and reduced to total obeisance. The moment was propitious for the state.

Until a decade or so ago it was not unusual for Haitian peasants to believe that Nord Alexis, the octogenarian general who ruled early in this century, was *still* president; the more educated spoke of Borno (1922-1930) as "sitting in the Palace." Such times are gone. The presence of Duvalier is not only known but felt in the remotest corners of Haiti. All *houngans* and *bocors* must acknowledge the existence of a superior authority within their own sphere of influence.

This is the real revolution of Duvalier: His armed militia is everywhere, but its chiefs hold only crumbs of power. None of them so far can hope to extend his control beyond a narrow territory. Recruited from the peasantry, the urban proletariat, and the expanding lower middle class, many militiamen and *macoutes* believe and practice Vodoun. Undoubtedly some of them belong to the Vodoun clergy. In them, politics have been amalgamated with religious faith and loyalty to a leader. This has created fanaticism, an attitude so uncommon in Haiti. The excessive zeal of the militia is directed toward one man, Duvalier, who derives from it both political and religious strength. The *houngans* of yesterday have consequently lost the control they long exercised upon their community. If they still hold some power it is for services rendered to the state or because they are willing to serve it. The triumph of Vodoun demands the submission of its clergy. The once independent religion is in chains. In a way it is the spouse of the state and performs her duties at command.

Although the economic debacle of Haiti and heavy taxes hinder the practice of Vodoun, ceremonies are organized, the drums beat and people dance, but the ritual is under government control. The government orders it and pays for it. Duvalier does not love Vodoun, he only uses it. To what purpose?

Clergymen, educated Haitians, foreigners, all miss the point when they try to denigrate Duvalier by accusing him of "voodooism." The attacks only enhance his stature among the masses and confirm his nationalism among his followers. His brand of nationalism is a special one that dictates a policy not guided by national interests but vitiated by ideological and doctrinal prejudices, precisely opposed to what a national policy should be.

But Duvalier cares little if the people are hungry, diseased, and illiterate. Perhaps he despises the Haitian people. He is that rare blend of dreamer and man of action who is fascinated by a theory which he holds to be the absolute truth. Haiti is Black and must be ruled by Blacks. Further, its ethnic cohesion must be strengthened by a religious symbol of its own, Vodoun. Haiti must have a National Faith and a national faith calls for a national head of the church: Duvalier. The idea is not a novel one if we remember Henry VIII of England or, without going back so far, Nazism.[14] If our thesis seems too far fetched, let us analyze a project of Duvalier. Late in 1957 he decided to change the Haitian flag from blue and red horizontal to black and red vertical, the black to the staff. Instead of the coat-of-arms designed by the mulatto president, Alexandre Pétion, Duvalier proposed that a guineafowl perched on a conch (the *lambi* which called the slaves to rebellion) was to stand at the upper left corner (dexter chief point). His proposal was greeted by a volley of protests, and since he had been in power only a few months, he withdrew his plans. It was said that the operation would be too costly. But in June 1964, the flag *was* changed; the full version with bird and shell going to the Army and a bastard one, keeping the old coat-of-arms, flying upon public buildings and embassies.

Historically there exists some doubts about the original colors of the flag; it might have been black and red. However, the blue and red horizontal was a symbol of national unity: Blacks and mulattos were supposedly equal, both sharing in state affairs (the staff). When the red is out on the black and red vertical flag it means that the Blacks are solely in control and the class struggle is won. But the bird signifies constant vigilance and the conch represents the call to massacre. There can be no clearer warning.

Lastly, in 1918, an esotericist of sorts, Arthur Holly, wrote a turgid book, *Les Daimons du culte voudo*, in which he advanced the thesis that the position of the colors of the national flag were in flagrant opposition to the esoteric forces. In order for Haiti to progress they should be set vertically. Dr. Duvalier probably smiles at such nonsense, but at the same time his decision to modify the flag expresses recognition of a political and social symbol. It gains him extra dividends: *houngans* and fanatic followers will have one more reason to believe in his wisdom and occult knowledge.

A president dressed in white tie is a common sight. It better suits the head of a national church to don more impressive trappings and to hold a more exclusive title. The title of Emperor is well associated with Vodoun. If Duvalier did wish to be crowned "Emperor," as it seems, it was not to satisfy his personal vanity, but for strictly political reasons. For the believers, he would have become equal to Dessalines, although for the bourgeoisie and the foreigners he would have been only a new Soulouque.

But whether Haiti under Duvalier ever becomes an Empire for the third time or not, her history will have gone full circle back to 1804, but with a qualitative difference. At the start of her independent life she was considered "out of place" because she had won her freedom against all expectations. The temporary isolation sought by her founder was motivated by the existence of real enemies; the subsequent failure of the responsible class confirmed that isolation. Today, Haiti is an anachronism, not because of a possible change in the form of government, but on account of a policy which condemns her people to live *en vase clos,* imposing on the peasants in the name of nationalism, the continuity of the very way of life which has denied them the benefits of health and education. By a cruel irony, a sector of the learned minority is responsible for the regression, this time not through failure to act but by deliberate choice. Here is a perfect example of what Julien Benda labeled *la trahison des clercs,* the treason of the learned. The honest attempt at rehabilitating Vodoun by searching for the truth about it was corrupted by selfish and narrow class interests and became a political nightmare. The Haitian *clercs* mistook their passionate interest in folklore for the active care they should have taken of their illiterate brothers. Folklore is beneficial to a country when it keeps esthetic values alive and is a mark of originality. But when it becomes the essence of a nation's behavior as it has in Haiti today, it can only obscure the prospects for positive change.

4 REACTION TO VODOUN

Though it is in bonds and under state control, Vodoun is at the height of its career. Its triumph over a century of Catholic opposition and over generation after generation of inimical Haitian writers, politicians, and scholars, however, is not due to its own dynamism. It is due, rather, to its powerful associations with politics, nationalism, and the class struggle. All during the long feud, Vodoun had the majority on its side, but until 1964, that majority had little of the organized'leadership which the opposition supposedly had. The story of the reaction to Vodoun is fraught with conformism, futility, irresponsibility, intolerance, and few instances of clearsightedness. In a word, an all too human episode.

During the last third of the nineteenth century and the first two decades of the twentieth, the Haitian intellectuals who took positions against the "primitive rituals" of the peasants did so for two reasons: (1) To defend their country from unfair and at times vicious attacks from abroad. Their patriotism conformed to the dominant European attitude of the period which considered everything non-white to be inferior. They had to lie piously about Vodoun by pretending that much of its reputed power over the masses was false or exaggerated. (2) To distinguish themselves from the ignorant peasantry, both Blacks and mulattos decried the barbaric practices. Those who had been educated in Europe, who were sincere Catholics, who spoke good French and knew their classics as well as any, were the true Haiti. This was a futile and cowardly defense.

From these two categories of *clercs* there were only a few who transformed their opposition to Vodoun into practical measures when they entered the field of politics. A couple of Ministers of Education tackled the problem the right way by launching programs of integral rural education. But their very initiative was their undoing. Men of such energy could aspire only to the presidency, so their career was usually brief. Illiterate generals do not trust intellectuals.

The surge of Negro culture in the nineteen twenties, the spread of jazz, the emergence of poets and novelists, the interest of white societies in the exotic and the unspoiled, the very movement which, in combination with nationalism, started the reappraisal of Vodoun in Haiti, did not disarm the adversaries of the African side of Haitian culture. In the name of Catholicism and of their French heritage, they repeatedly scored the demoralizing effect of Vodoun, associating it with backwardness and maintaining that all *houngans* were rogues.

The novel was the favorite form for such attacks. With little risk to the authors it could display sharp criticisms of the frequent associations of politicians and their wives with Vodoun. In order to drive the lesson home, the wives are usually seduced by the *houngans*. All very trite. These writers had more concern for the morality and proper behavior of the bourgeoisie than for the welfare of the rural and urban proletariat. A later group of novelists, belonging to a younger generation, are moderate in their criticism of Vodoun. They exploit it as a literary asset, but they emphasize the social change occurring among the peasants in order to predict the gradual disappearance of the religion.

In sum, the intellectuals on the side of Vodoun have been, for better or worse, more efficient than their opponents. Their task has been easier since with little critical sense they were also obeying the password given once more from abroad: Exalt your African heritage. In Africa, itself, the *clercs* have known how far to go. In Haiti the brakes failed.

If there is little wonder that individuals acting by the pen and without a program should have failed to dent the structure and power of Vodoun, it is astounding that an institution which is intrinsically committed to oppose a "pagan" religion should have made so little progress in the battle. Although the Catholic Church was poorly represented during the colonial period and the first sixty years of Haiti's independent life, its troubles were more basic. In the very beginning it adopted an inappropriate type of administration and its apostolic action lacked dynamism. While its clergy was ill-prepared to cope with "heathens possessed by the devil," they fought Vodoun in a more or less coherent fashion.

To achieve victory, however, the clergy needed sustained and wholehearted backing from the government and the collaboration of the learned class. But the authorities could not risk their slim popular support by attacking Vodoun openly; nor were they willing to risk giving a foreign clergy the means to gain much control over the masses. Since political instability made tenure in office precarious and short, there was a sore lack of continuity in policy. Furthermore, a new president was more apt to adopt an attitude towards Vodoun that was opposite to that of his predecessor. Finally, politicians in general (including members of the educated class) were either dependent upon Vodoun for support or in debt to it. The anti-Vodoun leagues, the pastoral letters, the local successes of individual priests consequently amounted to little.

During the American Occupation, official hostility to Vodoun could not be fully exploited by the Catholic clergy. The central issue for the Haitian was nationalism, but for the French priests the matter of cultural and religious influences was also at stake. The Occupation carried in its wake the danger of Protestantism and the adoption of new customs. The clergy preferred to side with the bourgeoisie which was chafing at the presence of a dominant foreign group, the Americans. It was not until 1941, under the presidency of Lescot, that Catholicism, for the first time in Haitian history, had a free hand to deal with Vodoun under ideal conditions, i.e., total collaboration with the government. At that time, "the anti-superstitious campaign" was launched, and its methods reached a high pitch of intolerance. Vodoun temples were sacked, the paraphernalia were burned and the believers were forced to "renounce" their faith.

The campaign took place, however, at the very moment when the war effort of the United States had required and obtained from the Haitian Government the means of starting a rubber production program. Peasant lands were expropriated and thoughtless destruction of fruit trees and cultivated plots took place. Faced with the menace of general discontent, the authorities had to stop the inquisitorial activities of the clergy. Thus the government which had given its blessing to the campaign had to come to the defense of Vodoun. In February 1942, shots fired in the Catholic chapel of Delmas during the Sunday Mass served notice to Catholicism that it had failed in its enterprise. The mistake of the Lescot government partly contributed to its downfall in 1946. Thereafter Vodoun was not molested officially.

Protestantism had begun to penetrate Haiti as early as 1830. Later, the immigration of Negroes from the United States who were invited by Haiti to help develop cotton plantations, gave Protestantism a broader foothold in the country. Its spread, even during the years of Occupation, was modest. But Protestantism holds a ponderous asset: it is not associated with Vodoun. It has remained immune to the syncretizing which had blended African and Catholic rituals from the beginning of the French rule of Haiti. The Vodounist believes in the Christian God as an almighty separate Being, but the saints have become closely associated with the *loas* or African spirits whenever their attributes, as they appear in images and sculptures, correspond to the age, functions, or symbols of their Vodoun counterparts.[15] Consequently, the believer who has failed in his obligation towards the spirits can expect little protection from Catholicism for these same spirits may be present in the place of worship. No line can be drawn in this respect.

Protestantism, however, uses no images. In its temples the fleeing Vodounist feels safer.[16] Protestantism is also much more strict about the behavior of its converts than Catholicism is. It admits no compromise with or tolerance of Vodoun. As a result the Protestant peasant develops a singular hatred for anything folkloric, such as tales, dancing, and drumming. He spends his free time singing hymns. The mechanical concept of refuge or protection explains some of the appeal of the numerous Protestant denominations for a limited sector of the Haitian peasantry, but we can go further. Escape from costly ceremonies to the *loas* and hope of actually recovering from illnesses might well move the bulk of converts, as Métraux explains.[17] Yet, another socio-cultural factor at work is non-conformism, *the reaction of Vodounists to Vodoun.* The ideas spread by agronomists, physicians, priests, ministers and the like about the possibility of a better life have found an echo among the more ambitious and progressive elements of the peasantry, few as they may be. They are ready to try fertilizers, contour cultivation, irrigation, new crops, and to learn to read and write. In a word, they want to break away from tradition, a tradition whose axis is Vodoun.

We do not mean to imply that Protestantism is the salvation of Haiti, nor the solution for its ailments. We have known Catholic ruralites who were as eager to follow the path of change in both religious and secular matters; who gave up polygamy as an uneconomical practice and laughed at Vodoun. By 1957, the cooperative movement which might have made decisive changes in Haiti, was beginning to bud in the countryside. The peasantry needed only a sustained official program of technical assistance to start moving steadily away from routine and the supernatural. Instead they got Duvalier. Instead of receiving agricultural guidance, schools, and clinics, they suffered the extortions of the militia and an overdose of Vodoun to kill their pains or to keep them in awe. Vodoun, which at times had been an instrument of union, became a tool of coercion, the whip of internal colonialism, a means for the exploitation of the Black by the Black. Such are the fruits of its triumph.

The *zombi*, the legendary soulless robot, once made Haiti infamous. Duvalier has *zombified* his country. According to folklore, the *zombi* must be fed salt in order to regain his faculties. When Duvalier goes, who will feed salt, the salt of life to a whole nation? In other words, what is the future of Haiti? We can only surmise that the recovery will be long and painful. Surely there will be a reaction against Vodoun. It has been discredited by being too closely associated with a destructive regime. Perhaps both Catholic and Protestant clergies will be chastened by their ordeal and with a newly gained cohesion they will set themselves resolutely to the task of providing the masses with material and spiritual help. May the *clercs*, cured of folklore at long last, learn the lesson from the progressive peasant and choose to lead the van.

Notes

1. Philip D. Curtin, *Two Jamaicas,* Cambridge: Harvard University Press, 1955, p. 36.
2. Alfred Métraux, *Voodoo in Haiti.* Translated by Hugo Charteris. New York: Oxford University Press, 1958, pp. 335–336.
3. C. Lévi-Strauss, *Tristes tropiques,* Paris: Librairie Plon, 1955, 462 pp.
4. J. S. Slotkin, *Social Anthropology,* New York: The Macmillan Company, 1950, pp. 182 ff.
5. Janheinz Jahn, *Muntu: An Outline of the New African Culture.* New York: Grove Press, 1961, p. 54.
6. A *houngan* is an initiate, a priest. The *bocor* is a magician or medicine man. *Houngans* do cure and practice magic, but no *bocor* officiates at Vodoun ceremonies. The word *bocor* has a sinister ring about it.
7. Odette Mennesson-Rigaud, "Vodou haitien: Quelques notes sur se réminiscences africanes." In *Afro-Américains: Memoires de l' Institut Français d' Afrique Noire,* No. 27. Dakar, 1953, p. 236.
8. The Vodoun pantheon increases with the passing of time and events. The United States Marine Corps left a *loa* in Haiti; when he possesses a believer (a

trance-like state) he asks, with an unmistakably American accent, for corned beef and whiskey, a rather expensive taste.

9. Robert H. Lowie, *Social Organization*, New York: Rinehart and Company, 1948, p. 317.

10. Duvalier's task was made easier by the ten months of political troubles which followed General Magloire's fall. As early as June 1957, the Chief of Staff, Antonio T. Kébrau, had purged the army of numerous privates and NCO's suspected of loyalty to Provisional President Daniel Fignolé whom he had overthrown.

11. Robert Debbs Heinl, Jr., "Terror in Haiti: A Case Study in Freedom," *The New Republic*, May 16, 1964, p. 19.

12. Dessalines, the Liberator of Haiti and its first Emperor, is best remembered by the common folk for his hatred of the "whites"—the French. Duvalier frequently compares his task with that which confronted the Emperor in 1803. His followers do not hesitate to put both men on the same level of greatness.

13. In his notebooks written during World War II and published posthumously, Lévy-Bruhl reneged on the theory of "Primitive mentality" to which he owed his celebrity.

14. Alfred Rosenberg, champion of the *Deutsche Glaubensbewegung*, was admiringly quoted by François Duvalier and the late Lorimer Denis, "L'Evolution stadiale du Vodou." *Bulletin* de Bureau d' Ethnologie d' Haiti, 3, Port-au-Prince, 1944, p. 32.

15. Michel Leiris, "Note sur l'usage des chromolithographies catholiques par les vodouisants d'Haïti," in *Les Afro-Américains, Mémoires de l'Institut Français d' Afrique Noire*, Dakar, 1953, pp. 201–207.

16. However, the Episcopalian cathedral of Port-au-Prince has been decorated by Haitian popular painters with a series of "frescoes" depicting scenes of the New Testament.

17. Métraux, 1958, pp. 311 ff. [pp. 351 ff. in Charteris' translation.—Ed.]

Vittorio Lanternari
RELIGIOUS MOVEMENTS IN JAMAICA

The revival of traditional African cults, a widespread phenomenon among Afro-Americans in this area, appears to have been started in Jamaica in 1783 by an ex-slave named George Lewis. The Native Baptist cult, which he established on an Afro-Christian pattern, was eventually to become an intrinsic part of local Negro culture and a redoubtable rival to Christianity. The Native Baptists showed their strength especially between 1840 and 1865, during the uprisings at Port Morant, when they fought strenuously against the missionaries who had banned all their traditional cults, customs, and celebrations.[1]

Another nativistic movement, called the Great Awakening, swept through the island in 1861. Even the missionaries viewed it with favor until they discovered that its manifestations were "inspired by the devil." The purpose of the Great Awakening was to restore spiritual links between the Jamaican Negroes and their African forebears,[2] and found its expression in the wildest forms of dancing, in collective trances, in sexual orgies, and in flagellations following upon public confession of sins.

In 1920 Alexander Bedward, an almost illiterate laborer from the Mona district who had joined the Methodist church and was extraordinarily eloquent and persuasive, caused an upheaval all over the island with a new cult which was called Bedwardism after his own name. His widespread following consisted of people who regarded him as a prophet and believed that he would soon be taken to Heaven like Elijah and would then return to select those who had earned their heavenly reward. He prophesied that after his second coming the whole earth would be destroyed by fire. Bedward was also a healer. He used water from the streams and the imposition of hands to invoke the power of the Almighty in his curative practices and called himself Christ, the Son of God. When his ascent to heaven failed to occur on December 31, 1920, according to his prophecy, Bedward announced that the Almighty had decided to delay the event until more of his followers had become worthy of eternal reward. Not long after this, he was arrested and committed to an institution for the insane,[3] but most of his followers continued to believe in him and revere him as their prophet.

In Jamaica, as elsewhere in the Caribbean, the most interesting forms of religious revival are found among the poverty-stricken populations of the cities. In such depressed areas as West Kingston, for instance, the

FROM PP. 159–165 OF *Religions of the Oppressed* BY VITTORIO LANTERNARI, TRANSLATED BY LISA SERGIO (NEW YORK: RANDOM HOUSE, 1963). COPYRIGHT © 1963 BY ALFRED A. KNOPF, INC. REPRINTED BY PERMISSISON OF THE PUBLISHER.

thousands of newly arrived Negroes provide fertile soil for any religious cult offering a hope of change. This new urban proletariat, which yesterday was fairly secure in the rural areas, is today struggling to find even a miserably underpaid job, and ekes out a bare living by resorting to petty larceny, prostitution, gambling, and other crimes. Any religious movement that raises its voice against the whites and the local upper class, or protests against the conditions to which the Negroes are subjected, is bound to gain a strong following among this pitiful segment of the population. Some of these cults, such as the Ras Tafari, have an anti-European objective; others, notably the Afro-Christian movements of older origin, are chiefly concerned with the social struggle.[4]

Tafarism, or the Ras Tafari movement, began to take shape in 1930. It stemmed from the evangelism of Marcus Garvey, the Jamaican Negro who, in 1918, had established the United Negro Improvement Association to better the lot of the Negroes in Africa, the Americas, and elsewhere.[5] Garvey advocated the mass migration of the American Negroes to Africa— a mass return to the homeland—which the Tafari movement also promotes through two of Garvey's most effective slogans: "Africa for Africans!" and "One God, One Goal, One Destiny!" "Marcus Garvey," said a Tafari preacher, "was an international figure. He brought a philosophy to the Black Man. Garvey laid the cornerstone and the foundation. . . . He was sent by Ras Tafari to cut and clear. . . ."[6]

West Kingston is the principal center of the Tafari cult, but the movement is widely diffused throughout the island. The cult promises the American Negroes freedom and salvation when they return to Africa. Because its followers, in general, are almost totally ignorant of geography, they regard Ethiopia as Africa and dream of returning to the kingdom of Haile Selassie. The identification of Africa with Ethiopia comes in part from the fact that Ethiopia avoided colonial rule and has always remained independent. Thus, for Jamaicans, as for many Africans, Ethiopia is the symbol of Negro freedom.

The following concepts constitute the fundamental teaching of the Ras Tafari movement: the Negroes are the reincarnation of the ancient tribes of Israel which were exiled to the West Indies in punishment for their transgression of the Law; the white man is inferior to the black man; Jamaica is the black man's hell on earth; Ethiopia is heaven; Haile Selassie is the living God; Haile Selassie will make it possible for all persons of African descent to return to their homeland; in the very near future the black man will be avenged by compelling the white man to become his servant.

The religious services held Sunday evenings begin with singing and are usually followed by this dialogue between the preacher and the congregation:

Speaker: How did we get here?
People: Slavery.

Speaker:	Who brought us from Ethiopia?
People:	The white man.
Speaker:	The white man tells us we are inferior, but we are not inferior. We are superior and he is inferior. The time has come for us to go home. In the near future we shall go back to Ethiopia and the white man shall be our servant. The white man says we are no good, yet David, Solomon, and the Queen of Sheba were black. The English are criminals and the black traitors [meaning the middle-class Jamaicans] are just as bad. There is no freedom in Jamaica. The black man who does not want to go back to Ethiopia doesn't want freedom. Ras Tafari started Mau Mau. Ras Tafari says: Death to the White Man!
People:	And to the Black Traitor! We believe in one God, one aim, one destiny. We believe in Africa for the Africans, at home and abroad![7]

The Tafari cult is not messianic and does not believe in visions or divine revelations. Its followers claim to have learned from direct personal experience the truths upon which their doctrine rests. Their position in regard to the religion of the whites is ambivalent: they favor it because it accepts the Bible and believes in a single God; they oppose it because of the policies pursued by the white man. They say: "Heaven is a scheme of the English to make the black man think that white men and black men will be equal in the sky, but on earth the white man isn't going to give the black man anything. Fraud has kept us back, the fraud of religion and politics." Tafari followers feel that colonial administrators and missionaries are one and the same thing: they regard the "police and the missionaries" as despicable people who have betrayed them and despise the whites as much for their politics as for their religion.[8] In 1953 there were at least a dozen different Tafari sects, each with its own leader or president, each administered by a deputy chief, a committee, and a secretary.

Tafari rituals are often conducted in the street: a red, gold, and green banner is carried aloft, flanked by a giant-sized photograph of Haile Selassie. Readings from the Bible are chosen largely for the antiwhite interpretations to which they lend themselves, the end of Babylon being regarded as symbolic of the end which will soon befall the white man's power. Their hymns are a call to action: "Africa awaken, morning is at hand. No more are thou forsaken Ethiopia now is free!"[9] The nativistic view of Judeo-Christian doctrine is revealed by the following prayer used at the conclusion of their worship: "Deliver us from the hands of our enemies, that we might prove fruitful for the last days. When our enemies are passed and decayed in the depths of the sea, in the depths of the earth or in the belly of a beast, oh, give us all a place in Thy Kingdom forever and ever. Selah."[10]

Tafarism, unlike many other cults, does not advocate political or military struggle to achieve its goals,[11] but holds out the promise that freedom will be found upon returning to African soil. It is, therefore, a typically *escapist* movement, rather than a revolutionary force. This is due in part to the historical fact that its followers are descendants of Africans brought to these islands by European slave traders, and in part to the nature of their current relationship to the white man, which makes the very idea of revolution unthinkable and unjustifiable.

Today, although the Jamaican Negroes are almost universally Christian, there is an intense revival of pagan-type religions, linked to old African traditions. Among those derived from Euro-American Christian inspiration are the Church of the Brethren, Christian Science, the Salvation Army, the Seventh-Day Adventists, the Society of Friends, Jehovah's Witnesses, the Pentacostal Church, the Mission Church of God, and the Bible Students. Their following proves that the natives are everywhere in quest of new religious ideas through which to demonstrate their independent choice of a church, in opposition to the strict orthodoxy required by the church of the whites.[12]

Other significant Afro-Christian cults include the Pocomania and the Zion Revival, different from each other only in ritual: the former emphasizes the reading and interpretation of Scripture, while the latter highlights ritual dancing, magical healing practices, and collective phenomena of possession.[13] Their deities are taken from ancient African polytheism and given Judeo-Christian names such as Michael, Gabriel, Samuel, Rachel, Jeremiah, Jesus Christ, Jehovah, Miriam, Satan, the Holy Ghost, Moses, Solomon, etc. This recalls a similar process characteristic of Negro-American polytheism in Haiti (Voodooism), in Cuba (the Santería), in Trinidad (the Shango), in Brazil (the Candomblé), at Porto Alegre (the Batuoue or Para) at Rio de Janeiro (the Macumba), at Pernambuco (the Zango).[14] The pagan names of the original African deities are no longer used, but both Pocomania and the Zion Revival are full of traditional pagan rituals from Africa, exploited by the Jamaican religious leaders to arouse popular protest against cultural and religious domination by the white man.[15]

The rituals of both Pocomania and the Zion Revival are performed in the open air around a pole sustaining a box which contains the Bible (Christianity), two wooden swords, a small ladder, and two wheels—the ladder for Jacob and Moses, the swords and wheels, weapons against alien tyranny. Both sects practice baptism by immersion within a pagan setting, and both have a clerical organization which includes several "equerries," called upon to restrain the faithful when convulsions and frenzy become excessive.[16]

In conclusion, the religious revival in Jamaica ranges from movements with political objectives, such as the Tafari cult, to sects which clothe their strictly aboriginal values and beliefs in Christian garb. All of them, however, take a definite anti-Western position which reflects the people's bitterness over religious persecution suffered at the hands of Protestant missionaries.[17]

Notes

1. G. E. Simpson: "Jamaican Revivalist Cults," *Soc. Ec. St.,* V, 4 (1956), pp. 334–5.

2. Ibid., pp. 335–6.

3. Ibid., p. 337.

4. Simpson: op. cit., pp. 343, 408; "Political Cultism in West Kingston, Jamaica," *Soc. Ec. St.,* IV, 2 (1955), p. 144.

5. G. Myrdal: *An American Dilemma: the Negro Problem and Modern Democracy* (New York, 1944), pp. 766 ff. According to R. L. Buell (*The Native Problem in Africa* [New York, 1928], p. 730), Garvey founded the United Negro Association in 1914.

6. Simpson: "Political Cultism in West Kingston, Jamaica," pp. 135–141.

7. Ibid., pp. 135–6.

8. Ibid., p. 137.

9. Ibid., pp. 133, 137–40.

10. Ibid., p. 140.

11. Ibid., p. 144.

12. Ibid., pp. 337–41.

13. Ibid., pp. 352–5, 417–18. For the interpretation of Christianity in the polytheistic setting, see pp. 430–3. See also my discussion of the Voodoo cult (Haiti).

14. Ibid., pp. 342–5.

15. Ibid., pp. 430–3.

16. Simpson: "Jamaican Revivalist Cults," pp. 360, 403, 466 ff.

17. Ibid., p. 408.

PART SIX
BLACK IDEOLOGY
AND BLACK POWER

Throughout the history of the black underclass in the Americas, there have been forms of resistance to the conditions and groups which oppress it. In order to be truly effective, however, resistance must be organized. The organization of resistance includes the groups involved and the ideologies that identify the aspects of social life to be attacked and justify action.

At one level of social life, this resistance is ubiquitous. These forms of resistance range from suicide to running away; refusal to work; and satire through song, narrative, and theater. The blues and work songs of the plantation worker and urban migrant in the United States express an attitude of resistance. In the West Indies, an equivalent role is played by calypso songs, as described by J. D. Elder. Music becomes an implicit part of political struggle. In Trinidad, where for a long time under colonialism the black underclass had no legitimate political means available to it, calypso songs and public drama articulated and expressed the conflicts inherent in that society.

Such forms of resistance, however, are by and large unorganized and without ideology, although they do indicate the people's awareness of the conflicts in society. The deprivation of education and literacy among the underclass means that the formulation of political ideology is often left to the literate. In the case of black society, this means middle class individuals with a racial awareness and a knowledge of the alternatives to the political and economic system that they share with the underclass.

C. L. R. James and Daniel Guérin take us through the history of racial and political ideology and of organized resistance in the Caribbean. James places the history of the West Indies in its world context. The rise and fall of Toussaint L'Ouverture, for example, is not an isolated episode of Haitian history; it is part of the Western tradition. Furthermore, in describing the realities of life under colonialism, writers articulate, in the words of the people themselves, the necessity for change. In the colonial context it is not strange to find a poet and a politician in the same person. James, himself, is an example of this proposition.

Guérin focuses on the development of labor organizations in the French and British West Indies, stressing the spontaneity of worker revolts and the role of the middle-class intellectuals. Guérin, too, points out that the growth of social and political consciousness goes hand-in-hand with expressions of black solidarity.

313

The attainment of black solidarity, however, is but a first step. In the United States, the demands of the black underclass are articulated by the poet-politicians of black nationalism. The racism, economic exploitation and political oppression they suffer, they also share with the underclass in other areas of the New World. Robert Blauner describes these relationships between the black ghettos and the national society as colonial relationships. As long as these relationships remain, meeting the demands for black control of black ghettos is obviated. This lesson is painfully learned in the Caribbean, where, in spite of political independence, countries such as Haiti, Jamaica, Trinidad are neo-colonies and dominated by foreign interests. Their impoverishment is a function of this domination.

The demands for change, then, have to be specific. As Robert Allen outlines, some Black Power groups want nothing more than black capitalism, under which the conditions of the black underclass are not likely to improve. Moreover, and at the opposite pole, those groups recognizing the necessity of solidarity not only among the black underclass, but among the underclass as a whole (and on a worldwide scale), will be seen as the most dangerous by a State desperately trying to maintain its hegemony over all the people as part of a social and economic system founded on a dehumanizing process of exploitation for private profit and perpetuated through racism.

J. D. Elder
COLOR, MUSIC, AND CONFLICT: A STUDY OF AGGRESSION IN TRINIDAD WITH REFERENCE TO THE ROLE OF TRADITIONAL MUSIC

This is a revised version of a paper read at a meeting of the Society for Ethnomusicology in November, 1961.

The island of Trinidad was discovered in 1498 by Columbus and remained part of the Spanish Empire until 1797 when it was captured by Abercromby during the French Napoleonic Wars for the English in whose hands it has remained since as a Crown Colony. The island is the second largest unit of the new West Indies Federation and is 1,684 sq. miles in extent and has a cosmopolitan population of nearly 80,000. According to the 1946 Census the racial pattern in the island stood as follows:—

African descent	261,485	(46.88%)
East. Ind. descent	195,747	(35.09%)
Mixed and colored	78,775	(14.12%)
White descent	15,283	(2.74%)
Chinese descent	5,641	(1.01%)
Other Asiatic	889	(0.16%)
Carib descent	124	(0.02%)

But far back in the year 1839, the country contained only 41,675 souls of whom 3,319 were White, 16,285 Colored, 762 Indian (Carib) and 21,302 Africans newly liberated from slavery. The small White minority stood in a position of economic and political superiority, while the majority group, the Africans and men of Amerindian descent living in the backwoods, had no voting status and were absolutely subordinate and subservient to the ruling White planter group which formed the core of the upper class and the elite in the society.

From that time to the present day, it is possible to trace an almost unbroken succession of clash and conflict of varying seriousness between White rulers and Colored subjects. In the early days when the upper class was identical with the White group, the conflict was no greater than today when many Coloreds have entered the upper class by virtue of their eco-

REPRINTED FROM *Ethnomusicology*, VOL. 8, 1964 BY PERMISSION. COPYRIGHT © 1964 BY THE SOCIETY FOR ETHNOMUSICOLOGY.

nomic prosperity and educational development. This was possible in a situation, where the main lines of differentiation in the total system were those of color and class. Class war evolved out of racial conflict and complicated the situation to a bewildering extent.

This conflict constitutes for the social historian a most fascinating drama, but it is far more tantalising for another reason—the fact that music forms for it a subtle background against which the action takes place, or through the medium of which the actors play their parts. Colonial governors, low class women of lax morals, African heroes, batoniers and tie-pins whose names adorn the history of Trinidad, strong men and Amazonians—all have had their role in a land where men of many racial origins struggle, in the crucible of race-mixture, towards something unique in history—towards a new nationhood which is gradually evolving out of this diversity.

The social problems of this community ring the changes all through the history of Trinidad. Slave whippings, hanging of maroons and vagrants, rebellions and riots on the sugar estates, intergroup clashes in the streets: this is the picture painted on the canvas of the centuries since Columbus discovered La Trinity—the triple land of conflict, music and color. This is the land of the deadly prussic acid of the Carib manioc roots, the hot vitriol of the satiric calypsoes, the maddening African Congo drums which the White man failed to silence; the long five foot Kalenda fighting stick. This is the land of the tamboo-bamboo bands. And this is a land of social protest against oppression, discrimination, crippling poverty, lack of true political equality, a land of the contrasted opulence of the Macaripe Beach Hotel and the squalor of Shanty Town and Sea Lots where human inhabitants mix with corbeaux and crow as they grovel and search in the "La Basse" for scraps of food among the rubbish dumps. This is the land where the minstrels who sang the old Ca-ie-soes lived in the backyard slums, in John John and LaCou Harpe, and where in recent times the musical geniuses among the unprivileged beat the first steel-pan music at Hell Yard, at 29 St. Joseph Road, and at the Hide-outs on Laventille Hills, at Prisoners Quarry and "Behind the Bridge."

In 1838 the Act of Emancipation became effective in Trinidad and what has been termed the "Colonial Society" began to take shape. The small White group wielded political as well as economic power in the land. They were the landed group—the rich Creoles who formed the aristocracy. As the ruling class they were concerned with preserving their power and position from encroachment. This was made possible by the availability of military forces and other less expensive means of coercion.

On the other hand, Negroes were kept in their place. Legislation and less legal methods were used to impress upon them the inferiority of their race, in ability, culture, and privilege. They throve on a subsistence wage. They lived on land which they worked either as day-laborers under the "truck-system" or as metayers eking out a miserable existence. It was illegal in those days for a Negro to own land. Any attempt to organize or to rally round a leader was deemed inimical to the Whites, and steps were taken to investigate and suppress it. In 1832, one of the most bloody slave risings took place at Plein Palais Estate, Pointe-a-Pierre. The 19th Regiment having been sent to suppress the rioters, the slaves burnt the plantation down before taking to the woods. In "Amber pond Marabella," the Kalinda singers have told in bitter lyrics how "mothers, sisters, and children were butchered and shot down." The "Nigger-grounds," the "Poor Niggers' Burial Lots" are visible evidences still present in many a rural village where the changing hand of industrialization has not yet reached.

Immediately after Emancipation Day trouble began. The deep rooted aggressions that had been smoldering for years now took tangible forms. The Negroes refused to submit to the Apprentice System which succeeded Emancipation as a tide-over measure conceded by the Imperial Government to the planters. The Negroes had been manumitting themselves long before Emancipation Day and they sent hundreds of petitions to the "Queen" requesting repatriation to Africa. The Planters opposed this movement, as well as any laws which tended to be ameliorative to Africans. The Africans retaliated with veiled hostility as well as open aggression. Risings on the estates became very common. Murder, arson, assaults on White overseers by Negro workers became the rule of the day. The reaction of the White group to this was ruthless and cruel. The sadism with which they meted out punishment has become notorious history. Even a character like the gallant Lord Picton has gone down in history for his alleged cruelty to Louisa Calderon, a quadroon whom, it is alleged, he tortured in order to extract from her evidence about a suspected Negro rebellion.

But for the purpose of this paper, the most remarkable incident was the Cannes Brule riot of 1881 (see L. M. Fraser, *Memorandum on history and origin of carnival.* Dispatch 5664, 1881). Lord Hamilton, who formed the Commission that inquired into the causes of the riot, quoting Fraser, Court Registrar and historian, reported that "for many years after Emancipation the Negroes celebrated the anniversary of their freedom on August Day by marching in organized bands in the streets and singing the *Kalinda* songs." The Negroes called their pageant *Cannes Brule* (in memory of the slavery days' cane-fires) and they dressed up like garden Negroes and came to be known as *Negre Jardin* by the French element. The celebrating bands were each headed by a mock King, a Queen, several Princesses and a galaxy of royal imitators. There were strong body-guards of armed batonniers each carrying a lighted flambeaux and a lethal looking hardwood five foot battling stick—two remarkable symbols for the newly freed slave. The Champion of each band walked ahead singing boastful Kalinda songs about himself and the victories and conquests of his followers. The bands were organised on parochial lines and very often clashed with rival bands which refused to recognise their supremacy. But often there was no free-for-all, the two leaders would close in to do battle with each other. In the circle would sit the drummers beating out drum language to direct the fighters. The supporting Chorus chanted the refrain to the

Kalinda songs led by the chantuelles. The music gave the warriors courage and the singers saw that the crude rules of the game were observed. No fighter, so long as he had fallen to the ground, was to be struck by his opponent. Once a challenger had blood drawn from his head by a blow, he was expected to with-draw from the fight, drain the blood from his head into the bloodhole in the middle of the ring, and then shake hands with the victor. (Many exponents have described the hole dug in the center of the fighting ring for receiving the blood from wounded scalps.) The two supporting bands could then move away peacefully to find new adventures during the day.

It was this Cannes Brule pageant of the Negroes which was brought in to Mardi Gras by the Africans although Fraser admits that "it is not easy to fix precisely when the addition was made to the Carnival." The Negroes argued that since Mardi Gras was a public holiday Cannes Brule could take place and "initiate the Carnival" without offence. But this invasion by Negroes of the Carnival of Mardi Gras, an upper class fete, was resented by the Whites, and stringent laws and Proclamations were passed in 1858 and active steps taken in 1859 in order to restrain the performance of Cannes Brule by Negroes on Mardi Gras. Matters came to a head when in 1881, the gallant Captain Baker, Intendant of Police, took to the street on Carnival Day with his Police to stop Kalinda and "put down this ribald Negro Saturnalia once and for all in Trinidad." Different historians have given differing accounts about the Riot which this attempt started. Briefly, the recorder relates that thousands were involved, and that "eighty men (four only mounted) armed with truncheons, cowed and overcame a mob of thousands." The militia, although called out, remained inactive. The prior Officer in Charge of Police had advised the Governor against the proclaimed interference with the Negro celebration.

The Roman Catholics had argued that the Negroes, as a pagan group, were desecrating a Christian Festival, while the upper class had protested against the entry of the Negro commonalty into what up to then was an upper class preserve. Even the "free men of color," according to Fraser, "although not forbidden to mask were subjected to stringent regulations and were never allowed to join in the amusements of the privileged class."

The harsh laws against Cannes Brule passed on the recommendation of Lord Hamilton, only served to drive Cannes Brule and Kalinda under ground. The emergence of leading stick men and kalinda singers went on untouched and legendary figures arose who carried on the movement, systematising the art of stick fighting and kalinda-singing to a fine point. (A random sampling of the batonniers or bois-men has yielded names such as Myler, Cobra, Secountan, Simewo, Toto, Shool, Banrye, Placide, Wambo, Semper, Lye, Fitzie Goonday, Maga Much, Bubull Tiger.) The songs worked their way into the woof of the cultural tradition, becoming more bitingly bitter with satire and hidden meaning, castigating the laxity of the high society with a viciousness and an effectiveness which would have been impossible without the assistance of the Negro domestics who worked in the wealthy "great houses" and saw at first hand the immorality and lechery of the ruling class. By 1881 there were backyards and village alleys by the score where the batoniers reigned King and practised the cult of Kalinda. Women fighters and chantuelles became common. Names like Sarah Jamaica, Long Body Ada, and Techselia are still words that Negro women use to frighten their naughty children. In 1884, another attempt was made by the Police to stamp out Kalinda and Cannes Brule in the small town of Arouca. The result was the brutal slaughter of the Police Inspector who was detailed to attack the bands. And, so, within fifty years, the attempt to stamp out Cannes Brule had cost Trinidad two Riots.

By the turn of the century it was clear that Cannes Brule was far from being stamped out in Trinidad. In fact members of the White group that had tried to suppress it had entered Cannes Brule, and so began the evolution of what has become present-day Carnival, the national annual Festival of Trinidad. In 1899, it is recorded that one Norman Le Blanc, a French aristocrat, set up the first Carnival Tent to which he invited the Negro singers to compose kalinda songs which were then beginning to be called "ca-i-so," later to be called "cal-y-so" although today they are called calypso. In fact Norman Le Blanc is remembered as the first man to sing a Calypso in the English tongue in Trinidad, "until then they were all sung in Patois French," a dialect introduced by the immigrants from Martinique, Dominica, and Guadeloupe, who were invited to settle in Trinidad under the famous Cedula of Population (Nov. 1783) of Roume de St. Laurent. (For more on calypso see D. J. Crowley in ETHNOMUSICOLOGY 5:57-65 and 117-24, 1959.)

The War of 1899 had just been over and the singers were able to vent their spleen on the common enemy—the Boers. Songs about the great Queen Victoria were common during this period. The object of persecution was no more confined to the White people, but to the rising middle-class to which the mulatto group so important in the stratification of Trinidad society was then moving, and who were by the time entering the occupational group of shop-clerks. Numerous old calypsoes castigating the mulatto group have been recorded in Trinidad. Due to the fact that the mulatto group was the result of race-mixture, and also because the members of this group despised the Negroes, the singers made life for mulattoes very uncomfortable by singing offensive songs about them as a group of persons "that did not belong"—whose grandmothers were rejected by them and whose grandfathers were ashamed of them.

The songs of this period are mostly about the alleged immoral life of the mulattoes, their duplicity and their ambition to enter the White group. On the other hand the bands which were allowed to parade the streets on Carnival day, provided they did not carry the old conch-shells and cow horns or beat the African drums, sang about the Wars. The chantuelles identified themselves with the heroes of war. The Leaders called themselves by names like: Iron Duke, Albany, Pharaoh, Duke of Marlborough, Black Prince, etc., and their bands carried names like: Artillery, Brigade,

Iere, Crescent, Morning Rose, White Rose, Black Ball, Mybone, True Blue.

One of the famous songs of this age has come down to us in the following form:

> Rule my Empire
> Is all I desire
> King Pharaoh—
> And no more:
> Run down the road
> And tell the Inventor:
> Run down the road
> And tell the Prosecutor:
> "Mauve 'anee pou ou." (i.e., bad year for you).

Another famous singer, known as Lord Executor, a Caucasian, and regarded as the greatest calypso singer of all times, has left us this song which is definitely composed with the idea of battle in his mind:

> Bend the angle on them
> Is to blow them down,
> Is to blow them down:
> But the bayonet charge
> Is the rod of correction—
> Kill them every one:
> The bay'net charge
> Is the rod of correction—
> Sans humanité.

The bands took on more socialized names like "White Rose," "Evening Bells," "Azalias," and the rivalry found release in the emphasis on wit and picong and on sharp *reparte*. The criticism became more veiled.

The leaders of bands were still fighters, but their fighting was only casual and occasional. For that matter, the carrying of sticks and weapons was illegal. The old African drums were still represented by a new invention—the Tambour-Bamboo—long pieces of bamboo to be struck on the ground like "stamping tubes" of the Yoruba as the band proceeded, as well as shorter pieces struck together as percussion instruments. The introduction of the trumpet and the clarinet was evidence of the compromise between purely African and purely European music that was taking place, and a testament to the fact that the two groups, Whites and non-Whites, were being provided with a common ground on which they could meet. Brierly lamented that " it is now possible to find young men from the White society joining in the ribaldry of the low class Negroes." He did not live to see the levelling of race and class barriers which was to take place through the medium of music during the next fifty years in Trinidad.

As the century got into swing and War threatened the British Empire, Negro and White were thrown together to defend, at home and on the battlefields abroad, the principles of democracy. The result was twofold. In the first place Negroes were, for the first time, able to correct some of their ideas about the racial superiority of the White race. They saw that "white dog could eat white dog," they saw that the White man could be poor, could be weak; that there were good White people besides those who had oppressed the slaves. Moreover another bug-bear, the German, was created for the songs of the calypsonians. The songs told of evil and vice as belonging to all men—not to some men only. The songs castigated the villains who had started the War. A calypso of this period runs:—

> Run your run Kaiser William
> Run your run:
> Lord Kitchener say—
> Cheer, boys cheer,
> With charity and fraternity
> We'll conquer Germany.

As the conquering troops came back home, the White Governor welcomed them. Praise was showered on Black and White veterans alike, and in the streets on the proclaimed holidays the calypsonians sang:

> Kaiser William run away
> Kaiser run away—
> Kaiser run into Ireland ma-ma!

It is of importance to note that the old Kalinda tunes were still in use although the texts were new and the subjects not as violent as they had been fifty years before. Typical of Cariso themes were those of the "King" of Morning Rose Band (L'hospice) who called himself the Duke of Kandahar (Candy Barricks) and sang about destroying the Boers of Kandahar, Pretoria, and how his band beat the enemy at Transvaal. The conflict was still there: the satire was still present, but it was turned on other things. It may be said that the conflict and the aggression were socialized.

During the last twenty years, the conflict we have been examining has taken a new turn, and the emergence of the "Steel Band" seems to be a most significant factor for our hypothesis that *"the old hatreds and blocked hostility have been alive in the land (of Trinidad) awaiting suitable conditions for their resurrection as a social problem."* Since the cessation of World War I, the island of Trinidad has been rapidly industrialised. The contrast between rich and poor has become very evident. The rapid increase of urban populations has intensified the housing problems: in fact the old slums have been cleared only to give rise, on the fringes of the urban districts, to Shanty Towns and concentrations of the poor, the depressed, and the frustrated. The age-group of 16-19 contains the most people in the island.

It was on these conditions that World War II descended, with the invasion of Trinidad in 1939 by the American service-man, his wealth, his power and his emphasis on success. The immediate result of this was the emergence of the "Sagga Boys"—a group of youths comparable with the Teddy Boys of England. Not only were they delinquent but they traded in vice. But far greater than all this was their hatred of the richer folk— anyone who was thought to belong to the monied class. They wore gaudy clothes, wore their hair long, wore jewels usually associated with females, and lived off the earnings of the prostitutes who carried on trade with the hundreds of American soldiers stationed in the military bases established at Carlsen Field, Chaguaramus, Waller Field, and Charlotteville. This group, in its organization and activities, resembled in many ways the old *tie-pins* and *batoniers* that arose in the 1840-1900 era, when members of the decent society in Trinidad, most of them White folk ("l'homme cami- sole"), entered the Jamette-Yards and supported the colored "Jamettes" and their male kalinda fighters who were retained for defense purposes in an age when the law was less harsh against soliciting.

It is from the ranks of the Sagga Boys, with their gaudy dress and their long, sharp stilettos and razors, that a new type of music arose. In the early days, mainly in 1938, young men had begun to sit on the dry em- bankment of the city of Port of Spain, idling. Those were the days of depression and low wages. This group could be seen experimenting with discarded motor-car parts, beating out what was mere rhythmic noise, under the tutelage of retired kalinda-men. In time, different lengths of iron were found to produce different pitches. Soon the group which met on that site came to be known as "Hell Yard Boys;" they called their orchestra "Iron Band." It took the duration of the war for the experiments to come to a head. (The names of the members of this "Hell Yard Band" remind us of the old Cannes Brule Bands. Among those I have collected are Hard Head, Scaly, Bonacky, Shool, Sweet Man, Wajank cock-eyed Bellonie, Short Blacks, Loolie, Sagiator, Manjo, Big Man, Geronymo.) By 1942, the young men were playing nursery rhymes and bass accompaniments to the calypso road marches of the Carnival. But since steel-scrap was valuable for the war it had become illegal to use old motor-car parts and the Hell Yard boys switched to dust-bins, lighter to carry "on the march" and of course, easily borrowed from anyone's yard. But when the Police instituted a campaign against dust-bin stealing, the percussionists turned to biscuit drums—so common in the War when other food was scarce. But even bis- cuit drums can be expensive for youths out of work and it seemed that the movement was doomed. At any rate by 1942, an oil company which started operations in Trinidad began to use steel drums in which to export crude oil and asphalt. This was a turning point for the movement. The "pan- men" began to use steel drums and "pan-music" was born.

It is not known who first beat out a tune on a *"pan"* as the instrument came to be known. There is much guess work about these questions, no one knows who first tuned a pan. No one can be pointed out as the one who introduced it as the marching orchestra for a Carnival Band. But without any reduction of its pace the Steel Band moved into the Carnival of Trini- dad, as the music to which hundreds of every social class "jump up" on the two frenzied days of Mardi Gras and Lundi Gras. The Steel Band filled a social role in the war years when, with money scarce, it was impossible for people to employ orchestras. Not only in the dance halls but in the social gatherings for christenings, birthday parties, and for marriages, the Steel Band became a necessity. By 1951 a Steel Band Association was formed on government initiative.

But the old characteristics of the Negre Jardin Cannes Brule are present as ever. The people among whom the Steel Band Movement arose were deviants in Trinidad society, the slum folk, the social isolates, the modern-day "Jamettes" (diamettes). And so the conflict between the elite and the low class has reared its head again in this most remarkable form. For the last decade the wounding of middle class people who have clashed with steel band men for one reason or another has assumed frightening proportions. Steel Bandsmen are usually armed to the teeth. Their hatred and suspicion of the upper class is so great that reprisals are usually waged against a whole upper class street in order to avenge the interference of one number of that district. The fantastic names: "Tokyo," "Casablanca," "All Stars," "Cross Fire," "Dixie Stars," and "Sun Valley," are reminiscent of the Cannes Brule bands, and reflect the preoccupation with militarism and power. The names of many of the notorious members of steel bands are interesting: Brains, Zigili, Scribo, Sunny Tail, Copper Head.

The inter-group rivalry and the deep seated aggression that exist between steel bands put the contests between the old Kalinda Bands in the shade. And yet there is a fascination in the steel band music for the upper class. In Trinidad today, the upper class has invaded this Movement. Convents have their steel band, and members of the White group and of the upper class not only employ steel bands to provide music for private parties but their children have formed steel bands for their own use and miniature pans called "mini-pans" are given to children as toys at Christmas. In 1952, during the Festival of Britain, TASPO went to England and played music on pans for celebrations.

But the old patterns are there. Inter-group street fights. Hatred for the upper class who once criticised them. Armed music makers. That is the pattern today. This strange phenomenon—this triple headed social problem in which the colored people struggle for spiritual security in a community shot through with conflicting forces in melodrama acted out against the maddening frenzied music of the steel band as back-ground just as the Old Cannes Brule Kalinda fighters struggled for acceptance and approval in the land where just a hundred years ago they had been slaves and chattels. It is as though the beating of the pans gave release to those who would punish men who offend and stand in the way of progress towards social security and emotional adjustment in the community.

C. L. R. James
FROM
TOUSSAINT L'OUVERTURE
TO FIDEL CASTRO

Toussaint L'Ouverture is not here linked to Fidel Castro because both led revolutions in the West Indies. Nor is the link a convenient or journalistic demarcation of historical time. What took place in French San Domingo in 1792-1804 reappeared in Cuba in 1958. The slave revolution of French San Domingo managed to emerge from

> . . . The pass and fell incensed points
> Of mighty opposites.

Five years later the people of Cuba are still struggling in the same toils.

Castro's revolution is of the twentieth century as much as Toussaint's was of the eighteenth. But despite the distance of over a century and a half, both are West Indian. The people who made them, the problems and the attempts to solve them, are peculiarly West Indian, the product of a peculiar origin and a peculiar history. West Indians first became aware of themselves as a people in the Haitian Revolution. Whatever its ultimate fate, the Cuban Revolution marks the ultimate stage of a Caribbean quest for national identity. In a scattered series of disparate islands the process consists of a series of unco-ordinated periods of drift, punctuated by spurts, leaps and catastrophes. But the inherent movement is clear and strong.

The history of the West Indies is governed by two factors, the sugar plantation and Negro slavery. That the majority of the population in Cuba was never slave does not affect the underlying social identity. Wherever the sugar plantation and slavery existed, they imposed a pattern. It is an original pattern, not European, not African, not a part of the American main, not native in any conceivable sense of that word, but West Indian, *sui generis,* with no parallel anywhere else.

The sugar plantation has been the most civilising as well as the most demoralising influence in West Indian development. When three centuries ago the slaves came to the West Indies, they entered directly into the large-scale agriculture of the sugar plantation, which was a modern system. It further required that the slaves live together in a social relation far closer than any proletariat of the time. The cane when reaped had to be rapidly transported to what was factory production. The product was shipped abroad for sale. Even the cloth the slaves wore and the food they

REPRINTED FROM *Black Jacobins* (NEW YORK: RANDOM HOUSE, 1963), PP. 391–418, BY PERMISSION OF THE PUBLISHER AND THE AUTHOR. COPYRIGHT © 1963 BY C. R. JAMES.

ate was imported. The Negroes, therefore, from the very start lived a life that was in its essence a modern life. That is their history—as far as I have been able to discover, a unique history.

In the first part of the seventeenth century, early settlers from Europe had made quite a success of individual production. The sugar plantation drove them out. The slaves saw around them a social life of a certain material culture and ease, the life of the sugar-plantation owners. The clever, the lucky and the illegitimate became domestics or artisans attached to the plantation or the factory. Long before the bus and the taxi, the small size of the islands made communication between the rural areas and the urban quick and easy. The plantation owners and the merchants lived an intense political life in which the ups and downs of sugar and in time the treatment and destiny of the slaves played a crucial and continuous role. The sugar plantation dominated the lives of the islands to such a degree that the white skin alone saved those who were not plantation owners or bureaucrats from the humiliations and hopelessness of the life of the slave. That was and is the pattern of West Indian life.

The West Indies between Toussaint L'Ouverture and Fidel Castro falls naturally into three periods: I. The Nineteenth Century; II. Between the Wars; III. After World War II.

I. THE NINETEENTH CENTURY

The nineteenth century in the Caribbean is the century of the abolition of slavery. But the passing of the years shows that the decisive patterns of Caribbean development took form in Haiti.

Toussaint could see no road for the Haitian economy but the sugar plantation. Dessalines was a barbarian. After Dessalines came Christophe, a man of conspicuous ability and within his circumstances an enlightened ruler. He also did his best (a cruel best) with the plantation. But with the abolition of slavery and the achievement of independence the plantation, indelibly associated with slavery, became unbearable. Pétion acquiesced in substituting subsistence production for the sugar plantation.

For the first century and a half of Haiti's existence there was no international opinion jealous of the independence of small nations; no body of similar states, ready to raise a hue and cry at any threat to one of their number; no theory of aid from the wealthy countries to the poorer ones. Subsistence production resulted in economic decay and every variety of political disorder. Yet it has preserved the national independence, and out of this has come something new which has captured a continent and holds its place in the institutions of the world.

This is what has happened. For over a century after independence the Haitians attempted to form a replica of European, i.e., French civilisation in the West Indies. Listen to the Haitian Ambassador, M. Constantin Mayard, in Paris in 1938:

French our institutions, French our public and civil legislation, French our literature, French our university, French the curriculum of our schools . . .

Today when one of us [a Haitian] appears in a circle of Frenchmen, "welcome smiles at him in every eye." The reason is without doubt that your nation, ladies and gentlemen, knows that within the scope of its colonial expansion it has given to the Antilles and above all to San Domingo all that it could give of itself and its substance . . . It has founded there, in the mould of its own national type, with its blood, with its language, its institutions, its spirit and its soil, a local type, an historic race, in which its sap still runs and where it is remade complete.

Generation after generation the best sons of the Haitian élite were educated in Paris. They won distinctions in the intellectual life of France. The burning race hatred of pre-independence days had vanished. But a line of investigators and travellers had held up to international ridicule the hollow pretensions of Haitian civilisation. In 1913 the ceaseless battering from foreign pens was reenforced by the bayonets of American Marines. Haiti had to find a national rallying-point. They looked for it where it can only be found, at home, more precisely, in their own backyard. They discovered what is known today as Negritude. It is the prevailing social ideology among politicians and intellectuals in every part of Africa. It is the subject of heated elaboration and disputation wherever Africa and Africans are discussed. But in its origin and development it is West Indian, and could not have been anything else but West Indian, the peculiar product of their peculiar history.

The Haitians did not know it as Negritude. To them it seemed purely Haitian. Two-thirds of the population of French San Domingo in Toussaint's time had made the Middle Passage. The whites had emigrated or been exterminated. The Mulattoes who were masters had their eyes fixed on Paris. Left to themselves, the Haitian peasantry resuscitated to a remarkable degree the lives they had lived in Africa. Their method of cultivation, their family relations and social practices, their drums, songs and music, such art as they practised and above all their religion which became famous, Vodun—all this was Africa in the West Indies. But it was Haitian, and the Haitian élite leapt at it. In 1926 Dr. Price Mars in his famous book, *Ainsi Parla L'Oncle* (This is What Uncle Said), described with loving care the way of life of the Haitian peasant. Rapidly, learned and scientific societies were formed. The African way of life of the Haitian peasant became the axis of Haitian literary creation. No plantation labourer, with free land to defend, rallied to the cause.

The Caribbean territories drifted along. At the end of the nineteenth century, Cuba produced a great revolution which bears the name "The Ten Years' War." It produced prodigies—no West Indian pantheon but will have among its most resplendent stars the names of José Martí the political leader and Maceo the soldier. They were men in the full tradition of Jefferson, Washington and Bolívar. That was their strength and that was their weakness. They were leaders of a national revolutionary party and a national revolutionary army. Toussaint L'Ouverture and Fidel Castro led a revolutionary people. The war for independence began again and ended in the Platt Amendment of 1904.

It was just one year after the Platt Amendment that there first appeared what has turned out to be a particular feature of West Indian life—the non-political writer devoted to the analysis and expression of West Indian society. The first was the greatest of them all, Fernando Ortiz. For over half a century, at home or in exile, he has been the tireless exponent of Cuban life and *Cubanidad,* the spirit of Cuba. The history of Spanish imperialism, sociology, anthropology, ethnology, all the related sciences are his medium of investigation into Cuban life, folklore, literature, music, art, education, criminality, everything Cuban. A most distinctive feature of his work is the number of solid volumes he has devoted to Negro and Mulatto life in Cuba. A quarter of a century before the Writers' Project of the New Deal began the discovery of the United States, Ortiz set out to discover his native land, a West Indian island. In essence it is the first and only comprehensive study of the West Indian people. Ortiz ushered the Caribbean into the thought of the twentieth century and kept it there.

II. BETWEEN THE WARS

Before World War I Haiti began to write another chapter in the record of the West Indian struggle for national independence. Claiming the need to recover debts and restore order, the Marines, as we have seen, invaded Haiti in 1913. The whole nation resisted. A general strike was organized and led by the literary intellectuals who had discovered the Africanism of their peasants as a means of national identity. The Marines left, and Negroes and Mulattoes resumed their fratricidal conflicts. But Haiti's image of itself had changed. "Goodbye to the Marseillaise," a famous phrase by one of the best-known of Haitian writers, signifies the substitution of Africa for France in the first independent West Indian state. Africa in the West Indies would seem to have been evoked by an empirical need and accidental circumstance. It was not so. Long before the Marines left Haiti, the role of Africa in the consciousness of the West Indies people had proved itself to be a stage in the development of the West Indian quest for a national identity.

The story is one of the strangest stories in any period of history. The individual facts are known. But no one has ever put them together and drawn to them the attention they deserve. Today the emancipation of Africa is one of the outstanding events of contemporary history. Between the wars when this emancipation was being prepared, the unquestioned leaders of the movement in every public sphere, in Africa itself, in Europe and in the United States, were not Africans but West Indians. First the unquestioned facts.

Two black West Indians using the ink of Negritude wrote their names imperishably on the front pages of the history of our time. Standing at the head is Marcus Garvey. Garvey, an immigrant from Jamaica, is the only Negro who has succeeded in building a mass movement among American Negroes. Arguments about the number of his followers dispute the number of millions. Garvey advocated the return of Africa to the Africans and people of African descent. He organised, very rashly and incompetently, the Black Star Line, a steamship company for transporting people of African descent from the New World back to Africa. Garvey did not last long. His movement took really effective form in about 1921, and by 1926 he was in a United States prison (some charge about misusing the mails); from prison he was deported home to Jamaica. But all this is only the frame and scaffolding. Garvey never set foot in Africa. He spoke no African language. His conceptions of Africa seemed to be a West Indian island and West Indian people multiplied a thousand times over. But Garvey managed to convey to Negroes everywhere (and to the rest of the world) his passionate belief that Africa was the home of a civilisation which had once been great and would be great again. When you bear in mind the slenderness of his resources, the vast material forces and the pervading social conceptions which automatically sought to destroy him, his achievement remains one of the propagandistic miracles of this century.

Garvey's voice reverberated inside Africa itself. The King of Swaziland told Mrs. Marcus Garvey that he knew the name of only two black men in the Western world: Jack Johnson, the boxer who defeated the white man Jim Jeffries, and Marcus Garvey. Jomo Kenyatta has related to this writer how in 1921 Kenya nationalists, unable to read, would gather round a reader of Garvey's newspaper, the *Negro World,* and listen to an article two or three times. Then they would run various ways through the forest, carefully to repeat the whole, which they had memorised, to Africans hungry for some doctrine which lifted them from the servile consciousness in which Africans lived. Dr. Nkrumah, a graduate student of history and philosophy at two American universities, has placed it on record that of all the writers who educated and influenced him, Marcus Garvey stands first. Garvey found the cause of Africans and of people of African descent not so much neglected as unworthy of consideration. In little more than half of ten years he had made it a part of the political consciousness of the world. He did not know the word Negritude but he knew the thing. With enthusiasm he would have welcomed the nomenclature, with justice claimed paternity.

The other British West Indian was from Trinidad, George Padmore. Padmore shook the dust of the cramping West Indies from his feet in the early 1920's and went to the United States. When he died in 1959, eight countries sent representatives to his funeral, which was held in London. His ashes were interred in Ghana; and all assert that in that country of political demonstrations, there never has been a political demonstration such as was evoked by these obsequies of Padmore. Peasants from remote areas who, it could have been thought, had never heard his name, found their way to Accra to pay the last tribute to this West Indian who had spent his life in their service.

Once in America he became an active Communist. He was moved to Moscow to head their Negro department of propaganda and organisation. In that post he became the best known and most trusted of agitators for African independence. In 1935, seeking alliances, the Kremlin separated Britain and France as "democratic imperialisms" from Germany and Japan, making the "Fascist imperialisms" the main target of Russian and Communist propaganda. This reduced activity for African emancipation to a farce: Germany and Japan had no colonies in Africa. Padmore broke instantly with the Kremlin. He went to London where, in a single room, he earned a meagre living by journalism, to be able to continue the work he had done in the Kremlin. He wrote books and pamphlets, attended all anti-imperialist meetings and spoke and moved resolutions wherever possible. He made and maintained an ever-increasing range of nationalist contacts in all sections of African society and the colonial world. He preached and taught Pan-Africanism and organised an African Bureau. He published a journal devoted to African emancipation (the present writer was its editor).

This is no place to attempt even a summary of the work and influence of the most striking West Indian creation between the wars, Padmore's African Bureau. Between the wars it was the only African organisation of its kind in existence. Of the seven members of the committee, five were West Indians, and they ran the organisation. Of them, only Padmore had ever visited Africa. It could not have been accidental that this West Indian attracted two of the most remarkable Africans of this or any other time. A founder-member and a simmering volcano of African nationalism was Jomo Kenyatta. But even better fortune was in store for us.

The present writer met Nkrumah, then a student at the University of Pennsylvania, and wrote to Padmore about him. Nkrumah came to England to study law and there formed an association with Padmore; they worked at the doctrines and premises of Pan-Africanism and elaborated the plans which culminated in Nkrumah's leading the people of the Gold Coast to the independence of Ghana. This revolution by the Gold Coast was the blow which made so many cracks in the piece of African colonialism that it proved impossible ever to stick them together again. With Nkrumah's victory the association did not cease. After independence was signed and sealed, Nkrumah sent for Padmore, installed him once more in an office devoted to African emancipation and, under the auspices of an African government, this West Indian, as he had done in 1931 under the auspices of the Kremlin, organised in Accra the first conference of independent African states, followed, twenty-five years after the first, by the second world conference of fighters for African freedom. Dr. Banda, Patrice Lumumba, Nyerere, Tom Mboya, were some of those who attended the conference. Jomo Kenyatta was not there only because he was in jail. NBC made a national telecast of the interment of his ashes in Christiansborg Castle, at which Padmore was designated the Father of African Emancipation, a distinction challenged by no one. To the degree that they had to deal with us in the period between the wars, many learned and important persons and institutions looked upon us and our plans and hopes for Africa as the fantasies of some politically illiterate West Indians. It was they who completely misconceived a continent, not we. They should have learned from that experience. They have not. The same myopic vision which failed to focus Africa is now peering at the West Indies.

The place of Africa in the West Indian development is documented as few historical visions are documented.

In 1939 a black West Indian from the French colony of Martinique published in Paris the finest and most famous poem ever written about Africa, *Cahier d'un retour au pays natal* (Statement of a Return to the Country Where I was Born). Aimé Césaire first describes Martinique, the poverty, misery and vices of the masses of the people, the lickspittle subservience of the coloured middle classes. But the poet's education has been consummated in Paris. As a West Indian he has nothing national to be aware of. He is overwhelmed by the gulf that separates him from the people where he was born. He feels that he must go there. He does so and discovers a new version of what the Haitians, as had Garvey and Padmore, had discovered: that salvation for the West Indies lies in Africa, the original home and ancestry of the West Indian people.

The poet gives us a view of Africans as he sees them.

> . . . my Negritude is not a stone, its
>   deafness a sounding board for
>   the noises of the day
> my Negritude is not a mere spot of
>   dead water on the dead eye of
>   the earth
> my Negritude is no tower, no cathedral
>
> it cleaves into the red flesh of the
>   teeming earth
> it cleaves into the glowing flesh of
>   the heavens
> it penetrates the seamless bondage of
>   my unbending patience
>
> Hoorah for those who never invented
>   anything
> for those who never explored anything
> for those who never mastered anything
>
> but who, possessed, give themselves up
>   to the essence of each thing
> ignorant of the coverings but possessed
>   by the pulse of things
> indifferent to mastering but taking the
>   chances of the world . . .

In contrast to this vision of the African unseparated from the world, from Nature, a living part of all that lives, Césaire immediately places the civilisation that has scorned and persecuted Africa and Africans.

> Listen to the white world
> its horrible exhaustion from its
>   immense labours
> its rebellious joints cracking under
>   the pitiless stars
> its blue steel rigidities, cutting
>   through the mysteries of the
>   flesh
> listen to their vainglorious conquests
>   trumpeting their defeats
> listen to the grandiose alibis of their
>   pitiful floundering

The poet wants to be an architect of this unique civilisation, a commissioner of its blood, a guardian of its refusal to accept.

> But in so doing, my heart, preserve
>   me from all hate
> do not turn me into a man of hate of
>   whom I think only with hate
> for in order to project myself into
>   this unique race
> you know the extent of my boundless
>   love
> you know that it is not from hatred
>   of other races
> that I seek to be cultivator of this
>   unique race . . .

He returns once more to the pitiful spectre of West Indian life, but now with hope.

> for it is not true that the work of man
>   is finished
> that man has nothing more to do in the
>   world but be a parasite in the world
> that all we now need is to keep in step
>   with the world
> but the work of man is only just beginning
>   and it remains to man to conquer all
>   the violence entrenched in the recesses
>   of his passion
> and no race possesses the monopoly of beauty,
>   of intelligence, of force, and there
>   is a place for all at the rendezvous
>   of victory . . .

Here is the centre of Césaire's poem. By neglecting it, Africans and the sympathetic of other races utter loud hurrahs that drown out common sense and reason. The work of man is not finished. Therefore the future of the African is not to continue not discovering anything. The monopoly of beauty, of intelligence, of force, is possessed by no race, certainly not by those who possess Negritude. Negritude is what one race brings to the common rendezvous where all will strive for the new world of the poet's vision. The vision of the poet is not economics or politics, it is poetic, *sui generis,* true unto itself and needing no other truth. But it would be the most vulgar racism not to see here a poetic incarnation of Marx's famous sentence, "The real history of humanity will begin."

From Césaire's strictly poetic affinities* we have to turn our faces if even with distinct loss to our larger general purpose. But *Cahier* has united elements in modern thought which seemed destined to remain asunder. These has better be enumerated.

1. He has made a union of the African sphere of existence with existence in the Western world.

2. The past of mankind and the future of mankind are historically and logically linked.

3. No longer from external stimulus but from their own self-generated and independent being and motion will Africa and Africans move towards an integrated humanity.

It is the Anglo-Saxon poet who has seen for the world in general what the West Indian has seen concretely for Africa.

> Here the impossible union
> Of spheres of existence is actual,
> Here the past and future
> Are conquered, and reconciled,
> Where action were otherwise movement
> Of that which is only moved
> And has in its no source of movement—

Mr. Eliot's conclusion is "Incarnation"; Césaire's, Negritude.

Cahier appeared in 1938 in Paris. A year before that *The Black Jacobins* had appeared in London. The writer had made the forward step of resurrecting not the decadence but the grandeur of the West Indian people. But as is obvious all through the book and particularly in the last pages, it is Africa and African emancipation that he has in mind.

Today (but only today) we can define what motivated this West Indian preoccupation with Africa between the wars. The West Indians were and had always been Western-educated. West Indian society confined black men to a very narrow strip of social territory. The first step to

---

* Baudelaire and Rimbaud, Rilke and D. H. Lawrence. Jean-Paul Sartre has done the finest of critical appreciations of *Cahier* as poetry, but his explanation of what he conceives Negritude to mean is a disaster.

freedom was to go abroad. *Before they could begin to see themselves as a free and independent people they had to clear from minds the stigma that anything African was inherently inferior and degraded.* The road to West Indian national identity lay through Africa.

The West Indian national community constantly evades racial categorisation. After Ortiz, it was another white West Indian who in the same period proved himself to be the greatest politician in the democratic tradition whom the West Indies has ever known.

Arthur Andrew Cipriani was a French Creole in the island of Trinidad who came into public life as an officer in a West Indian contingent in World War I. It was in the army that many of the soldiers, a medley from all the British West Indian islands, for the first time wore shoes consistently. But they were the product of their peculiar history. The speed with which they adjusted themselves to the spiritual and material requirements of a modern war amazed all observers, from General Allenby down. Cipriani made a reputation for himself by his militant defence of the regiment against all prejudice, official and unofficial. To the end of his days he spoke constantly of the recognition they had won. By profession a trainer of horses, it was only after much persuasion that, on his return home after the war, already a man over forty, he entered politics. He at once put himself forward as the champion of the common people, in his own phrase, "the barefooted man." Before very long this white man was acknowledged as leader by hundreds of thousands of black people and East Indians. An utterly fearless man, he never left the colonial government in any doubt as to what it was up against. All who ever heard him speak remember his raising of his right hand and his slow enunciation of the phrase, "If I raise my little finger . . ." Against tremendous odds he forced the government to capitulate on workmen's compensation, the eight-hour day, trade union legislation and other elementary constituents of democracy. Year after year he was elected mayor of the capital city. He made the mayoralty a centre of opposition to the British Colonial Office and all its works.

Cipriani always treated West Indians as a modern contemporary people. He declared himself to be a socialist and day in and day out, inside and outside of the legislature, he attacked capitalists and capitalism. He attached his party to the British Labour Party and scrupulously kept his followers aware of their privileges and responsibilities as members of the international labour movement. Cipriani was that rare type of politician to whom words expressed realities. Long before any of the other territories of the colonial empires, he not only raised the slogans of national independence and federation of the British West Indian territories, he went tirelessly from island to island mobilising public opinion in general and the labour movement in particular in support of these slogans. He died in 1945. The islands had never seen before and have not seen since anything or anybody like him.

The West Indian masses jumped ahead even of Cipriani. In 1937, among the oil field workers in Trinidad, the largest proletarian grouping in the West Indies, a strike began. Like a fire along a tinder track, it spread to the entire island, then from island to island, ending in an upheaval at the other end of the curve, in Jamaica, thousands of miles away. The colonial government in Jamaica collapsed completely and two local popular leaders had to take over the responsibility of restoring some sort of social order. The heads of the government in Trinidad and Tobago saved their administrations (but earned the wrath of the imperial government) by expressing sympathy with the revolt. The British Government sent a Royal Commission, which took much evidence, discovered long-standing evils, and made proposals by no means unintelligent or reactionary. As usual they were late, they were slow. Had Cipriani been the man he was ten years earlier, self-government, federation and economic regeneration, which he had advocated so strenuously and so long, could have been initiated then. But the old warrior was nearly seventy. He flinched at the mass upheavals which he more than anyone else had prepared, and the opportunity was lost. But he had destroyed a legend and established once and for all that the West Indian people were ready to follow the most advanced theories of an uncompromising leadership.

III. AFTER WORLD WAR II

Cipriani had built soundly and he left behind a Caribbean Labour Congress devoted to federation, independence and the creation of an enlightened peasantry. But what has happened to Castro's Cuba is inherent in these unfortunate islands. In 1945 the Congress, genuinely West Indian, joined the World Federation of Trade Unions. But in 1948 that body split into the World Federation of Trade Unions of the East and the International Confederation of Free Trade Unions of the West. The split in the international split the Caribbean Labour Congress and it lost its place as the leader and inspirer of a genuinely West Indian movement. The British Colonial Office took the coloured middle class under its wing. These gradually filled the Civil Service and related organisations; they took over the political parties, and with the parties, the old colonial system.

What is this old colonial system? It is the oldest Western relic of the seventeenth century still alive in the world today, surrounded on all sides by a modern population.

The West Indies has never been a traditional colonial territory with clearly distinguished economic and political relations between two different cultures. Native culture there was none. The aboriginal Amerindian civilisation had been destroyed. Every succeeding year, therefore, saw the labouring population, slave or free, incorporating into itself more and more of the language, customs, aims and outlook of its masters. It steadily grew in numbers until it became a terrifying majority of the total population. The ruling minority therefore was in the position of the father who produced children and had to guard against being supplanted by them.

There was only one way out, to seek strength abroad. This beginning has lasted unchanged to this very day.

The dominant industrial structure has been the sugar plantation. For over two hundred years the sugar industry has tottered on the brink of disaster, remaining alive by an unending succession of last-minute rescues by gifts, concessions, quotas from the metropolitan power or powers.

SUGAR MANUFACTURERS' "GRIM FUTURE"
From our Correspondent

Georgetown, Sept. 3

The British West Indies Sugar Association's chairman, Sir Robert Kirkwood, has stated here that cane sugar manufacturers were facing a grim future and the position was reaching a stage where beet sugar production should be restricted to provide cane manufacturers with an enlarged market. Sir Robert pointed out that Britain's participation in the European Common Market should be no threat to sugar manufacturers in the region provided preferences under the Commonwealth sugar agreement were preserved.

You would be able to read the same in any European newspaper at regular intervals during the last two hundred years. Recent official reports on the life and labour of the plantation labourer are moved to language remarkably similar to that of the non-conformist agitators against plantation slavery. There are economists and scientists today in the West Indies who believe that the most fortunate economic occurrence would be a blight that would destroy the sugar cane completely and thus compel some new type of economic development.*

As they have been from the first days of slavery, financial power and its mechanism are today entirely in the hands of metropolitan organisations and their agents.

Such a Westernized population needs quantities of pots, pans, plates, spoons, knives, forks, paper, pencils, pens, cloth, bicycles, buses for public transport, automobiles, all the elementary appurtenances of civilisation which the islands do not manufacture, not forgetting Mercedes-Benzes, Bentleys, Jaguars and Lincolns. In this type of commerce the dominating elements are the foreign manufacturers and the foreign banks. The most revealing feature of this trade and the oldest is the still massive importation of food, including fresh vegetables.

The few industries of importance, such as oil and bauxite, are completely in the hands of foreign firms, and the local politicians run a ferocious competition with each other in offering inducements to similar firms to establish new industries here and not there.

As with material, so with intellectual necessities. In island after island the daily newspaper is entirely in the hands of foreign firms. Radio and television cannot evade the fate of newspapers.

---

* None will dare to say so publicly. He or she would be driven out of the territory.

In 1963 the old colonial system is not what it was in 1863; in 1863 it was not what it had been in 1763 or 1663. The fundamentals outlined above, however, have not changed. But for the first time the system is now threatened, not from without but from within, not by communism, not by socialism, but by plain, simple parliamentary democracy. The old colonial system in the West Indies was not a democratic system, was not born as such. It cannot live with democracy. Within a West Indian island the old colonial system and democracy are incompatible. One has to go. That is the logic of development of every West Indian territory, Cuba, the Dominican Republic, Haiti, the former British colonies, the former French colonies, and even Puerto Rico, the poor relation of the wealthy United States.

The supreme wrong of West Indian politics is that the old colonial system has so isolated the ruling classes from the national community that plain, ordinary parliamentary democracy, *suffused with a sense of national identity,* can remake the islands.

Statistics of production and the calculations of votes together form the surest road towards misunderstanding the West Indies. To which for good measure add the antagonism of races. The people of the West Indies were born in the seventeenth century, in a Westernized productive and social system. Members of different African tribes were carefully split up to lessen conspiracy, and they were therefore compelled to master the European languages, highly complex products of centuries of civilisation. From the start there had been the gap, constantly growing, between the rudimentary conditions of the life of the slave and the language he used. There was therefore in West Indian society an inherent antagonism between the consciousness of the black masses and the reality of their lives, inherent in that it was constantly produced and reproduced not by agitators but by the very conditions of the society itself. It is the modern media of mass communication which have made essence into existence. For an insignificant sum per month, the black masses can hear on the radio news of Dr. Nkrumah, Jomo Kenyatta, Dr. Julius Banda, Prime Minister Nehru, events and personalities of the United Nations and all the capitals of the world. They can wrestle with what the West thinks of the East and what the East thinks of the West. The cinema presents actualities and not infrequently stirs the imagination with the cinematic masterpieces of the world. Every hour on the hour all variations of food, clothing, household necessities and luxuries are presented as absolutely essential to a civilised existence. All this to a population which over large areas still lives in conditions little removed from slavery.

The high material civilisation of the white minority is now fortified by the concentration of the coloured middle classes on making salaries and fees do the work of incomes. Sometimes a quarter of the population is crowded into the capital city, the masses irresistibly attracted by the contrast between what they see and hear and the lives they live. This was the tinder to which Castro placed a match. Historical tradition, education in the sense of grappling with the national past, there is none. History as taught is what it always has been, propaganda for those, whoever they may be, who administer the old colonial system. Power here is more naked than in any other part of the world. Hence the brutality, savagery, even personal cruelties of the régimes of Trujillo and Duvalier, and the power of the Cuban Revolution.

This is the instrument on which perform all West Indian soloists, foreign or native. Take the French West Indian islands of Martinique and Guadeloupe. The colonial administration declared and acted for Vichy, the mass of the population for the Resistance. Vichy defeated, the islands whole-heartedly became departments of France, anxious to be assimilated into French civilisation. But the hand of the Paris administration, notoriously heavy in the provincial administrations of France itself, is a crushing weight on any attempt to change the old colonial system. To-day the mass of the population, disillusioned, is demanding independence. Their students in Paris are leading the struggle with blood, with boldness and with brilliance available to all who use the French language.

The British system, unlike the French, does not crush the quest for a national identity. Instead, it stifles it. It formed a federation of its Caribbean colonies. But the old colonial system consisted of insular economies, each with its financial and economic capital in London. A federation meant that the economic line of direction should no longer be from island to London, but from island to island. But that involved the break-up of the old colonial system. The West Indian politicians preferred the break-up of the Federation. Two of the islands have actually been granted independence. The Queen of England is their queen. They receive royal visits; their legislatures begin with prayers; their legislative bills are read three times; a mace has been presented to each of these distant infants by the Mother of Parliaments; their prominent citizens can receive an assortment of letters after their names, and in time the prefix "Sir." This no longer lessens but intensifies the battle between the old colonial system and democracy. Long before the actual independence was granted, large numbers of the middle classes, including their politicians, wanted it put off as far into the distance as possible. For the cruiser in the offing and the prospect of financial gifts and loans, they turn longing eyes and itching feet towards the United States.

The Caribbean is now an American sea. Puerto Rico is its show piece. Puerto Rican society has the near-celestial privilege of free entry into the United States for their unemployed and their ambitious. The United States returns to the Puerto Rican Government all duty collected on such staple imports as rum and cigars. American money for investment and American loans and gifts should create the Caribbean paradise. But if the United States had the Puerto Rican density of population, it would contain all the people in the world. Puerto Rico is just another West Indian island.

In the Dominican Republic there is no need to go beyond saying that Trujillo had gained power by the help of the United States Marines and all through the more than quarter-century of his infamous dictatorship he was understood to enjoy the friendship of Washington. Before the recent election of his successor, Sr. Juan Bosch, the French newspapers stated as an item of news that members of the left in the Dominican Republic (names were given) were deported to Paris by the local police, who were assisted in this operation by members of the FBI. Trujillo gone, Duvalier of Haiti is the uncrowned king of Latin American barbarism. It is widely believed that despite the corruption and impertinence of his régime, it is American support which keeps him in power: better Duvalier than another Castro.

Such a mass of ignorance and falsehood has surrounded these islands for so many centuries that obvious truths sound like revelations. Contrary to the general belief, the Caribbean territories taken as a whole are not sunk in irremediable poverty. When he was Principal of the University of the West Indies in Jamaica, Professor Arthur Lewis, former head of the faculty of economics at Manchester University and at the time of writing due to head the same faculty at Princeton, tried to remove some cobwebs from the eyes of his fellow West Indians:

> This opinion that the West Indies can raise all the capital it needs from its own resources is bound to shock many people, because West Indians like to feel that ours is a poor community. But the fact of the matter is that at least half of the people in the world are poorer than we are. The standard of living in the West Indies is higher than the standard of living in India, or China, in most of the countries of Asia, and in most of the countries of Africa. The West Indies is not a poor community; it is in the upper bracket of world income. It is capable of producing the extra 5 or 6 per cent of resources which is required for this job, just as Ceylon and Ghana are finding the money they need for development by taxing themselves. It is not necessary for us to send our statesmen around the world begging for help. If help is given to us let us accept it, but let us not sit down and say nothing can be done until the rest of the world out of its goodness of heart is willing to grant us charity.*

The economic road they have to travel is a broad highway on which the sign posts have long been erected. Sr. Juan Bosch began his campaign by promising to distribute the land confiscated from the baronial plunder of the Trujillo family. His supporters rapidly transformed this into: "A house and land for every Dominican." Not only popular demand and modern economists, but British Royal Commissions during the last sixty years, have indicated (cautiously but clearly enough) that the way out of the West Indian morass is the abolition of the plantation labourer and the substitution, instead, of individual landowning peasants. Scientists and economists have indicated that an effective industry is possible, based on the scientific and planned use of raw material produced on the islands. I

---

* Study Conference of Economic Development in Underdeveloped Countries, August 5–15, 1957, University of the West Indies, Jamaica.

have written in vain if I have not made it clear that of all formerly colonial coloured peoples, the West Indian masses are the most highly experienced in the ways of Western civilisation and most receptive to its requirements in the twentieth century. To realise themselves they will have to break out of the shackles of the old colonial system.

I do not propose to plunge . . . into the turbulent waters of controversy about Cuba. I have written about the West Indies in general and Cuba is the most West Indian island in the West Indies. That suffices.

One more question remains—the most realistic and most pregnant question of all. Toussaint L'Ouverture and the Haitian slaves brought into the world more than the abolition of slavery. When Latin Americans saw that small and insignificant Haiti could win and keep independence they began to think that they ought to be able to do the same. Pétion, the ruler of Haiti, nursed back to health the sick and defeated Bolivar, gave him money, arms and a printing press to help in the campaign which ended in the freedom of the Five States. What will happen to what Fidel Castro has brought new to the world no one can say. But what is waiting in the West Indies to be born, what emerged from the womb in July 1958, is to be seen elsewhere in the West Indies, not so confused with the pass and fell incensed points of mighty opposites. I speak now of a section of the West Indies of which I have had during the past five years intimate and personal experience of the writers and the people. But this time the people first, for if the ideologists have moved closer towards the people, the people have caught up with the ideologists and the national identity is a national fact.

In Trinidad in 1957, before there was any hint of a revolution in Cuba, the ruling political party suddenly declared, contrary to the declaration of policy with which it had won the election, that during the war the British Government of Sir Winston Churchill had given away Trinidad property and it should be returned. What happened is one of the greatest events in the history of the West Indies. The people rose to the call. Mass meetings and mass demonstrations, political passion such as the island had never known, swept through the population. Inside the chains of the old colonial system, the people of the West Indies are a national community. The middle classes looked on with some uncertainty but with a growing approval. The local whites are not like whites in a foreign civilisation. They are West Indians and, under a strong impulse, think of themselves as such. Many of them quietly made known their sympathy with the cause. The political leader was uncompromising in his demand for the return. "I shall break Chaguaramas or it will break me," he declared, and the words sprouted wings. He publicly asserted to mass meetings of many thousands that if the State Department, backed by the Colonial Office, continued to refuse to discuss the return of the base, he would take Trinidad not only out of the West Indian Federation but out of the British association altogether; he would establish the independence of the island, all previous treaties entered into under the colonial régime would automatically become null and void, and thus he would deal with the Americans. He forbade them to use the Trinidad airport for their military planes. In a magnificent address, "From Slavery to Chaguaramas," he said that for centuries the West Indies had been bases, military footballs of warring imperialist powers, and the time had come to finish with it. It is the present writer's opinion (he was for the crucial period editor of the party journal) that it was the response of the population which sent the political leader so far upon a perilous road. They showed simply that they thought the Americans should quit the base and return it to the people. This was all the more remarkable in that the Trinidad people freely admitted that Trinidad had never enjoyed such financial opulence as when the Americans were there during the war. America was undoubtedly the potential source of economic and financial aid. But they were ready for any sacrifices needed for the return of the base. They were indeed ready for anything, and the political leadership had to take great care to do or say nothing which would precipitate any untoward mass intervention.

What was perhaps the most striking feature of this powerful national upheaval was its concentration on the national issues and its disregard for all others. There was not the slightest trace of anti-American feeling; though the British Colonial Office was portrayed as the ally of the State Department and the demand for political independence was well on the way, there was equally no trace of anti-British feeling. There was no inclination towards non-alignment, not even, despite the pressure for independence, anti-imperialism. The masses of the people of Trinidad and Tobago looked upon the return of the base as the first and primary stage in their quest for national identity. That they were prepared to suffer for, if need be (of this I am as certain as one can be of such things) to fight and die for. But in the usual accompaniments of a struggle against a foreign base, they were not in any way concerned. Not that they did now know. They most certainly knew. But they had had a long experience of international relations and they knew precisely what they wanted. Right up the islands, the population responded in the same way to what they felt was a West Indian matter. The press conference of the political leader was the most popular radio programme in the West Indian islands. It was 1937-38 all over again. "Free is how you is from the start, an' when it look different you got to move, just move, an' when you movin' say that is a natural freedom make you move." * Though the British flag still blew above them, in their demands and demonstrations for Chaguaramas they were free, freer than they might be for a long time.

The West Indian national identity is more easily to be glimpsed in the published writings of West Indian authors.

Vic Reid of Jamaica is the only West Indian novelist who lives in the West Indies. That presumably is why he sets his scene in Africa. An

---

* *Season of Adventure,* by George Lamming.

African who knows the West Indies well assures me that there is nothing African about Reid's story. It is the West Indies in African dress. Whatever it is, the novel is a *tour-de-force*. African or West Indian, it reduces the human problems of under-developed countries to a common denominator. The distinctive tone of the new West Indian orchestra is not loud but it is clear. Reid is not unconcerned about the fate of his characters. The political passions are sharp and locked in murderous conflict. But Reid is detached as no European or African writer is or can be detached, as Garvey, Padmore, Césaire were not and could not be detached. The origin of his detachment appears very clearly in the most powerful and far-ranging of the West Indian school, George Lamming of Barbados.

Confining ourselves strictly to our purpose, we shall limit ourselves to citing only one episode from the latest of his four powerful novels.

Powell, a character in *Season of Adventure*, is a murderer, rapist and altogether criminal member of West Indian society. Suddenly, after nine-tenths of the book, the author injects three pages headed "Author's Note." Writing in the first person he accounts for Powell.

> Until the age of ten Powell and I had lived together, equal in the affection of two mothers. Powell had made my dreams; and I had lived his passions. Identical in years, and stage by stage, Powell and I were taught in the same primary school.
>
> And then the division came. I got a public scholarship which started my migration into another world, a world whose roots were the same, but whose style of living was entirely different from what my childhood knew. It had earned me a privilege which now shut Powell and the whole *tonelle* right out of my future. I had lived as near to Powell as my skin to the hand it darkens. And yet! Yet I forgot the *tonelle* as men forget a war, and attached myself to that new world which was so recent and so slight beside the weight of what had gone before. Instinctively I attached myself to that new privilege; and in spite of all my effort, I am not free of its embrace to this day.
>
> I believe deep in my bones that the mad impulse which drove Powell to his criminal defeat was largely my doing. I will not have this explained away by talk about environment; nor can I allow my own moral infirmity to be transferred to a foreign conscience, labelled imperalist. I shall go beyond my grave in the knowledge that I am responsible for what happened to my brother.
>
> Powell still resides somewhere in my heart, with a dubious love, some strange, nameless shadow of regret; and yet with the deepest nostalgia. For I have never felt myself to be an honest part of anything since the world of his childhood deserted me.

This is something new in the voluminous literature of anti-colonialism. The West Indian of this generation accepts complete responsibility for the West Indies.

Vidia Naipaul of Trinidad does the same. His Mr. Biswas writes his first article for a newspaper.

DADDY COMES HOME IN A COFFIN

U.S. Explorer's Last Journey
On Ice by M. Biswas

. . . Less than a year ago Daddy—George Elmer Edman, the celebrated
traveller and explorer—left home to explore the Amazon.
    Well, I have news for you, kiddies.
    Daddy is on his way home.
    Yesterday he passed through Trinidad.
In a coffin.

This earns Mr. Biswas, former agricultural labourer and keeper of a
small shop, a job on the staff of this paper.

Mr. Biswas wrote a letter of protest. It took him two weeks. It was
eight typewritten pages long. After many rewritings the letter developed into
a broad philosophical essay on the nature of man; his son goes to a secondary school and together they hunt through Shakespeare for quotations and
find a rich harvest in *Measure for Measure*. The foreigner may miss this
bland reproduction of the *modus operandi* of the well-greased West Indian
journalist, politician, prime minister.

Mr. Biswas is now a man of letters. He is invited to a session of local
literati. Mr. Biswas, whose poetic peak is Ella Wheeler Wilcox, is
bewildered by whisky and talk about Lorca, Eliot, Auden. Every member
of the group must submit a poem. One night after looking at the sky
through the window Mr. Biswas finds his theme.

> He addressed his mother. He did not think of rhythm; he used no
> cheating abstract words. He wrote of coming up to the brow of the hill,
> seeing the black, forked earth, the marks of the spade, the indentations of
> the fork prongs. He wrote of the journey he had made a long time before.
> He was tired; she made him rest. He was hungry; she gave him food. He
> had nowhere to go; she welcomed him . . .
>   "It is a poem," Mr. Biswas announced. "In prose."
>
> . . . "There is no title," he said. And, as he had expected, this was re-
> ceived with satisfaction.
>   Then he disgraced himself. Thinking himself free of what he had
> written, he ventured on his poem boldly, and even with a touch of self-
> mockery. But as he read, his hands began to shake, the paper rustled; and
> when he spoke of the journey his voice failed. It cracked and kept on
> cracking; his eyes tickled. But he went on, and his emotion was such
> that at the end no one said a word . . .

The West Indian had made a fool of himself imitating American
journalism, Shakespeare, T. S. Eliot, Lorca. He had arrived at truth when
he wrote about his own West Indian childhood, his West Indian mother
and the West Indian landscape. Naipaul is an East Indian. Mr. Biswas
is an East Indian. But the East Indian problem in the West Indies is a
creation of politicians of both races, seeking means to avoid attacking the

old colonial system. The East Indian has become as West Indian as all the other expatriates.

The latest West Indian novelist is one of the strangest of living novelists. Beginning in 1958 he has just concluded a quartet of novels.* He is from British Guiana, which is a part of the South American continent. There are nearly 40,000 square miles of mountains, plateaux, forest, jungle, savannah, the highest waterfalls in the world, native Amerindians, settled communities of escaped African slaves—all largely unexplored. For fifteen years, over this new territory, Wilson Harris worked as a land surveyor. He is a member of a typical West Indian society of 600,000 people which inhabits a thin strip of coastline. Harris sets the final seal on the West Indian conception of itself as a national identity. On the run from the police a young Guianese, half-Chinese, half-Negro, discovers that all previous generations, Dutch, English, French, capitalists, slaves, freed slaves, white and black, were expatriates.

> ". . . All the restless wayward spirits of all the aeons (who it was thought had been embalmed for good) are returning to roost in our blood. And we have to start all over again where they began to explore. We've got to pick up the seeds again where they left off. It's no use worshipping the rottenest tacouba and tree-trunk in the historic topsoil. There's a whole world of branches and sensations we've missed, and we've got to start again from the roots up even if they look like nothing. Blood, sap, flesh, veins, arteries, lungs, heart, the heartland, Sharon. *We're the first potential parents who can contain the ancestral house.* Too young? I don't know. Too much responsibility? Time will tell. We've got to face it. Or else it will be too late to stop everything and everyone from running away and tumbling down. And then All the King's Horses and all the King's Men won't be able to put us together again. Like all the bananas and the plantains and the coffee trees near Charity. Not far from here, you know. A small wind comes and everything comes out of the ground. Because the soil is unstable. Just pegasse. Looks rich on top but that's about all. What do you think they say when it happens, when the crops run away? They shrug and say they're expendable crops. They can't begin to see that it's *us,* our blood, running away all the time, in the river and in the sea, everywhere, staining the bush. *Now* is the time to make a new-born stand, Sharon; you and me; it's up to us, even if we fall on our knees and *creep* to anchor ourselves before we get up."

There is no space here to deal with the poet in the literary tradition, or the ballad singer. In dance, in the innovation in musical instruments, in popular ballad singing unrivalled anywhere in the world, the mass of the people are not seeking a national identity, they are expressing one. The West Indian writers have discovered the West Indies and West Indians, a people of the middle of our disturbed century, concerned with the discovery of themselves, determined to discover themselves, but with-

---

* *Palace of the Peacock, The Far Journey of Oudin, The Whole Armour, The Secret Ladder.* London: Faber & Faber.

out hatred or malice against the foreigner, even the bitter imperialist past. To be welcomed into the comity of nations a new nation must bring something new. Otherwise it is a mere administrative convenience or necessity. The West Indians have brought something new.

Albion too was once
a colony like ours . . .

. . . deranged
By foaming channels, and the vain
expanse
Of bitter faction.
All in compassion ends.
So differently from what the heart
arranged.

Passion not spent but turned inward. Toussaint tried and paid for it with his life. Torn, twisted, stretched to the limits of agony, injected with poisonous patent medicines, it lives in the state which Fidel started. It is of the West Indies West Indian. For it, Toussaint, the first and greatest of West Indians, paid with his life.

Daniel Guérin
THE DAWNING OF
A SOCIAL CONSCIOUSNESS

A SANE HISTORICAL DESTINATION

The achievement of racial consciousness and of social consciousness are closely interwoven; the former was the first to occur in the West Indies and set the stage for the latter. For the sake of clarity, I have thought it best to treat them separately. I should like now to describe the birth and earliest phases of a simultaneously political and trade-union movement with a more or less socialist or communist bent.

As formerly in Europe, the initial spark was given to this movement by a fraction of the middle class which detached itself from the rest of the bourgeoisie in order to make common cause with the people. Every observer has noted the deepening rift between the 'conformist' right wing and the 'rebel' left wing of the Caribbean middle class. 'The rebellion against this racial-economic dichotomy is strongest among the brown intellectuals,' Paul Blanshard writes. 'From these intellectuals rather than from the proletarian masses are coming the agitators who understand the meaning of their own subjection in the system.'[1]

Jacques Roumain, who founded communism in Haiti and who spent years in jail because of his ideas, was a member of Port-au-Prince's mulatto élite—which was evident enough to me when I paid a visit to his widow who lives in an elegant home in the section where Haitian aristocracy's 'better' families reside; his brother-in-law, a 'conformist', is a renowned university teacher, and the most bourgeois of the mulattos have always had a secret indulgence for Roumain, that *enfant terrible* bred within their own circle and still its child. . . .

Meanwhile, as a fraction of the half-caste upper layer was 'descending' towards the people, a black petty bourgeoisie was starting to rise and acquire the means whereby it could give its children a university education. In due time, from the ranks emerged a handful of dark-skinned intellectuals, all impatient to put an end to a social régime which insulted and ridiculed men of their colour. Mulattos who had deserted their class and young Negroes in revolt met, combined their resources, formed the backbone of the social emancipation movement: Aimé Césaire joined forces with Jacques Roumain.*

* Nevertheless, within the progressive movements the fusion of these two elements is still not total. In Haiti, in Martinique, a certain defiance exists between mulatto and Negro militants. In Jamaica, the lower middle class Negroes who back Norman Manley's party have inherited from Marcus Garvey their prejudice against lighter-skinned leaders, *gentlemen* soaked in British culture and somewhat contemptuous of their own following.[2]

REPRINTED FROM *The West Indies and Their Future* (LONDON: DENNIS DOBSON, 1961) BY PERMISSION OF THE AUTHOR. COPYRIGHT © 1961 BY DANIEL GUÉRIN.

At the outset the movement did not place the accent upon fighting for specifically working-class ends. It was originally the creation of some trail-blazers who had come from the middle class: men like Boisneuf in Guadeloupe, 'Captain' Cipriani in Trinidad, Marryshaw in Grenada, Juan Gualberto Gomez in Cuba, etc., and its programme (more political than economic) rather more reflected the aspirations of the petty bourgeoisie than the needs of the workers. But its character was soon to undergo a radical change. Towards 1935–8 in the British West Indies, 1940 in Puerto Rico, from 1944 in the French Antilles, 1946 in Haiti, we witness the birth of a new kind of movement: the middle class continues to play a certain role in it (often a cautionary role) but the middle class no longer provides the driving-force; workers' demands move to the fore, trade union action and political action team up in close harmony, and the programme adopts anti-capitalist overtones. To be sure, the tags and the labels are different from one island to the next, indeed they may be antagonistic. In the French West Indies communists and socialists vie for influence (the position of the communists, at least up to Césaire's split, was stronger in Martinique than in Guadeloupe, the socialists are a little less given to betraying their own doctrine in Guadeloupe than in Martinique). In the British West Indies and in Puerto Rico we come upon a reformist labour movement which is here more and there less influenced by the Marxist ferment. In Haiti, it is a juncture of liberal, syndicalist, socialist and communist elements which makes a brilliant although brief appearance upon the political scene from 1946 to 1949 before being overthrown, temporarily, by a military dictatorship.

But the real aims and contents of the movement vary much less, from one island to another, than party labels would lead one to suppose. The movement everywhere expresses a dual awareness, firstly racial, then social, a common revolt against the supremacy of the white sugar planters; and its militants are more preoccupied by the immediate and peculiarly Caribbean aspects of their struggle than by extra-Caribbean ideologies, by the socialist and communist internationals their leaders belong to. As Blanshard remarks, 'it is not possible to draw any sharp line between communist and non-communist influence. As representatives of oppressed peoples [the natives] tend to seek the most revolutionary power group available, whether they agree with it completely or not.'[3]

The moderate labourite Chief Minister of Jamaica, Norman Manley, may ignore or repudiate the communist deputy from Martinique, Aimé Césaire, and *vice versa*. The fact remains that, appearances notwithstanding, the two movements have the same family resemblance. Regardless of whether one declares himself a reformist and the other a revolutionary, they are both, basically, prisoners of the same contradiction: authority has been delegated to both, they hold office, one on the governmental plane, the other on the departmental and municipal planes, but within the framework of the colonial capitalist régime: their common problem is *how to do anything to relieve the poverty of the masses without being yet able to take measures to render the sugar plutocrats harmless.* The 'cold war' which split the Caribbean into two camps just as it did the whole world has managed to drive the two men towards opposite poles: they will meet again along the same road leading to the same historical destination.

• • •

MARTINIQUE

Let us then journey about the islands, looking at them one by one. Martinique's drift towards the far left began only ten years ago. Visiting the island in 1935, Marthe Oulié came home to announce that she'd seen neither hide nor hair of racial or class conflict in Martinique. If one takes her word for it, there was, to be sure, a lot of anti-'Factory' talk during the electoral campaigns but, the voting once over with, everything settled back to normal again. 'The Communist Party,' she wrote, 'has never been able to get more than sixty or eighty members.'[4] Although that frivolous journalist seems to have introduced overmuch of sweetness and light into her description of the situation, her reportage still contains a certain amount of truth, and it serves as a yardstick to measure what has been accomplished since then.

The French West Indies' evolution to the far left was given added impetus by an historical accident: the military dictatorship which, in the name of the Vichy Government, Admiral Robert bestowed upon the islands. They have preserved a stinging memory of that individual's tyranny, of the white mayors he appointed, of the racism of some ten thousand sailors who invaded Fort-de-France for several years,[5] of the severe privations caused by the allied naval forces' blockade of the islands. André Breton's little book and, in a more recent writing, Claude Lévi-Strauss, give an idea of the atmosphere which reigned in Martinique at the time.[6] Needless to say, the powers of social conservatism—planters and priests—unstintingly backed the Vichy régime, for which, even today, they have a nostalgia: 'What these islands need,' a *béké* recently confided to a visitor, 'is a firm hand, and that's what they got during the war, under Admiral Robert. Whereas now—'[7] Paul Blanshard very aptly remarks that 'The post-war position of the small ruling class was not made more tenable by the fact that many leaders of that class were inordinately friendly to the Vichy régime . . .' which explains 'Martinique's sharp swing to the left at the end of the war.'[8] There were massive popular demonstrations in Martinique during July and August of 1943, and it was then that the proletariat marched on to the stage. 'Martinique,' writes Fanon, 'was in the act of systematizing its political consciousness for the first time.' And, he goes on, 'it is perfectly logical that, in the elections which followed the Liberation, two of the three deputies sent to Paris were communists.'[9] It was a left-wing landslide. Césaire entered the National Assembly. Of the thirty-six seats in the island's Conseil Général, the communists won fourteen and the socialists a dozen, while Césaire was elected mayor of Fort-de-France. In the 1951 legislative elections, despite the shameful cheating of the authorities, the Communist Party obtained, thanks to Césaire's personal prestige, over 60 per cent of the votes cast and seated two deputies, Césaire and Bissol*—and, in the elections of January 2, 1956, Communist Party strength rose to just above 62 per cent.

Not long ago, *Le Monde* conceded that communism appeared to be 'the one organized and living political force in the island.'[10] Thanks to the struggle it has waged, to the ideas it has clarified and broadcast, the Communist Party may justly claim to have awakened the working-class in the cities, and even more so, in the country.[11] The day Bissol was elected to the Conseil Général I was in Le Vauclin and I have an imperishable recollection of that old Martiniquaise who, so humbly dressed the moment before, suddenly came out in all her finery: madras, bright scarf, necklace. When I enquired the reason for this abrupt metamorphosis, she declared in a tone of proud assurance I cannot hope to transcribe: *'Why indeed, sir, I am on my way to the polls!'*

As for the socialists, directly the war ended they went over to the camp of the 'Factory',[12] and the discredit they have fallen into is one of the causes of the Communist Party's preponderance.

Having failed to find any other device by which to hold the Communist Party in check, the colonial administration was perfectly willing to tamper with the election machinery and doctor the results. And that was what was done during the cantonal elections of 1953: the Prefect fetched over the urns from the François commune, filched out communist ballots, substituted others for them, and ended up proclaiming the victory of a socialist.

As regards the development of trade unions, the results have been no less impressive. Headed by an extraordinarily dynamic union leader, Crétinoir, a stonemason, the workers on the plantations at the northern part of the island have declared war on their employers. In the Basse-Pointe district, one strike lasted three months (in 1944–5). In March 1948, under the reign of a socialist prefect, Trouillé, three strikers who had come to pick up back pay were provoked and then killed by the police at Carbet. In 1950, at Basse-Pointe, a white overseer, Guy de Fabrique, having threatened the strikers with his revolver even though he was protected by a police escort, was lynched by the workers who then disarmed the police. The administration tried to take advantage of this dramatic incident in order to torpedo the trade union movement by getting rid of its leaders. Sixteen of them were arrested, spent two years in prison awaiting trial, and were finally acquitted at Bordeaux.

In the course of a virtually general stoppage that lasted for three months, from January to March of 1954, the police and the C.R.S. were sent into the countryside, villages were placed under martial law, thirty-

* The third deputy elected, Véry, a socialist, got in thanks to an anti-communist *bloc*.

nine unionists were jailed.[13] When at Fort-de-France, I met Victor Lamon, the present secretary of the C.G.T. Union des Syndicats; Lamon, a dedicated, energetic and realistic man, sober in manner, told me that his organization has 10,000 members (out of 30,000 wage-earners) and that, in the Social Security elections, the C.G.T. list, with 24,000 votes, got thirteen of the fifteen seats.

At the end of 1956 there was a sudden and sweeping change in the political scene in Martinique. On October 24, in a masterfully written letter addressed to Maurice Thorez, Secretary-General of the French Communist Party, Aimé Césaire announced his resignation from the Party. The letter (published at once in French and, in February 1957, in English) and the gesture had immediate repercussions: in order to provoke new municipal elections, Césaire also resigned his post as Mayor of Fort-de-France: on February 10, 1957 he was triumphantly re-elected, his list winning 82.5 per cent of the vote. The Communist Party had opposed him in the campaign, and was routed, obtaining not a single seat in the City Council. Hitherto tied to Stalinism's apron-strings, the movement towards racial and social emancipation in Martinique has assumed the form of a kind of national communism: but now slightly adrift.

GUADELOUPE

Starting right after the Liberation, Guadeloupe has had a parallel evolution. In 1946 the communists obtained 47.3 per cent of the vote and two seats in the French National Assembly (Mlle Gerty Archimède and Dr. Rosan Girard), the socialists 39 per cent of the vote and one seat (Paul Valentino). In the 1951 general elections the respective percentages of the two parties were 44.4 and 22.9 per cent; in 1956, 45 and 22.1 per cent. In 1951 the well-co-ordinated forces of reaction defeated Mlle Archimède, whose seat went to Furcie Tirolien, a counter-revolutionary, but the other two deputies were returned. The majority of the island's Conseil Général is today composed of socialists and communists. The latter administer some important municipalities, including Basse-Terre, the capital town, Capesterre, Saint-Louis, Bouillante. The administrative performance of Mayor Lacavé of Capesterre has won admiration from all sides. In the Social Security elections, the C.G.T. Union des Syndicats list won fourteen out of fifteen seats. Often eventful strikes have been repeatedly called on the sugar-cane plantations, notably in 1945 and 1952. During the 1952 strike, the Prefect, Villéger (who, since then, has gone to exercise his talents in Martinique*), had the town of Le Moule occupied by the C.R.S. who, given a free hand, literally ran amok, murdering four workers and gravely wounding thirteen others.

The next Prefect, Jacques Brunel, acquired a melancholy reputation by inaugurating 'prefabricated elections' on the Algerian model. Having

---

* A very minor example: he *forbade* Radio-Martinique to announce the lecture I gave in Fort-de-France in April 1955.

taken a hand in the Sainte-Rose commune's municipal elections where, by means of fraud and violence, he stopped the communists, he repeated the exploit in the Le Moule commune on April 26, 1953. Le Moule is, as a matter of fact, an important strategic point on the island's class-struggle battlefield. Its population is harshly exploited by the Gardel sugar factory owned by the family of that Martiniquais magnate, Aubéry. It is, further-more, the electoral stronghold of the energetic Rosan Girard who occupies the two offices of mayor and communist deputy. The Prefect opened the game with the democratic gambit: against the communists he tried to whip together an anti-communist coalition of every party in sight, including the socialists. That operation failed. Whereupon the metropolitan govern-ment's minion got up a colonialist ticket headed by the Gardel factory book-keeper. On election-day the police marched into the city hall, used rifle butts on the voters, worked over the persons charged with supervising the balloting; meanwhile, some 'gangsters' (wearing arm-bands, they avoided the clubbing being meted out to everyone else) made off with one of the urns, deposited it in a jeep belonging to the police, and off the police drove. Only one thing had been overlooked: the signed registry of voters, thanks to which Dr. Girard could lawfully proclaim the communist list elected. But no, the Prefect wouldn't have it: he suspended the mayor, annulled his proclamation, and named a 'delegation' of three reactionary souls to administer the commune temporarily. This triumvirate of usurpers organized rigged elections for July 5. The results allowed the communists two seats on the city council, the colonialists awarding themselves fifteen and passing out ten to the socialists.

And this was only the start. His appetite whetted, M. Brunel swung into action against the Conseil Général itself. At Le Moule the socialists hadn't played ball with the Prefect when he had sought to paste an anti-communist front together . . . for Brunel had not, for his part, wished to guarantee the socialists an absolute majority which would have given them control of the Le Moule city hall. Nettled, they had decided to ally them-selves in the island's Conseil Général with the communists and against the Prefect, blaming him not only for his election stunts, but for the sanctions he had decreed against civil servants gone out on strike.[14] And, on July 16, the majority (socialists and communists) of the Conseil had passed a resolution condemning Brunel's 'illegal and anti-republican machinations', declaring that 'a profound divorce [exists] between the dictatorial meth-ods of his administration and the population of this department' and demanding his recall. Well, the Prefect had *this* resolution annulled by the French Conseil d'Etat. On November 28, 1953 the Guadeloupe Conseil Général chose a socialist president for itself. Toribio was elected by the coalition of the two workers' parties. Raising a technical point of order, the Prefect, his counter-revolutionary minority at his heels, stalked out of the chamber, signed a decree invalidating the session, and sent to the Minister of the Interior at Paris for a writ dissolving the Conseil Général of Guadeloupe. The writ was granted.

One need not search far to detect a correlation between the sugar plutocracy's interests and this 'get tough' policy. These events transpired on the eve of the sugar harvest. Had the socialists and communists remained allies in the Conseil Général, the employers would have been forced to listen to the workers' demands.[15] On February 23, 1954, in the speech introducing his bill before the National Assembly, Furcie Tirolien let the cat out of the bag when he explained that 'as a consequence of this dissolution, access to the tribune of the Conseil Général is as of now blocked to the trouble-makers who, every year, employ it to serve partisan and revolutionary purposes, *regularly exciting the workers to strike at the start of the sugar-harvesting season.*'

In order to give some ideas of the gravity of the Prefect's and the government's strong-arm gesture, one might mention that never, since 1874, had the French Government pronounced the dissolution of a Conseil Général. The government pronounced it, moreover, without even taking the trouble to justify the measure. And Guadeloupe stayed without a Conseil Général for *nearly one year.*

But the tug-of-war Brunel had launched ended in his defeat. He was recalled in January 1954* and the ensuing elections (held on October 24, 1954) returned a socialist-communist majority (ten socialists, eight communists) to the Conseil. The common front forged in the struggle has not been broken since then. Guadeloupe's Conseil Général is still presided over by Toribio who enjoys the two workers parties' support and a prestige that has only been enhanced by his courageous resistance to the dictatorial Prefect.

But his successor, Ravail, did nothing to halt the repetition of the fraudulent and violent election practices initiated by Brunel. The commune of Le Moule was prevented from choosing its city councillors in the October 1954 elections. Falsification of the electoral lists paved the way for provoking fist-fights during which the urns were now simply smashed: the ballots, consequently, could not be counted this time. I was in the West Indies when, on April 17, 1955, the voters of Le Moule were once again invited to designate their municipal councillors. More frauds, more falsifications, more interference with the voting procedure were committed in the presence and under the protective supervision of the police and the gendarmerie; and the outcome was that, in this commune, overwhelmingly composed of workers and communists, the two seats at stake were given to the counter-revolutionary list. In those polling places where the voting went on in an atmosphere of freedom, the Communist Party obtained from 68 to 83 per cent of the suffrages; whilst in others where the reaction handled the count, the Communist Party did rather less well: getting between 6 and 10 per cent of the vote.

* The socialist president of the National Assembly, M. André le Troquer, could think of no better way of employing this undesirable civil servant than as the director of his cabinet.[16]

JAMAICA

In the British West Indies, the social movement began prior to World War II. Why this head-start over the French islands? Probably because the repercussions of the international economic depression were more acutely felt, particularly in the form of unemployment, in these islands, larger and less backward than the French holdings. Also because, as long ago as the twenties, Jamaica's Marcus Garvey had ignited the spark that was to lead to racial consciousness. And, finally, because the close ties, established as a result of emigration, between the American Negro community and the British West Indies, particularly between Harlem and Jamaica, drew the West Indies into the current of social progress and rebellion which, at that time, was flowing so powerfully in the United States. The return to native soil of emigrants coming home either from the United States or elsewhere, either voluntarily or perforce, as a consequence either of economic troubles or of measures taken to expel them, brought a wave of discontent to the islands, and also brought the desire for improved political and social conditions. These prodigal sons returned with new ideas, with new demands, for they had become habituated to a higher standard of living and were no longer willing to tolerate the sordid living conditions in which the West Indies were rotting. They spearheaded the revolt.[17]

Another cause of the explosion in Jamaica was the swift rise in urban population. We have already alluded to the great speed with which Kingston grew. This mass of people, poorly fed, paid and housed, was ripe for leftist political and social ideas. A sociologist has compared this group in its political importance with that of the Parisian populace in French politics, and attributed some of the political changes since 1938 to the presence and growing self-consciousness of this pressure group at the site of the central government.[18]

On May 2, 1938 the workers on the great Frome sugar-cane plantation, belonging to the English firm of Tate and Lyle, struck and mauled their bosses. The police opened fire: four workers dead, nine wounded. Several days later the Kingston dock-workers joined the fight and on the 23rd a general strike was called in the capital whilst the aroused workers staged demonstrations in the streets, attacked shops and tramways. The repression was brutal. The combined forces of the police and the army killed eight persons, injured 171 and made 700 arrests while a warship dashed at full speed from Bermuda.

The whole privileged structure of their interests suddenly imperilled, the planters saw the ground yawn beneath their feet. For a moment they believed some sort of 'Bloody Wednesday' was upon them and they rushed to put their families in places of safety.

The rebellion had been entirely spontaneous. No leaders prepared it. But then a leader stepped forward and was accepted. Alexander Bustamante (his real name was Clarke) was a most unusual figure. An almost white-skinned Jamaican mulatto, an orphan from birth, he had early expatriated himself, knocked around almost everywhere, done all sorts of jobs, simultaneously organized the New York dockers and made a pretty penny from stockmarket speculations; and, since his return to Jamaica, his fame derived mainly from his career as a money-lender. An untaught and uncouth histrionic, he spoke a bad English, but he had uncommon gifts as an orator and political agitator and, his eyes flashing, waving his arms, he would harangue the crowd in a voice of thunder. His blatant demagogy, his mephistophelean silhouette, his verbal extravagances enabled him to impress a populace which still lacked political education and to which, like one inspired, he would cry: 'Believe in me and I shall save you!'[19] He was thrown into prison. The strikers made his release the first condition of any going back to work, and they finally had their way.

The next year—in 1939—Bustamante decreed another general strike. Fifty thousand workers walked out. The British governor replied by proclaiming martial law. Later, during the war, Bustamante, without trial, was sent to an internment camp where he remained for seventeen months for having once again incited the Kingston dock-workers to strike.*

Thus, the 1938 revolt was the opening shot that touched off a vast movement of social and national liberation. Its immediate consequence was to multiply the island's trade unions. In July of that year Bustamante had created a workers' organization which he may be reproached for having turned into his personal fief, and to which he lent his own name: the *Bustamante Industrial Trade Union*. He designated himself its president, gave himself life tenure, and in its statutes included clauses stipulating that his directorial functions could not be revoked save if he were to become insane or were to leave the island for good! He furthermore established himself as a one-man committee in charge of the union's finances. Despite his hardly democratic behaviour, this union rapidly acquired 50,000 members and developed into the most powerful labour organization in the British West Indies. One cannot deny Alexandre Bustamante the historical merit of having been the first to awaken the Jamaican workers' class consciousness and to have forged the weapons wherewith they could fight for the emancipation they had been for so long deprived of. Neither his flaws of character, nor his later reversals of position, can nullify his outstanding achievements.

The 1938 revolt had another, a parallel, an almost immediate consequence: the founding of a political party dedicated to national liberation: the People's National Party (P.N.P.). Impossible to imagine two more dissimilar personalities than its founder, Norman Manley, and the rabble-rousing Bustamante (the two men are close cousins for all that). Manley,

---

* Bustamante was not the only labour leader to undergo the hardships of internment. Seven other labour leaders underwent the same fate, and Roger Mais, a writer, was sentenced to six months on a prison farm for having written a courageous article in the paper of the People's National Party, *Public Opinion*, where he lashed out at Winston Churchill and British imperialism. (He has, incidentally, related his experiences in a fine book.)[20] Mais died prematurely in 1955.

an eminent lawyer, educated at Oxford where he formed ties of friendship with Sir Stafford Cripps, has derived his impeccable manners and his broad culture from the English leisure class. A mild although forceful speaker, flexible and reassuring, a born mediator, skilled at winning the confidence of the wealthy and the esteem of the colonial administration, with a fondness for order and a deep respect for protocol, hostile to violence and irregularity but at the same time profoundly sympathetic and humane, animated by a sincere passion for social reform, endowed with a brilliant intelligence and a subtle wit and with an aristocratic power of seduction, there is much about him that reminds us of Léon Blum. It was in September of 1938 that, in the course of a meeting held in the presence of Sir Stafford Cripps, Manley founded the P.N.P. on a moderate labourite programme. The year before, this firm believer in collaboration between classes had concluded an agreement with the powerful American trust, United Fruit, which controls Jamaican banana production; according to the terms of this agreement, United Fruit agreed to pay ten cents extra for each bunch of bananas exported. The money thus accumulated was deposited in a welfare fund managed by Manley himself and used notably to subsidize agricultural co-operatives. During the 1938 disorders, Manley represented the strikers in the negotiations with the administration and the employers, and he did so with success. He also succeeded in obtaining Bustamante's release every time his turbulent cousin landed himself behind bars.

But it was not long before the two men were at odds. In 1943–4, owing to the intervention of Manley and the P.N.P., the British governor abandoned his policy of toughness, restored Bustamante to freedom, and granted universal suffrage to Jamaica. In the 1944 elections, suddenly converting his labour organization into a new political party, the Jamaica Labour Party, Bustamante handed Manley and his followers a stunning defeat. Looking for revenge, the P.N.P. founded a rival union, the Trade Union Council, organized on a democratic basis in contrast with the dictatorial structure of Bustamante's labour federations.*

Once in power, Bustamante inaugurated, and for almost ten years (from 1945 to the end of 1954) maintained, a simultaneously authoritarian and venal régime, with undisguised heavy-handedness muzzling his political and union adversaries, dealing just as crudely with his own party all of whose candidates he himself named, and governing by corruption. At the same time, under a gloss of syndicalist demagogy, he adopted and expressed increasingly reactionary ideas, storming against communism and praising British imperialism to the skies. Little by little the working masses lost their faith in him as he, in the meantime, gained favour amongst the planters. The 1949 elections kept him in power, but considerably whittled

---

* On March 31, 1952 nearly 100,000 of Jamaica's workers were union members, and half of them were paying their dues. (At that time, the island had a total of 319,000 wage-earners.) I don't know how many of these workers drifted back and forth between the two rival labour organizations; I only know that, in 1952, Bustamante's had lost a sizable number of its adherents to the T.U.C.

down his parliamentary majority, and the number of votes he obtained was smaller than the P.N.P.'s total. The 1954 elections saw him routed. While the P.N.P. collected 51 per cent of the votes and eighteen seats, Bustamante got only 38 per cent and fourteen seats. Norman Manley came to power; he still heads Jamaica's government. When I sat in the visitors' gallery of the Legislative Assembly I saw the new Chief Minister direct affairs with an authority that belied his modest stature, plead his case masterfully, and defend his policy against an inconsistent and hateful, sardonic and sneering marionette: cousin Bustamante, reduced in rank to leader of the opposition.

It is still too early to form a judgement on the 'Manley experiment', which is only in its initial stages. We may however try to distinguish some of its positive and negative aspects. First of all, the personality of the leader. Whereas Bustamante is no more than a vulgar and mediocre politician, Manley has been favoured with an exceptional mind and the equipment and air of a statesman. His vision is keen and ambitious. It is not confined to the narrow perimeters of Jamaica, nor even of the British West Indies. He is, and we shall have subsequent evidence of it, one of the rare Caribbean leaders who, if one may so phrase it, thinks 'Caribbeanly'. Moreover, his P.N.P. is organized in so remarkable a fashion that, to its great credit, it may truly be considered a party that represents the masses, enjoying the wholehearted confidence and the enthusiastic backing of the great majority of the island's workers. Its local sections are very strong and their meetings frequent. It is run along relatively democratic lines. And, finally, the P.N.P. has helped organize quite powerful trade unions with which it keeps in close touch.

The P.N.P. has what in European terms would qualify as a more or less radical past. In 1940 it proclaimed itself socialist. It adhered to a Caribbean Labour Congress, founded in 1945, which, through a programme calling for the nationalization of the sugar industry and public services, land reform and agricultural co-operatives, grouped together the entirety of the British West Indies' labour organizations. Directly after the war, in September 1945, this association convened at Barbados and Manley sent one of his collaborators as his representative, a young Kingston Marxist, Richard Hart, of whom, in an accrediting letter, he spoke with the warmest praise.

But, as they neared power, Manley and his party had swerved sharply to the right. Like any other national freedom movement, the P.N.P. has a forward-going wing composed of unionized workers, and, opposite it, a relatively conservative wing emanating from the middle classes (business men, small planters, members of the professions). Between the two there had already been clashes, harbingers of a class-struggle in the making. However, both sides sensed the necessity to present a solid front against British colonialism, and this had preserved the party's unity; it was Manley who, from his moderate's position, had arbitrated the two factions' differences.

But, by the end of 1952, the party's leader was overwhelmed by its right wing. How did that happen? As Bustamante's prestige had progressively declined, the workers had deserted his union and come over to swell the ranks of the P.N.P., of, that is to say, its left, thus affecting the balance of forces inside the party. Seeing the scales being tipped against it, the right, panic-stricken, lent a more attentive ear to Bustamante's calumnies which centred around the notion that the P.N.P. was a communist-dominated, at the very least a communist-infiltrated, movement. The conservatives fancied that, in order to wean votes away from the adversary, tangible proof of 'anti-communism' had to be furnished. Apart from that, the cold war had reached Jamaica's shores. The labour unions in the West Indies, as elsewhere, found themselves torn between the two world federations inspired by the two antagonistic empires. The right wing finally decided that it would be wise policy, in this over-populated and under-developed island already partially enthralled by American trusts, and hunting for a new capital, to pawn itself to Uncle Sam.

And so, after having unsuccessfully tried to cook up a union to rival the one which had the party's official support, the right wing obliged Manley to deliver the left wing's scalp. The union leaders were exposed to a 'witch-hunt' under the shoddy pretext that they had been responsible for circulating educational literature that smacked of Marxism, and they were summarily expelled from the P.N.P. The union stood by these scapegoats. The whole operation had a very ugly smell; and it was, to put it very mildly, based upon an exaggeration. Afterwards, it was fully evident that, if one of the expelled leaders, Richard Hart, made no bones about his communist sympathies, the union's secretary, Ken Hill, was nothing but a trade unionist, and could hardly be said to have been indoctrinated with Marxist ideology.[21]

By beheading its left wing, Manley has deprived his party of its workers' flank; and he has himself become the prisoner of a bourgeois right wing. At his home near Kingston, during a dinner to which he most kindly invited me, I was tactless enough to bring the conversation round to this painful affair. The unexpected vehemence with which this perfect gentleman sought to justify his conduct led me to suspect that it was not without an inner distress he had adopted it and that it still weighed on his conscience.*

Since the excisions performed at the end of 1952, the P.N.P. has significantly changed its tune. The nationalization plank fell clear out of its 1954 electoral platform and, instead, the P.N.P. campaigned for Christianity and declared itself resolutely opposed not only to communism, but

* After the schism, Manley tried to re-establish the equilibrium he had himself destroyed by artificially creating another—a third!—labour organization whose direction he entrusted to his son, called home from England where he was completing his studies. At the time I was in Jamaica with his father, at the head of the government, the younger Manley was directing a strike of 10,000 of the workers on the island's two biggest sugar plantations!

all forms of 'constraint', 'coercion' and 'expropriation'. At the same time, trying to lure capital to Jamaica, it has been flashing tender glances and making all sorts of promises to foreign investors. Manley likes to cite the example of Puerto Rico's reformist governor, Luis Muñoz Marin, and, like him, is endeavouring to absorb unemployment by means of a plan for industrializing, for which Uncle Sam is to act as the banker.* But despite his capacity and his goodwill, I doubt whether he is going to succeed in pulling Jamaica out of the quagmire if not so much as a finger is to be laid on the masters of the sugar plantations.

Following the first federal election of March 1958, in which Busta-mante supporters gained twice as many seats as the P.N.P., the latter improved its organization, particularly in the rural areas where it was weak; and in July 1959, in the first election under the new constitution, the P.N.P. won 30 seats in the new House of Representatives, the Jamaica Labour Party 15.

TRINIDAD

Barbados apart, Trinidad was the first of the West Indies to evolve politically. Both historic and economic factors were responsible for this head-start. The island was, comparatively speaking, not much marked by slavery's usual stigmata. African slaves did not begin to arrive there until 1783; and no more came after 1807, the date when the slave trade was prohibited. As early as 1834 slaves in the British possessions were given their liberty. Thereupon, free, they colonized the interior of Trinidad and, so as not to fall back into the clutches of the planters, refused to work for them. For manpower the planters had to rely on indentured workers im-ported from India. Sugar monoculture, moreover, was less prevalent in Trinidad than in the other Caribbean islands, and the cultivation of cocoa permitted a small independent peasantry to develop; and, finally, the dis-covery of extensive oilfields gave Trinidad, in so far as industrialization goes, a certain lead over the other islands. One ought also to mention the influence exerted by neighbouring Venezuela, a rich and modernized country.

·The Trinidad worker became aware of his dignity as a man long before his comrades living elsewhere in the Caribbean. As early as 1919 the Port of Spain dockers had set off a general strike and marines had to be landed to break their grip upon the capital.[22] During my stay in the island I was struck at once by the forthright carriage and the fine presence of the natives. Almost no signs of inferiority complexes in these people.

Just as in 'France's' Madagascar, where it was a metropolitan colonist —the admirable Paul Dussac[23]—who supplied the impulse that resulted

---

* Manley's government has been assisted by a United Nations technical adviser named Cadbury. British by nationality, a member of the chocolate-manufacturing family, he looked to me to be on good terms with certain American business circles.

in the birth of a national independence movement, so A. A. Cipriani, a white and Corsican by origin, guided Trinidad's first steps along the road to freedom. A horse-trainer by trade, he had served as an officer in World War I, and had defended coloured soldiers against racial discrimination: whence his legendary nickname, 'Captain'.[24] Having returned to civilian life, he became the animator of a labour party which, at its peak, had a membership numbering a quarter of the island's population.[25] Many a Trinidad labour organizer and labour leader was schooled by 'the Captain'. Taking up arms in defence of the 'barefooted man' he made universal suffrage the prime objective of the battle. Cipriani succeeded in getting himself elected mayor of Port of Spain and a member of the island's legislature.

But towards the end of his career he became more conservative and his movement was eclipsed, especially in the south, in the oilfields, by new political and trade union organizations, radical in tendency and dominated by the working class.

A first explosion occurred in February 1935; a short-lived strike of oil-workers was followed by a 'hunger march' on Port of Spain. At the head of the movement was one of Cipriani's one-time lieutenants, a Negro, Uriah Butler, who had become familiar with the meaning of the oil companies' exploitation. This self-educated man derived his principles from both the Bible and Karl Marx; but he was moved by a great sincerity and endowed with formidable talents as an orator.

In June 1937 there was a second outburst. The high cost of living, low rates of pay, and above all the racial discrimination the white employers practised, set fire to the powder-keg or, more precisely, to the oil wells. Following the American-style sit-down strike, the strikers' action included occupying one of the oil properties. While Butler was delivering an impassioned speech to a seething crowd of strikers, the unfortunate idea of arresting him occurred to the authorities. They were assaulted directly they arrived upon the scene, then ejected, while one policeman (a Negro) was beaten to death and his body burned. When the police tried to arrest the murderers, they were greeted by stones and gunfire.

The riots lasted several days, spread through the larger towns where the shops had to close, reached the sugar plantations, and rapidly assumed the look of a general insurrection. Rioters attacked commercial buildings and tried to seize a munitions train. The governor sent a S O S to His Majesty's Fleet in the Bermudas; marines landed, restoring Trinidad to 'order' once again: this was achieved by killing fourteen natives, wounding fifty-nine more, and throwing hundreds of others into prison. The planters had been given a terrific scare; the working class, for its part, had got its first taste of fire in the class war. Trade unions mushroomed everywhere, and Marxist ideology penetrated the masses.[26]

When World War II broke out, like Bustamante in Jamaica, Butler, 'for safety sake', was interned without trial for the duration of the hostilities.

A third explosion took place—once again on the oilfields—at the beginning of 1947. In the course of a new labour conflict, strikers set fire to the biggest oil wells and emptied the storage tanks. The Governor decreed a state of emergency and imposed a curfew.

Today, relations between the oil company management and its exploited employees are a little less convulsive, the former having finally been forced to deal on an equitable basis with a powerful labour union to which two-thirds of the workers belong. Accompanied by its president, Rojas, I had occasion to visit the Pointe-à-Pierre refinery, and I was impressed both by the deference shown Rojas by company officials and by the plain-spoken frankness he used when announcing to them what he had on his mind. The Oil-workers Union (numbering 10,000) was for a long time affiliated with the World Federation of Trade Unions, and only recently was blackmailed into leaving this organization, the Trinidad Government having threatened otherwise to dissolve the Union.

But, in the last few years, Trinidad had lost some of the lead it held on the political and social front. Universal suffrage was put into effect for the first time in June 1946, and the elections transpired amidst the most extreme confusion. Owing chiefly to the defects in the constitution which inhibit the free functioning of the island's parliamentary system, no party emerged with a majority. There were in fact no parties, only personalities. Racial animosities and personal ambitions alone distinguished one candidate from the next. It must be pointed out that Trinidad's political battles are complicated by the presence of a large number of inhabitants (37 per cent of the population) who originally came from India. This ethnical minority clings together, forming a separate, intact *bloc*. Under the aegis of a High Commissioner accredited by the Indian Government, it has its own parties, its own unions, its own religions (Hindu and Moslem), its own fields of economic activity (sugar plantations, transport—buses and taxis), and it is—or at least its political chiefs are—on rather bad terms with the Negro majority.* Furthermore, Trinidad seems to hold the record for rotten, cynical, turncoat politicians. The most typical (and, simultaneously, the most corpulent) of these renegades is the former minister, Mr. Albert Gomes, Portuguese by ancestry: he, after having been the left's spokesman, simply transformed himself into the bourgeoisie's valet. Repeated betrayals have made the people exceedingly wary of any kind of political action, and the founders of new parties have great trouble winning their confidence.

However, that is what Eric Williams has dared to undertake. He has succeeded in providing his little country with a seriously organized political party comparable to Jamaica's P.N.P., founded on an essentially democratic programme calling for an end to corruption and misgovernment, for

---

* At the Bandung Conference, China made important concessions to Indonesia regarding the two million Chinese living upon the latter's soil.[27] It is to be hoped that India, faithful to the spirit of Bandung, will be moved to follow this example in her relations with Trinidad.

political education, for social and economic reforms, for the abolition of racial discrimination in employment, for a slum-clearance programme, for an improved system of education, for the integration of all races and creeds into the community.[28] And in the general election held on September 24, 1956, the People's National Movement achieved a large victory. It won thirteen of the Legislative Assembly's twenty-four elected seats. Invited by the Governor to form a new government, Eric Williams accepted but upon condition that the Governor agree to appoint *on his proposal* two of the five nominated members of the Assembly. Thus assured of a parliamentary majority and finding himself in a free position to govern, Williams is the Chief Minister of Trinidad today.

BARBADOS

The 1937 rash of disturbances which shook Trinidad infected the little nearby island of Barbados almost at once. The germ was carried by a friend and labour associate of Uriah Butler, the fiery Clement Payne. After centuries of economic servitude, of racial oppression and of suppressed discontent, it needed only a spark to set the island ablaze. The Governor having decided to deport Payne, his followers marched to the courthouse. The riot began. Automobiles were pushed into the sea, shops were stoned, the police assaulted; 'order' was re-established at the price of making sixty victims.

The Barbadian George Lamming's novel, *In the Castle of My Skin,* contains a vivid description of the feeling in Barbados in those years when the sugar plantation labourers formed themselves both into a sturdy trade union and into a socialistically orientated political party. In 1945, during a bitter controversy over cane-cutting wages, more than 2,500 acres of cane —enough to have yielded 30,000 tons of sugar—were burned by the strikers.

Today, the Barbados Labour Party, formerly led by Grantley H. Adams and now by H. G. H. Cummins, is in power,* but the closed caste of white planters, though more and more hemmed in, still dominates the island.[29] In Barbados, as everywhere else, the two forces remain squared off in a precarious equilibrium which cannot last for ever.

HAITI

Haiti's social and political awakening can be said to date from 1946. If this little state gained its independence a century and a half ago, the obstacles that have impeded its development have been just as great as those that have paralysed the captive West Indies. Former slaves turned impromptu soldiers were the Republic's founders. They went to their task

---

* At the general election of December 7, 1956 Adams's party won fifteen out of twenty-four parliamentary seats.

unequipped with any political, administrative or technical education; they had no historical precedent, nor the example of any immediate neighbour to guide them in building a free state. Worse still, the war of independence had wrecked the country's economy and the indemnity France required as a price for withdrawal encumbered its finances. And, as climax to the situation, the new free state remained in a prolonged quarantine imposed by the major imperialist powers who dreaded an epidemic of uprisings inspired by ideas harboured in this hot-bed of anti-slavery.[30] In its infancy, Haiti found nothing at hand but the political tradition of San Domingo's old colonial system, and it was this that survived in the form of military dictatorships run by Negro captains who took the places vacated by white tyrants, and interrupted now and then by attempts at liberal government under the leadership of mulattos who had received a European education. These liberal régimes never endured long, and the country would soon pass back into the grip of black soldiers, despotic, uncultivated, but ardent defenders of Haitian independence. The people, ignorant and poverty-ridden, were left completely out of the political picture: no one, neither half-caste élite nor gold-braided black officers, cared a fig for the masses.[31]

Certain spirits, pointing to the sorry spectacle offered by Haiti, take it as an opportunity to regret the French departure from San Domingo and to deplore (in a perhaps not altogether disinterested manner) the fact that the old colonial system was not 'saved' by judicious nick-of-time concessions.[32] Aggrieved by one fact, they neglect another: that the Haitians, poor and misruled as they may well have been, have inherited a priceless and irreplaceable treasure: the love of freedom.[33] Alfred Métraux informs me that, today, the average Haitian peasant *does not even remember that his ancestors were slaves*. As Professor Revert writes, 'Haiti is free. . . . It has a future.'[34] And the Haitian novelist Jacques Stephen Alexis confirms it: 'In spite of everything, the people sing, they laugh.'[35] Haiti may trail far behind the other West Indies in so far as material values are concerned, but with regard to spiritual values she is doubtless in first place. Haiti is the one Caribbean territory where I for one did not find a depressing atmosphere. I came into touch with a people in rags, yes, but overflowing with vitality and verve and personality, and the impression I had was of cheerfulness. I sensed nothing of the sort anywhere else.

Nearly two decades of American military occupation only intensified this love of freedom. The oppression, ham-fisted and cruel, lasted from 1915 to 1934, and gave birth to a national liberation movement where bourgeois rubbed elbows with revolutionaries. Jacques Roumain won his first political spurs in the resistance. In 1929–30, after a sensational trial which had enormous repercussions and during which his blood literally flowed in the courtroom, Roumain was sentenced to prison for something he had written in the Press. In 1934, the same year as the Americans evacuated Haiti, he broke with the bourgeois nationalists and founded the Haitian Communist Party. Judged by a military tribunal, he was sentenced to three years in jail. He came out, his health broken, and died prematurely in 1945, shortly before the second awakening of Haitian political consciousness.[36]

It was, as a matter of fact, on January 7, 1946 that a students' strike gave the signal for an uprising against the unpopular government of President Lescot, the mulatto élite's creature. The movement had been prepared and directed by a 'Unified Democratic Front' in which liberal politicians and violently racist anti-mulatto Negroes stood side by side with unionized workers and Marxists. But this embryonic revolution was quickly nipped in the bud by a junta of Negro officers. A compromise was eventually worked out between the civil and military elements; it paved the way for the accession, in August, of Dumarsais Estimé to the presidency. The régime he inaugurated was distinctly progressive. The while battling against colour bigotry and endeavouring to restore the Negro's prestige, he helped the working classes (for the first time in Haitian history) to realize some of their objectives. He tolerated—and even encouraged—a flowering of trade unions and of political parties with socialist leanings. But, seconded by Uncle Sam, the propertied class (Negroes and mulattos who had composed their differences to unite against the Marxist *avant-garde* and the intransigent Negro racists) grew worried about the rather too radical turn the Estimé administration was taking. Under their pressure, the President, in 1949, had to swing sharply against the left—had to dissolve the parties, to ban the newspapers. But these concessions were judged insufficient by the junta and, in 1950, it deposed the presidential puppet and replaced him with one of their number, Colonel (later General) Paul Magloire.[37] Magloire subjected Haiti to an ironclad military dictatorship: all of the leftist parties have been outlawed, their newspapers silenced, the leftist Press smashed, leftist leadership hunted or jailed, the trade unions tamed. While I was in Haiti, on April 12, 1955 I heard the President go on the air and the state radio's broadcasting system brought us bellowed imprecations and horrible threats aimed against a gagged opposition. But the spirit of the January 7, 1946 revolution was not dead, it stole abroad in disguise, lived on in silence and only awaited the propitious moment to manifest itself openly once again.

It did in December 1956. The military dictator had long been unpopular, and had only maintained himself in power thanks to the support he received from the United States. That support finally failed when his money-lenders one day noticed that no appreciable results had been obtained from the thirty million dollars which, in theory, had been invested in a hydro-electric project and which, actually, had gone into the pockets and Swiss bank accounts of Magloire and his clique. The American creditors called for a reckoning; they did not obtain satisfaction. Deprived of their backing, the General was revealed as a bedraggled marionette suspended in mid-air. Nevertheless, and in violation of the constitution, he undertook to have his presidential mandate (expiring on December 6) renewed. Whereupon a general strike of merchants, workers and students paralysed the capital and annihilated Magloire's ambitions.

All that remained was for a few young officers, machine-guns in hand, to ferret the dictator from his palace and load him aboard an aeroplane heading for Jamaica. Since then the Republic of Haiti has passed through a period of instability and confusion; but there are hopes that the spirit of the January 7, 1946 revolution has not been extinguished.

Notes

1. Blanchard, Paul, *Democracy and Empire in the Caribbean*, New York, 1947, p. 57.

2. Hart, Richard, *The National Movement Forward to Freedom*, Kingston, Jamaica, 1925, p. 17.

3. Blanchard, *op. cit.*, p. 57.

4. Oulié, Marthe, *Les Antilles Filles de France*, Paris, 1935, p. 131.

5. Fanon, F., "Antillais et Africains," *Espirit*, Paris, February, 1955.

6. Breton, André and André Masson, *Martinique charmeuse de serpents*, Paris, 1948: Lévi-Strauss, Claude, *Tristes Tropiques*, Paris, 1956.

7. Fermore, Patrick Leigh, *The Traveller's Tree*, London, 1950, p. 29.

8. Blanchard, *op. cit.*, pp. 252, 256, 263.

9. Fanon, 'Antillais . . .', *op. cit.*, p. 267.

10. *Le Monde*, Paris, January 19, 1954.

11. *Justice*, Fort-de-France, Martinique, March 24, 1955.

12. Revert, *La Martinique*, p. 450.

13. Césaire, Assemblée Nationale, *Journal Officiel*, Paris, March 27, 1954, p. 1317.

14. Cf. Auger, *L'Observateur d'aujourd'hui*, Paris, December 17, 1953.

15. Rousseau Nadir, Henri, *Réalitiés Coloniales*, Paris, 1954, pp. 46–47.

16. *Le Monde*, Paris, February 17, 1956.

17. Macmillan, W. M., *Warning from the West Indies*, London, Penguin Books, 1938, p. 98; Cumper, George, *The Social Structure of Jamaica*, Kingston, Jamaica, undated, p. 17.

18. *Ibid.*, pp. 22–23.

19. Kerr, Madeleine, *Personality and Conflict in Jamaica*, Liverpool, 1952, p. 159; Makin, William J., *Caribbean Nights*, London, 1939, *passim*.

20. Mais, Roger, *The Hills Were Joyful Together*, London, 1953.

21. Cf. *Public Opinion*, Kingston, Jamaica, March 3, 1952; Hart, *op. cit.*; Padmore, George, *Pan-Africanism or Communism?*, London, 1956, p. 344.

22. James, C. L. R., *History of Negro Revolt*, London, 1938, p. 75.

23. Cf. Guérin, Daniel, *Au Service des Colonisés*, Paris, 1954, pp. 160–166.

24. James, C. L. R., *The Life of Captain Cipriani*, Port of Spain, Trinidad, 1932.

25. Arthur Lewis, *Labour in the West Indies*. London, 1939, p. 19.

26. James, *History . . .*, pp. 77–79; Lewis, *Labour . . .*, pp. 21–24; Blanchard, *op. cit.*, pp. 23–24.

27. Wright, *The Colour Curtain*, p. 137.

28. *People's National Movement, Election Manifesto*, September 24, 1956.

29. Blanchard, *op. cit.*, pp. 25, 151–154.

30. Charlier, Étienne D., *Aperçu sur la formation historique de la nation haïtienne*, Port-au-Prince, Haiti, 1954.

31. Leyburn, James G., *The Haitian People*, London, 1941, *passim*.

32. Cf. Viatte, Auguste, "Saint-Domingue pouvait être sauvée," *Le Monde*, Paris, August 9, 1955.

33. Leyburn, *op. cit., passim.*

34. Revert, *Les Antilles,* p. 58.

35. Alexis, Jacques Stephen, *Compère général Soleil,* Paris, 1955.

36. Jacques Roumain, *Analyse Schématique,* Port-au-Prince, 1934, pp. 1–2; biographical sketch prefixed to *Gouverneurs de la Rosée,* Paris, 1950.

37. Cf. Rodman, Selden, *Haiti: The Black Republic,* New York, 1954, pp. 28–31; Charlier, "Analyse Étienne, Schématique de la crise de 1946," *La Nation,* Port-au-Prince, December 18–23, 1950.

Robert Blauner
INTERNAL COLONIALISM
AND GHETTO REVOLT

It is becoming almost fashionable to analyze American racial conflict today in terms of the colonial analogy. I shall argue in this paper that the utility of this perspective depends upon a distinction between colonization as a process and colonialism as a social, economic, and political system. It is the experience of colonization that Afro-Americans share with many of the non-white people of the world. But this subjugation has taken place in a societal context that differs in important respects from the situation of "classical colonialism." In the body of this essay I shall look at some major developments in Black protest—the urban riots, cultural nationalism, and the movement for ghetto control—as collective responses to colonized status. Viewing our domestic situation as a special form of colonization outside a context of a colonial system will help explain some of the dilemmas and ambiguities within these movements.

The present crisis in American life has brought about changes in social perspectives and the questioning of long accepted frameworks. Intellectuals and social scientists have been forced by the pressure of events to look at old definitions of the character of our society, the role of racism, and the workings of basic institutions. The depth and volatility of contemporary racial conflict challenge sociologists in particular to question the adequacy of theoretical models by which we have explained American race relations in the past.

For a long time the distinctiveness of the Negro situation among the ethnic minorities was placed in terms of color, and the systematic discrimination that follows from our deep-seated racial prejudices. This was sometimes called the caste theory, and while provocative, it missed essential and dynamic features of American race relations. In the past ten years there has been a tendency to view Afro-Americans as another ethnic group not basically different in experience from previous ethnics and whose "immigration" condition in the North would in time follow their upward course. The inadequacy of this model is now clear—even the Kerner Report devotes a chapter to criticizing this analogy. A more recent (though hardly new) approach views the essence of racial subordination in economic class terms: Black people as an underclass are to a degree specially exploited and to a degree economically dispensable in an automating society. Important as are economic factors, the power of race and racism in America cannot be sufficiently explained through class analysis. Into this theory

REPRINTED FROM *Social Problems*, VOL. 16, 1969 BY PERMISSION OF THE SOCIETY FOR THE STUDY OF SOCIAL PROBLEMS AND THE AUTHOR.[1]

vacuum steps the model of internal colonialism. Problematic and imprecise as it is, it gives hope of becoming a framework that can integrate the insights of caste and racism, ethnicity, culture, and economic exploitation into an overall conceptual scheme. At the same time, the danger of the colonial model is the imposition of an artificial analogy which might keep us from facing up to the fact (to quote Harold Cruse) that "the American black and white social phenomenon is a uniquely new world thing."[2]

During the late 1950's, identification with African nations and other colonial or formerly colonized peoples grew in importance among Black militants.[3] As a result the U. S. was increasingly seen as a colonial power and the concept of domestic colonialism was introduced into the political analysis and rhetoric of militant nationalists. During the same period Black social theorists began developing this frame of reference for explaining American realities. As early as 1962, Cruse characterized race relations in this country as "domestic colonialism."[4] Three years later in *Dark Ghetto*, Kenneth Clark demonstrated how the political, economic, and social structure of Harlem was essentially that of a colony.[5] Finally in 1967, a full-blown elaboration of "internal colonialism" provided the theoretical framework for Carmichael and Hamilton's widely read *Black Power*.[6] The following year the colonial analogy gained currency and new "respectability" when Senator McCarthy habitually referred to Black Americans as a colonized people during his campaign. While the rhetoric of internal colonialism was catching on, other social scientists began to raise questions about its appropriateness as a scheme of analysis.

The colonial analysis has been rejected as obscurantist and misleading by scholars who point to the significant differences in history and social-political conditions between our domestic patterns and what took place in Africa and India. Colonialism traditionally refers to the establishment of domination over a geographically external political unit, most often inhabited by people of a different race and culture, where this domination is political and economic, and the colony exists subordinated to and dependent upon the mother country. Typically the colonizers exploit the land, the raw materials, the labor, and other resources of the colonized nation; in addition a formal recognition is given to the difference in power, autonomy, and political status, and various agencies are set up to maintain this subordination. Seemingly the analogy must be stretched beyond usefulness if the American version is to be forced into this model. For here we are talking about group relations within a society; the mother country—colony separation in geography is absent. Though whites certainly colonized the territory of the original Americans, internal colonization of Afro-Americans did not involve the settlement of whites in any land that was unequivocally Black. And unlike the colonial situation, there has been no formal recognition of differing power since slavery was abolished outside the South. Classic colonialism involved the control and exploitation of the majority of a nation by a minority of outsiders. Whereas in America the people who are oppressed were themselves originally outsiders and are a numerical minority.

This conventional critique of "internal colonialism" is useful in pointing to the differences between our domestic patterns and the overseas situation. But in its bold attack it tends to lose sight of common experiences that have been historically shared by the most subjugated racial minorities in America and non-white peoples in some other parts of the world. For understanding the most dramatic recent developments on the race scene, this common core element—which I shall call colonization—may be more important than the undeniable divergences between the two contexts.

The common features ultimately relate to the fact that the classical colonialism of the imperialist era and American racism developed out of the same historical situation and reflected a common world economic and power stratification. The slave trade for the most part preceded the imperialist partition and economic exploitation of Africa, and in fact may have been a necessary prerequisite for colonial conquest—since it helped deplete and pacify Africa, undermining the resistance to direct occupation. Slavery contributed one of the basic raw materials for the textile industry which provided much of the capital for the West's industrial development and need for economic expansionism. The essential condition for both American slavery and European colonialism was the power domination and the technological superiority of the Western world in its relation to peoples of non-Western and non-white origins. This objective supremacy in technology and military power buttressed the West's sense of cultural superiority, laying the basis for racist ideologies that were elaborated to justify control and exploitation of non-white people. Thus because classical colonialism and America's internal version developed out of a similar balance of technological, cultural, and power relations, a common *process* of social oppression characterized the racial patterns in the two contexts—despite the variation in political and social structure.

There appear to be four basic components of the colonization complex. The first refers to how the racial group enters into the dominant society (whether colonial power or not). Colonization begins with a forced, involuntary entry. Second, there is an impact on the culture and social organization of the colonized people which is more than just a result of such "natural" processes as contact and acculturation. The colonizing power carries out a policy which constrains, transforms, or destroys indigenous values, orientations, and ways of life. Third, colonization involves a relationship by which members of the colonized group tend to be administered by representatives of the dominant power. There is an experience of being managed and manipulated by outsiders in terms of ethnic status.

A final fundament of colonization is racism. Racism is a principle of social domination by which a group seen as inferior or different in terms of alleged biological characteristics is exploited, controlled, and oppressed socially and psychically by a superordinate group. Except for the marginal case of Japanese imperialism, the major examples of colonialism have involved the subjugation of non-white Asian, African, and Latin American peoples by white European powers. Thus racism has generally accompanied colonialism. Race prejudice can exist without colonization—the experience of Asian-American minorities is a case in point—but racism as a system of domination is part of the complex of colonization.

The concept of colonization stresses the enormous fatefulness of the historical factor, namely the manner in which a minority group becomes a part of the dominant society.[7] The crucial difference between the colonized Americans an dthe ethnic immigrant minorities is that the latter have always been able to operate fairly competitively within that relatively open section of the social and economic order because these groups came voluntarily in search of a better life, because their movements in society were not administratively controlled, and because they transformed their culture at their own pace—giving up ethnic values and institutions when it was seen as a desirable exchange for improvements in social position.

In present-day America, a major device of Black colonization is the powerless ghetto. As Kenneth Clark describes the situation:

> Ghettoes are the consequence of the imposition of external power and the institutionalization of powerlessness. In this respect, they are in fact social, political, educational, and above all—economic colonies. Those confined within the ghetto walls are subject peoples. They are victims of the greed, cruelty, insensitivity, guilt and fear of their masters. . . .
>
> The community can best be described in terms of the analogy of a powerless colony. Its political leadership is divided, and all but one or two of its political leaders are shortsighted and dependent upon the larger political power structure. Its social agencies are financially precarious and dependent upon sources of support outside the community. Its churches are isolated or dependent. Its economy is dominated by small businesses which are largely owned by absentee owners, and its tenements and other real property are also owned by absentee landlords.
>
> Under a system of centralization, Harlem's schools are controlled by forces outside of the community. Programs and policies are supervised and determined by individuals who do not live in the community . . .[8]

Of course many ethnic groups in America have lived in ghettoes. What make the Black ghettoes an expression of colonized status are three special features. First, the ethnic ghettoes arose more from voluntary choice, both in the sense of the choice to immigrate to America and the decision to live among one's fellow ethnics. Second, the immigrant ghettoes tended to be a one and two generation phenomenon; they were actually way-stations in the process of acculturation and assimilation. When they continue to persist as in the case of San Francisco's Chinatown, it is because they are big business for the ethnics themselves and there is a new stream of immigrants. The Black ghetto on the other hand has been a more permanent phenomenon, although some individuals do escape it. But most relevant is the third point. European ethnic groups like the Poles, Italians, and Jews generally only experienced a brief period, often less than a generation, during which their residential buildings, commercial stores, and other enterprises were owned by outsiders. The Chinese and Japanese faced handicaps of color prejudice that were almost as strong as the Blacks faced, but very soon gained control of their internal communities, because their traditional ethnic culture and social organization had not been destroyed by slavery and internal colonization. But Afro-Americans are distinct in the extent to which their segregated communities have remained controlled economically, politically, and administratively from the outside. One indicator of this difference is the estimate that the "income of Chinese-Americans from Chinese-owned businesses is in proportion to their numbers 45 times as great as the income of Negroes from Negro owned businesses."[9] But what is true of business is also true for the other social institutions that operate within the ghetto. The educators, policemen, social workers, politicians, and others who administer the affairs of ghetto residents are typically whites who live outside the Black community. Thus the ghetto plays a strategic role as the focus for the administration by outsiders which is also essential to the structure of overseas colonialism.[10]

The colonial status of the Negro community goes beyond the issue of ownership and decision-making within Black neighborhoods. The Afro-American population in most cities has very little influence on the power structure and institutions of the larger metropolis, despite the fact that in numerical terms, Blacks tend to be the most sizeable of the various interest groups. A recent analysis of policy-making in Chicago estimates that "Negroes really hold less than 1 percent of the effective power in the Chicago metropolitan area. [Negroes are 20 percent of Cook County's population.] Realistically the power structure of Chicago is hardly less white than that of Mississippi."[11]

Colonization outside of a traditional colonial structure has its own special conditions. The group culture and social structure of the colonized in America is less developed; it is also less autonomous. In addition, the colonized are a numerical minority, and furthermore they are ghettoized more totally and are more dispersed than people under classic colonialism. Though these realities affect the magnitude and direction of response, it is my basic thesis that the most important expressions of protest in the Black community during the recent years reflect the colonized status of Afro-America. Riots, programs of separation, politics of community control, the Black revolutionary movements, and cultural nationalism each represent a different strategy of attack on domestic colonialism in America. Let us now examine some of these movements.

RIOT OR REVOLT?

The so-called riots are being increasingly recognized as a preliminary if primitive form of mass rebellion against a colonial status. There is still a tendency to absorb their meaning within the conventional scope of assimilation-integration politics: some commentators stress the material motives involved in looting as a sign that the rioters want to join America's middle-class affluence just like everyone else. That motives are mixed and often unconscious, that Black people want good furniture and television sets like whites is beside the point. The guiding impulse in most major outbreaks has not been integration with American society, but an attempt to stake out a sphere of control by moving against that society and destroying the symbols of its oppression.

In my critique of the McCone report I observed that the rioters were asserting a claim to territoriality, an unorganized and rather inchoate attempt to gain control over their community or "turf."[12] In succeeding disorders also the thrust of the action has been the attempt to clear out an alien presence, white men and officials, rather than a drive to kill whites as in a conventional race riot. The main attacks have been directed at the property of white business men and at the police who operate in the Black community "like an army of occupation" protecting the interests of outside exploiters and maintaining the domination over the ghetto by the central metropolitan power structure.[13] The Kerner report misleads when it attempts to explain riots in terms of integration: "What the rioters appear to be seeking was fuller participation in the social order and the material benefits enjoyed by the majority of American citizens. Rather than rejecting the American system, they were anxious to obtain a place for themselves in it."[14] More accurately, the revolts pointed to alienation from this system on the part of many poor and also not-so-poor Blacks. The sacredness of private property, that unconsciously accepted bulwark of our social arrangements, was rejected; people who looted apparently without guilt generally remarked that they were taking things that "really belonged" to them anyway.[15] Obviously the society's bases of legitimacy and authority have been attacked. Law and order has long been viewed as the white man's law and order by Afro-Americans; but now this perspective characteristic of a colonized people is out in the open. And the Kerner Report's own data question how well ghetto rebels are buying the system: In Newark only 33 percent of self-reported rioters said they thought this country was worth fighting for in the event of a major war; in the Detroit sample the figure was 55 percent.[16]

One of the most significant consequences of the process of colonization is a weakening of the colonized's individual and collective will to resist his oppression. It has been easier to contain and control Black ghettoes because communal bonds and group solidarity have been weakened through divisions among leadership, failures of organization, and a general disspiritment that accompanies social oppression. The riots are a signal that the will to resist has broken the mold of accommodation. In some cities as in Watts they also represented nascent movements toward community identity. In several riot-torn ghettoes the outbursts have stimulated new organizations and movements. If it is true that the riot phenomenon of 1964-68 has passed its peak, its historical import may be more for the "internal" organizing momentum generated than for any profound "external" response of the larger society facing up to underlying causes.

Despite the appeal of Frantz Fanon to young Black revolutionaries, America is not Algeria. It is difficult to foresee how riots in our cities can play a role equivalent to rioting in the colonial situation as an integral phase in a movement for national liberation. In 1968 some militant groups (for example, the Black Panther Party in Oakland) had concluded that ghetto riots were self-defeating of the lives and interests of Black people in the present balance of organization and gunpower, though they had served a role to stimulate both Black consciousness and white awareness of the depths of racial crisis. Such militants have been influential in "cooling" their communities during periods of high riot potential. Theoretically oriented Black radicals see riots as spontaneous mass behavior which must be replaced by a revolutionary organization and consciousness. But despite the differences in objective conditions, the violence of the 1960's seems to serve the same psychic function, assertions of dignity and manhood for young Blacks in urban ghettoes, as it did for the colonized of North Africa described by Fanon and Memmi.[17]

CULTURAL NATIONALISM

Cultural conflict is generic to the colonial relation because colonization involves the domination of Western technological values over the more communal cultures of non-Western peoples. Colonialism played havoc with the national integrity of the peoples it brought under its sway. Of course, all traditional cultures are threatened by industrialism, the city, and modernization in communication, transportation, health, and education. What is special are the political and administrative decisions of colonizers in managing and controlling colonized peoples. The boundaries of African colonies, for example, were drawn to suit the political conveniences of the European nations without regard to the social organization and cultures of African tribes and kingdoms. Thus Nigeria as blocked out by the British included the Yorubas and the Ibos, whose civil war today is a residuum of the colonialist's disrespect for the integrity of indigenous cultures.

The most total destruction of culture in the colonization process took place not in traditional colonialism but in America. As Frazier stressed, the integral cultures of the diverse African peoples who furnished the slave trade were destroyed because slaves from different tribes, kingdoms, and linguistic groups were purposely separated to maximize domination and control. Thus language, religion, and national loyalties were lost in North America much more completely than in the Caribbean and Brazil where slavery developed somewhat differently. Thus on this key point America's internal colonization has been more total and extreme than situations of classic colonialism. For the British in India and the European powers in Africa were not able—as outnumbered minorities—to destroy the national and tribal cultures of the colonized. Recall that American slavery lasted 250 years and its racist aftermath another 100. Colonial dependency in the case of British Kenya and French Algeria lasted only 77 and 125 years respectively. In the wake of this more drastic uprooting and destruction of culture and social organization, much more powerful agencies of social, political, and psychological domination developed in the American case.

> Colonial control of many peoples inhabiting the colonies was more a goal than a fact, and at Independence there were undoubtedly fairly large numbers of Africans who had never seen a colonial administrator. The gradual process of extension of control from the administrative center on the African coast contrasts sharply with the total uprooting involved in the slave trade and the totalitarian aspects of slavery in the United States. Whether or not Elkins is correct in treating slavery as a total institution, it undoubtedly had a far more radical and pervasive impact on American slaves than did colonialism on the vast majority of Africans.[18]

Yet a similar cultural process unfolds in both contexts of colonialism. To the extent that they are involved in the larger society and economy, the colonized are caught up in a conflict between two cultures. Fanon has described how the assimilation-oriented schools of Martinique taught him to reject his own culture and Blackness in favor of Westernized, French, and white values.[19] Both the colonized elites under traditional colonialism and perhaps the majority of Afro-Americans today experience a parallel split in identity, cultural loyalty, and political orientation.[20]

The colonizers use their culture to socialize the colonized elites (intellectuals, politicians, and middle class) into an identification with the colonial system. Because Western culture has the prestige, the power, and the key to open the limited opportunity that a minority of the colonized may achieve, the first reaction seems to be an acceptance of the dominant values. Call it brainwashing as the Black Muslims put it; call it identifying with the aggressor if you prefer Freudian terminology; call it a natural response to the hope and belief that integration and democratization can really take place if you favor a more commonsense explanation, this initial acceptance in time crumbles on the realities of racism and colonialism. The colonized, seeing that his success within colonialism is at the expense of his group and his own inner identity, moves radically toward a rejection of the Western culture and develops a nationalist outlook that celebrates his people and their traditions. As Memmi describes it:

> Assimilation being abandoned, the colonized's liberation must be carried out through a recovery of self and of autonomous dignity. Attempts at imitating the colonizer required self-denial; the colonizer's rejection is the indispensible prelude to self-discovery. That accusing and annihilating image must be shaken off; oppression must be attacked

boldly since it is impossible to go around it. After having been rejected for so long by the colonizer, the day has come when it is the colonized who must refuse the colonizer.[21]

Memmi's book, *The Colonizer and the Colonized*, is based on his experience as a Tunisian Jew in a marginal position between the French and the colonized Arab majority. The uncanny parallels between the North African situation he describes and the course of Black-white relations in our society is the best impressionist argument I know for the thesis that we have a colonized group and a colonizing system in America. His discussion of why even the most radical French anti-colonialist cannot participate in the struggle of the colonized is directly applicable to the situation of the white liberal and radical vis-à-vis the Black movement. His portrait of the colonized is as good an analysis of the psychology behind Black Power and Black nationalism as anything that has been written in the U.S. Consider for example:

> Considered *en bloc* as *them, they,* or *those,* different from every point of view, homogeneous in a radical heterogeneity, the colonized reacts by rejecting all the colonizers *en bloc.* The distinction between deed and intent has no great significance in the colonial situation. In the eyes of the colonized, all Europeans in the colonies are de facto colonizers, and whether they want to be or not, they are colonizers in some ways. By their privileged economic position, by belonging to the political system of oppression, or by participating in an effectively negative complex toward the colonized, they are colonizers. . . . They are supporters or at least unconscious accomplices of that great collective aggression of Europe.[22]
>
> The same passion which made him admire and absorb Europe shall make him assert his differences; since those differences, after all, are within him and correctly constitute his true self.[23]
>
> The important thing now is to rebuild his people, whatever be their authentic nature; to reforge their unity, communicate with it, and to feel that they belong.[24]

Cultural revitalization movements play a key role in anti-colonial movements. They follow an inner necessity and logic of their own that comes from the consequences of colonialism on groups and personal identities; they are also essential to provide the solidarity which the political or military phase of the anti-colonial revolution requires. In the U.S. an Afro-American culture has been developing since slavery out of the ingredients of African world-views, the experience of bondage, Southern values and customs, migration and the Northern lower-class ghettoes, and most importantly, the political history of the Black population in its struggle against racism.[25] That Afro-Americans are moving toward cultural nationalism in a period when ethnic loyalties tend to be weak (and perhaps on the decline) in this country is another confirmation of the unique colonized position of the Black group. (A similar nationalism seems to be growing among American Indians and Mexican-Americans.)

THE MOVEMENT FOR GHETTO CONTROL

The call for Black Power unites a number of varied movements and tendencies.[26] Though no clear-cut program has yet emerged, the most important emphasis seems to be the movement for control of the ghetto. Black leaders and organizations are increasingly concerned with owning and controlling those institutions that exist within or impinge upon their community. The colonial model provides a key to the understanding of this movement, and indeed ghetto control advocates have increasingly invoked the language of colonialism in pressing for local home rule. The framework of anti-colonialism explains why the struggle for poor people's or community control of poverty programs has been more central in many cities than the content of these programs and why it has been crucial to exclude whites from leadership positions in Black organizations.

The key institutions that anti-colonialists want to take over or control are business, social services, schools, and the police. Though many spokesmen have advocated the exclusion of white landlords and small businessmen from the ghetto, this program has evidently not struck fire with the Black population and little concrete movement toward economic expropriation has yet developed. Welfare recipients have organized in many cities to protect their rights and gain a greater voice in the decisions that affect them, but whole communities have not yet been able to mount direct action against welfare colonialism. Thus schools and the police seem now to be the burning issues of ghetto control politics.

During the past few years there has been a dramatic shift from educational integration as the primary goal to that of community control of the schools. Afro-Americans are demanding their own school boards, with the power to hire and fire principals and teachers and to construct a curriculum which would be relevant to the special needs and culture style of ghetto youth. Especially active in high schools and colleges have been Black students, whose protests have centered on the incorporation of Black Power and Black culture into the educational system. Consider how similar is the spirit behind these developments to the attitude of the colonized North African toward European education:

> He will prefer a long period of educational mistakes to the continuance of the colonizer's school organization. He will choose institutional disorder in order to destroy the institutions built by the colonizer as soon as possible. There we will see, indeed a reactive drive of profound protest. He will no longer owe anything to the colonizer and will have definitely broken with him.[27]

Protest and institutional disorder over the issue of school control came to a head in 1968 in New York City. The procrastination in the Albany State legislature, the several crippling strikes called by the teachers union, and the almost frenzied response of Jewish organizations makes it clear that decolonization of education faces the resistance of powerful vested interests.[28] The situation is too dynamic at present to assess probable future results. However, it can be safely predicted that some form of school decentralization will be institutionalized in New York, and the movement for community control of education will spread to more cities.

This movement reflects some of the problems and ambiguities that stem from the situation of colonization outside an immediate colonial context. The Afro-American community is not parallel in structure to the communities of colonized nations under traditional colonialism. The significant difference here is the lack of fully developed indigenous institutions besides the church. Outside of some areas of the South there is really no Black economy, and most Afro-Americans are inevitably caught up in the larger society's structure of occupations, education, and mass communication. Thus the ethnic nationalist orientation which reflects the reality of colonization exists alongside an integrationist orientation which corresponds to the reality that the institutions of the larger society are much more developed than those of the incipient nation.[29] As would be expected the movement for school control reflects both tendencies. The militant leaders who spearhead such local movements may be primarily motivated by the desire to gain control over the community's institutions—they are anti-colonialists first and foremost. Many parents who support them may share this goal also, but the majority are probably more concerned about creating a new education that will enable their children to "make it" in the society and the economy as a whole—they know that the present school system fails ghetto children and does not prepare them for participation in American life.

There is a growing recognition that the police are the most crucial institution maintaining the colonized status of Black Americans. And of all establishment institutions, police departments probably include the highest proportion of individual racists. This is no accident since central to the workings of racism (an essential component of colonization) are attacks on the humanity and dignity of the subject group. Through their normal routines the police constrict Afro-Americans to Black neighborhoods by harassing and questioning them when found outside the ghetto; they break up groups of youth congregating on corners or in cars without any provocation; and they continue to use offensive and racist language no matter how many inter-group understanding seminars have been built into the police academy. They also shoot to kill ghetto residents for alleged crimes such as car thefts and running from police officers.[30]

Police are key agents in the power equation as well as the drama of dehumanization. In the final analysis they do the dirty work for the larger system by restricting the striking back of Black rebels to skirmishes inside the ghetto, thus deflecting energies and attacks from the communities and institutions of the larger power structure. In a historical review, Gary Marx notes that since the French revolution, police and other authorities have killed large numbers of demonstrators and rioters; the rebellious "rabble" rarely destroys human life. The same pattern has been repeated in America's recent revolts.[31] Journalistic accounts appearing in the press recently suggest that police see themselves as defending the interests of white people against a tide of Black insurgence; furthermore the majority of whites appear to view "blue power" in this light. There is probably no other opinion on which the races are as far apart today as they are on the question of attitudes toward the police.

In many cases set off by a confrontation between a policeman and a Black citizen, the ghetto uprisings have dramatized the role of law enforcement and the issue of police brutality. In their aftermath, movements have arisen to contain police activity. One of the first was the Community Alert Patrol in Los Angeles, a method of policing the police in order to keep them honest and constrain their violations of personal dignity. This was the first tactic of the Black Panther Party which originated in Oakland, perhaps the most significant group to challenge the police role in maintaining the ghetto as a colony. The Panther's later policy of openly carrying guns (a legally protected right) and their intention of defending themselves against police aggression has brought on a series of confrontations with the Oakland police department. All indications are that the authorities intend to destroy the Panthers by shooting, framing up, or legally harassing their leadership—diverting the group's energies away from its primary purpose of self-defense and organization of the Black community to that of legal defense and gaining support in the white community.

There are three major approaches to "police colonialism" that correspond to reformist and revolutionary readings of the situation. The most elementary and also superficial sees colonialism in the fact that ghettoes are overwhelmingly patrolled by white rather than by Black officers. The proposal—supported today by many police departments—to increase the number of Blacks on local forces to something like their distribution in the city would then make it possible to reduce the use of white cops in the ghetto. This reform should be supported, for a variety of obvious reasons, but it does not get to the heart of the police role as agents of colonization.

The Kerner Report documents the fact that in some cases Black policemen can be as brutal as their white counterparts. The Report does not tell us who polices the ghetto, but they have compiled the proportion of Negroes on the forces of the major cities. In some cities the disparity is so striking that white police inevitably dominate ghetto patrols. (In Oakland 31 percent of the population and only 4 percent of the police are Black; in Detroit the figures are 39 percent and 5 percent; and in New Orleans 41 and 4.) In other cities, however, the proportion of Black cops is approaching the distribution in the city: Philadelphia 29 percent and 20 percent; Chicago 27 percent and 17 percent.[32] These figures also suggest that both the extent and the pattern of colonization may vary from one city to another. It would be useful to study how Black communities differ in degree of control over internal institutions as well as in economic and political power in the metropolitan area.

A second demand which gets more to the issue is that police should live in the communities they patrol. The idea here is that Black cops who lived in the ghetto would have to be accountable to the community; if they came on like white cops then "the brothers would take care of business" and make their lives miserable. The third or maximalist position is based on the premise that the police play no positive role in the ghettoes. It calls for the withdrawal of metropolitan officers from Black communities and the substitution of an autonomous indigenous force that would maintain order without oppressing the population. The precise relationship between such an independent police, the city and county law enforcement agencies, a ghetto governing body that would supervise and finance it, and especially the law itself is yet unclear. It is unlikely that we will soon face these problems directly as they have arisen in the case of New York's schools. Of all the programs of decolonization, police autonomy will be most resisted. It gets to the heart of how the state functions to control and contain the Black community through delegating the legitimate use of violence to police authority.

The various "Black Power" programs that are aimed at gaining control of individual ghettoes—buying up property and businesses, running the schools through community boards, taking over anti-poverty programs and other social agencies, diminishing the arbitrary power of the police— can serve to revitalize the institutions of the ghetto and build up an economic, professional, and political power base. These programs seem limited; we do not know at present if they are enough in themselves to end colonized status.[33] But they are certainly a necessary first step.

THE ROLE OF WHITES

What makes the Kerner Report a less-than-radical document is its superficial treatment of racism and its reluctance to confront the colonized relationship between Black people and the larger society. The Report emphasizes the attitudes and feelings that make up white racism, rather than the system of privilege and control which is the heart of the matter.[34] With all its discussion of the ghetto and its problems, it never faces the question of the stake that white Americans have in racism and ghettoization.

This is not a simple question, but this paper should not end with the impression that police are the major villains. All white Americans gain some privileges and advantage from the colonization of Black communities.[35] The majority of whites also lose something from this oppression and division in society. Serious research should be directed to the ways in which white individuals and institutions are tied into the ghetto. In closing let me suggest some possible parameters.

1. It is my guess that only a small minority of whites make a direct economic profit from ghetto colonization. This is hopeful in that the ouster of white businessmen may become politically feasible. Much more signifi-

cant, however, are the private and corporate interests in the land and residential property of the Black community; their holdings and influence on urban decision-making must be exposed and combated.

2. A much larger minority have occupational and professional interests in the present arrangements. The Kerner Commission reports that 1.3 million non-white men would have to be upgraded occupationally in order to make the Black job distribution roughly similar to the white. They advocate this without mentioning that 1.3 million specially privileged white workers would lose in the bargain.[36] In addition there are those professionals who carry out what Lee Rainwater has called the "dirty work" of administering the lives of the ghetto poor: the social workers, the school teachers, the urban development people, and of course the police.[37] The social problems of the Black community will ultimately be solved only by people and organizations from that community; thus the emphasis within these professions must shift toward training such a cadre of minority personnel. Social scientists who teach and study problems of race and poverty likewise have an obligation to replace themselves by bringing into the graduate schools and college faculties men of color who will become the future experts in these areas. For cultural and intellectual imperialism is as real as welfare colonialism, though it is currently screened behind such unassailable shibboleths as universalism and the objectivity of scientific inquiry.

3. Without downgrading the vested interests of profit and profession, the real nitty-gritty elements of the white stake are political power and bureaucratic security. Whereas few whites have much understanding of the realities of race relations and ghetto life, I think most give tacit or at least subconscious support for the containment and control of the Black population. Whereas most whites have extremely distorted images of Black Power, many—if not most—would still be frightened by actual Black political power. Racial groups and identities are real in American life; white Americans sense they are on top, and they fear possible reprisals or disruptions were power to be more equalized. There seems to be a paranoid fear in the white psyche of Black dominance; the belief that Black autonomy would mean unbridled license is so ingrained that such reasonable outcomes as Black political majorities and independent Black police forces will be bitterly resisted.

On this level the major mass bulwark of colonization is the administrative need for bureaucratic security so that the middle classes can go about their life and business in peace and quiet. The Black militant movement is a threat to the orderly procedures by which bureaucracies and suburbs manage their existence, and I think today there are more people who feel a stake in conventional procedures than there are those who gain directly from racism. For in their fight for institutional control, the colonized will not play by the white rules of the game. These administrative rules have kept them down and out of the system; therefore they have no necessary intention of running institutions in the image of the white middle class.

The liberal, humanist value that violence is the worst sin cannot be defended today if one is committed squarely against racism and for self-determination. For some violence is almost inevitable in the decolonization process; unfortunately racism in America has been so effective that the greatest power Afro-Americans (and perhaps also Mexican-Americans) wield today is the power to disrupt. If we are going to swing with these revolutionary times and at least respond positively to the anti-colonial movement, we will have to learn to live with conflict, confrontation, constant change, and what may be real or apparent chaos and disorder.

A positive response from the white majority needs to be in two major directions at the same time. First, community liberation movements should be supported in every way by pulling out white instruments of direct control and exploitation and substituting technical assistance to the community when this is asked for. But it is not enough to relate affirmatively to the nationalist movement for ghetto control without at the same time radically opening doors for full participation in the institutions of the mainstream. Otherwise the liberal and radical position is little different than the traditional segregationist. Freedom in the special conditions of American colonization means that the colonized must have the choice between participation in the larger society and in their own independent structures.

Notes

1. This is a revised version of a paper delivered at the University of California Centennial Program, "Studies in Violence," Los Angeles, June 1, 1968. For criticisms and ideas that have improved an earlier draft, I am indebted to Robert Wood, Lincoln Bergman, and Gary Marx. As a good colonialist I have probably restated (read: stolen) more ideas from the writings of Kenneth Clark, Stokely Carmichael, Frantz Fanon, and especially such contributors to the Black Panther Party (Oakland) newspaper as Huey Newton, Bobby Seale, Eldridge Cleaver, and Kathleen Cleaver than I have appropriately credited or generated myself. In self-defense I should state that I began working somewhat independently on a colonial analysis of American race relations in the fall of 1965; see my "Whitewash Over Watts: The Failure of the McCone Report," *Trans-action*, 3 (March-April, 1966), pp. 3–9, 54.

2. Harold Cruse, *Rebellion or Revolution*, New York: 1968, p. 214.

3. Nationalism, including an orientation toward Africa, is no new development. It has been a constant tendency within Afro-American politics. See Cruse, *ibid.*, esp. chaps. 5–7.

4. This was six years before the publication of *The Crisis of the Negro Intellectual*, New York: Morrow, 1968, which brought Cruse into prominence. Thus the 1962 article was not widely read until its reprinting in Cruse's essays, *Rebellion or Revolution, op. cit.*

5. Kenneth Clark, *Dark Ghetto*, New York: Harper and Row, 1965. Clark's analysis first appeared a year earlier in *Youth in the Ghetto*, New York: Haryou Associates, 1964.

6. Stokely Carmichael and Charles Hamilton, *Black Power*, New York: Random, 1967.

7. As Eldridge Cleaver reminds us, "Black people are a stolen people held in a colonial status on stolen land, and any analysis which does not acknowledge the

colonial status of black people cannot hope to deal with the real problem." "The Land Question," *Ramparts,* 6 (May, 1968), p. 51.

8. *Youth in the Ghetto, op. cit.,* pp. 10–11; 79–80.

9. N. Glazer and D. P. Moynihan, *Beyond the Melting Pot,* Cambridge, Mass.: M.I.T., 1963, p. 37.

10. "When we speak of Negro social disabilities under capitalism, . . . we refer to the fact that he does not own anything—*even what is ownable in his own community.* Thus to fight for black liberation *is to fight for his right to own.* The Negro is politically compromised today because he owns nothing. He has little voice in the affairs of state because he owns nothing. The fundamental reason why the Negro bourgeois-democratic revolution has been aborted is because American capitalism has prevented the development of a black class of capitalist owners of institutions and economic tools. To take one crucial example, Negro radicals today are severely hampered in their tasks of educating the black masses on political issues because Negroes do not own any of the necessary means of propaganda and communication. The Negro owns no printing presses, he has no stake in the networks of the means of communication. Inside his own communities he does not own the house he lives in, the property he lives on, nor the wholesale and retail sources from which he buys his commodities. He does not own the edifices in which he enjoys culture and entertainment or in which he socializes. In capitalist society, an individual or group that does not own anything is powerless." H. Cruse, "Behind the Black Power Slogan," in Cruse, *Rebellion or Revolution, op. cit.,* pp. 238–39.

11. Harold M. Baron, "Black Powerlessness in Chicago," *Trans-action,* 6 (Nov., 1968), pp. 27–33.

12. R. Blauner, "Whitewash Over Watts," *op. cit.*

13. "The police function to support and enforce the interests of the dominant political, social, and economic interests of the town" is a statement made by a former police scholar and official, according to A. Neiderhoffer, *Behind the Shield,* New York: Doubleday, 1967 as cited by Gary T. Marx, "Civil Disorder and the Agents of Control," *Journal of Social Issues,* forthcoming.

14. Report of the National Advisory Commission on Civil Disorders, N.Y.: Bantam, March, 1968, p. 7.

15. This kind of attitude has a long history among American Negroes. During slavery, Blacks used the same rationalization to justify stealing from their masters. Appropriating things from the master was viewed as *"taking* part of his property for the benefit of another part; whereas *stealing* referred to appropriating something from another slave, an offense that was not condoned." Kenneth Stampp, *The Peculiar Institution,* Vintage, 1956, p. 127.

16. Report of the National Advisory Commission on Civil Disorders, *op. cit.,* p. 178.

17. Frantz Fanon, *Wretched of the Earth,* New York: Grove, 1963; Albert Memmi, *The Colonizer and the Colonized,* Boston: Beacon, 1967.

18. Robert Wood, "Colonialism in Africa and America: Some Conceptual Considerations," December, 1967, unpublished paper.

19. F. Fanon, *Black Skins, White Masks,* New York: Grove, 1967.

20. Harold Cruse has described how these two themes of integration with the larger society and identification with ethnic nationality have struggled within the political and cultural movements of Negro Americans. *The Crisis of the Negro Intellectual, op. cit.*

21. Memmi, *op. cit.,* p. 128.

22. *Ibid.* p. 130.

23. *Ibid.,* p. 132.

24. *Ibid.,* p. 134.

25. In another essay, I argue against the standard sociological position that denies the existence of an ethnic Afro-American culture and I expand on the above themes. The concept of "Soul" is astonishingly parallel in content to the mystique of "Negritude" in Africa; the Pan-African culture movement has its parallel in the burgeoning Black culture mood in Afro-American communities. See "Black Culture: Myth or Reality" in Peter Rose, editor, *Americans From Africa,* Atherton, 1969.

26. Scholars and social commentators, Black and white alike, disagree in interpreting the contemporary Black Power movement. The issues concern whether this is a new development in Black protest or an old tendency revised; whether the movement is radical, revolutionary, reformist, or conservative; and whether this orientation is unique to Afro-Americans or essentially a Black parallel to other ethnic group strategies for collective mobility. For an interesting discussion of Black Power as a modernized version of Booker T. Washington's separatism and economism, see Harold Cruse, *Rebellion or Revolution, op. cit.,* pp. 193–258.

27. Memmi, *op. cit.,* pp. 137–138.

28. For the New York school conflict see Jason Epstein, "The Politics of School Decentralization," *New York Review of Books,* June 6, 1968, pp. 26–32; and "The New York City School Revolt," *ibid.,* 11, no. 6, pp. 37–41.

29. This dual split in the politics and psyche of the Black American was poetically described by Du Bois in his *Souls of Black Folk,* and more recently has been insightfully analyzed by Harold Cruse in *The Crisis of the Negro Intellectual, op. cit.* Cruse has also characterized the problem of the Black community as that of underdevelopment.

30. A recent survey of police finds "that in the predominantly Negro areas of several large cities, many of the police perceive the residents as basically hostile, especially the youth and adolescents. A lack of public support—from citizens, from courts, and from laws—is the policeman's major complaint. But some of the public criticism can be traced to the activities in which he engages day by day, and perhaps to the tone in which he enforces the "law" in the Negro neighborhoods. Most frequently he is 'called upon' to intervene in domestic quarrels and break up loitering groups. He stops and frisks two or three times as many people as are carrying dangerous weapons or are actual criminals, and almost half of these don't wish to cooperate with the policeman's efforts." Peter Rossi *et al.,* "Between Black and White—The Faces of American Institutions and the Ghetto," in Supplemental Studies for The National Advisory Commission on Civil Disorders, July 1968, p. 114.

31. "In the Gordon Riots of 1780 demonstrators destroyed property and freed prisoners, but did not seem to kill anyone, while authorities killed several hundred rioters and hung an additional 25. In the Rebellion Riots of the French Revolution, though several hundred rioters were killed, they killed no one. Up to the end of the Summer of 1967, this pattern had clearly been repeated, as police, not rioters, were responsible for most of the more than 100 deaths that have occurred. Similarly, in a related context, the more than 100 civil rights murders of recent years have been matched by almost no murders of racist whites." G. Marx, "Civil Disorders and the Agents of Social Control," *op. cit.*

32. Report of the National Advisory Commission on Civil Disorders, *op. cit.,* p. 321. That Black officers nevertheless would make a difference is suggested by data from one of the supplemental studies to the Kerner Report. They found Negro policemen working in the ghettoes considerably more sympathetic to the community and its social problems than their white counterparts. Peter Rossi *et al.,* "Between Black and White—The Faces of American Institutions in the Ghetto," *op. cit.,* chap. 6.

33. Eldridge Cleaver has called this first stage of the anti-colonial movement *community* liberation in contrast to a more long-range goal of *national* liberation. E. Cleaver, "Community Imperialism," Black Panther Party newspaper, 2 (May 18, 1968).

34. For a discussion of this failure to deal with racism, see Gary T. Marx, "Report of the National Commission: The Analysis of Disorder or Disorderly Analysis," 1968, unpublished paper.

35. Such a statement is easier to assert than to document but I am attempting the latter in a forthcoming book tentatively titled *White Racism, Black Culture,* to be published by Little Brown, 1970.

36. Report of the National Advisory Commission on Civil Disorders, *op. cit.,* pp. 253–256.

37. Lee Rainwater, "The Revolt of the Dirty-Workers," *Trans-action,* 5 (Nov., 1967), pp. 2, 64.

Robert Allen
THE DIALECTICS
OF BLACK POWER

THE POLITICS OF BLACK POWER

From Civil Rights to Black Power. The Southern-based nonviolent civil rights movement is dead. It died a victim of the intransigent U.S. racism which sparked the first fiery urban rebellions in Northern black ghettos. From the ashes of these early revolts came the angry cry of black power.

Now, that same racism, as solidly entrenched as ever, and the growing intensity and breadth of urban convulsions may be sounding the death knell of the black power movement as it has been known up until now. Repression, co-optation and deepening alienation of the urban masses has posed a crisis that has splintered the black power movement and presented an obstacle which much of the present leadership appears unable to surmount.

Among some of these leaders and spokesmen there is increasing fear that "the man" is about to apply the "final solution" to the ghettos. Others more soberly conclude that only militant black leaders and organizations are to be the targets. They expect to be jailed or assassinated and their groups disbanded or co-opted as neocolonial rulers of the troublesome natives who populate urban black colonies. A few genuine radicals, the feeling is, perhaps even the fragments of an organization, will survive to carry on the liberation struggle.

Which way any given individual or organization will go is almost anybody's guess.

Black power is and always has been a maze of contradictions, a jumble of conflicting goals and strategies. This stems in part from basic differences in ideology among black militants and partly from the contradictory status of black people in the U.S. Further, the interweaving of these two factors generated new and, to some, more confusing permutations, resulting in a latticework umbrella ambiguously labeled black power.

This confusion has deep-reaching roots. In a sense, black power may be viewed as simply the latest swing in the pendulum which marks the perennial oscillation between integration on one side and separatism-nationalism on the other. This unresolved conflict in goals has plagued the black movement since slavery days.

But black power represented an innovation in the old debate. The innovation was found in the fact that the new slogan made a nationalist appeal without employing the religious demagoguery, seen for example in

REPRINTED FROM THE *Guardian*, MAY 25, 1968 BY PERMISSION OF THE AUTHOR AND THE PUBLISHER.

the Black Muslims, which tends to alienate intellectuals and cynical young ghetto dwellers alike. Secondly, the black power movement, unlike earlier nationalist movements, ignores the question of land, whether of the back-to-Africa or five-states-in-the South variety. Thus, it avoided becoming involved in endless and diversionary hassles over how to get back to Africa or which states were suitable. Instead, it focused the attention of militants on the problem of how to achieve power in this land with the black population dispersed as it is.

The almost organic attraction which black power, like other nationalisms, held for the black masses, lay in its ability to give to ordinary black people a sense of self-worth and identity, no matter how fleeting or vague. The increasingly alienated blacks who clung to existence in the slums recognized, as many early activists did not, that the civil rights movement was intended to benefit middle-class blacks, and that integration meant assimilation into white society and the submergence of whatever separate black culture existed. But the slogan of black power coupled a conscious sense of pride in blackness with the one term which all Americans, particularly the oppressed, view as a positive value: power.

Dilemma. For the frustrated and rebellious ghetto youth, black power was at once a ray of hope and the final angry cry to be uttered when the torch was set to a white store. Stokely Carmichael, then chairman of the Student Nonviolent Coordinating Committee (SNCC), wrote in the spring of 1967 that the black power movement "could speak to the growing militancy of young black people in the urban ghetto." The difficulty is that in the ghetto hope and despair chase each other at breakneck speed in a vicious circle, creating an impulse to action which quickly turns to nihilism. This poses a grave dilemma for the radical organizer, a dilemma which has now trapped Carmichael.

To a degree black power was a reaction to the nonviolence doctrine and white paternalism which characterized the civil rights movement. As this movement came North it confronted black people living in ghettos where nonviolence is understandably equated with lack of mother wit. As it penetrated the South it encountered overt and covert enforcers of the Southern Code for whom nonviolence was not a moral force but simply red carpeting on the path to broken heads, broken bodies and dead bodies. Unable to come through with the material advancement or moral uplift it promised, the nonviolent civil rights movement became discredited.

At about the same time young black activists attacked the paternalistic aspects of that movement. They turned inward and began talking of race pride, black consciousness, black history and culture. In short, they laid the basis for the cultural nationalism which has become characteristic of the black power movement.

This, like other elements of the militant movement, has become distorted and co-opted. Natural hair-styles, African robes, shirts, dresses and sandals have become standard equipment for the well-dressed black militant. Even middle-class hipsters have gone "Afro," and a business firm advertises a hair spray especially suited for natural styles. Needless to say, much of this public display simply alienates ordinary blacks, North and South, and makes it easier for "the man" to identify budding militants.

Cultural Nationalism. This is not to imply that there is no role for cultural nationalism. Revolutionary nationalists would probably agree with imprisoned Black Panther leader Huey P. Newton's position, expressed in an interview last March:

"We believe that it's important for us to recognize our origins and to identify with the revolutionary black people of Africa and people of color throughout the world. But as far as returning, per se, to the ancient customs, we don't see any necessity in this. And also, we say that the only culture that is worth holding on to is revolutionary culture, for change, for the better."

Black power as originally articulated by SNCC in 1966 was antiracist. It attacked white paternalism, but urged whites to go into their own communities to work against institutionalized racism while black activists organized in black communities to assault the same enemy. But white activists, by and large, moved into antiwar action instead of attacking domestic racism, thus in some measure precipitating bitter tirades by black militants against the white left. On the other hand, while most serious black militants remain antiracist, some have fallen victim to the latent (and not so latent) antiwhite and antisemitic sentiments which exploitation has bred in the ghettos. For others, frustration with the white left and antiwhite sentiment have fed into each other, fueling the racism which does indeed permeate U.S. society.

Politically, the black power movement is at once reformist and radical, nationalist and internationalist, depending on the individual militant or organization in question. Even the same individual, viewing the black struggle first from one perspective and then from another, may give contradictory definitions of the term.

As originally formulated by SNCC, black power implied several things, not all of which were mutually congruent. In the broadest sense it implied black control of black communities. This control was to be exercised through economic cooperatives, election of black politicians, community control of local school boards, etc. There were calls for middle-class blacks to return to the ghettos, bringing with them their skills and resources to be made available to the community at large. This aspect is something like an idealized model of traditional ethnic politics and ethnic group assimilation into the American mainstream.

A second part of this original formulation viewed U.S. blacks as a colonized people and called for revolutionary action to implement self-determination or national liberation and the establishment of links with the third world. This was radical rhetoric, but it stood in conflict with the first conception of black power which SNCC also embraced.

At the root of this conflict, however, is the fact that the situation of black people is simultaneously like that of an ethnic subculture within U.S. society and, on the other hand, like an oppressed colony standing outside that same society. This contradiction underlies, in a real sense, many of the divisions which have developed within the black power movement. The Black Panther Party for Self Defense is perhaps the only militant group to recognize this contradiction and to attempt to deal with it in their program.

Finally, SNCC threw whites out of the organization and repudiated nonviolence as an absolute principle in implementing its new black power orientation. It was this which the bourgeois press latched onto in a hysterical way, and effectively prevented any rational discussion of black power for at least a year.

Jim Forman, head of SNCC's international affairs commission and movement strategist and theoretician, offered an explanation of this phenomenon in his pamphlet, "1967: High Tide of Black Resistance": "Not surprisingly accusations of 'extremism' and 'racism in reverse' filled the air. Those accusations reflected the fact that the slogan 'Black Power' was frightening to white Americans in general and the U.S. government in particular because of its revolutionary implications. That government knows that whites have power and blacks do not. Therefore, the idea of poor black people, especially in the cities of the United States, uniting for power on the basis of independent political action—and against the foreign wars of the United States—represented a type of revolution."

FORMULATIONS OF BLACK POWER

By the time of the Newark Black Power Conference in July, 1967, it was clear that black power meant different things to different people, and the divisions in the political spectrum which black power represented became manifest at that historic meeting.

Within this spectrum five different formulations of black power can be roughly distinguished. All of them are permeated by varying degrees of cultural nationalism, and there is a good bit of overlapping between categories. In addition, orthodox black nationalists, being a political potpourri, can be found in all five categories. Moving from the political right to the political left in this spectrum, we can distinguish:

(1) Black power as black capitalism. This is espoused, for example, by the nationalist Black Muslims who urge blacks to set up businesses, factories and independent farming operations. Whitney Young, executive director of the National Urban League, essentially endorsed this formulation in his recent call for "ghetto power." Another exponent is Dr. Thomas W. Matthew, a black neurosurgeon and president of the National Economic Growth and Reconstruction Organization (NEGRO), who in a speech Feb. 1, 1968, before a Young Americans for Freedom audience eschewed government handouts and called instead for whites to provide capital to black businessmen through loans.

The most recent supporter of black capitalism is presidential aspirant Richard M. Nixon. In a speech April 25, 1968, Nixon called for a move away from massive government-financed social welfare programs to "more black ownership, black pride, black jobs . . . black power in the most constructive sense." Black militants, according to Nixon, should seek to become capitalists—"to have a share of the wealth."

(2) Black power as more black politicians. Several years ago electoral politics was endorsed by SNCC as a means to achieving power. SNCC urged that black people organize independent parties, such as the Lowndes County (Alabama) Freedom party, which can place in office black men who will remain responsible to their people. This was ethnic politics. But it soon was distorted into integration politics. For example, the January, 1968, issue of Ebony magazine, which is integration-oriented and aimed at the black middle class, described the election of Negro mayors in Gary, Ind., and Cleveland, Ohio, as "Black power at the polls." But in those elections and their aftermaths the essential ingredients of ethnic group loyalty were missing. As militants have said time and again, "A black face in office is not black power."

In addition to these examples, electoral politics as a means of realizing black power has taken some unexpected turns, particularly in Newark. In a city with a growing black majority population but run by an Italian minority government, one has a situation comparable with the classic colonial model.

Ballot vs. Bullet. LeRoi Jones, well-known black nationalist and member of the United Brothers, Newark's black united front which is seeking control of the city, actively sought to cool out the riots which developed after the murder of Rev. Martin Luther King Jr. Jones believes that control can be won through the ballot, not the bullet.

On April 12, 1968, Jones participated in an interview with Newark police captain Charles Kinney and Anthony Imperiale, leader of a local right-wing white organization. During the interview Jones suggested that white leftists were responsible for instigating the riots. The policeman then named Students for a Democratic Society and the Newark Community Union Project (NCUP) as being behind the riots. Jones did not make this specific charge but the inference was that he agreed. Later in the interview it was suggested that Jones and Imperiale would be working together with the cops to maintain the peace.

A week later Jones elaborated on his position in an interview with the Washington Post. "Our aim is to bring about black self-government in Newark by 1970," Jones said. "We have a membership that embraces every social area in Newark. It is a wide cross-section of business, professional and political life.

"I'm in favor of black people taking power by the quickest, easiest, most successful means they can employ. Malcolm X said the ballot or the bullet. Newark is a particular situation where the ballot seems to be advantageous. I believe we have to survive. I didn't invent the white man. What we're trying to do is deal with him in the best way we can . . .

"Black men are not murderers . . . What we don't want to be are die-ers."

Jones added that he had "more respect for Imperiale, because he doesn't lie, like white liberals." Imperiale, he said, "had the mistaken understanding that we wanted to come up to his territory and do something. That was the basic clarification. We don't want to be bothered and I'm sure he doesn't want to be bothered."

White Provocateurs. From other such fragmentary evidence the explanation of Jones's new tactics appears to be complex but instructive. It should be noted parenthetically that a factor which confuses the matter further is found in unconfirmed reports, originating with neither the police, right wingers or nationalists, that certain whites actually were attempting to distribute molotov cocktails to blacks during the riots.

In Newark the opportunity exists for militant black nationalists to gain control of the city, assuming that they can avoid being wiped out by the police or right wingers. From their point of view, then, it is of crucial importance to buy time and maintain the peace until a nonviolent transfer of power can be effected, hopefully in the 1970 municipal elections. A violent confrontation right now, the nationalists might argue, would be disastrous for their young and still relatively weak organization.

In the meantime, during this period of stalemate, and with the real power of the city government and right-wing whites on the wane as their supporters emigrate from the city, every effort would be made to unify the black community around the aspiring new leaders and to eliminate potentially "disruptive" elements. Such elements may derive from two sources: independent political operations which have some black support, particularly one such as NCUP which also controls one of the city's eight antipoverty boards, and, on the other hand, groups which advocate arming and what may be regarded as premature violence against the establishment. Both sources exist in Newark and the essential question at issue is not that they are white or black; right, left or apolitical. The point is that they're working in the black community but are independent of the group which is seeking control, and because they, too, may grow in strength, unlike the white establishment, they could pose a long-term, even immediate threat.

Of course, as far as the police and Imperiale were concerned, Jones's statements were very useful since they publicly set one group of militants in the black community against another. The cops and Imperiale are also playing a waiting game: waiting to exploit what they hope is a growing rift among Newark's militant groups. But the situation is very much in flux, and it remains to be seen whether Jones will maintain the position he has taken.

What is strongly suggested when this dynamic is examined is that problems such as this may be expected to arise in other metropolitan areas

as more and more U.S. cities find themselves with black majority populations, and the struggle for power is transformed from militant rhetoric into
actual practice.

Since 1968 is a presidential election year it is natural to ask what kind
of policy black militants have adopted. The answer is that no uniform
strategy has been agreed upon. Some groups advocate abstention, others
support Socialist Workers party candidates and still others are allied with
the various Peace and Freedom party campaigns. The Black Panther party
is running Eldridge Cleaver for President. Assorted nationalist groups have
called for a write-in vote for exiled militant Robert F. Williams, and
to top matters off, comedian-activist Dick Gregory is running his own
spirited campaign.

All of this adds up to a lack of political direction which may well
make it easier for establishment politicians to co-opt many black militants.
Sen. Robert F. Kennedy was successful in getting militants in Indiana to
campaign for him, and it is not beyond the realm of possibility that one of
the major party candidates may receive the tacit or explicit support of one
of the militant national organizations.

Richard Nixon, for example, recently proclaimed a new political
alignment which includes Republicans, the "new South," "new liberals"
and black militants. According to The New York Times of May 17, Roy
Innis, associate national director of the Congress of Racial Equality,
described Nixon as the only presidential candidate who understood
black aspirations.

(3) Black power as group integration. Nathan Wright, chairman of
the Newark Black Power Conference, expressed this view most clearly in
his book, "Black Power and Urban Unrest." Wright urges black people to
band together as a group to seek entry into the American mainstream. For
example, he calls for organized efforts by blacks "to seek executive
positions in corporations, bishoprics, deanships of cathedrals, superin-
tendencies of schools, and high-management positions in banks, stores,
investment houses, legal firms, civic and government agencies and
factories." Wright's position differs from black capitalism or integration
politics in that he calls for an organized group effort, instead of individual
effort, to win entry into the American system. This might be regarded as
simply another version of ethnic politics.

(4) Black power as black control of black communities. This is the
political center of the black power spectrum and the most widely accepted
formulation. It is what SNCC, in part, originally meant by the term and
how the Congress of Racial Equality (CORE) views black power today. It
implies a group effort to seize total control of black communities from the
white governing structure and business interests.

"Black people," said Floyd McKissick, national director of CORE in a
speech July 31, 1967, outlining the group's program, "seek to control the
educational system, the political-economic system and the administration of

their own communities. They must control their own courts and their own police . . .

"Ownership of businesses in the ghetto must be transferred to black people—either individually or collectively."

The difficulty with this program is that it overlooks conflicting interests within the black community. It doesn't specify who is to control or in whose interest. Thus, it is open to co-optation by the power structure or may degenerate into black capitalism.

In the 1930s and '40s the Communist party supported black separatism under the slogan, "Self-determination in the black belt areas of Negro majority." Party theorists argued that black people formed a colony and that the fundamental task of the black liberation movement was to "complete the bourgeois-democratic revolution" (i.e., the Civil War) by forming a separate black nation in the Southern states, thus ending white domination and the semi-feudal status of Southern blacks. The party recognized that the Negro petty-bourgeois class, attempting to play the role of a black bourgeoisie or ruling class, has traditionally been the "most aggressive carrier of nationalism," but it thought that the proletarian and nationalist revolutions could occur simultaneously, resulting in the creation of a separate proletarian black state. At the time this might have been termed working class control of the black community.

The party later changed its line and became integrationist.

Black Administrators. The underlying logic of the Communists' arguments, however, appears to be motivating white ruling-class efforts to co-opt black power and forestall further urban revolts. The power structure has apparently concluded that direct white rule of the ghettos, at least in some instances, is no longer operating satisfactorily. It is instead seeking out appropriate black groups to administer the colonies. Traditional Negro leaders are not acceptable, having been discredited both within and without the black communities and obviously exercising no real control.

Therefore it is the new black elite, which ironically was created by both the successes and failures of the civil rights movement, to which the power structure must now turn. Some of the members of this group are militant nationalists, even separatists. They tend to be drawn from the traditional black petty-bourgeois class or to be upwardly mobile members of the working class whose mobility in some measure was made possible by early civil rights victories.

But they share a common frustration with the failures of the civil rights movement and often exhibit a genuine desire to improve the lot of black people. Because they are committed militants they also enjoy a certain credibility and acceptance in the ghetto.

It is these factors which make this group ideal administrators of the ghetto. They seek improvement, not revolution. Having moved up on the social ladder they do not share the nihilism of the youthful ghetto resident. Because they are accepted, they also have the potential to restore ghetto peace and tranquility. Even the more opportunistic members of this group have their use since they will work for "law and order" in return for the right to control and exploit the ghetto.

In short, black control of the black community is slowly being transformed into black elite control of the black community, and the bourgeois-democratic revolution is being completed, but in a manner designed to buttress the power of the white establishment over the black ghettos.

Internal Colony. (5) Black power as black liberation within the context of a U.S. revolution. This wing of the black power movement, represented by the Black Panthers, many members of SNCC and various local groups, views black people as a dispersed internal colony of the U.S., exploited both materially and culturally. It advocates an anticolonial struggle for self-determination which must go hand-in-hand with a general revolution throughout the U.S. It urges alliances with white radicals and other potentially revolutionary segments of the white population since, according to its analysis, genuine self-determination for blacks cannot be achieved in the framework of the present capitalist imperialism and racism which characterize the U.S. Links with the revolutionary third world are also stressed since the black struggle will supposedly be anticolonialist like other national liberation movements, and directed against a common enemy: U.S. imperialism.

But the black radicals, with some exceptions, have been unable to apply this analysis concretely or transform it into a program for struggle. There is a widespread feeling among militants that this is the way things ought to be, but few are sure as to why or how to make it reality.

For example, there has been no elaboration of the relationship between a general U.S. revolution and the black national liberation struggle. Only the theories of the orthodox white left are available, but these are explicitly rejected by black militants.

The question of third world link-ups has also presented difficulties. Aside from trips to third world countries or meetings with third world representatives, the only program developed for a direct link-up is found in the Panthers' call for a UN-supervised black plebiscite and the stationing of UN observers in U.S. cities. And even this is simply a variation on Malcolm X's plan in 1964 to secure UN intervention.

An indirect link to the third world exists in the black antiwar movement. Most militant black antiwar activists openly endorse revolutionary liberation struggles around the world while opposing imperialist wars of aggression. These activists also have a potential base from which to operate. For example, two days before President Johnson announced his non-candidacy, the Philadelphia Tribune, a black community newspaper, completed a seven-week "Vietnam Ballot" in which 84.5% of those polled favored a "get out of Vietnam" position. Only 11% favored a "stop the bombing—negotiate" position, and fewer than 5% supported what was then U.S. policy.

Unfortunately, this sentiment by and large has not been transformed into organization or action. The black antiwar movement has suffered from opportunism and weak or ineffective organizing efforts. A new group, the National Black Antiwar Antidraft Union, headed by SNCC's John Wilson, hopes to solve some of these problems, but it is still too young to have had any noticeable effect.

Aside from these problems the pressure of events is also overtaking black radicals. On the one side they are facing the prospect of increasing repression, on the other there is the escalating anger and nihilism in the ghettos. Black power did in some sense speak to the anger and frustration of urban masses and increased their militance. Their response has been bigger and better rebellions. The outbreaks are political in that they clearly challenge property rights, but black power militants have not brought this political undertone into conscious focus, except among black students, nor have they been able to deal with the resulting repression and co-optation. Instead, those who have not been co-opted, jailed or killed have tended to yield to nihilism and fatalism.

The inability of the white left to seriously deal with racism and repression has accelerated this process. Many black militants increasingly believe that there simply are no effective revolutionary elements in the white population. White students have largely confined themselves to the campuses, where the left has grown stronger, and have not organized poor whites or white workers, groups which have simply persisted in their support of U.S. racism and imperialism. The older middle-class white left has opted out by joining with itself in a middle-class antiwar movement or thrown in with the liberals in supporting McCarthy. A handful of white leftists maintain the proper rhetorical posture vis-a-vis the blacks, but they aren't able to produce the goods.

So, Stokely Carmichael, under these conflicting pressures, announces that whites are the enemy or, at best, irrelevant. He organizes black united fronts, whose unity consists in shared blackness and concern for survival. And survival quickly becomes the uppermost concern.

Socialism becomes irrelevant for Carmichael because he foresees a race war: black against white. He does not anticipate any class struggle in the orthodox sense, hence class analysis has no use. To Carmichael all blacks form one class: the hunted. All whites form another class: the hunters and their accomplices.

Not all militant leaders have yielded to these pressures. Even within the same organization there are differences. H. Rap Brown, present chairman of SNCC and a veteran of white America's jails, contends that it is not possible to judge a revolutionary by the color of his skin. At last October's Guardian meeting Brown expressed his position: "We don't need [white] liberals, we need revolutionaries . . . So the question really becomes whether you choose to be an oppressor or a revolutionary. And if you choose to be an oppressor then you are my enemy. Not because you are white but because you choose to oppress me."

Brown, a man who has ample reason to be bitter against whites, has nevertheless frequently contended, and still does, that the revolutionary forces and their allies must be judged by the same standards: commitment and action. But these are tough standards to meet and Brown, too, is known to have growing doubts about the existence of revolutionary forces both within and without the black communities.

Fear of Genocide. Carmichael believes the blacks will win the projected race war, but there is an ominously growing concern with death, genocide and extermination among black militants. King's assassination added new weight to this concern.

Shortly after King's death and only a few hours before he was to be shot and jailed, Eldridge Cleaver, minister of information of the Black Panthers, said: "The death of Dr. King signals the end of an era and the beginning of a terrible and bloody chapter that may remain unwritten, because there may be no scribe left to capture on paper the holocaust to come."

Earlier Cleaver had expressed a widespread view when he wrote in the May issue of Ramparts: "If the white mother country is to have victory over the black colony, it is the duty of black revolutionaries to insure that the imperialists receive no more than a Pyrrhic victory, written in the blood of what America might have become."

National Organization Needed. It is not possible to say with certainty what will become of the black liberation movement in the coming months and years. It may develop that fear of massive or selective repression was overrated. At this point the signs are unclear.

Despite these gloomy prognostications it should not be overlooked, as one militant commented recently, that "the black power movement and the urban revolts have insured that there are few black men today who are not politically conscious." The same comment applies to cultural awareness and activities. In black communities today cultural activities rival the Harlem renaissance of the 1920s. Certainly cultural nationalism, as a factor within the political struggle, has been a positive force.

Already, here and there, are signs pointing toward the post black-power era. There is increased thinking about creating or forging one of the existing black groups into a national organization with a consistent radical or revolutionary program and real roots in black communities. For black radicals the strategic problem to be solved lies in finding the right relationship between the national and class aspects of the black movement. In the past, radicals have swung from one pole to another, but it is becoming ever clearer that at neither extreme can a winning strategy or an effective program for the black liberation movement be found.

It is the recognition of this fact which underlies the thinking of the Black Panthers. "We recognize," said Eldridge Cleaver in an interview with this writer published in the Guardian April 13, 1968, "the problem presented to black people by the economic system—the capitalist economic system. We repudiate the capitalist economic system. We recognize the class nature of the capitalist economic system and we recognize the dynamics involved in the capitalist system. At the same time we recognize the national character of our struggle. We recognize the fact that we have been oppressed because we are black people even though we know this oppression was for the purpose of exploitation. We have to deal with both exploitation and racial oppression, and we don't think you can achieve a proper balance by neglecting one or the other."

Because of the stress laid on the national question the Panthers are potentially able to mobilize a very wide spectrum of the black population. Because they also understand the nature of class exploitation in U.S. society, the Panthers have been able to work with allies outside the black community and identify enemies within it.

The Panther strategy and organization are far from perfect. The group is also being systematically harassed and destroyed by the Oakland police. The Panthers may well be wiped out, but the history of struggles in other countries suggests that after a certain point a liberation struggle develops a continuity which is independent of individuals or organizations.

This is what Jim Forman meant when he recently wrote: "The technical destruction of a single organization such as SNCC would be unfortunate but it can no more stop the black liberation movement than the murder of Che Guevara can stem the tide of liberation in Latin America. We do not despair or fear the future. Too many brothers have taken up the cry: Freedom or Death."

FURTHER READINGS

This bibliography attempts to provide up-to-date references for an elaboration on the selections in this volume and an introductory list for the interested or beginning student. It is not meant to be exhaustive, and many classic works are mentioned in the readings rather than here.

More detailed bibliographies can be found in:

Comitas, Lambros. *Caribbeana: A Topical Bibliography*. Seattle: University of Washington Press, 1968.

Miller, Elizabeth. *The Negro in America: A Bibliography*. Cambridge: Harvard University Press, 1966.

Franklin, John Hope. *From Slavery to Freedom*. 3rd ed. New York: Random House, Vintage Books, 1969. (The best comparative history.)

A. PREFACE

Background and support for the many assertions which I make in the Preface can be found under the following headings.

Anthropology

Fried, M. (ed.). *Readings in Anthropology, Volume II*. New York: Thomas Y. Crowell, 1968. (Articles on cultural and social anthropology.)

Gough, Kathleen. "World Revolution and the Science of Man." In Theodore Roszak, ed., *The Dissenting Academy*. New York: Random House, Pantheon Books, 1968. (A critique of anthropology by an anthropologist.)

Wolf, Eric. *Anthropology*. Englewood Cliffs, N.J.: Prentice-Hall, 1964. (A lucid statement on present anthropological interests.)

Origins and Nature of Capitalism

Dobb, M. *Studies in the Development of Capitalism*. Rev. ed. New York: International Publishers, 1963. (A basic source.)

Frank, A. G. *Capitalism and Underdevelopment in Latin America*. New York: Monthly Review Press, 1967. (Underdevelopment as a function of development.)

Magdoff, H. "Problems of United States Capitalism." In R. Milliband and J. Saville, eds., *Socialist Register*. New York: Monthly Review Press, 1965.

Marx, Karl. *Capital*. Centennial Ed. New York: International Publishers, 1967. (The basic source.)

Colonization and European Expansion

Parry, J. H. *The Establishment of the European Hegemony.* New York: Harper and Row, Harper Torchbooks, 1961.

Rochester, Anna. *American Capitalism 1607–1800.* New York: International Publishers, 1949.

Culture Heterogeneity of Afro-America

Documentation for this point can be found in novels and autobiographies by Black authors as well as in the anthropological literature.

Brown, Claude. *Manchild in the Promised Land.* New York: Macmillan, 1965. (American ghetto life.)

Ellison, F. P. *Brazil's New Novel: Four Northeastern Masters.* Berkeley: University of California Press, 1954.

Lamming, George. *In the Castle of My Skin.* New York: McGraw-Hill, 1953. (About Barbados.)

Patterson, Orlando. *The Children of Sysyphus.* London: New Authors, 1964. (The slums of Kingston, Jamaica.)

Roumain, Jacques. *Masters of the Dew.* London: Regnal and Hitchcock, 1964. (The French West Indies.)

Whitten, N. and J. Szwed (eds.). *Afro-American Anthropology.* New York: Free Press, 1970. (A recent and important compilation of studies.)

X, Malcolm. *The Autobiography of Malcolm X.* New York: Grove Press, 1964. (American ghetto life.)

B. SLAVERY

Anthologies

Most of the classic and most recent works on slavery are found in these collections.

Foner, L. and E. Genovese (eds.). *Slavery in the New World: A Reader in Comparative History.* Englewood Cliffs, N.J.: Prentice-Hall, 1969.

Weinstein, A. and O. Gatell (eds.). *American Negro Slavery: A Modern Reader.* New York: Oxford University Press, 1968.

Woodman, H. (ed.). *Slavery and the Southern Economy.* New York: Harcourt, Brace and World, 1966.

Descriptions of Slave Societies

Bluestone, D. M. "Marxism Without Marx: The Consensus-Conflict of Eugene Genovese." *Science and Society,* Vol. 33 (1969). (A review of *The Political Economy of Slavery.*)

Genovese, E. *The Political Economy of Slavery.* New York: Random House, Pantheon Books, 1965.

———. *The World the Slaveholders Made.* New York: Random House, Pantheon Books, 1969.

Goveia, Elsa. *Slave Society in the Leeward Islands at the End of the Eighteenth Century*. New Haven: Yale University Press, 1965.

Patterson, Orlando. *The Sociology of Slavery: An Analysis of . . . Negro Slave Society in Jamaica*. London: MacGibbon and Kee, 1967.

Prado Junior, Caio. *The Colonial Background of Modern Brazil*. Berkeley: University of California Press, 1967.

Slave Revolts

Aptheker, H. *American Negro Slave Revolts*. New York: International Publishers, 1963.

————. *Nat Turner's Slave Rebellion*. New York: Humanities Press, 1966.

Carneiro, Edison. *Guerras de los Palmares*. Mexico: Fondon de Cultura Economica, 1946. (The Negro republic of Palmares, c. 1630.)

James, C. L. R. *The Black Jacobins*. New York: Random House, Vintage Books. (The Haitian revolution.)

Ramos, A. "The Negro Republic of Palmares." In *The Negro in Brazil*. Washington: The Associated Publishers, 1951.

C. RELATIONS OF PRODUCTION

Plantations and the Black Rural Proletariat

Guerra y Sanchez, R. *Sugar and Society in the Caribbean*. New Haven: Yale University Press, 1964. (Primarily concerned with changes in the Cuban plantation system.)

Handler, J. Aspects of Work Organization on Sugar Plantations in Barbados. *Ethnology*, Vol. 4 (1965).

Jayawardena, C. *Conflict and Solidarity on a Guianese Plantation*. London: Athlone Press, 1967.

Johnson, C. *Shadow of the Plantation*. Chicago: University of Chicago Press, 1934. (American South.)

Marshall, W. K. "Metayage in the Sugar Industry of the British Windward Islands, 1838–1865." *Jamaica Historical Review*, Vol. 5 (1965). (A history of sharecropping.)

Mintz, S. "The Folk-Urban Continuum and the Rural Proletarian Community." *American Journal of Sociology*, Vol. 59 (1953).

Ortiz, F. *Cuban Counterpoint*. New York: Alfred A. Knopf, 1947. (Discusses the production of sugar and tobacco and their social correlates.)

Pan American Union. *Plantation Systems of the New World*. Washington, 1959. (A basic source.)

Perlo, V. *The Negro in Southern Agriculture*. New York: International Publishers, 1953. (Important discussion of sharecropping.)

Powdermaker, H. *After Freedom*. New York: Viking Press, 1939. (American South.)

Rubin, M. *Plantation County*. Chapel Hill, N.C.: University of North Carolina Press, 1951. (American South.)

Steward, J. (ed.). *The People of Puerto Rico*. Urbana, Ill.: University of Illinois Press, 1956. (Chapters on plantation and peasant production and society.)

Vance, R. *Human Factors in Cotton Culture*. Chapel Hill, N.C.: University of North Carolina Press, 1929. (American South.)

Wolf, E. and S. Mintz. "Haciendas and Plantations in Middle America and the Antilles." *Social and Economic Studies*, Vol. 6 (1957). (A basic source.)

Black Peasantry

Harris, M. *Town and Country in Brazil*. New York: Columbia University Press, 1956.

Herskovits, M. and F. Herskovits. *Trinidad Village*. New York: Alfred A. Knopf, 1947.

Horowitz, M. M. "A Typology of Rural Community Forms in the Caribbean." *Anthropological Quarterly*, Vol. 33 (1960).

————. *Morne-Paysan: Peasant Village in Martinique*. New York: Holt, Rinehart and Winston, 1967.

Katzin, M. "The Jamaican Country Higgler." *Social and Economic Studies*, Vol. 8 (1959). (Internal marketing system of Jamaica.)

Marshall, W. K. "Peasant Development in the West Indies Since 1838." *Social and Economic Studies*, Vol. 17 (1968).

Métraux, A. *Making a Living in the Marbial Valley*. Paris: UNESCO, 1951. (Haitian peasantry.)

Mintz, S. "The Question of Caribbean Peasantries: A Comment." *Caribbean Studies*, Vol. 1 (1961).

Mintz, S. and V. Carroll. "A Selective Social Science Bibliography of the Republic of Haiti." *Revista Interamericana de Ciencias Sociales*, Vol. 2 (1963).

Mintz, S. and D. Hall. "The Origins of the Jamaican Internal Marketing System." *Yale University Publications in Anthropology*, Vol. 57 (1960).

Pierson, D. *Cruz das Almas, A Brazilian Village*. Washington: Smithsonian Institution, 1951.

Smith, M. G. *Kinship and Community in Carriacou*. New Haven: Yale University Press, 1962. (Windward Islands, West Indies.)

Smith, R. T. "Ethnic Difference and Peasant Economy in British Guiana." In R. Firth and B. Yamey, eds., *Capital, Savings and Credit in Peasant Societies*. London: George Allen and Unwin, 1964.

Wolf, Eric. *Peasants*. Englewood Cliffs, N.J.: Prentice-Hall, 1966. (A basic source.)

Black Proletariat: Urban and Industrial

Batchelder, A. "Poverty: The Special Case of the Negro." *American Economic Review* (May 1965). (The "value" of Negro money.)

Broom, L. and N. Glenn. *Transformation of the Negro American.* New York: Harper and Row, 1967. (See especially chapter on occupations and incomes.)

Clark, K. *Dark Ghetto.* New York: Harper and Row, 1965. (About Harlem, New York City.)

Drake, St. C. and Horace Cayton. *Black Metropolis.* New York: Harcourt, Brace and World, 1945. (About Chicago.)

Du Bois, W. E. B. *The Philadelphia Negro.* Philadelphia: University of Pennsylvania Press, 1899.

Ferman, L., J. Kornbluh, and J. Miller (eds.). *Negroes and Jobs: A Book of Readings.* Ann Arbor, Mich.: University of Michigan Press, 1968.

Hunter, Guy (ed.). *Industrialization and Race Relations.* London: Oxford University Press, 1965. (See especially chapters on the U.S.)

Kain, J. (ed.). *Race and Poverty.* Englewood Cliffs, N.J.: Prentice-Hall, 1969.

Myrdal, G. *An American Dilemma.* New York: Harper and Bros., 1944.

National Advisory Committee on Civil Disorders. *Report of the National Advisory Committee on Civil Disorders.* New York: E. P. Dutton, 1968. (Good for statistics.)

Nearing, S. *Black America.* New York: Schocken Books, 1969. (Originally published in 1929.)

Patterson, S. *Immigrants in Industry.* London: Oxford University Press, 1968. (Black workers in Britain.)

Wright, P. *The Coloured Worker in British Industry.* London: Oxford University Press, 1968.

D. RACE AND CLASS RELATIONS

General and Comparative

Banton, M. *Race Relations.* London: Tavistock Publications, 1967. (Social anthropological perspectives.)

Benedict, R. *Race, Science and Politics.* New York: Viking Press, 1945. (On race and racism.)

Brace, C. L. *et al.* "On the Race Concept." *Current Anthropology,* Vol. 5 (1964). (Debate among human biologists.)

Comas, J. *et al. The Race Question in Modern Science.* Paris: UNESCO, 1956.

Cox, O. C. *Caste, Class and Race.* New York: Monthly Review Press, 1969. (A Marxist-sociological perspective.)

Morner, M. *Race Mixture in the History of Latin America.* Boston: Little, Brown and Co., 1967. (Despite the title, a good introduction to race and class in Latin America.)

Thompson, E. T. (ed.). *Race Relations and the Race Problem.* New York: Greenwood Press, 1968. (A republication of essays, some outdated, but many still relevant.)

Van Den Berghe, P. *Race and Racism.* New York: John Wiley, 1967. (A recent sociological survey.)

Wagley, C. and M. Harris. *Minorities in the New World.* New York: Columbia University Press, 1958. (Cultural anthropological perspectives.)

United States

Frazier, E. F. *Black Burgeoisie.* Glencoe, Ill.: Free Press, 1957.

Hare, N. *The Black Anglo-Saxons.* New York: Marzani and Munsell, 1966.

Killian, L. and C. Grigg. "Race Relations in an Urbanized South." *Journal of Social Issues,* Vol. 22 (1966).

Pinkney, A. *Black Americans.* Englewood Cliffs, N.J.: Prentice-Hall, 1969.

Silberman, C. *Crisis in Black and White.* New York: Random House, 1964.

Walker, H. J. "Changes in the Status of the Negro in American Society." *International Social Science Bulletin,* Vol. 9 (1957).

Wilhelm, S. "Red Man, Black Man and White America: The Constitutional Approach to Genocide." *Catalyst,* Vol. 4 (Spring 1969). (An important argument concerning the changing expressions of racism.)

Caribbean

Braithwaite, L. "Social Stratification in Trinidad." *Social and Economic Studies,* Vol. 2 (1953).

————. "Social Stratification and Cultural Pluralism." In V. Rubin, ed., *Social and Cultural Pluralism in the Caribbean.* New York: New York Academy of Sciences, 1960.

Hoetink, H. *The Two Variants in Caribbean Race Relations.* London: Oxford University Press, 1967.

Lewis, G. *The Making of the Modern West Indies.* New York: Monthly Review Press, 1968.

Lowenthal, D. "Race and Color in the West Indies." *Daedalus,* Vol. 96 (Fall 1967).

Smith, M. G. *The Plural Society in the British West Indies.* Berkeley: University of California Press, 1965.

————. *Stratification in Grenada.* Berkeley: University of California Press, 1965.

Brazil

Bastide, R. "Race Relations in Brazil." *International Social Science Bulletin,* Vol. 9 (1957).

Fernandes, Florestan. Phyllis B. Eveleth, ed., *The Negro in Brazilian Society.* Translated by Jacqueline D. Skiles, A. Brunel, and Arthur Rothwell. New York: Columbia University Press, 1969.

Harris, M. and C. Kottak. "The Structural Significance of Brazilian Racial Categories." *Sociologia,* Vol. 25 (1963).

Pierson, D. *Negroes in Brazil; A Study of Race Contact at Bahia.* Carbondale, Ill.: Southern Illinois University Press, 1967.

Wagley, C. (ed.). *Race and Class in Rural Brazil.* Paris: UNESCO, 1963.

Britain

Banton, M. *White and Coloured*. London: Jonathan Cape, 1959.
Griffith, J. *et al. Coloured Immigrants in Britain*. London: Oxford University Press, 1960.
Patterson, S. *Dark Strangers*. London: Tavistock Publications, 1963.
Peach, C. *West Indian Migration to Britain*. London: Oxford University Press, 1968.

E. FAMILY AND INTERPERSONAL RELATIONS

R. T. Smith's articles refer to works up to 1963. I have listed here only some of the most important references since then, as well as one or two other articles which should be read.

Adams, R. N. "An Inquiry into the Nature of the Family." In G. Dole and R. Carneiro, eds., *Essays in the Science of Culture*. New York: Thomas Y. Crowell, 1960.
Cohen, Y. "Four Categories of Interpersonal Relationships in the Family and Community in a Jamaican Village." *Anthropological Quarterly*, Vol. 3 (1955).
Feagin, J. R. "The Kinship Ties of Negro Urbanites." *Social Science Quarterly*, Vol. 49 (1968).
Frazier, E. F. *The Negro Family in the United States*. Revised Ed. Chicago: Phoenix Books, 1966.
Gonzalez, N. *Black Carib Household Structure*. Seattle: University of Washington Press, 1969. (A recent and important discussion of the "matrifocal" family by an anthropologist.)
Keiser, R. L. *The Vice Lords*. New York: Holt, Rinehart and Winston, 1969. (About a Black teen-age gang in Chicago.)
Kunstadter, P. "A Survey of the Consanguine or Matrifocal Family." *American Anthropologist*, Vol. 65 (1963).
Moynihan, D. F. *The Negro Family: The Case for National Action*. Washington: U.S. Government Printing Office, 1965. (See also Rainwater and Yancey.)
Otterbein, K. F. "Caribbean Family Organization: A Comparative Analysis." *American Anthropologist*, Vol. 67 (1965).
Rainwater, L. "Crucible of Identity: The Negro Lower Class Family." *Daedalus*, Vol. 95 (Winter 1966).
Rainwater, L. and W. Yancey (eds.). *The Moynihan Report and the Politics of Controversy*. Cambridge: M.I.T. Press, 1967.
Schulz, D. *Coming Up Black: Patterns of Ghetto Socialization*. Englewood Cliffs, N.J.: Prentice-Hall, 1969.
Stack, C. "The Kindred of Viola Jackson: Residence and Family Organization of an Urban Black American Family." N. Whitten and J. Szwed, eds., In *Afro-American Anthropology*. New York: The Free Press, 1970.

F. RELIGION

Bascom, W. "The Focus on Cuban Santería." *Southwestern Journal of Anthropology,* Vol. 6 (1952).

Bastide, R. *Le Condomblé de Bahia.* The Hague: Mouton, 1958.

——. *Les Religions Africaines au Brésil.* Paris: Presses Universitaires de France, 1961.

Essien-Udom, E. U. *Black Nationalism.* Chicago: University of Chicago Press, 1962. (About the Black Muslims.)

Frazier, E. F. *The Negro Church in America.* New York: Schocken Books, 1963.

Glenn, N. "Negro Religion and Negro Status in the United States." In Louis Schneider, ed., *Religion, Culture and Society.* New York: John Wiley, 1964. (A good sociological survey.)

Herskovits, M. "African Gods and Catholic Saints in New World Negro Belief." *American Anthropologist,* Vol. 39 (1937). (On syncretic religions.)

Lincoln, C. E. *The Black Muslims in America.* Boston: Beacon Press, 1961.

Metraux, A. *Voodoo in Haiti.* New York: Oxford University Press, 1959.

Simpson, G. E. *The Shango Cult in Trinidad.* Rio Piedras: University of Puerto Rico, 1965. (Institute of Caribbean Studies).

Smith, M. G., R. Augier and R. Nettleford. *The Ras Tafari Movement in Kingston, Jamaica.* Mona: University of the West Indies, 1960 (Institute of Social and Economic Studies).

Thrupp, S. (ed.). *Millennial Dreams in Action.* The Hague: Mouton, 1962. (A basic source on millenarian religious movements.)

G. BLACK IDEOLOGY AND BLACK POWER

Ideology and Culture

Abrahams, R. *Positively Black.* Englewood Cliffs, N.J.: Prentice-Hall, 1970. (Black American folklore and culture.)

Bastien, R. "The Role of the Intellectual in Haitian Plural Society." In V. Rubin, ed., *Social and Cultural Pluralism in the Caribbean.* New York: New York Academy of Sciences, 1960.

Blauner, R. "Black Culture: Myth or Reality?" In N. Whitten and J. Szwed, eds., *Afro-American Anthropology.* New York: The Free Press, 1970.

Cleaver, E. *Soul on Ice.* New York: Dell Publishing Co., 1968.

Coulthard, G. R. *Race and Colour in Caribbean Literature.* London: Oxford University Press, 1962.

Fanon, F. *Black Skin, White Masks.* New York: Grove Press, 1967. (On being Black in a white world.)

Hill, E. (ed.). *The Artist in West Indian Society.* Mona: University of the West Indies, 1963. (Department of Extra-mural Studies).

Hill, H. (ed.). *Anger and Beyond: The Negro Writer in the United States.* New York: Harper and Row, 1968.

Hughes, D. (ed.). *From a Black Perspective: Contemporary Black Essays.* New York: Holt, Rinehart and Winston, 1970.

James, L. (ed.). *The Islands in Between.* London: Oxford University Press, 1968. (Critical essays by West Indians on West Indian literature.)

Jones, Le Roi. *Blues People.* New York: William Morrow, 1963. (A sociology of music.)

Kelley, W. M. "The Roots of Soul." *Negro Digest* (May 1968).

Szwed, J. "Afro-American Musical Adaptation." In N. Whitten and J. Szwed, eds. *Afro-American Anthropology.* New York: The Free Press, 1970.

Power and Politics

Adler, F. H. "Black Power." In R. Milliband and J. Saville, eds., *The Socialist Register, 1968.* New York: Monthly Review Press, 1968.

Allen, R. *Black Awakening in Capitalist America.* New York: Doubleday, 1969. (An important book.)

Breitman, G. *The Last Year of Malcolm X.* New York: Schocken Books, 1967.

Carmichael, S. and C. Hamilton. *Black Power: The Politics of Liberation in America.* New York: Random House, Vintage Books, 1967.

Clarke, J. H. "The New Afro-American Nationalism." *Freedomways* (Fall 1961).

Cleaver, E. "Three Notes from Exile." *Ramparts,* Vol. 8 (September 1969).

Dratch, H. "The Emergence of Black Power." *International Socialist Journal,* Vol. 5 (July 1968).

Du Bois, W. E. B. *The Souls of Black Folk.* New York: Fawcett, 1961.

Eaton, G. E. "Trade Union Development in Jamaica." *Caribbean Quarterly,* Vol. 8 (1962).

Fanon, F. *The Wretched of the Earth.* New York: Grove Press, 1966.

Franklin, R. S. "The Political Economy of Black Power." *Social Problems,* Vol. 16 (1969).

Grant, J. (ed.). *Black Protest: History, Documents and Analyses, 1619 to the Present.* Greenwich: Fawcett, 1965. (A good source book.)

Hahn, H. "Ghetto Sentiments on Violence." *Science and Society,* Vol. 33 (1969).

Hewitt, C. N. "The Peasant Movement of Pernambuco, 1961–1964." In H. A. Landsberger, ed., *Latin American Peasant Movements.* Ithaca, N.Y.: Cornell University Press, 1969. (Peasant political reaction in the Northeast.)

Jagan, C. *Forbidden Freedom.* London: Lawrence and Wishart, 1954. (The struggles of anti-colonialism in British Guiana.)

James, C. L. R. "Parties, Politics and Economics in the Caribbean." *Freedomways,* Vol. 4 (Summer 1964).

Kaiser, E. "Recent Literature on Black Liberation Struggles." *Science and Society,* Vol. 33 (1969). (A basic source.)

Lewis, G. *The Growth of the Modern West Indies.* New York: Monthly Review Press, 1968.

Lewis, W. A. *Labour in the West Indies: The Birth of a Workers' Movement.* London: V. Gollancz, 1939.

Ofari, E. *Black Liberation: Cultural and Revolutionary Nationalism.* Ann Arbor, Mich.: Radical Education Project. Undated.

Oxaal, R. *Black Intellectuals Come to Power: The Rise of Creole Nationalism in Trinidad and Tobago.* Cambridge: Schenkman Publishing Co., 1968.

Rudwick, E. "The Niagara Movement." *Journal of Negro History,* Vol. 42 (1957). (An early twentieth-century Black political movement.)

Zeitlin, M. *Revolutionary Politics and the Cuban Working Class.* New York: Harper and Row, Harper Torchbooks, 1970.

The Colonial Situation

Balandier, G. "The Colonial Situation: A Theoretical Approach." In I. Wallerstein, ed., *Social Change: The Colonial Situation.* New York: John Wiley, 1966. (A basic source.)

Caute, D. *The Decline of the West.* New York: Macmillan, 1966. (A novel describing colonialism in Africa and the United States.)

Fanon, F. *A Dying Colonialism.* New York: Grove Press, 1967.

Kennedy, R. "The Colonial Crisis and the Future." In R. Linton, ed., *The Science of Man in the World Crisis.* New York: Columbia University Press, 1945.

Lenin, V. I. *On the National and Colonial Questions.* Peking: Foreign Languages Press, 1967.

Memmi, A. *The Colonizer and the Colonized.* Boston: Beacon Press, 1965. (On the psychological and existential dilemmas of both.)

Viet Report. "Colonialism and Liberation in America." Special issue of *Viet Report,* Vol. 3 (Summer 1968).

Wallerstein, E. (ed.). *Social Change: The Colonial Situation.* New York: John Wiley, 1966. (A wide-ranging compilation of articles.)

Woddis, J. *Introduction to Neo-colonialism.* New York: International Publishers, 1967. (An important source.)